The Emerging Contours of the Medium

thinking|media

series editors:
bernd herzogenrath
patricia pisters

The Emerging Contours of the Medium

Literature and Mediality

Edited by
Richard Müller

BLOOMSBURY ACADEMIC
NEW YORK • LONDON • OXFORD • NEW DELHI • SYDNEY

BLOOMSBURY ACADEMIC
Bloomsbury Publishing Inc, 1359 Broadway, New York, NY 10018, USA
Bloomsbury Publishing Plc, 50 Bedford Square, London, WC1B 3DP, UK
Bloomsbury Publishing Ireland, 29 Earlsfort Terrace, Dublin 2, D02 AY28, Ireland

BLOOMSBURY, BLOOMSBURY ACADEMIC and the Diana logo are trademarks of
Bloomsbury Publishing Plc

First published in the United States of America 2024
Paperback edition published 2025

Editor © Richard Müller, 2024

© Institute of Czech Literature of the CAS, 2024

Each chapter © Richard Müller, Tomáš Chudý, Alice Jedličková, Stanislava Fedrová, Josef
Šebek, Pavel Šidák, Josef Vojvodík, and Martin Ritter, 2024

Translated by Peter Gaffney except for Chapters 10 and 11, which were translated by
Nicholas Orsillo.

For legal purposes the Acknowledgements on p. xvii constitute an extension of this
copyright page.

During the work on this book, use was made of Czech Literary Bibliography resources
(ORJ identifier: 90243).

Published by Bloomsbury Publishing Inc, and the Institute of Czech Literature of the
Czech Academy of Sciences.

This book was published with support from the Czech Academy of Sciences and created
with support of Research Development Program RVO 68378068.

Cover design: Daniel Benneworth-Gray
Cover image © Paolo Sanfifilippo

All rights reserved. No part of this publication may be: i) reproduced or transmitted in any
form, electronic or mechanical, including photocopying, recording or by means of any
information storage or retrieval system without prior permission in writing from the publishers;
or ii) used or reproduced in any way for the training, development or operation of artificial
intelligence (AI) technologies, including generative AI technologies. The rights holders expressly
reserve this publication from the text and data mining exception as per Article 4(3) of the
Digital Single Market Directive (EU) 2019/790.

Bloomsbury Publishing Inc does not have any control over, or responsibility for, any third-
party websites referred to or in this book. All internet addresses given in this book were
correct at the time of going to press. The author and publisher regret any inconvenience
caused if addresses have changed or sites have ceased to exist, but can accept no
responsibility for any such changes.

Library of Congress Control Number: 2023031408

ISBNs of the Bloomsbury Editions

HB: 978-1-5013-9867-4
PB: 978-1-5013-9871-1
ePDF: 978-1-5013-9869-8
eBook: 978-1-5013-9868-1

ISBNs of the Institute of Czech Literature of the CAS Editions

HB: 978-8-0765-8068-8
ePDF: 978-8-0765-8069-5
eBook: 978-8-0765-8070-1

Series: Thinking Media

Typeset by Deanta Global Publishing Services, Chennai, India

For product safety related questions contact productsafety@bloomsbury.com.

To find out more about our authors and books visit www.bloomsbury.com and sign up
for our newsletters.

[. . .] information [. . .] is a difference which makes a difference.
　　　　　　　　Gregory Bateson, *Steps to an Ecology of Mind*, 1972

[. . .] aus dem Telephon nichts und nichts zu hören bekam, als einen traurigen, mächtigen, wortlosen Gesang und das Rauschen des Meeres. Ich begriff wohl, daß es für Menschenstimmen nicht möglich war, sich durch diese Töne zu drängen, aber ich ließ nicht ab und ging nicht weg.
　　　　　　　　　　　　　　　　　Franz Kafka to Felice Bauer, 1913

Contents

List of figures	xiii
List of tables and diagrams	xiv
Author profiles	xv
Acknowledgements	xvii

Introduction: Genealogy of the concept of the medium and literary studies *Richard Müller* — 1
  1. Integrating literary and media study: In search of principles — 1
    Starting from an absence — 1
    Defining the subject — 3
    Genealogy of the concept and genealogy as a method — 5
    Constitutive questions and issues — 9
  2. The emerging contours of the medium: Outline — 10

1 The 'medium': Concept and history *Tomáš Chudý* — 19
  1. Conceptual (pre-)history of the medium — 19
    Delimiting the 'medium': Functional perspective — 19
    Evidence and records of concept and function — 22
    A functional definition of media in light of its conceptual (pre-)history — 29
  2. Aspects of media evolution — 31
  3. The medium as an environment *and* as a means/tool – a unified concept? — 37

2 Reflections of mediality in Prague School thinking *Richard Müller and Pavel Šidák* — 45
  1. Defining the problem — 45
  2. Structuralism's turn to medial thinking under the influence of film — 48
  3. How the theorization of architecture transforms the aesthetic function into a 'mediating' function — 54

	4. Problems of semiosis in connection with theatre	59
	The unifying principle of meaning and unintentionality in the theatre	60
	5. Conclusions	63

3	The media philosophy of Walter Benjamin *Martin Ritter*	69
	1. Concept of the medium	70
	2. The age of the masses	74
	3. The problem of mastering emancipated technology	76
	4. Media of the world's self-givenness	77
	5. Benjamin's media thinking	79

4	'Let the ghosts come back': Modern spectrology and its media *Josef Vojvodík*	83
	1. Film: The double 'image-ghost of man'	86
	2. Technics as 'open form'	87
	3. Humanity as a 'medial event'	88
	4. 'Place of image'	90
	5. 'Being a skull': Cube, crystal and black box	92
	6. Negativity, indeterminacy, ambiguity: The modalities of negative anthropology	94
	7. The science of spectres, or spectrology	97
	8. 'A shadowy semblance with a certain intimation of being': Photo-technics and *fantomachia*	102
	9. A posthumous photograph and a death mask: The media of imprinting and disappearing	106
	10. (G)HOSTage: to be held hostage by ghosts	113

5	Gesture and its (proto-)medial thresholds *Richard Müller*	127
	1. The mediality of the semantic gesture and unintentionality	131
	The medial 'symptomaticity' of semantic gesture	131
	Intentionality and unintentionality as media phenomena	135
	The protomedial thresholds of gesture	138
	2. The mediality of communication between gesture and speech	140
	Gesture, speech, rhythm and graphism	140

	On the origin of the medial differentiation of the sign ('mythogram')	144
	Double unintentionality?	147
3.	Gesture and intentionality in 'The Vane Sisters' (1951)	152

6 Openness: The information (cybernetics) moment in literary theory and experimental poetry of the 1950–60s *Richard Müller*   167
    1. Prelude: I wish you had heard his 'Nevermore'   168
    2. The cybernetic turn   170
    3. From entropy to perceiver   172
       Jakobson: The first mediator   172
       Between information theory and cybernetics   176
       Eco: *The Open Work* and its 'legacy'   184
       Problems of *The Open Work*   189
       Communication models and the birth of the reader   198
       Červenka: The process and organization of a literary work, aesthetic function and focus on the *univers de discours*   199
    4. The Czech 'poetry of new consciousness' in the Information Age   206
       A sense of crisis and cultural breakdown   208
       Inherent problems of media classification   209
       Different conceptual and ideational sources and goals   214
       Machine poetry and the construction of scienticity: The meaning effect   217
       New modes of reading and perception   220
    5. The information (cybernetics) moment from the perspective of experimental poetry (and vice versa)   222

7 Technics and media *Tomáš Chudý*   229
    1. The technological unconscious as shift in the role of media (Kapp, Thrift, Ihde, McLuhan)   229
       Ernst Kapp, Nigel Thrift and technics theory after Gilbert Simondon   231
       Don Ihde and the phenomenology of technics   236
       The recursive loop and Erhard Schüttpelz   238
       The narcotization of media: McLuhan (and successors inspired by semiotics: Winkler)   241

	2. Processing, manipulation and discursive economics	246
	Manovich: The persistence of representations	246
	Kittler: Manipulation without the concept of a sign	248
	Winkler: Processing and discursive economics	254
	3. Infogenic man and the software explosion	262
	Conclusion	269
8	Communication, solution and mediality: The paradoxical character of Williams's thinking on the medium *Josef Šebek*	279
	1. Culture and communication	280
	2. Technique, technology and cultural form: The medium and technological determinism	284
	3. Solution: The medium within social signification systems	289
	4. A media theory of literature?	297
9	Social systems theory and the medium *Tomáš Chudý*	303
	1. The improbability of communication and double contingency	303
	2. The medium of the 'artwork' and the code of art	310
	Epilogue: Media forms	319
10	Poetics – semiosphere – medium: Lotman's cultural semiotics at the crossroads *Richard Müller*	327
	1. Points of departure	327
	2. Lotman's crossroads and borders	331
	Prologue: Uncertainty and the dream as a (pre-)media phenomenon	331
	Towards cultural dynamics	333
	The semiosphere and the mediality of memory	344
	Commentary from a media-genealogical perspective	346
	3. Lotman's semiotics and technology	350
	The memory function and the technological *dispositif*	350
	The creative function and text generation by neural networks	351
	Appendix 1: The phantom of interactivity and the dimensions of immersion (Marie-Laure Ryan)	358
	A hologram or the simultaneity of media (un)awareness?	360

	Media diversity as a corrective of the dichotomy of 'interactivity' and 'immersion'	361
	Appendix 2: A return to Iser: Reading, image and indeterminacy	364
	The image as *metaxy* and the reading process	365
11	The theory of intermediality: Apparentness of relations, elusiveness of medium *Stanislava Fedrová and Alice Jedličková*	373
	1. The genealogy of intermediality	373
	Prehistory: The paradigm of art and the concept of *ut pictura poesis*	374
	Proto-intermediality: An overlooked member of the family tree	379
	Pre-intermediality: Comparative arts, interart studies	383
	2. Intermediality: The systemization of theory and the establishment of the discipline	391
	Motivations for change: The state of culture and the academic discourse	391
	The background of intertextuality: An expanding scope under the influence of visual studies	392
	Seeking a perfect model: Literature-centred intermediality	394
	3. An established discipline	402
	Critiques of existing models and new emphases	402
	Searching for an umbrella term	404
	Stimuli and competition: Narratology, transmedia storytelling and adaptation studies	406
	Finally, a definition of *medium*: The concept of modality	412
	4. The identity of research: Flexibility and continuity	415
	Parallel disciplines: Intermediality and multimodality	415
	A concept as an argument: Media transformation	419
	Processuality and materiality: Latency and presence once again	422
	Prospects for the future: Across, inter, in-between, in?	425

Polylogue: Steps to a media theory of literature *Richard Müller, Tomáš Chudý, Alice Jedličková, Josef Šebek and Stanislava Fedrová* 433

Media and media processes, defining 'medium' and conceptual
  genealogy 434
Art and media, and the veiled mediality of literature: A lesson
  in (and to) intermediality 437
Media archaeology, media evolution? 439
Communication, its aporias and limits, literature, medium
  and culture 441
Technics 446
Literature and the medium of speech, culture and
  (contemporary infogenic) society 447

References 453
Index 489

Figures

2.1	Vítězslav Nezval: O, from *The Alphabet*, 1926	47
4.1	Victor Regnault: Untitled, c. 1850, calotype	103
4.2	Jaroslav Rössler: posthumous photograph of Bohumil Kubišta, 1918	107
4.3	Bohumil Kubišta: *Pozůstatky padlého* (Remains of the Fallen), 1918, linocut, 10 × 16 cm, National Gallery in Prague	108
4.4	Bohumil Kubišta: *Hlava* (Head), c. 1904, ink drawing, paper, 54 × 37 cm	108
4.5	Death mask of Jindřich Štyrský, 1942	110
4.6	Jindřich Štyrský: From the cycle *Muž s klapkami na očích* (The Man with Blinkers), 1934, photograph, 32 × 28.5 cm	111
4.7	Jindřich Štyrský: *Náhrobní kámen* (Gravestone), oil, canvas, 115 × 70 cm, period photograph of the painting with the attached mask	112
4.8	Jindřich Štyrský: *Na hrobě* (On the Grave), 1939, oil on canvas, 64 × 58 cm	114
4.9	Jindřich Štyrský: *Lautréamont*, 1939, collage, paper, 15.5 × 12.5 cm	115
4.10	Jindřich Štyrský: *Dar* (Gift), 1937, oil on canvas, 54 × 42 cm	117
5.1	Vítězslav Nezval: *Soví muž* (Owl Man), gouache	134
5.2	Robert Capa: *Muerte de un miliciano*, gelatin silver print, 18.1 × 23.8 cm, 1936	151
6.1	Hans G. Markert: Rectangle, square, 1964, concrete poem	167
6.2	Jiří Kolář: *Sólo pro kuličkové pero* (Solo for a Ballpoint Pen), 1982, collage (chiasmage, music sheet), 30 × 40 cm	211
6.3	Ladislav Nebeský: from the collection *Zaplňování prázdna* (Filling the Void), 2007	212
6.4	Josef Honys: *Rozvoj vize* (The Development of Vision), c. 1964–8, ink drawing, 29.8 × 21.8 cm	213

Part divider images (in order of appearance)
'Pheasant Pen' from the Traces series by Běla Kolářová © Martin Helcl (1961). Reproduced with the permission of DILIA Agency Z.S.
'Untitled' from the Traces series by Běla Kolářová © Martin Helcl (1961). Reproduced with the permission of DILIA Agency Z.S.
'Untitled' from the Traces series by Běla Kolářová © Martin Helcl (1961). Reproduced with the permission of DILIA Agency Z.S.
'Fragment of the Moon' from the Traces series by Běla Kolářová. Reproduced with the permission of DILIA Agency Z.S.

Tables and Diagrams

Tables

1.1	Three stages of media evolution according to Régis Debray (1991)	40
11.1	Claus Clüver, Leo H. Hoek and Eric Vos 1997	396
11.2	Hans Lund 2002	398
11.3	Irina O. Rajewsky 2002	400

Diagrams

6.1	Illustration of a general communication system (M stands for 'message'); a combination of schemes	180
10.1	The transformation of text T1 within the space of conventionally correlated codes (K{1, 2, . . ., n})	336
11.1	Werner Wolf 2002, revised 2018	399
11.2	Lars Elleström's model of transmediation	420

Author profiles

Tomáš Chudý works as an independent researcher, translator (Kittler, Luhmann, Taylor, etc.) and lawyer for the Czech National Bank. His research interests include media philosophy and the interrelation of technical and humanist paradigms by means of working with signs, as well as interlinking social and economic aspects in technically mediated communication. He has published in scholarly journals, such as *Social Studies*, and he is the co-author, with Richard Müller et al., of the Czech edition of *The Emerging Contours of the Medium* (2020).*

Stanislava Fedrová is Head of the Department of Art Historiography and Theory at the Institute of Art History at the Czech Academy of Sciences, Czech Republic, researcher at the Institute of Czech Literature of the Czech Academy of Sciences, Czech Republic, and Assistant Professor of Literature and Intercultural Communication at Masaryk University, Czech Republic. Her scholarly interests include literary theory, art theory, visual culture and intermedial research, with a focus on the relations between verbal and visual media. She is co-author, with Alice Jedličková, of *Visible Descriptions: Visuality, Suggestivity and Intermediality of Literary Description* (2016).

Alice Jedličková is Senior Researcher at the Institute of Czech Literature of the Czech Academy of Sciences, Czech Republic, and Associate Professor of Literature and Intercultural Communication at Masaryk University, Czech Republic. Her research interests include intermedial studies (socio-spatial relations of cultural representations) and its history, literary theory, diachronic poetics and the theory of narrative. She is the co-author, with Stanislava Fedrová, of the interdisciplinary enquiry *Visible Descriptions: Visuality, Suggestivity and Intermediality of Literary Description* (2016). She is also the editor of, and principal contributor to, *Narrative Modes of Nineteenth-Century Czech Prose* (2022). She has published on transmediation as a marker of cultural continuity and on the potential of intermedial approach in education recently.

Richard Müller is Senior Researcher at the Institute of Czech Literature of the Czech Academy of Sciences, Czech Republic, Assistant Professor of Comparative Literature at New York University in Prague, Czech Republic, and Assistant Professor of Literary Criticism and Writing at the Prague School of Creative Communication, Czech Republic. His research interests include

---

* Unless noted otherwise, all publications mentioned are in Czech.

the contextual transformations of literary mediality, the history of semiotics, (post)structuralism and cultural materialism, the genealogies of literary and media theory and the writings of Franz Kafka. He is the editor of the scholarly journal *Czech Literature*, co-author, with Pavel Šidák et al., of *The Dictionary of Modern Literary Theory* (2011), and co-author, with Tomáš Chudý et al., of the Czech edition of *The Emerging Contours of the Medium* (2020).

Martin Ritter is Senior Researcher at the Institute of Philosophy of the Czech Academy of Sciences, Czech Republic. His research interests lie in phenomenology, critical theory, philosophy of technology and media philosophy. As editor and translator, he has prepared a three-volume edition of Walter Benjamin's work, and is author of *Walter Benjamin's Philosophy of Language* (2009). His most recent book is *Into the World: The Movement of Patočka's Phenomenology* (2019, in English).

Josef Šebek is Assistant Professor of Czech and Comparative Literature at the Faculty of Arts of Charles University in Prague, Czech Republic. His research concerns cultural materialism, the sociology of Pierre Bourdieu and current French sociology of literature. He also works on contemporary theory of discourse and rhetoric, media theory of literature, genres of life writing and queer studies. He is the editor of the scholarly journal *Word & Sense* and author of *Literature and the Social: Bourdieu, Williams, and Their Successors* (2019).

Pavel Šidák is Assistant Professor of Literary Criticism and Writing at the Prague School of Creative Communication, Czech Republic, researcher at the Institute of Czech Literature of the Czech Academy of Sciences, Czech Republic, and editor-in-chief of the scholarly journal *Czech Literature*. His research interests include literary theory, literary genology and the relation between literature and folklore. He is the co-author, with Richard Müller et al., of *The Dictionary of Modern Literary Theory* (2011) and author of *Introduction into the Study of Genres* (2018).

Josef Vojvodík is Professor of Czech and Comparative Literature at the Faculty of Arts at Charles University in Prague, Czech Republic. His research focuses on modern literature and visual arts (specifically, symbolicist and post-symbolicist modernism and the avant-garde movements of the 1920s–30s with 'transhistoric' links to Mannerism and Baroque), as well as German and French media, social and cultural anthropology, and phenomenology. He is the author of *Surface, Latency, Ambivalence: Mannerism, Baroque and the (Czech) Avant-Garde* (2008) and *Pathos in Czech Art, Poetry and Artistic-Aesthetic Thinking of the 1940s* (2014).

Acknowledgements

This book is the work of a collective of authors led by Richard Müller, and was conceived as early as 2015 in detailed discussions with Tomáš Chudý. The core of our approach was further elaborated in discussions with Alice Jedličková, Stanislava Fedrová, Josef Šebek and Pavel Šidák (Institute of Czech Literature, Czech Academy of Sciences), and expanded in conversations with Josef Vojvodík and Miroslav Petříček (Department of Czech and Comparative Literature, Faculty of Arts, Charles University, and Institute of Philosophy and Religious Studies, Faculty of Arts, Charles University) and Martin Ritter (Institute of Philosophy, Czech Academy of Sciences). Our joint work over the period 2016–20 led to the Czech edition, *Za obrysy média: Literatura a medialita*.

The effort to adapt this work into an English edition was motivated by our sense of the vital urgency of the topic (as well as encouraged by reviews from Jakub Vaněk, Mariana Prouzová, Marek Debnár, David Vichnar and Vít Gvoždiak). Bloomsbury and its Thinking Media series strike us as the ideal platform for raising questions today about the mediality of literature. The book has been slimmed down; in the process, two chapters were cut, one on nineteenth-century Czech aesthetics by Pavel Šidák, the other by Miroslav Petříček on the context of French philosophy and literature in the 1950s and 1960s from a media philosophical perspective. It has also been adapted for an English-language readership (including contextualization of phenomena and sources used) and selectively updated in terms of latest research and newly emerging topics (large language models, for example, from the point of view of Lotman's semiotics, the relationship between intermediality and multimodality, etc.).

We would like to thank the translators Peter Gaffney and Nicholas Orsillo for rising to their arduous task. The whole process has confirmed to us that artificial intelligence has yet to replace the human element in translating between natural languages.

Both Czech and English versions of the text were supported by many people. First of all, we must thank the reviewers John Guillory and Lars Ellestrôm, not only for providing consultation at several moments of this project but also for their conceptual work in the field, which served and supported us throughout. Sadly, Lars Ellestrôm, with whom some of us had developed a bond of friendship, passed away suddenly in 2021.

We have to thank the readers of the Czech version, Tomáš Dvořák and Bogumiła Suwara, for their invaluable suggestions. We would also like to thank Lisa Gitelman, Leif Weatherby, Clifford Siskin and other members of the Digital Theory Lab at New York University for their feedback during the presentation of various parts of the project, and to Beate Schirrmacher for her detailed comments on Chapter 11. We are grateful to a number of other colleagues for their suggestions and help: Irina O. Rajewsky, Kateřina Krtilová, Kateřina Svatoňová, Michal Jareš, Karel Piorecký, Petr Kaderka, Josef Hrdlička and Libuše Heczková. We are also grateful to the anonymous reviewers of studies that served as the basis in whole or in part of Chapters 2, 5, 6, 8 and 9. I thank Gregory Currie and Emily Troscianko for their suggestions at the colloquium *The Power of Analysis and the Impossibility of Understanding: Lessons from Kafka*, held in Prague in 2017.

Several members of our team participated in the international mobility project 'Boundaries of Literary Science: Literary Communication and Cultural Transfer' (Ministry of Education, Youth and Sport of the Czech Republic), which provided an important opportunity to engage in sustained critical discussion of our work with peers at the Freie Universität Berlin, New York University, Lund University, Linnaeus University and the Linnaeus Centre for Intermedial and Multimodal Studies.

The Thinking Media series editors, Bernd Herzogenrath and Patricia Pisters, provided invaluable assistance and support, and we also thank Katie Gallof, Bloomsbury Publisher in Film and Media Studies. We are very grateful to our colleagues from the Editorial and Textological Department, Lucie Kořínková, Michal Kosák and Kateřina Bínová, for securing financing and administration for the project, and to Jakub Foršt for handling the rights to illustrations. Additional thanks to Daniela Straková, Matěj Kos, Tereza Vondrášková and Josef Šebek for their valued assistance in editing the text.

The two principal contributors thank their dear wives Eliška and Paia for support – to Eliška, moreover, for her vital editorial help – and their children, Beátka and Benjamín, and Filípek, Anička and Madlenka for being.

Richard Müller
Prague, Czech Republic, 14 August 2023

Introduction

Genealogy of the concept of the medium and literary studies

Richard Müller

1. Integrating literary and media study: In search of principles

Starting from an absence

The primary aim of this book is to develop a common basis for the study of literature and media and their respective fields. Such an effort is less straightforward than at first it might appear. We could characterize the dialogue between the two disciplines thus far, briefly but concisely, by each side's long-standing reluctance to listen to the other. This is partly due to the fact that media studies was born precisely out of an effort to radically differentiate its field from the established frameworks of literary disciplines. ('For the "content" of a medium', writes McLuhan in *Understanding Media*, 'is like the juicy piece of meat carried by the burglar to distract the watchdog of the mind.') It remains unclear what 'mediality' means in the context of literary studies, and when this and related issues are raised, they tend to derive from, or remain focused almost exclusively on the questions of digital and network forms of literature. The field of media studies, whose initial 'dissident' tendencies have been succeeded by the self-confidence of a socially necessary discipline, seems little concerned, for its part, with the study of an 'old medium' like literature. This is paradoxical, since its 'founding fathers' Marshall McLuhan and Friedrich Kittler took literature as a natural, even if radically estranged starting point. Today, when words on the page no longer 'quiver with sensuality', and many would prefer to 'hallucinate' (as Kittler might put it) on the computer – perhaps even artificial intelligence – to print forms, has literature become an obscure medium? Or has our fascination with the new merely obscured the mediality of literature from our view?

Even those who, like Friedrich Kittler, feel no need to 'exorcize the spirit' from the humanities (or *Geisteswissenschaften*) will understand that our project – the concurrent differentiation and integration of 'literary' and 'non-literary' mediality – poses formidable challenges. In spite of various encouraging signs – the fact that many of the pioneers of media research came from the field of literary studies, early prefigurings such as *Literatur- und Medienanalyse* and word-and-image studies in the 1980s, as well as the founding of 'literature-centred' intermedial studies in the 1990s, and more recently the emergence at the margins of such approaches as systems theory and actor-network theory (and their extension into literary studies) – this project has made little progress. What we see instead is how the former representatives of these trends have gradually shifted the scope of research to *exclude* literature. Instead of systematic dialogue, what we find is mutual resistance, indifference, or at best partiality.

The renewed effort to integrate these disciplines is motivated by a number of unresolved issues in literary studies: the *unclear* status of the 'material' in literature; the *ambiguous* extent to which new media has had an impact on literary-cultural processes, including such long-established practices as reading and writing; and the difficulty of conceptualizing the role of technics that far *exceeds* the history of written cultures. It is this situation that shapes our methodology from the outset. How do the (initial) conditions of media discourse come into being? How do these conditions affect the basic perspectives of literary study? Our line of enquiry thus takes its starting point from a certain *absence*: *Why* did it take so long for the concept of the medium to emerge, and why has it always remained *latent* in literary fields and related disciplines? Why did it emerge only gradually, during the twentieth century, expanding from media studies proper to other fields, to the point where it could no longer be dismissed – a nagging presence impossible to ignore? Questions like these lead to a host of others, though we may begin with the most basic: What is the medium and what is mediality? How has the long absence of this concept, its latency and emergence – as well as the changes and reversals by which it came to assume its current form – affected the very manner in which literary studies and the humanities formulate related lines of enquiry? In what various forms do we find media studies and its theories today, and how can we choose from among the nearly inexhaustible number of concepts and positions?

Does the reluctance, in the end, to accept literature *as a medium* mean its mediality is somehow not self-evident? We find certain reasons to regard literature in this way, including the imaginative and theoretical fictions that weigh in on the motif of its end: Ray Bradbury's novel *Fahrenheit 451*, for example, where books are burned and replaced by (televisual) simulacra; Kittler's eschatological vision of history, as it 'rewinds to the beginning' to form a loop; predictions about the end of (the concept of) the medium at the dawn of the computer age. Should we think of literature as a medium whose mediality was obscured 'from the beginning' and which 'at the end' will once more cease to be a medium?

Defining the subject

For the reasons outlined above, we must return to earlier stages of the discipline – carried out in such fields as structuralism, semiotics, reader-response theory and post-structuralism – and to its latent assumptions and discoveries regarding mediality (see Chapters 2, 3, 5, 6, 8, 10 and 11). Through this preliminary step, we shall be able to formulate criteria for assessing individual fields in terms of how effectively each one might serve as a point of departure for the mutual integration of literary and media studies. Conversely, media philosophy (*Medienphilosophie*) may also help us work out the best principles and conditions for carrying out this integration. In the pages that follow, we will also look closely at the field in the German context, which provides a specific and relatively recent example of media thinking, as well as a particular philosophical perspective on various issues that would not otherwise be accessible or even thinkable (see Chapters 3 and 4).

Two points should be emphasized about this effort: First, we do not present a collection of essays on the emerging forms of literary media and related methods of enquiry (as do Ensslin, Round and Bronwen 2023), but a collectively developed proposition of a *systematic approach* growing out of an evaluation of the past *and* present of the discipline, its subject and related fields. Second, with this evaluation we propose an assimilation of Anglo-American with German and French (literary, media, cultural and philosophical) theory, while meanwhile maintaining a concurrent focal point in the Central-Eastern European context (Structuralism before and after the Second World War, cultural semiotics). It is the concept of the medium that allows us to draw back into the analysis of literature the various layers that have usually been excluded (the material and technical 'exteriority' of signs, for example; cf. Gumbrecht 1988), or relegated to other disciplines (descriptive and later material bibliography), without thereby losing sight of its other aspects. However, as we will see, such an all-encompassing view of the medium (its 'inner plurality') is difficult to capture, and individual aspects tend to receive more or less emphasis as interests change and analysis shifts focus. Adopting the concept of the medium also entails a media-comparative point of view (see Chapter 11), even where literary criticism once maintained – and still maintains – its monomedia anamnesis. This anamnesis is also explained by the wider media perspective – as a legacy of its (now very shaken) position as a culturally hegemonic 'medium of sense' and the (artistic) medium most thoroughly emancipated, as Hegel argues in his aesthetics, from matter.

Looking at the media studies landscape today, comprised as it is of various individual fields – new media, the theory of intermediality, the theory, history and philosophy of media, *Medienwissenschaft*, media anthropology, comparative media studies, the archaeology, geology and ecology of media, and the theory of individual media or groups of media and so on – we find a vast diversity of contexts and situations in which the terms 'medium' and 'mediality' are deployed. This has partly to do with the different geneses of the study of media across different vernacular contexts, such as media *studies* in the Anglo-American context and media *science* (*Medienwissenschaft*) in Germany. More fundamentally, its very aims and methods may compel us to rethink the conventional division between the hard sciences and humanities (a division that already appears to be called into question by the use of the term *Wissenschaft*). Our first task must therefore be to orient ourselves in the interdisciplinary field from the historical-conceptual as well as cultural-philological perspectives. It remains unclear, however, which theoretical domains should govern the introduction of 'medium' and 'mediality' to the field of literary studies. What is evident is that we should aim to free the concept of the medium from the limits imposed by specific kinds or categories of media, such as the mass media, media technologies or artistic media. Yet there is a strong tendency to project specific media characteristics onto the concept of the medium in general, resulting in a certain 'media blindness' (as Liv Hausken puts it) which is harder to overcome than may first appear. This is not only, as we shall see, because such a tendency has a long historical tradition (with such notable exceptions as Lessing's *Laocoon*, for instance). One starting point is offered by taking account of the functions that media have gradually acquired (as Chapter 1 suggests): to make appear, represent, communicate, store, disseminate, process data and so on. It may also be that our initial efforts to avoid reductive approaches will lead us to other outcomes: an emphasis on the essentially negative character of media, for example, or their relationship to 'appearing' (and 'disappearing'). Or it may lead us to certain discoveries regarding human existence in general, so that a specific question arises regarding the relationship between the mediality of media and that of 'human orientation' (see Chapter 4). Alternatively, the negativity of media may be explained with regard to the way it stimulates the unconscious – we may regard this as its central function – giving rise in turn to specific configurations of desire (desire to capture reality 'as it is', in the first place). This brings us back to the processes mentioned above, and to developments characterized by their multiplication and stratification. Media can do more and more; *and yet something still eludes them (and us) in the act of mediation.*

Genealogy of the concept and genealogy as a method

Throughout this volume, our intention is not (only) to write a history of the concept of the medium, nor (only) some discrete segment in the history of the humanities and social sciences. We certainly do share some of the initial beliefs of these kinds of historiographies: for example, that in order to understand a certain state of the discipline, one must know its early stages and motivations. To what extent then may we overcome the preconceptions imposed by our contemporary perspective? This question, however, does not apply to us, since we are compelled to build on the media system at its current stage of development. Our thinking here thus relies heavily on *genealogy*, a concept that already suggests a retrospective point of view. Just as it is only possible to trace a family history starting from the present and working backwards in time, so too we find it necessary to work through the genealogy of media by first recognizing the contemporary situation. It is not simply a matter of relocating some aspect of the past that now lies deep beneath the surface, waiting to be discovered. We are reminded here of Yuri Lotman's noteworthy remarks on historical method in the context of his search for the principles of an historical semiotics: 'history is a strange film that, when it is run backwards, will *not* get us back to the first frame'. (We therefore use the term 'genealogy' with only indirect reference to Foucault's concept; more apt would be an analysis of his genealogical position within media theory – one that Friedrich Kittler, in his own way, has already carried out.)

It follows from Lotman's remark that history *is not* like a film; some processes are simply irreversible, and the same is true of history and historiography. However, isn't it precisely media that introduce a special 'partial reversibility' into the live event, one moreover that can be mutually translated, combined, layered, or – often not entirely – deleted? Lotman's historical semiotics, however, also shows us how these transformations are themselves irreversible if they include what he calls a 'generative' aspect (see Chapter 10). A genealogy of the concept of the medium needs to be carried out with reference to the development of media as such.

By taking the 'verbal functions' of the medium as our point of departure, as suggested earlier, we consciously contain this moment of backwards projection (in the manner of a 'circular argument'). In this case it is precisely media and their development that give rise to functions and operations that we may then retroactively identify in their older (more rudimentary) form. In cinema, for example, it can be said that we first become aware of that aspect of media processing Friedrich Kittler later called 'editing'. From there, however, it begins to appear as something much older, something that has been part of aesthetic practices and poetics since time immemorial, and as such appearing also 'after cinema', in the poetic and artistic works of Jiří Kolář, for example (see Chapter 6).

The development and genealogy of the concept cannot therefore be separated from the development of media, although there is probably no causal link, especially if media themselves are linked to one another not only materially and technologically, but above all by virtue of their semiotic and self-reflexive potential. In the final analysis, the 'media' character of media only emerges once they have forged a deeper involvement with culture: the moment their functions grow more expansive, when they integrate with older media and define themselves with regard to them, when they differentiate their various forms and formats, and when they give rise to social circles made up of their recipients and creators.

Perhaps, unlike tools and cultural techniques, media can be defined by their capacity for (self-)reflexivity, that is, their tendency to appear reproduced in themselves and in one another. While even this definition is the subject of ongoing discussion (Bernhard Siegert is among those who argue that cultural techniques are equally self-reflexive), it provides us with a starting point that seems historically necessary from the perspective of literary studies – the starting point and perspective of communication broadly conceived, or 'sign systems'. As Claude Lévi-Strauss has shown, cooking only becomes possible as a (social) practice insofar as it constitutes certain structural differences. However, the real problem arises when we want to reveal, or communicate this self-reflexivity (in a weak sense), or else put it into circulation. It is no wonder that Bernhard Siegert did not carry out his analysis by cooking (although it is not entirely inconceivable), and that we most often convey certain distinctions using such techniques as writing and reading. It could be said that cultural techniques, in the most basic sense, constitute the underlying precondition for the event of communication, indeed determining whether it will take place at all. But that does not mean that this moment is the sole constituting or determining factor. Why not? The simple but compelling answer is that there is always a plurality of techniques (or media) – a range of alternatives – for 'constituting' reality. There is always yet another semi-translatable 'ontic operation'. The evasiveness of the Real is itself evidence of the invariably secondary nature of cultural techniques (see Chapters 5 and 7).

We will note that in literary studies, the first significant changes brought about vis-à-vis media thinking took place with the introduction of the concept of communication and the question of its *boundaries*. A particularly telling example of this can be found in Czech structuralism and structural semiotics, which we deal with in Chapter 2. As Jan Mukařovský observes, it is not only literary works that engage in processes of communication, but also buildings and paintings: the 'diffuse' manner in which a building organizes the space of human activity, for instance. After all, the absence of linguistically articulated signs can be seen as marking the origins of modern poetry. The Prague School, for its part, also contributed to the modern theory of communication – and, of course, to the theory of signs. Yet it seems specific to media that they can challenge established oppositions, for example between image and verbal message. What processes of mediation (including technical development) lead to a situation in which the accepted distinctions are presently exceeded? Every media relationship also indicates the *limits* of what can be considered a sign, a general model or manner in which to articulate a sign. As Roman Jakobson points out in his essay 'Is the Film in Decline?' (1933), even though the basic condition of the film sign is that of an articulation (editing and montage), it is not the same as the linguistic sign. But even Jakobson – a keen observer of modernity – does not seem certain about how far this difference goes (see Chapters 2 and 6).

Mediality thus seems to emerge only when it makes perceptible that which was previously beyond the horizon of perception; notably, this is often – even if not only – in the contact and competition that arises among actual (emerging) media. There is evidently a persistent tension here between the concept of the medium as a means of 'communication' and mediality in the broader sense; this too will inevitably play a role in our reflections.

By turning our attention to the development of media, and inevitably also to media as a reflection or making of history, we see how the effects of media and technology in human society are multidirectional and cannot be traced to a single source, not even to the cultural techniques that seem (but only seem) to serve as their groundwork. Every technique, as Erhard Schüttpelz aptly points out, is always already cultural. Similarly, anthropologist Pierre Lemonnier demonstrates that no practice or technique – what André Leroi-Gourhan calls 'operational chains' – can be transferred from one culture to another without undergoing a process of transformation (quite often a fundamental one). What this suggests is that techniques are not really the constitutive factor; rather, it is culture or society as a whole that plays this role, much more so than any of its individual parts or factors. Starting from this premise we might logically conclude that the evolution of media is characterized by its essentially contingent nature. But there are other lines of thought that lead us to understand this evolution as a function of unconscious desires and wishes (see Chapter 7). Put another way, if 'medial conditions' can, on the one hand, be extended to include the pre-reflexive assumptions of perceptions themselves (see also Chapter 5), these same conditions, on the other hand, belong to the horizons of a thing so complex that, as in meteorology, our deterministic models and predictions are not likely to have any real prognostic value. Several chapters offer different (but related) conceptualizations of this complex of connections, from the point of view of 'culture and society' (Chapter 8), 'social systems' (Chapter 9) and Lotman's 'semiosphere' (Chapter 10). As we will see, especially in the last two chapters (10 and 11), institutional environments can also serve as a microcosm for analysing the conditions of media and mediality in the broadest sense.

A genealogical reconstruction of the concept of the medium may draw on a number of previous studies. We are especially inspired, however, by the work of Georg Christoph Tholen, John Guillory, Stefan Hoffmann and Jens Schröter. One of the most important findings of Guillory's article 'Genesis of the Media Concept' (2010) is that if the Western philosophical tradition was under pressure to grasp the medium of communication in theoretical terms, this had something to do with the discourses of the arts – 'arts', that is, in the sense of *technai*, including 'mechanical arts' and such historical disciplines as grammar, dialectic and rhetoric (i.e. the medieval *trivium*), as well as 'fine arts' in the contemporary sense. According to Guillory, the notion of media emerged in the late nineteenth century in response to 'the proliferation of new technical media – such as the telegraph and phonograph – that could not be assimilated to the older system of the arts'. As a consequence, these new technical media 'perplexed thereafter the relation between the traditional arts and media of any kind'. It was the 'emergence of new technical media', Guillory argues, that 'seemed to reposition the traditional arts as ambiguously both media and precursors to the media' (Guillory 2010: 321–2). This way of reconstructing the concept of the medium shows how a certain kind of mediality becomes visible in the process of 'remediation', or 'transmediation', and how the emergence of new media technologies typically leads to the recognition of their latent presence in older means of communication and representation – just as the invention of the letterpress led to considerations about the latent presence of printing techniques in the process of writing by hand (as Francis Bacon suggests in *Novum Organum*).

One of the basic features of the genealogical model is that the history of theoretical thinking on the concept of the medium is connected with specific medial conditions. We should notice, however, another feature of media development here: the opposition to, and critique of, technology and media along cultural and eschatological lines, the motivating factors of which are clearly not limited to the reactionary tendency. In the context of artistic and critical reflections on the disembodying yet technically materialized modern media, such themes as the body, images, dreams and the knowledge of death (as anthropological phenomena) are more intensively discussed and represented. This is accompanied by a rise in the belief in various paraphenomena. In these acts of imagination and critique, 'reality itself' acquires a certain spectral aspect; ghosts, conversely, seem to become real. Chapter 4 raises the question of where this resistance to media comes from and what kind of 'negativity' (as understood by later media philosophy) it implies.

We must also take into account the ways in which the (accelerating) development of communication *dispositifs* represent a process of democratization (see Chapters 1, 7 and 8), as they expand opportunities for an increasingly diverse range of actors to engage in 'content creation'. This involves, on the one hand, the need to establish corresponding processes of inculturation, and to master the relevant media competencies. On the other hand, a certain inert power on the part of media and media technologies arises in this context. While one could reasonably argue that the foundations of Western civilization (as elsewhere) are built on certain structures of inequality that the expansion of communication *dispositifs* has helped in part to redress – in particular, by expanding access to the possibilities and means of communication – we also notice how these same media technologies inevitably become part of the systems through which access is regulated. Think of today's willing engagement of users to provide feedback (even if unknowingly) to improve current large language models, possibly contributing to the oligopolization of AI by Big Tech.

Constitutive questions and issues

Returning now to our point of departure – the current situation and genealogy of the concept of the medium – we find it is not possible to reduce the fully developed stage of this concept, nor the whole range of media theories proper to a single set of characteristics. It may be useful, however, to enumerate a network of topics by which theories on media and mediality in their more recent stages of development – that is, from the 1960s to the present – relate to one another as their fundamental questions and issues. By a fully developed concept of the medium we do not mean to suggest any unified or unifying concept (which does not exist), but rather a concept that is strategically central (as in McLuhan's oft-quoted statement that 'the medium is the message'). We present this network of subjects with the disadvantage that many individual points are based on different, sometimes even directly opposite, assumptions; others, conversely, are based on assumptions that partially overlap. They include the following in particular:

1. the interconnectedness of all media and of art as a whole (media are not just 'mass media', as they are commonly understood), that is, the

inevitable mutual relations that are formed among the various means of recording, reproduction, distribution and data processing;
2. the migration of contents, forms and structures across various media; simultaneously, the competition between 'old' and 'new' media, as well as the various substitutions and adaptations that take place between them (between novel and film, for example); remediation processes and their effects (the manner in which media tend to remove themselves from the experiences they make possible, while simultaneously highlighting their presence), media integration and accumulation;
3. issues related to the material and corporeal realization of signs, representation and communication, and to criteria for differentiating between their technicality, materiality and/or corporeality;
4. questions regarding logic and dynamics within the development of communication and media technologies, together with their multilateral influence (e.g. in the sense of 'recursive operational chains'), as well as 'cultural techniques' that establish the very conditions of possibility for the culture/nature distinction;
5. the heterogeneity of reception circuits within a single medium, or across various media, and reshaping of the recipients' communities in the overall cultural context;
6. awareness of the limits of extending monomedia paradigms to other media fields, and of the limits of applying categories based on written cultures to non-written cultural practices and techniques, as well as imposing the parameters pertaining to one kind of media on others;
7. issues regarding collective creative processes, shaped or made possible by media; the way this encroaches on the very essence of the artefact, and related changes in the concept of reception (e.g. interactivity), the work (hypertext) and so on;
8. the capacity of a medium to perform several functions simultaneously, such as data transmission, recording, processing and manipulation;
9. the structural gap inherent to processes of 'inscription', communication, imagining and thinking; media difference as a precondition inscribed within the very core of being in the world.

2. The emerging contours of the medium: Outline

Developed by eight authors on the basis of regular discussions, readings and mutual review of one another's contributions, *The Emerging Contours of the Medium* is both an edited volume and a work of collaborative writing.

Introduction 11

The principles for a media theory of literature are elaborated within three main research areas, which are reflected in the major focus of each of the three parts of the book: (1) the prehistory of media thinking, (2) media philosophy and negative media anthropology, and (3) intersections between media and literary theory with a view to developing a shared basis. The division of the volume into three parts, in fact, reflects a certain proposal for how to structure the concept of the medium itself. The first part raises basic questions regarding the genealogical definition and conceptualization of media evolution. It also engages the prehistory of media thinking, as well as what is recognized as one of the key moments in the emergence of media awareness in literary thinking: the Prague School's engagement with mediality from late 1920s to 1940s. The second part then emphasizes various fundamental dimensions of the medium concept that are difficult to subsume under any evolutionary framework, and demonstrates from various new angles how (the history of) media thinking is shaped in large part by its lacunae and negativity. The third part deals more directly with the ways media, as *dispositifs* that *articulate* various modes of perception and communication, provide a basis for identifying more general phenomena that arise either between media (in their mutual synergy or contradictions), between media artefacts, or between man and apparatus. The relationship between mediality and literature, like the question of literature as a medium in particular, is an ongoing issue throughout the volume and the specific concern of several chapters.

The following outline describes individual chapters in terms of their central lines of enquiry, questions and motivations. Numerous thematic and methodological connections between the chapters are indicated by cross-references, the further exploration of which we leave to the discretion of the reader.

Chapter 1 asks, What is a medium?, following a genealogical-etymological approach to identify various semantic layers that make up the term as we find it today. In this way, it seeks to identify those characteristics which have emerged in close connection to the development of media, in particular those processes – or 'verbal functions' – that the medium makes possible. These are also the subject of key theories on the evolution of media. Within this framework, Chapter 1 focuses on the varying relationships between the technical and social aspects of the medium, explaining how wider access involved the expansion of certain media competencies: the ability to create and work with the relevant signs, for example. The question arises here: How can we reconcile the two apparently irreconcilable global aspects within a single term – that is, the 'medium' both as *means* and *environment*?

In the context of the Prague School's classical period, we will be searching for traces of a more systematic reflection on mediality. Crucial here is a conjunction between the premise that all arts communicate and signify, albeit differently (the communication via signs premise), and the rapid transformation of art forms and materials (including film technology). The Prague School thus came under certain pressure to provide new definitions for the sphere of the arts. What were the basic theoretical consequences of adopting a comparative approach to the layering of time in film (as an emerging medium), epic poetry and theatre? How is (functionalist) architecture reflected in Jan Mukařovský's concept of the aesthetic function, especially in light of a certain tension between linguistic and architectural functionalism? In the Prague School's reflections on theatre, what changes can we see in the concept of the actor, and in the relationship between sign and thing? Mediality begins to appear here as a latent concept, which takes shape specifically at the intersection of Structuralist thinking and the artistic avant-garde and its utopias, especially in its synthetic dimension.

In Chapter 3, the same context leads on the author to consider Walter Benjamin's media philosophy as a crucial component of his thinking. In Benjamin, the medium cannot be identified with technology; rather, it comprises the manner in which human perception is organized, in relation to the influence of both nature and history. He proceeds to discuss the continuity of Benjamin's thought, tracing the connections between, on one hand, his late reflections on film, architecture and the modern city (the problem of dispersed and tactile perception), and, on the other, his early preoccupations with fantasy, language and translation (the paradoxical immediacy of the medium). What Benjamin offers is an exploration of the problem of the medium in modern society from what can be considered in hindsight as a visionary perspective.

Chapter 4 draws attention to what we earlier described as 'resistance' to media, turning to its negativity in the context of modern German (and French) cultural, social and philosophical anthropology – the eschatological critiques of new technologies in the interwar and post-war periods (by Günther Anders, e.g.), as well as their mythological invocations (as resurrections of the 'archaic vision', for instance). Critical reflections on the new modern media, framing it as both disembodying and technically materialized, are shown to have implications beyond that of a generally reactionary attitude. In this context, as in art, the liminal phenomena associated with physical human existence and its disappearance (body impressions, ashes, tears, spectres) become subject to representation. The chapter aims to explain how this, together with the colonization of the human image by digital media (Hans Belting), is related to the more fundamental character of the image as double, and how the mediality of the medium is configured along these lines. To this end, it takes into account several symptomatic art works, death masks and post-mortem photographies (Alberto Giacometti, Jindřich Štyrský and Bohumil Kubišta).

The fifth chapter partly follows the findings of Chapters 2 and 4, exploring the limits of signification as they arise in relationship to the *gesture*. It is explained how gesture can be conceived simultaneously as social object-image and physical or semantic movement, as well as a staging of the connection between (communication) technology and the body. Serving here as the first point of departure is Jan Mukařovský's concept of *semantic gesture* and *unintentionality*. What conclusions may we draw from the fact that the 'planes' of the literary work which come together in the semantic gesture are concurrently generated by it – that they are born 'in contact with it'? It is with an interest in addressing this question in broader terms that the argument turns, in the second part, to André Leroi-Gourhan's concept of the 'mythogram'. On its basis, how can we understand the embryonic form of media that transcends the idea of writing, and even the opposition between word and image? How to understand the exteriority of the sign? In its third and final part, a number of topics from earlier in the chapter are re-examined in the context of Vladimir Nabokov's short story 'The Vane Sisters' (1951). The story stages a paradoxical duality of the hiddenness and visibility of sense (in the image and in writing). But couldn't Nabokov's story also be related to the broader conditions of a certain type of writing and literature?

If Chapter 2 deals primarily with the semiotic theories of communication in their initial stages, Chapter 6 picks up on one of their common threads: new trends in the field of semiotics in the post-war era through the 1960s, under the influence of information theory and cybernetics. What implications to the study of media have emerged in this context? How did the cybernetic and information transmission models change when confronted with the literary work as form of communication and with semiotic thinking? In this context, the chapter traces the thinking of Roman Jakobson, Max Bense, Umberto Eco and Miroslav Červenka to the point where the complexities of literary and artistic communication cause the original information theory and cybernetics inspiration to 'implode'. At the same time, this approach gives birth to the 'paradigm' of openness, which emerged explicitly in the context of elucidating experimental art and literature of the period. How did the concept of 'openness' influence or prefigure the concept of the reader – one of Umberto Eco's central concerns in his later work? How should we understand the concept of 'noise' in the context of non-technical communication? In what way was the original Structuralist conception of the aesthetic function transformed in this context? Thinking through these questions leads us to the final part of Chapter 6, which addresses Czech experimental poetry of the 1960s, and, in particular, a specific trajectory of the artistic post-avant-garde, whose works were shaped by the information-aesthetic understanding of creativity, while at the same time exceeding it. How did the influence of cybernetics and information aesthetics differ within the field of experimental poetry? What is the legacy of this 'moment' for the conception of literature as a medium?

The discussion then turns to technics and technology via two partly complementary, partly opposing frameworks. Chapter 7 analyses the medium as a technical apparatus in the context of the philosophy and theory of technics (and their genealogy), beginning with Ernst Kapp and the idea of technology as an extension of the unconscious, and working through the transformation of this concept to the present. How exactly are we to understand the relationship between human activity and technical aids? Erhard Schüttpelz's position fittingly emphasizes here the need to focus on the alternating process of mutual determination that joins technology and man at the pre-individual level. What insight do we find in Marshall McLuhan's distinction between 'hot' and 'cold' media, taking into account related media competencies on the part of their users and audiences? We proceed by working through Hartmut Winkler's semiotic reconstruction of McLuhan's theses before turning to the topic of data manipulation (Friedrich Kittler and Lev Manovich) as a prerequisite for artistic creation (and a characteristic feature of contemporary media). Winkler's notion of media as 'de-contextualization machines' raises several further questions: How should we understand the economy of signs and discourses? What insights does this framework bring to the domain of literature? The chapter ends with the question: How can we distinguish between data, information, signs and messages, and between information and communication? (Here we examine Manfred Faßler's concept of 'infogenic man'.) This sets the stage for Chapter 9, which discusses literature in the context of a systems theory of the medium.

Chapter 8 examines some of the paradoxes within Raymond Williams's media thinking, which he develops in the context of cultural theory and cultural materialism. This context provides an important counterexample to the anti-humanist tendencies of Kittler's concept of technics discussed in the previous chapter. It also provides us with a perspective on the social causes and effects of media phenomena (already anticipated in Chapter 2 with Walter Benjamin). The chapter follows three main lines of enquiry. First, it examines a certain (dis)continuity in Williams's thinking about the medium in works published from the late 1950s to the early 1980s. How does Williams's key notion of communication relate to issues of media, especially as it may be understood in a world-making sense encompassing both artistic and non-artistic communication? Another area of concern is Williams's relation to

McLuhan's theory. What are the specific points of Williams's critique of 'technological determinism'? Are the two approaches really so incompatible? A third line of consideration focuses on the topics of dissolution, solution, precipitate and structures of feeling as a framework for contextualizing Williams's works in relation to media. What model does Williams propose for the interrelationship of such disparate spheres as literature, art, politics and economics? What are its merits and shortcomings?

Parallels can be found in Williams's thinking to both Luhmann's systems theory and Lotman's semiotics of culture, to which the following two chapters are devoted. Chapter 9 provides analysis of the concept of media through the lens of a sociologically oriented systems theory, picking up on the discussion of media evolution raised in Chapter 1. Systems theory is based in large part on the notion of the 'improbability of communication' and the process of functional differentiation of communication systems in modern societies (Niklas Luhmann). The aim here is to better understand the way symbolically generalized communication media play the role of what Luhmann calls 'uncertainty absorption', and the underlying mutual conversion of differences (information) that this involves. Considering art as a functional social system, we ask: What is the (symbolically generalized) medium of art? This line of enquiry sheds light on various problems we face in trying to define the system's code; to a greater extent than other systems, there is a tendency here to invert the relations of traditions, functions and performance techniques. Following this line of reasoning, we arrive at the question, with reference to Rainer Leschke's theory and David Mitchell's *Cloud Atlas* (2004) as a case study: How should we understand 'forms' in relation to media and how should we distinguish (between various kinds of) media within their movement?

Having explored several ways in which medial issues intersect with the development of semiotics in Chapters 2, 6 and 7, there are several features – namely, a regard for different kinds of sign systems and the limits of sign processes, the discovery of systemic complexity, as well as a peculiar literary and cultural-historical approach – that motivate us in Chapter 10 to examine the works of Yuri Lotman. Our aim here is to understand what new insights Lotman's cultural semiotics brings to literary-media thinking. Lotman's point of departure is the distinction between various functions of culture (or 'semiotic objects') – its memory, creative and transmissive functions – and in the incompatibility of differently constructed codes or orientations of communication. Such incongruity is understood as culturally generative. The chapter further explores the role played in culture by the collision of different sets of codes (as distinct media regimes). It is then shown how these questions lead Lotman to the concept of the 'semiosphere' as semiotic continuum. This raises the question: What approach should we take to overcome the characteristic technical blindness of cultural semiotics? Do Lotman's observations provide us with an effective principle for conceptualizing artificial intelligence – and the automatic processes in literature? This last point turns our attention to Mary-Laure Ryan's dichotomy between immersion and interactivity as basic modalities of experiencing art and literature, and to Wolfgang Iser's work *The Act of Reading* as a possible (even if insufficient) corrective to her concept.

Genealogy proves to be an especially effective methodology in Chapter 11: the family tree of ideas, attitudes, approaches and schools that preceded intermedial studies is extremely rich. The survey of prehistory and history of the discipline (comprising proto- and pre-intermedial concepts) suggests that one of the key factors in the evolution of intermedial thinking has been the idea of comparing arts (however diverse the reasons of such activity). We therefore ask what possibilities were opened up, and what limits in turn were established by this tradition? What were the consequences of taking art and its properties so long for granted? Mapping the intermedial landscape allows us to observe the gradual emergence of the medium. Nevertheless, the question arises why has it taken so long to arrive at a clear definition of medium? Why was it preceded by a typology of intermedial relations? What was/is the role of literature in this context? Which media relations defined the interests of intermedial studies and why? Which other methodologies and disciplines exercised significant influence on intermedial research? Does intermedial studies have a chance to become a methodology underlying any and all cultural study? Or is just one of numerous disciplines enquiring into the processes of meaning-making and aspiring to control the landscape of cultural representation and communication?

The joint reflection that makes up the final chapter of the book is an attempt to concentrate and confront the key findings of individual chapters, with respect to the horizon of a media theory of literature, the elaboration of which seems essential for literary (but also media) disciplines. The chapter is thus presented in the form of a polylogue, born from a series of discussions by all the authors together.

1

The 'medium': Concept and history

Tomáš Chudý

1. Conceptual (pre-)history of the medium

Delimiting the 'medium': Functional perspective

In search of the concept of the medium, it is a good idea to first distinguish it from related concepts. Let's begin with two, on the understanding that they are not necessarily the only two possible: the medium is not merely a tool, nor is it merely a form. It is not entirely identifiable with a hammer or pliers, for example, nor is it only a specific form of communication.[1] We might also add that it is not identical with a machine, though this belongs rather to the analysis of new media and technics. The medium is used for a certain spectrum of activities[2] that are usually referred to collectively as 'cultural production', in contrast to natural mediators, such as air for the transmission of (culturally insignificant) sound. An important distinction emerges, moreover, between the simple uncoded mediation of meaning, on one hand, and encoded forms of media, on the other, that therefore require a sophisticated interface for translating deeply embedded code into a user surface.

As we trace these two conceptual constituents of the medium, which we might define provisionally as that which is not-merely-tool and not-merely-form, it will also be necessary to clarify which processes or functions we are tracing. In this respect, we will not proceed from general substantive features (social institutions, materiality, instrumentality, transportation) or prepositions (*meta*, *dia* or *über*, cf. Mersch 2010), but from verbs that characterize the kinds of operations that media ought to serve. In fact, there are different possible approaches, including a nominal-adverbial approach, which draws on spatial prepositions, and a verbal approach, which deals on the contrary with time and processuality, and in which media are assigned meaning on the basis of verbs, or functions. It is the latter, however, which better captures what is generally understood as a medium (not only in media theory), whereas prepositions, understood as they are largely in the abstract, lead to the extension of the concept to phenomena that are intuitively difficult to classify, often without providing sufficient basis for distinguishing between 'medium' and 'art', and thereby obscuring the analysis of common 'medial' features. Substantive qualifiers are also problematic in that they often cannot fully comprise the functions which will be necessary to define: technical apparatuses per se do not define mediality until communication, storage, manipulation and so on are attributed to them (without that, they are mere machines: for example, a milling machine), nor even do material supports (it depends on what they support). As for the medium as a set of institutions, they too are constituted by their function, as we will see when we deal with the origins of media theory and theory of social organization. Conversely, contextually determined media (cf. Chapter 11, pp. 414–15)[3] permit us to work with contexts that capture a certain function, but they do not involve the functional aspect as a primary focus, and this prevents us from using them to fully analyse its potential. It is essential to bring to light the dynamics of change that the operations go through, and eventually also the reciprocal relationship between the operations and the medium.

Obviously, the functions of media may refer to different actions. For example, dissemination, paradoxically, is also a kind of bringing near (the further information is disseminated, the closer a source comes to its addressee). The notion of the medium as something that extends the body, as McLuhan conceives of it, may refer however to any technology, illustrated par excellence by the prefix *tele-* (Hörisch 2001: 63). It is not enough merely to indicate whether the action is adverbially far or near, since it is communication that is actually the heart of the matter. If we neglect it, a hyperinflation of the concept of the medium occurs, to the point that it may equally refer to a bicycle and a dress (in a non-semiotic sense, considered simply as an extension of the skin).

In addition, the functional-verbal aspect can also be found in the German classics (not only) of media theory, especially the works of Niklas Luhmann and Friedrich Kittler, who distinguish between dissemination media (*Verbreitungsmedien*), recording media (*Speichermedien*) and media that allow for the editing, manipulation and rearrangement of content (giving rise to a certain reflexive potential within a medium in relation to itself, unlike a telephone, for example),[4] communication media, and eventually mass media and technological media (as opposed, for example, to sheer sound, i.e. sound that is not captured as a written score, a gramophone record, a CD or music roll). These categories partially overlap, but not completely – and that is essential.

As mentioned above, one alternative is offered by Dieter Mersch, for example, with the prepositions *meta* and *dia*, which point to a certain topology, or make certain relationships visible. To this extent, they enrich the theoretical consideration of media, but their aim is not to isolate a particular function. Indeed, Mersch resorts to such differences when he summarizes what these prepositions imply: pure processuality (Georg Christoph Tholen), or the function epitomized by the Latin word *experire*, highlighting both the 'experimental' and 'per-formative' inclination (or pressure) of the media. *Experire, performare* – these are the kinds of functions that involve pressing into a form, but also the 'experience of experiment', which, as suggested by the Indo-European root *per-yo* (in Latin *periri*), also means 'to try' or 'to test', and therefore to transition to something yet unknown, to create and experience difference as a definition of information (regarding that which is transmitted by media as well as the media themselves and their invention). (On experimentation, see also Chapter 6, p. 187 and p. 220.) Media are thus intrinsically connected with the act of testing and inventing, and so also with the notion of the 'technological a priori' (esp. Kittler). Yet this act is always carried out with a particular aim, even if it may shift or develop in a new and unintended direction – indeed, it is precisely in this aspect that the function of the medium is revealed. Topological prepositions thus bring us back to what media specifically can and should do.

The relevant verbs are therefore: *to communicate, represent, store* and *preserve, accelerate* (data exchange), *draw into proximity, edit, disseminate* (messages), *mass distribute*, but also *code, transmit* and *calculate* in the technological sense. All these senses are usually mixed together, however, which raises issues for theories that specialize in only one or more such verbs (functions). While the dominant sense is often that of *mediation*, at least in a certain branch of research, this is more often a source of misunderstanding – that is, when lacking a detailed definition of other functions – than a clarifying feature. Generally speaking, it is necessary to clarify which functions we have in mind before media can be (functionally) compared.[5] As a result, the characteristics and connections we attribute to 'media' do not apply to, or properly characterize, all media. The prehistory of the medium concept then traces its emergence *avant la lettre*, but is biased by the specific verb/function we choose. For example, we may be interested in the way information (news, messages) is transmitted, disseminated, processed or stored.

But how did these operational functions reveal themselves in the first place? Currently, media history and, more recently, media archaeology are often practiced in response to this question. We will later highlight approaches in these fields to the evolution of media. First, however, it will be necessary to examine some crucial phases of the prehistory of the *concept*, as this would allow us to trace those conceptual elements to which use of the word 'medium' has gradually been extended.

No sooner do we start out in this direction, however, than we begin running into various hidden assumptions. We are compelled to ask: *Which elements?* But the answer depends on the particular media function we were tracing. The circle is complete. To break out of it, we may consider our line of enquiry primarily to concern technical (or technological) media, which, roughly speaking, began to dominate the world of media in the nineteenth century: '"Technique" was no longer understood in the sense of a technique of representation or rhetoric, as a technique of forms or art of writing, but as a machine, an objectified technology – already with letterpress and binding techniques, but finally also with photography, telegraphy, gramophone records, radio, film and television (and essentially also later with digital media)' (Faulstich 2006: 61). It is a long arc of history, however, that leads to this moment. As we retrace it we attempt to outline a certain dichotomy in the 'medium', and then to map it precisely onto the background of that differentiating effort.

Evidence and records of concept and function

At the beginning, we find Aristotle's *Poetics* on artistic communication, and specifically those places where most translations choose the term 'means' (and some even 'medium'). However, the Greek original is much more terse: *ἐν ἑτέροις* ('in various'), and eventually as a recapitulation in 1448a, *ἐν οἷς* ('in which'). It is always the function of a pronoun, used with the preposition *ἐν* ('in'), invariably referring in a broad sense to the environment, that is, to 'that *in* which'. That it has not yet come to refer to the instrument or means is confirmed by the preposition, given that the Greek third case in its instrumental function would have to be used without any preposition. At the same time, this 'environment' is not just an empty space, but one that serves to mediate something, namely *mimesis* (as paint applied to canvas, for example, or rhythm to voice). It is therefore neither merely a *means* (nothing prevents us here from using the term *organon*) nor merely an indeterminate *environment* (*χώρα*). Rather, it is 'something in between', which does not yet have a name and can only be expressed by a prepositional phrase.

Moving on now to the actual term 'medium', we find that the original Latin meaning includes the sense of an 'abstract public'[6] ('rem in medium vocare', 'cogitationes evocat in medium', 'pellitur e medio sapientia'), and of a 'commonality' or 'community' ('in medium consulere, consultare', 'laudem conferentes potium in medium quam ex communi ad se trahentes', 'in medium mors omnis abit'), and also of a 'neutrality' or something 'left undecided'. From this last sense arises the aspect of indifference towards the *contents* of the medium – an approach often criticized by those (esp. McLuhan) who understand the contents precisely as something the medium predetermines.

It can be noted in passing that already in the classical Roman period the word 'communication' (from the Latin *communicō*) acquires the common meaning of 'sharing ideas',[7] 'information' and 'plans',[8] and even of 'consulting and talking with an audience',[9] 'connecting different parts' (surviving today in the notion of 'communication' as a 'connecting channel, line or passage'), but also 'to share material goods'.

It is only in this connection between the concept of the medium and communication, revealing a symbiosis between them, that certain aspects of mediality, such as the social function of the media, begin to be fully manifested. Thus, we might say provisionally that what we now mean by the term 'media' is always also *communication* media (while its other early references, 'ether' for example, are not implied). This is because we understand both media and communication to involve sharing (a shared understanding of signs, selection of contents, act of communication, etc.) – a fact that is also evident in Guillory's (2010) treatment of the topic. We are here referring to verbal forms of communication, but later also purely audio or visual forms, that is, signs in the broadest sense. When defining media, it is therefore important to define that which persists from the concept of communication (but which concept – ancient or modern, or both?) and remains latent in the concept of the 'medium'.

Further indications can be found in medieval Latin, where the term 'medium' carries the sense – at this point still non-technological – of a mediator of sensory perceptions (the Latin translation of Avicenna;[10] and abundantly in Thomas Aquinas' comments on Aristotle's *De anima*; cf. Hagen 2008), but also the general meaning of 'mediation', or, more specifically, means in relation to institutions or to God. The difference lies between immediacy and mediation by which something from the outside is communicated to the soul. And with this, we move from the medium as environment towards an instrumental conception.

We may further argue that, in addition to the aesthetic variant (the medium through which the image passes before it is perceived), which reveals the materiality of the medium (*medium diaphanum*, a transparent medium that is present but remains in the background), there is also, from Paracelsus onwards (cf. Schröter 2014: 15), the metaphorical extension of this sense to mean 'that through which a supernatural phenomenon appears', which persists to the nineteenth-century phenomenon of the 'spiritual medium'. Other metaphors – the dream as a medium, for example – de-emphasize the material aspect, and thus also the sensory perceptibility of the medium.

Even here, however, that which is communicated consists of signs (also in the sense of good and bad signs, i.e. 'omens').

The notion of the medium in connection to perceptibility lasted practically until the onset of the founding age of media (Kittler). In the French context, we find the functionally equivalent term *milieu* in the early seventeenth century with Mersenne and Descartes (or, according to some, later with Boulainvilliers), a term that maintains the meaning of a material through which something passes (air, water, etc. – cf. Newton (1730/1704: 195, 205 and 229) who includes ether as an 'ambient medium').[11] D'Alembert includes the entry 'milieu' in the *Encyclopédie*, which 'in Mechanical Philosophy, means a material space through which a body passes in its motion, or [. . .] in which a body is placed' (incidentally, the entry for 'medium' redirects to 'milieu' as the more common term). During the nineteenth century, in the context of the natural sciences (botany, zoology), the term 'milieu' refers to the local determination of a set of conditions that affect an organism. Here – as in the investigation of optical phenomena – the emphasis is on the environment as a determined space in which something can take place, perhaps also because the expression *moyen* soon comes into use as a standard designation for 'means'.[12] Charles Bonnet (1720–94) uses the term 'milieu' to refer to the senses through which the soul perceives.[13]

Other evolutions are more familiar. As the classic media theorist Raymond Williams (1983/1976: 203–4) suggests, the concept of the medium has shifted from the general designation for a means (spoken and written language, for example) to a more technical meaning, wherein the mediating role is amplified by increasing the dimensions of communication (mass media). This, of course, is the second part of the development whose beginnings we wish to trace. What did this development look like? As concerns the instrumental sense of 'medium', the turning point took place between the fifteenth and sixteenth centuries with the development of technologies first in the optical and acoustic fields (the lens and later *camera obscura*, as well as telescope and sound pipes implanted in the hidden parts of buildings). With the advent of the natural sciences at the turn of the seventeenth and eighteenth centuries (introduction of the concept of force, rising interest in electricity), the originally mechanical concept of the medium extends into psychology, though in some cases it will be replaced altogether (by the concept of the electromagnetic 'field' in the nineteenth century, for example). Nevertheless, the expansion of its use is noticeable, until finally it acquires almost universal currency in connection with spiritual and natural mediating processes.[14]

In John Guillory's (2010) retracing of the development of the term, the first major milestone thinker he examines in detail is Francis Bacon. Bacon's significance, according to Guillory, is that he puts material technologies generally speaking (including paper and the compass) into the same context as instruments (what he calls 'organs of tradition'), and thus approaches the essential meaning of the term medium in its present-day polyvalence. Even so, Bacon's 'by the medium of words'[15] does not yet sufficiently connect the two. Next it was John Wilkins, who sought a technological solution to overcome the communicative shortcomings of language (Guillory 2010: 481) – an episode to which we shall later return. Focusing on literature as a way of capturing written language, we will need to consider how the invention of the printing press was viewed in its own time. As for the thing itself, Martin Luther (1912: 523) was one of the first in the German environment to express his praise for typography. The printing press is also referred to eschatologically as 'the last flame before the world is extinguished'. Yet another milestone is represented by Enlightenment connection between printing and scientific progress, the classical example of which is, prior to Condorcet, the entry for '*imprimerie*' in the *Encyclopédie* (Diderot and D'Alembert 1765: 607).

Historically, therefore, with the development of technics (which took place without the concept of the 'medium'), one can trace the shift of its meaning from the sense of an 'ambient quality' to that of a 'means', by way of a 'middle and environment of perception'. At first, the sense is that of 'within', locating a particular operation in a particular environment, which as a 'middle term' or 'means' then takes on the sense of an instrument or tool. This development would continue further, so that the instrumental sense of 'medium' dominates in common usage today, essentially synonymous in English (since the seventeenth century) with 'means', in French with *moyens* (as in *moyens de communication*), and in German with *Kommunikationsmittel*. In this common usage, the instrumental manner appears separately from the sense of 'in which'.

We will need to go deeper in search of glimpses of media functions. Communication theory, which we have for now taken as the main context for theories of media, is concerned with two basic topics: coding and speed. Again it was John Wilkins who pioneered these topics in his book *Mercury: Or the Secret and Swift Messenger* (1694/1641), where he outlines a theory of communication, describes the effects of writing, and analyses distance in space and time, as well as the connection between secrecy and speed. Guillory describes the contrasting views of Locke and Wilkins in terms of the difference between two concepts of the medium: one as a communication defect and the other as a material technology. In a certain sense, this key difference has been decisive to this day (at least in the background). As Guillory points out, it's not so much that Wilkins anticipates binary code (which Bacon had already done before him) but that 'Wilkins's communication at a great distance is possible only by recourse to the same device – code – that is otherwise the means to *frustrate* communication. Putting Locke and Wilkins together, we see that whether communication fails (Locke) or is deliberately frustrated (Wilkins), the effect is to bring the medium into greater visibility' (Guillory 2010: 338). Although Wilkins (1641) significantly predates Locke (1689), his conception is technologically more prophetic, if not more informed. From the perspective of Locke's idealism, signs (words) represent an obstacle to communication; Wilkins, on the other hand, sees coding as a tool to bring it to the limits of its possibilities. To think of communication without coding is impossible for Wilkins, and would amount to a completely different field of activity.

It is particularly remarkable that Wilkins (after having explored the limited possibilities of transmitting visual and ready-made signs) proposes to achieve the combined secrecy and speed of communication by means of *sound* (Wilkins 1694/1641: 131–46), and this is because unlike visual transmission, it can even be transmitted through walls. Moreover,

> Whatever is capable of a competent difference, perceptible to any sense, may be a sufficient means, whereby to express the Cogitations. It is more convenient indeed, that these differences should be of as great variety as the letters of the Alphabet; but it is sufficient if they be but twofold, because two alone may, with somewhat more labour and time, be well enough contrived to express all the rest. (Wilkins 1694/1641: 131–2)

In short, sound is able to overcome barriers that visual signs cannot, and may also be used to transmit abstract (in case of emergency, binary) code. Wilkins adds:

> But now if these inarticulate sounds be contrived for the expression, not of *words* and *letters*, but of *things* and *notions*, (as was before explained, concerning the universal Character) then might there be such a general Language, as should be equally speakable by all People and Nations; and so we might be restored from the second general curse, which is yet manifested, not only in the confusion of *writing*, but also of *speech*. (Wilkins 1694/1641: 145)

That these 'inarticulate sounds' could be used to overcome a range of communication barriers, including great distances, would eventually be demonstrated by Samuel Morse and his famous code. With Wilkins, the effort that guides the invention of technological media in the modern age is already evident here: how to facilitate the widest possible communication of information to the largest possible group of addressees (for this purpose he even considers magnetism, the science of which, however, was not yet sufficiently understood to give rise to the first analogue media). Wilkins's approach to these issues nonetheless inspired an inventive effort that – first in a material and later in a conceptual sense – would lead to the creation of the 'medium'.

We might take this one step further. The Jesuit Athanasius Kircher, a contemporary of Wilkins, was the first to differentiate measurable properties (tone) from the physical environment (air) as two kinds of media, the second of which has an exclusively technical meaning involving an effort to produce, transmit and manipulate sound (amplification, for instance, with the use of echo).[16] The meaning of optical and acoustic research can then be summarized as 'optical and acoustic media and the analytical models of perception promoted with them draw attention, on one hand, to the clear technical splitting of the perception process, originally described as naturally analogue, and on the other hand, to improving mediating capabilities' (Schröter 2014: 16). Since then, the deceptive effects of the medium have also become much more significant, as the resistance given by the material nature of the technical medium comes to the fore in more detail (Schröter 2014: 16). Simultaneously, the element of instrumentality – beyond that which is represented by words printed on paper – comes to be more pronounced.

A very specific category of forerunners for the technical development of the media comprises prophetic works of artistic creation (especially literature, but also mixed forms, such as opera). By virtue of a poetic license, these works are often the first to announce individual inventions, albeit primarily in a somewhat hallucinatory mode. Kittler is the most exemplary collector of such prophetic motifs (his book *Gramophone Film Typewriter* is interspersed with samples of short stories and poems that anticipate nineteenth- and twentieth-century inventions – sometimes prematurely). There are various works we are compelled to add to this collection: the opera *Der Telegraph oder die Fernschreibmaschine* ('The telegraph, or teletype machine'), for example, written by Joseph Chudy and first performed on 3 January 1796 (Zielinski 2006: 183 f.). While neither the libretto nor score survives, the work nonetheless provides an important testimony. At the end of the eighteenth century – while Condorcet, in his *Esquisse d'un tableau historique des progrès de l'esprit humain* (*Outline of an historical view of the progress of the human mind*), was exploring the role of the printing press in communicating to dispersed peoples (Condorcet 1796/1795: 146) – people across Europe were feverishly trying to solve the problem of how to transmit messages quickly over long distances, more quickly, that is than delivering printed matter (Zielinski 2006: 181 f.). It was as if theoretical reflections on media (Condorcet) were lagging behind actual inventions, while at the same time being pregnant with them. Yet we also see, indirectly, that these reflections are dependent on the possibility of transforming the contents communicated (the influence of new media on how much, what, how quickly, and to how many people something may be communicated), and this in turn is dependent on technical progress. While inventors, from Francis Bacon to Claude Chappe were only inventing code, which was still technically transmitted by rudimentary lamps, semaphores or the sound of bells (shots, drums), there was no discussion of the transformation of communication by media in McLuhan's sense, nor therefore of media in general. It is safe to say that change slowly but surely began to take place in 1837 and 1838 when Morse invented the electric telegraph.

A detailed history of inventions and the discussions about them would be virtually endless. Let us therefore focus on mapping out the more marked shifts in the concept of the 'medium'.

It took on a completely new dimension with the enormous technological advance that began at the turn of the eighteenth and nineteenth centuries. The first modern (English) use of 'medium' in the sense of (mass-) communication dates back to around 1850, but this acceptation is only common starting in the 1920s.[17] If, as discussed earlier, an effective approach to the subject focuses primarily on what the medium does – that is, on a verb that expresses how we expect it to function (store, record, distribute, disseminate, exchange, communicate, possibly manipulate the content, etc.) – it is not insignificant that among the many possible meanings of the word 'medium' listed in the *Oxford English Dictionary*, the common sense of an *instrument* or *channel* applies to a diversity of specific activities – exchange, circulation,[18] fine arts, communication and physical recording – all in one subcategory. Another subcategory includes the *intervening* or *surrounding* substances through which forces act and sensations are transmitted, and in which an organism lives (also in the sense of the 'environment', including, since 1865, the social environment).[19] We thus see that activities (record, communicate, manipulate, perceive) put flesh on the two basic senses, the locative and the instrumental.

In the cases mentioned above, there is a noticeable shift away from the basic sense of a 'middle' (together with the environment it implies) towards a concept in which the medium acquires an instrumental meaning. In some cases, these two senses are combined, as with a thing in the middle through or by which another thing is perceived, which from another perspective simultaneously represents that which surrounds it, that is, the overall space in which something is located, the 'environment'. First, it is a signifying environment or 'medium of words' (Bacon), which can also be understood as an environment of words, or what McLuhan, Luhmann and

Mitchell would later consider a 'habitat'[20] in which sign forms are formed. Yet, we should not speak of an *opposition* between the instrumental and locative (i.e. as grammatical cases) – indeed both were already present, in certain contexts, within the Greek dative. Rather, we ought to note how their difference depends on the point of view determined by the relevant verbs. It was in the 1920s, as Guillory writes, that 'The latency of the media concept is superseded by the era of its ubiquity' (Guillory 2010: 348). Even then, however, the two different senses that made up the germinal components of this concept would continue to appear in varying proportions.

A functional definition of media in light of its conceptual (pre-)history

By approaching media from the perspective of the verbs that express their functions we gain insight on their dynamics, revealing certain features that were already evident in the preceding historical-etymological discursive analysis. Early on, they serve a mediating function (perception, communication), but not yet dissemination, and therefore involve a relatively limited purpose or circle of communicants (officials of the first palace states used writing within a limited range of activities, for instance, and Charles Cros invented the phonograph for the deaf and dumb). Only gradually, as they expand to include a mass audience, do they acquire the sense of a 'middle' of communication – its 'centre of gravity', as it were. From the meaning that 'medium' gradually came to occupy, but which was apparently not its earliest meaning (i.e. the environment, that from which the form is just beginning to emerge as centre of interest and attention), it moves 'to the middle'. Media become the centre of attention – and likewise media theory (McLuhan's effort to turn our attention to the medium itself can be seen as the foundational gesture of media studies, a field that fixes our attention precisely on that which was always overlooked as non-signifying).

These principles underlying the shifting life of media do not mean that the older meanings fade into oblivion – on the contrary, those meanings persist (the possibility of a simple record, for example, continues even with the expanding potential for its manipulation). This accounts for the extreme polymorphism and ambiguity of the concept of the medium, to the point where it can accommodate certain striking contradictions. For example, it conveys the sense of an *environment*, that is, that which recedes into the background, but also of a *middle*, that is, that which comes to the fore. The medium is that which is neutral to the message – a 'messenger' who is indifferent to what is delivered – and at the same time that which embodies the message (Régis Debray) – a 'mediator' outside of which the message does not exist, and which decisively dictates what the message can be. The polymorphic concept of the medium, encompassing all these polarities, as well as the various shades between them (from the nebulous background to the contours of the framework for a message), makes it rather exceptional; few concepts are polymorphic to this degree.

The individual functions will be shown in more detail in the next explanation, when we will continue by introducing the concept of the medium evolution and also the technical concept of the medium. But before that, let us approach the function of social communication. Here it is Charles Cooley (*Social Organisation, a Study of the Larger Mind*, 1909) who best grasps the concept's implicit meanings – those same meanings that serve as components of the concept of the medium as we have been tracing it here. Cooley's claim is that 'the zeal for diffusion which springs from communication and sympathy has in it much that is not directly favorable to the finer sorts of production' (Cooley 1909: 174).[21] He goes on:

> If one were to analyse the mechanism of intercourse, he might, perhaps, distinguish four factors that mainly contribute to its efficiency, namely:
> Expressiveness, or the range of ideas and feelings it is competent to carry.
> Permanence of record, or the overcoming of time.
> Swiftness, or the overcoming of space.
> Diffusion, or access to all classes of men. (Cooley 1909: 80)

These points can be compared to those proposed by Manfred Faßler nearly a century later:

- Media arise in the human cognitive and signifying performance of differentiation [*Unterscheidungsleistungen*]. They are the disembodied 'external representation' of the sensory, neurophysiological and cognitive performance of differentiation.[22]
- Media arise by splitting off from the body, but that entails certain convergence with the body through cybernetic, media-enabled implants, wearable technology and so on.[23]
- Media make it possible for information to function independently of individuals, that is, as a social or cultural flow of information.[24]
- Media favour increasing complexity in the self-organization of forms of human coexistence.[25]
- Media favour expansion in the areas of the artificial/artistic [*künstlichen*], inanimate and fictional references to life.[26] (Faßler 2008: 124)

Faßler's points are evidently based on advances in media theory, while Cooley, who does not even refer to the medium as such, is guided by the concept of communication practices. We see then that attention is first given to the fact of communication; only later, with the emergence of more and more means of communication, would the field become one of the dominant meanings of the 'medium'. By that point, the field had already been shaped by Cooley's formulation (and others like it). Cooley's focus on communication is crucial; after all, the communication process has been at the base of media since Aristotle.

2. Aspects of media evolution

Starting with the history of the concept we arrive at the history of media as such, though it is not initially labelled as such. Here too, we are confronted by those same basic functions, even if in a roundabout way. We need not always trace media back to military origins (Kittler), that is, the race to improve technical means in order to defeat an adversary; we might trace them instead to the economic context (the need for trade and tax records motivated the development of writing, for example, and the circulation of data by telegraph initially served business purposes – Hörisch 2001: 322). Similarly, it can be argued that the medium is only given its name when it is transferred from the military (*Funk*) to civilian context (*Rundfunk*), since only then does it exhibit its generally expanding function.[27] Sometimes there is more than one origin: for the computer there is Alan Turing (the race to decode the German military's Enigma) *and* John von Neumann (commercial research in the United States). Technical innovations become media only after business models are available for their dissemination, at which point they begin to be institutionalized, and a certain non-negligible positive social function is attributed to them (cf. Faulstich 2006). This variety of sources is further multiplied by the variety of additional uses of the medium.

Generally speaking, evolution is a stochastic process, susceptible to random or contingent factors (Stöber 2013: 418). By extrapolating from the history of inventions, however, it is possible to draw general models for the development of media as such. An example would be the 'innovation model', proceeding in three phases – invention, innovation and diffusion – and it is only with this last that the laws and *dispositifs* governing the use of a medium are established (Stöber 2013: 419 f.).[28] This model can effectively account for the unintended, new effects of a medium, and even introduces two possible reactions: *adaptation* and *exaptation* (where improvements come to be considered as new functions; Stöber 2013: 446). At the same time, the history of media shows at least three tendencies (Faulstich): differentiation of forms (in printed newspapers, for instance), syncretism of functions (film) and the limited scope of 'transitional media' (the telegraph, and perhaps even e-mail today; Faulstich 2006: 59).

Yet there is an inescapable regularity in the mutual influence exerted by one medium on another: according to McLuhan, as well as Jay David Bolter and Richard Grusin (1999), media development must be seen as a process of constant remediation. With each step of this process, there is a pronounced effort to improve on existing media and their functions.

In their book *Remediation* (1999), Bolter and Grusin define the medium simply as 'that which remediates' (1999: 65). But this also means that the medium only becomes apparent in its plurality (1999: 65; cf. Kittler 1999/1986: 5–7), who also claims that as long as writing was the only means of communication, the term 'medium' was not used in connection with communication).

As long as interest in using media is limited to a group of professionals (priests, monks and others writing in the Middle Ages, officials using writing and printing technique in China), the medium remains in its 'premedia phase': while it already exists in terms of its technical constitution, the medium has not yet acquired a social *dispositif* which would allow its function to be fully developed and theorized (cf. Stöber 2013: 413). This latter moment can only logically begin once media are already in practical use, but it is often preceded by an understanding of their function, since this motivates the search for a new concept. The free competition of other media also usually shows that the spread of the signal is in principle democratically permissible and desirable (which is why the beginning of media studies is often dated to the Chicago School and to Dewey, Cooley and Mead).

Remediation liberates writing from its status as a monomedia: 'since the early modern period, the Lutheran Reformation legitimized and supported rational information processing and monomedia communication without interaction' (Giesecke 1999: 188). Yet older media do not disappear, but remain part of an (increasingly complex) media landscape, according to a principle first formulated by Wolfgang Riepl in 1913 ('Riepl's Law'):

> as a principle law of the development of communication, it emerges that the most basic means, forms and methods, if once established and found efficient will never, not even by the most accomplished and highly developed, be completely and permanently replaced and will never become obsolete but will exist parallel to them. They only might have to look for new fields and usages. (Riepl 1913: 5)[29]

Media development therefore has the character of evolution rather than revolution, however 'at a certain price: old media must change their function, their aura, their prestige and their areas of application neck and neck with their newfangled competition' (Hörisch 2001: 76, in agreement with Bolter and Grusin).

The foundations of the theory of media evolution, made famous by Marshall McLuhan, were thus laid by Wolfgang Riepl, without any need to use the term 'medium' (it is almost completely subsumed in his *Nachrichtenmittel*, or 'means of communication'):

> not only are the means of communication constantly multiplying and intensifying, but also the field of their application and use is constantly expanding and deepening. It seems that some areas of this field compete with each other, but in the ongoing process of the division of labour, they find enough space and tasks alongside each other to develop, reclaim lost territories and conquer new ones. To cite just one example, the oral transmission of messages, which stands at the beginning of this line of development, has been overtaken, if not completely supplanted by written and later telegraphic transmission and yet in the last three decades, with the help of the telephone, it has regained much territory without for that matter displacing written or telegraphic transmission, or even reducing their activity. (Riepl 1913: 5)

Let us now attempt to generalize some aspects of media evolution – keeping in mind the fundamental plurality of sources, directions and purposes – and to examine those aspects in more detail. To begin with, the cycle of media evolution (Stöber 2013: 417–18) refers not only to a medium's technical development, but also to the development of its use and functional forms. When one of these forms faces a crisis – due to a lag in development, for instance – it takes refuge in specialized niches: new journalistic-economic niches are thus constantly developing as new relevant markets or journalistic (sub)genres (Stöber 2013: 418). These considerations lead us to the next law of media evolution: new media may only instigate deep cultural transformation on the condition of their otherness. It is only to the extent that printed books differed from manuscript, for example, that they were enthusiastically received and ultimately prevailed (Giesecke 1999: 196). This goes along with another rule, however, which is the corollary to this: following the introduction phase, the fact that a new medium has yet to find its business model leads to a crisis (Stöber 2013: 416).

Oblivion and marked attention (enthusiasm/shock) are the two poles between which media oscillate in society. For a long time (until recently, cf. Faulstich 1997: 22–4) newer media were met with contempt from the perspective of high art and high culture, so that to be highly cultured one must despise the mass media (or ignore them completely), reject cinema as a 'proletarian' diversion, and shun computer games as a waste of time;[30] when media first come on the scene (including print media), they have the flavour of something secondary, quaint or irrelevant. This also corresponds to 'primary intermediality', which refers to an initial reaction of mistrust within individual fields of art theory based on the prioritization of (the forms of) the existing media *dispositif* (film borrows from theatre forms, radio distributes other media outputs, etc.; Leschke 2003: 23 f., cf. Hörisch 2001: 70–1). (For the relationship between theatre and film, see also Chapter 2, p. 53 and elsewhere.)

The importance of discovering not only one's own *dispositif* or 'language' but, more broadly, one's own social functions is aptly conveyed in the examples listed by Stöber:

> Gutenberg's invention would have been the ideal book copyist's tool, electric telegraphy only enhancement of the state intelligence system of optical telegraphy, moving photographs would have been another fairground amusement, wireless would have improved wire telegraphy (one to one). The function of television would have been exhausted in the videophone, the internet would have remained a computer network for the simple purpose of time-sharing. (Stöber 2004)

In this context, some mention must be made of the differentiation of media (as a phase of development) into primary, secondary and tertiary media, as first proposed by Harry Pross (1972) and later adopted by Werner Faulstich. What distinguishes each category is the relationship between the communication process and its technical requirements: primary media can be found in communication processes that do not require any technical innovations (a baby crying, face-to-face interaction); secondary media involve technical applications for generating and transmitting messages, but not yet for receiving or decoding them (letterpress, manuscript, photography). Tertiary media require an apparatus on the side of both sender and receiver (first with telegraphy for symbolic signals, and phonography/telephony for acoustic signals; today with information technology for all manner of communication; Hörisch 2001: 76–7). These distinctions do not fully overlap with the division between 'old' and 'new' media. New media do mark a certain technical breakthrough that is not fully accomplished until the transition from mass media (television, radio) to interactive media. Moreover, whereas the former involve a one-to-one or one-to-many sender-receiver relationship (the letter or letterpress, respectively), the latter can be addressed many-to-many.

The relevant *dispositif* and social function thus also raise the question of the accessibility and use of media across broad strata of the population. Perhaps the true face of media and mediality throughout their history was not recording or communication in and of themselves, but the way they involve user processing, that is, the access they provide to potentially anyone to edit content. This suggests a more nuanced concept of the medium, one that would apply only to the most recent and – strangely enough – the very earliest inventions. Cave painting basically meets the same high standard of accessibility (to those who could be counted as its addressees), as software culture of the recent present. Throughout the intervening period, access to new achievements was limited either to a narrow circle of people with sufficient *economic* means (again, monasteries in the Middle Ages, and more generally the educated class throughout the entire period of history – perhaps with the exception of a certain period of generally media-saturated ancient culture (cf. Chartier 1995/1993: 14–15)), or to those who had means and *technical* know-how (after literacy had become more or less universal, around 1800 (Kittler 1995/1985), there was a brief 'open' medial period (with open access to paper and code), interrupted by the invention of photography, telegraphy and other media, which placed access once more beyond the means of broad sections of the population).

The accelerating intervals between popular expansion of mass media then cause what some authors call a 'vortex effect' (Hörisch 2001: 388), by which each revolution (the internet, for example) is accompanied by greater democratization – greater freedom to engage in communication, commentary and co-creation of media contents – and this leaves its mark in turn on older media as well. The application of media cannot be separated from social conditions, which also means that media (and their functions) cannot be blindly projected into the future, but only into specific contexts. One theorist who has systematically applied such an approach is Régis Debray (1996/1994, cf. Debray 1991: 534–5), who divides media development into three stages, spanning the entire breadth of culture: logosphere, graphosphere and videosphere (see Table 1.1).

Debray also assumes (like Leschke and others) that the cultural effect of a medium must be distinguished from the moment of its invention, and that it requires a change in the media image of culture (Debray 1996/1994: 14 ff.). The 'medium-milieu' – a socio-technological complex that conditions the expansion of possibilities – emerges only with the acquisition of necessary media competences and democratization of each medium, that is, with the acquisition of a certain 'modicum', or – a critical mass of competent users (see also Chapter 7, esp. p. 238).

It is not difficult to see how crucial it is for a technical medium to establish a corresponding social practice – by looking, for example, at the embarrassment caused by use of a telephone (even in 1912):

The most perfect telephone is nothing more than a child's toy, and its effects depend very much on the imagination. The evidence of this can be found in the fact that it is not easy for us to talk on the phone, except with persons whose voices are familiar to us, and about familiar things. When the person on the other end names a third person, we are compelled to ask him to repeat himself. (Štěpánek 1912)

This illustrates the social horizon of messages sent and received across the 'logic of custom or use' (Debray 1996/1994: 16). Lisa Gitelman sees something similar in the 'protocols' that invariably accompany every medium (Gitelman 2006: 7).

In retrospect, we can identify any number of socio-cultural aspects involved in media development. But what can this process of evolution tell us about the future? Here again we must consider the motivations. In one approach, media history is seen as a process of *Wunschgeschichte*, or 'wish history' (Winkler 2004; Schröter 2014): new media technologies respond to desires born out of previous media-technological developments, with the 'fulfilment' existing primarily in the form of a utopian dream, thus giving rise to new desires: 'the creation of technically captured images (i.e. film) at the end of the nineteenth century responds to the "crisis of speech" (*Sprachkrise*) [...] just as the development of digital media responds, in turn, to the feeling that the promise of concreteness/concretion of technological images remains unfulfilled' (Schröter 2014: 147; cf. Winkler 2004: 142).

Winkler thus characterizes new media as 'desire machines' (*Wunschmaschine*; 2002/1997: 11). Explicitly technological wishes have their roots in possible operations – in the desire to continue following links to infinity, for example, which is fulfilled to some degree by hypertext internet culture (in contrast to the function of a book). The fact that media are themselves the message is then only a derivative consequence of the fact that they cannot effectively fulfil their true mission: namely, to recede so far into the background that they are only naked 'phantasms' without any expression. All media are explicitly based on a certain technological advance, that is, on the pioneering effort of the inventor to capture the signal in a particular way. In other words, there is an inevitable tendency with technical media – in spite of their own persistent efforts to make possible, at last, the direct transmission of cognitive contents – to draw attention to themselves. This is in contrast to other types of expression, which, being long-established, do not need to advertise their 'technical novelty', and which tend more effectively to hide their media character.

In the Information Age, the models of media history mentioned here (Stöber, Debray, Kittler and Winkler, to which we may add McLuhan) may be supplemented with an historical approach based on models of information processing. According to the most prominent theorist of infogenic potential, the Frankfurt-based cultural anthropologist Manfred Faßler (2008: 124), this development occurs through four distinct information revolutions, each one accompanied by the relevant process of cultural evolution: the invention of information as artificial, abstract signs; the Renaissance (development of sciences, letterpress, microscope and telescope; emergence of automata endowed with information logic, linear perspective); the public circulation of signs and their industrial mass production, with the purpose of movement, not information storage (telegraph, telephone); and finally, the artificial information universe (computer-driven, non-trivial handling of information, including automated manipulation).

Even the fulfilment of infogenic potential is not in itself any clearer than other functional perspectives, which brings us back to the notion of evolution, with its unintentional moments (on which, see Chapter 7, esp. pp. 233–6 and 240–1) – a notion Faßler himself does not reject: 'Each medium is [. . .] an applied technology of thought, storage, and transmission. [. . .] But the same applies here: the processes of their creation disappear in the results, and effects once more become causes. In other words: That which is stored not only influences the users, but is also changed in the newly initiated processes.' (Faßler 2005: 68–9)

3. The medium as an environment *and* as a means/tool – a unified concept?[31]

Having summarized the medium's conceptual prehistory and discussed aspects of media evolution, we can now return to the concept of the medium. We have stated that the medium is neither exclusively a tool nor exclusively an environment. On a fundamental level, we can approach a unified concept via the notion of *possibility*: a medium is an environment of possibilities. The possibilities of a medium are determined by the way it is used (as an instrument), depending on the particular functions we choose (communication, recording, manipulation, etc.).

One of the most general definitions of 'medium' can therefore draw on its instrumentality, meaning *that with which something happens* (during communication), whether we are speaking of an environment affected by an event within it, or of a means, such as means of communication, in which there is evidently an element of instrumentality. This is because, whether the sense given is *that with which* (instrumental) or *that in which* (locative) something happens, we are also dealing with an action that happens (immediately or through a particular form) *to* this 'something'. It is in this sense that the question 'What is happening *to* me?' converges with another: 'What is going on *with* me?'

In this context, Niklas Luhmann's concept of the medium is perhaps the most precise (though difficult to grasp): the communication medium is an operative use (specific arrangement) of the difference between media substrate and form (Luhmann 2012/1997: 116). In other words, the obverse of the communication medium is not 'its' content; rather, the medium is itself an operation of the difference between the substrate and the (operative) form this substrate takes. The medium is not an identity but a difference, and it always affects the form (that is, what we might otherwise call the content of the message). Luhmann clarifies that although the term 'communication medium' is commonly applied to the operative use of the difference as a whole, he himself understands 'medium' in the narrower sense of the media substrate. The media substrate of communication is a certain free connection of elements, or 'loose coupling', from which forms emerge only by virtue of their close connection, or 'tight coupling'. This substrate circulates, which is to say that it is repeatedly connected and disconnected to/from forms. It is, moreover, indispensable for the creation of forms and vice versa: forms are what the medium repeatedly makes visible. One does not exist without the other. It therefore serves *at the same time* as environment and means for forms *qua* substrate. In the context of the circulation of the media substrate, technical devices (Luhmann 2012/1997: 180 ff.) make various manners of tight connection possible: a telephone operating in the medium of electromagnetic signals, for example, or letterpress operating in the medium of writing. The creation of forms in the medium may also take place by 'remediation', but *this is not the only way it takes place.*

The different senses of the medium as environment and as means also converge wherever technological media exceed the limits of man's original plans and become second nature (McLuhan). Tools thus tend to become the medium that man moves in: that is, they transcend him. (This tendency is discussed in numerous contexts: Marx's analysis of factory production with regard to complex machines; Bergson's (1963/1932) understanding of machines as an extension of the organism, yet enclosing it within boundaries unforeseen at the moment of their invention; and the current debate on cyborgs.) We will return to this aspect of technological media in the chapters that follow (see Chapter 7, pp. 230–1 and 236–7;[32] cf. Chapter 5, pp. 149–50, and Chapter 8, pp. 292–7). For now, we may simply consider how tools that are highly complex at both 'ends' (input and output) become an environment as they incorporate more and more meaningful aspects of 'life'. No longer do technologies serve as extensions of the (human) body; now it is the body (the human individual) that serves as an extension of technology, wedged inside it, wrapping itself up in the machine, and that by his/her own doing.

This raises a more general line of enquiry on the topic of 'environment'. In today's technologically saturated environment, we may ask exactly what has changed. Does the medium become second nature by virtue of the fact that it does not cross the threshold of perception, that its effects have been (imperfectly) naturalized?[33] After McLuhan, it was Kittler (following Lacan) who described the subperceptive effects of media, scrutinizing their slightest traces in the cerebral cortex. The idea of the medium as an environment signals that the concept may cease to be useful when a certain media technology comes to fulfil too many social or 'life' functions.

What can we conclude from this? Let us now try to address some of the implications of the conceptual distinctions we have made to this point.

The medium as a means must be distinguished from tools, as it serves not only work as such, but also ('leisurely' or 'entertainment') communication. It is precisely the aspect of entertainment which most characterizes recording media,[34] but not the telephone (and yet we would classify it among media, not tools). Could it be said that there are some media functions, such as recording, which diverge to some extent from pure instrumentality, and which carry the concept of the medium to its completion?[35] Aleida Assmann offers one possible answer: unlike a tool or mere invention, the medium serves to create the world, representing a more complex meaning structure than the one-sided use of a tool.[36] In Luhmann's terminology, a medium must always have the property of free connection (and thus ample possibilities of recombination) of its elements, from which also arises its multifunctionality. A tool, by contrast, is typically characterized by its 'tight' connections, which is to say its monofunctionality (a hammer ceases to be a hammer when it is used for another purpose).

The dialectic of means and environment also spurs the debate on the direction of determination: whether man determines the medium or the medium determines man. Each side has its representatives, with Raymond Williams on one side and Marshall McLuhan on the other (see Chapter 8, pp. 285–7). But how is this relevant in the age of posthumanist and cybernetics paradigms (Actor-Network Theory, Deleuze and Guattari, Luhmann)?

As an alternative, we therefore propose an approach that proceeds by tracing media functions.[37] It is increasingly apparent, moreover, that the key lies in working with signs, from presentation (that which does not show, does not mediate), through dissemination (letterpress and all telemedia), to manipulation. It is then possible to ask which function demands too much of media, without getting bogged down in a latent humanism. In the concept of functions outlined here, one can start with rudimentary functions (to define the medium it suffices to ask if it expresses at all), and come eventually to subtler ones (who expresses, and to whom?; with what distortion and how quickly or easily?).

It is only with these subtler forms that the dilemma concerning the human determination by media becomes more acute. Is it due to representation? Transmission? Coding? Communication? Manipulation? Entertainment? To what extent do media themselves lay claim to these functions (and thus become the subject of history)? That is, to what extent do they delimit what it means to represent, transmit, encode, communicate or entertain? The answer to this question naturally changes as media evolve, a process from which, at least for the time being, humans are not excluded.

Table 1.1 Three stages of media evolution according to Régis Debray (1991)

	Logosphere (Writing)	**Graphosphere (Print)**	**Videosphere (Audiovisual)**
Group ideal; political tendency	The One (City, Empire, Kingdom); absolutism	All (Nation, People, State); nationalism and totalitarianism	Each (population, society, world); individualism and anomie
Figure of time; vector	Circle (the Eternal, repetition); past-oriented	Line (history, Progress); future-oriented	Point (current events); self-oriented: cult of the present
Canonical generation	Elder	Adult	Youth
Spiritual class	Church (prophets, clerics)	Intelligentsia (professors, doctors)	Media (broadcasters, producers)
Legitimating reference	The divine (because it's sacred)	The ideal (because it's true)	The effective (because it works)
Driving force	Faith (fanaticism)	Law (dogmatism)	Opinion (relativism)
Status of the individual	Subject (to be commanded)	Citizen (to be persuaded)	Consumer (to be seduced)
Identifying myth	The saint	The hero	The celebrity
Maxim for personal authority	'God told me'	'I read it'	'I saw it on TV'
Basis of symbolic authority	The invisible	The legible	The visible
Subjective centre of gravity	The soul	The consciousness	The body

Source: Debray 1996: 171.

Notes

1 A theorist like Hartmut Winkler (2008: 214), however, regards medium as a form when he postulates the necessity of its semiotic function. Marshall McLuhan's broad definition of media as an extension of man, by contrast, also comprises those tools which somehow extend human ability (the hammer, for example).
2 Not necessarily man-operated; it would be more accurate to speak of a 'spectrum of agency'.
3 See also Elleström 2010: 24 f. In this context, it should be specified that Elleström's semiotic modality basically only develops a communication function.
4 Cf. Kittler 1993 and secondary literature, such as Krämer 2006, Winkler 2015 and the literature cited there.
5 The comparison between literature and telephony or e-mail communication, for example, does not take into account the storage/recording function in which their mutual difference lies, etc.
6 *Oxford Latin Dictionary* (1968), entry for 'medium'. The other references that follow are also taken from the *Oxford Latin Dictionary*.
7 Pliny the Younger, *Epistulae*, Book IV, Letter 24.
8 Suetonius, *De vita Caesarum*, Book III – Tiberius, Part 18.
9 Cicero, *De Oratore*, Book III, 204.
10 *Novum Glossarium mediae latinitatis* (1961), entry for 'medium'. Cf. also Ficino, *Theologia platonica*, Book X, Chapter VIII.
11 As Littré states, the keyword is '*milieu*' (http://www.littre.org/definition/milieu).
12 Jean Froissart (1336–1405), *Chroniques*, Book I, Part I, Chapter CXLIV; written in vernacular Middle French.
13 Charles Bonnet, *Contemplation de la nature*, Part V, Chapter V: Le Tempéramment; Littré, keyword '*milieu*'. Cf., similarly: 'Moses [...] wrought [...] by the medium of mens affections', Walter Raleigh, *The History of the World*, Part II, Chapter V, Section X (1614).
14 This also increases the appeal of the term for metaphorical usage (Schröter 2014: 16).
15 Francis Bacon, *The Advancement of Learning*, Book II, Chapter XVI, Paragraph 2 (1605).
16 'Duplex hoc loco medium considerandum est, Physicum & Mathematicum. Physicum medium est spatium illud aereum, per quod vox propagatur, diversaeque qualitatis & constitutionis est. Mathematicum medium est magnitudo, vel parvitas intervalli propagatae vocis durationem metientis, de utroque breviter hac praelusione tractabimus a medio Mathematico initium facturi' (Kircher 1673: 12). See Hoffmann 2002: 66 f. for further analysis. In addition to this, Kircher – like Wilkins – also counts among the first to identify one of the leading themes of the media history, namely secrecy; cf. Kircher 1673: 99.

17 'Mass media represents the most economical way of getting the story over the new and wider market in the least time', G. Snow, in Noble T. Praigg, *Advertising and Selling* (1923), p. 240 (*Oxford English Dictionary* online).
18 'Money is become the Medium of all Commerce' (1695), and the 'medium of Exchange' (1714).
19 'You cannot thus abstract any man from the social medium by which he is surrounded.'
20 Similarly, Winkler (2008: 213) conceives of the medium as a biotope for semiosis.
21 This understanding of the influence of the masses will remind us of what Benjamin wrote several decades later, as well as what Cooley describes as a loss of 'distinction' that characterizes mass production, and that represents, for those content to 'cast their lives heartily on the general current' the source of a 'diffuse joy' (Cooley 1909: 175).
22 A view typical of Friedrich Kittler.
23 A view typical of Marshall McLuhan and again Friedrich Kittler. Here, disembodied means unbound from the (phenomenological) primacy of the human body, which, on the other hand, does not prevent their characterization as artificial organs that incorporate the human body into a cybernetic loop.
24 A view typical of Yuri Lotman and Hartmut Winkler.
25 A view typical of Niklas Luhmann.
26 A view typical of Hartmut Winkler, Lev Manovich and others, including literary theorists, chief among them researchers in the field of intermediality.
27 This transition, incidentally, is illustrated by Kittler himself (1999/1986: esp. 95–114): from what was originally exclusively military technics, through its 'abuse', to a situation in which 'all the powers [...] strive to reduce the "population's leadership vacuum" to zero' (1999/1986: 94).
28 Stöber's elaborate model takes a number of aspects – politics, economics, power – into account.
29 For example, the theatre persists, even after the advent of cinema, and television (albeit in digitized form) in spite of the advent of the internet.
30 Cf. the turn in how games are represented in Steven Spielberg's film *Ready Player One* (2018).
31 Cf. Schröter (2014: 14) as it concerns *Werkzeug* and *Milieu*: 'It is now a matter of combining both signifying aspects; the suppression of one of them leads to characteristic asymmetries that can be seen in the works of some authors.'
32 The recursive loop and McLuhan's narcosis also represent a certain fusion of both aspects into a unity.
33 Bernard Stiegler or W. J. T. Mitchell have addressed this topic; see also Chapter 7, pp. 230–1 and pp. 234–5, and Chapter 8, pp. 289–93.
34 Incidentally, we must also understand the medium concept that may be extrapolated from Aristotle's *Poetics* as recording – that is, as a form of communication recorded 'in something'.

35 In search of the first connection between theories of collective memory and media theories, Winkler (2002/1997: 82–3), notices that traditional definitions of mass media do not include any relationship to memory, or indeed any recording function whatsoever, instead referring only to a mass transmission function. It is only with the advent of the computer and increased attention to writing that a shift took place, with an emphasis on the recording function as one of its logical dimensions. This is confirmed by the fact that Kittler's *Gramophone* was published in 1986, when computers (together with the corresponding user software) had already safely penetrated into common usage by the general public.

36 Various functions are included within this characteristic: perception, communication and dissemination of messages, as well as their storage and manipulation, coding, decoding and computing operations.

37 Certain German theorists (Khurana 1998) similarly look for a structural constant that may be called 'mediality' and define it on the basis of functions.

2

Reflections of mediality in Prague School thinking

Richard Müller and Pavel Šidák

1. Defining the problem

The Prague School, in addition to its seminal contributions to linguistics, developed one of the first comprehensive systems of modern literary thinking. Extensive studies on its work in this field emphasize its independent methodological and aesthetic-philosophical starting points (its original notion of structure, open dialectic and solution for overcoming the opposition between Kant's formalist and Hegel's conceptual aesthetics), noting as well how the Prague School differs from French structuralism of the 1960s (especially with reference to its concept of structural dynamics and interest in the issue of diachrony in language and literature). In this last regard, it can even be said that the Prague School anticipated certain post-structuralist concerns. While we will inevitably deal with some of these observations in the pages that follow, our main focus lies elsewhere: to explore why and how a notion of mediality *avant la lettre* arises in the Prague School. We can begin by pointing out that it was not directly related to attempts to confront the issue of new media technologies. Nor did Prague School thinkers identify various forms of art as different media in the full sense (although they did tend to compare them). Rather, their thinking on issues of mediality resulted, as we shall see, from an interest in the rapidly changing conditions, functions, and materials of modern linguistic and artistic practice, and more generally, from their structuralist concern for *relations*, rather than essences or isolated entities. In this way their enquiries were inspired into communication and signs, and the shifting boundaries of these aspects within the field of contemporary (and earlier) art, as well as the influence of social and technological development. In the same way more general questions concerning the relationship between *aesthetic* and *non-aesthetic* functions, norms and values rose.

Guillory's (2010) conceptual genealogy (see also Introduction here, p. 8) suggests that we may situate the classical period of Czech structuralism at the end of a long epoch during which the concept of the communication medium was absent, and yet before the emergence of media discourse in the true sense of the term. This chapter may therefore be seen as a contribution to the broader exploration of this 'transitional context'.

The first important genealogical insight is that the theory of (modern) art and literature formulated by the Prague School is for the first time combined with the concept of linguistic and non-linguistic communication.[1] The aesthetic quality of a work of art is not conceived of in terms of beauty, but rather as something which fulfils a certain communication and signifying function, thus serving to transform everything in the work into part of a specific kind of communication sign. At the same time, aesthetic function is latently present, to a greater or lesser degree, in any and all practice; in the arts, however, it dominates. As we shall see, this pushes the boundaries of both the theoretical concept of the sign and generally accepted notions of communication, leading to certain changes in the way they are conceptualized. In this chapter, we argue that thinkers in the Prague School – not only Jan Mukařovský and Roman Jakobson, who are most commonly referred to in this context – were themselves compelled to deal with these shifting boundaries, due in part to their efforts to further develop aesthetic thinking through a reflection on the creative practices of the artistic avant-garde. To some extent, it is this turn to the avant-garde that would come to characterize the 'transitional phase of the concept of the medium' during the period in question.

This is particularly evident with those elements of the avant-garde that expressed a certain 'techno-optimism' vis-à-vis advances in human civilization, as we find, for example, in early Poetism. In this context, the work of art (as well as manifestos and other related non-artistic production) is imbued with ecstatic references and internal ties to cinema, photography, film, the telegraph and telephone, variety shows, pantomime, ballet, folk festivals, cabarets, circuses, and music halls, as well as sports, cars, airplanes, factories, electricity and city streets. The avant-garde drew attention to the image and shape of letters and fonts, just as it rendered sensible the decomposability of the image. Their fascination with the changing attributes of the modern world would lead ultimately to the disruption of the medium of language itself;[2] different artistic disciplines would come to influence one another by way of their media realizations (see Figure 2.1). Surrealism emphasized the juxtaposition and mutual influence of different discourses within a single poem (often marked by different typefaces), foreseeing the potential for the transformation of society in the deep sources of imagination and dreams (cf.

O

dráha komety znamení astronomovo
Elipsa nekonečnosti též zvon
Zas věčnost? Po Einsteinovi? Tajemství Ahasverovo
Ó ano každá rovnice má svoji neznámou

Figure 2.1 Vítězslav Nezval: O, from *The Alphabet*, 1926, dance composition by Milča Mayerová, photomontage and typography by Karel Teige, photography by Karel Maria Paspa.

Nezval's development of the paranoid-critical method). The avant-garde thus undertook a major reorganization of the concept and function of art, and did so in various ways – not only expanding the palette of possible artistic materials, but mixing together disparate forms of media, expanding the influence of artistic creation across all social strata, emphasizing the materiality of the material and assaulting the unconscious regions of the psyche. Their attitude was that art should spill over into all of society and contribute to its transformation – possibly contributing, in the process, to a rising scepticism about the future.

In its classic period (from the late 1920s to the 1940s), the development of the Prague School was closely linked to the avant-garde.[3] Mutual ties were generational and personal (poetic works were in some cases dedicated to particular theorists) as well as theoretical (the mutual influence between Teige and Jakobson, for instance). Furthermore, these ties had a generally ideological or political character, as with the modernist notion of collective labour and exchange of ideas, and implications of social engagement (cf. Toman 1995). Structuralists closely followed and reflected on the development of avant-garde currents in a number of fields.

Some theorists of the avant-garde (Aage A. Hansen-Löve, Renate Lachmann) distinguish two concurrent tendencies of the avant-garde:

analytical and synthetic. It is the latter that characterizes the Prague School, especially in the case of Mukařovský. As Josef Vojvodík puts it,

> If the basic principle of the analytical avant-garde (Cubo-Futurism, Futurism, Constructivism, Dadaism, Poetism and Surrealism) is that of discontinuity and rupture, specialization and innovation, deformation, function and mechanics, that of the synthetic pole (Acmeism, Neoplasticism, Abstraction-Création, and to a certain extent New Objectivity) has to do with adopting the cultural tradition and its new vision, the principle of fulfilment and teleology, essentialism and organicism.

Mukařovský's aim, he goes on, was 'to develop an aesthetic philosophy within the avant-garde itself; an aesthetics that would make it possible [. . .] to reinterpret traditional categories of philosophy and aesthetics, including sense, individual, individuality, value and norm, as well as various questions concerning metaphysics, artistic noetics and the anthropology of art. It is through this effort that Mukařovský's thinking approaches an aesthetic and artistic syntheticism' (Vojvodík 2004).

An important aspect of structuralism in its initial stages is that it dealt with a wide range of research dealing with a diverse range of topics, including the theory and analysis of language, literature, theatre, film, architecture and visual arts, the aesthetics and general theory of art, comparative art theory and comparative semiotics of art. It was in this way that these fields confronted the old with the new, in addition to an interweaving and mutual engagement with philosophy of language, anthropology and ethnography – and in the background of much of this, the development of communication theory.[4] Much attention was paid to non-artistic and non-aesthetic phenomena as well, while the concept of 'function' emphasized the dynamics of change and development.

In what way then did the Prague School understand the concept of the medium *avant la lettre*? What influenced the emergence of this problem, and how? What inspiration, if any, does it offer for contemporary media thinking?

2. Structuralism's turn to medial thinking under the influence of film

Media historians see film as a paradigmatic example of the process through which a new medium comes to be established, undergoing rapid changes in its status (from scientific-technical invention to novelty/attraction to art form). Yet film was never called a 'medium' during this formative period, and it is only in retrospect that it may be properly understood as such. The medial significance of early film and early discussions about film can be better understood when we note how the new medium – much like photography before it – created and further intensified pressure on the concept of art, from the 'outside' as it were. It also (somewhat inadvertently) raised questions regarding the relationship between technology and art (cf. Benjamin 2010/1935). In the 1930s, the artistic status of film and role of technology became central topics in structuralist (and structuralist-inspired) thinking on cinema.[5]

Mukařovský and Jakobson joined the Czech debate on film at the beginning of the 1930s. It was a critical moment marked by a rich diversity of discussions on film and developments within the medium itself. Silent film was gradually being replaced by 'talkies', with the former regarded more and more as a residue of the past and the latter still searching for an expression proper to synchronized sound. Meanwhile, film had become an established cultural institution in Czechoslovakia with an advanced production and distribution infrastructure and comparatively densest network of cinemas in Europe (Szczepanik and Anděl 2008: 42).

Mukařovský's three articles on film, along with Jakobson's essay from the early 1930s,[6] undoubtedly represent the first formulations of structuralist thinking on film, characterized by an effort to avoid a predominantly speculative and prescriptive approach. Indeed, it is with the aim of redressing this tendency, as Mukařovský writes at the beginning of his article on Chaplin and *City Lights*, that structuralism approaches the work of art as 'a system of components aesthetically deautomatized and organized into a complex hierarchy that is unified by the prevalence of one component over the others' (Mukařovský 2016a/1931: 192). In his analysis of Chaplin's 'Tramp' character, Mukařovský takes a semiostructuralist approach, while in his second essay he considers the phenomenology of film space and time; Jakobson takes a functional and semiotic approach discussing the relationship between silent and sound film. Both thinkers, in this way, approach the medium within the context of general aesthetics and comparative art theory, also taking into account a technical changeability that contributed to the intense proliferation of aesthetic standards and an unprecedented openness of artistic possibilities: film makes it possible to see the very embryonic stages of the emergence of an art form.

These contributions can therefore be seen as part of the historical transition of film theory from ontological to methodological: that is, from the effort to capture film's essence to that of identifying a general method for its conceptualization as a cultural phenomenon (Kokeš 2018). The question that interests us here, however, is how (if at all) film – as an emerging art (or medium) – influenced the development of structuralist methodology.

This influence, indeed, comes at several moments. First, there is Jakobson's somewhat surprising framing of the film's *material*. If the material of poetry is language and that of theatre human action, then the 'specific material of cinematic art', according to Jakobson, is 'things (visual and auditory), transformed into signs' (Jakobson 1976/1933: 146). In this sense, dialogue on the theatre stage is yet another manifestation of human action, while dialogue in the synchronized-sound film is an 'auditory object' alongside 'the buzzing of a fly or the babbling of a brook, the clamor of machines' (Jakobson 1976/1933: 148). For Jakobson, the specificity of film seems to be that it reverses the physical shape and imprint of reality in signs, which is conditioned by the synergy of recording technology (the capture of sound waves on a phonograph cylinder, light waves on a photosensitive layer), the perceptual continuity of movement ('A dog barks at dogs on film because the material of the cinema is a real thing' – but not at the painting of a dog), as well as editing and montage. It is telling that Jakobson, faced with the mediality of film, comes to regard its sign as having a direct relation with the phenomenal world; he never thought of the linguistic sign in such a way. However, while his studies on the *iconicity of language* lie beyond the scope of this chapter, we suggest that they be read as a return to the same problem, as if from the opposite side. Jakobson seems to have been fascinated by iconicity, how linguistic signs, despite the immanently discrete nature of the elements from which they (and thus the text) are composed, acquire certain qualities that are *analogous* to those inherent in the things signified, or else take on the contours of their own distinctive order. At the same time, Jakobson's proposal is precisely not to subordinate studies on film dialogue to the perspective of linguistics: here speech is a sub-component of the sound plan in the entire hierarchy of the film structure.

Second, the extent to which film is considered as an art form widely varies. Mukařovský clearly regards it as such in the introduction to his article on the formation of film space. Later, however, although he notes that film aspires to this status (with reference to the works of Dziga Vertov, Sergei Eisenstein and Charlie Chaplin), it is, on the other hand, primarily an 'industry', since it tends to 'immediately and passively assimilate each advance in its technical machine base' (Mukařovský 1971a/1936: 16).[7] In yet a later essay (Mukařovský 2000/1943), he reverses his view once more, designating film as an art form. Such examples of the shifting status of film correspond to the changeable aspect of the phenomenon itself. This shifting status, however, takes on methodological-developmental significance as it is connected to issues regarding the aesthetic function and social effect of art by way of aesthetic values and norms. It is, indeed, the *in-between* status of film that prompts Mukařovský to rethink the relationship between aesthetic and non-aesthetic functions, leading him to make more general observations about the principles of the norm-forming and value-forming cultural process. (We will see a similar process in the case of architecture.) He thus finds (1978b/1935) that the antinomy between art and the social order intensifies in modern times: art is no longer connected to any specific social stratum, in this way diverging from the widely differentiated structure of society, and therefore of the audiences themselves. Cinema compensates by aiming to appeal to the widest possible audience, as we see, for example, in the case of Chaplin's comedy films. It is also by virtue of the transitional status of film that we see how aesthetic norms spill over and permeate non-artistic spheres. In the specific case of film, the artistic gesture is generated within the framework of an intensive norm-forming artistic activity that may directly permeate everyday life, where it acquires a more binding validity as the true measure of value. The aesthetic norm is thus projected through the film image into the body habitus itself. It is in film, unique among modern art forms, that the capacity to transform the human habitus across different social strata manifests itself. As Mukařovský notes, 'over a period of several years there emerged before our eyes [. . .] an entire system of feminine gestures, starting with a certain manner of walking, and ending with the smallest movement, such as opening a powder case, or the play of muscles across the face' (Mukařovský 1971a/1936: 32). (On the ability of film to transform human behaviour and perception, see Chapter 3, pp. 75–7.)

Film makes up for its ephemeral status (Mukařovský points here to the new medium's technical base and thus its passive dependence on industrial-technological development) by a potential to influence everyday life. His hesitation here concerning film's status as an art form – from the genealogical perspective – appears symptomatic of a general uncertainty about how to fit the new medium into the older system of art, and the pressure it exerted on the aesthetic and poetic tradition. This pressure is apparent in Mukařovský's article 'Čas ve filmu' ('Time in Film'), which, alongside Jakobson's contribution, was to be included in the collection *Předpoklady českého filmu* (The Grounds of Czech Film), but would not be published until 1966. In this article, Mukařovský compares the function of time across three media – the literary epic, film and theatre – with the aim of developing 'a more precise characterization of time in the arts of action [storytelling arts] in general' (Mukařovský 2008a/1933: 262). His observations on time in film lead him to modify his original idea about temporal layers. With regard to the literary epic and theatre, he had previously identified a double temporal order: that of the plot and that of the perceiving subject (in the epic, there is an emphasis on plot; in theatre, on a concurrence of both orders). Only in film does a third layer become (literally) visible: the movement of film through the projector, or 'image-time'. Mukařovský here gives the example of a montage sequence in which marching feet are juxtaposed to a landscape that changes with the seasons, underscored by a single continuous song, in this way signifying a journey lasting many months.[8] As with the staging of a play, the film image flows simultaneously with the time of the viewer; unlike a play, however, this image is not identical to the time of the plot. Rather, the relationship between film image and plot is that of a message (or record); in this respect, film is more analogous to the literary epic.[9] Mukařovský then generalizes this third intermediate time order as the temporal domain of the work-sign, one that runs parallel in all narrative media to the time of the perceiving subject, but which is technically *only concretized in film*. Mukařovský's aesthetic concept is essentially phenomenological, and this third order, which we could understand as the time of the signifier, appears in most other media to be connected with the experience of the perceiving subject: that is, it is given as a *quality* (Mukařovský speaks of 'tempo'). With film, however, this third order takes on a concrete, *measurable* existence, since 'the temporal extent of the work is based on the mechanically regular motion of the projector' (2008a/1933: 269). This represents a significant moment within the development of the concept of the medium, insofar as film (the movement of projected images) makes visible the mediating *time* of the work's signifier. Mukařovský, whose thinking is based on phenomenology (i.e. on an 'intentional' conception of the sign), aims here to reconcile his perspective with the technical reality of a new medium that phenomenology is ill-suited to account for. We should note as well that Mukařovský disregards the temporal dimension in which the sign (in any medium) actually 'unfolds': in the case of the literary epic (the narrative), it makes no difference 'how much time we spend reading; we can read a novel continuously or intermittently, in a week or in two hours' (Mukařovský 2008a/1933: 263). Starting from such a perspective, however, it is impossible to take into account the external technical analogy between, for instance, a page of text and single frame of film, which involves a fundamental difference in perception (the perceiving subject cannot see the film frame). Where classical semiotics tends to disregard those dimensions of the sign that are determined by its material support, considering them too tangential to the emergence of meaning, the approach will be radically altered by its encounter with the film medium. Here, the material support (what Mukařovský calls, in passing, the film's 'technical base') shifts all attention to the issue of its *mediality*, revealing it as a fundamental condition of the *manipulation* of signs. In later communication models inspired by information theory (Jakobson's famous model of the late 1950s, for instance), this 'technical base' comes to be situated in the transmission or communication channel (see Chapter 7, pp. 168–70 and 172–4).

Jindřich Honzl takes a similar approach in his article 'K diskusi o řeči ve filmu 1' (1935, 'Contribution to the Discussion of Speech in Film 1', 2018), drawing on technical aspects of the sound apparatus to demonstrate the *imagery* of the spoken word in cinema. In particular, he considers how certain limitations within this apparatus (in terms of units of kilohertz) eliminate and distort the characteristic colour of spoken language, giving the reproduced sounds their own distinct character. The sound film, he argues, directly *displays* words and sentences, drawing attention to some of the more abstract and striking features of their intonation, division and rhythm. In this way, film offers new possibilities for freeing up means of expression by technically dividing the process of reproduction into two separate components: sound and image.

In early discussions of the *relationship between theatre and film*, it was typical – not only for the Prague School – to try to make a comparative distinction between them. If the transition from silent to sound film raised questions regarding the simultaneity of sensory stimuli, it also created the conditions for looking more closely – from the genealogical perspective – at the human sensory apparatus in the context of theatre. In Jakobson's view, what is emphasized by the new, technically based art cinema is a *process* that transforms things into signs (whereas this process, in the case of language, has been all but forgotten). Film smoothes over the 'constructedness' of a certain perceptual illusion – of the fact that it is made up of signs (a real dog barks at dogs on film) – while at the same time, paradoxically, emphasizing the technical construction of the sign. This constructedness is a function of the apparatus, which can be seen before or after the illusion is in place, and becomes itself an object of fascination (in contrast to theatre, where it is almost impossible to separate the technicity of acting from the interpretation of the theatre sign). The abrupt reshuffling of relations among various media, together with the attendant expansion of material boundaries in modern art and the artistic avant-garde, had a notable impact on the aesthetic concept of the sign. This also influenced theories on the signifying function of human actions in theatre (see Section 4). We might simply point out the tension between two distinct conceptions of the 'material' that signification involves: material as part of the sign and material as that which (in very non-Saussurian fashion) sticks out conspicuously and resists the sign as such – a situation that foreshadows the problem of 'unintentionality'.

3. How the theorization of architecture transforms the aesthetic function into a 'mediating' function

In the mid-1920s, the Prague School developed a general linguistic functionalism (language as a system of functional means of expression or functional languages whose 'repertoires of elements' partly overlap) that helped to overcome the strict Formalist opposition between poetic and everyday language. At the same time, a general theory of functions begins to take shape in this context, which, as we will show, has important cultural-anthropological implications. The intersection between these two lines of enquiry is the category of the sign, and the assumption that signification arises from repeated use (function) and from the resulting social consensus, which is maintained within the intangible form of the 'collective consciousness'. Yet it seems that a certain tension appears, in Mukařovský's essays on functions, between general linguistic functionalism and the general theory of functions. At times, Mukařovský opposes aesthetic function to practical functions that are diverse and inexhaustible by a single typology (Mukařovský 1971a/1936; 1978c/1937). At other times, he presents the aesthetic function simply as a negation of communicative functions. We see this, for example, in the 1936 essay 'Poetic Designation and the Aesthetic Function of Language' (1977a/1936), in which he uses Bühler's organon model of language to define the aesthetic function as the opposite, and negation of, the other communicative functions of the sign, i.e. representational (i.e. referential), expressive and appellative (Bühler 1990/1934). Prague School approaches to the fields of culture and art were not simply an extension of their language communication model. The idea of a functional approach in which function is defined against substance (as with Ernst Cassirer) resonated with the 'thought structure of the time' (Bohumil Trnka, cited in Daneš 2001: 11), and could be found in any number of scholarly fields at the beginning of the twentieth century, from biology to logic, anthropology and philosophy (cf. Wutsdorff 2011: 72; also Schmidová 2011/1997).

If we follow the genesis of the concept of aesthetic function in Mukařovský, a significant role is played by his reflections on architecture (namely 'K problému funkcí v architektuře', 1937, 'On the Problem of Functions in Architecture', 1978, and 'Člověk ve světě funkcí', Man in the World of Functions, 1946),[10] especially as they are influenced by his engagement with the often stormy discussions on architectural functionalism from the 1920s to the 1940s.

How does modern architecture come to be related to mediality and in what sense is architecture a medium? We said above that the new technological means of recording and communication intensified the pressure on the older system of art. In the sense that modern and modernist trends in architecture were partly motivated by recent technological developments and the unprecedented possibilities offered by such materials as steel, concrete, and machine-made plate glass, we can say that it was caught up in the same 'civilizational movement' as film. Mukařovský's definition of architecture is telling in this respect. The fluctuating status of film as an art form – which is also evident in his writings – can be linked to the filmic medium's passive absorption of developments in its 'technological base' as it continued to search for a material system, and to the gradual development of a tradition of filmic norms and means of expression. In the case of architecture, by contrast, he observes how 'it is impossible for the aesthetic function to prevail – as in the other arts – or at least to reach the extreme limit of possibility in this direction. Here practical functions can never be fully subordinated to the aesthetic function so that a building becomes an aesthetically autonomous creation' (Mukařovský 1978c/1937: 246). It seems that architecture, by its very definition – as opposed to film, whose transitional status is merely temporary – *represents a sphere of oscillation* between aesthetic function and values on the one hand, and non-aesthetic functions and values on the other. In other words: 'Architecture, so firmly rooted in material culture, unlike the other arts, is the first to become a bridge over which the conquests of art cross directly into everyday life' (Mukařovský 1978c/1937: 282); architecture is situated in the system of art *'at their centre or at their base'* (Mukařovský 2008b/1939–40: 122; italics added). In the modern era, characterized by the differentiation of functions (we will return to this later) and the gradual fusion of the means of communication and recording, architecture emerges as the *proto-medium*, the oldest 'medium' of *environment formation*[11] (let us recall the lowly place assigned to architecture by Hegel in his *Aesthetics*). This concept contains within it the two main aspects of the medium in its fully developed, contemporary conception: architecture is both a means of expression and an environment.[12] Similarly, we can say that it was only with the invention of synchronized sound in cinema that the protomediality of theatre became visible, as an art form that addresses all senses of the perceiving subject.

The tacit analogy between film and architecture may have come to Mukařovský's mind by way of other avant-garde efforts to draw connections between such disparate fields as architecture, urbanism, film and music. Thus, in the neo-constructivist view of the architect Vít Obrtel, film makes it possible to give value to temporary forms. It is an architecture of temporary beauty, an architecture of images that coincides with the vision of the project – which, after all, often remains unrealized in practice. This is also evident in

Jan Kučera's film *Stavba* ('Building'), which documents the 1932 construction of the General Pension Institute, the largest functionalist architectural realization in Czechoslovakia, designed by Josef Havlíček and Karel Honzík. For Kučera, the film 'is able to capture alive [. . .] the formative labors, the process of crystallization, and the work of the people' (Kučera 2008/1933: 186).[13] In addition to their more immediate impact on everyday life, what architecture and film share in common is a collective creative process (Mukařovský gives the example of the Gothic cathedral, which brings the whole community together in its construction; Mukařovský 2008b/1939–40).

How are the specific characteristics of architecture – in the context of modern and avant-garde architecture and, above all, the various currents and forms of functionalist architecture – directly implied in the concept of the aesthetic function? What is the medial-genealogical meaning, if any, of this influence? We might first recall that, according to Mukařovský, the aesthetic function may focus on the sign itself but does not for that matter lose sight of the *object* of signification, which is taken up as a component of the overall structure of the work. This referential relationship is simultaneously weakened and intensified: 'weakened in the sense that the work does not point to the reality it directly depicts; it is reinforced, however, in such a way that the work of art, as a sign, acquires an indirect (figurative) relationship to the lived reality of the perceiver and, through it, to the perceiver's entire universe as a set of values' (Mukařovský 1971a/1936: 53). The internal structure of the sign comprises a network of links, interpolating the value position of the perceiver – one that, due to its mediation by signs, necessarily has a *social nature*. Mukařovský elsewhere goes so far as to characterize the ambiguous reality that the work of art points to as the 'total context of so-called social phenomena' (Mukařovský 1978a/1934: 84). In this way, through the unique totality of the work, the aesthetic function activates a set of non-aesthetic meanings and values, while the relationship between signs and their intended meanings is actualized and regenerated. This tendency culminates in the essay 'Aesthetic Function, Norm and Value as a Social Fact', where Mukařovský describes the work of art at last as

> An actual collection of extra-aesthetic values and nothing else. The material components of the artistic artefact, and the manner in which they are used as artistic means, assume the role of mere conductors of energies introduced by extra-aesthetic values. If we ask ourselves at this point what has happened to aesthetic value, it appears that it has dissolved into individual extra-aesthetic values, and is really nothing but a general term for the dynamic totality of their mutual interrelationships. (Mukařovský 1971a/1936: 60–1)

This is the much-discussed *transparency* of aesthetic value (see, for example, Červenka 1973: 177–8; Kalivoda 1984). As we shall see, this also defines the aesthetic function itself, the effect of which – *in and through the work* – is 'only' a specific arrangement, rearrangement and linking together of non-aesthetic meanings and values.

In the important article on architecture mentioned earlier, Mukařovský (1978c/1937) suddenly makes a similar claim about the aesthetic function and its relationship to other functions. Extra-aesthetic functions are not straightforwardly defined here as the negation of communication functions. Certainly, as in other non-figurative arts (music, dance), a work of architecture has its own 'diffuse communicative element' (Mukařovský 1978a/1934: 85). This is especially pronounced in those designs where certain functions are made to 'simulate' the function of another building type, as we find in the case of an apartment building with a palace façade. However, the aesthetic function in architecture is built on the negation of *practical*, rather than *communication*, functions. It is evident that the practical functions of a building may never be fully negated (architecture without practical functions, Mukařovský points out, is simply another name for sculpture). In architecture the aesthetic function appears rather as a *specific arrangement of practical functions* that the building fulfils, giving a particular order to the inhabitant's living space – not only as a negation of other sets of functions and of functionality in general, but as the *functional negation of functionality*. In this lies the central insight gleaned by Mukařovský from discussions on Czechoslovakian functionalist architecture, which dealt with the application and extent of basic architectural functions ('hygienic', 'working', etc.), the possibilities of their rational organization, and eventually the need to supplement architectural thinking with a systematic treatment of 'psycho-ideological' and emotional functions and so on (Vít Obrtel, Karel Honzík, Josef Havlíček, Bedřich Feuerstein, etc.; see Švácha 1998). In those art forms where the power of communication, according to Mukařovský, is unmarked (literature and painting), negation of the communication function results in a paradoxical *amplification* of the message. What such negation accomplishes is nothing less than the experimental transformation of the realm of signs, a transformation of the perceiver's very intuitions about the world. In architecture, the tendency to negate practical functions results in the reshaping of 'the basic foundations of everyday life' (Mukařovský 1978c/1937: 248; translation modified), that is, at its very interior, the centre of the human action, its ebb and flow. It is a centre that is increasingly automated[14] but capable of being revived. And if avant-garde architects eventually came to the consensus that man is the measure of all things[15] – that architecture organizes space in relation to the entire range of human action and 'appeals to man in his entirety' (Mukařovský 1978c/1937: 243) – they were yet surprised by

Mukařovský's emphasis on the *variability of the creative work's functions and of functional relationships*. Not only does architecture provide a striking example of the polyfunctional character of human creations, goals and needs. The aesthetic function also carries out or induces a rearrangement of the functions of the work (including the entire architectural type) and substitution of its dominant function. The ancient Roman basilica, for example, which could be found in the design of marketplaces and courtrooms, was later appropriated in the construction of Christian churches. The aesthetic function appears as a *mediator of both development and conservation*: on the one hand a 'harbinger of change', it may also replace other functions or preserve a thing or act that has lost its original meaning. Examples from the fields of ethnography, architecture and literature point to the aesthetic colouring of practices and objects that have lost their original (magical or practical) functions: a ritual, ruin or historical work read today as literature. In summary, *aesthetic function and value are mediators between all other functions and values*. This can also be seen in the discipline of literature. After all, the aesthetic function is a linguistic function only to the extent that it always acquires the character of the function to which it is attached (Mukařovský 1977a/1936). Because of this mediating capacity, the aesthetic function, as we will now see, should also have fundamentally anthropological implications.

In the 1940s (1978d/1942, 1971b/1946), Mukařovský elaborated the connection between his general aesthetics and anthropological cultural theory, conceived in terms of the functions carried out by human material culture (see Schmid 1997). Starting with primitive societies, where undifferentiated functions were typically grouped around a particular act or object (scarification and tattoos, for example, which might have aesthetic, magico-religious and erotic functions), he traces the differentiation of functions, their gradual intensification through history, and culmination in the differentiation and autonomization of functions during the industrial-technological boom of the nineteenth century. In addition to primitive societies,[16] this process is also typical of children's speech[17] and folkloric traditions,[18] in each case developing from undifferentiated functions to their maximum differentiation, the model of which is the machine (functionalism, Le Corbusier's house as a 'machine for living in'). It is precisely through the developmental negation of this differentiation that, according to Mukařovský, human society once again realizes and recognizes the polyfunctionality of human action, together with the multiplicity of the subject as a living source of functions. Following the stage of 'pure functionalism', under the pressure of the machine's feedback on and regulation of human activity, the functional balance and concept of man as a versatile bearer of functions is rediscovered in architecture as well (e.g. cosiness). By the same token, the 'very material fact that the architect shapes' (building materials, light, air; Mukařovský 1971b/1946: 286) generates pressure on the form with its own complex regularity, and awareness of man as a measure of all things is renewed (Honzík's 'anthropometricism'; Mukařovský 1971b/1946: 286). In this way, Mukařovský takes critical account of his humanistic functionalist conception, both within the logical conceit of his aesthetic theory (in the direction of a general cultural theory of functions), and in contact with contemporary avant-garde thinking of a distinctly utopian persuasion, as well perhaps as the appalling dehumanization of man and his technologies by the ongoing war. It is under these influences that Mukařovský came to a new understanding of technological development, which had been a source of optimism for the left-wing intelligentsia, especially in the 1920s. Thus, in the post-war commentary on Honzík's book, we read that there is no way back from 'machine culture' and the escalated state of functions: all that remains is '*to think functionalism through*' (Mukařovský 1971b/1946: 286; italics added).

4. Problems of semiosis in connection with theatre

Earlier in this chapter, we looked at structuralist thinking on film, touching on its implications for theatre and problematics of the sign – both being of theoretical importance within the Prague School during the period in question. It was at this time that Prague School thinkers began to expand their efforts beyond the field of linguistic signs with a particular interest in symbols, turning to iconicity and 'iconic signs' ('things' in theatre), as well as unconventional signs (colour in painting). These theoretical approaches to theatre also raised questions concerning the limits of semiosis more broadly: the issue of when a theatrical sign is a sign properly so-called, and when it retains the character of a thing (as in Jakobson's deliberations on signs in film, mentioned above). Petr Bogatyrev similarly takes note of the varying conventionality of the theatrical sign in the case of puppet theatre: the puppet itself is conventional, but 'like living people' it speaks real language, which is unconventional (Bogatyrev 2016b/1938: 105). Finally, Mukařovský's notions of intentionality and unintentionality are also closely related to the shifting conceptual boundaries of semiosis – a problematic we will return to below.

Published in 1931, 'The Aesthetics of Dramatic Art' (*Estetika dramatického umění*) by Otakar Zich had a significant influence on the Prague School. They were particularly interested in Zich's distinction between the 'actor's figure' (*herecká postava*) and 'dramatic persona' (*dramatická osobnost*): the first referring to the technical notion of a 'formed actor' as perceived from backstage, the second to the same thing as a mental representation from the audience's point of view (Zich 1931: 56). In other words, the *signifier* and the *signified*. These are then distinguished from a third term: the actor (*herec*), considered in his or her actuality as a human being.

Mukařovský considers this dichotomy to refer to the 'artefact' (a sign comprising an objectively existing figure on the stage) and 'aesthetic object' (the meaning of this sign; Mukařovský 1933). Two problems follow from this distinction. Jiří Veltruský was first to point out the resistance of stage acting to any straightforward application of the concept of the sign as signifier/signified (*signifiant/signifié*), arguing that 'in any given moment of a performance it is often difficult [. . .] to determine what belongs to the [performer] figure and what to the [dramatic] person' (Veltruský 1994/1981: 23). The boundary separating the two is often ambiguous, with various aspects belonging as easily to one as to the other. The second problem goes back to Zich's proposal. In theoretical circles of the time, attempts to introduce the real actor into the semiotic framework were met with controversy, and ultimately failure, with some theorists arguing that the real actor should be excluded from this framework (as it was overshadowed by its relevance as a sign), and others that it could not be dismissed or rendered transparent. The real actor invariably remained visible on the stage – and a thorn in the side of theatrical semiotics. According to Veltruský (Veltruský 1994/1981: 20), the actor is the main engine of theatrical semiosis ('everything that takes place during the performance revolves around the actor'; Veltruský 1994/1981: 20), all other components being 'less real' by comparison. The counterpart of the actor is the viewer; with this statement, however, Veltruský seems to remove (or partially extract) the actor from the realm of signs and place him in the empirical world. Influenced by Veltruský and the Prague School, a similar ambivalence was expressed by a number of other theorists: Elaine Aston and George Savona (1999) regard the actor as 'top of the hierarchy of theatrical components' (cited in Ambros 2001: 463), while at the same time emphasizing its empirical being: 'the identity of the performer plays an important role' (Ambros 2001: 463). We are thus confronted, in addition to signifier and signified, with a third component.

The unifying principle of meaning and unintentionality in the theatre

With Otakar Zich we come upon the idea of 'coupling' sound and language components: one has no meaning without the other. This merger of disparate elements over time and by virtue of a particular process can be found as well in Honzl's 1940 essay 'Pohyb divadelního znaku' ('The Mobility of the Theatrical Sign', 2016). He expounds here on the idea of 'variability of the sign' ('its ability to "change its garb"', Honzl 2016/1940: 139) – that is to say, the changeability of theatrical components, when the stage can be the bearer of the action, the actor can be the bearer of the music and so on. The semantic variability of the sign is united by the dramatic action. This same (simultaneous) doubling of the function of the thing can be found in the works of Olga Srbová (see especially Stehlíková 2016: 184). All these ideas may be traced back, even if indirectly, to the concept of a unifying principle – what Mukařovský calls a 'semantic gesture': a content-nonspecific flux of meaning, constantly linking all layers of the work into a dynamic unity, one that may however only be evoked from the perceiver's perspective.

Mukařovský's notion of 'unintentionality' (referring to that part of every work that remains semantically ununified) serves as another example of a concept originally modelled on linguistic material as a phenomenon of literary poetics, and subsequently – nearly simultaneously – applied to another medium. The concept also gives theoretical consistency to the tension between the work as a sign (intentional) and as a thing (unintentional) (for a more detailed analysis, see Section 1 of Chapter 5, pp. 131–40). Discussions on theatre and its theory also thoroughly worked through these concepts, without explicitly relating them to Mukařovský.

Petr Bogatyrev who provided extensive insight into these phenomena does not explicitly acknowledge the role of unintentionality in the theatre. His view is that everything here serves as a sign of some kind, and he identifies three possible semiotic types. First, there is the 'sign of the thing itself': the set piece of a house, for instance, serves as the sign of a house (sets and props in the ordinary sense are of this type). Second, there is the 'sign of a sign of a thing': the set piece of a house may serve as a sign (or connotation) of wealth, nationality and so on. Further elaborating on the semiotic behaviour of things, he describes this as their 'representation function'. Yet he claims that 'theatrical signs [. . .] do not always have a *representational* functions', suggesting a third type which he calls 'real things' (Bogatyrev 2016b/1938: 100). These theatrical signs – that is, certain gestures, movements, the proscenium itself – serve neither as the sign of a thing nor as the sign of a sign. He will repeat this thesis two years later in the book 'Czech and Slovak Folk Theatre' (*Lidové divadlo české a slovenské*). Here, in connection with the actors' movements, he distinguishes between those things which have a 'representation' function, that is, signs (characterizing the dramatic character), and those which are 'purely theatrical'. These last do not necessarily have the character of a sign; as Bogatyrev writes, they 'do not necessarily have the aim of representation, and can sometimes directly contradict the person's character', including certain gestures, movements and facial expressions (Bogatyrev 1940: 123–8). He maintains, however, his basic thesis that all things in theatre serve as a sign of some kind: 'Not only costumes and decorations are used on the stage [. . .] but also real things. Even these real objects, however, are not viewed by the audience as real things, but as signs of signs or signs of things' (Bogatyrev 2016b/1938: 140). In the conclusion of the study, however, he makes an exception in the case of actors. Bogatyrev seems to be working here with a double definition of the sign: as that which represents something else (first and second types), and as that which represents itself (third type). However, even signs of the third type actually represent something else: the proscenium, for example, serving as an indication that we are in a theatre.

Veltruský similarly considers that 'not all the components of the actor's performance are purposive; some of them are simply determined by physiological necessity (for instance, various automatic reflexes)'. Yet the viewer, he argues, understands 'even these non-purposive components of the actor's performance as signs. This is what makes the stage figure [Veltruský's version of the actor's figure concept] more complex and richer – we are tempted to say more concrete – as compared to the other carriers of signs. In addition to its sign character it also has the character of reality. And the latter is precisely the force that attracts all the meanings towards the actor' (Veltruský 2016/1940: 149).

In a 1940 review of Bogatyrev's book, Jindřich Honzl turns a critical eye to the idea of absolute signification – that everything in the theatre is a sign. According to Honzl, all theatrical signs also have the aspect of a *thing*, and the viewer perceives both aspects – the sign *and* reality of its bearer – simultaneously. There is no need, as with Bogatyrev, to distinguish between signs of things and signs of signs. 'I believe that theatrical perception is a special case of the perception of signs,' Honzl writes, 'because the perceiver's attention here is not completely focused on the sign, but is simultaneously turned to the thing whose properties serve the viewer (perceiver) as signs – for instance, the viewer's attention is not only focused on the sign of Hamlet (carried by Eduard Kohout) but also on Eduard Kohout himself' (Honzl 1940: 110).

While Honzl's conceptualization of sign-thing duality borrows from Zich's distinction between 'general' and 'technical' ideas (Zich 1931: 56), it represents an important shift away from the opposition between two discrete things, in favour of a processual oscillation between two different perceptions of the same thing: as sign-thing and as sign-sign. This conceptual shift brings us nearly all the way to Mukařovský's concept.

5. Conclusions

What more general conclusions can be drawn? Let us begin by examining the relationship between 'art' and 'media'. During the period in question, where we would most likely use the term 'medium' today, we find 'art' – and question of its boundaries – or 'technics'. While there is a certain tension between the terms art and technics, most striking are the efforts to synthesize them, as we find, for instance, in Mukařovský's consideration of time in the literary epic, theatre and film. The dominant position of the concept of art, which had already gone through phases in which its autonomy was recognized and confirmed (from Baumgarten and Kant to the Russian formalists, by varying approaches), allowed it to open in new directions, due in large part to the emergence of new technologies for the reproduction of sound and images, and rise of the artistic avant-garde. Indeed, in the new context, the concept of art would transcend the autonomist definition of 'art' on which the earlier formalist poetics and aesthetics had been built.

Approaching Mukařovský's work from a genealogical perspective, the aesthetic function itself can be seen to have a medial quality, one that most likely came about through contact with the artistic avant-garde, its inner reflection of civilizational processes and their acceleration (including technologies that drove it), and with avid expansion of the range of materials available to artistic processes. This last especially would become the object of increased attention, as well as the impetus for revisiting and correcting earlier aesthetic theories. In Mukařovský's view, the aesthetic function has no essence of its own and is not determined by any specific set of means or materials, but is instead capable of making use of any and all materials in arbitrary fashion. It is thus able to join itself to functions and values of any type at all – social, non-aesthetic, practical, communication and so on – through which, by reassigning and regrouping them, it is itself manifested and realized. In this way it presents a tentative schema of functions and values, which acquires an intense relationship to reality precisely – and paradoxically – because the *direct* connection of the sign to the object, perceiver and creator, is delayed and interrupted. We can now express the paradox of the aesthetic function more clearly: its role, as function of the negation of all functions in general, is to bring closer by zooming out – in other words, to achieve *an intense contact* between the work (sign) and perceiver through the processes of *layered mediation*.

It is not surprising then that, having explored the distinctive mediality of the aesthetic function[19] in the case of functionalist architecture, Mukařovský would then apply the same characteristics 'retroactively' in his understanding of poetry (following on the works of Prague School linguistics theorists Bohuslav Havránek and Vilém Mathesius).[20] In a comprehensive 1940 study on poetic language, he argues that language focused on signification itself (its aesthetic function) is adapted to the task of 'constantly reviving man's attitude toward language and the relation of language to reality, for constantly revealing in new ways the internal organization of the linguistic sign, and for showing new possibilities of its use' (Mukařovský 1977b/1940: 6). Unlike other functional languages, language in the aesthetic mode can draw on the resources of any linguistic layer, even one that is otherwise limited to a single function (an argotic expression, for instance, may add colour to a character, serve as a parodic element, etc.): 'This both distinguishes poetic language from other linguistic levels [. . .] and closely connects it to them because poetic language is *the mediator of their interrelations and interpenetration*' (1977b/1940: 7; italics added). In this aspect of the aesthetic function – its 'mediating potential' – we can see a connection with the utopian-programmatic thinking of the avant-garde, namely its 'synthetic' pole. It is not necessarily art, but the aesthetic quality as such – or else the function that a work acquires depending on social conditions and the development of norms – that (paradoxically) represents a means of renewing the relationship of the sign to reality by focusing on the sign itself.

Film and architecture were often associated in avant-garde thinking and artistic production with the possibilities and requirements of a 'new vision' of reality, indeed, of a new stage of civilization in which human societies already found themselves. Urban space came to be seen not from the individual subject's point of view, but from that of a camera, rendering visible the automatized movements of the modern masses and technologies. Mukařovský remarks on 'how [architecture] forms a space for man's eye and his movement. Its own function is considered only insofar as it manifests itself in this organization' (Mukařovský 1978c/1937: 240). Perhaps it is Vít Obrtel who best illustrates this view on the alliance of architecture and film, in progressive thinking, with his idea of film as artistic medium of a temporary architecture: an ideal means for combining functionality with fantasy.

In Mukařovský's later thinking, aesthetic function and value come to occupy a medial position vis-à-vis other functions and values, reorganizing and reorienting them in the contact between the work of art and perceiving subject, freeing them from their immediate context; interfacing (in the case of values) with the worlds of human experience. In a similar fashion, film and architecture came to occupy a mediating position, during the period in question, between the arts and non-artistic fields of human social and cultural activity.

Significantly, Mukařovský considers a number of directions and (re)orientations within the avant-garde architecture of the 1920s and 1930s all under the rubric of 'functionalism', including purism, constructivism, and 'scientific' and 'emotional functionalism'. It was not long before parallel trends in functionalism and technicism would clash dramatically and fuse together with organic (Obrtel) and naturalistic architecture (Žák), as well as Neoclassicism (Fragner, later Gočár). The disparity between architectural/urban visions and their eventual realizations, which determined the development of architecture in the 1920s through the 1940s, also has its theoretical counterpart in Mukařovský's thinking, namely at the *general level of the dialectical opposition between functionality and the negation of functionality*. It is here that the aesthetic function plays the role of mediator or operator, turning the relation of negation into the mode of a *strengthened bond between the perceiver (social world) and the work*, and of a *renewed relationship between sign and thing*. Mukařovský does not develop the key concepts of function, norms and values within a specific aesthetic programme or comparative theory of art, but aiming at a *synthetic approach as an open system of general aesthetics*.

We see then how the aesthetic function exceeds the concept of art, without, for that matter, formulating a set of medial questions in the full sense of the word. However, its elaboration vis-à-vis the material of modern theatre, literature, architecture, visual arts, ethnography and film (to name the most significant) necessarily raises questions concerning the relationship between art and practice, as well as technology, materiality[21] and the formation and reshaping of the human environment. The contours of the *cultural-anthropological theory of functions*, which thus appear to Mukařovský and other structuralists of the classical period, make it possible to grasp the points of contact between older forms of art and everyday life with the innovations of avant-garde expression.[22] Thanks to the relationalist methodological basis of Structuralism, older art forms – from folk theatre to Realist prose – can be compared to the emerging forms of communication and representation, all of which we would call media today. The context of all media and technology as a totality, however, represents something of a blind spot. Mukařovský's sketch of the civilizational development of technology and the human, from the point of view of later trends in media theory, appears to be intrinsically connected to a particular *stage of avant-garde-anthropological thinking*. Keeping in mind the view of Hans Günther, for example, who (like Robert Kalivoda) succinctly interprets Mukařovský's aesthetic function as 'a notion of humanizing multifunctionality' and the aesthetic effect as an empty, variable value – the expression of the essential need to humanize reality – we can now better understand how Mukařovský's concept belongs to a different phase of thinking on art and media than that which came to be dominated by post-humanist and antihumanist tendencies, from the 1960s onwards, among which the notion of interconnected media systems has taken a central place under mounting pressure to deal with the fusion of technology, action and thought. Looking back at the period in question, however, it appears nonetheless possible to establish, once more, a new starting point.

Notes

1. As Mukařovský claims: 'Poetry and painting usually contain a message; even if in some periods of their development the communication function is reduced to a zero degree [. . .], this reduction appears as a refutation of the normal state. In a very similar way, modern linguistics speaks of the "zero ending"' (Mukařovský 1971a/1936: 50–1).
2. See, for example, Jaroslav Seifert's poems from the collection *Na vlnách T.S.F.* ('On the Waves of TSF', 1925) and Nezval's *Abeceda* ('Alphabet', 1926).
3. See, for example, Drozd, Kačer and Sparling 2016; Vojvodík 2004; 2011; Toman 1995; Fabian 2005; Winner 1994; and Chvatík 1970.
4. See, for instance, Kokeš 2018; Drozd, Kačer and Sparling 2016; Šlaisová 2016; Volek 2004; Doležel 1995; Ulver 1991; Veltruský 1994/1981; Matejka and Titunik 1977.
5. Including Mukařovský 2016a/1931; 2008a/1933; 2016b/1933; Jakobson 1976/1933; Honzl 2018/1935; Bogatyrev 2008/1938; Kučera 2008/1933; Vančura 2008/1935; Weingart 2008/1935; Burian 2016/1936.
6. I.e. Mukařovský 2016a/1931; 2008a/1933; 2016b/1933; Jakobson 1976/1933.
7. An English translation was published in 1979 as *Aesthetic Function, Norm, and Value as Social Facts* (University of Michigan Press, trans. M. E. Suino). In this volume, we quote directly from the original Czech text.
8. Mukařovský draws this example from Vasily F. Fyodorov's 1932 film *Mertvÿĭ dom* (Dead House).
9. We should add that in film, a visual record of the event is constituted through the step-by-step work of a cameraman, director, editor, and so on – a process that precludes its status as 'discourse time' (as later defined by narratology). The 'collective creator' position in film thus marks a difference to that of the epic narrator.
10. Also the lecture series 'Aesthetics of Architecture' (Mukařovský 2008b/1939–40) and several passages in Mukařovský 1971a/1936.
11. The phrase is first used in a 1943 study by Czech functionalist architect Karel Honzík.
12. Compare to Bernhard Siegert: 'The essence of the archaeological-media method [. . .] is not related to the excavation of media – on the contrary,

media are perceived as the environment in which we conduct excavations' (Siegert and Krtilová 2016: 158). Also compare to the genealogical definition of the term in Chapter 1, pp. 22–9 and pp. 37–40 (Section 3).
13 We should also mention Arnošt Hošek (1885–1941), an architect, urban planner, and acoustics expert who used 'musicalistic images' (musical and visual systems of expression) and 'melody of space' (building acoustics) as a tool for forging mutual connections among different senses and art forms, as well as the permeation and harmonization of external and internal spaces.
14 This automation of human movement – the movement of the masses – was uniquely captured in such experimental films as Walter Ruttmann's *Berlin: Symphony of a Metropolis* (1927) and Dziga Vertov's *Man with a Cinema Camera* (1929).
15 See Švácha 1994/1985. This consensus may have also been motivated by the consequences of the Great Crash, which strengthened the left-wing orientation of the avant-garde.
16 'For a primitive', Mukařovský writes 'every practical act and creation has at the same time and with equal importance a symbolic significance' (Mukařovský 1978d/1942: 44) and 'every act is accompanied by a whole cluster of functions' (Mukařovský 1978d/1942: 39).
17 The word merges with the objective world: 'a cloud is called a cloud because it is grey, an umbrella is called an umbrella because someone can jab us with it – Piaget' (Mukařovský 1978d/1942: 45).
18 Cf. Bogatyrev's essay on folk costume (Bogatyrev 2016a/1936).
19 The medial aspect of the aesthetic function was adumbrated as early as the Prague School's Theses of 1929.
20 See, for example, Havránek's article 'Mácha's Language' in the anthology *Torzo a tajemství Máchova díla* (The Torso and the Secret of Mácha's Work, 1938).
21 According to Mukařovský, different 'materials' are where artistic disciplines begin to differentiate themselves.
22 Some of the typical features of avant-garde scenography, which could be regarded as an anti-traditional innovation, directly follow the tradition of older folk theatre (conversely, Petr Bogatyrev's conceives of folk theatre as having a close connection with that of the contemporary avant-garde). This is especially the case with Jindřich Honzl and E. F. Burian (for instance, in his *První* and *Druhá lidová suita*, 1938 and 1939, First and Second Folk Suite). These features include genre syncretism, breaking of the fourth wall, a moving stage, the indication of space using gesture or dialogue (Šlaisová 2016: 75–7, Kouřil 1978: 211).

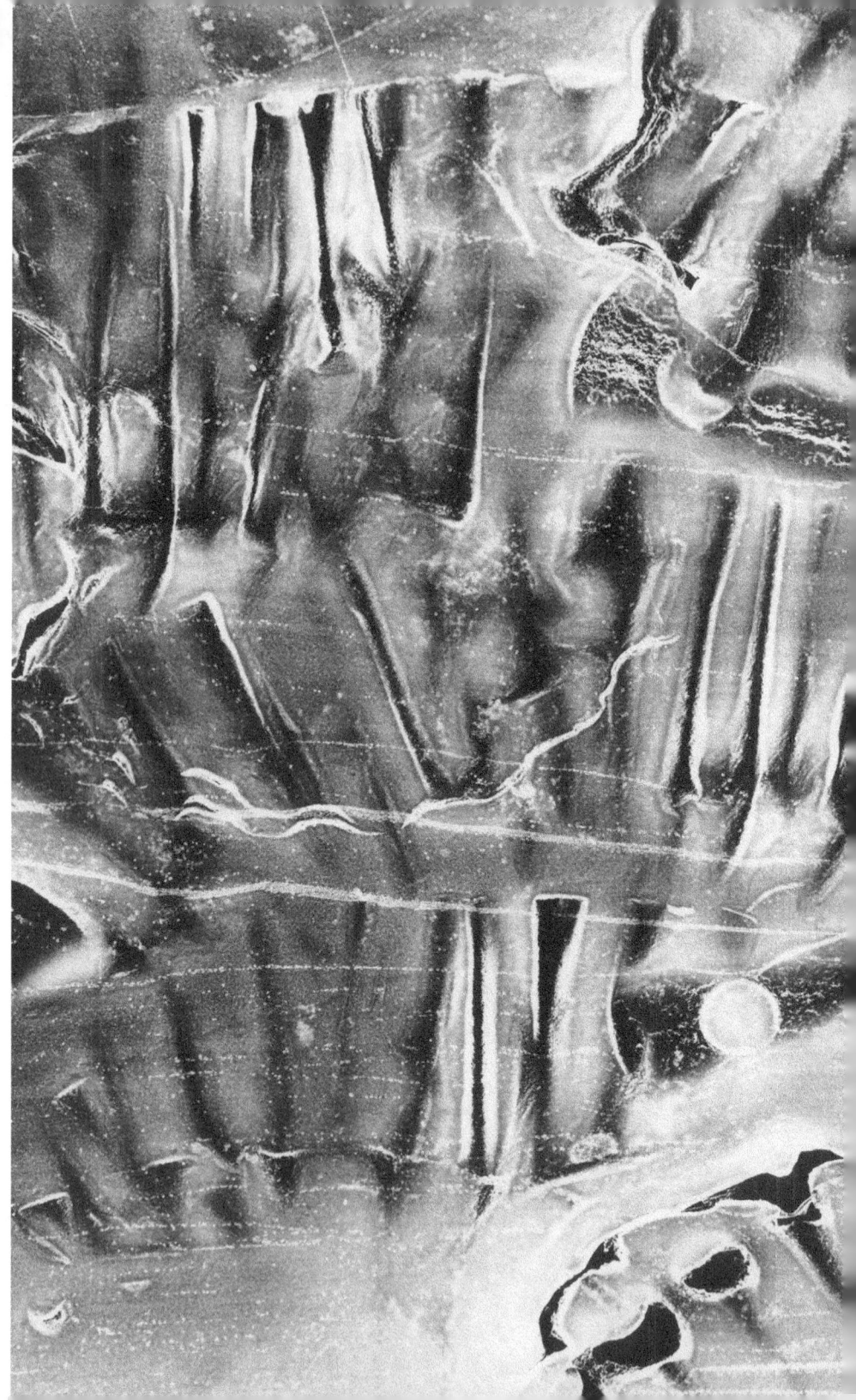

3

The media philosophy of Walter Benjamin

Martin Ritter

This chapter aims to show how media philosophy is an essential aspect of Walter Benjamin's thinking, in the strict sense of *philosophy* as opposed to the theory or theories of individual media, or media history. While scholarship on the history and theory of media is typically restricted to the character and functioning of specific media, or else generalizes the findings on these topics, media philosophy focuses on the investigation of mediality as such: that is, on 'mediation' as non-instrumentally enabling media 'effects'. In other words, media philosophy explores the conditionality of being in the world, indeed the conditionality of the world itself, of 'things themselves' – this conditionality cannot be captured by generalizing the findings on individual media.

I will not here reconstruct Benjamin's influence on contemporary thinking on mediality. In this regard, let it be said simply that a more comprehensive understanding of Benjamin's thinking has been predicated on getting past the idea that media serve primarily as means of communication. While the medium certainly can serve as such a means – that is, as that which conditions communication – Benjamin's interest lies elsewhere, namely in the medium as that which conditions the way we perceive the world. As he writes in his essay 'The Work of Art in the Age of Its Technological Reproducibility', '[t]he way in which human perception is organized – the medium in which it occurs – is conditioned not only by nature but by history' (Benjamin 2010/1935: 15).

For Benjamin, the concept of the medium does not deal primarily with specific technical or artistic means, but instead with the 'atmosphere' in which the immediate perception of the world takes place. Of course, it is pertinent to consider how and to what extent this atmosphere is conditioned by the technologies associated with it. However, it is one of the main goals of this chapter to demonstrate that Benjamin does not reduce mediality to technicality, even in his thoughts on the age of technological reproducibility.

1. Concept of the medium

While media theorists typically focus on Benjamin's late essay on technological reproducibility, the concept of the medium figures much more prominently in his earlier texts. Let me begin with his dialogue 'The Rainbow' (Benjamin 2011/1915), in which Benjamin reflects on colour and the imagination.

According to Benjamin, the 'pure' perception of colour[1] allows the subject to merge with the medium of the imagination, which is understood as a medium precisely to the extent that it is asubjective. The medium of the imagination is imbued not only with a power of its own, but with its own logic, which Benjamin conceives essentially in material terms: it is *in* colours themselves, not outside of them.[2] It would make no sense to say that the subject constructs this logic. On the contrary, it may even merge with it, or else (much like shapes) dissolve in it. A person who yields to the sensation of colour merges with the medium of the imagination, in which subjectivity itself 'disappears' (a more detailed discussion of Benjamin's concept can be found in Ritter 2016; also see Somaini 2016b: 12–14; and Böhme – Ehrenspeck 2007: esp. 446–9).

Benjamin's reflections on colour and the imagination can be read as part of a more broadly conceived ontology (and cosmology) in which *all that exists* is language. Benjamin outlines this ontology in his article 'On Language as Such and on the Language of Man', in which all is language because 'it is in the nature of all to communicate their mental meanings [seinen geistigen Inhalt mitzuteilen]' (Benjamin 1979a/1916: 107). The 'essence' of language – what makes it language in the first place – lies in an ability to *immediately* convey what it conveys, to be 'expressive' in this sense. As Benjamin himself puts it, 'all language communicates itself *in* itself; it is in the purest sense the "medium" of the communication. Mediation, which is the immediacy of all mental communication [die Un*mittel*barkeit aller geistigen Mitteilung], is the fundamental problem of linguistic theory, and if one chooses to call this immediacy magic, then the primary problem of language is its magic' (Benjamin 1979a/1916: 109).

To put it very simply,[3] when Benjamin speaks of the mediality of language what he means is the mediality of *everything*, insofar as everything that exists also reveals and discloses itself. Things in the world are not mere givens; rather, each thing, by virtue of its existence, is also an act of self-expression. Benjamin thus critiques the notion of language as a means of communication, as it fails to account for a more *basic* linguisticity, a more *basic* mediality. Surely, anything can come to serve as a vehicle for conveying anything else – in the case of language, an arbitrary sign that conveys meaning – and yet each thing intrinsically has a certain *expression* that is non-arbitrary, or indeed 'intrinsic'. We see here, however, an important duality – or even ambiguity – in Benjamin's concept of mediality: while the notion of mediality necessarily implies mediation, Benjamin conceives of this mediation, paradoxically, as having the character of immediacy (we'll return to this paradox later).

In the essay 'On Language', Benjamin presents the world not as a place for the 'democratic' multiplicity of equal things/languages but, on the contrary, as a hierarchical structure – a place in which the mute language of things is created by the Word of God. The things demand to be named by man, who is the only one capable of *fully* expressing their spiritual essences, which they themselves are not capable of expressing.[4] Indeed, to express the essence of things requires a name that only man (Adam) is capable of pronouncing. As Benjamin comments: 'Man can call name the language of language (if the genitive refers to the relationship not of a means but of a medium) and in this sense certainly, because he speaks in name, man is the speaker of language, and for this very reason its only speaker' (Benjamin 1979a/1916: 111).

A name is an expression of the *truth* of a thing, and as such it has an internally contradictory character: it expresses the truth of something other than what it is, but it does so precisely because of the complete identity between the expression and the expressed. In other words, the name is – unlike the entity whose truth it expresses – completely transparent. It has perfect mediality, if we can even talk about mediality in this case.

Be that as it may, Benjamin's essay 'On Language' has, as it were, two faces. On the one hand, we can read it as an extremely speculative text: a linguistic-philosophical retelling of the biblical description of creation with all its metaphysical elements. On the other hand, it is clear that Benjamin does not conceive of human language as a miraculous identification of a true name (along the lines of Adamic naming), but as a process of *transformation*: human language is a reshaping of what man perceives in the world, rather than an *identification* of a truth that has been expressed in things 'since the beginning of the world'. To interpret Benjamin's text requires a certain effort to combine these two 'sides' of his conception, or in any case to accept them simultaneously. To view it from a different perspective: one must simultaneously accept the metaphysical nature of Benjamin's conception *and* its emphasis on concrete phenomena.

In several later texts, Benjamin further develops his ideas from 'On Language'. Before turning to them, however, we must consider Benjamin's dissertation 'The Concept of Art Criticism in German Romanticism' (1919).[5] Here, Benjamin starts with an analysis of Fichte's philosophical system, proceeding from there – drawing particularly on Friedrich Schlegel – to reveal the philosophical foundations of the Romantic understanding of art criticism. For these foundations, the concept of the medium is absolutely central. To put it briefly, Benjamin shows that for the Romantics, criticism involves judging a work not from the outside, but rather with an eye to its internal development, a notion that makes sense against the background of a broader ontology in which all that exists resides in the 'medium of reflection' (*Reflexionsmedium*).

We find a number of analogies between the linguisticity of all things that Benjamin describes in 'On Language' and the reflexivity that is elaborated in his dissertation. If we accept that reflection broadly understood is intrinsic to *everything*, then everything is also part of a single whole in which every part, every individual thing is able to 'reflect' a larger or smaller 'range' of the whole, that is, the overall context, without for that matter being a subject with the *ability* of reflection. Rather, we must think of all things as specific instances or 'formations' of reflection itself. This idea is logically consistent with the thesis of 'On Language' that everything participates in language, in the sense that it communicates (its) 'mental meaning'. We must therefore also attribute a 'greater or lesser degree of consciousness' (Benjamin 1979a/1916: 107) to everything: to participate in language means participating in reflection, that is, in the 'capacity' for (linguistic) reflection/expression.

What this implies essentially – and paradoxically – is that, due to the 'inclusion' of everything in the medium of reflection, it is possible to talk about knowing things *immediately*. The Romantics theoretically 'ensure' this immediacy by conceiving of knowledge not as a relationship between consciousness (i.e. subject) and its object, but as a relationship between reflection and the reflection of reflection, that is, as an *intrareflexive* relationship. In addition to the immediacy of knowledge, the Romantics also cared about its *infinity*. Here, according to Benjamin, they deviated from Fichte's conception, in which infinity was something that needed to be eliminated. The Romantics, on the contrary, welcomed it, but only because they conceived of it not as the infinity of progress but as the 'full infinitude of interconnection' (Benjamin 1996b/1919: 126). This 'proper' infinity does not imply continuation *ad infinitum*, but rather the capture of an infinite connection concentrated in one 'point' or moment. Of course, even this kind of expression needs its own medium.

As mentioned earlier, Benjamin develops the ideas formulated in 'On Language' in several texts, namely 'The Task of the Translator' (1923), the 'Epistemo-Critical Foreword' to his book on the baroque mourning play (1924), and two short texts on the mimetic faculty (1933). Each of these texts develops a different topic already implied by the essay 'On Language'. 'The Task of the Translator', for example, follows the motif of the biblical fall of languages into a state of multiplicity, and proceeds to develop a concept that a specifically conceived translation – one that raises the text into a 'higher and purer linguistic air' (Benjamin 1996c/1923: 257) – facilitates the development of languages towards their messianic end. By contrast, the essays 'On the Mimetic Faculty' (1979d/1933) and 'Doctrine of the Similar' (1979c/1933) do not deal with the notion of a true Adamic language, but rather with the emergence of language through *mimesis*, and more specifically with the idea that language is 'a medium into which the earlier powers of mimetic production and comprehension have passed without residue' (Benjamin 1979d/1933: 163).

A central theme in all the linguistic-philosophical texts mentioned earlier is the irreducibility of linguistic phenomena to their *semiotic* dimension. In the text 'On the Mimetic Faculty', for example, Benjamin argues that 'the mimetic element in language can, like a flame, manifest itself only through a kind of bearer. This bearer is the semiotic element' (Benjamin 1979d/1933: 162). The 'Epistemo-Critical Foreword' thematizes the duality of conceptual knowledge and truth: just as language is irreducible to semantics, truth is irreducible to concepts, that is, to the conceptual grasp of phenomena. (On the limits of semiosis, cf. Chapter 2, pp. 60–2, and Section 1 of Chapter 5, pp. 131–40.)

In fact, there are two aspects of truth as Benjamin defines it in the 'Foreword' that are difficult to reconcile with one another. On the one hand, truth must be mediated insofar as it needs to be made present: it appears exclusively in its presentation, and thus medially. In other words, it emerges through the very act of its presentation, its 'performance'. On the other hand, Benjamin identifies his concept of truth with the Platonic doctrine of ideas,[6] in a way that echoes his evocation in the essay 'On Language' of the biblical notion of Adam giving things their *true* names, which is to say, the names expressing the truth. The truth is thus given through a medium, and hence mediated, but Benjamin attributes this act of representation to the *truth itself*: the way of 'presenting' the truth, he writes, 'is, for truth, presentation of itself and therefore is given together with it as form. This form is suited not to a connection internal to consciousness [. . .] but rather to being' (Benjamin 2019/1924: 4).

Looking at the development of Benjamin's thinking in the period after his book on the *Trauerspiel*, we can identify certain new emphases. What is particularly important for the present discussion is that he no longer posits proper names as *grounding* phenomena. He now focuses his attention on the very *conditionality* of the world's appearing – on phenomena as fundamentally conditioned – without referring to the idea of a *true* foundation or *fundamental* medium, that is, the medium of truth itself. In addition, Benjamin's theoretical attention, more so than in previous writings, turns not only to works of art as important media of truth, but also directly to the 'external' world.

In this regard, we can undoubtedly talk about the *politicization* of Benjamin's thought, starting with his work *One-Way Street*, written between 1925 and 1927. We already see here his interest in the modern metropolis, which will remain thereafter the fundamental 'object' of Benjamin's attention. In this context, it is important to note the significance of his 'memories' of Berlin (*Berlin Childhood around 1900*), and especially of the *Arcades Project*, where he aims to interpret Paris as the capital of the nineteenth century. In all these works, memory plays a crucial role, though he understands it 'not [as] an instrument for exploring the past, but rather [as] a medium. It is the medium of that which is experienced, just as the earth is the medium in which ancient cities lie buried' (Benjamin 1996e/1932: 576).

2. The age of the masses

The concept of the medium features more prominently (and explicitly) in the early phase of Benjamin's thinking. In spite of this, it is his later reflections on media that have received the most interest, in particular his seminal text 'The Work of Art in the Age of Technological Reproducibility' (first version published in 1935). Is this interest justified? And do the ideas conveyed in these later works pick up on Benjamin's earlier discussions on mediality, or do they represent a markedly different approach?

In the essay on technological reproducibility, Benjamin distinguishes between the 'cult' and 'exhibition' value of artworks. He argues that in an age characterized by advances in technological reproduction, not only can we see how art has long been 'parasitizing' on ritual (through its cult value). We can also choose to reject this function and emphasize instead the 'social function of art' connected with politics. If Benjamin talks about the need to connect art with politics, it is not in the sense of subordinating it to a given political agenda, nor is his aim to relegate art to a mere instrument for the realization of externally prescribed goals. Rather, he calls for the *democratization* of art – a reorientation of art vis-à-vis everyone (the entire *polis*) – at the same time wishing to highlight its social significance.

The artwork essay is an attempt 'to redefine the social meaning of art in the face of fascism and the rapid development of new technologies and mass culture' (Böhme and Ehrenspeck 2007: 475). We have already mentioned that Benjamin was keenly interested in the city, a subject inseparably connected with the existence of the masses moving through urban space.[7] If his key thesis – that '[t]he way in which human perception is organized – the medium in which it occurs – is conditioned not only by nature but by history' (Benjamin 2010/1935: 15) – is important from the point of view of media philosophy, it is equally important that he connects this transformation with '*the entire mode of existence of human collectives*' (Benjamin 2010/1935: 15), which is to say, with social life rather than individual human existence.

Benjamin argues that '[t]he alignment [Ausrichtung] of reality with the masses and of the masses with reality is a process of immeasurable importance for both thinking and perception' (Benjamin 2010/1935: 16). According to Astrid Deuber-Mankowsky, Benjamin conceives of reality, much like Siegfried Kracauer, as something constructed by the masses. Unlike Kracauer, however, Benjamin approaches this problematic in terms of movement, rather than seeing it from an optical perspective (cf. Deuber-Mankowsky 2009: 59–61). He connects the decay of the aura with the rise of the masses, and with a mode of perception in which the object is no longer grasped as occupying a unique time and place, but as something essentially repeatable. As they are in constant motion, the masses are no longer able to perceive the world in a focused, concentrated manner. Whereas to perceive the aura requires a certain kind of contemplation, Benjamin identifies a marked shift across all spheres of contemporary art towards a 'distracted' form of perception.[8]

In fact, certain artforms have always been perceived in this distracted way. This is particularly evident in the case of architecture, which for Benjamin represents 'the prototype of an artwork that is received in a state of distraction and through the collective' (Benjamin 2010/1935: 33).[9] For Benjamin, architecture is remarkable to the extent that it is perceived not only optically, but above all tactilely, the distinction being that '[t]actile reception comes about not so much by way of attention as by way of habit' (Benjamin 2010/1935: 34). In other words, we do not meditate on architecture, we habituate ourselves to it. While optical perception involves attentive observation, tactile perception implies the passive mode of being affected. 'Under certain circumstances', Benjamin argues, 'this form of reception shaped by architecture acquires canonical value. For the tasks which face the human apparatus of perception at historical turning points cannot be performed solely by optical means – that is, by way of contemplation. They are mastered gradually – taking their cue from tactile reception – through habit' (Benjamin 2010/1935: 34).

At this point, film comes into play in a fundamental way: '*Reception in distraction* [. . .] *finds in the cinemas its central place*. And there, where the collective seeks distraction, the tactically [taktisch] dominant element that rules over the regrouping of apperception is by no means lacking' (Benjamin 2010/1935: 34). According to Benjamin, film shows the tension of the present precisely by virtue of the fact that 'this tactically dominant element asserts itself in optics itself [. . .] through the shock effect of its image sequences'

(Benjamin 2010/1935: 34). This is also why film is 'the most important subject matter, at present, for the theory of perception that the Greeks called aesthetics' (Benjamin 2010/1935: 34). 'Film is the art form corresponding to [. . .] profound changes in the apparatus of apperception – changes that are experienced on the scale of private existence by each passerby in big city traffic, and on the scale of world history by each fighter against the present social order' (Benjamin 2010/1935: 33). (On the connection between architecture and film, cf. Chapter 2, pp. 50–1, 55–6, 64.)

3. The problem of mastering emancipated technology

Based on the preceding discussion, it should be clear that Benjamin's essay on the work of art does not only address the question of how technologies of reproduction have transformed art. Behind this question lies a more fundamental problem regarding the relationship between technology and human (collective) existence broadly speaking.

Benjamin does not conceive of technology in opposition to humanity. On the contrary, as he writes in the final aphorism of *One-Way Street*, 'In technology a *physis* is being organized through which mankind's contact with the cosmos takes a new and different form from that which it had in nations and families' (Benjamin 1979b/1928: 104). Writing ten years before the essay on technological reproducibility, Benjamin considers here the whole of humanity as the only subject capable of renewing the human relationship to the world, of restoring its interaction with the cosmos, while technology itself is understood as a means or medium for mastering the 'relation between nature and man'.

In this context, he emphatically rejects the idea that technology serves as a tool for mastering nature, echoing certain passages in his essay 'On Language' that criticize the notion that language serves as a communication tool based on arbitrary convention – a notion he considers 'bourgeois' (Benjamin 1979a/1916: 111, 116). In *One-Way Street*, he rejects the idea that technology is a tool for mastering nature, calling it imperialistic: 'The mastery of nature, so the imperialists teach, is the purpose of all technology. But who would trust a cane wielder who proclaimed the mastery of children by adults to be the purpose of education?' (Benjamin 1979b/1928: 104). In a way that will remind us of his essay on technological reproducibility, Benjamin connects the problem of unmastered technology, and thus of the unmastered relationship between nature and man, with war: 'But because the lust for profit of the ruling class sought satisfaction through it, technology betrayed man and turned the bridal bed [of humanity and cosmos] into a bloodbath' (Benjamin 1979b/1928: 104).

In the essay on technological reproducibility, we read more specifically that, unlike prehistoric societies in which technology (together with art) was closely linked to ritual, today's technology is emancipated. Yet in this emancipation it stands in relation to society 'as a second nature [. . .] no less elemental than that given to primeval society' (Benjamin 2010/1935: 18). According to Benjamin, one must literally *learn* to master this element. This is why film is so important:

> art once again places itself at the service of such an apprenticeship – and in particular film. Film serves to train human beings in those new apperceptions and reactions demanded by interaction with an apparatus whose role in their lives is expanding almost daily. To make the enormous technological apparatus of our time an object of human innervation – that is the historical task in whose service film finds its true meaning. (Benjamin 2010/1935: 19)

Benjamin's notion in *One-Way Street* that '[i]n technology a *physis* is being organized' resonates with his claim in 'The Work of Art' that perception is organized historically, that is, through technology. Technology is thus an organ of the 'physical' (but not immutable) being in the world, whose 'subject' is not the individual but a collective – a 'social reality' (Benjamin 1996d/1930: 312).

4. Media of the world's self-givenness

It should already be clear that even while Benjamin acknowledges the importance of new artistic media, it is not the media themselves that interest him, but the extent to which they correspond to a new, immediate way of perceiving the world, one which humans have to assimilate. It is precisely this effort to assimilate the new mode of perception that film serves.

Let us recall the formulation mentioned earlier, according to which film is 'the art form corresponding to [. . .] profound changes in the apparatus of apperception – changes that are experienced on the scale of private existence by each passerby in big city traffic, and on the scale of world history by each fighter against the present social order' (Benjamin 2010/1935: 33). It is no accident that Benjamin draws heavily on analogies between the way we experience film and the way we experience architecture. It could even be argued that the architecture of the city is itself a technology for managing the relationship between man and nature; as such, it co-determines the organization of perception. However, in contrast to film, which provides a context in which to practice new apperceptions, the city determines our 'medium of perception' – that is, our relation to the world – in a non-artistic and not-so-playful fashion.

It should be even more obvious in the case of the city than that of film that what 'determines' the medium of perception is not so much the objective technologies that characterize the urban setting, but rather the setting itself, the specific environment of movement in the 'atmosphere' of the city. In other words, the big city conditions perception not through 'its' technologies, but directly through what Benjamin sometimes refers to as its 'physiognomy'. It is also in this broader sense that we may understand Benjamin's references to architecture in his essay on technological reproducibility, namely as the (determinative) physiognomy of the city. From the point of view of the urban pedestrian, the city is not so much an *object* of perception; rather, through its architecture and by virtue of his habituation to the city, the pedestrian assimilates the city into his own physiognomy, his own organism. To use Benjamin's own terms, the city is assimilated as part of the pedestrian's own perceptual organization: the city-as-technology becomes his or her *organ*. At the same time, however, it disappears in its performance of mediation, to the point that it acts immediately.

Hence, it seems problematic to classify Benjamin's media philosophy in the tradition of 'media diaphana', which originates with Aristotle and continues up to the present day (Somaini 2016a: 19–25).[10] Benjamin undoubtedly regards the medium neither as a technical tool, nor as a form of representation, nor as a means of communication (Somaini 2016a: 19). In the tradition of media diaphana, however, the medium is defined as the intermediating substance between two objects, that is, between subject and object. Benjamin's conception of the medium diverges here insofar as it challenges the subject-object dichotomy itself.[11] Let us recall how this conception in various contexts – the imagination, language and (Romantic) reflection – places the medium *outside* such a dichotomy, suggesting that the 'givenness' of things does not lie in their self-identity, but rather in a form of mediation irreducible to that between subject(s) and/or object(s).[12] This is true as well for Benjamin's later reflections on the medium of perception. In accordance with the concept of technology as an organization of the *physis* (of humankind), and therefore as an organ, the medium of perception is also directly on the 'body' of humanity, as it were, not between it and the objectivity of the world. In more radical terms, if Benjamin emphasizes the mediality of perception, it is not in the sense of the perception of a subject through which an object is given, but rather in the articulation of reality itself.

5. Benjamin's media thinking

We can now return to the question of whether the disproportionate attention given to Benjamin's later writings on mediality is justified, and whether commonalities can be found between his early and late thinking in this context. Based on the argument presented here, I claim that any non-reductive interpretation of Benjamin's essay on technological reproducibility must necessarily take his earlier ideas into account. Benjamin does not reduce the medium to something else (technology, for instance). On the contrary, he reveals its (paradoxical) fundamentality. As a consequence, Benjamin's concept of the medium is based neither on a model in which objectively graspable technology is the *a priori* basis of everything, nor on one in which the medium is only a tool for the transmission of what is essential (the communication of a message, for example). Instead, he forces us to think of the medium as a kind of *immediate mediator*, and of mediation as the *immediacy of giving* irreducible to absolute givenness.

Sybille Krämer has rightly pointed out that '[t]he discovery of the formational power of media parallels the "linguistic turn" that took place [. . .] through the work of Austin, Ryle and Wittgenstein, who determined that linguisticality was a basic condition of our relation to the world' (Krämer 2015: 28). The analogy between media thinking and the linguistic turn is that 'in both cases it involves a reflexive figure whose goal is to reconstruct the opacity and autonomy of transitory and secondary phenomena, thereby showing that something considered derivative and inferior actually has the power to define structures and systems' (Krämer 2015: 29). In Benjamin, we find both 'turns', and the claim can be made (though its elaboration lies beyond the scope of this chapter) that reflections on the concept of the medium represent a specific transformation of his earlier reflections on the concept of language. The key feature in both cases is that Benjamin does not consider language or the medium primarily as a semantic or symbolic instrument, but precisely as a *medium of the immediate* (cf. also Rautzenberg 2009: 348). Changes in technology, like changes in the 'physiognomy' of the city, interest him insofar as they are connected with the 'functioning' of a new immediacy. As we have already seen, this applies as well to Benjamin's attitude towards technologies of reproduction, whose reproductive function does not figure in his writings as a mediator of the same but, rather, as a medium corresponding to the transformation of immediacy, to a new form of immediate perception.

Benjamin formulated his reflections on mediality around the same time that the philosophy of media was first coming on the scene, a time when no methods or corresponding disciplines had yet been established for dealing with the concept. We must therefore consider his writings on the subject as truly avant-garde,[13] in the sense that they involve pioneering the field itself, paving the way for new approaches. Benjamin's reader is therefore confronted by a tangle of open roads, and so also by an open question regarding the core or unifying principle of his philosophical position.[14] Without wishing to downplay the significance of his theological and Marxist influences, I would argue that Benjamin's media thinking, his thinking on the medium, is already present in his reflections on language, and that it can be understood as a fundamental dimension of his approach as a whole. Benjamin's late thinking then clearly shows that this foundation is never absolute – never fundamental in the strong sense of the word – but always historically concrete. Accordingly, while there is no single true language, no one true medium, mediality is a universal characteristic of being in the world.

If, in recent decades, media thinking has reached the insight that discrete approaches to individual media are not sufficient – that it will be necessary on the contrary to open media studies to philosophical questions, while simultaneously reworking philosophy (to whatever extent the task remains) through a reflection on its own mediality – then it is precisely among this constellation of considerations that Benjamin's media philosophy appears utterly current, even if it has never had anything to do with today's pervasive media and technologies. At the same time, the essay on technological reproducibility is only one of Benjamin's contributions to media thinking: a contribution with a specific political agenda. A full understanding of Benjamin's writings on mediality presupposes consideration of his work as a whole.

Notes

1 Benjamin makes a sharp distinction between the way adults and children perceive colour. While adults perceive colour as the quality of a substance, allowing them to track things in space-time, children can perceive colours as such.
2 Benjamin takes exception with Kant's separation between sensuality and rationality logic.
3 A more comprehensive interpretation of Benjamin's philosophy of language can be found in Ritter 2007. See also Menninghaus 1980 and Menke 1991.
4 Böhme and Ehrenspeck (2007: 450–1) describe this 'limitedness' of things as follows: 'Things do not speak; their being is linguistic.'
5 The relationship between Benjamin and German romanticism, as well as the question of affinity between romanticism and Benjamin's philosophical

approach is discussed in several of the studies collected in Benjamin and Hanssen (2002).

6   In this context, Böhme and Ehrenspeck argue that Benjamin's emphasis on the inseparability of truth from representation 'hardly surprises us today [. . .] In the 1920s, by contrast, it was scandalous. What surprises us today is that Benjamin found it necessary to resort to pure Platonism in order to safeguard his thought system' (Böhme and Ehrenspeck 2007: 461).

7   Coming across another of Benjamin's (and Baudelaire's) favourite figures: the *flâneur*. On the significance of this figure, see for example Böhme and Ehrenspeck 2007: 468–74.

8   Benjamin speaks literally of the 'Rezeption in der Zerstreuung' ('reception in distraction'). Perhaps it is worth mentioning that, in addition to 'distraction' and 'entertainment', the term *Zerstreuung* also refers to the notion of 'dispersal', whether of doubts or protesters, with an evident connection to the masses.

9   Benjamin uses the following image to illustrate the difference between contemplative and distracted perception: 'A person who concentrates before a work of art is absorbed by it; he enters into the work, just as, according to legend, a Chinese painter entered his completed painting while beholding it. By contrast, the distracted masses absorb the work of art into themselves. Their waves lap around it; they encompass it with their tide' (Benjamin 2010/1935: 33).

10 A brief discussion of the Aristotelian concept can be found in Krämer 2015: 32–4.

11 Benjamin states this explicitly in his 1918 work 'On the Program of the Coming Philosophy' (Benjamin 1996a/1918).

12 It is for the same reason that it can be misleading to work with the metaphor of a 'constructed reality', or more specifically with the idea that reality is constructed by the masses (*pace* Deuber-Mankowsky 2009).

13 Tobias Wilke's definition of the avant-garde seems particularly apt: 'From the beginning [. . .] avant-garde art movements have taken up the image of small bands of "troops," marching like pioneers ahead of broader social formations to come. And they have gone on to expand this metaphor of territorial exploration and military mobility to elucidate both the function and the peculiar character of avant-garde aesthetic practices' (Wilke 2010: 43).

14 It is no accident that many studies on Benjamin, even those which focus on a particular text or aspect of Benjamin's thinking, are so fascinated with the difficulty of solving this problem. From my point of view, the condition for the possibility of a truly articulate solution is to be found in the careful reconstruction of the unchanging conceptual structures that can be traced throughout the entire span of Benjamin's thought. A systematic reconstruction of this kind is offered, for example, by Menke (1991).

4

'Let the ghosts come back'

Modern spectrology and its media

Josef Vojvodík

'You don't need to feel afraid if a ghost actually turns up.'
'Oh, that's only a secondary fear. The real fear is a fear of what caused the apparition.'

Franz Kafka, 'Unhappiness', 1912

'Modern technology, contrary to appearances, although it is scientific, increases tenfold the power of ghosts. The future belongs to ghosts.'

Jacques Derrida in *Echographies of Television*, 1996

Both pre-realist and post-realist epistemes are developing within an optical paradigm whose interpretation involves speculation on invisible phenomena.

Renate Lachmann, *Erzählte Phantastik*, 2002

The psychiatrist Erwin W. Straus, in his reflections on the 'upright posture', mentions the case of a patient who was admitted to a clinic because, upset by certain perceived insinuations, he shot his television. 'It is perhaps one of the principal features of the paranoid schizophrenic' writes Straus, 'that he is no longer able to maintain the distance of his regard in the presence of actual events' (Straus 1965/1963: 687). In his seminal work *Die Antiquiertheit des Menschen* (1956, The Antiquatedness of the Human Being), Günther Anders regards this inability to maintain the distance of one's regard as a phantom effect of image and projection technologies, especially television and radio, which have transformed the world into a phantom and simulation phenomenon. With television, ghosts have entered the living room and become part of everyday life: 'When [the world] becomes socially important only in its form of reproduction, i.e. as an image, the difference between being and appearance, between reality and image is eliminated' (Anders 1985/1956: 111). In spite of its pervasively apocalyptic undertone, characteristic of a post-war era in the grip of Hiroshima and post-historical thought, Anders's book (especially the chapter 'The World as Phantom and Matrix') introduces various topics that would later be followed up by Marshall McLuhan and other prominent media theorists: his thesis, for example, on the 'ontological ambiguity' of media phenomena (Anders 1985/1956: 131). However, this chapter does not only deal with the critique of the media in its technical aspect. Indeed, in the introductory sections (1–3), it outlines positive attitudes towards this technical aspect, primarily as this concerns the notion of man as 'homo pictor' (Hans Jonas), creating images, simulacra and simulations in part because he himself – as a 'being of appearances', as Wilhelm Weischedel writes (1960a: 165) – is subject to the power of images. The image is 'paradoxically double', in the primary sense that its essence consists in the 'absorption of nearness and distance', from which emerges the paradox of an 'absent presence' (*ungegenwärtige Anwesenheit*) created through pictorial representation. This is the inner duality of the image, corresponding to the duality of the thing the image re-presents: by its appearance (*Erscheinen*), the image refers to another phenomenon that appears in itself. All that exists, according to Weischedel, exists only in the images of its being – 'We always see the world in the image of the world' (1960a: 162) – and he points to Nicolai Hartmann's description of the image as 'a necessary element of the essence of the relation of knowledge' from his *Grundzüge einer Metaphysik der Erkenntnis* (1921, Foundations of a Metaphysics of Knowledge). We are subject to the power of the image, at once aware of this power and at the same time seeking to escape it. We are subject to the power of appearance because in our own essence we exist at a distance from the truth. Only in appearance do we approach the truth: 'Truth reveals itself, but by doing so hides in its appearance' (Weische 1960a: 165).

On the one hand, the human individual longs to escape this paradoxical duality of the medial and longs to break the 'beautiful appearance of the image', all the time remaining aware of the unreality of this act: 'Man longs for appearance, because he hates both being and not-being, because he himself is a being of appearance' (1960a: 165). The things that a painting represents are indeed present in the painting, but at the same time unreal, present only in the mode of appearance. For Weischedel, the 'ontological weakness' (*ontologische Schwäche*) of the image lies in this broken relationship to reality, bestowing on it a unique power. Man is subjected to this power, and he suffers from it, but he is able to resist that power by creating his own simulacra.

That the notion of 'simulacrum' has garnered so much attention of late, argues Wolfgang Iser, has to do with the fact that it allows us to grasp something, as a representation of what is absent, that 'mimesis', focused as it is on the object, fails to express (Iser 1998: 676). Iser regards simulation, simulacrum and phantasm as 'emergent phenomena' that represent the transformation of 'a complex system of imitation of nature' (Iser 1998: 682), which is to say the transformation of a mimesis that leaves its mark in simulation. In all these emergent phenomena there is an inherent element constant in all variants, namely 'being of the nature of an image' (*Bildhaftigkeit*), whether the image is a representation or idea: 'In the imitation of nature the image is a representation, in the simulation an "as if" (*Als Ob*), in the simulacrum a revelation of deception, and in the phantasm the figuration of unreality' (Iser 1998: 683).

The last sections of this chapter (9–10) discuss the relationship between the image and death, taking as starting point a posthumous photograph of the painter Bohumil Kubišta and another photograph depicting the death mask of painter Jindřich Štyrský. Roland Barthes has written with extraordinary subtlety not only on the relationship between the image, the photographic image and death, but also on photography and grief, pointing out that the advent of the medium of photography brought with it something unknown at the time: the visibility of mortality. Unlike fine art, photography is never completely fictitious or fantastic. Whatever is in front of the camera lens is always in a certain sense that which has been (Barthes calls this mode of existence *ça-a-été*).

> Photography must have some historical relation with what Edgar Morin calls the 'crisis of death' beginning in the second half of the nineteenth century. [...] For Death must be somewhere in a society; if it is no longer (or less intensely) in religion, it must be elsewhere; perhaps in this image which produces Death while trying to preserve life. Contemporary with the withdrawal of rites, Photography may correspond to the intrusion, in our modern society, of an asymbolic Death, outside of religion, outside of ritual, a kind of abrupt dive into literal Death. *Life / Death*: the paradigm is reduced to a simple click, the one separating the initial pose from the final print. (Barthes 1981/1980: 90, 92)

Barthes also names one of the key events of modernity: the disappearance of ritual as a result of the process of secularization and modernization, and resulting affinity between modernity – its artistic and poetic expressions – and grief. This last is paradigmatically conveyed by the motto of Eliot's *The Waste Land*, taken from Petronius's *Satyricon*, in which Trimalchio says at his feast: 'For I saw Sibyl at Cumae with my own eyes. She was hanging in a bottle, and when the guys asked her, "What do you want, Sybil?" she replied, "I want to die'" (Petronius 2000: 35). The experience of the First World War, rapidly developing process of modernization, vision of a modern city where ghosts of the dead mingle with the living, and representations of ritual burial and mourning in key texts of the period reveal and reflect a 'thanatoid' element proper to modernity (cf. Section 3 of Chapter 5, pp. 152–65). The 'simple click' that Barthes writes about involves the fixation of a ghostly (because already mortified) moment, of that which may never return (we will discuss the ghostliness of the photographic image later in Section 8).

Yet it is the image in general, the power of the image, that Jacques Derrida (writing on the death of his friend, the art historian and philosopher Louis Marin, in 1993) understands as the 'power of death'. Here the image speaks to us of absence itself: 'death, which is expressed, in sum, by all the other absences as absences, is what gives painting its greatest force' (Derrida 2001: 154). We will return to this topic in Section 7.

1. Film: The double 'image-ghost of man'

In his sociological-anthropological interpretation of cinema, *Le cinéma ou l'homme imaginaire* (1956, *The Cinema, or the Imaginary Man*, 2005), Edgar Morin recalls the surreal scenario of Jacques Prévert and Georges Ribemont-Dessaignes's play *Le métro fantôme* (1951, The Phantom Metro), originally written for radio, in which a photograph drains the life from a man and turns him into a ghost. 'The world of images', says Morin, 'constantly doubles life' (Morin 2005/1956: 29). What film presents to the viewer, above all, is a magical play of phantom images, which the viewer, sitting in the dark cinema, perceives as his doubles, as 'the image-ghost of man' (Morin 2005/1956: 25): 'This image is projected, alienated, objectivized to such a degree that it appears as an autonomous ghost, endowed with an absolute reality. This absolute reality is at the same time an absolute superreality: the double is the focal point of all the needs of the individual, as if they were realized there, especially his most madly subjective need: immortality' (Morin 2005/1956: 25). The double has a 'magical power': 'The archaic person is literally *doubled* [...] throughout his life, to finally be left, as remains, a corpse, upon his death. Once the flesh is destroyed, the decomposition complete, the double frees itself definitively to become a specter, *a ghost*, a spirit' (Morin 2005/1956: 34).

Indeed, Morin not only considers that the world of film has a certain proximity to the archaic image and perception of the world but also directly represents the 'resurrection of the archaic vision of the world' (Morin 2005/1956: 154). Film animates the fantastic, the dream, the 'spectacle of nature', and is therefore akin to the cave drawings in Altamira or Lascaux, just as 'the scribblings of children, the frescoes of Michelangelo, sacred and profane representations, myths, legends' (Morin 2005/1956: 217). Yet never have these images been so alive as with the filmic image, this 'avant-garde of the world of technology' (Morin 2005/1956: 213).

That which represents a symptom of the crisis of the modern world, culture and the inflationary 'colonization' of the image by digital media for such thinkers as Max Picard, Günther Anders and Hans Belting (who we will discuss further on) is for Morin an important part of the development of civilizational modernity, since film as a modern medium is not only an 'anthropological mirror' (Morin 2005/1956: 212) but also a 'mirror of human participation' in the reality of the modern epoch (Morin 2005/1956: 218). (On the fluctuation between 'media trance' and 'stimulation' cf. Chapter 7, esp. pp. 142–4, and Chapter 9, p. 230 and *passim*.) This enthusiastic theory of film as a medium of imaginary anthropology, and even the technical realization of certain ideas already existing in the spiritual sphere – Morin writes that it was the specificity of film that was 'so searched for in the platonic sky of essences' (Morin 2005/1956: 217) – ultimately leads to the defence of technics as a field of culture. This defence had already been advanced, albeit from a different philosophical and conceptual perspective, by Ernst Cassirer, one of those thinkers who, uniquely among his contemporaries, defended the positive meaning of technics as one of the 'fundamental powers of the spirit' – and this at a time when the prevailing attitude was to demonize (Ludwig Klages) or pathologize it (Husserl's *Crisis of European Sciences*). For Cassirer, the question of the value of technics cannot be decided by assessing its mutual pros and cons. Here 'it is not about like or dislike, happiness or pain, but about freedom and unfreedom' (Cassirer 2004: 172).[1] We find the direct embodiment of these three instances of Western culture – science, technics and art – in the figure of Leonardo da Vinci, in his scientific experiments, technical inventions and artistic projects.

2. Technics as 'open form'

In October 1932, Helmuth Plessner gave a keynote lecture in Weimar with the title 'Wiedergeburt der Form im technischen Zeitalter' (The Revival of Form in the Age of Technology), as part of an event commemorating the twenty-fifth anniversary of the founding of the *Deutscher Werkbund*, an association of leading architects, artists, designers, industrialists and artisans. In the lecture, Plessner emphasizes a marked strengthening of artistic consciousness that developed alongside the explosion of technics during the first decades of the nineteenth century. It was as if the creation of new artistic forms and relations – form referring above all, as Plessner points out, to relations and order – was meant to buttress against the immensely chaotic and disruptive influence of modern technology, as it was perceived. Indeed, it was as early as 1924 that Plessner, in his essay 'Die Utopie in der Maschine' (Utopia in the Machine), wrote (prophetically):

> To escape from machines and return to nature is impossible. They won't let us go and we won't let them go. By virtue of a mysterious violence they are in us and we are in them. We must proceed yet further, following their law, until they show us at some higher stage [...] the very limits of the control of nature. (Plessner 1985/1924: 31–40)

In his 1932 lecture, Plessner asks whether the development of technics brings with it the development of a new style or new forms, and thus the emergence of a new industrial aesthetic. Four years later, in his lecture 'Das Problem der Klassizität für unsere Zeit' (The Problem of Classicism in Our Time), which he delivered in exile at the International School for Philosophy in Amersfoort, Netherlands, Plessner was already more sceptical about the importance of technics for art and culture. In 1932, however, he still saw considerable hope in this connection: namely, in a new form that arises from the spirit of technics, in interaction with it, rather than taking up a romanticized and therefore false opposition to it. According to Plessner, the creative interplay of technics, art and lifestyle grows out of an awareness of the positive potential of technology, the measure and model of which is what Plessner calls the ideal of 'open form' (in opposition to the past ideal of closed form). As Peter Bernhard has demonstrated (2007: 237–52), Plessner's lecture – which was only recently published by his estate in 2001 – is fairly remarkable, built on anthropological-philosophical foundations that contain the early beginnings of a philosophy of technics. Plessner's concept of 'open form' revolves around the idea that man does not inhabit a rigid, determined, circumscribed world, but a space of open and unlimited possibilities. This also corresponds to the idea of the openness of technics and its endless potential.

3. Humanity as a 'medial event'

More recently, Cassirer's cultural anthropology has been taken up by Ernst Wolfgang Orth, who attributes a medial character to the intentionality of human consciousness. The human concept of and approach to the world, he argues, is mediated at the level of sensory perception – that is, through media – which is what allows for social and cultural communication and orientation. This mediation includes not only modern technological media, but the natural world and intersubjective (person-to-person) communication; this includes formation of individual social bonds and complex forms of cultural performance, such as art and literature, as well as cultural and religious practices, and so on. Orth defines this kind of mediality as an 'anthropological radical' (*anthropologisches Radikal*) of human orientation, referring to a complex set of empirical, practical-pragmatic, time-space actions and theoretical, spiritual, but also aesthetic motives and contents (Orth 1991: 272). He further develops one of the basic theses of (Kantian) philosophical anthropology: that man is a being who must productively and projectively give shape to his identity. Man is a creative and imaginative 'creator' (*Bildner*) with respect to both the world and himself. The work of art, as a function of this creative subjectivity, is not only an aesthetic but also a 'practical' expression, that is, in relation to his being. The human capacity for creative constitution of oneself and the world comprises not only works of fantasy and fiction but the production of illusions.

Orth understands media as 'sensory substrates' (*sinnliche Substrate*) functioning as actual or potential bearers of meanings (*Bedeutungsträger*). In this context, he writes about the 'mediality of human orientation' in the world (Orth 1996: 167). Orientation is a 'paradigmatic metaphor' in the sense that it makes up the constitutive moment of culture as a particular form of orientation. Among the paradigmatic metaphors of this kind, Orth also classifies knowledge, experience, image, speech, reading and so on. For Orth, one of the essential characteristics of cultural anthropology is that primary subject-centred concepts ('intentions', for example) cannot be substituted by mere relations, just as it is not possible to substitute the concept of an 'act' (*Handlung*) with that of an 'operation'. Nor is it the case that the category of the human being, or man as empirical-transcendental subject, may be replaced, even in the world of technical media by a new type of 'user'. As Orth reminds us, man cannot slough off his 'transcendental shadow' even in the 'posthuman' era. Notwithstanding frequent claims of the 'death of man' and 'death of the subject', he remains an irreducible centre of cultural, aesthetic, medial and technical practices and events.

Following Max Scheler's work in anthropology and Cassirer's philosophy of culture, Orth elaborates three basic theses in his cultural anthropology: (1) Man himself is a 'medial event' (*Medienereignis*) as an organism that is at once meaningful (*bedeutsamer*) and meaning-giving (*be-deutender*), and is thus able to exist in both self-relation and reflexive self-distance (Orth 2006: 29–42); (2) The human body, in its specific 'mediality' and cultivation, is always already culturally disposed and 'formed' and in this sense also represents – in Ernst Cassirer's term – a 'symbolic form'; (3) Orth's understanding of culture as 'the world of man' represents a rehabilitation of both the subject and subjectivity as a fully concrete cultural event (*Ereignis*). In Orth's anthropology, the subject always represents concrete humanity in its situatedness in the world. The human individual, who does not simply live but exists as a subject in its 'potentiality' (*Seinkönnen*), manifests itself as a plurality of personal individualities. This model of subjectivity has a universal character; what a culture is primarily concerned with is its concrete subjectivity, just as the world itself is always first and foremost the world of the subject.

4. 'Place of image'

For his anthropology of the image in *Bild-Anthropologie* (2001, *Anthropology of Images*, 2011), Hans Belting proceeds from the idea that the image of the human *body* as a metonymy of the *image* of man was consistently 'colonized' by technical and digital media during the nineteenth and twentieth centuries, transformed by analogy into a technically and later digitally reproduced image. The representation of man, in each case, 'represents a being (*Sein*) that can only be conveyed as an appearance (*Schein*). It conveys a person through the image in which he appears. This image once more acts on the representation of the body, which is staged [by the image] in such a way that the body will then provide the expected evidence' (Belting 2001: 89). The cultural history of the image is analogously reflected in the cultural history of the body. According to Belting, however, this concerns not only the theory of the image but also a broader philosophy, one that would be centred not on the image '*an sich*' but on its philosophical implications and related issues as these concern man, and on the basic question, *What is man?*

According to Belting, we find ourselves today in a paradoxical situation: no epoch in human history has been accompanied by such an excessive production and ubiquity of images, which, however, results in an iconoclastic anesthetization of the image. This also affects the past, collective memory and the human body: 'Today, on the contrary, due to a discontinuity with the past, we are experiencing "the end of the identity between history and memory", as Pierre Nora writes. The disappearance of official and collective memory is compensated and at the same time accelerated by the blind purchase of commemorative material in the technical memories of archives and media' (Belting 2001: 67). In an analogous manner, today's 'iconomania' is accompanied by the disappearance of the body (Belting 2001: 196). The dominance of the semiotic-hermeneutic tradition in the twentieth century, which focused on abstractly spiritual *sense* and *meaning*, and which marginalized the status of the body and corporeality, has played a role in this. Belting writes about the 'flight of the body':

> Today's flight of the body provides new evidence of the connection between perception of the image and perception of the body. Fleeing into the body and fleeing from the body are just two opposing forms of dealing with the body, and of defining oneself either through it or against it. Today, the immanence and transcendence of the body are confirmed by the images we use to impose this contrary tendency. Today's digital media, like all technical media before them, change our perception, yet this perception remains bound to the body. Only through images do we vicariously free ourselves from our bodies, from which we distance ourselves with our gaze. Electronic mirrors show us how we want to be [shown] but also how we are not. They show us *artificial bodies* that cannot die, thus fulfilling our utopian wishes *in effigy*. (Belting 2001: 23)

Certain aspects of Belting's anti-semiotic anthropology of the image are susceptible to criticism, including its very broadly conceived concepts of the image and body, apodictic nature of various claims, and insufficient (and unclear) distinction between the 'external' and 'internal' image, that is, between the material side of visual artefacts and the fantasy images of the consciousness that imagines them (Wiesing 2005: 24). Yet Belting's work remains valid in a number of other aspects, in particular its critique of the usurpation and virtualization of man by technical media. It should also be emphasized that he understands his anthropology of the image and already declares it in the subtitle of the book as an *Entwurf* ('draft' or 'project'), which remains open, and not as a conclusive work on the subject. One of the main theses of Belting's anthropology is especially important, namely that the primal condition for the creation of images, the pictorial presentation of absence, is a ritual processing of the consciousness of death. This comprises the experience and perception of the other *as other in his lived presence*, as if conditioned by an awareness of the other's disappearance. This sense of presence carries within it a prefiguration of that which is to come: the other's disappearance even before the moment of physical death – the presence and perception of the other as a 'departing' other, as Iris Därmann writes in her interpretation of the mediality of the image in *Tod und Bild* (Death and the Image), 'always indicates that the possibility of mourning the other on this side of the grave, before and beyond his (actual) death, has already been evoked and taken place' (Därmann 1995: 450).

Belting asks what role death plays in the emergence of the image, in the creation of images and for the analogy between image and death, which is as old as the image itself: 'The contradiction between presence and absence, which we still find in images today, has its root in the experience of the death of the other. We have images before our eyes, just as we have the dead who are no longer here' (Belting 2001: 143). He recalls that among the pre-ceramic Neolithic, the very first posthumous masks of the cult of the dead represented the skull. Like a painting, a mask also lives on the basis of an absence, which it replaces with a vicarious presence.

5. 'Being a skull': Cube, crystal and black box

The logic of dead heads, if we can call it that, appears indeed to be a paradoxical logic of *de-signification*: once the face is dead, what remains of it is at the same time an 'insignificant object' and an object of terror. But there exists another way to 'de-signify' faces, and to make objects of them, any old objects that are however heavy with fright. This is the way of the *Cube*. (Didi-Huberman 2015/1993: 74–5)

Georges Didi-Huberman is referring here to Alberto Giacometti's 1934 sculpture *Le cube* (*Pavillon nocturne*) (Cube (Nocturnal Pavilion)), a monolithic polyhedron, reminiscent of a crystal, in which the French philosopher sees 'an object of latent death' (Didi-Huberman 2015/1993: 75). The sculpture presents the viewer with an unsettling geometric shape and volume: a polyhedron that, in spite of its (apparent) fullness, contains and reveals only emptiness – or, more precisely, an experience of emptiness that characterizes the cenotaph. Giacometti's *Cube* occupies a unique place in the chronology of his work. Didi-Huberman recalls two events that had a fateful significance in the creation of the *Cube*: the death in June 1933 of the artist's father – the painter Giovanni Giacometti – precisely at the time when Alberto Giacometti was exhibiting his *La table surréaliste* (Surrealist Table), and devoting himself intensively to Dürer's engraving *Melencolia I*, which was being shown at the Petit Palais in Paris during the spring and summer of 1933. In this context, Giacometti set to work on the *Cube* as on an image and object of grief – 'a crystal of absence and a crystal of spacing' (Didi-Huberman 2015/1993: 134) – which accounts for a peculiar tension arising in the work between pure geometric space and problematic portrait, between 'father and son' (Didi-Huberman 2015/1993: 157). It is a cube, in other words, that takes on anthropomorphic features in order to demonstrate the absence of a face – 'humanity in absentia' (*humanité par défaut*; Didi-Huberman 1992: 102) – thus disturbing our gaze with the missing dimension of the human. 'Humanity' is present here, but only in a state of dissemblance, or as evidence and trace of a missing person. What is missing here is a person, 'faces and bodies' (Didi-Huberman 1992: 101). From this perspective, it is possible to see in Giacometti's *Cube* a gravestone or cenotaph for a lost loved one. Instead of the human body, what emerges here is an empty cube or geometric body, similar to the strictly geometric cubes made of modern materials by American minimalists: Tony Smith's 'Black Boxes', for instance, which quite deliberately evoke the archaic forms of ancient Egyptian sacred buildings – a problematic anthropomorphism that Didi-Huberman discusses in his book *Ce que nous voyons, ce qui nous regarde* (What We See Looks at Us, 1992).

Cube, crystal, head, skull – these are images and associations to which Giacometti returns again and again. As Didi-Huberman quotes the artist:

> One day, while I wanted to draw a young girl, something struck me, I mean that, suddenly, I saw that the only thing that remained alive, was the gaze. What remained, the head that was transforming into a skull, was becoming almost the equivalent of the skull of the dead person. That which marked the difference between the dead and the person was the gaze. So I asked myself – and I have thought about it since – if, basically, it would not be interesting to sculpt the skull of a dead person. We try to make the sculpture of a living person, but in the living person, without a doubt, what makes the living person is his gaze. (Didi-Huberman 2015/1993: 72)

The cube represents the manifestation of a crystal and latency of a skull; we must therefore understand this play of forms, this composition of edges and facets, this play of the crystal projected onto the head, writes Didi-Huberman, as a 'scintillating play of death' (2015/1993: 79).[2] Let us return, however, to Belting's postulate that image theory should also focus on philosophical implications and questions that are related to humankind, with the underlying question of what it means to be human. Belting's critique aims to counter technical media in its monopoly on the image, which he sees primarily as the image and place of man. Through the mutual permeation of the artificial and the natural, the technical and the living, the automaton and the acting subject, the relative distance modern life from nature and decentring of human self-experience, the order of nature, once founded on ontology, has lost its binding force. Man has become, as Gerhard Gamm (2004) writes, 'indeterminate'.

6. Negativity, indeterminacy, ambiguity: The modalities of negative anthropology

Over the last three decades, Gerhard Gamm has been developing the logic and semantics of indeterminacy as an alternative theory – and the underlying character – of modernity. According to Gamm, indeterminacy and the negative perspective represent the basic symptoms of all self-descriptions of modernity that aim to think and define itself precisely from this position. Yet Gamm also conceives of an approach that would 'make the negative positive', that is, a way to interpret negativity and ambivalence not as a deficit, but as the potential for interpreting anew the main themes of the philosophy of modernity. At the beginning of his book *Nicht nichts. Studien zu einer Semantik des Unbestimmten* (2000, Never Nothing: A Study on the Semantics of the Indeterminate), Gamm writes:

> The uncertainty and working through of all determinations of knowledge and action appear to be an important dimension of modern relations to oneself and to the world. Indeterminacy can be demonstrated by the failure of all anthropological attempts to determine the essence of man, as well as by the antinomic structures of moral principles or by the difficulties that arise in the natural sciences (up to the re-examination of the foundations of individual disciplines) from the principled indeterminacy of their subject matter. (Gamm 2000: 7)

(On the notion of indeterminacy, see also Chapter 6, esp. pp. 194–5.) In this context, however, negativity does not refer so much to 'nothing' or 'nothingness' as to the double movement of indeterminacy and that which cannot be refuted: a complex interplay of presence and absence, seen and unseen, of that which recedes, disappears and escapes, as well as exerting a certain attraction in and through it. Evidently, this is not a new nihilism but, rather, an effort to conceptualize ambivalence without recourse to the notion of deficit, namely, as the possibility of an alternative interpretation of the main themes of philosophy and philosophical anthropology of modernity.

In what sense is man 'indeterminate'? According to Gamm, the human body, in the age of 'technical reproducibility' (especially since the early 1970s), has become the object of various regimes – scientific, technological, biotechnical, molecular-genetic and so on – that have their root in a rising interest in corporeality and longevity, a phenomenon that is corollary to the 'fading' (Christian) belief in the soul and its immortality (Gamm 2004: 41). Yet Gamm considers the most striking and characteristic to be today's near fanatical effort to find new and for the most part positive definitions (Gamm

2004: 51). He refers here to Helmuth Plessner's idea – one he advanced as early as the 1920s – that man exists in a 'relation of indeterminacy to himself'. Plessner thus characterizes man's position in the world as 'excentric', in the sense that his 'centre' is not firmly determined; he bears the full weight of this excentric position, along with an awareness of the precarious state of his existence.[3] Rather than diligently searching for positive definitions, Gamm argues that these negative aspects – the 'loss of a centre', indeterminacy, 'inexplicability' – should compel us to consider whether it is not precisely in this inexplicability as it concerns the 'artificial nature' of human subjectivity that we find the very fulcrum of the self-interpretation of modernity as a whole (Gamm 2004: 53), accompanied by scenarios of the disappearance of the subject and disappearance of the human. It was already in the mid-1960s that Hans Blumenberg formulated his thesis of the indeterminacy and ambivalence of the work of art (or 'aesthetic object') as trademark of modernity in general. In his essay 'Die essentielle Vieldeutigkeit des ästhetischen Gegenstandes' (The Essential Multiplicity of the Aesthetic Object, 1966), Blumenberg asks:

> Does aesthetic subjectivity really only and primarily lie within the subject, or is the aesthetic object in itself and essentially ambiguous, in such a way that this ambiguity does not constitute its deficiency with comparison to the theoretical object, but rather makes its aesthetic function possible in the first place? Ambiguity is virtually the index under which the concreteness of the aesthetic identifies itself. (Blumenberg 2001b/1966: 112)

According to Blumenberg, ambiguity even implies 'the non-correctability of a given interpretation by another, more evident one' (Blumenberg 2001b/1966: 114). Here, the philosopher of metaphorology follows up on his 1964 study concerning one of the key aesthetic-philosophical tropes of artistic ambiguity, that is, of that which cannot be clearly defined but which occupies our thinking precisely by virtue of its ambivalence and indeterminacy: the *objet ambigu*. Taking the perspective of the aesthetics of reception, Blumenberg considers how the work of art as *objet ambigu* – a concept he borrows from Paul Valéry's dialogue *Eupalinos ou l'architecte* (1923, *Eupalinos, or the Architect*)[4] – becomes a central topic around which the common and entrenched view of things may be challenged. The reality of the *objet ambigu* thus lies in the unmanageable and inexplicable quality of its ambiguity, raising unanswered questions that cannot be dispelled. Is it a work of nature or an artefact? Does one build (*construire*) or know (*connaître*)? (Valéry 1960/1923: 33). For Valéry, the work of art, as both *mimesis* and *poiesis*, is itself of an 'ambiguous' nature. As Blumenberg (2001a/1964: 96) points out, however, the concept of imitation has a rather unconventional meaning in Valéry's aesthetics. The essence of the beautiful is precisely that which is provocatively ambiguous, indeterminate or indeterminable, polyvalent or straightforwardly unnameable. It is not by chance then that the concept of the *objet ambigu* has been applied to one of the main problems for the theory and practice of art in the twentieth century, standing for the duality and ambivalence between key oppositions: between artefact and spontaneous work of nature, artefact and thing, intentionality and unintentionality, function/purposefulness and nonpurposefulness/value, mechanical and organic, spirit and organism, body and soul, transparency and opaqueness, finitude/form and infinity/formlessness. Gamm returns to Blumenberg's interpretation of Valéry's *Eupalinos*, and to the idea of indeterminacy: In his consciousness of his own finitude and of the indifference of nature, Blumenberg observes, man feels humiliated by the domination of nature, to which he can only respond by building the sphere of culture as a 'phantom body' (*Phantomleib*), providing refuge and 'relief' (*Entlastung*) from 'absolute pressure': 'As an organic system resulting from the mechanism of evolution, "man" breaks free from the pressure exerted by this mechanism by placing something like a phantom body in its way. This is the sphere of culture' (Blumenberg 1990/1979: 182). This sphere comprises not only of institutions and their respective cultural techniques but also of art. Man's confrontation with the natural world shifts into the sphere of culture and art; in its 'painful indeterminacy', art remains 'the pleasure-giving indecipherability of human work' (Blumenberg 2001b/1966: 119). Gamm develops the thesis that the disintegration of the subject and subjectivity characteristic of modernity, originating in German romanticism and idealism, has its counterpart in the idea of maximally expanding the boundaries of art, to the point of self-loss and dissolution, whether in life, knowledge, politics or religion (Gamm 2006: 50). For Gamm, this tendency of radical self-realization in art, like that of the self-liberation of the subject, resulted in a vicious circle of the tautological 'art for art's sake', aporia and loss of the self.

Around the time of the First World War, Russian formalism was postulating a form of artistic production that emphasized the 'transparency of processes', media of 'construction' and 'constructive principles' of the work of art as 'things', using spoken and written language, materials, media of representation and their structures, colour and form, sound and voice as media for explaining the relationship to the world. Gamm shows how, in parallel with the weakening and constant blurring – or outright negation – of subjectivity and individuality, there was a growing awareness of the control exerted by 'objective structures', systems and functions, and he indicates various attendant phenomena of this development: the unconscious, chance, functionalism and automatism, the erasure of distinctions between everyday life and artistic stylizations of life practice, and between art and non-art, the reduction of a work of art to a mere object, artefact, design, incompleteness, fragmentariness and so on (Gamm 2006: 59).

7. The science of spectres, or spectrology

In 1934, the German-Swiss psychiatrist and critic of modern culture Max Picard published his book *Die Flucht vor Gott* (Flight from God, 1951), in which he considers film not as a modern medium of visual art, but as the perfect medium of escape for modern man:

> The cinema – there is the perfect Flight. [. . .] Like one in a hurry who drops his luggage, the figures have laid down their bodily substance somewhere in the background, while they themselves make off in the foreground of the screen, outlines only of their bodies. [. . .] Here in the cinema it is as if there were no more men, as if the real men were somewhere in safety, had for long been in safety, and as if these shadows had been left behind simply to flee in place of the real men. They only pretend to be in flight and even the men who sit in front of the screen in order to gaze at the shadows there seem nothing but dummies, arranged to complete the illusion, while the real men have long since departed. (Picard 1951/1934: 8–9)

Already in *Das Menschengesicht* (1929, *The Human Face*, 1931), Picard had described the face in modern times as the ghostly face of the cinema, the face of the film screen:

> today the human face does not imitate the face on the film screen, but the other way around: the face on the film screen approximates the human face of today. The moving, hurried, provisional, disappearing face of today is transferred to the mechanical: this is the face of cinema. [. . .] It is here only so long as it moves, at every moment producing only this: simply that it is here, or rather, that it is only here – without being, without presence. (Picard 1955/1929: 47)

Picard's critique of cinema and modern technical media from the metaphysical-Christian perspective may sound rather apocalyptic, conservative or pessimistic today, yet it anticipates some of the underlying motifs set forth by later media theorists, such as Günther Anders, Vilém Flusser, Jean Baudrillard and Paul Virilio. It was in the immediate aftermath of the First World War and dissolution of the concept of 'life' in European thinking, as well as an expression of departure from the idealistic conception of the absolute (Schnädelbach 1999/1983: 23), that Picard published *Der letzte Mensch* (1921, The Last Man). The former vision of a 'resurrected Adam' had been left in tatters by the bloodshed and trenches of the world war, and the enthusiastic vision of a new man had been turned into a catastrophic and ghostly vision of the last:

> Once, when I was standing in a queue, I saw a ghost standing next to me, a ghost with a body, as if it were a being just like me! Alas, it would seem that there are magicians even among the beings that are permitted to look like humans, magicians who can be helpful, that even ghosts take on human appearances. Alas, even ghosts must now help to fill up space against nightmarishness. Do you remember the creatures killed by poisonous gas in the trenches? They didn't look human anymore, and still they were there: dead, rifle in hand, pointing beyond the rifle at this or that target [...] We are permitted to exist only as ghosts for the world of this new being. [...] And so it is that whoever wants to be a ghost must look human. [...] Anyone who doesn't look like a human can't frighten anyone. Ghosts that look like people have made everything spooky in their own way. There is no other way than to haunt in human form. (Picard 1988: 12–16)

For Picard, modern technology amounts to no more than the perfection of escape, ultimately contributing to the dehumanization and disappearance of man, whose image has become shadowy and ghostly. This is the dark side of media as 'tools' that bring about the dissociation of humanity, so that it no longer knows duration but only the chaos of discontinuous moments: an existence without substance, a 'shadowy' pseudo-existence.

Yet it is in this same period – the 1920s and 1930s – that we find a renewed interest in the 'image of man', specifically the human face and physiognomy, related no doubt to the growing influence of such new (technical) media as photography and film. The sudden increase during this period of works on the human face and image of man reflects a deepening tension between surface and depth, face and mask, inner and outer world, part and whole, partiality and totality of the world and man's place in it, the Christian interpretation of which, as the image of God, had been ravaged by the war.[5] It was also in the early 1920s that Picard's friend, the writer and philosopher of culture Rudolf Kassner – who was also in contact with Hugo von Hofmannsthal and Rainer

Maria Rilke (Rilke's eighth 'Duino Elegy' is dedicated to Kassner) – published his *Die Grundlagen der Physiognomik* (1922, Fundamentals of Physiognomy), later returning to the topic in several other treatises. Kassner, like Picard, perceives modernity as a profound crisis of culture; this crisis is reflected in the human face, where it leaves traces of alienation and uprooting. What is particularly remarkable about his thinking on the 'physiognomic image of the world' is the way he combines the concepts of vision and visage with that of an imagination focused on the face, suggesting the possibility of apprehending the 'face of the world' as a shape, that is 'the world [as] shape and face' (*Gestalt und Gesicht*; Kassner 1951/1932: 196).[6]

Picard's comparison of the (filmic) image to a ghost has its roots in the expressionist 'sense of the world', accompanied by a notion of unreality and ghostliness. With his criticism of cinema as a phantomatic medium, Picard formulated the notion of the phantom image, a notion that, following the Second World War, would become one of the main lines of critique of technology and image media in a work by Günther Anders – incidentally a student of Husserl – *The Antiquatedness of the Human Being* (1956). In the chapter 'Die Welt als Phantom und Matrize: Philosophische Betrachtungen über Rundfunk und Fernsehen' (The World as Phantom and Matrix: Philosophical Reflections on Radio and Television), Anders, like Picard, criticizes the invasion of the media, of television and radio, into the intimate space of the household as a spectralization of the reality of the home (*Heim*), transforming it into a space that is alien and uncanny (*unheimlich*; Anders 1985/1956: 105–6): 'The family is now restructured as an audience in miniature, the living room as a miniature viewing room, and the cinema as a model of the home' (Anders 1985/1956: 106). According to Anders, phantom images (*Phantombilder*) are characterized precisely by the fact that they do not serve as representations:

> [T]he question 'Are we present or absent?' is not relevant here, not because the answer 'image' (and thus 'absent') is self-explanatory, but because what is peculiar to the situation created by the transference is its *ontological ambiguity*; because broadcast events are at once both present and absent, both real and merely apparent, both there and not there, in short: because they are phantoms. (Anders 1985/1956: 131)

When Jacques Derrida, in his interview with Bernard Stiegler, says that 'the future belongs to ghosts', he questions the viewer's trust in images (mainly television) mediated by the technical medium: 'Technics will never produce a testimony. [. . .] [W]hoever testifies and takes an oath pledges, not only to tell the truth, "me, now, here, before you," but to repeat and confirm this truth right away, tomorrow, and ad infinitum. [. . .] [T]o bear witness is always to speak, to engage in and uphold, to sign a discourse' (Derrida and Stiegler 2002/1996: 94). Derrida considers the relationship of technology to historical heritage (and inheritance), memory and testimony, arguing that technology will never produce testimony, but rather engages it in a more complicated, aporetic relationship: while technology cannot mediate testimony, testimony makes use of technology 'in secret'. At the same time, 'pure technics' destroys inheritance, and yet without technics there is no inheritance (Derrida and Stiegler 2002/1996: 87). What is conveyed by television and film, as well as the photographic image, is a 'spectrographic' image, a ghostly and spectre-inducing medium.

Ghosts as phantomatic beings are characterized by this ontological ambiguity: they are an apparent unreality, or else real in an unreal way. Anders (1985/1956: 134) speaks here of the erasure of the boundary between two presences, with reference to the principle of simultaneity in modern poetry of the early twentieth century, specifically Apollinaire and his polythematic work *Zone*. Inspired by Cubist and Futurist painting, *Zone* is created on the simultaneous principle of the modern *tableau parisien* and montage, combining amimetic images from childhood memory with recent experiences and impressions from his travels around Europe. These fragmentary impressions, captured as if in a snapshot or sequence of film shots and cuts, form a kaleidoscopic image of memory and perception, of the Self that simultaneously remembers and perceives, speaks and is spoken to. It is an image in which various temporal and spatial layers are superimposed – lived experience, the imaginary and remembered past, the worlds of myth and of civilizational modernity – and of the world through which the poet-*flâneur* wanders. It is not only a world in fragments that *Zone* depicts, but fragmentariness as a poetics and as determinant aspect of the means of expression, the trademark feature of its modernity (Szondi 1978: 414–25). This modern world of fragments and discontinuity, which strives to create a new unity and identity in multiplicity, is the stage on which the poetic Self lives and experiences that which figures in Apollinaire's poem as its thematic horizon (Stierle 1982: 92–104). Anders understands this simultaneity as a formula for conjuring the 'ubiquitous moment of the now' and inducing a state of 'artificial schizophrenia', and as a splitting the Self and attempt to summon 'metaphysical magic' (Anders 1985/1956: 135–7).

For Derrida, the essential moment involves the relationship of the (filmic) image to death and phantoms. Yet he means this in the opposite sense than that suggested by Edgar Morin thirty years earlier. In 1983, Derrida appeared in a short sequence in the experimental film *Ghost Dance* (1983), in which the actress Pascale Ogier asks him if he believes in ghosts, to which he replies,

'To be haunted by a ghost is to remember what one has never lived in the present, to remember what, in essence, has never had the form of presence. Film is a "phantomachia." Let the ghosts come back. [...] Modern technology, contrary to appearances, although it is scientific, increases tenfold the power of ghosts. The future belongs to ghosts' (Derrida and Stiegler 2002/1996: 115). At the end of this improvisation, Derrida asks the actress, in turn, 'And do you believe in ghosts now?' She replies, 'Yes, now I do, yes.' It was only a few months after filming the scene that the 26 year-old Ogier died suddenly, and when Derrida screened this scene from *Ghost Dance* years later to a class in Texas, he felt like he was seeing a ghost:

> Suddenly I saw Pascale's face, which I knew was a dead woman's face, come onto the screen. [...] I had the unnerving sense of the return of her specter, the specter of her specter coming back to say to me – to me here, now: 'Now . . . now . . . now, that is to say, in this dark room on another continent, in another world, here, now, yes, believe me, I believe in ghosts.' (Derrida and Stiegler 2002/1996: 120)

In relation to film and photography, Derrida speaks of the 'logic of the specter', consistently distinguishing between this term and 'ghost' (Derrida and Stiegler 2002/1996: 115). As with television, the cinema screen is a phantomatic medium for Derrida. A spectre is characterized by a specific ambivalence: it is 'both visible and invisible, both phenomenal and nonphenomenal' (Derrida and Stiegler 2002/1996: 117). It is an in-between phenomenon.

For Edmund Husserl the image is endowed with a special property that involves the fantastic power to make present the absent and disappeared, which returns like a spectre from the grave. He considers images, and especially photographs, to be 'engines of memory' (*Erinnerungs-Motoren*), which serve through the associative function as 'aids to memory', providing the memory with 'more complete image presentation' of the object (Husserl 2006/1980: 38, 56). Husserl describes this 're-presentation', which is the unique property of the image, by way of strikingly funereal metaphor: it makes it possible for a 'dead shape' to emerge from the 'retentional grave' and into living presence – this, however, requires an 'affective awakening' (Husserl 2001/1966: 358–9, 407, 506).

This sepulchral metaphor of re-presentation through the image is strange and remarkable. Existing somewhere between the past and the present, the living and the inanimate, the image is marked by an unsettling ambivalence, as close to life as it is to death. Images of death anticipate death and the disappearance (of the other), but at the same time – and paradoxically –

they save what has been mortified, what has disappeared, from definitive erasure.

It is precisely this feeling that Derrida contemplates in a lecture he gave in January 1993, on the occasion of the death of the art historian and philosopher Louis Marin, with the title 'À force de deuil' (The Force of Grief). The grief that follows death, he observes, is a feeling of this kind: the manifestation of a certain strength that coexists with a certain weakness. For Marin, the power and strength of the image – the subject of his last and posthumous book *Des pouvoirs de l'image* (The Powers of the Image) – lies precisely in the fact that it is a re-presentation of death, that it re-presents to the living the disappeared or the dead. The dead, as Marin (1993: 12) writes, appear in their grave and yet, by virtue of the painter's gesture – following Husserl's funeral metaphor – they seem to 'rise from their graves'. The 'being of the image' (*l'être de l'image*) that Marin investigates coexists – much like strength with weakness and power with impotence – with a 'being-toward-death'. Derrida makes use of the Heideggerian concept, but, as he adds, without Heideggerian connotations, since

> the *being-to-death* of an image [...] has the force, that is *nothing other than* the force, *to resist, to consist, and to exist* in death, precisely there where it does not insist in being or in the presence of being. [...] For it would be from death, from what might be called the *point of view of death*, or more precisely, of the dead, the dead man or woman, or more precisely still, from the point of view of the *face* of the dead in their portraiture, that an image would give seeing, that is, not only would give itself to be seen but would give insofar as it sees, as if it were seeing as much as seen. (Derrida 2001: 147–8)

8. 'A shadowy semblance with a certain intimation of being': Photo-technics and *fantomachia*

The famous chemist and amateur photographer Henri Victor Regnault (1810–78) took a studio photograph of his wife with her sister in 1850. Behind them on the right is an empty space, illuminated and covered with a fine granular dust, through which *something* shines or radiates, without for that matter being light: 'A self-enclosed aura, perhaps an emerging form, or more likely a form that is falling into the light and *disappearing* again. Something like a phantom: a demon of dissimilarity, a gift of veiling' (Didi-Huberman 1998: 60). This 'supernatural light' is actually pulverized carbon pencil that Regnault overlaid on the photographic negative, producing a

'Let the Ghosts Come Back'   103

Figure 4.1 Victor Regnault: Untitled, c. 1850, calotype, Paris, French Society of Photography.

'halo of white dust' on the developed print (Didi-Huberman 1998: 61). A false and paradoxical light, as Georges Didi-Huberman notes in his beautiful essay 'Superstition'. Who is hidden by this 'spectral veil' (see Figure 4.1)?

We learn in this case that Regnault often photographed his two sons, and may have even taken one of the first unedited private photographs of one of his sons asleep in his crib. The boy had grown a bit older when he posed for the 1850 photo, but he failed to stand still for the camera, and his blurred image thus seemed to disturb the 'exactness of photographic art'. We do not know which of his sons is smudged out under graphite dust.

Regnault took a pencil to the sensitive negative to blacken the already blurry portrait 'without realizing the vengeful significance of his own act' (Didi-Huberman 1998: 62). One of the sons later went mad, and 'liked to roll in ash'. The other, whom 'Mallarmé amicably called "Piccolino colourist", died in 1870 in the dust of the battlefield, face to the ground, with a bullet in his right temple' (Didi-Huberman 1998: 62). Regnault's wife died as early as 1866, followed by her sister:

Behind the tears, I imagine the irrevocable, quavering gaze. *Here it is* – in the memory of a child's face, blurred, suffocated under the dust of a child stiff and buried. The negative aura gave light to the image, but this light destroyed the bodies. It bore within it erasure and disappearance. When the bodies disappeared, the light remained, and it remains to this day in the form of this glowing dust, which must be called by its Latin name, a word that is ancient from time immemorial: *superstes*, or 'survivor'. (Didi-Huberman 1998: 63)

Ironically, the light that had been meant to give rise to the image destroyed it in the end. Didi-Huberman first published his essay in a 1987 issue of the journal *Antigone: Revue littéraire de photographie*, and later included it in his book *Phasmes: Essais sur l'apparition* (1998, Ghosts: Essays on Apparitions), the common theme of which is the phantasmic quality – or, more precisely, the ontological ambiguity – of those phenomena, things, artefacts and pictorial objects that Husserl touches on in his lectures on fantasy, pictorial consciousness and memory: 'Transparent phenomena. Vague, fluctuating. [. . .] The image object here is different from a normal image object. It appears as a shadowy semblance with a certain intimation of being' (Husserl 2006/1980: 76). Didi-Huberman's essay on Regnault's 1850 photograph is a fine example of the birth of (modern) ghosts from the spirit of technology, as Roland Barthes contemplates in *Camera Lucida*. It is of little surprise that the realism of the 1850s to 1880s should provide the literary- and cultural-historical background for this development of modern phantoms.

The explosion of technical (especially visual) media made it possible to look at and perceive the external world in new ways, meanwhile revealing aspects hitherto invisible to the naked eye. This development went hand in hand with an extraordinary interest in spiritualism, occultism, somnambulism and other paraphenomena. The early realism of the 1850s was already accompanied by fluctuations between rational psychologism (or so-called physiologism) and the fantastic, the natural and supernatural realms, technology and magic, scepticism and emotional pathos; meanwhile the border between these dichotomies was becoming more permeable. Fascination with the occult was not mutually exclusive with the teachings of Darwinism, positivism, naturalistic monism, and so on.[7]

Renate Lachmann describes this phenomenon as 'realistische Fantastik' (Lachmann 1998: 217), with reference to a certain development in the literature and visual arts of the 1870s and 1880s in which the term 'realism' itself acquires a dialectical meaning, through an opposing position (Preisendanz 1977: 221): the fantastic elements in an otherwise realistic text or image.[8] Here Lachmann turns to Turgenev's 1882 novella *Clara Militch* (written with the working title 'Après la mort'), in which the photographic image of the dead singer and actress – her 'photoimage' – plays a key role. The story is inspired by an event Turgenev learned about in letters sent to him by his friends in Moscow: the case of a well-known opera singer and actress of her time, who committed suicide by poison on an open stage (allegedly out of unrequited love). An acquaintance of Turgenev who was a member of the Moscow elite, and who had seen the actress only once on stage, was driven by her death into an ecstatic state, punctuated by the amorous outburst 'stronger than death' (and from there into psychosis). After the actress's death, her admirer also acquired an ominous photograph, which acts as the story's 'narrative and semantic core' (Lachmann 1998: 235). According to Lachmann, Turgenev's literary treatment of this case represents a special precision 'in the rehabilitation of the phantasm' as well as a certain rigour 'in the subversion of realistic poetics' (Lachmann 1998: 221). In his effort to make his 'enjoyment of the delusion' as perfect as possible, the protagonist begins to develop photo-technical activities, namely by means of a stereoscope. We will recall here Jonathan Crary's observations on the stereoscope: 'There is no longer the possibility of perspective under such a technique of beholding. The relation of observer to image is no longer to an object quantified in relation to a position in space, but rather to two dissimilar images whose position simulates the anatomical structure of the observer's body. [. . .] The prehistory of the spectacle *and* the "pure perception" of modernism are lodged in the newly discovered territory of a fully embodied viewer, but the eventual triumph of both depends on the denial of the body, its pulsings and phantasms, as the ground of vision' (Crary 1990: 128, 136).

As Lachmann shows, Turgenev's *Clara Militch* participates, in the (romantic) tradition of the relationship between *eros* and *thanatos*. What is important here, however, is the writer's interpretation of the medium in connection with magic, and Lachmann's incisive grasp of the medial rivalry between photography and writing, in which it is only through the transgression of writing that photography become legible. The protagonist of the story is unable to write a biography of the dead, and only falls more profoundly under the spell of the hallucination caused by the phantom image, which ultimately brings him to ruin: '[P]hotographic reality actually only reveals the phantom character of realism, which remains silent in its "conscious" poetics' (Lachmann 1998: 263).

When Lachmann reflects on the presence of the phantasm in a realist text, she finds, on the one hand, that it 'seeks to free itself from the mimetic bond; on the other hand, it is dependent on the mimetic parameters in which it can manifest itself. However, while mimeticism permits its own transcendence in phantasm (anti-mimeticism), its depiction falls back on quasi-realist strategies, introducing a topic that legitimates it, in an attempt to mediate between the two poles of the explicable and inexplicable, the likely and impossible. The phantasm is a mimetic bastard' (Lachmann 1998: 261–2). Realism unites both models, which have a common goal: the illumination of the invisible, the unknown, the unexplained, preferably with the use of technical achievements and possibilities.

However, there are phenomena and *realities* that defy measurability, visibility, representation, thus opening up a fissure into which the fantastic penetrates, making the 'cultural unconscious' unsettlingly apparent (Lachmann 2004: 46).

9. A posthumous photograph and a death mask: The media of imprinting and disappearing

In 1918, one month after the Czechoslovak Declaration of Independence, the painter Bohumil Kubišta died in the military hospital on Prague's Charles Square from the effects of the Spanish flu at the age of thirty-four. Jaroslav Rössler, who was sixteen at the time, and who worked as a laboratory assistant in the photography studio of František Drtikol, was apparently summoned, at the request of Jan Zrzavý, to take a photograph of the deceased in the hospital morgue. Rössler, a future member of Devětsil and one of the most prominent figures of Czech avant-garde photography, captured the painter's face in a photograph – the portrait of a painter whose work, as Karel Teige wrote, 'was one of the pinnacles of modern Czech painting, [. . .] a beacon illuminating the path to come' (Teige 1994/1949: 385). In the photograph, Kubišta's head is resting on a draped white canvas, tilted diagonally and to the left, similar to the head in Kubišta's woodcut *Prosba* (1915, The Supplication). His lips are slightly parted, as if to imply smile, and his left eye is slightly open, creating the illusion of a man who is only asleep (see Figure 4.2).

Rössler cropped the original photograph, a detail of Kubišta's head, into a circular frame, and then set it – as Karel Srp observes (Srp 2014: 31) – into a square that is 'waning'. The upper part of the circle forms a black section, as if an aura of nothingness were radiating from behind Kubišta's head, similar to the overlay of graphite dust that obscures the face of the living-dead in Regnault's 1850 photograph. Photography is illumination, traces of light, in this case tracing the presence of death in life, but also absence in presence. At that moment, when the dying man lets go his final breath, he 'begins *to resemble himself'*– this is how Maurice Blanchot (1982/1955: 257) describes the transition from presence to absence, from living to unliving and death. The cadaver at once remains and ceases to be the body of the living. Starting in 1912, with the paintings *Zátiší s lebkou* (Still Life With a Skull) and *Polibek*

'Let the Ghosts Come Back' 107

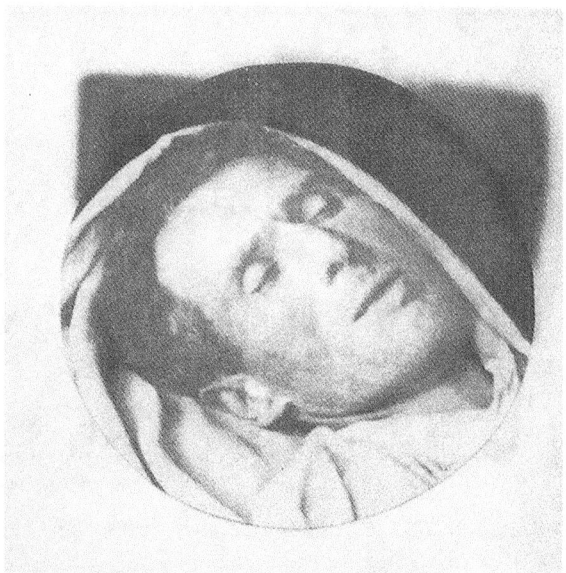

Figure 4.2 Jaroslav Rössler: posthumous photograph of Bohumil Kubišta, 1918, private collection.

smrti (The Kiss of Death) – two paintings that revolve around death as both *nature morte* and allegory – Kubišta returned repeatedly to visualizations of death on canvas: *Oběšený* (The Hanged Man, 1915) and, in the year of his own death, the linocut *Pozůstatky padlého* (Remains of the Fallen, 1918; see Figure 4.3). Blanchot points out that the image 'does not, at first glance, resemble the corpse, but the cadaver's strangeness is perhaps also that of the image' (1982/1955: 256); the same could be said of Kubišta's posthumous photograph. The canvas on which Kubišta painted the parable of death returns in the post-mortem photograph as an allegory and allusion, when the painter's body is wrapped in the white cloth that makes up the background of the photographic image. At the same time, this image lends to the body of the dead, as it disappears, the paradoxical constant 'presence' of life.

One of Kubišta's oldest drawings, created around 1904 by the then twenty-year-old artist, is that of a head or mask (possibly a death mask) rendered in pencil and based on plaster models (see Figure 4.4). It serves then as a kind of book end, anticipating that of the posthumous photo taken of Kubišta, the final portrait that closed his work and life. Indeed, photography in general might be seen to serve as a mask, and as a form of imprinting or impressing. In his *Historia naturalis*, Pliny claims that the history of art begins with the

Figure 4.3 Bohumil Kubišta: *Pozůstatky padlého* (Remains of the Fallen), 1918, linocut, 10 × 16 cm, National Gallery in Prague.

Figure 4.4 Bohumil Kubišta: *Hlava* (Head), *c.* 1904, ink drawing, paper, 54 × 37 cm, Gallery of Modern Art in Hradec Králové.

ritual imprinting of death masks. With Kubišta, however, it is a drawing of a death mask, so that a work of visual art imitates a work of sculpture: the subject of lively sixteenth-century debates called *paragone* on whether painting or sculpture was the more 'perfect' artistic medium (cf. Chapter 11, esp. pp. 377–9). According to Benedetto Varchi, painting can feign plastic three-dimensionality on the canvas surface, and is thus more 'artistic' than the actual three-dimensionality of sculpture. What unites the impression of a death mask with a photograph of the dead, on the one hand, is their immediate proximity to death, and on the other, the moment of the imprint and of touch. Touching and tactility as a modality of sensory perception, as Niklaus Largier (2008: 43–8) considers it, is present in every sensory act, that is, also in the gaze and in vision.

In his cosmology of the senses, Eugène Minkowski writes about touch as a basic, if not the most basic sensory quality, insofar as touching involves an ability to 'introduce coherence into the world and thus "complete" all sensory qualities. [. . .] Could we perceive an object, approach it, reach out to it, "touch it with our gaze", if touch did not reveal to us a deep sense of tactility in general?' (Minkowski 1999/1936: 180–1). 'Touch', for Minkowski as well as Largier, significantly exceeds the sense of touch, since everything 'that affirms its being in life can touch or be touched' (Minkowski 1999/1936: 181). It is this element of reciprocity that distinguishes touch from the other senses: the individual soul affirms its being in life, writes Minkowski, 'primarily as an emotional soul capable of touching and being touched' (Minkowski 1999/1936: 182).

The sense of touch, moreover, involves the materiality of the body, skin and so on in a totally unique form. Largier deals with touch and touching in relation to medieval texts, in the context of which he discusses the practice of prayer, but also kissing, embracing and the experience of pain. He shows how in medieval mysticism the sense of touch is considered to serve as a medium for 'touching', 'afflicting' and affectivity between man and God. This does not involve 'direct contact' so much as a format in which it is possible to model sensory perception. Touch is the medium through which the soul acquires its form – or, as Largier writes, borrowing an expression from Robert Musil's *Man without Qualities*, a 'sense of the possible' (*Möglichkeitssinn*). This is not the 'authenticity' and immediacy of experience, but precisely the possibility of modelling sensory perception in its 'non-originality', that is, in its indirectness and obscurity (Largier 2008: 48).

When Jindřich Štyrský died on 21 March 1942, Vincenc Makovský created his death mask (see Figure 4.5). What is the relationship between the posthumous photograph of Kubišta's face and Štyrský's death mask? What is evident here is not only a relationship between image and death, but also

Figure 4.5 Death mask of Jindřich Štyrský, 1942.

between media: as a modern artistic medium, photographs can be traced back to the archaic art of casting, Roman effigies and death masks. According to Martin Heidegger, photography is capable of showing much more than what is photographed:

> Now the photograph, however, can also show how something like a death mask appears in general. In turn, the death mask can show in general how something like the face of a dead human being appears. But an individual corpse itself can also show this. And similarly, the mask itself can also show how a death mask in general appears, just as the photograph shows not only how what is photographed, but also how a photograph in general, appears. (Heidegger 1997/1991: 66)

Photography thus represents the reincarnation of the much older art of casting death masks, summoning into modern times an ancient medium for preserving that which has already passed. What the photograph and death mask share in common is a form of 'touching' and imprinting, to the extent that the effect of light on the photographic negative could be regarded as a kind of *impression*. Both the photograph and the death mask preserve the form of the dead and are in this way a 'testimony' of his former presence, but also a testimony of a specific moment in which this imprint was taken, whether by light or plaster. At the same time, both the photograph and the death mask figure as 'documents' of disappearance and loss.

Both the photograph and the death mask capture a face as it disappears. The relationship – including the medial relationship – between the photographic image and the face/mask in the context of death and disappearance is one of the main themes of Štyrský's work. In *Emilie přichází ke mně ve snu* (1933, *Emilie Comes to Me in a Dream*, 1997), Štyrský describes this moment of loss and disappearance *sub specie mortis*: 'Life is one long waste of time. Every day death nibbles away at what we call life and life constantly consumes our longing for trivialities. The idea of the kiss dies before ever the lips meet and every portrait pales before we can look at it' (Štyrský 1997/1933: 3–4).

In 1934, Štyrský produced a series of photographs featuring gravestones and funeral parlour display windows. The same year, he created a photograph of a white mask attached to the upper frame of a door or cabinet (see Figure 4.6), including it his cycle *Muž s klapkami na očích* (The Man with Blinkers, 1934). A photo of Štyrský's *Náhrobní kámen* (Gravestone, 1934), as it appeared at the First Exhibition of the Surrealist Group in Czechoslovakia, shows a similar mask attached to the upper frame of the painting (see Figure 4.7). This is then

Figure 4.6 Jindřich Štyrský: From the cycle *Muž s klapkami na očích* (The Man with Blinkers), 1934, photograph, 32 × 28.5 cm, Museum of Decorative Arts in Prague.

Figure 4.7 Jindřich Štyrský: *Náhrobní kámen* (Gravestone), oil, canvas, 115 × 70 cm, period photograph of the painting with the attached mask.

an artist who dealt intensively in paintings and photographs with gravestones, objects directly related to death, as well as masks juxtaposed to gravestones. In addition, by affixing the mask, he gave not only a three-dimensional plasticity to the flat image, but also a 'face' to the gravestone – a metonymy of death – thus conferring to its image an anthropomorphic quality. This produces a certain *mise en abyme*, the effect of multiplying a certain element, motif or medium in the microstructure of the same element/medium which is its matrix. *Mise en abyme* figures both as a genuine phenomenon of aesthetic self-reference and as an interdisciplinary and intermedial chiasmatic crossing of artistic production and aesthetic reception/reflection: image and text, drawing and writing, sculpture and drawing, art and theory, life and art, life and artwork.

Just like Štyrský, the sculptor Alberto Giacometti drew a mask on the right edge of a 1932 sketch of his studio (*Dessin de mon atelier*), just above a studio door. Writing on Giacometti's drawing and his *Cube*, Didi-Huberman observes that the mask is not a face, only an empty mass of plaster, with openings to simulate the eyes and mouth:

> Neither presence, nor absence, this false face evokes both a theatrical mask to be worn by no one, and the prepared mold for someone who will

be forever absent. It evokes, in any case, very precisely, the mask or the mold that Giacometti had shown in his drawing from 1932, dominating like the face of a commander all of the other objects in the studio. It evokes a funerary *imago*, like those the Romans hung in their atria, or a ghost that has escaped from its body. It gives the impression of being alone in the enjoyment of being able to bear the presence of the object, looking only from its absence of a face. (Didi-Huberman 2015/1993: 60)

We will recall that Kubišta too created the sketch of a plaster (death) mask sometime around 1904.

Štyrský was attracted to the oscillation between the inanimate medium of the image (canvas), dead material and the artistic resurrection of that which it depicts. One might say that for Štyrský, the painting was akin to the 'phantom body' (*Phantomleib*) in Hans Blumenberg's conception. The body, consecrated to disappear, remains present as the phantom body of the image.

10. (G)HOSTage: to be held hostage by ghosts

Štyrský returned to the theme of faces/masks once more in 1939, when he created the painting *Na hrobě* (On the Grave) and a collage for the bibliophile edition of Miloš Marten's essay on Lautréamont, 'Zastřený profil' (1909, Veiled Profile). 'On the Grave' depicts a kind of painted stone or skeletal portrait in cool silver-grey tones. It appears to be made of skeletal remains, with an empty hole instead of an eye: a perforated face that seems to materialize before the viewer's eyes, or else a mask placed on a shape conveyed by darker shades of grey and black that seem to form the top of the head.[9] It is as if we were watching the strange transformation of originally organic matter into an alien phantom object – in the manner of 'grave sculpture' – one that unsettles and disturbs the viewer who is unable to make out its identity. In the lower part of the painting, in a saffron yellow that evokes fire or heat, we find a number of enigmatic, inscrutable urn-like vessels, broken as if by the heat and covered in ashes (see Figure 4.8).

These objects form a strange chain, culminating in a phantom head. The head and mask are rendered in various hues of greyish paint, which strike the eye as 'colourless' and 'closed', due to a distancing effect in relation to the light and the viewer's gaze, thus enhancing the alien impression of the objects depicted. At its minimum light intensity, the grey conveys something oppressively menacing, macabre, the colour of life cut short and hopes extinguished (Sedlmayr 1957: 33). In a book dedicated to the doctrine of immortality in Orphic theology, Johann Jakob Bachofen mentions the urn

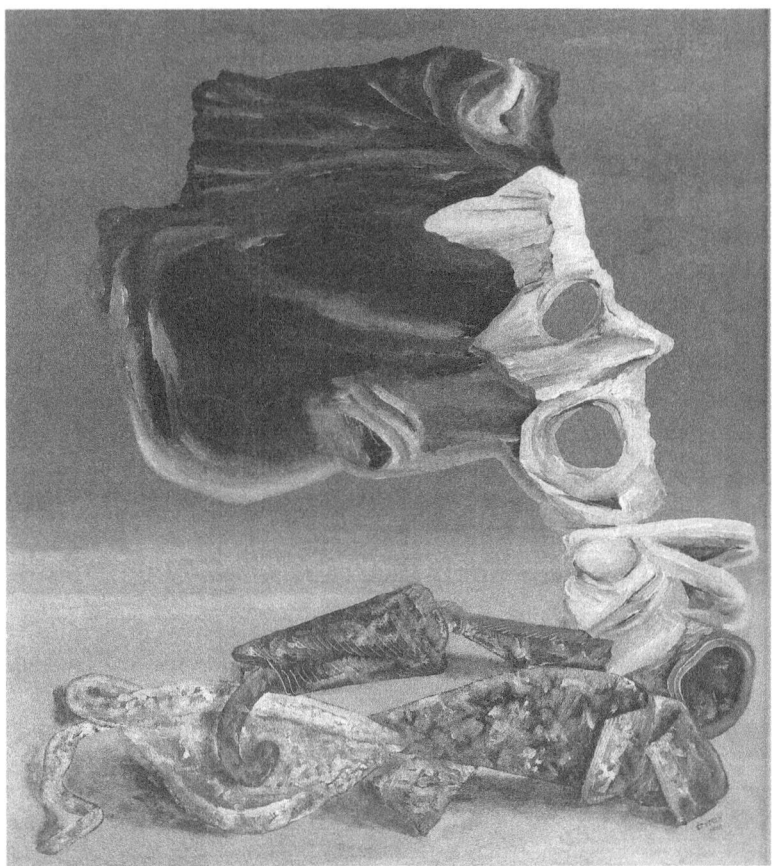

Figure 4.8 Jindřich Štyrský: *Na hrobě* (On the Grave), 1939, oil on canvas, 64 × 58 cm, National Gallery in Prague.

motif (*urna feralis*) that appears on ancient Roman gravestones as a symbol of rebirth and the transformation of the mortal body into the immortal soul. The act of rebirth was often represented by a winged Bacchic boy (reminiscent of a Christian cherub) emerging from the opening of the urn. An overturned, emptied urn turned to the viewer was meant to represent the completion of this process of transformation (Bachofen 1958: 154–6, 219). In Štyrský's painting, by contrast, transformation seems to give rise only to oppressive, hallucinatory ghosts, reflecting the disaster erupting in Europe at the time it was painted.

Štyrský's collage for Marten's 'Veiled Profile' depicts a head in profile with its skin removed, taken from a book of anatomical drawings. In the

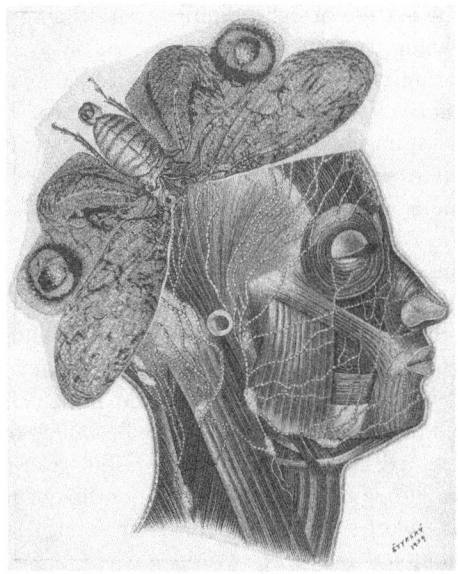

Figure 4.9 Jindřich Štyrský: *Lautréamont*, 1939, collage, paper, 15.5 × 12.5 cm, private collection in Paris.

place where we would expect a human brain, Štyrský has affixed part of a zoological illustration showing the moth-like wings and abdomen of a tropical fulgorid insect or 'planthopper' (*Fulgora laternaria*; Bydžovská and Srp 2007: 465; see Figure 4.9). Between 1939 and 1940, Štyrský created several collages and drawings on the motif of butterflies (*Severní točna, Bez názvu, Alabastrová ručička* (North Pole, Untitled, Alabaster Hand), 1940), as well as *Sen o motýlech* (Dream of Butterflies) in his book of *Dreams* (1941). We can trace the motif back to classical antiquity, where the butterfly was associated with the *psukhē*, or 'soul', and metamorphosis, an Apollonian insect straddling the spheres of nature and culture, matter and spirit. In this context, the butterfly is a bearer of signs, hidden and apparent, manifested directly on the surface of its wings. In the Apollonian aesthetic, the butterfly (and its metamorphosis) symbolizes camouflage, deceptive, false, veiled identity and decoy. Štyrský's imaginary portrait of the author Lautréamont is characterized by a similar ambivalence: a surface that is at once exposed (*écorché* or skinned) and hidden, without a face or identity, a head that serves only as an anatomical preparation. The portrait also conveys the connection between the spheres of man and nature, represented by a tropical insect whose Latin name ('laternaria') co-constitutes the lexeme of light, illumination, leading in turn back to Apollonian mythology.

At the beginning of 1940, in Bern, Paul Klee painted one of his last paintings *Tod und Feuer* (Death and Fire). At the centre of the painting, Klee presents us with a strangely deformed skull or mask, lying white-hot in fire. Basic geometric lines suggest a body on whose shoulder rests a ball that may fall to the ground at any moment, symbolizing the capriciousness of fate, according to Otto Pöggeler (2002: 146). In this orb, the heat of the fire is particularly strong, and three black lines reach aggressively and perilously into the image from above. On the right, another figure seems to be walking directly towards this place of danger and destruction, holding a kind of spear with which it might mean to defend its life. These elements also make up the letters of the word *tod*, or 'death'. In the title of the painting, this word is juxtaposed to 'fire', representing at once the beginning of the world and its end – the fire of a disastrous war in which (as Pöggeler reminds us) had already engulfed Europe as Klee was working on this painting. Here Klee seems to be coping, like Štyrský, with his own impending death at the time of the great conflagration of the Second World War.

These two paintings are connected not only by the motifs of fire and death, but also, both explicitly and implicitly, by that of cinders or ashes – residues of destruction and disappearance, or as Derrida writes in his polyphonic essay *Feu la cendre* (1987, *Cinders*, 2014), 'the best paradigm for the trace' of the form of a world that has disappeared (Derrida 2014/1987: 25). As the 'residue' of this form, he argues, the cinder is an indication of its impermanence and imperceptibility, as a 'remainder' and as something 'preserved', the symbol of 'pure substantiality' (Conrad-Martius 1923: 332): The cinder can be found exactly where 'someone vanished but something preserved her trace and at the same time lost it, the cinder. There the cinder is: that which preserves in order no longer to preserve' (Derrida 2014/1987: 15–17). Ashes and cinders are a reminder, a memory, a trace, but they are also an ontological motif.

'Everything the poet forsakes turns grey, turns to ash,' wrote Štyrský in the opening passage of his essay 'Kraj markýze de Sade' (1933, The Land of the Marquis de Sade). Ashes and cinders are both a remainder and a trace of what has disappeared, at the same time leading back to the cause of their being, to fire – 'No cinder without fire' ('Pas de cendre sans feu'; Derrida 2014/1987: 19). Ash blurs the distinction between matter and form, so that in a 'realontological' sense, as Hedwig Conrad-Martius writes, it is 'already completely inflammable', incombustible (Conrad-Martius 1923: 332). For Štyrský, similarly to Derrida, it is connected with time and disappearance, but also with preservation.

'Let the Ghosts Come Back' 117

In 1937, Štyrský created a painting with the almost Derridian-Lévinasian title *Dar* (Gift): a charred, flesh-coloured book, whose fire-twisted pages 'reveal' the profile of what appears to be a male head, featuring a realistically painted ear that seems to grow out of the book's front cover (see Figure 4.10). Or, as Jan Mukařovský puts it, 'there is a face here that is simultaneously a burnt book' (Mukařovský 1966/1938: 310). The 'veiled profile' motif

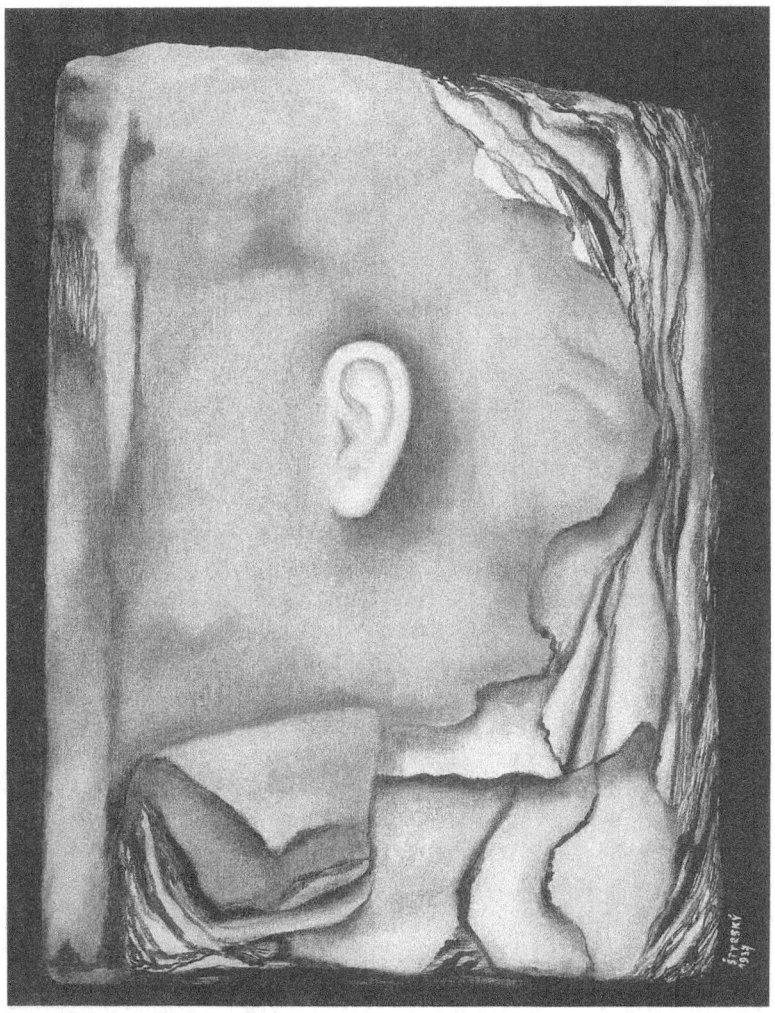

Figure 4.10 Jindřich Štyrský: *Dar* (Gift), 1937, oil on canvas, 54 × 42 cm, private collection in Paris.

already appears in this painting, and the motif of fire, ash and cinders from which a phantom faces seem to rise (which we discussed with Štyrský's 'On the Grave') appears here as well. The notion of a charred book evokes the destruction of text, of writing by fire. The painting suggests an equivalence between the body and the book, between literality/scripturality and vocality/auditivity, the latter conspicuously brought to our attention by the ear that protrudes from its centre. While the inspiration for 'Gift' came to Štyrský in a dream, according to the painter's dream diary (Štyrský 1970: 85), the title of the painting raises the question: *What gift, and to whom is it to be given?* In the dream diary, we read that Štyrský wants to buy a book for Toyen from a second-hand bookseller before her train leaves Paris, to help her pass the time. The outline of the male head in profile together with the detail of the ear presents a kind of trace or contour of an absently present subject, one who *is given* to the other – or, more precisely, who *gives himself* to the other in the Lévinasian sense of 'obliging others to give themselves'. In this way, the subject is 'given as a hostage to the other' (*d'otage livré en don à l'autre*; Lévinas 1974: 193). According to Emmanuel Lévinas, the connection of corporeality and the gift (the gifting of oneself) is the key moment of 'affection by others'. It is a gift in the shadow of death, which Štyrský almost succumbed to during a joint visit with Toyen to Paris in the summer of 1935. Finally, the painting as a work of art is itself a gift: a painting as a charred book, and both representing a body to be 'read' as a book and seen as an image.

After recovering from a sustained cerebral embolism in June 1935, to the point that he could paint again, Štyrský created *Trauma zrození* (Trauma of Birth, 1936). Despite the allusion to Otto Rank's psychoanalytical study of the same name, which Štyrský knew, this was the first in a series of paintings on the topic of death. 'Gift' occupies an exceptional position here.

Štyrský's burnt book seems to foreshadow the books covered in smoke and soot, and inverted shadows cast by books in the installations of Italian artist Claudio Parmiggiani. From the 1970s to the 1990s, Parmiggiani produce his *Delocazioni* using the smoke, ash and soot from burning tires as it passes through bookshelves to make shadowy imprints on the wall behind: a charred-black 'silent book' (*Libro muto*, 1976) that calls to mind the burning of the Library of Alexandria – or, in the words of Didi-Huberman, 'a work that sculpts the absence of things in the material of their volatile ashes' (Didi-Huberman 2001: 88).

In Štyrský's collection of poems, *Poesie* (probably dating from the late 1930s, but first published posthumously in 1946 with a reproduction of Štyrský's death mask on the frontispiece), we find a poem with the title 'Hledal jsem popel v popelu' (I was looking for ashes in the ashes), which ends with the lines: 'I walked over the peaks / Which were only mountains of ash / Into which I fell' (Štyrský 1992/1946: 19). Ashes figure as one of the main elements in the through-line of Štyrský's pictorial and literary work: grave – stone – ashes. The paintings *Gravestone* (1934) and *On the Grave* (1939), together with his drawing *Pohřbené kameny* (Buried Stones, 1939) and drawings for *Sen o Matce-zemi* (Dream of Mother Earth, 1940) all serve as graves for images as well as images of the grave.

Disappearance (of the other), imprints, traces, ashes and dust can all be seen as media of inaccessibility and loss. We see this as well in František Halas's poem 'Rukojmí' (Hostage, from the collection *Hořec* (Gentiana), 1933, later included in the fourth edition of the collection *Tvář* (Face)), dedicated to Egon Hostovský, a work that revolves around issues of vision, the gaze, the dialectic of seeing and being seen, the relationship to the other as an ontological-ethical problem, phantomality and the (Lévinasian) notion of the hostage.

> *I once saw a coffin*
> *and a weeping candle*
> *and then the noble mouth of one*
> *so repentant*
>
> *and the dead gaze a coiled serpent*
> *in its cold twisting*
> *he only looked, perhaps only with apprehension*
> *on what was clutching me*
> *like an idea that means to stay hidden*
> *he persisted unmoved in himself*
> *You who are dead what does that mean*
> *I know I am your hostage and time wasted swelling*
>
> (Halas 1957: 198)

The *syuzhet* of Halas's poem leads from seeing, through vision and thought, to knowing: from 'I saw' in the first line to 'I know' in the last. Through the poem, the poetic self arrives at a certain insight, which is also a response to the gaze it feels exposed to: namely, the dead, whose 'dead gaze' calls for a response. The candle light in the second line of the first stanza also alludes to this context; it is what makes possible – as a *medium* – not only vision ('I saw') but insight and understanding.

To be at the mercy of another's otherness, to endure the challenge of the 'guest', to act as his host and become his 'hostage', it is in this way that we can understand the main theme of Halas's poem. Lévinas dwells on the notion of the 'hostage' (*otage*) in 1967 in relation to the idea of a claim or right to which we are exposed *face to face* with the other, which 'imposes itself on me as a demand (*exigence*)' and at the same time as a call for a response (Lévinas 2007/1961: 207). The term 'hostage' radically expresses the fundamental ethical situation not only of humanity, but of existence in general.

The principle of 'hospitality' is for Derrida, following Lévinas, the very principle of ethics in its entirety (Derrida 1999/1997: 50). But the technologization of public space and contemporary life, the dramatically increasing influence of the media, the place they occupy in our privacy, lead Derrida to think about 'hospitality' from this perspective as well: a stranger in a foreign land carries with him two desires and two wistful memories: his mother tongue and the dead. Derrida quotes Lévinas's formulation: 'the essence of language is goodness, [. . .] friendship and hospitality' (Lévinas 2007/1961: 305). Exile can take many forms, but the exile always keeps his mother tongue, which serves in the end as his home. As Derrida writes in his book *De l'hospitalité* (1997, *Of Hospitality*, 2000), it is the most mobile of all mobile phones, faxes and emails because we always have it with us (Derrida 2000/1997: 47, 91). One's mother tongue is endowed with the power to resist the technology that invades our homes, dislocating and uprooting us. Yet one's mother tongue is also a ghost that 'disappears', remaining with the speaker only when it is spoken. Birth and death, the mother's womb, one's mother tongue, 'mother earth' as a grave – this makes up the semantic line on which Derrida's thinking on foreignness/hospitality unfolds. We carry our mother tongue with us from the cradle to the grave: 'the foreigner is a foreigner by birth, is a born foreigner. Here, rather, it is the experience of death and mourning, it is first of all the law of burial that becomes – let us say the word – determining. The question of the foreigner concerns what happens at death and when the traveler is laid to rest in a foreign land' (Derrida 2000/1997: 87). What kind of hospitality, Derrida asks, would it be that was not prepared to be extended to the dead, the ghost (Derrida 2000/1997: 93–5)?

In Halas's poem, the view of the dead is 'like an idea that means to stay hidden': it binds, holds, claims the living man by entrusting to him what 'means to stay hidden' – and in Czech 'to entrust' (*svěřit*) is a near homophone of 'to clench' (*sevřít*). This, however, is a connection the living explicitly acknowledges: 'I know I am your hostage.' But, as Derrida notes, hospitality is not hospitable without remembering, and there would be no remembering if it did not belong to the dead (Derrida 2000/1997: 107). Halas's 'Hostage' is also introduced by a memory: 'I once saw a coffin / and a weeping candle / and then the noble mouth of one / so repentant.' Repentance presupposes the offense of transgression, which in this poem seems to be related to the motif of the serpent, the 'seduction' and fall into original sin, and thus into the captivity of death.

Yet 'Hostage' also presents us with an oxymoron: 'the dead gaze coiled serpent' nevertheless gazes 'on what was clutching me'. It is the snake-gaze-thought 'that means to stay hidden'. Here, the snake is not only a metaphor for fate (beginning and end, life and death, consciousness and the unconscious), but – above all – it is also connected with vision and thought, with the realm of the spiritual and thus also with the process of knowledge, which culminates in 'I know'. The hypnotizing gaze of the dead is also an act of initiation, a figuration of being 'stung' by the gaze, awakening an awareness regarding the hostage's life and death as 'time wasted swelling'. This awareness leads us back to the initial lines of the poem, to the poem as a whole, to the tears (the liquid with which the poem is 'written') of the 'weeping candle', to the 'noble mouth' that repents and speaks. It is the emergence of the poem, in written and spoken form. In the face of the dead, however, this awareness of life is weighed against 'time wasted swelling'.

In October 1990, Derrida wrote an essay for the opening of an exhibition at the Louvre, with the title *Mémoires d'aveugle: L'autoportrait et autres ruines* (translated and published three years later as *Memoirs of the Blind: The Self-Portrait and Other Ruins*). It is an examination of the relationship between the self-portrait and symbolic, transcendental, spiritual blindness, of seeing beyond the borders of vision, and of the sense of sight but also of tears as a medium of vision. Derrida asks why vision or enlightenment in painting is so often thematized as blindness or blinding. The artist, he argues, creates in a state of symbolic blindness: he does not see what he depicts, because it comes from memory and for memory. There is, moreover, a complementary relationship between vision and blindness that deeply affects our being in the world, that intercedes in the visibility and knowability of the world, at the same time shaping the relationship between faith and knowledge. Derrida also notes the link between words and tears, *logoi* and *lacrimae*: tears as a fluid, with which text both visible and invisible is written. Tears enable a different, spiritual vision of the world, covering it with a 'veil of tears' while at the same time revealing another, hidden reality: 'Between seeing and weeping, he sees between and catches a glimpse of the difference, he keeps it, looks after it in memory – and this is the veil of tears – until finally, and from or with the "same eyes", the tears see' (Derrida 1993/1990: 128).

Tears appear in Halas's poem 'Hostage', metaphorically, as the flowing wax of a candle and 'noble mouth of one / so repentant', that is, as unspoken repentance. The poem is dedicated to Egon Hostovský, whose name contains both 'guest' and 'host', and also – according to the etymology of the Greek *xénos* – 'foreigner', which describes Hostovský's status in American exile, as well as the protagonist of his novella *Cizinec hledá byt* (A Foreigner Is in Search of an Apartment, 1947), a *hostage* of death who searches fruitlessly in a foreign city for a place where he could finish his work, and finally dying in a foreign country.

In his poem 'Tränen' ('Tears'), Friedrich Hölderlin addresses the fiery tears of love, turned to ash: 'The fiery that are full of ash' (*Ihr feurgen, die voll Asche sind*). In Otokar Březina's poem 'Píseň o slunci, zemi, vodách a tajemství ohně' ('Song of the Sun, Earth, Waters and the Secret of Fire', 1897), tears are like 'burning light' (*hořící světlo*). At the end of Balzac's short story 'Gambara', the brilliant but insane composer Gambara touches his tears and utters, 'Water is burnt flesh'. If ash represents a material substantiality that has been rendered 'unburnable', tears 'burning with light' may represent the revelation of a metaphysical substantiality.

This brings us once more to fire, ashes and tears. It is likely that Štyrský's painting *On the Grave*, under which title it has been presented since the painter's first posthumous exhibition in 1946, is actually *Na hrobě Astoleny* (On the Grave of Astolena), a painting that Štyrský mentions in a diary entry of 1939 (Štyrský 1996: 134). It is inspired by the character of Astolena from Maurice Maeterlinck's original puppet play *Alladine and Palomides* (1894). In this play, which was performed in mid-December 1939, the character of Palomid the knight says: 'I saw tears that came not from the eyes, but from far beyond' (Maeterlinck 1917/1894: 180). Tears as a fluid medium, or secretion, carry a secret: of life, death and poetry, as the 'wine of the eyes' – *Augenwein* – a rare essence that the poet must press again and again, like the winemakers in Paul Celan's poem of that title ('Die Winzer', 1953), and transform it into the word.

Notes

1   Two years into the First World War, when Cassirer published *Freiheit und Form* (1916, Freedom and Form), one of his intentions was to contribute to the discussion of that period on the relationship between culture and civilization. Tracing the development of German spiritual history, Cassirer comes to situate its ideological centre in the figure and work of Johann Wolfgang von Goethe, as well as Kant's concept of autonomy, spontaneity and the laws of spirit. Freedom increases with the deepening awareness of form and power to create forms, and Cassirer comes to regard these aspects as the anthropological determination of man: 'The free individual exists as a form only by giving form to itself' (Cassirer 1993/1939: 249).
2   Didi-Huberman deals with this topic in his collection of short essays *Être crâne: Lieu, contact, pensée, sculpture* (2000, *Being a Skull: Place, Contact, Thought, Sculpture*, 2016), where he traces the historical fascination with the 'miracle box', from Leonardo da Vinci and Albrecht Dürer to Giuseppe

Penone, the sculptor and prominent representative of the Italian group of artists Arte Povera. Didi-Huberman draws certain relationships that emerge in connection with the sculptural object: between the tactile object and object of thought, between the plasticity of the skull and organ of thought, and between the shape and its artistic-philosophical reflection.

3 As early as 1928, in his book *Die Stufen des Organischen und der Mensch* (*Levels of Organic Life and the Human*, 2019), Helmuth Plessner presents his well-known thesis about the *excentric positionality* of the human being. Here he distinguishes three regularities proper to the human in order to convey the manner and human 'form of being' in the world (*Daseinsform*), which he defines precisely as positionally-excentric (Plessner 2019/1928: 271). This is due to the fact that the human being is characterized by his 'natural artificiality' (*natürliche Künstlichkeit*). 'Only because the human is naturally partial and thus stands above himself is artificiality the means to find a balance with himself and the world' (Plessner 2019/1928: 298). Artificiality is an integral aspect of human existence, because without it – that is, without culture – he could not exist. The human position in the world is also characterized by 'constitutive homelessness' and 'the law of the utopian standpoint', which forces us to constantly search for balance. The third basic anthropological law, according to Plessner, is the law of 'mediated immediacy' (*vermittelte Unmittelbarkeit*): the human individual is neither exclusively interior nor exclusively exterior. Man *has* a body (*Körper*), but it is by virtue of his body (*Leib*) and by his work that he *is*; his essence thus includes 'expression'. 'Expression' also belongs to the role that the human individual assumes as part of a community of other human individuals.

4 *Eupalinos: Or, The Architect* is a dialogue set in the Underworld on the topic of art, especially architecture and music. The discussion revolves around the distinction between *construire*, or 'building' (art), and *connaître*, or 'knowing' (philosophy). Phaedrus tells Socrates about the buildings created by the architect Eupalinos, which he saw in Piraeus. The goal of Eupalinos's extraordinarily disciplined creative effort is to transform disordered material into an ordered whole that would be subject to the laws of symmetry, laws of a higher order, and thus transformed into a perfect work of art (in Valéry's theory of art, the poet does the same). In the middle of the dialogue, Socrates speaks of an episode from his youth, when – at the age of eighteen, while walking along the seashore – he discovered a 'wretched object' washed up on the sand. He describes it as a 'white thing' (*une chose blanche*): hard, smooth and light, it was also the most ambiguous object in the world, on the border between water and land. It is this ineffable quality that gave Socrates, he recalls, 'cause for doubt', and to vacillate between building/art and knowing/philosophy (he decided on the latter). Was it a whim of nature? A fish bone? A carved piece of ivory? Or even the likeness of some unknown deity? Was it formed by the 'eternal work of the waves', by the action of infinite time – a work of blind chance, in other words, which the artist could only imitate

with concentrated effort (Valéry 1960/1923: 118–19). Confronted with the mysterious object, an object for which thinking can form no representation (in the Platonic idea of the world such an object cannot exist; Valéry's dialogue rejects this in favour of the Aristotelian worldview), Valéry's young Socrates throws it back in the sea. The very existence of such an ambiguous object is unbearable for Socrates, and he considers the difference between 'natural' and 'human' productivity, represented in its purest form by the artist/*artifex*. Nature creates by constant metamorphosis – indeed, nature *is* metamorphosis. The creative person strives to objectify his creation in an enduring work.

5   In his book on the 'limits of physiognomics' (*Die Grenzen der Physiognomik*, 1937), Picard discusses Matthias Grünewald's depiction of the crucifixion, in which Christ is rendered in human form. Picard interprets this as the ultimate impact of the human form, arguing that 'from this point on, he would actually have to stop looking human. It is presumptuous to look human when God has dared to do so and failed. [. . .] In Grünewald's paintings, the human form appears strained, almost ruptured, because it can no longer bear to be human, as it was at the death of Christ. It [. . .] is on the verge of abandoning [man]' (Picard 1937: 179).

6   Siegfried Kracauer also deals with these topics – the psychology of appearance, surface and movement – in essays he wrote during the 1920s, which were collected and published in *Das Ornament der Masse* (1927, *The Mass Ornament*, 1975). In the 1920s, the concept of physiognomy has been imported into social and cultural relations from the field of anthropology. For Kassner, Picard, Kracauer, Benjamin, Jünger and others, this process is a manifestation and consequence of the technical dynamics of the surface and its movement: an expression of dependence on technical means, in which interiority and exteriority are inverted.

7   The doctor and psychiatrist Albert von Schrenck-Notzing (1862–1929), for example, was a member of the Psychological Society (founded in 1886), whose aim was to develop a scientific justification for spiritualism. Schrenck-Notzing held séances with mediums through which the dead materialized and announced themselves, carrying 'messages' from beyond the grave. An important aspect of these séances was the camera, which was thought to capture photographic evidence of 'teleplasm', a mysterious substance through which the dead were supposed to materialize. The mysterious 'teleplasm' actually consisted of bits of tulle and gauze fabric that Schrenck-Notzing's mediums would produce from their mouths for the camera (they were kept concealed on the medium's person) (Imorde 2005: 361–84). The motif of teleplasm also appears in Nabokov's 'spectrological' short story 'The Vane Sisters' (see Section 3 of Chapter 5, pp. 152–65).

8   For Lachmann, fantastic literature also represents the 'opposite side of culture': culture's otherness as something hidden or forbidden – but also (secretly) desired – that 'falls victim to exclusion' (Lachmann 2004: 46). In

her cultural-anthropological interpretation of literary fantasy, Lachmann sets out from the idea that 'fantastic literature tells of the meeting between culture and its forgotten aspect. [. . .] And yet if this forgetting which the fantastic reproaches culture allows that which has been erased and displaced to rise again in its own discovered and invented images – the fantastic as a mnemonic institution of culture – it may serve, on the other hand, as the motor of arbitrary creations which allow for a valid, remembering imaginary to cover over or erase counter-images (*Gegenbilder*) – fiction as *ars oblivionalis*. For a space is needed, made possible by a counter-memory, in which are stored the *imagines* of the unseen, the unthinkable' (Lachmann 2002: 11).

9 In 1944, Roland Kuhn, a psychiatrist in Basel, published *Maskendeutungen im Rorschachschen Versuch* (Interpretation of Masks in the Rorschach Experiment), a work that is still read and discussed today. Kuhn is interested in the question: *What does it mean if someone sees a mask in Rorschach blots?* The mask evokes a fascinating horror, one that the subject fears and resists but cannot escape, and so begins to imagine masked figures in order to face this terror.

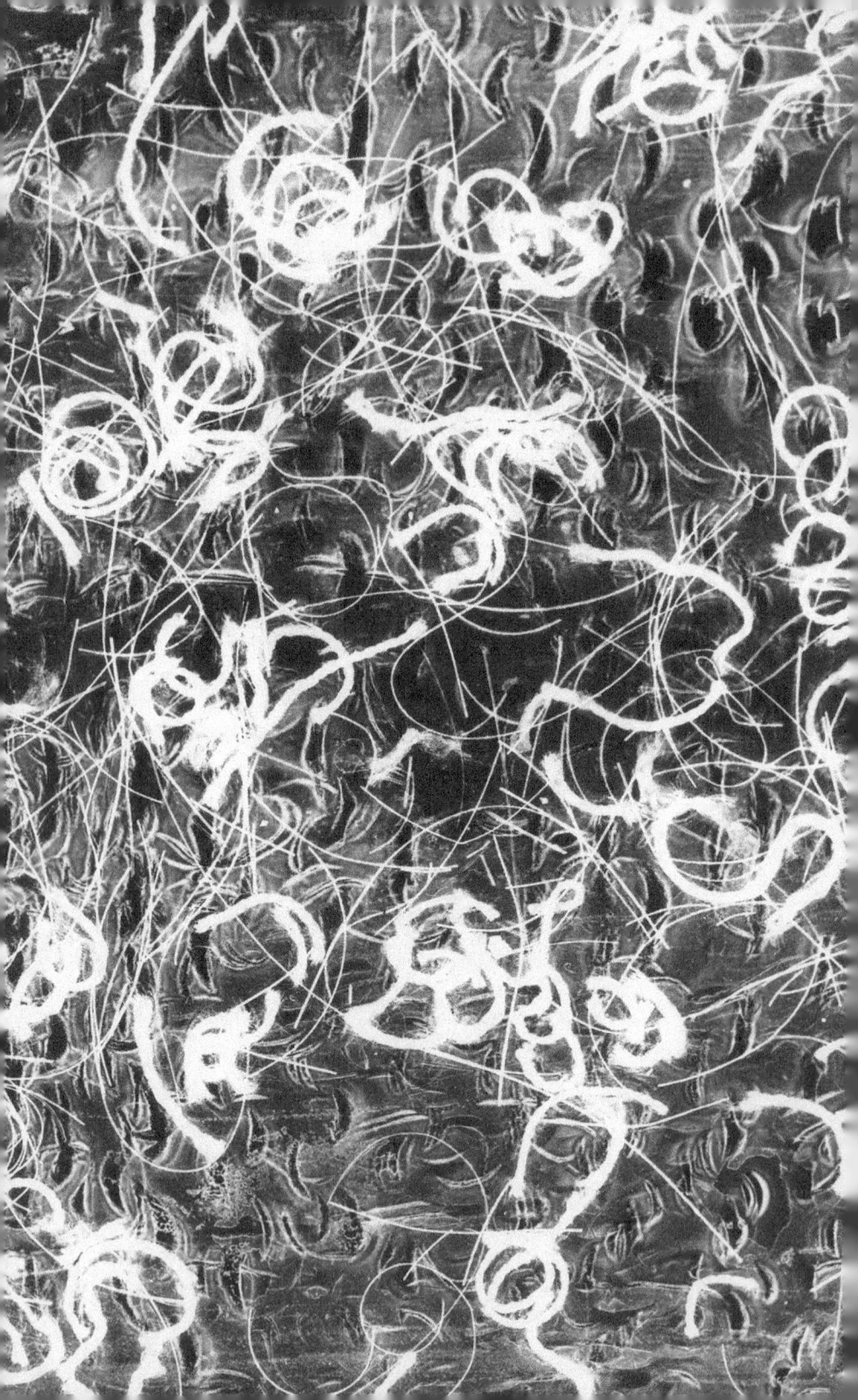

5

Gesture and its (proto-)medial thresholds

Richard Müller

If we consider the communicative components of a literary work (and literature as a specific kind of communication), what does 'gesture' mean and how does it manifest itself in this context? The term is widely prevalent in theory, but it has a number of possible references in common usage as well. 'Gesture'[1] may be used to refer to the gestural body movements that accompany spoken language, with consciously expressive aims. But there is also a hint of the involuntary in this case which arises from the connection of gesture to human physicality and the body, and which prevents us from using the body as a freely intentional means of communication. In eye expression, as with other gestures, we often wish to see something that goes beyond what is spoken. While this may be true of all communication, the issue of immediacy in face-to-face conversation has a special urgency. Consequently, the term 'gesture' may convey the authenticity of an act or attitude (e.g. 'a gesture of generosity'), or, on the contrary, a superficial action meant to hide the lack of authenticity ('it was only a gesture').[2]

In the field of linguistics (and elsewhere) there has long been a defining concept according to which gestures (i.e. gestural movements) supplement or stand in for spoken language. They communicate, but only visually, and are therefore 'parasitic formations' (John Lotz), conceptualized much in the same way as writing (Edward Sapir, Roman Jakobson). The view on gesture in its contemporary cognitive and developmental-psychology conceptions has undergone considerable reassessment, especially in the field of gesture studies. While its leading representatives (Adam Kendon, David McNeill, more recently Susan Goldin-Meadow; see C. Müller 2018) have not yet come to terms with the relationship between gestures and signs, or the degree to which gestures represent signs (the degree to which they are linguistic in nature), they agree that gestures are not merely substitutes or supplements to the spoken word, but an integral and inseparable part of language and language learning. McNeill, for example, argues that speech and gesture always occur together, even among variously bodily disadvantaged persons.

More fundamentally, gestures represent the evolutionary co-foundation of speech as such, and it is by virtue of their unity that speech developed in its particular form: an ability that involves simultaneously thinking and speaking 'in real time'. According to McNeill, at a certain moment in the evolution of communication, an evolutionary adaptation took place in early humans known as 'Mead's Loop' (after cultural anthropologist Margaret Mead), by which the functional orientation of mirror neurons was 'twisted'. As a consequence, these neurons began to respond to one's own gestures *as if they belonged to someone else*. Gestures thus become 'social objects' – a state of affairs that McNeill considers to be the beginning of human language. He argues that voice and gesture are inseparable, and that they are controlled, as more recent neuroimaging technology (fMRI) confirms, by contiguous areas of the brain.

We will proceed from the view that, in terms of the development of language, gesture and spoken language are intrinsically connected, and perhaps even that human speech begins only with their mutual articulation. Furthermore, there are indications here that gesture contains both a movement and image component. Does this not directly imply a need to grasp this connection from the medial perspective? Does this not of itself suggest that the medial 'identity' of spoken language – and so also gestures – is not self-identical, not uniform, but on the contrary breaks down into multiple, most likely variable elements or dimensions? Is it not then precisely the media – and more broadly the environment as such and different types of perception – that allows the various aspects of gesture and speech to be variously separated and recomposed? If the answers are not negative, we will have to look at gesture from other perspectives than those defined by the context of gesture studies.

Let us return to literature and the literary work to point out some preliminary considerations. Gestures – that is, gestures in the straightforward sense, as a means of nonverbal communication and expressive movement – have their place in spoken language when translating a dramatic text into a theatrical performance, for example, and in the recitation more broadly of written texts. A common way to convey gestures in literature is by description. We have only to recall the work of Franz Kafka, for instance, where moments of gesture, as Walter Benjamin first pointed out, take on extraordinary meaning. Hyun Kang Kim writes about this in his insightful commentary on Benjamin's concept of gesture, representing 'crystalline images of movement', 'sudden standstills' and 'the minimal difference between event and form' (Kim 2014: 120).

The Czech theorist of aesthetics Jan Mukařovský conceptualized gesture along yet other lines, considering the 'semantic gesture' as a singular way of shaping and unifying the meaning of a literary work. In the sphere of literature, as he understood it, the term 'gesture' was primarily meant metaphorically. Tracing the genesis of this concept, however, we come across a remarkable clue in the author's early work from the mid-1920s on motor events (*motorické dění*) in poetry. With his rather intuitive concept of motor events, or else gesture, Mukařovský means to capture (and subject to analysis) an intense impression of the unifying movement induced by the poetic text. It is an impression that begins, as Mukařovský observes, with the *sound* layer and sound-motor ideation of the movement of forces, which in turn becomes meaning.

It is already evident that the concept of (semantic) gesture in literature is medially ambiguous and symptomatic. In a certain sense, gesture seems to exist only at the margins, but also – considering that the initial stages of what we now call literature involve oral utterances, rhythmic and ritualized annunciations from celebratory songs to oracles – at its early beginnings. How then, in the modern understanding of 'literature', whose forms are (still) predominantly linked to printed distribution, may we understand the metaphorical nature of this term? (On the transfer of literature to the computerized environment, see Appendix 1 in Chapter 10, pp. 358–64, and Chapter 7, esp. pp. 267–9.) How to think of gesture in its *various* – that is, corporeal and non-corporeal, linguistic and non-linguistic – medial dimensions?

The work of French paleoanthropologist (and 'paleontologist of art') André Leroi-Gourhan provides clear indications about how these questions may be answered, especially in his two-volume work *Le geste et la parole* (1964, 1965, *Gesture and Speech*, 1993). According to Leroi-Gourhan, a gesture is defined on one side by the *connection between hand and tool, or technique*, and on the other by the connection between hand and symbol (the symbol here denoting both a certain expression or movement, and its recording); the human body and intelligence thus extend through speech and gesture into physical and cultural space (all the various 'components' above are simultaneously defined through this process). *Gesture is co-evolutionarily linked to speech*, both of these arising from the same source, and their mutual articulation makes up the driving evolutionary force of man and society.[3]

Around the same time as Marshall McLuhan – and with clear parallels to his work – Leroi-Gourhan developed his conception of technology as the exteriorization of the human body, a notion that is still influential today not only in media theory but also in social ethnology and anthropology. According to Leroi-Gourhan, the memory of the 'operational gestures' of using and making tools is exteriorized together with speech, so that in the latter as well as in tools and technology, the species and socio-ethnic memory and thinking, feeling and the entire nervous apparatus of man are all gradually exteriorized. Keeping in mind his later critics, it is worth exploring the media dimensions of Leroi-Gourhan's concepts of gesture and speech, as this would help us to better understand how, along with aspects of communication (signification) and embodiment that play a decisive role in both gesture and speech, we may proceed to think of their technically 'exteriorizing' aspect. Incidentally, this aspect of the metaphor of the gesture can also be found in Mukařovský: the gesture as the manifest intention of meaning, and an impulse for the extension of meaning in a *printed* text. In this way, what follows can also be said to serve as a reflection on the partial foundations of the broader field – that is, research on gesture as a component not only of literary communication but of communication in general, in connection with its *dispositifs*.

As we saw in Chapter 2, technological motifs permeated the thinking of the Prague School, primarily through contact with the artistic avant-garde. It was in this context that the aesthetic function acquired its characteristic tendency of counterbalancing the one-sided, mechanistic differentiation and isolation of functions. Mukařovský notes (1971d/1946: 286) the inevitable rise of 'machine culture', and a certain anthropological and culturally humanistic perspective, even an ideal, is built into his basic structuralist points of departure (human actions and man-made objects are necessarily multifunctional). Leroi-Gourhan's concern about the rise of audiovisual media in the 1950s and 1960s (see below) is motivated by a similar impulse; according to him, the massively increasing number of people are being turned into passive 'organs of assimilation', disturbing the balance between sensorimotor and symbolizing activities, which until now are thought to have been the driving force of human evolution. However, in Mukařovský's writing on the 'machine' and machine functions, where the aesthetic function is defined in relation to them, he is still largely thinking within the paradigm of classical 'first' machines. (See Chapter 2, esp. pp. 58–9 and Chapter 7, pp. 229–30.) As we shall see, Leroi-Gourhan had already absorbed a quite different discourse in his paleoanthropological theory (or philosophy) of technology – as his use of the term 'operational' earlier suggests – namely the discourse of cybernetics. We may search here, in the tension between humanistic foundations and cybernetic principles, for the cause of a certain ambiguity, a shade of doubt and the suggestion of a certain eschatology that permeates Leroi-Gourhan's notes on the theory of technics. It is here that we will find one of the main keys to interpreting his concept of technics.

What follows consists in three parts. In the first of these, we deal with the concept of the semantic gesture and unintentionality in the literary aesthetics and poetics of Jan Mukařovský. In the second, we work through

Leroi-Gourhan's approach, while continuously considering what it means for a media concept of gesture. In the third part, building on the concept of gesture and its variations as they emerge from the previous interpretation, we consider these findings in the light of a remarkable short story by Vladimir Nabokov, written in 1951 but first published only eight years later (chronologically, the last story by the author to be published): namely, 'The Vane Sisters'.

1. The mediality of the semantic gesture and unintentionality

The medial 'symptomaticity' of semantic gesture

The concept of 'semantic gesture' was originally formulated in the context of specific, author-oriented literary-semantic analyses, but it opened up a wide range of aesthetic and semiotic aspects from within this framework. For Mukařovský, 'semantic gesture' refers to the unifying principle of the construction of meaning in a particular literary work or corpus of a particular author, by which all components and levels – rhythm and sound, tropes, themes and motifs, sentence structure and composition, and so on – are integrated into or 'caught up in' (*strhávány*) a unifying stream or current. The semantic gesture is, in other words, a meaning-creating principle: a 'concrete' but 'content-undetermined' semantic event in which we encounter the meaning of the work, or rather its *genetics*, its formation. It manifests itself through a recurring impulse to the semantic linking and integration of the work's components across its various levels, in this sense also including the necessary 'resistance', namely to the communicative function of the text as this is commonly understood. What remains non-manifest here is meaning, or information, and speech itself presents something of an unusual 'reversed' face. It is not a predetermined idea or pure form, nor is it quite apt here to speak of a distinction between form and content. Rather, it implies a certain *individualized but re-invocable attitude towards reality and its semiotic mediation*, which emerges through the dynamic interplay of the various levels of the literary work (cf. also Jankovič 2005).

Mukařovský's notion of the semantic gesture first appears in his study 'On Poetic Language' (1940). He had already posited the notion of a common denominator for the different layers of a literary work in his earlier analyses (1925 and 1928) of Božena Němcová's *Babička* (*The Grandmother*) and Mácha's *Máj* (*May*), but above all in O motorickém dění v poezii (On Motor Events in Poetry, written 1926–7), which we will later explore in detail. He would continue searching for a semantic-gestural principle in his work on Mácha's poetry, on Nezval's Surrealist collection from 1937 and on Vančura's prose (the first two essays from 1938, the last from mid-1940s). In his essay on Karel Čapek's epic writing, Mukařovský adumbrates for the first time the importance of the reader: 'the meaning-making process by which the work was created and which the reading evokes in the reader' (Mukařovský 2001b/1939: 451). In a study on artistic intentionality and unintentionality (1943), the participation of the perceiver becomes crucial: 'often the perceiver appreciably modifies the semantic gesture of a work contrary to the author's original intention' (Mukařovský 1978e/1943: 111).

There are various perspectives from which the concept of the semantic gesture may strike us as a media symptom: its direct application in the field of literature; its extended application to various other artistic and media types; and finally, its genesis. Mukařovský elaborates his idea of a movement that unifies different levels of the work in *On Motor Events in Poetry* (1926–7, not published until 1985). Here, he follows on from Henri Bremond's concept of pure poetry and *le courant poétique*, and certain episodes in a relatively large field of French psychological theory regarding the motor/kinetic understanding of mental activity (Théodule-Armand Ribot, Pierre Janet and Marcel Jousse).[4] Mukařovský then stipulates that this is not a mere sound characteristic but a unified *internal* unfolding of movement 'which is carried by all the components of a poetic work' (Mukařovský 1985/1926–7: 24). Among these he mentions sound qualities (euphony, rhythm, melody), and grammatical and stylistic means, as well as thematic and mental aspects ('thoughts and ideas'). Nonetheless, the impression given by the poetic text and its subsequent analysis – mostly in the case of Czech poets of the nineteenth and twentieth centuries – begin with the 'sound movement'. It is 'the sound component of a poem [. . .] that most clearly manifests (or rather induces most intensively) the poet's motor gesture' (Mukařovský 1985/1926–7: 47). The motor event is conceived here as a manifestation of the posited motor gesture – a semantic-movement tendency – in the mind of the poet, and induced once more in the mind of the reader. If, outside of art, the movement of ideas, images and linguistic means is primarily determined from the outside, by the practical focus of the message, in poetry it becomes autonomous and unified, subordinating all components of expression. (Jakobson and Mukařovský will later, in this context, speak of the *poetic* or, alternatively, *aesthetic function*.) The sound qualities, especially as they involve expiration and intonation in relation to the choice of word order, can be reflected in the movement of the speech organs (the speaker's motor activity) as well as body movements and gesture; all this can point towards revealing the current that is 'solidified' into a specific verbal form.

In this case, however, body movements remain a mere external image – Mukařovský distances himself here from Eduard Sievers and Karl Groos with their 'empirical-subjectivist' interpretation of the sound forms in verse – an internal movement, which tends to subordinate all components of linguistic (and secondarily also bodily) expression to its own energy.[5]

In a text that remained unpublished during his lifetime, Mukařovský indicates how motor events represent a specific, aesthetically oriented semantic extension of a kind of germinal (imagined) sound-motor action, that is, of a stream of ideas and images and the corresponding movement of vocal and articulatory organs. At the earliest stages of the literary work, one would thus find this *germinal movement tendency, which seeks its development (unfolding) in a concrete form*. Mukařovský already suggests here, in his early pre-structuralist conception, the existence of a level of meaning, sound and gesture on which their individual distinctions, differently manifest in spoken and written language, are not yet determinate or remain open – what Milan Jankovič calls the 'genesis of sense' (*genetika smyslu*). Through the poetic work, we may come into contact with this provisionally indivisible *potentiality of sense* that arises from *sensorially yet undetermined 'planes'* – or, one might say, *medially yet undefined modalities*.

What Mukařovský seeks – though never in these terms – is a certain transmedial, or more precisely *protomedial* level, which in his later conceptualizations concerns the relationship between gesture and image, and between image and word. The mutual interpenetration of the (artistic or photographic) image with the poetic word, and, indirectly, image with gesture, is the subject of a study from 1938 on the poetics of Nezval's collection *Absolutní hrobař* (1937, *The Absolute Gravedigger*, 2016). Mukařovský does not directly speak here of the semantic gesture, but seeks precisely this kind of 'basic meaning-making principle' for the light it might shed on Nezval's poetic output during his Surrealist period.[6] Using a series of detailed observations, Mukařovský demonstrates that the generative principle of these works is a process in which optical perception and figurative naming coincide and intermingle; the very boundary between the imaginary and the literal is deliberately blurred. An optical illusion gives rise to a naive, often violently forceful poetic image ('Harvesters / crawl on their knees across the field / Which is ebbing / [. . .] / They writhe like people drowning'; cited in Mukařovský 2001a/1938: 381),[7] which acquires its own reality as it gradually branches out. The consistent, manifold development of this principle produces a kind of 'return wave', a reverse intermedial link in which 'poetry, which gave its tropes some time ago to the art of painting, borrows [. . .] this inventory back in the shape that painting has supplied out of its own material' (Mukařovský 2001a/1938: 395). The invention of this principle was influenced not only by elements of Surrealist painting and a cycle of photographs by Jindřich Štyrský, as Mukařovský mentions, but also by Dalí's 'paranoid-critical method' and his illustrated book *La femme visible* (1930), in which the painter offers poetic interpretations of his paintings.

Arcimboldo's paintings are the inspiration behind the poems in the section 'Muž který skládá z předmětů svou podobiznu' ('Man Who Composes His Likeness out of Objects'). Nezval also elaborates in his own unique way the method of decalcomania, under the influence of Max Ernst and Jindřich Štyrský; photographic reproductions of six of these works are included in the 'Decalcomania' cycle (see Figure 5.1). The resulting images, or *décalques*, made by pressing black gouache between sheets of paper, present a kind of enigma to the poet, who begins a composition with various shape associations, thereby introducing, in accordance with the requirements of Surrealist poetics, an instance of unintentionality – though Mukařovský

Figure 5.1 Vítězslav Nezval: Soví muž (Owl Man), gouache, from the *Absolute Undertaker* collection, 1937.

does not yet use the term – not only during the reception process, which is briefly mentioned, but already, necessarily, during its genesis. It is worth noting that the *décalques* are printed as photographic reproductions in the original edition on chalk paper, and with certain flattening and technical noise effects (notably distorting contrast), which unsurprisingly remains outside the purview of Mukařovský's analysis. It is also worth noting the fact that in the reproductions included in the present volume – the images you see before you now – the analogue noise of the photograph is substantially transformed by its digital conversion (which is directly evident when the reproduction is enlarged), and in its printed form. Later, we will consider the consequences of these technical transformations with regard to the problem of unintentionality and gesture.

Intentionality and unintentionality as media phenomena

Avant-garde art, however, gives perceptible form to the invisible and the instantaneous, in ways that are not always connected to photographic technique or other technologically determined means. It is along these lines that Mukařovský analyses a characteristic of Picasso's work that was singled out by André Breton in the essay 'Picasso dans son élément' (1933, 'Picasso in His Element', 1999). With its help, the Czech theorist demonstrates the variability of aesthetic value in contemporary art, at the same time foreshadowing his concept of unintentionality (Mukařovský 1971b/1936). According to Breton, the yellowing of newspaper clippings, fading and crinkling of blue and pink paper, 'low-grade' guitar wood and so on in Picasso's *papiers collés* must be understood as premeditated, intentional. The processes of deformation to which these materials are intrinsically susceptible, as Breton argues (and Mukařovský concurs), are accentuated and emphasized as part of the work and its concept. Creation is conceived as a mere *moment of contact between subject and world*, and is – to use Mukařovský's later terminology – 'intentionally unintentional', putting on display the striking temporality of the medium's material modality, its inevitable physical degradation, a characteristic that art materials share in some way with the human body.

It is by emphasizing this counterthrust to the semantic unification of the work (i.e. to intentionality) that the work conveys a refreshing touch to human perception, as Breton illustrates with the example of a butterfly that remains 'forever immobilized next to a dry leaf' in one of Picasso's paintings, and that delights Breton in the manner of the 'sparkling patches through which the radiant river sings of its triumph over the obstacle it had set itself' (Breton 1999/1933: 111). Mukařovský later transposes this method of exposing and drawing attention to unintentionality, with appropriate variations, to his views on the development of art and to his broader conceptualization of the conflict between intentionality and unintentionality. We see then that, while unintentionality figures as a certain limit of semiostructural thinking (which deals primarily with signs and sign relations as rule-based and intentional phenomena), it is drawn into the thinking of Czech structuralists at those moments when the material and corporeal aspect of (aesthetic) sign creation appears irreducible, emerging rather as an integral part of reception and the creative process, albeit in the sense of a dialectically incomplete negation. The relevance of avant-garde artistic production in this context may also be connected to the fact that, by uncovering the materiality and corporeality of the sign, it is as if the artistic avant-garde were aiming to take back that which the rise of mass technical culture had irrevocably stripped from the human individual, namely the disposition to 'multifunctional' activity (hence the aestheticization of activities and objects that are not proper to the artistic sphere) and lived experience vis-à-vis the surrounding world of objects such as it is constructed under these constraints.

In May of 1943, when Mukařovský elaborates on the principle of intentionality and unintentionality in art in a lecture for the Prague Linguistic Circle, using these terms for the first time, he also refers back to his *idée fixe* of gesture. But the emphasis here has significantly shifted. Intentionality – the semantic gesture – appears here as the potential of the semantic energy stored within the work of art for the 'concrete but undetermined' unification of its various levels and components, a *process that can only be actualized by the perceiver*: 'over the course of its duration, the semantic gesture is gradually filled with specific contents, without it being possible to say that these contents approach from the outside: they are simply born within the range and sphere of the semantic gesture, which directly forms them as it is born' (Mukařovský 1978e/1943: 111; translation modified). As it follows from this formulation, the dynamics of unification is therefore a direct consequence of the attitude and efforts of the perceiver; 'at moments when [the artist] regards his creation from the standpoint of pure intentionality in an effort (conscious and subconscious) to introduce traces of this intentionality into its organization, he acts as a perceiver'; 'only from the perceiver's viewpoint does this tendency towards semantic unification manifest itself in all its intensity and untarnished clarity' (Mukařovský 1978e/1943: 97; translation modified). However, where Mukařovský's aim in earlier reflections on the unifying power of gesture was to point out how unexpected connections are born between otherwise disjointed planes, *as if invisibly reaching out towards one another*, here he alludes to the fact that sooner or later a crack appears, the impression of a disruption – unintentionality. One might even say that the intensity of the 'impact of non-sign reality' is proportionate to the impulse to unify the work-sign. At this point in its reception, the work begins to behave differently: it ceases to appear as a supersign and takes on the features of a mysterious 'thing', one whose determination we cannot know. According to Mukařovský, it is precisely in this immediate 'thingness' that the work most profoundly affects the perceiver, stirring something within his very life experience, exposing him to a shock – one, however, that is directly dependent on the perceiver's effort to induce a unifying gesture within a hitherto controlled and distanced aesthetic stance.

We have already pointed out how Mukařovský's thinking relates to the context of mechanized production and technical media, as well as a certain ambivalent reaction to this context on the part of modern art and the avant-garde. His thoughts on function might well be affected by the intensification of weapons development during the second half of the 1930s and war years, which shed a stark light on the functionalization of human behaviour. However this may be the case, when we place his reflections in a historical context we notice that he himself subjects the antinomy of intentionality and unintentionality to a historical contextualization. For him, unintentionality is perceived as a disruption only in the context of a certain concept of art that developed between the Renaissance and the nineteenth century, wherein the meaningful unification (intentionality) of a work of art is understood as a normative ideal. In addition to the medieval and folk traditions mentioned by Mukařovský, we find counterexamples to this concept of art and its emphasis on artistic intentionality in certain features of Baroque culture and Romanticism. Mukařovský also considers that historical factors influence *which* components are perceived as most immediately disruptive (in terms of unintentionality) as a work survives its time and is taken up in various new reception contexts. Citing various period-specific cases of the reception of Mácha's work as well as other examples, Mukařovský demonstrates how it is precisely those seemingly inappropriate, artless or unintentional aspects of the work (often leading to its rejection or ridicule) that have the effect of disrupting aesthetic enjoyment and contemplation, and account for that irritating quality within the work whereby it seems to take the place of unmediated reality. This actually involves a *moment* of the work, or rather that moment of its perception which cannot be integrated into an oriented semantic event, with the result that one component is displaced from the structure of the work, 'the component which *opposes* all the others' (Mukařovský 1978e/1943: 112), and thus appears to the perceiver as unintentional. These examples also make it clear that, over the course of the history of a work's reception, various of its components may take on this unintentional character: the conflict in Mácha's *May*, for instance, between the lyric of nature and thought on one hand and 'a metaphysical nihilism' on the other; thematic incoherence; or, a lack of sufficient motivation in various elements of the plot. That which originally appeared as inappropriately immediate, arousing displeasure, is reassimilated into the structure of the work, over time, as its *internal* antithesis. Moreover, if in its intentional, semiotic unification 'the work ultimately appeals always to what is socially and temporally determined in [man]', it is precisely in its unintentional aspect that the work appears as a thing with existential implications and affects 'what is generally human in man', 'penetrating through its action to the deepest layers of the perceiver's individuality' (Mukařovský 1978e/1943: 128; translation modified). These conclusions also underscore the humanistic basis of Mukařovský's concept in connection to various utopian aspects of avant-garde thinking. We would argue that this anticipates the commencement of a new period in semiotic thinking, in which it will begin to deal with *the very limits of sign mediation*. Mukařovský's study of intentionality and unintentionality in art comes at the end of a long arc in this thinking that would make him return to and reconsider the psychological conceptions of art, and aesthetics of emotionalism and the subconscious (with references to Stephan Witasek, Théodule-Armand Ribot, Frédéric Paulhan and Pierre Janet), some of which had already influenced his thinking on 'motor events'. The result was that he would now separate the polarity of intentionality/unintentionality from the polarity of consciousness/subconscious on the basis of semiotic theory, at the same time pushing this semiotic theory to its limits.

The protomedial thresholds of gesture

Where in this reconstruction of Mukařovský's thinking do we find the figure of mediality? We said earlier that gesture – now intentionality, as extended to all artistic disciplines – was originally conceived in the literary context as a semantic tendency suggesting a specific line of sense running through the various levels and components of a work. The overall outline for this model of levels and components is based on linguistics (cf. Mukařovský's study 'O jazyce básnickém', 1940, 'On Poetic Language', 1977, where the concept of the semantic gesture appears for the first time).[8] For literary study, to start from linguistic models of language and its levels is quite natural; this forms the systemic basis of poetic language. In the context of gesture, however, something else begins to show itself: the delimitation of language *levels*, which has a *differential* character, reaches its limit precisely in the semantic tendency of gesture. In a specific text, or rather, in the specific act of its creation or reception, it is not possible to model the scope of these levels in advance, since gesture – even in the abstract sense of the conditions or systemic basis of 'poetic language' – has to do precisely with the fact that they are *in flux*, that is, in a state of transformation or *'birth'*. Just as the *mutual relations* of language levels (specific contents) are born and take form *only 'within the range and vicinity'* of the semantic gesture, their boundaries may only be formed and shaped simultaneously with the manner in which they are *connected (and transcended)* within the perception and reception of the work. Levels and components may indeed appear as different types of 'sub-coding', in themselves variously complex and combinable,[9] consisting of different types of relations, as well as both *continuous and discrete* elements. At the same time, however, they are *only constituted* – at least partially, *in the line of their connection* – within a given act of reception. It is only in contact with the gesture – that is, in contact between the material and consciousness of the receiver – that they acquire a certain passability, the movement towards a certain aim, context of a tendency or thrust, or tendency to unfold in a certain direction. As media thresholds, these layers (levels, components) are therefore 'weakly charged' or characterized by different degrees of 'conducivity', and they suggest only various potentialities for fulfilling different media types, or indicate the existence of a 'transmedia' level, of media features that remain to be determined. This would mean that, in the semantic gesture, the work falls back on a kind of 'pre-mediality' that (according to Yuri Lotman, for example) is characteristic of dreams (see Chapter 10, pp. 331–3). From the point of view of the development of media, however, one can ask: Is this concept not in fact preconditioned by the medial situation, in which disparate materials *resist conversion* from one to another? Would this not in turn have the consequence that in an environment dominated by *binary-numeric coding* and interface, which *absorbs* any media at will, this notion of gesture *loses its footing*? If we return to the 1940s, however, we will find a direct intermedial example – with special genealogical significance for our retracing of the contours of mediality – in which unintentionality arises not only on the border between sign and reality, but on the medial thresholds between sculpture and painting and their respective materials. Mukařovský is referring here to the work of the remarkable quattrocento painter Andrea Mantegna (1430–1506), who depicts figures, robes and dresses, landscapes, leaves and fruit, and so on, all with the appearance of rock, marble and crystal, of something made from metal or glass. As often repeated in the history of art – by his teacher Francesco Squarcione, Giorgio Vasari, the German art historian Richard Muther and others – it is a manner of depiction that produces the intense effect of intrinsic hardness and sharpness. Mantegna, who also pioneered copper engraving and *trompe l'oeil* ceiling painting (the *Camera degli Sposi*, for example, in the Palazzo Ducale of Mantua) that would inspire Baroque painters and architects, makes implicit references to the 'inappropriate' material characteristics of one media type in another, in this way deliberately introducing the influence of ancient sculpture, which was more perfect in his eyes than reality. These characteristics suggest the transferability of sculpture to painting, while also hinting at the phantasmic possibilities of the implied material transformations; 'leaves, which no breeze could disturb, hang fast as steel from the branches' (Muther, cited in Mukařovský 1978e/1943: 109). As Mukařovský adds, '[T]he painting exceeds the limits of its semiotic range and becomes something other than a sign. Its individual parts suggest realities which do not belong to the semantic realm of the work, and they thus acquire the nature of a peculiar, phantasmal objectivity' (Mukařovský 1978e/1943: 109; translation modified).

To summarize our preliminary findings, we see that there are actually three different *modalities of unintentionality*: (1) between media and various materials; (2) between a sign and manifest reality (material, social or psychological); and (3) in the case of photographic reproduction, between the sign and its 'purely' technical implementation. In Nezval's photo reproductions of his *décalques*, that is, we are also confronted with an *impression of alienness*, but one that has its origin in the technical mediating effect of a kind of noise or grain that seems to exceed all relationality to aesthetic experience (intentional or unintentional), even in the negative sense. It is clear that this alienness does not arise from any diversity of reception or search for meaning, nor even from the way materials are processed (or their resistance to processing), but from a kind of 'inhuman' or completely meaningless aspect: the opposite side of consciousness or 'disorienting dark' of the unconscious,[10] or else something that detaches itself from meaning (in relation to man) in a hostile manner – or that is simply not worth talking about.[11] We will later return to the question of whether the transition to the sphere of *technical mediality* can be counted among the 'media' or 'protomedia thresholds', as we have considered them here, and how to define this sphere. We will also return to the question of whether the 'semantic gesture' may have experienced a decline in the networked media environment.

2. The mediality of communication between gesture and speech

Gesture, speech, rhythm and graphism

Convincing evidence for the fact that written and spoken forms of language are in principle media-mixed forms, and above all that image, writing, gesture and rhythm are connected on some deeper, primal level, can be found in André Leroi-Gourhan's famous work on paleoanthropology *Gesture and*

Speech.[12] This and other works by the French thinker were soon recognized as a fundamental contribution to the theory and philosophy of technology, and ultimately, by way of his reception among such French post-structuralists as Jacques Derrida and Gilles Deleuze, adopted in contemporary media thinking. According to Leroi-Gourhan, evolution is determined by a series of liberations and exteriorizations, by which the hands 'exude' technics just as speech organs produce speech, while technics contains in itself more and more of its own operational programme (it is involved in the entire operational chain, as discussed below). Evolution thus proceeds by the ever more rigorous technical exteriorization of the human sensory and nervous apparatus. The operational syntax of tool production and use has its direct parallel in the operational syntaxes of speech genesis and use. The critical link to Leroi-Gourhan's notion of the 'operational chain' (*la chaîne opératoire*) is the point of origin for the concept of 'recursive operational chains' (Bruno Latour and others). Various critical points of view have shown how the process of exteriorization must be consistently described as non-cumulative, since every new technique is generated and used in an environment that is always already socially and technically mediated, that is, in an environment of multidirectional feedback co-determining the use and impacts of technology and speech.[13]

It would be impossible here to trace Leroi-Gourhan's paleoanthropological argument in all its detail. For our purposes, however, it will suffice to examine his thinking on graphism, rhythmicity, and the relationship between writing and image within the framework of his own media thinking, as this could indicate ways to rework Mukařovský's 'semantic gesture' and unintentionality into a fully medial concept. Above all, we do not wish to lose sight of the possibility of a theoretical-interpretive application of the concept of gesture in the field of literature, or overlook its implications for the process of understanding and 'hermeneutics', since this context makes its way to Leroi-Gourhan's work merely in the form of 'reading' archaeological findings (rather than in the form of theory).

Thus, according to Leroi-Gourhan, human evolution begins with and is made possible by the simultaneous, coevolutionary liberation of the 'anterior field' of hands and mouths in service of the production of tools and phonic symbols, as well as graphic expression.[14] By the term 'gesture', he does not primarily mean movements of the hand with a communication function, but rather the structural connection of hand movements to a tool, made possible – as with the connection of operational memory to the tool with the help of speech – by freeing the anterior field from locomotor functions. The hand gradually evolutionarily exteriorizes itself in its tools, and these in turn anticipate and temporarily establish the operational sequences for their future use. However, the way a tool is produced and used is not imprinted in a person's genetic make-up, that is, in their biological memory. Rather, the operational programme of technology is stored, with the help of speech, in the collective (socio-ethnic) memory, and increasingly, over the course of human evolution, in the technology itself (mechanical memory). This latter process, in modern times, takes on quite dramatic proportions.[15] And just as there is no discovery in which our oldest (pre-)human ancestors[16] were not surrounded by a particular set of tools, it is certain, as Leroi-Gourhan argues, that these closest ancestors (and companions) of the genus Homo inevitably used sound symbols, even if no archaeological evidence has been found to confirm this: 'tools and language are neurologically linked and cannot be dissociated within the social structure of humankind'; 'language [. . .] sprang from the same source as technics' (Leroi-Gourhan 1993/1964, 1965: 114, 115). Just as the separation of tool and hand readies one for the other's use, so too does the differentiation of signal and symbol enable integrating symbols into operational chains, while simultaneously making it possible to consolidate or adapt the given operational syntax.

The aspect of Leroi-Gourhan's anthropology of technology that coincides with contemporaneous and modern-day media is particularly noteworthy, and his thoughts on the audiovisual media of his time carry some of the darker undertones of his conception. Here, the gap between 'the symbol and its contents' narrows, so that 'the spectator has absolutely no possibility of intervening actively in the "real" situation thus recreated'. The organs of vision, movement and hearing are addressed simultaneously, and the entire sphere of perception is forced into passive participation (Leroi-Gourhan 1993/1964, 1965: 213). He anticipates, however, that the development will go on replacing and 'exteriorizing' the operations of memory and logical judgement with artificial intelligence. (With the rise of computer-based interactive media, in fact, this passivity could only be transformed into a more complete integration of the human vis-à-vis the demands of the artificial environment, and a more perfect illusion of participation; the development of artificial intelligence, then, is not constrained to the symbolic, logic-oriented approach.) With regard to the 'recursive effects' mentioned earlier, it would be more precise to say that human cognitive operations and social relations develop both with the help of their partial transfer to the sphere of 'tools' (automatic computer evaluation, for example), and at the same time by deviating from the areas and functions to which they were thus delegated. According to Leroi-Gourhan, the first step in the 'exteriorization of the cerebral cortex' was card catalogue systems, which made it possible to project the simplified content of a vast body of written material into a supplementary structure. However, the file system still required the involvement of the 'visual and manual operating field' of its users. With the invention of the punch card system, in which the binary computing mechanism is already at work, the way was opened to the emergence of the 'electronic integrator' and a capability that transcends that of the human brain: to link any recollection with any other:[17] 'To refuse to see that machines will soon overtake the human brain in operations involving memory and rational judgment is to be [. . .] like the Homeric bard who would have dismissed writing as a mnemonic trick without any future' (Leroi-Gourhan 1993/1964, 1965: 265).

Technology and speech are therefore aspects of the same phenomenon. Yet the gesture does not only have a technical function, but also a communication function; it is here that Leroi-Gourhan begins to speak of 'graphism'. Given that the empirical evidence is limited here to archaeological findings, it is entirely understandable that he focuses on those expressive gestures which are imprinted in a material.[18] Graphic expression and spoken language balance each other, so that 'The gesture [graphic expression] interprets the word, and the word comments upon graphic expression' (Leroi-Gourhan 1993/1964, 1965: 210). With the emergence of graphism, 'The hand has its language, with a sight-related form of expression, and the face has its own, which relates to hearing' (Leroi-Gourhan 1993/1964, 1965). The fact that the development of graphism 'is connected with the development of the gesture-coordinating [cortical] areas' (Leroi-Gourhan 1993/1964, 1965: 195), gives it a specific character that is more difficult to perceive from the modern perspective. The oldest known traces of this type, dating from the end of the Mousterian and the beginning of the Châtelperron period, do not, as Leroi-Gourhan notes, have any figural character. The equidistant notches and lines engraved in bone or stone, according to Leroi-Gourhan, do not represent 'hunting tallies' as they are sometimes interpreted, but rather a rhythm or rhythmic process associated with a related verbal component, perhaps even part of 'a rhythmic system of an incantatory or declamatory nature' (Leroi-Gourhan 1993/1964, 1965: 188).

The dating of what Leroi-Gourhan called graphism has moved backwards with new findings and new combined methods of determining their age. The oldest figurative representations known today have been dated to before 40000 BCE (see Aubert et al. 2018; Conard 2009), and the oldest graphic marks from Blombos Cave in South Africa, a cross-hatched pattern etched with ochre in silcrete, to before 70000 BCE (Henshilwood et al. 2018). Remarkably, these findings only confirm Leroi-Gourhan's argument that 'graphism did not begin with naive representations of reality but with abstraction' (Leroi-Gourhan 1993/1964, 1965: 188), and give new relevance to his insight that graphism did not begin by 'reproducing reality in a slavishly photographic manner', but developed 'from signs which [. . .] initially expressed rhythms rather than forms' (Leroi-Gourhan 1993/1964, 1965: 190). Though based only on the archaeological evidence available at the time, Leroi-Gourhan's thesis has a more profound and enduring validity. What we understand today as figural representation seems to have been associated at its origins with speech, with which it established a certain *rhythmic process*, and was 'much closer to writing (in the broadest sense) than to what we understand by a work of [visual] art' (Leroi-Gourhan 1993/1964, 1965: 190). Writing and painting have the same origin – graphism – and the development of figurative art first arises through a bifurcation within a single line.

The 'radial representation of thought' thus rests on the connection between the graphic sign and the rhythmic stream of speech. Yet this rhythmic pairing of phonation and graphic expression is hard to imagine for a person embedded within a culture of writing, and especially, as Leroi-Gourhan observes, of linear, phonetic writing. From this 'mythography', in Leroi-Gourhan's terminology, it nevertheless follows that 'from the beginning' there existed a multidimensionality in systems of expression, by virtue of the combination of the temporal dimension of speech with the radiality of graphic expression and their rhythmic connection. Leroi-Gourhan also substantiates part of this thesis with more recent pictographs, including examples from Alaskan Inuit and Native North American cultures: a pictograph implying a narrative line invariably and without exception appears as the result of contact with a civilization based on written language (Leroi-Gourhan 1993/1964, 1965: 192, 197).

On the origin of the medial differentiation of the sign ('mythogram')

The paleontological concept of graphism thus refutes the idea of the medial unity of text and written speech, but also spoken language, as well as image. In his *Of Grammatology*, Derrida borrows from this concept in his critique of phonocentrism (the secondary status of writing), while at the same time introducing interesting turns and shifts into Leroi-Gourhan's thinking. For Derrida, writing is as primary as spoken language, and spoken language is as artificial as writing, and he is primarily concerned with overcoming the opposition between them ('Actually, the peoples said to be "without writing" lack only a certain type of writing'; Derrida 1998/1967: 83). By drawing on Leroi-Gourhan's work, he is able to posit a special instance or level of communication and perception anterior to the differentiation of written and spoken language. He uses various terms for this, including *archi-écriture* ('arche-writing' or 'proto-writing'), and *l'écriture généralisée* ('generalized writing'). Prior to the differentiation between linguistic forms and substances, this level acts as a kind of pure difference beyond the opposition of the material and immaterial but also as an event of differentiation, its movement. Indeed, it is this *archi-écriture*, and graphism generally speaking, that serves as the very condition for the expression of something as something, of which the expression itself (in any form or substance) is necessarily a trace or indication, referring to itself only in its own absence. In the framework of Derrida's philosophical project, the assumption of this most general difference is of fundamental importance, shaping his theoretical project in ways that we are too numerous to trace here. Especially notable, however, is the way Derrida is able to make strategic use of Leroi-Gourhan's notion of the 'mythogram' as 'a writing that spells its symbols pluri-dimensionally; there the meaning is not subjected to successivity, to the order of a logical time or to the irreversible temporality of sound' (Derrida 1998/1967: 85). This allows him to delineate an alternative conception of 'writing' to counter an age-old war waged in the name of 'linearization', of phonetic writing and printing, and of all the far-reaching cultural consequences that the linear arrangement of speech and the associated organization and conception of knowledge in the Western world entails.

Miroslav Petříček engages with Derrida's view on this most general possible difference as condition for a conceivable difference within language, that is, as common ground of the spoken and written sign (as Hans Jørgen Uldall puts it, 'stream of air, stream of ink'):

> It is here that we may build on Derrida's work while at the same time departing from it (only because he himself did not proceed in this direction); [. . .] if glossematics places the greatest emphasis on the independence (of a sign) from a substance [. . .], then the question naturally arises: why limit what the sign is independent of to different kinds of linguistic substances [. . .]? Should we proceed further in this direction, we will arrive [. . .] at a notion of difference on a level that precedes not only the opposition between spoken and written language, but also that between word and image. (Petříček 2006: 35)

Here, Petříček proceeds to the generalized concept of line as a boundary, a pure difference, and as a stroke, tendency, inclination; it also clearly approaches quite close to the concept of gesture as it appears among the Prague structuralists. This is where our close reading of *Gesture and Speech* and Leroi-Gourhan's argumentation pays off: he was able to demonstrate that graphism is oriented towards the differentiation of image and writing through the expression and articulation of *rhythm*, with the suggestion that the interconnection between speech and gesture through rhythm has an invaluable developmental, even evolutionary, significance. (For Leroi-Gourhan, rhythm can be imprinted in a figure whose specifically spread lines can be traversed in different ways; rhythm is 'spatialized', delinearized.) *The communication disposition of man and, by extension, of human communities is multidimensional from the beginning.* Leroi-Gourhan therefore indicates the existence – speaking more to the primal, 'immemorial' conditions of communication and instrumentality, than to their early phases – not only of a level of difference that precedes that which exists between writing and image, but also of a kind of differentiation between grapheme, image, sound, gesture, touch and rhythm that cannot be traced back to a specific moment.

That is not all, of course. Leroi-Gourhan's work also clearly shows the open *technical* nature of man. Here it is precisely the human disposition to multidimensional communication that necessarily underlies the tendency to technical 'exteriorization'; the development of expressive means and modes on one side, and technical 'exteriorization' on the other is a *concurrent* and interconnected movement, by which that which is externalized is simultaneously differentiated and created. The implications of this link for our understanding of consciousness and memory are far-reaching. Yet it is also necessary here to combine this principle with the concepts of communication and sign. It turns out that the communication means and signs that media work with are interconnected on some basic level, or more aptly, they develop on the basis of the *fundamental condition of mutual correlation*. The interrelation among basic means of communication (speech, gesture, graphic expression) is primal (constitutive) and *cannot be attributed to any special technical turn or media invention*; on the contrary, it is *inseparable from technics (the technical gesture)*.[19] Communication is constituted on the potentiality of transferring between various means, between expressions formulated by the various means necessary (made possible through 'externalization') to address the reception apparatus of the 'collective'. Recalling the limit of the concept of sign that we encountered in the case of Mukařovský, this limit seems to lie precisely on the border that characterizes its exteriority. There is no reason to understand this as a kind of material or technical 'outside' – indeed, we should not understand it this way, but as an 'empty cipher' that allows something to be expressed – and understood – in yet another way, *without giving this possibility a positive determination* (this necessarily applies as well to reception). At the same time, however, this empty cipher is *actually externalized* in the materiality of the signifier, since such an inevitable, precarious exteriority of the sign cannot be directly represented in the sign (even if it offers the evidence to our senses), being *inseparable from its mediating function*.

We can now more clearly grasp the level on which the *indeterminacy (openness) of media modalities*, which are 'theoretically' mutually translatable or combinable, arises as a fundamental condition of communication. We have also found reason to support the claim that this condition in some way accounts for media development and cannot be cancelled by, or reduced to, any new media or particular technology.

Double unintentionality?

The cybernetic subtext of Leroi-Gourhan's work can already be seen to emerge from the analysis above. It is implied within the concepts of 'programme' and 'operation', and arises unmistakably in the idea of the successive steps of exteriorization; it is in the last stage that these steps, with the electronic computer and promise of artificial intelligence, accede to the very 'control centre'. We see this subtext as well in the concept of operational behaviour, which involves a kind of programme (not only in humans, but also in higher mammals) preserved largely through mechanical operations in social memory, and in processes of imitation and imitative learning. In humans, Leroi-Gourhan argues, this process is most intensively reoriented by way of 'lucid' phases, that is, through the intervention of language and symbolic representations, which make it possible to continuously adapt the connections between the links of the operational sequence and 'organize [them] consciously toward the creation of new processes' (Leroi-Gourhan 1993/1964, 1965: 233).

The cybernetic discourse that permeates Leroi-Gourhan's work, and that is so typical of the time, provides a universal media framework, but it also stokes uncertainty regarding the nature and origin of the connection between technology and human consciousness. It is the same with the instinctive behaviour that Leroi-Gourhan describes characteristically in terms of 'automatic aspects', and which in man, as in all living things, is 'programmed'. For Leroi-Gourhan, this leads to a certain apprehensiveness: What are the consequences of that constitutive technical aspect in humans?

As Leroi-Gourhan observes with concern, the transfer of skilled movements into the apparatuses themselves and into machine-defined control gestures, the steady rise of fields in which technical and programming gestures overlap or replace communicative and physical gestures (photography and electronic music, for instance), have already had their effect on humankind. And while this development may coincide with the cybernetic moment of Leroi-Gourhan's conception mentioned above, he himself sees the disconnection of technical intelligence from the hand in rather ominous terms:

The dwindling importance of the makeshift organ that is our hand would not matter a great deal if there were not overwhelming evidence to prove that its activity is closely related to the balance of the brain areas with which it is connected. [...] Not having to 'think with one's fingers' is equivalent to lacking a part of one's normally, phylogenetically human mind. (Leroi-Gourhan 1993/1964, 1965: 255; 1965: 62)

There are several good reasons not to subscribe to the 'technology pessimism' that underscores these words. Some of these reasons are identified by Leroi-Gourhan himself. Above all, as Walter Benjamin suggests, it is necessary to emphasize the indeterminacy with which human society makes use of a certain technology. In the same vein, as Raymond Williams (1989/1983) also points out, *the introduction of a technology always brings with it moments of choice* (see Chapter 8, e.g. pp. 287–9). Hartmut Winkler's thinking on media (which otherwise significantly diverges) leads him to similar conclusions: it is impossible to theorize the materiality or technicality of media without regard to their use, relevance and context (see Chapter 7, esp. pp. 256–8). Thanks to Leroi-Gourhan's work, we can now consider as established fact that speech and gesture are also in some sense 'teletechnics' (*Tele-Techniken*), and that the means of communication are in some sense always already 'at a distance' (cf. Tholen 2005: 160). Yet many contemporary media theorists do not consider language to be a medium: according to them, the medium must have the technical ability to record and store, and mediality necessarily includes the possibility of converting data given on a timeline into spatial articulations, that is, the possibility of technical reproduction. But even from this point of view, gesture and speech exhibit their *transitional position*: gesture with its 'detachable' pictorial component (this is already evident in 'graphism'), and speech with its traditional mnemonic techniques, such as rhythmization and repetition, which applies as well to oral traditions.

Media do not only include '(modern) technical media' but also that 'in which perception, feeling and thinking find their characteristic forms, and presentations' (Hartmut Böhme, Klaus R. Scherpe, cited in Tholen 2005: 159). (Cf. also Chapter 3, pp. 76–8.) There can be no doubt, however, that it is only the development of modern technical media that *made visible* the medial processes inherent in writing and printing, thus making it possible to think about the *mediality* of spoken language and the linguistic sign – just as writing, according to Walter J. Ong (2002/1982), made it possible to think about the word as a sign (or visible *signum*), and the invention of letterpress, according to John Guillory (2010), opened the problem of the technological nature of writing.

To summarize our conclusions thus far, we have observed an important cybernetic subtext in Leroi-Gourhan's thinking on gesture, one that provides the conceptual background for understanding how the protomediality of thresholds is constitutive of the development of speech and gesture – and so also of media. We can say, moreover, that the possibility of expressing or giving shape to something rests on the *condition of the possibility of transmediation and translation, which is primary*. We have also taken account of a half-forgotten influence on Mukařovský's concept of the semantic gesture and unintentionality, namely visual arts (and in Section 4 of Chapter 2, pp. 59–62, also theatre). Leroi-Gourhan's main contribution, I would argue, is his discovery of *the inner, inescapable technicality of the human gesture and symbol*. Yet returning to his paleoanthropological work is also instructive for addressing the *changing spectrum of media differences* – not every technique is like writing – and at the same time giving an intimation of their origins. His understanding that the earliest graphic expressions are records of rhythm and, above all, his thoughts on the multidimensionality of communication that arises from the pairing of rhythm/sound with a graphic symbol, helps us to conceptualize the gestural dimension of literature by recalling that level of meaning (sense) at which specific sensory and semiotic characteristics are not yet determined, and which serve as a germinal impulse to movement that only acquires its semantic fulfilment and complexity in the act of reception.

The line of reason that proceeds from the semantic gesture to the technical gesture and back again thus allows us to consider the foundations of differences on which the diverse elements and levels of the work are formed, and which are in fact a necessary condition for the movement of their 'unification'.

There is yet another lesson to learn from this connection between the semantic gesture – the impulse to unify the meaning of a complex literary work – and gesture and speech as fundamental parts of the memory and material evolutionary process of human societies, in Leroi-Gourhan's conception. For Mukařovský, the concept of gesture also implies that, in the genesis of a literary work, a large amount of meaning is embedded within the recorded expression by virtue of a unique orientation or tendency. Slightly shifting our perspective, we may say that it 'exteriorizes itself' (thus becoming, for the reader, the author's trace). It is especially clear in this case that 'exteriorization' does not refer to a unidirectional or isolated process. If such a case of complex 'exteriorization' – the process of creation and perception of meaning, as represented by the 'semantic gesture' – is possible at all – it is one that is conditioned and accompanied by the existence and development of entire sets of long-standing cultural techniques, as well as social, educational and cultural institutions. It is these techniques and institutions that maintain and support the 'codes' of gesture, whether or not in progressive terms (in Walter Benjamin's sense). Thus, even in the case of 'institutions' and 'codes', this is never a one-way process, insofar as it is connected with various kinds of internalization through the acquisition of competences, enculturated dispositions and embodied habits. Any change in this network of relations implies a change as well in the conditions of the conception of the (semantic) gesture. It cannot, for this reason, be considered a universal concept. In other words, *intentionality* presupposes a number of factors, including a certain *media competence* and *willingness* (or openness) on the part of the *perceiver*, a process of *'forgetting'* the unintentional, the possibility of *returning* to the text (repeat reading), and perhaps even a certain *stability of the recording*. Is it not the case then that intentionality *in this sense* loses the very conditions of its possibility, in the current 'network environment' of unstable traces and accelerated, as well as automated communication?

Turning our attention once more to the specifically asubjective and technical 'modality' of unintentionality, we notice that it maintains a uniquely *lateral* relationship to unintentionality in the original sense, which arises always in relation to an intentional instance – that is, to sense and the unifying movement of a work. 'Technical intentionality' arises instead as a result of the seemingly insignificant situation of technical mediation (of the work), which, much like the material aspects of the sign, can emerge in a disruptive way against the background of semantic processes. This suggests, in turn, that unintentionality is actually a single phenomenon, its different types arising only in the context of a certain *historically specific understanding of technics,* and that *'double unintentionality'* is in fact always only a *symptom of the discrepancy between older and newer understandings of technics*. At the same time, technical unintentionality may shift as it develops to aspects of stylization, or else a willingness may arise, in the perceiver's mind, to be affected by the impression of a (technical) crack.

Such effects can include – in analogue photography, for example – the impression of documentary fidelity or traumatic 'presence of the past', as Roland Barthes discusses in his work *La chambre claire: Note sur la photographie* (1980, *Camera Lucida: Reflections on Photography*, 1981), albeit without the technical side of photography in mind. As an example, we can refer to Robert Capa's *Muerte de un miliciano* (known as *Falling Soldier*),[20] which captures the moment in which a member of the Spanish Republican Army is shot dead in a skirmish with Francoist forces (see Figure 5.2). The body of the soldier seems to be arrested mid-fall, his legs bent and body slightly reclined – a figure that can no longer be restored to balance – while the right arm extends as if to voluntarily put down his rifle, the eyes close, the head bows. The soldier in this photograph seems no longer alive but not yet

Figure 5.2 Robert Capa: *Muerte de un miliciano*, gelatin silver print, 18.1 × 23.8 cm, 1936, New York, The Museum of Modern Art.

dead – he is, in this sense, a 'spectre'.[21] Robert Capa (Endre Ernő Friedmann) made this photograph during the Spanish Civil War on 5 September 1936, in the vicinity of Cerro Muriano. That the authenticity of this famous war photo has been questioned and defended many times is significant, with respect to the relationship of photography to the past, as well as that between man and technology. Its relationship to the past is peculiarly opaque: the moment captured is intensely singular, but also irretrievably past, and the consciousness of the figure it depicts as multifariously inaccessible at this moment of perfect (delayed) ambiguity. At the same time, however, this inaccessibility (of consciousness and the past) is immediately present, it materialized in the form of a photograph. This effect is also due to the fact that every photograph, even in the analogue context, is always already in some sense a copy (cf. Batchen 2018), just as the immediate moment, in the gesture of presenting itself, is always already in the past. *Technical graininess may inadvertently accentuate and foreground this 'perfect ambiguity'*.

In literature, a 'low-tech' artistic and communication medium whose identity was established by the spread of literacy and intertwined with manuscript and oral traditions, technical modifications are traditionally considered marginal, if not overlooked altogether. We may well ask whether the (often tacit) humanist inclination or impression is justified: Can literature really hold a mirror to technics, create the conditions for its self-alienation or counter its automation with a humanizing influence? We might be inclined to answer in the affirmative were it not for the evidence presented here that the gesture necessarily includes a (more or less hidden) technical aspect. But is it not rather that the technical aspect of mediation is a necessary condition for such a 'mirror'? This raises a similar question: Is there a human tendency to try to recuperate by means of the semantic gesture that which technology has taken away? This would only be the case in the context of a certain literary-aesthetic concept, according to which the individual internalizes him- or herself in literary speech precisely by and through what otherwise makes that individual – as a subject of communication – 'external'. However, it is hardly possible that the primary or only motivation for such an aesthetic concept could be found in techno-evolutionary causes.

3. Gesture and intentionality in 'The Vane Sisters' (1951)

In the final part of this chapter, we will consider various aspects of the concept of gesture by way of an interpretation of Vladimir Nabokov's short story 'The Vane Sisters'. The story was written in 1951 but not published until 1959, in New York's *Hudson Review*, and the same year in London-based literary magazine *Encounter*.[22] Let us start (quite traditionally) with a synopsis. The narrator, a professor of French literature at an unnamed college located between Albany and Boston,[23] recounts with a certain detached fascination how the path of his life intersected with that of the Vane sisters, and how the younger sister, Sibyl Vane, took her own life after an unhappy affair with a married professor, the narrator's colleague D., after leaving a suicide note in an exam paper for the narrator's class. The narrator, acting as its messenger, delivers the note to the elder sister Cynthia. The narrator soon begins to frequent Cynthia, and mocks her in his narration for her mystical belief in spiritualism and 'theory of intervenient auras' – secret coded messages in 'old books' and literary texts, as well as the strange series of signs and spectral interventions in the everyday experiences of the living. According to Cynthia's theory, the manner of these interventions reflects the personality of the departed. With amused irony, the narrator himself participates in private spiritualist séances (though not those involving 'paid mediums'; Nabokov 1958–9: 499) conducted by Cynthia and two owners of a print shop, who are brothers (and Cynthia's lovers), and who, as the narrator mentions in passing, possess 'considerable wit and culture' (Nabokov 1958–9: 499). These sessions are visited upon, via messages rapped out on a table (and other signs), by the spirits of 'Oscar Wilde', 'Leo Tolstoy' and several other disembodied beings. The narrator is not sexually attracted to Cynthia, at least not consciously, and though she is considered beautiful, he is put off by her style and appearance: 'in the stark lamplight of her studio, you could see the pores of her thirty-two-year-old face fairly gaping at you like something in an aquarium'; 'I glimpsed, with a secret shudder, the higgledy-piggledy striation of black hairs that showed all along her pale shins through the nylon of her stockings with the scientific distinctness of a preparation flattened under glass' (Nabokov 1958–9: 495).[24] The narrator is drawn to Cynthia rather by her paintings, 'those honest and poetical pictures', among which he particularly appreciates '"Seen Through a Windshield" – a windshield partly covered with rime, with a brilliant trickle [. . .] across its transparent part and, through it all, the sapphire flame of the sky and a green and white fir tree' (Nabokov 1958–9: 499). The narrator's visual sensitivity (accompanied by his disparaging view of the human exterior) is on full display at the beginning of the story. Here he recounts his observations, on a Sunday walk through town, of glistening water as it trickled from melting snow and droplets falling from icicles on the eaves. He did not at first see the shadows of the droplets, and when he finally glimpsed one, it seemed to run, like 'the dot of an exclamation mark', faster than its source (notice that this is a graphic symbol). Moments later, a coloured shadow caught his attention: 'The lean ghost, the elongated umbra cast by a parking meter upon some damp snow, had a strange ruddy tinge; this I made out to be due to the tawny red light of the restaurant sign above the sidewalk' (Nabokov 1958–9: 492). By way of these observations, he comes to the places where his former colleague D. lived and learns about Cynthia's sudden death.

As we read at the end of the story (sections six and seven), this news surprisingly shakes the narrator's self-confidence. He passes a sleepless night idly searching for acrostics in Shakespeare's *Sonnets*, listens with a tingle to a furtive crackling sound in his quiet, dark apartment, imagines the mischievous presence of Cynthia's ghost and retraces the history of spiritualist hoaxes. In the morning, with the sun's rays coming through the 'tawny' window shades, he falls into a restless sleep and dreams of Cynthia. When he awakes, however, he is unable to recall them: 'I could isolate, consciously, little. Everything seemed blurred, yellow-clouded, yielding nothing tangible. Her inept acrostics, maudlin evasions, theopathies—every recollection formed ripples of mysterious meaning. Everything seemed yellowly blurred, illusive, lost' (Nabokov 1958–9: 503). The first words of this last paragraph, as an improbably perceptive or perhaps repeat reader may notice – and to which the text itself provides clues on several occasions – form a secret message, an acrostic: 'IciclEsbycyntHiameterfrommEsybil'. This suggests a kind of mysterious participation of the two dead sisters, undetected by the narrator, in his own mediation of their story, and suggests the possibility that the visual spells at the beginning of the narrative were related to their operation, with the intention perhaps, of leading the narrator to receive the incriminating message, or establish a strange, unconscious contact with them, or as a gift hidden in plain sight.

The whole story thus acquires another layer of mystery; an interference seeps into the narrator's voice, of which he himself is not aware. Yet the literary text, constructed in this way, does not simply invite us to believe in ghosts. The narrator's objections to Cynthia's superstitious notions – "'Ah, that's Paul,"' she would say when the soup spitefully boiled over' (Nabokov 1958–9: 497) – are rational and well-founded. It becomes apparent that this pedantic and somewhat aloof narrator, who observes others a bit like specimens under glass slides, is *a bad medium (and reader)* of Sibyl's dying note and the story of the Vane sisters, of the message scribbled on the exam, as well as those messages that *become legible in the 'script' of his mediation*. It is this invisibility and blindness, paradoxically, that is anticipated by the visual play at the beginning of the story, and likewise a mutual non-transparency between the narrator and the narrated that is signalled in the final acrostic. A strange opacity thus emerges, quite *literally* – or indeed, *in the letters*. The story as a whole appears to be witnessed as if through a frosted glass – 'a car windshield partially covered with rime' – and the fictional painting by Cynthia becomes a trope (another kind of image) for the way the story is told, and for the split between its telling and its sense. The final acrostic (though it is only one of several devices, as we shall see) serves as an analogy for that transparent trickle, the possibility of crossing the threshold between one world and another, between narration and meaning, or perhaps between image and word. In those thirty-two letters, another, tacit sense is imprinted, which we glimpse from the margins of the narrator's mental and verbal mediation of the narrated world. Yet it is precisely the narrator's artistic and pictorial sensitivity that enables *contact* between the two impenetrable 'worlds', a contact that arises from the constitutive supplement to verbal communication, or, in Derridian terms, its graphic representation or spatialization – that is, from *écriture*.

But this requires further clarification: what worlds exactly are we speaking of here, and what kind of contact is being negotiated – by whom and for whom? Can we use the concepts of gesture and unintentionality, or does this case suggest the need for their further modification?

The effectiveness of 'The Vane Sisters' depends on the fact that the narrator does not really see what he sees, and at the same time, conversely, that his visual perceptiveness predisposes him to a certain understanding of the story, an understanding, however, that remains below the threshold of consciousness. The narrator provides hints of hidden messages, the shadows of things, highlighting the thresholds between various modes of meaning – the words we read, his intentions and the conception of events as the reader is meant to infer from his words – while simultaneously establishing the passage and connection between these thresholds. The visual effects with which the narrative opens convey something of the same fateful tendency to make connections – the interventions of the dead in accordance with their individual personalities or destinies – that the narrator himself elsewhere ridicules. With Cynthia, who seems to intervene in the narrator's life, it is as much about her irrational spectrological theories as her paintings, as if the influence of ghosts in the background as shadows of a 'tame metaphysics' really were at hand.[25]

After all, Nabokov's intention, as he explained in a letter to the board of editors at *New Yorker* magazine (to whom he offered the story), seems to have been that the narrator is not aware of certain connections. Nabokov himself held the text in high esteem and was rather disappointed (and, judging by the tone of the letter, not a little irritated) when the otherwise favourable editor Katharine White, on behalf of the board, turned him down. Coincidentally, 'The Vane Sisters' was the last of his stories to be published. In a later commentary, the author explains that 'the narrator is supposed to be unaware that his last paragraph has been used acrostically by two dead girls to assert their mysterious participation in the story' (Nabokov 1975: 218), and writes in his letter to Katharine White of the 'inner scheme of my story' (Nabokov 1989: 117) and the 'webs of style' (Nabokov 1989: 115) in this work that induce unusual ways of reading it. 'Most of the stories I am contemplating and some I have written in the past [. . .]', adds the author, 'will be composed on these lines, according to this system wherein a second (main) story is woven into, or placed behind, the superficial semitransparent one' (Nabokov 1989: 117). In response, Katharine White writes that 'a web can also be a trap when it gets snarled or becomes too involved, and readers can die like flies in a writer's style if it is unsuitable for its matter' (Nabokov 1989: 118).[26] Another *New Yorker* editor, Harold Ross, according to Nabokov's recollection, is said to have declared: 'We don't publish acrostics' (cited in Kupsch 2010: 301).

Even more remarkable – and more salient, perhaps, for our understanding of gesture and unintentionality in the case of Nabokov's story – is that the inhibited, stuttering mediation is not limited to the tension between the story's meaning and its visuality or 'writing' (*écriture*). A wide range of *cultural and literary references and allusions* appear in the narrator's discourse, of which, however, the narrator himself seems to be largely – but *only partially* – unaware. He evidently misses the fact that Sibyl Vane has her literary prototype in the eponymous character of Wilde's novel *The Picture of Dorian Gray* (1891) with allusion to its theme of an essence or message hidden in a work of art or in aestheticized visual perception, and to a certain confusion between surface and reality. Dorian's moral ruin is revealed in the image of his portrait, just as Sybil's beauty lies in her acting: 'Without your art, you are nothing,' Dorian fatally tells her (Wilde 2006/1891: 75). In Nabokov, too, an inner contact (between the narrator and the two sisters) is established through images, as we see in the narrator's affinity for Cynthia's paintings, as well as the visual charm of melting ice and snow, dripping and trickling water and play of light and shadow. The kinship between the two literary Sibyls is primarily inscribed, however, in their shared manner of death, and in the motif of their aesthetic shortcomings. Wilde's Sibyl commits suicide after failing in her acting role and being rejected by Dorian. In Nabokov's story, the narrator mercilessly observes Sybil Vane's faults in French grammar and handwriting. She also commits suicide following a jilted love affair, in this case with the narrator's colleague D. It is striking then that the narrator fails to quip that the 'ghost' of Oscar Wilde, wherever his voice comes from, speaks precisely to this coincidence of (not only) names.[27] Beyond the horizons of his awareness, moreover, the name Sybil evokes a long mythological tradition of divination and mediation between the realm of *Dīs Pater* (Hades) and the world of the living, as well as the motif of difficult to read letters and scrambled notation associated with the figure of the Cumean Sibyl in Virgil's *Aeneid* (*c*. 29–19 BCE),[28] for example, or the Sybil's near immortality, aging body and lingering voice in Ovid's *Metamorphoses* (8 BCE),[29] or even – moving to the modern context – in Eliot's *The Waste Land* (1922).[30] By evoking this connection between modernity and ancient myth, Nabokov elaborates one of the distinctive traits of Anglo-American modernism.

We may develop this line of enquiry even further. Even though the narrator himself recalls the central river motifs of Joyce's 'work in progress', the prose of *Anna Livia Plurabelle* (1928, 1930), and Coleridge's *Kubla Khan: or A Vision in a Dream* (1816),[31] he fails to see that the same thematic layer is joined by the motifs of flowing water and the trickle across the windshield, which take on special shades of meaning associated with the dialectic of seeing and not seeing, and passing between the solid and the liquid state and life-in-death existence evoked by allusions to *The Rime* (rime, rhyme) *of the Ancient Mariner* (1798), as well as with the rivers of the Greek and Roman underworld, the intermediate spaces of outflow, transition and contact between the realm of the dead and the living, and perhaps also with motifs of freezing waters in the lowest circles of Dante's *Inferno*. Similarly, while the narrator draws attention to the literary stylization of Coleridge's alleged inspiration in the opium dream, he seems to ignore that the name Porlock in his narrative is an echo of the 'person on business from Porlock' who, Coleridge alleges, disrupted his ecstatic state of inspiration while composing

Kubla Khan – a situation which thus resonates with the narrator's own supremely sceptical attitude towards Cynthia's spiritualist fantasies.

There are various established categories of narrative theory and poetics that might help to shed light on the nature of the narrator's paradoxical blindness. We might consider, for example, the 'implied author' concept: the hypothetical text-constructing subject whose implications lie beyond the horizon of the narrator's awareness. Yet this approach, I believe, would only bring us farther afield. What is essential for the reader effect in this case is precisely the fact that *the narrator himself* provides the clues that should indicate to him that something else is at work behind his words – *the vast unseen arc of language, or perhaps the world of ghosts* – perhaps a different intention or conception of events that the reader has to deduce from the words on the page. This thesis is supported by the fact that at times it is the narrator's intention to introduce intertextual references – his allusion to the feast from Plato's *Symposium*, for example (Nabokov 1958–9: 500), or rivers in the works of Joyce and Coleridge – while at other times he appears not to see, or hear, these connections. The boundary between conscious and unconscious intertextuality thus splits his discourse somewhere in the middle. Above all, this reading is supported by the fact that the narrator's professional interest is precisely the field of literature, specifically one of the Romance literatures (quite aside from his own French origins). Nabokov – the authorial subject – seems to indicate, through an intertextual tangle of allusions, a kind of secret kinship between himself, the multi-layered realm of classical and modern literature and culture, and the world of ghosts from which the Sybil Vane speaks in fragments. If the play of shadows, water and light at the beginning of the narrative resembles the influence of the departed on the fate and (unconscious) experience of the living, the authorial subject suggests that the narrator's fate and speech are also determined by a dense tangle of invisible cultural traces, so that *both spirits and author* seem to *emanate from the same realm of not quite material inscriptions*. Would this not also imply a hidden kinship between the narrator and 'authorial subject'? This is perhaps where the effect of *unintentionality* comes into play. One of the more impressive aspects of Nabokov's story, in my opinion, has precisely to do with an uncertainty, a grey area of contradiction that is implied in the narrator's words themselves, suggesting the unclear kinship between the narrator and 'implied author'. It is a kinship comprised by their shared background in the sphere of literature, their literary and visual aestheticism, as well as a certain ironic, perhaps even haughty tendency and derisive undertone, one that leads Nabokov himself (his literary personality) to a certain way of constructing the narrator, a certain way of treating him. (In the letter to Katharine White quoted here, the author characteristically describes the narrator as 'a somewhat obtuse scholar', Nabokov 1989: 116.) Nabokov's authorial subject thus begins to share common features with the narrator – or, seen from a different angle, we might say that the classification and division of subjects of communication or the layers of the narrative indicated here somehow miss their mark or go awry, when the effect lies somewhere in the transitions and mediation between them – in the work of the semantic gesture – leading to these not fully intentional breaks in the narrator's discourse. There is a certain ambiguity in the effect, perhaps not entirely intentional,[32] which precludes any straightforward interpretation of spectral intervention, while making it equally impossible to establish a clear boundary between the narrator's conscious and unconscious intercessions in the network of cultural references, or categorically dismiss a certain level of – unintentional – kinship between the 'implied author' and nameless narrator.

Perhaps the most convenient way to account for this contradiction in the text is from the perspective of operationally divided phases of reading. (This also implies the need to read the text more than once.) On the 'first reading', according to this schema, it is as if the reader should join in the narrator's haughty scepticism of Cynthia's spiritualist activities and beliefs – errors such as 'plagiatisme' reveal their human, all too human agents. Immediately on the 'second reading', however, the reader notes with concern that the messages 'from beyond the grave' may carry a deeper meaning, one that the narrator does not understand. On the 'third reading', something else begins to emerge: a certain resonance or parallel between the author's stylization of the narrator ('a somewhat obtuse scholar') and the high-minded, ironic distance with which the narrator sees everything around him, and above all his fellow human beings – with the exception, that is, of Cynthia's paintings (which he admires), and the visual signs of spectral intervention (which elude him). This interpretation (and application of the concepts of gesture and unintentionality) is supported by yet another discursive layer of the story, consisting in the heavy use of figures of speech and tropes interwoven into the narrator's discourse, which include the rich application of acronyms,[33] paronyms, puns,[34] parechesis,[35] metagrams,[36] consonance and assonance,[37] paronomasia, *figurae etymologicae* and alliteration.[38] If this dense material is completely in line with the ironic and intellectually aloof stylization of the narrator's personality, it is also clear that a schism opens up between conscious and unconscious discursive play; through that schism, it is as if we heard the *whisper* of an altogether different message than the one the narrator means to convey. While these devices seem to fall into the mode of conscious and sovereign language play, there are a number of others – in addition to the final acrostic, a riddle,[39] the homophony of 'Vane' and 'vain',[40] and motifs of dying, death and the afterlife[41] – that elude the narrator's conscious reflections and produce a certain resonance with the possible spectral interventions that appear at the beginning of the narrative. In the middle of the story, at the end of the fourth part, a hidden self-referential key to the final paragraph of the short story is inserted,[42] to which the narrator also remains blind, paradoxically so, in spite of his keen visual sense – or precisely because of it.

These figures and tropes intensify the theme of doubling, reflection, echo, form and spectre, and of essences appearing through the surface while simultaneously hiding behind it. The motif of doubling and duplicity is repeated: the sisters, who resemble each other in hair and eye colour, bad skin and premature death (and its veiled mediation); the brothers Podgy and Pudgy, who are owners of a printing house and Cynthia's lovers; Corcoran, Cynthia's acquaintance and art dealer, who saves two drowning people on separate occasions, both named Corcoran.

The narrator also refers frequently – and, it seems, consciously – to architectural and artistic styles (the classical fluting printed on the dustbins, the 'cubist pattern' of scars on Sibyl's face), and to antiquity generally (Elysium, Plato's *Symposium*, c. 385–370 BCE). Woven throughout his speech, finally, is the vast multi-layered etymological matrix of English words, dating back to various stages of Greek, and above all Latin, English and French (recalling the narrator's origins). Glossing Cynthia's theory of the afterlife with amused disdain, he describes the ever present parallel world of ghosts as a 'solarium', a word echoing the Latin *sōlārium* (from *sōl*, or 'sun'). Already in Homer's epic, the Elysium is a place permanently bathed in the sun, where 'there is made the easiest life for mortals' (Homer 1999/1967: 79). But this also (probably unconsciously) resonates with the rays of sun the narrator observes at the beginning and end of the story, and with the seventh poem from the fourth book of the *Elegies* by Propertius (50–15 BCE), where the ghost of Cynthia, a quarrelsome deceased lover, appears to the poet at his bedside: 'Spirits [*Manes*] do exist. Death doesn't end it all: / a pale ghost [*luridaque . . . umbra*] has escaped the conquering pyre. / For Cynthia appeared, leaning over my pillow, / who was recently buried at the bustling roadside' (Propertius 2004: 385). In addition to a possible namesake for Cynthia Vane, we find similar motifs of yellow (*luridaque*), associated with the unfaithful Roman woman, the nocturnal wanderings of spirits and shadows (*Manes, umbra*), the river Lethe (Propertius 2004: 385), and 'dreams that come through the portals of truth' (Propertius 2004: 391).

Finally, a number of references to the techniques of reproduction and communication can be found in this play of surface and meaning, appearances and depths, intentionality and unintentionality, as well as their actual usage: among the various techniques and technics we undoubtedly need to count the above mentioned rhetorical, poetic and intertextual devices.

Sibyl leaves her last message, as mentioned, in a handwritten note on a French literature exam. However, its external signs reveal more than its contents, and the real message seems to be hidden in various unintentional traces: in addition to various errors ('*Cette examain est finie*'), there is evident alternation of writing tools (hard-leaded and soft-leaded pencil, 'charcoal', fountain pen), and an array of accidental signs (an embossed effect on the reverse side of the exam, varying thickness of pencil lead, traces of lipstick caused by 'sucking the blunt point' of the pencil), as well as gratuitous underscores and footnotes. The narrator carefully notes all these inscriptions, traces and residues, but from his limited pedagogical perspective sees only symptoms of carelessness and incompetence that he is possessed with a blind urge to correct. He speaks ironically of Cynthia's admiration for what a college literature teacher might be expected to appreciate, namely Sybil's inventive puns,[43] and he is equally blind to the perhaps not unintentional 'examain', which could suggest the externalization (Greek *éxō*) of hand (French *main*), or handwriting. Constrained to his pedantic view, the narrator sees only linguistic and aesthetic lapses where there are possible signs of intelligence, to say nothing of agitation and affect.

There are furthermore allusions to photography and printing (by way of Cynthia's lovers), mirrors ('gorged with reflections'), telegraphy and spiritualistic media – and, of course, literature. At the end of the story, the narrator also invokes the phonograph: 'I lay in bed, thinking my dream over and listening to the sparrows outside: Who knows, if recorded and played backward, those bird sounds might not become human speech, voiced words, just as the latter become a twitter when reversed?' (Nabokov 1958–9: 503). It is not only a foreshadowing of the coming acrostic, but also a reminder of the hidden message that reproduction may carry within itself, and a parallel to the medial capacity of a written text to create *non-linear, horizontal and diagonal text layers and phonetic chains*.

Clumsy handwriting, related unintentionally to artistic expression; audio recording played backwards; puns, rhetorical figures and tropes, recalling (as if from beyond the grave) and mirroring the etymological layers of language; intricately intersecting intertextual and cultural references. Do the communication and reproduction techniques mentioned here share a set of characteristics in common? Do they point to a certain interrelatedness? It would appear that these media, *on the reverse side* of their capacity to record, convey a message that defies literal expression, as if the hidden symptoms of the sign lay dormant precisely in the possibilities for rearranging and regrouping it, that is, in the inherent conditions of its reproduction: manipulation and transmission. And yet no one of these possibilities makes sense *on its own, without prior memory traces or traditions and without the ability or willingness to hear and see*. All these media references, moreover, are made in the context of a highly stylized literary text whose own means are not radically new. This is also true of its visual, and also sound aspects that were not directly mentioned in the preceding argument: the specific semantic and intonation rhythm of long sentences, in which the details and information are often superimposed, one on top of the other, in such a way that they do not culminate, in terms of intonation and content, in any significant climax.

What we may conclude from these last paragraphs, which touch on the phenomenon of *media (self)reflexivity*, is that the 'medialization' of the concept of gesture, as we have seen in this reading of 'The Vane Sisters', is connected to the fact that a text must also be situated media-historically and engage the concept of gesture in a corresponding manner. It was during this period that Nabokov's writing technique underwent significant changes. With regard to writing instruments, Nabokov had been using a pencil and pen for literary creation; typescripts served in the editing and publishing process, and were assisted by his wife Vera, while the author dictated (Boyd 1991: 201, 225, 374, 577). However, around the time he wrote 'The Vane Sisters' – from 1950, while beginning work on what would later become *Lolita* – the author began using *index cards* (Boyd 1991: 169, 189, 201, 211, 251, 407). This practice, which he had previously used for notes on his lepidopterological findings, he now adopted for literary writing itself, and for organizing preliminary notes. Nabokov's creative method here suggests something of a scientific, even electronic, method of data storage. It was during the same period that Isidore Isou and Maurice Lemaître carried out the first literary experiments in *lettrism*, a movement that may be seen as a continuation of the French pre-war avant-garde, or else as the early beginnings of visual poetry akin to Eugen Gomringer's concurrent first experiments in concrete poetry. These latter trends, which began between the early and mid-1950s, explored new possibilities of expression in the relationship of word and image, as well as various ways of loosening the ties between literary work and authorial subject.

In the following chapter we will discuss experimental literature in more detail. As we conclude this chapter, however, we are left with a question: Is it not the case that the precipitous rise of technical images – which, at the turn of the 1940s and 1950s had become ubiquitous to the point of intrusive (the new heyday of film and rise of the television in American households) – together with the advancing 'technicalization' of communication (coinciding with the development of scientific and technical communication models in cybernetics and information theory) put the *mystical power of writing*, a medium so close to Nabokov's heart, in a very new light – one that weakened precisely the densely layered and stylized writing that we have discussed here, maybe even inadvertently demystified it? Is it not the case, after all, that Nabokov wrote the 'swan song' on this kind of literature, whose effect derives from the use and recognition of a rich texture of allusions and cultural references to ancient and modern (European) authors, and to send it off – along with the fictional apparition of one Sibyl – with an anticipatory and 'prophetic' last goodbye?

Notes

1. From medieval Latin *gestūra*, which comes from *gerĕre*, to carry.
2. Both examples are listed in the *OED* in the sense, apparently derived from the French *geste*, of 'a move or course of action undertaken as an expression of feeling or as a formality'.
3. Some of today's recognized cognitivist approaches and resulting concepts of speech evolution (e.g. Fadiga et al. 2006) support the thesis that the neural basis for human speech evolved out of regions of the brain responsible for gesture recognition. Cognitivists consistently understand gestures as means of communication. Leroi-Gourhan also (primarily) conceived of them as a means of production; however, the intersection with Leroi-Gourhan's concept is the assumptions regarding the existence of a *socio-imaginary* and *kinetic* aspect of gesture, and the integration of speech and gesture in *shared cortical circuits*.
4. The remarkable work of Marcel Jousse (1886–1961) in the field of the anthropology of gesture and gestural mnemonics of oral traditions (in the Hebrew and Aramaic, as well as Native American traditions) only came to be fully known through the posthumous publication in three volumes of his synthetic project *L'anthropologie du geste* (1974–8). Walter J. Ong (2002/1982) refers to Jousse's work on oral style as well as the notion of *verbomoteur* as an important precursor to the work of Milman Parry and Erik Havelock, and what could be described as the rediscovery of oral cultures.
5. As Milan Jankovič points out, the overall tendency towards movement is related 'to Bergson's central concept of *élan vital*, even if the author of the study does not follow it directly, but indirectly, through the stimuli of the cited psychological works' (Jankovič 1985: 128).
6. He does not therefore assume this kind of meaning-creating principle here to characterize the poet's life and work in its entirety, but only a certain creative period.
7. 'Ženci / plouží se na kolenou po poli / Kterého ubývá / [. . .] / Zmítají se jako utopenci.'
8. In this work, Mukařovský divides poetic speech into two large categories: sound and meaning. The first includes such aspects as speech sound sequences and euphony, syllables, intonation, exhalation intensity, vocal

timbre, tempo and pauses. In the second category, analysis proceeds from morpheme and word, word meaning and poetic designation to the syntactic and semantic construction of the sentence, and then to higher levels of description that go beyond grammar, i.e. compositional and thematic formations of meaning and to monologue and dialogue as well as to 'hidden meaning' at the border of language and the psychic event. However, an important prerequisite for the theory of poetry is '[t]he congruity of the semantic structure of the sentence with the structure of higher semantic units, indeed, even with that of the entire text' (Mukařovský 1977b/1940: 54).

9 Various levels will typically appear in this breakdown of levels and components, including syntactic connections, sentence semantics, compositional relationships, formation of motif complexes, thematic and intertextual connections, sound layer, figurative and literal designation, and so on.

10 Cf. the notion of technics and media as extensions of the unconscious that is discussed intermittently throughout Chapter 7.

11 One may raise the objection against Mukařovský that unintentionality always operates differently, and that we can never agree on what aspect of a given work, place or context comprises it, and that his own analysis to some extent negates this radical singularity.

12 The first volume is subtitled *Technique et langage* (1964, 'Technics and Language'), the second *La mémoire et les rythmes* (1965, 'Memory and Rhythms').

13 Cultural ethnologists such as Pierre Lemonnier, who works directly with Leroi-Gourhan's concept, start for example from the finding that 'operational chains' of the same tools are never transferable from one culture to another (cf. Lemonnier 2012; Latour 2014). Bernhard Siegert follows on from 'recursive operation chains' with the concept of cultural techniques; as ontic operations, cultural techniques simultaneously establish both a certain difference and the thing they differentiate (the difference between analogue and digital, for instance; Siegert and Winthrop-Young 2015). Stiegler developed his critical philosophy of technology through a deconstructivist approach that focuses precisely on Leroi-Gourhan's concept. One of Stiegler's starting points is the notion of 'second origin', which he critiques as a paradox arising from the manner in which Leroi-Gourhan's conception, despite all evidence to the contrary, emphasizes cognitive activity over technology. For Stiegler, this represents the metaphysical residues of Leroi-Gourhan's attempt, between the lines, as it were, to save the human soul from 'technical animality' (Stiegler 1998/1994: 185); cf. also Ingold 1999.

14 Therein lies the ambiguity: a graphic expression can be associated with a gestural movement that is seen and interpreted, or – and this is what Leroi-Gourhan is primarily concerned with – it can be imprinted in a material substrate. We return to the topic of graphism later in this chapter.

15 If the hand first freed itself for technics, technics later freed itself from the hand; thus the exteriorization of the human nervous system in technology increases exponentially. This process also accounts, however, for the desensitization of the gesture by which the evolutionary engine is thrown off balance. Up to this point it had been kept running as well by the fact that man 'thought with his hands': 'the evolution of the human being – a living fossil in the context of the present conditions of life – must ultimately follow a non-neuronal path if it is to continue' (Leroi-Gourhan 1993/1964, 1965: 265). Compare to the critique by Hörl (2013).

16 That is, *Paranthropus* (*Australopithecus*) *boisei* – or, in Leroi-Gourhan's terminology '*Les Australanthropes*' and '*Le Zinjanthrope*'.

17 More aptly, perhaps, one might consider the organic mind in its ability to conduct 'simultaneous processing' and – what is likely a related phenomenon – the power of intuitive knowledge, and to try to grasp its specific functional condition in the ability to choose and forget.

18 Leroi-Gourhan's observations have also been linked to the context of image theory (cf. Hildebrandt 2011).

19 It reveals, in Derridian terms, a 'gap' at the heart of the 'natural', and the very structural possibility of its technical extension or expansion. As Derrida aptly writes: '[I]t is difficult to avoid the mechanist, technicist and teleological language at the very moment when it is precisely a question of retrieving the origin and the possibility of movement, of the machine, of the techne, of orientation in general' (Derrida 1998/1967: 84–5).

20 An alternative name is *El miliciano muerto*.

21 For the relationship between a spectre and image, as it was grasped especially by social and philosophical anthropology of the twentieth century after the First World War and later, see Chapter 4.

22 It was then included in the collection *Nabokov's Quartet* (1966). See below for the pre-publication history of the text.

23 Nabokov himself taught at Wellesley College.

24 The persuasive vividness (*enargeia*) of these descriptions, in classical rhetorical terms, resists the interpretation that the narrator is concealing a sexual relationship with Cynthia.

25 This is how the narrator refers to Cynthia's spiritualist faith (Nabokov 1958–9: 497).

26 The editors of the magazine supposedly have agreed that the fate of the girls does not really arouse the reader's interest.

27 The message conveys the accusation that Cynthia's (and Sybil's) parents have committed *plagiatisme* ('plagiarism'). The narrator, a native of France, only laughs at this artless ruse.

28 The Sibyl acts as Aeneas's guide to the underworld in the sixth book of the epic: a prophetess who composes her divinations from letters written on leaves, which may subsequently be scattered by the wind. When Aeneas beseeches her to divine his fate, the god Phoibos (Apollo) speaks to him

through the Sibyl's mouth and the hundred mouths of her cavern. In contrast to the Greek tradition, with its dense network of oracles, the Roman tradition consists only in quotations and legends about the lost *Sibylline Books* (*Libri Sibyllini*). In the temple of the goddess Fortuna, the use of Praenestian lots was reserved to the poorer classes; single letters as well as entire sentences were written on oak tablets (Vidman 1997: 98–9).

29 In the fourteenth book of the *Metamorphoses*, Sybil tells Aeneas how Phoibos has given her as many years of life as there are grains in a handful of dust. Since the Sybil rejected his love, however, and since she neglected to ask for eternal youth, the god has allowed her body to age, and she knows that the only thing left of her, in the end, will be her *voice*.

30 The words of the drunk Trimalchion from Petronius's *Satyricon* can be heard in the motto for Eliot's composition. The Sibyl, living in a 'bottle' (*ampulla*), wants nothing more than to die.

31 Coleridge 1912. Cf. the name of the 1817 'Collection of Poems' *Sybilline Leaves*.

32 This does not mean that Nabokov himself (in the sense of a concrete historical figure) could not have had this in mind, but rather that it may only arise with such intensity in the act of reception – or, to put it another way, it is only here that it seems suddenly, and with a disturbing effect, to be uncontrolled.

33 Cynthia's interpretation of the river Alph in the poem by Coleridge.

34 Hither – Hitler; Corcoran – Coransky – Cochran.

35 Examples include 'odds and ids' and 'higgledy-piggledy'.

36 'Podgy and Pudgy', as the narrator nicknames Cynthia's two lovers.

37 E.g. 'raw awareness'.

38 Such as 'twinned twinkle', 'observed and observant things', tawny (from the Old French *taner*, 'to turn hide into leather, tan') – tan, scion – Cynthia, chance – choice, flaw – flower, and drip-dripping.

39 The message from one séance reads: 'What is this—a conjuror's rabbit, / Or a flawy but genuine gleam— / Which can check the perilous habit / And dispel the dolorous dream?' (Nabokov 1958–9: 499). The narrator wryly notes that the rhyme oddly resembles Cynthia's own 'fugitive productions'. In actuality, the poem seems to refer to the visual wonders at the beginning as well as the acrostic at the end (the 'flawy but genuine gleam').

40 The Vane sisters bear witness, in vain and to the somewhat vain narrator, to their own life and death.

41 Examples include 'dead snow', 'delicately dying sky', 'mummified guinea pig', 'dead traffic' and 'lean ghost'.

42 'And I regret that I cannot remember that novel or short story (I suspect by some contemporary author) in which, without the author's knowledge, the first letters of the words in its last paragraph formed – as deciphered by Cynthia, a message from his dead mother' (Nabokov 1958–9: 499).

43 'Death was not better than D minus, but definitely better than Life minus D' (Nabokov 1958–9: 494).

6

Openness

The information (cybernetics) moment in literary theory and experimental poetry of the 1950–60s

Richard Müller

How many sunrises and sunsets did Titov and Glenn see in just a few hours?

'It's me. Listen, you! We are here!'

Or have you never seen swarming ants? Swarming bees? Writhing worms? A moving crowd? Bosch and Brueghel. Don't we find the divine with the one, and the human cut-up with the other? And what is a city, and what the world?[1]

```
the ef            p o s s i b i l i t i e
                  s    o f    a    w h i t e
fect o            s q u a r e    w h i c h
                  i s    a l r e a d y      m
f a wh            o v i n g      a w a y      f
ite re            r o m    t h e    p h l e
ctangl            g m a t i c      f i e l d
e on a
n area
whichi
t over
lapped
```

1. Prelude: I wish you had heard his 'Nevermore'

Roman Jakobson begins his 1949 article 'Language in Operation' with an anecdote: 'Recently, aboard a train, I overheard a scrap of conversation. A man said to a young lady, "They were playing 'The Raven' on the radio. An old record of a London actor dead for years. I wish you had heard his *Nevermore*"' (Jakobson 1981a/1949: 7).

Based on this incident, Jakobson proceeds to extract a system of 'transmitters' and 'senders', 'relays' and 'reproduction devices', which successively set in motion a single message: 'Nevermore', relayed from one to another in a series of nodes: the raven's 'master' – the raven – the lyrical hero – the poet (Poe) – the actor – the radio station – the stranger on the train – Jakobson himself. Let's recall the situation from Poe's narrative poem: the lyrical hero, affected by the loss of his mistress Lenore, is surprised in his room by an unexpected guest: the titular raven. The man engages the raven in dialogue, but only seemingly, as it gives the same mechanical response to each of his questions: 'Nevermore'. It is obvious that the raven only vacuously repeats the word, learned by rote from its previous 'unhappy master' – or so concludes the hero. In actuality, or perhaps in addition to this, the word 'Nevermore' seems to arise in the poem simply by virtue of the fact that it resonates with the final word in each of the first seven stanzas ('nothing more', 'for evermore'). It may even be that the echo curiously precedes the message; the poem does indeed exhibit the characteristics of 'verbal hallucination' (Jakobson 1981a/1949: 10).[2] However, in spite of the poem's hallucinatory aspect, Jakobson reconstitutes the entire sequence of communication largely in linear fashion, using such terms as 'transmission', 'relay', 'broadcast', 'reception' and 'recording'. The various effects of repetition are in fact *orchestrated* from a particular link in the chain, namely 'from the end' – 'the poem may be said to have its beginning – at the end' (Poe, cited in Jakobson 1981a/1949: 12). It is the author, the poet himself, who gives them direction and who incorporates disparate elements into complicated sound-semantic figures that mirror one another.

Jakobson does not arrive at the conclusion adumbrated by his (near) contemporaries in the philosophy of culture and philosophical anthropology (e.g. Max Picard and Günther Anders; see Chapter 4, pp. 97–9): that radio broadcasting has a special way of multiplying the *hallucinatory* character of the repetition that thus underlies the whole system. Instead, he places the successive transferences that make up the situation, as well as the 'internal' communication represented in and implied by 'The Raven', into the *framework of information and communication theory*. According to Jakobson, what first appears as a wholly *unpredictable* situation (a raven responding to a rhetorical question) turns out to be one of complete *predictability* (the incessant repetition of the word 'Nevermore'), so that, in probabilistic terms, the utterances of the lyrical subject become *inversely proportional* to a statement emitted by a non-human source. What the lyrical subject provides – in the manner of linguistic 'regressive assimilation'– is the ever-changing semantic and emotional shades of, and potential sound variations on, one and the same word, as well as similar phonemic and morphematic configurations (most concentrated in the mirror pair *raven–never*).

We believe, as this chapter will demonstrate in various contexts, that there is a tension in Jakobson's analysis between three somewhat different – though not disparate – types of communication modelling: (1) the transmission model of communication; (2) the probabilistic modelling of the process of communication (or communication act) and (3) a model based on the internal communication structure or texture of the text. The third type accounts for such factors as who (or what) is speaking and from which textual level, and all ensuing variations and semantic transformations of the utterance. Jakobson imagines that it is in the instance of the poet that these transformations are most intense – indeed, that it is the poet who plays the central role in the construction and control of the text. Significantly, he gives full credence to Poe's own well-known analysis of 'The Raven', 'The Philosophy of Composition', and ridicules the sentimental rejection of Poe's instructions on how to construct a poem with all its 'wheels and pinions' (Poe, cited in Jakobson 1981a/1949: 15). The third model in this sense is similar to the first, except that the first model does not deal with communication within the work itself, but communication involving the work in the broader context. Above all, as Jakobson explicitly points out, inner speech represents a form of dialogue that cannot be very effectively transposed onto the model of *one-dimensional, linearly transmitted information* – onto a chain of signals – without taking into account the different levels of speech, the process and situation of their perception and creation, and other considerations regarding their intention, intonation potential and various multiple origins (cf. Bakhtin's notion of *heteroglossia*, which was elaborated in the 1960s – somewhat surprisingly – into the extensive field of intertextuality theory.) To this list we must add *the function of the work in various areas of reception*. It is in light of these many considerations that the 'transmission communication system' elaborated by Jakobson at the beginning of 'Language in Operation' cannot be adequately modelled as a 'whole sequence of transmitters' (Jakobson 1981a/1949: 8).

Each node in the series – including Jakobson's interpretation – serves as more than a mere point of transmission, suggesting at least a different type of origin, a different kind of ambiguity, different conditions of perception, different expectations, a different scope of reception, as well as other semantic effects. Each node is a point of 'multiple entry'. From a perceptual point of view, for example, only the subject's psychic distress can explain his compulsive tendency to simultaneously inspire, anticipate and receive the raven's responses; only the situation of analytical control à la Poe and Jakobson leads to a reading 'from the end'; only the tuning of the radio dial – which also implies a certain kind of perception – allows the man on the train to be enchanted by the voice of a long-dead actor, and so on.

Without cutting its 'native' ties to structural linguistics and poetics, Jakobson's analysis of 'The Raven' clearly belongs – though not without internal tensions and contradictions – to what was essentially the nascent 'cybernetic' theory of communication and information (e.g. Norbert Wiener, Donald MacKay, John von Neumann, Gregory Bateson, Heinz von Foerster, Warren McCulloch, Walter Pitts) and related concepts of communication and control, as well as the simultaneous publication of 'A Mathematical Theory of Communication' by Claude Shannon (1948). The birth of communication theories in the United States (and, indirectly, Europe) during the late 1940s and early 1950s thus enters our field of view.

2. The cybernetic turn

The prelude by Jakobson introduces our main theme. The pages that follow deal with the proliferation of elements of information theory and cybernetics into literary theory, aesthetics, art theory and intellectual experimentation, as well as the Czech experimental works of the late 1950s and 1960s (characteristically multimedia in nature, far exceeding the concept of 'literature') and their transformation in this context. In the 1950s and 1960s, information and communication theory and cybernetics all had a profound influence on attitudes in many disciplines and fields of the humanities, social sciences, natural and technical sciences (from linguistics to philosophy, from anthropology to neurophysiology, from mathematics to communication engineering) and a number of different creative activities. While there have been considerable differences in information-cybernetics discourse, even contradictions,[3] general features of the (cybernetics) communication model can be set out as follows: communication (information) input, output and feedback, joined together in a circuit; a quantified and dematerialized concept of information; a system concept of continuous communication exchange in which individual, human and non-human components perform certain correlative functions in the overall process. This shows a broader turn that is epistemological in scope, so that Jean-François Lyotard will consider the integration of linguistics and cybernetics to be a pivotal moment in the birth of the 'postmodern situation' (Iuli 2013: 226), and Katherine Hayles will later count these features among the motivating factors of the self-concept in 'How We Became Posthuman' (Hayles 1999). The emergence and development of cybernetics and information technology was simultaneously associated with certain *dispositifs* (Geoghegan 2011) that came to influence the material and institutional structures of research after the Second World War (support from the Rockefeller Foundation, for example, which also gave funding to Jakobson). As Cristina Iuli notes, the epistemological transformation that is associated (among other things) with the birth of cybernetics brought, on the one hand, a conceptual transformation in aesthetics, art and literature 'from object to process, from static to performative, and from closed to open system' (Iuli 2013: 228). On the other hand, 'the discourse of cybernetics cannot be fully disarticulated from fantasies of technical total control spurred by the unexpected success of Wiener's bestseller *Cybernetics, or Control and Communication in the Animal and the Machine* (1948), whose title reinforced the association between cybernetics, control and the techno-military infrastructural complex that Wiener partly wrote against' (Iuli 2013: 231).

We will focus on those moments when models of the information circuit (and transmission) were connected to semiotics, or fundamentally changed in their confrontation with the literary work as communication. We will first look at the influence on Roman Jakobson's conception of semiotics and communication theory. We will then take a close look at Umberto Eco's famous treatise on modern aesthetics *Opera aperta* (1997/1962, The Open Work),[4] and the remarkable work by 'Second-Wave' Czech structuralist Miroslav Červenka, *Významová výstavba literárního díla* (1968, The Semantic Organization of a Work of Literature). In this context, we will work through several fundamental transformations of the original inspiration, especially when interpreting emerging ideas about the literary work as process, the participation of the perceiver in its movement and the 'role of the reader' in Eco's later thinking (taking his cues, in an interestingly negative sense, from *The Open Work*). More generally, we will look at information aesthetics and literary semiotics in Czechoslovakia, Germany, France and Italy during the 1950s and 1960s. This will lead us inevitably to consider related trends of the same period in the experimental poetry of the Czech neo- and post-avant-garde. Here we will be compelled to ask: how was its international dimension established; to what extent did experimental poetry take inspiration from information science and cybernetics; what role did these new fields play in this context, and in connection to what other lines of development and ideological influences? What, conversely, set these new fields apart?

In the shadow of 'suppressed hallucinations' and a deliberate move towards the exact sciences, the influence of information theory and cybernetics in the fields of information poetics and literary semiotics, as we will see, has led to several consequences: (1) an emphasis on the openness of the work with regard to its (semantic) movement and process; (2) an emphasis on the reader (perceiver) as starting point of the literary process; and most surprisingly, (3) the confirmation – but also modification – of the concept of the structure of literary communication. The experimental work, in its very self-concept, then comes up against its own limits, as well as those of art and literature.

It also finds itself up against, and moving beyond, the limits of media. This is crucial for us, both because this moment is clearly not motivated by the recognition of the concept of the medium, and because it specifically connects the development of computer and media technologies with the prehistory of media studies, *bringing them to the threshold of their own history*. This will show us the special status of the birth of information theory and cybernetics in the context of the genealogy of 'media thinking'.

We are interested in this period not only because it is the effective starting point for the development of the information technologies that now literally surround us, but to a greater extent because it is within literary theory and the arts that the limits of information theory as a foundation for communication theory were discovered – limits that are of greater importance today than ever before.

If the fascination with information theory and cybernetics can best be understood within its specific historical context, then outlining the ways in which visual and experimental 'poetry' are linked to this epistemological and media moment – or rather to this series of moments – also means providing at least one possible explanation of the sense, both historical and developmental, that these moments have for us today.

3. From entropy to perceiver

Jakobson: The first mediator

The influence of information theory

Roman Jakobson was undoubtedly one of the first to integrate information theory, semiotics and structuralism, working out the preliminaries of this approach. Jakobson landed in New York in June 1941, and in the spring of the following year he began lecturing at the École libre des hautes études. During the war, he is thought to have made the acquaintance of several members of the Cybernetics Group (such as anthropologist Margaret Mead), and in March 1948, he was invited to the fifth of the celebrated cybernetics conferences supported by the Macy Foundation (1946–53). In 1949 he was already acquainted with both Shannon's 'Mathematical Theory of Communication' (Geoghegan 2011) and Wiener's *Cybernetics* (Kline 2015: 141). In the same year he moved to MIT at Cambridge. In his own research, as well as his correspondence with Warren Weaver and Charles Fahs, who held leading positions at the Rockefeller Foundation, Jakobson expressed his support for the methodological integration of structural linguistics, information theory and cybernetics. Meanwhile, during the war and in cooperation with the American administration, there was growing interest in the field of communication engineering, a field organized primarily around the development of methods of coding and error-free data transmission, encryption and decryption of secret messages and development of anti-aircraft systems.

In the exciting field of communication engineering theory, Jakobson, as is well known, reinterpreted the concepts of *langue* and *parole* as 'code' and 'message'. From this new perspective, he then came to understand, for example, how a phonological system functions on the basis of a binary divider mechanism, the distribution of distinctive features in appropriate 'bundles' (phonemes) and the formation of permissible sequences – that is to say, a selection process that passes through nodes of dichotomous situations to form combinations of units. The operational linguistic behaviour of both the receiver of the message and the speaker was supposed to have this binary, disjunctive decision-making process in the background. Incidentally, in 1944, he had organized an excursion with the Linguistic Circle of New York to the AT&T auditorium in Manhattan where engineers from Bell Laboratories gave a presentation of its Voder (Voice Operating Demonstrator). The Voder synthesized speech by decomposing it into discrete units distributed over time and reassembling them with the help of a phonetic keyboard (Geoghegan 2011: 105). Similarly, he was fascinated by the way Bell's engineers were able to transpose speech onto special frequency graphs (Geoghegan 2011: 105), i.e. 'spectrograms' that captured the frequency spectrum of signals as they changed over time. For Jakobson, this supported his assertion that speech analysis should be carried out only on the basis of acoustic (rather than acoustic-articulation) variations. More generally, Jakobson was able to confirm the phonological principles he had developed during his structuralist period, while at the same time significantly altering his approach to the study of communication engineering.

Parallels

Of course the expansion of information theory into linguistics and poetics had its own intrinsic motivations. We see in Jakobson's case that it came about not only because of the inherent appeal of cross-disciplinary research (and perhaps even a degree of acute geopolitical instinct), but also and above all because of actual parallels between certain principles of the new discipline and those of Structuralist semiotics, however at times superficial or imprecise.

The goal-directedness of a cybernetic organism or mechanism is not exactly teleological in the Structuralist sense – not quite the same as the target function of an element within a structure (in the conception of the Prague Linguistic Circle, which regarded language as a system of functional means). An element can fulfil various functions (as in the grammatical meanings of a suffix, for instance), just as, conversely, a function can be implemented by various elements (as in synonymy). Even a subsystem (in Structuralism) can have teleological features: it correlates with other systems while retaining its autonomy. The cybernetic system, on the other hand, at the moment of 'information exhaustion', will return to the last working branch of alternatives. *Its continuity is of a different nature.* The system of input, output and feedback (or self-referential 're-entry') is not identical with dialogue, which (1) does not form a system, and (2) does not lead to a state of equilibrium.[5] The alignment of intentions in communication does not correspond to the system's tendency towards equilibrium, not least because these intentions can be numerous – to align, but also to persuade, deceive, extract information, take pleasure and so on – and are not necessarily mutual. Dialogue is a model that demonstrates how communication does not always reach the level of a new starting point. Moreover, the mode in which a person may be 'goal-directed' (Jakobson 1971c/1970: 686) differs radically from that in which a language may be so, a difference that is made strikingly evident in the case of a mental disorder, which has no equivalent in the linguistic system. This disparity can also be manifest in a speaker's decision *not* to communicate. The behaviour of a person who refuses to react is not analogous to the breakdown of a Homeostat; it is a communication strategy. To liken it to 'negative feedback' is inaccurate, because – once again – dialogue is not necessarily conducted like a system aiming towards equilibrium. Furthermore, the cybernetic organism operates with the help of cycles of inputs and outputs, as if it were itself on the border between them. It is a system in the sense of an operational process. The language system in the Saussurian sense, on the other hand, is a system of *internal* differences: that is, differences generated *purely* from within the system (the whole).

Linguistics, semiotics, communication: all paths of communication lead to (spoken) language

In this way, Jakobson gradually begins to conceive of linguistics as a special field of 'general semiotics', 'the whole theory of signs' and at the same time as a theory of communication (Jakobson 1981b/1958; see also Eco 1987/1977). This leads him to distinguish between various types and structures of signs, on the basis of their comparability as well as their resistance to transferability, and with respect to the means specific to a particular artistic discipline, and conversely those that are shared across different disciplines or sign systems. However, relationships do not form between sign systems on the same level (the idea of the *Iliad* and *Odyssey* in the form of comic books strikes him as 'ludicrous'; Jakobson 1981b/1958: 19). Verbal communication is the basic model for communication in general, and linguistics is a scientific discourse built on the description of *the most complex and the only universal communication sign system*; hence also *'linguistici a me alienum puto'* (Jakobson 1971a/1952).

As Jakobson claims, 'any human communication of nonverbal messages presupposes a circuit of verbal messages, without a reverse implication' (Jakobson 1971c/1970: 662). Even more specifically, it is *the spoken language* for Jakobson that constitutes the core of all semiotic systems, while written language is merely an auxiliary or substitute system. Gestures and 'idiomorphic systems' are similarly supplementary, as corroborated by the thesis that children acquire gestural communication only as a *consequence* of learning spoken language.

We will take a closer look at media shortcomings within the legacy of semiotics in the sections that follow, but let us make a few preliminary observations here. While gestural communication is included among the general interests of semiotics, it is situated in a marginal position compared to linguistics (Jakobson 1971b/1968: 698). Yet if we consider gestural and bodily communication as an *integral, germinal* part of speech, the relationship between verbal and nonverbal communication takes the character of a fundamental synergy and basis for the model of phylogenetic and ontogenetic co-evolution of the means of communication. This in turn will affect the way we think about all verbal and nonverbal forms of communication, including written language, which no longer appears 'auxiliary' or 'supplementary' to spoken language, however much it can be said to 'follow' it. (For further discussion, see Chapter 5, pp. 127–8 and 144–7.)

Additionally, when Jakobson characterizes the purely auditory and temporal features of spoken language and music as granular structures composed of discrete elements, he seems to be influenced by a notion of phonology based on the parameters of the established techniques by which music and spoken language were reproduced (writing systems and musical notation, and later the modes of electronic binary notation) into the meta-description of their constituent structures and the way they function. According to Jakobson, if technical mediation can be the subject of linguistic or sociological research, it's because the relevant communication situation affects the source, receiver and construction of the message; however, 'the sign pattern remains the same' (Jakobson 1971b/1968: 701). What falls outside the scope of Jakobson's theory is identifying changes in the sign's structure by virtue of its technical construction and mediation (cf. here Chapter 7, pp. 254–62; for more, including the position of Peirce's semiotics, see Chudý and Müller 2023).

Finally, Jakobson's model assumes the adaptive behaviour of the communication system, and a movement of forces leading to dynamic equilibrium, or homeostasis. As we shall see, there are parallels here as well with the natural sciences (or Lévi-Strauss's anthropology). These assumptions can be questioned or limited in various ways and from various perspectives: the 'economy of symbolic goods', for example, in the post-structural sociology of Pierre Bourdieu, or post-structural text theory of Roland Barthes and Julia Kristeva; text as production, play of signs, *écriture* and so on; and Lotman's theory of cultural dynamics (discussed in Chapter 10). With Lotman, a fundamental reversal of perspective occurs: from a hierarchical and concentric model of communication, to a model in which the coexistence and confrontation of diverse semiotic mechanisms generates culture in an autocommunication process.

Between information theory and cybernetics

'Channel theory', the birth of media theory and the universality of the information-cybernetic model

As Erhard Schüttpelz has shown, information theory, communication theory and variants of cybernetics discourse were all part of a broader set of early 'communication studies' during the late 1940s and early 1950s that can be characterized as 'channel theory'. The concept of communication here coincided with the existing media: the telegraph provided a solution to the problem of code optimization; the telephone network exposed the problem of its congestion (solved in turn by the switchboard), as well as acoustic fidelity, or capacity of the channel; radio (and, starting in the 1950s, television) revealed the problem of ensuring 'reception flow', that is, providing persuasive broadcast content to listeners.

So it was not yet, properly speaking, a 'media theory'; this would arise only later, with a certain shift. As Schüttpelz writes,

> While the 'channel theory' in all its US-American variants identified with the observer who observes communication on a recipient, i.e., from the point of view of the circle, for an optimal linearization of the (physical and psychological) channel and an optimal centralization of the coupling with the 'observer', Carpenter and McLuhan identified rigorously with the location of the recipient and particularly with his 'space'. They also made the scientific observer and each producer into precisely such a 'recipient' who was no longer bound to any linearized specifications. Rather, he was bound to the circularity of his or her perceptual control (which had been a fundamental field of studies especially in cybernetics from the beginning) and of the perception of the different channels reciprocally disrupting each other. (Schüttpelz 2010: 134)

Until the 1960s, communication theories based on information-cybernetic discourse shared certain assumptions, such as (most commonly): that communication can be modelled through the process of information looping rather than the interpretation of meaning; that information is a statistically measurable quantity; and that the value of the information is systemic, not individual or contextual (referential). This had two consequences (as Cristina Iuli has shown). First, every system is expressible in the universal language of information; humans and machines show operational behaviour, the common denominator being the systemic looping of information (input, output and feedback). Second, following the fundamentals of information-communication theory, it should have been possible to formulate the groundwork for a mutual understanding between the different disciplines (if not a truly universal scientific language uniting natural, technological and social sciences). Many of the founders of cybernetics did not have universalist ambitions, however, and perceived cybernetics as a radical 'interdiscipline' (rather than a meta-discipline) (Kline 2015: 62).

Information, feedback loop, entropy, noise

Central to cybernetics is the idea of 'circular causality': a feedback loop in the communication circuit. When this idea was given practical application in various contexts – anti-aircraft systems (Wiener, Bigelow, Rosenblueth), circuitry with sensors, switches and so on (Shannon's mouse Theseus, Ashby's Homeostat, Wiener's 'hearing glove'), the computational and mathematical modelling of neural ('nervous') systems (McCulloch, Pitts)

– the specifics of the models had to be substantially changed. Similarly, when the idea of circular causality was brought to the context of artificial human creations traditionally defined as art, it would have the consequence of determining a specifically dematerialized and disembodied form of (artistic) communication, and this was later seen to be problematic. Paradoxically, it also seemed to coincide with a certain idealistic heritage that characterizes art theory and the humanities in general. In this context, a specific concern was the position of the observer, and whether (and in what way) metacommunication phenomena should fall into the circle of causality. Accepting that they do in fact have a causal role, our perspective shifts to *systems theory*. Here too the position of the observer is understood to be involved in a circular system of communication feedback, as in, for example, Bateson's theory of 'second-order cybernetics'. In the case of Poe's 'The Raven', Jakobson models the *internal* communication of the poem at least in part as a circularly causal structure: an element of speech which is known in advance functions retroactively, by way of 'verbal hallucination', to generate a series of new statements by a lyrical speaker (Jakobson's key concept here is 'reverse assimilation', which belongs to the field of linguistics – originally phonetics – not cybernetics). At the same time, however, he assumes positions of control and observation (author, interpreter) on other, 'higher-level' circuits of communication, with some of his analyses following the linear model of transmission. Had he included these within the circle of causality, it would have led him to significantly reconsider and emphasize his own self-reflexive attitude: by identifying his expectations, for example, as well as previous readings – considering in precise terms the pragmatic aspects of his interpretations and choice of a methodological framework, and so on. Later, we will touch on these and other conceptual changes (observer, interpretation, 'systemic consideration') in connection with the development of Eco's literary semiotics.

Before moving on, we should clarify how the concept of information is most often understood in information theory and cybernetics.

It has often been pointed out that Shannon conceived of information not as a transferable quantum of content, but as a measure of freedom (or uncertainty) in the selection of information from a source (Weaver) – or, in other words, 'a measure of the difficulty in transmitting the sequences that are produced by some information source' (Shannon cited in Kline 2015: 60). It is also well known that Shannon acted as a cryptographer during the Second World War, acquainting him with the perspective of the 'enemy cryptanalyst': the assumption that a message will be intercepted, and care taken to encode it as efficiently as possible with respect to all individual links in the chain. From this perspective a new idea began to take shape: to work with information as a measure of uncertainty in selecting a message from an information source. This source would then consist in a set of possible messages, or a set of symbols/signals in a discrete or continuous system, typically with an uneven probability distribution. In this context, the 'meaning' of the symbols – that is, what the given symbols (or set of messages) represent in the world or with respect to it – can be disregarded: 'Frequently the messages [. . .] refer to or are correlated according to some system with certain physical or conceptual entities. These semantic aspects of communication are irrelevant to the engineering problem' (Shannon and Weaver 1964/1949: 31).

Wiener's conception of information is quite similar, while presenting several general – but essential – differences. In his *Cybernetics*, Wiener (like Shannon) defines information as the selection of one among a number of possible messages: a quantity determined by the relative 'organization' of the set of all possible messages. Thus, for both Wiener and Shannon, the notion of information comes very close to that of entropy (as originally conceived in physics): a measure of (un)predictability concerning the state of a particular (communication) system. For Shannon, it was practical to model information as the highest possible measure of evenly distributed probability states, taking into account the corresponding capacity of the transmission channel when constructing a suitable coding of the original signal (see Diagram 6.1). Wiener's approach, by contrast, makes an analogy between processes of information loss and processes in which entropy increases: the more organized the process of selecting a message in a communication system, the more information. He therefore arrives at a notion of information defined as 'negentropy' (unlike Shannon, who defines it as entropy; Shannon's approach 'made sense intuitively', argues Kline, since 'the more *uncertain* we are of what message will be selected, the more information we receive'; 2015: 16). They were in agreement, however, that this difference – the difference in sign – was only a mathematical formality (Kline 2015: 16). In other respects, however, this difference can have rather significant consequences.

A trace of physicality is latent in Wiener's reasoning. In a sealed gas-filled container, the probability distribution for the occurrence of a certain particle at a certain place becomes increasingly uniform over time, approaching molecular chaos. Such a system is characterized by ever higher entropy, an ever higher degree of unpredictability regarding the next state of the system. It is in this context that the Austrian physicist Ludwig Boltzmann struck on the idea that the behaviour of a physical system could be examined by a logarithmic interpretation of the relationship between entropy and probability (kinetic theory of gases). Later, in connection to the question of how to use a disorganized system to do work, a combination of entropy and information emerged (the first instance of this was in 1929). Leó Szilárd,

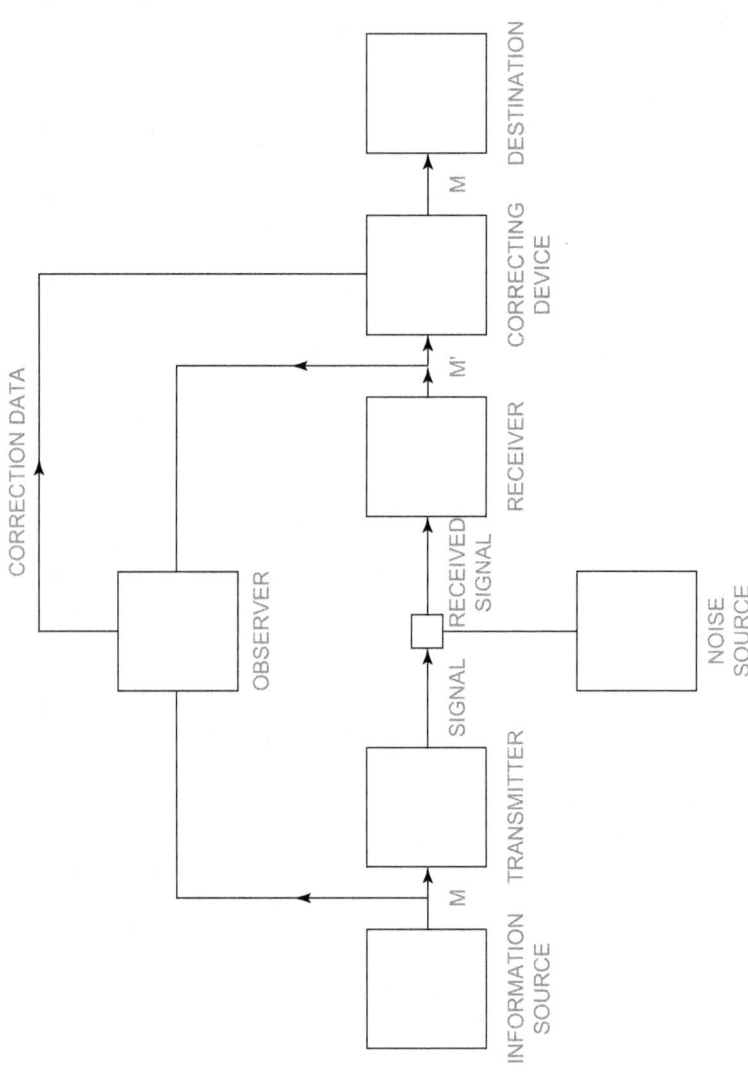

Diagram 6.1 Illustration of a general communication system (M stands for 'message'); a combination of schemes. *Source*: Shannon and Weaver 1964/1949: 34, 68.

Léon Brillouin and others came to the conclusion (while working through the well-known thought experiment 'Maxwell's demon') that being able to classify individual particles in a vessel is analogous to having information about them. It was then possible to show that the energy expended to obtain information about each individual particle is in principle higher than the energy that can potentially be obtained from their organization. This results in an indirect proportion between entropy and information.

Although Wiener would refine his mathematical solutions to the problems of statistical prediction, filtering, detection and signal analysis, he did not (unlike Shannon) shy away from the loftier abstraction of cybernetic principles. He arrived in this way at his ontological conception of information as something that is neither energy nor matter, and to the generalization of processes of information exchange between organism and environment, as well as the conception of society as a communication system and various other socio-philosophical implications of his theories. Certain traces remain of the original physicalist subtext: in nature, processes lead to an even distribution of states, high entropy (exhaustion and thermal death) and the dissipation of information. Transmission of information depends on differential probability distributions. In Wiener's own words, 'We are but whirlpools in a river of ever-flowing water. We are not stuff that abides, but patterns that perpetuate themselves' (Wiener, cited in Hayles 1999: 104).

Shannon, whose perspective retained something of his cryptographic origins, was compelled to include in his concept of information the notion that every message requires a channel. In real conditions, this channel is disrupted by interference and noise, whether with certain physical parameters, such as white or thermal noise (definable in terms of spectral density), part of an external signal or other transmission frequencies and random elements. However, by selecting a suitable encoding method, the effects of interference and noise can be mitigated. Starting from this observation, Shannon arrives at an ingeniously simple solution to safeguard the message from both noise and enemy code breakers. If information is a measure of uncertainty in the selection of a sign (message), then noise can also be thought of as a kind of information. One can then proceed with remarkable efficiency; rather than increasing the redundancy of the message, repeating the signal, increasing the power of the transmitter, improving insulation of the circuit and so on, one has only to model the average values that necessarily result from the very existence of the transmission channel. The source is then described globally in statistical terms, so that the coding parameters, 'transmission rate' and channel capacity of the message – including relative entropy – are reciprocally constructed for the entire circuit of transmission (see Diagram 6.1).

As Kittler puts it, 'signals, whenever possible, mimic interferences. [. . .] Information without matter and matter without information are coupled just like the two ways of reading a picture puzzle' (Kittler 1988: 344–5). With Shannon, information and transmission material are converted to statistical values, thereby reducing them to a single operation only in order to be able to uncouple them again.

Communication thus takes place invariably in the presence of noise: in the first place because the channel itself always emits noise, but also because the message itself can be generated statistically (randomly) by filtering or selecting from noise. Shannon develops a procedure for approximating a text in a certain language using statistical processes (zero-order, first-order, second-order, third-order, etc.); by generating random characters (using Markov chains) it is possible to approach the text of natural language, producing something that at first glance – but only the most cursory glance – looks like an excerpt from Joyce's *Finnegan's Wake*,[6] or perhaps a stream of consciousness in a state of delirium – the mutterings of the castaway in the radio play *Der Monolog der Terry Jo* (1968), written by Max Bense and Ludwig Harig (cf. Siegert 2014: 13–14).[7]

Based on the conditions of constructing a code, Shannon was then able to draw a strict analogy between entropy and information. Within this framework, the occurrence of a symbol prescribed by the code is likely; the occurrence of an error (or random character) and other deviations from the structure given by the code are unlikely. We can thus situate Shannon's concept in close proximity to the poetics of the Russian formalists, or in any case certain notions that they put forward (automatization and defamiliarization, for example). These parallels remained more or less tacitly in the background with the advent of experimental and neo-avant-garde interpretations of mathematical information theory.

Bense, information aesthetics, statistical innovation and the problem with the 'birth of the code'

In the mid-1950s, Max Bense and Abraham André Moles, the founders of two different versions of information aesthetics, began to advance the idea that the principles of information theory find their proper application in the field of aesthetics. A German philosopher and mathematician, Bense believed in bringing together the natural sciences and humanities, and promoted the (metaphysical) concept of 'beautiful programming'. He was also a founder of the experimental Stuttgart Group. Bense's thinking would transition from Hegel's view of the *Geistesgeschichte der Mathematik* ('intellectual history of mathematics') and the notion of art as a teleological epistemic process,[8] to cybernetics, information theory and Peircian semiotics.

In the spirit of Norbert Wiener and Gotthard Günther, Bense understands signs to be a kind of information, and information in turn as the place of contact between phenomenological consciousness and material substance, something 'exactly on the border between consciousness and the outside world' (Bense 1967/1962: 15). This corresponds to the universality of information models discussed earlier in this chapter. However, experimental creators (of concrete poetry, for example) could simultaneously confirm and deny this by hybridizing and manipulating material elements from various artistic systems. What is revealing in Bense's thought system is his exaggeration of the discrepancy between aesthetic and semantic information, or meaning. If it can be said that meaning reproduces what is already known, relying solely on code or convention (important for Bense in this regard is Wittgenstein's *Philosophical Investigations*), aesthetic information, by contrast, *depends only on statistical innovation* – that is, on the unlikely use of signs. It refers to a kind of information that, in the strict sense, cannot be interpreted: 'Properly speaking [...] aesthetic information may only be realized by deriving other aesthetic information from it' (Bense 1967/1962: 124). Here we find a logical flaw in Bense's communication concept of sign. While the sign (following in the footsteps of Peirce) has a 'trivalent function', always involving vehicle, object and interpreter, art supposedly defies interpretation to reach a point where there is no longer any distinction between *novelty* and *disintegration of the code*. Aesthetic information is statistically measurable, because the monitored sets are reduced to simple volumes of *syntactic* elements (in the sense given by Charles W. Morris), and by disregarding the *semantic* and *pragmatic* dimensions of the message, its relations to the (represented) world, and to the users of the message.

An aesthetic message conceived only by means of information and statistics might conceivably be likened to a return to an 'Edenic language' and its transformations – a thought experiment carried out by Umberto Eco in his essay 'On the Possibility of Generating Aesthetic Messages in an Edenic Language', appearing in *The Open Work*. Here, Eco describes how God gave to Adam and Eve an extremely simple and perfectly symmetrical code. He then proceeds to show how the discovery of a contradiction in the semantic universe brings unrest to the conventional construction of the code, causing it to *turn in on itself*. Its expressions and contents, the essential correspondence between them, begin to shift, triggering a process of differentiation that soon spreads throughout the code. The semantic interpretation of the world thus begins to diversify; *the 'aesthetic game' begins*. Admittedly, Eco's thought experiment suffers from certain shortcomings: the assumption, for example, that 'in the beginning' there was code. In fact, the code is never given in advance, before the communication act: the relationship between communication act and code is mutual, circular. Moreover, Eco presumes a discrete composition of the code, with the suggestion that the prototype of all codes consists in graphic symbols. Still, the essay demonstrates compellingly how the 'birth' of the code is *irreversible*. Each further differentiation of contents and expressions, each mutual separation of forms and substances carries with it variously distributed and layered traces of their previous states. Eco thus brings something new to the semiotics of information: it is not possible to return either to the original chaos (traces and memory persist), or to the homogeneous state of the code, where the universe appears without contradictions and the code has yet to extend along lines of metaphoricity and connotation – that is, to a state before the event of the 'factual judgment' of God, which inadvertently 'provides people with the means [to] disrupt the whole code' (Eco 1997/1962: 293, 297).

In spite of such shortcomings, the theoretical material produces several key breakthroughs. In Bense's *Theorie der Texte* (Theory of Texts, 1962)[9] the problem of structuring and measuring an aesthetic text (using the term 'text', rather presciently, to refer to any kind of message in any medium) arises with the notion of 'supersigns'. The supersign, as a step towards the internal structuring of a text, introduces another kind of uncertainty, and demonstrates how even meaning can be distributed in an unlikely manner: '[S]upersigns as signs of a higher order arise from the fixed forms of a priori elementary signs' (Bense 1967/1962: 48), in an artistic literary text, for example, it is a collection of 'simultaneously perceptible words', metaphors and so on. Higher-order supersigns 'give new information', creating the conditions for 'subjective gain of redundancy in perception' and 'new repertory of aesthetic information' (Bense 1967/1962: 48–9), and so on. We thus find, in these passages from *Theory of Texts*, how *style* may (for the first time) become a source of *new aesthetic information*. What has to this point been understood as redundancy (i.e. style) either helps provide the conditions for obtaining new information (the new phenomenon can only be perceived with appropriate measures of redundancy) or it can itself become the basis of new combinatorics.

Eco: *The Open Work* and its 'legacy'

Even if the ideas found within information theory and cybernetics provide the unmistakable subtext and source material for Eco's well-known early treatise *The Open Work* (1962), Eco's work has significantly advanced (and altered) them in the context of poetics and aesthetics.[10] *The Open Work* also played a pivotal role in the development of Eco's own thinking, which came to combine principles of communication theory with aspects of (pragmatic) semiotics and structuralism. To whom or what is the work open? If the openness of the work inevitably includes the effect of the work on the perceiver, the question arises: to what extent and in what direction did this partly 'pre-semiotic' work (as Eco came to think about it) contribute to, or provide certain preconditions for, his later interest in the semiotic theory of the 'role of the reader'?

The politics of the open form and context of the Italian avant-garde

The Open Work emerged out of a spirit of self-reflection by the Italian artistic neo-avant-garde, and from considerations about their socio-political implications by non-conformist intellectuals.[11] Eco was member of a group centred around the Milan magazine *Il Verri* (founded in 1956). This would later make up the core of Gruppo 63, whose origins are sometimes connected with the publication of *I Novissimi*, a collection of experimental poetry (1961). Eco collaborated with Luciano Berio on the radio polyphonic composition *Thema (Omaggio a Joyce)* (Theme: Homage to Joyce), which consisted of recitations and electroacoustic manipulations of the opening of the 'Sirens' chapter from Joyce's *Ulysses* read in three languages (in the second version, Berio reduced the intertwining voices to pure audio effects; Eco 1997/1962: 5; Caesar 2009: 143). Eco also wrote an article introducing the catalogue of the notable Milan exhibition *Arte programmata: Arte cinetica, opere moltiplicate, opera aperta* (Programmed Art: Kinetic Art, Multiplied Works, Open Work), which featured works by artists and groups such as Bruno Munari, Enzo Mari, Gruppo T and Gruppo N (Munari and Soavi 1962; Bondanella 1997: 21). This context also includes Eco's work in 1954–9 at the cultural editorial office of the public television station RAI.

Eco's reflections on the new poetics revolve around the need to reflect on the social and collective meaning and impact of open works, advocating for formal experimentation, to the ire of 'the neorealist [...] left' (Eco 1997/1962: 7). His main task is to explain how works that␣␣–␣seemingly␣–␣break all ties with the outside world and their content, as well as all earlier systems of expression, were in fact earnest and accurate statements about the contemporary world. While the many references in *The Open Work* to recent discoveries in the formal and exact sciences, from quantum mechanics to information theory and cybernetics, may have only a metaphorical significance, they also speak to an imminent process of transformation in the Western world calling for a corresponding creative and intellectual response. On the one hand, the perceptual demands of the 'work in movement' can be 'construed by the consumer of art as a solicitation of his freedom and responsibility, habituated as he is to all the tricks of anaesthetic communication and psychological seduction exercised by commercial film, advertising, television, of simplistic theatre productions that include catharsis in the admission price (against which Brecht fought) and the decadent melodiousness played in high fidelity' (Eco 1997/1962: 8). (On the similar motif of 'narcosis', see Chapter 7, pp. 243–4, and Chapter 10, pp. 363–4.) On the other hand, Eco points out how the open work, by virtue of its techniques, can reproduce 'in artistic structures the crisis of our worldview' (Eco 1997/1962: 9), representing 'an epiphenomenon of crisis, which is connected with this crisis to such an extent that it has no liberating power, but appears to the consumer rather as an opportunity for intellectual alienation' (Eco 1997/1962: 9). Everything is tailor-made for this kind of reproduction and fed into the pathological situation of culture – even the methodology proposed by the intellectual – so that any solution that is offered inevitably bears its stamp.

Thus, according to the 'Marxian' Eco, the individual experiences alienation from others and from humanity not only in the process of production but also in relation to the objects produced (in the new industrial society, this alienation is simultaneously multiplied and 'masked', as in the emotional relationship to a car). But he also understands it in the Hegelian sense of (a natural and inevitable process of) externalization. In this tension, one finds precisely the possibility that the creative, formative act – the act of giving form to a particular medium (*modo di formare*) – may become an 'engaged relation to reality' by which objects that have gained the upper hand over people as a result of an alienating process of production (this is the aim of industrial design) can be transformed into instruments of liberation. According to Eco, however, this is only possible in an 'anti-human' and apparently 'impersonal' manner: that is, through artistic experimentation. Alienation in this sense cannot be simply eliminated; one must instead change social structures to eliminate the specifically economic forms of alienation, in this way laying the foundations for liberating work. Similarly, human communication can be transformed through actions of a 'formative' nature: 'I do violence to language because I refuse to express with it a false integrity that is no longer ours. At the same time, however, I risk expressing and accepting the very dissociation born of the crisis of integrity, which I had sought to dominate by speaking. Yet there is no alternative to this dialectic, nothing else but to cast light on this alienation by turning it on itself, objectifying it in a form that reproduces it' (Eco 1997/1962: 285).[12]

Eco is interested in a similar knot of problems in his introduction to the catalogue of *Programmed Art*, an exhibit held notably in the showroom of the Italian information technology company Olivetti, a manufacturer of typewriters, calculators and computers – 'the nexus', as Cristina Iuli puts it, 'at the beginning of a national industry of calculating machines and kinetic art in Italy' (Iuli 2013: 230). If Eco distinguishes here between, on the one hand, the new art of perfect form with its hidden geometric and mathematical law, and, on the other, innovators working in the art of materials and formlessness, he concludes that their political and aesthetic schism is only temporary. Their common goal, according to Eco, is 'to expand the area of what is perceptible and applicable to people today' (Eco 1962: [2]). At the same time, however, the scientific perfection of form leads inevitably to the subsuming of all innovation into the 'forms of mainstream industrial society' (Eco 1962: [2]), while the anarchists who work to destroy form want to be worshiped as artists precisely by that society they protest against, or else proudly exclude themselves from it. Eco sees a way forward from these reactions, or as he puts it, from the 'neocapitalist conversion of artistic rebellion' (Eco 1997/1962: 265 n.), as well as the avant-garde tendency towards exclusion and 'aristocratism' (creating works exclusively for a 'future society') and complicity with (capitalist, technological) industrial production (not being a Marxist, his proposals do not return to the notion of the 'base'). He holds this view because, according to him, the principles on which technological consumer society is based can be turned against consumer society itself. One such principle states that random chance may be simulated mathematically. This concept, borrowed from the new disciplines in science, such as quantum theory and cybernetics – the 'field of possible states', suggests a kind of intrinsic (real) relationship between the openness of the system (social or natural) and the openness of artistic works. If Eco ultimately appears to be an 'aesthetic-technological optimist', it may therefore be because he believes it is not technology but art (in its more progressive manifestations) that cultivates perception, bringing about new ways of thinking, seeing and feeling. Or, more precisely, a technology *discovered* through artistic experimentation. In his 1965 article, Helmut Heißenbüttel draws attention to the initial moment of speculation and creativity that can be found in the most skilfully organized physics experiment *precisely in the spirit of the neo-avant-garde*, and in a form of 'technological art' that counters the rigidity of scientific knowledge (Heißenbüttel 1967/1965). Even in a society engulfed by an 'anaesthetic communication' served by technology (and perhaps that comes about, at the same time, as a result of technology), it remains possible to awaken society, both in art and the speculative horizons of scientific and technical knowledge.

Eco's later postmodern medieval detective story, *The Name of the Rose* (as well as an earlier parody of the history of philosophy, *Filosofi in libertà*, which had fascinated his publisher Bompiani), can be seen in this light as finding a way out of a problem that the neo-avant-garde had failed to overcome: namely, through the application of certain generic structures in which there is a central deviation (a procedure that can itself become a bit of a generic structure), and through the postmodern technique of integrating consumer-friendliness with sophistication.

Two kinds of openness

It is the curious tendency of avant-garde and neo-avant-garde works to engender a search for their modern and pre-modern predecessors. According to Eco, such works compel us to provide explanations for their openness, and because a work of art is always open and polyvalent in *some* sense, it is necessary to speak of 'openness of the second order'. A work of this kind no longer involves a core of meaning, but is radically ambiguous from the outset, either because it consists of polyvalent signifiers (as in *Finnegan's Wake*, Eco 1997/1962: e.g. 91–2), or because it is composed of several variable parts – or doesn't have any permanent shape at all, and is set perpetually 'in movement' by the perceiver's interventions into its material form. Eco gives several examples of this kind of work: Mallarmé's unfinished project *Le Livre*, Boulez's *Third Sonata for Piano* (based on the free combinability of parts and pages of the score) and Pousseur's electronic composition *Scambi* (with thirty-two sequences and instructions for the way they may be combined, including playing them at the same time), as well as various works in kinetic and optical art – mobiles, 'found objects', moving constellations and structures (by Group T, Dieter Roth, Jesús Rafael Soto, Jean Tinguely and so on) – that present the viewer simultaneously with a multitude of mutually exclusive spatial perspectives. Each work is a 'field of possibilities' that is not vaguely suggested but defined and real; as Eco points out, 'there are no two moments in time when the mutual position of work and viewer is reproduced in precisely the same way' (Eco 1997/1962: 157).

How is it that Eco, in search of an appropriate language for reflecting on these 'open works of the second order', comes to choose statistical information theory? Undoubtedly, it responds to a certain inclination – on the part of both theorist and experimental artist – to take a scientific approach to poetics. In this context, statistical concepts help shed light on various connections among phenomena and processes that would otherwise resist our efforts to understand them: the destruction of style, for example, which is effectively a form of 'redundancy reduction'; the form of the work, which in practice necessarily entails the notion of predictability; and noise/entropy, which provides a model for unpredictability.

This value, this kind of second-order openness that contemporary art aims at, could be defined as an increase and multiplication of the possible meanings of a message. But the term lends itself to misunderstanding, since few would be willing to speak of "meaning" when it comes to the kind of communication at play in a non-figurative pictorial sign or constellation of sounds. We will therefore define this sort of openness as an increase of *information*. (Eco 1997/1962: 93)

And what is meant by 'increase in information', we will recall, is the non-human variety. A certain line of aesthetics involving statistical and quantum openness begins here, though it is clear in retrospect that this is only one aspect of neo-avant-garde experimentation, and one moreover that is difficult to project into the past. In the broader perspective, however, it is of considerable importance: both artists and theorists of the avant-garde – a number of them, in any case – will consciously accept the non-humanity (the 'anti-human') that Eco evoked in his introduction to *Programmed Art* (1962).

Problems of *The Open Work*

The transposition of scientific categories creates certain tensions in *The Open Work*, of which the author – judging by the extent to which he undertook to revise successive editions – was more and more aware. For one, Eco encounters a number of difficulties in his effort to reformulate information theory within the context of (literary) aesthetics. He is evidently at pains to preserve that most ingenious aspect of the model by which information is measured against entropy (uncertainty). Yet he must reconcile it with that aspect by which redundancy helps to reduce the probability that noise will interfere with the signal, while at the same time reducing the informational value of the message, since more elements carry the same information. This leads him to emphasize the pre-existence of *code* as an *organizing mechanism with its own inertia*. In *The Open Work*, deformation and openness – especially the more radical 'second-order' openness – do seem to increase entropy, yet redundancy, as the introduction of the probability of what is expected, serves here as a necessary complementary force (Abraham Moles advances the same view, albeit on the perceptual level.) The issue requires a certain 'dialectical' view of the 'layering' of the situation: it is only when we look at the improbability of the occurrence of a certain element from the perspective of an already established order (code) that it makes sense to speak about increases in the information of a message alongside increases in its disorganization. If there was no previous structure of codes, there would be nothing to 'measure' against. In poetic communication, 'we are examining [. . .] the possibility of conveying information that is not "meaning" in the habitual sense *by using conventional structures of language that defy the laws of probability governing language from within'* (Eco 1997/1962: 111).

We have already indicated some of the weaknesses of this approach. Meaning here appears as quantifiable information formulated in relation to a particular code (rather than continuously formed representation schemata, for example). Furthermore, Eco conceives of codes vaguely as probability matrices, without working through the particular manner of their emergence (or decay), preservation or development. He draws here on several competing concepts of communication – physicalistic, transmission and aesthetic – be it the idea of the information circuit, transmission of information, the transition between information states (to reach temporary equilibrium), construction and selection of the message, or the act of forming or shaping (what Eco refers to as *il modo di formare*). He then passes freely in his interpretation from one link in the 'communication exchange' to the next, modelling it everywhere as an information source. Grasping the aesthetic message in these terms, he considers its course of reception in probabilistic terms, assessing its difficulty, resistance and shock. Turning then to a set of possible messages, he models the creative possibilities as a determinable field of information possibilities (in a work of art, however, it is a matter of shifting this field rather than calculating it in relation to a definable set). Finally, taking the code as a source of information, he views the aesthetic increase of information as the purposeful deviations in the areas of expression and content.

In other words, while the message and individual sign (signal) are treated similarly in computational theories, communication theory proper makes a necessary distinction: the message (in this case, the work), unlike the sign, is hierarchically structured, having a certain communicative autonomy and relative integrity.

In his '1966 postscript' to *The Open Work* (Eco 1997/1962: 125–30), Eco returns to his original (refreshingly unorthodox) position to describe some of its problems. Returning to its general starting points, he provides us with the following corrections (we enumerate them here for the sake of clarity): (1) When the concept of information is applied to the message itself as a source of information, information theory becomes a *theory of communication*. This can be understood to mean that the moment a message is related to a set of other possibilities, it begins to undergo a process of interpretation, in terms of its relevance or reason, for instance. At that point, however, it is no longer a measurable quantity. (2) When information is transmitted between people, it is charged with 'connotation phenomena', and the signal is enveloped in their 'echoes'. (3) A polyvalent message puts the recipient in a state of excitement and interpretative suspense. (4) The message is the initial disorganization (which emerges from the order situated within the overall state of disorder), and as such requires the filtering of meanings in order to become a new message, an interpreted work – that is, it requires *interpretation*. (5) As it is applied in the context of communication, information theory takes on a different categorical schema and loses its algorithmic system. (6) At a certain moment, information theory has nothing more to say, leaving room for semiology and semantics. (7) The open works themselves challenge us to search for inspiration in the relations described by information theory.

The apparent media universality of the concept of information

Before considering how the themes and problems of *The Open Work* might be transposed to another work by Eco that deals with the semiotics of communication, we must ask what *The Open Work* tells us about mediality: which of its latent conceptions does it bring to the fore?

In a letter of 1931 quoted by Eco, Anton (von) Webern writes to the poet and painter Hildegard Jone (Webern 1959: 17–18):

> I have found a series (that is, twelve tones) which already contains in itself very complex relations (among these twelve tones). Perhaps it's a bit like this old palindrome:
>
> S A T O R
> A R E P O
> T E N E T
> O P E R A
> R O T A S

Webern then describes (and draws out) all the horizontal and vertical directions in which the cryptogram can be read to produce identical strings of letters. The quote exemplifies the formal affinity of different material systems in avant-garde experimentation (other similar models also served as the inspiration for concretism). For Eco, it is not just that the compositional possibilities of twelve-tone music are homologous to those of a limited repertory of spatially interconnected letters. The implications of this structural agreement point to a much broader plan, namely the global possibility of applying statistical information theory (and field theory) to any work of art within the framework of an 'aesthetics of openness'. Whether Eco turns his analysis to a literary (musical, artistic, cinematic) work or television broadcast, whether it is in regard to a medieval (baroque, classical) or modern work, whatever cell he isolates in the information circuit as source of a probability matrix – they all hang together in reference to a single point, and that is the concept of information. Or, to be more precise, it is a *particular* concept of information that is universal in communication and media: if we accept that the concept of information can be applied to any system of expression, that means it must be *dematerialized* and *destructured* to a single unit: a bit. Just as a broad range of contemporary scholarly disciplines have taken up information as a media-universal concept, so also did a certain number of the neo-avant-garde. Yet the universality of the notion of information across a wide variety of (communication) media leads to a certain 'antimediality', so that even while the approach sheds light on experimentation, it does so only by obscuring its 'media specificity', which can play a significant (and significantly different) role in neo-avant-garde practice, drawing attention to specific media forms and materials in one work, dramatically blending them in another.

Thus, if Eco's analyses of the (immaterial) dialectic of form and deformation in modern art represent, in a certain sense, the return of a formalist way of thinking, the concept of information and probabilistic models suggest radically new conditions for its return: the search for a universal scientific language, (apparent) universality of communication forms and a general 'inflation' of communication.

The critical and avant-garde character of Eco's work, however, remains in the background. When Eco considers the degree of formal improvisation in real time that is allowed on live television, he wonders (even here) how to open up the 'work'. During the broadcast of a football match, for example, the director immediately follows the shot of a goal being scored with that of the cheering crowd. Eco sketches an alternative approach: 'he could suddenly show, ingeniously and controversially, a glimpse of the adjacent street (women in the window occupied with the daily routine, cats curled up in the sun)' (1997/1962: 203). Such a distracting gloss, drawing the viewer out of his state of hypnotic fascination (where he has been drawn by the action), would thus serve as an 'alienation' device: an interruption of passive attention that provides the impetus to free oneself from the seductive power of the television screen. It is McLuhan who turns to the 'viewer's space' and speaks of the different conditions for the mesmerizing and hallucinatory power of media, but similar experiments lie beyond the scope of his interests. In short, where McLuhan considers the *medium to be the message*, Eco considers the *form to be the medium*. Yet it is the 'information-quantum' universality of the concept of the open work that accounts for its power to invoke the ideal and ethos of liberation.

From 'cybernetic' transaction to interpretive cooperation, from disposition capacity to strategy

In one part of *The Open Book* (written for the second, 1967 edition), Eco turns his attention to the subject of transactional and genetic-structural psychology

(F. P. Kilpatrick, Jean Piaget) in order to demonstrate the open nature of perception and intelligence, emphasize once more this openness in the case of neo-avant-garde works, and outline a new interpretive model that would make these aspects more apparent. The implications of this 'process- oriented' psychology, which coincide with – or draw directly from – the discoveries of cybernetic principles, lead Eco to make a certain observation: Gestalt psychology sets out (mistakenly) by defining perception as an always already organized and directed configuration of stimuli, by virtue of a fundamental isomorphism between the psychophysical structures of the perceiving subject and structures of the object perceived. By contrast, the schools of psychology on which Eco bases his ideas model cognitive experience as an open-ended process. Certain dispositions of the subject (memories, unconscious preconceptions, assimilated culture) play a formative role in perception, while form is shaped together with value in relation to the *goals* that the perceiver is pursuing (Eco 1997/1962: 133). Although perception and intelligence (according to Piaget) represent processes that differ in their structure, they are both characterized by their *open nature*. Moreover, the search for balance that one finds in this process, and that is reminiscent of cybernetics, allows for a predictive and at the same time infinitely variable assimilation process: 'The reason for the interactions between object and subject seems quite different from that which the founders of Gestalt theory borrowed from phenomenology. The notion of perceptual equilibrium suggested by the facts is not that of a physical field in which the forces at play automatically and meticulously seek balance, but rather that of an *active compensation on the part of the subject as it seeks to moderate exterior disturbances*' (Piaget, cited in Eco 1997/1962: 135 n. 29; emphasis added); 'the subject endlessly constructs new schemata during its development and assimilates the perceived objects into them, without determinable limits between the properties of the assimilated object and structures of the subject that assimilates it' (cited in Eco 1997/1962: 135 n. 29). This provides the basis for Eco's understanding of the communicative relationship between the unusual art objects of the neo-avant-garde and the interpretive effort they encourage: 'the relationship between message and receiver, in which the interpretive decision of the receiver constitutes the effective value of possible information' (Eco 1997/1962: 131). This also suggests a transition from the quantitative to qualitative concept of information, similar to the transition that appears in the work of Miroslav Červenka, as we will see later. Eco is fascinated by the transactional interpretation of the neo-avant-garde, which sets itself apart from more common ways of perceiving and knowing for the fact that the 'search for balance' takes place here under *consciously accepted conditions of crisis* – it involves an expectation of the unforeseen, and a complementarity of the lines of perception vis-à-vis the work of art (Eco 1997/1962: 147).

The cybernetics-information model is also taken up by American musicologist and aesthetician Leonard B. Meyer, who models the reception of the meaning of a work as a continuous process carried out by transitioning between probability systems. According to Meyer, musical 'meaning' arises in moments of deviation from the probable, when latent expectations become active: in other words, when the most probable course (perception) of the composition – in terms of its tonality, for example – is somehow disturbed. This whole process is by nature continuous and multi-layered. Deviations from what is expected or probable fall into several different categories, such as the delay of a probable solution, the ambiguity of an initial (antecedent) situation and the unexpectedness (improbability) that may arise in a certain context. The process of perceiving musical meaning is itself structured, consisting in various 'curves', systems or series of probabilities with respect to the different layers (for example, melodies and musical structure are governed by different systems of probabilities). For Eco, this represents more than a simple analogy between the perception of a musical work and the act of reading a text: rather, it provides a general model for the perception of any work of art. Regarding this analogy, we could point out that: (1) disturbances manifest what Wolfgang Iser, after Ingarden, calls 'places of indeterminacy' (*Unbestimmtheitsstellen*) (on the 'cybernetic' aspect of reading, see Chapter 10, pp. 364–5); (2) Meyer and Eco model these disturbances in terms of the 'uncertainty' of an information source; (3) the text (the act of reading) presents an analogy to a musical composition, since the perception of the work (always) takes place in time, but the material and spatiotemporal nature of the stimulus is not recognized; (4) the notion of stratification (Meyer's 'architectonics') appears once more in the context of Červenka's thinking about the process – the structure and perception – of a literary work.

In Meyer's application of information theory, the structure or series of dispositions that allows a listener to recognize specific musical styles is defined as an individual series of different channels of varying capacity, different for each individual. Meyer builds this model on the assumption that the structure of dispositions depends on the acquired cultural model, but at one point – as Eco observes – he makes a 'gestaltic return' to the view that assimilation schemes are immutable or universal. And this is where it is necessary to distinguish (precisely in the spirit of Warren Weaver)[13] between desirable and undesirable forms of uncertainty: desirable uncertainty 'arises within and as a result of the structured probabilities of a style system in which a finite number of antecedents and consequents become mutually relevant through the habits, beliefs, and attitudes of a group of listeners'

(Meyer 1957: 420-1); undesirable uncertainty can be understood as an unknown probability that arises from reactions based on ignorance of style (cultural noise; the listener has 'zero expectations') or from external acoustic interference (acoustic noise): 'Cultural noise, as I shall use the term, refers to disparities which may exist between the habitual responses required by the musical style and those which a given individual actually possesses' (Meyer 1957: 420).

Eco's project, however, is to argue for the value of neo-avant-garde works, in which the perceiver's ability to predict the next state is difficult by design ('intentional uncertainty'), resulting in a profusion of 'cultural noise': a conflict between the artist's assumptions about the structure of dispositions and the specific profile of dispositions for a given perceiver. For the early Eco, this is precisely the effect of second-order openness he so highly values. Meyer writes: 'the redundancy rate of this music is at times so low as to be unable to counteract the cultural noise which is always present in a communication situation. [. . .] in their zeal to "pack" music full of meaning some contemporary composers have perhaps so overloaded the channel capacity of the audience that one meaning obscures another in the ensuing overflow' (Meyer 1957: 420). Eco sees things differently: contemporary art, from serial music to kinetic installations, 'indicates to modern man a possibility of recuperation and autonomy' (1997/1962: 151). In practice, however, it could lead in the opposite direction, towards a loss of its audience, and its exclusion as a field of production.

As we have seen, Eco grasps the concept of code in (the first edition of) *The Open Work*, somewhat vaguely, as a probability field based on fixed conventions. He tries to redress this problem in his article 'On the Possibility of Generating Aesthetic Messages in an Edenic Language' (1971), mentioned earlier in this chapter. Yet Eco's work in semiotics in the 1960s and 1970s would amount to one of the most sophisticated general theories of its time on semiotics and the text, culminating in his *Trattato di semiotica generale* (1975, *A Theory of Semiotics*, 1976). In a related work of 1979 in the field of textual semiotics and pragmatics, *Lector in fabula: La cooperazione interpretativa nei testi narrativi*, Eco develops the concept of 'interpretive cooperation'.[14] The question here is: How did Eco's thinking change as it evolved from *The Open Work* to the communication model presented in *Lector in fabula* (a title which suggests the reader is situated literally *within* the story)?

Eco's earlier concept of 'second-order openness' drew attention to the *process of interpretation*, indicating the necessary interplay of many *different* interpretations. As Eco writes in his introduction to *Lector in fabula*: 'It could be said [. . .] that all the studies I conducted from 1963 to 1975 aimed (if not solely at least in large part) at seeking out the semiotic foundations of the experience I had described as "openness" but for which I had not laid down the rules in *The Open Work* (Eco 1979: 8). For Eco, the narrative literary text is not a pleasure-producing mechanism (à la Barthes) but a 'lazy (or economic)' one, living off the 'surplus value of meaning' (Eco 1979: 52), which draws the reader into interpretive cooperation. In *Lector in fabula*, Eco describes a number of textual codes and subcodes, as well as rules and ways to apply them, various structural levels of the text (discursive, narrative, actantial, ideological), extensional operations summoned by the text (the construction of worlds, inferences), and all other levels and operations of the text by which it guides and seduces the reader to cooperate in the interpretive process (vis-à-vis the 'intention of the text'). Between a particular author and the reader, two intermediaries are built into the text that make this process possible: the 'model author' and 'model reader'. These positions are globally implicit text strategies; at the same time, however, they represent hypotheses about the role of the sender and receiver that are asymmetrical (the process by which the reader makes a hypothesis about the author is not symmetrical with the one in which the author makes a hypothesis about the reader) and irreversible once realized (cf. Müller R. 2011). Eco confines his argument in *Lector in fabula* to the search for the limits and rules of interpretation, choosing not to focus on 'opening' the work or the transgressive pleasure of the text. The boundaries between the interior and exterior of the text are clearly defined, and the empirical reader, like the empirical author, approaches from the outside, where the text is susceptible to 'free usage' – that is, the empirical reader may choose to use the text merely to confirm his or her own personal experience, rather than submitting it to interpretation in the strict sense of the word. However, by using the text in this way, which may take the form of under-interpretation, over-interpretation or various associative conjectures and 'abuses', the empirical reader moves away from the given text and field of interpretation, thus betraying the established rules of the text game – the mechanism of cooperation. The mechanism, for its part, may be designed with various 'tricks', intentional dead ends and 'shortcuts' (for example, by using generic formulae to raise expectations only to disrupt them later in the text). Eco's terms *intentio operis*, *intentio lectoris* and *intentio auctoris*, which appear primarily in his work *The Limits of Interpretation* (1994/1990), elaborate the same structure of boundaries.

By comparison to *The Open Work*, which illustrates Eco's wide-ranging interest in a variety of media, the focus of *Lector in fabula* is markedly narrow. This is due perhaps not only to his more focused objective – to provide a more rigorous description of a single medium (narrative text) and its functioning – but also certain 'monomedia' tendencies in the field of textual semiotics itself. These tendencies were premised (just like in information theory) on the dematerialization of central concepts – of information and the sign – and generally by a certain disregard for many of the material, social and technical aspects of communication processes. For example, the term 'encyclopaedia' represents a semiotic model for generating propositions in the constantly modified and infinitely variable network of a semantic universe. As such, it tends to obfuscate certain questions: In what ways does a particular individual situated in a certain physical and social space acquire an encyclopaedia? Can access to the encyclopaedia be variously enabled and controlled? How, by whom and for whom is the encyclopaedia constructed and handed down?

Eco's notions of (1) the model reader and (2) empirical reader can be seen to correspond, retrospectively, to the (1) presumed structure of dispositions in the recognition of style within an art form, and (2) dispositions available to a particular perceiver. The concept of the channel in information theory – which laid the stage for what we would today call *the medium* – is split in Meyer's model of the reception process into two categories, as he found it necessary to distinguish between 'cultural noise' and the appropriate response. Eco rejects this split in *The Open Work*, arguing that the open work wilfully transgresses the boundaries of what is and is not an appropriate response. As a result, his concept of the channel (or medium) spans the entire set of actual and presumed perceptual dispositions. If it can be said that the form *is* the medium for Eco, this set of dispositions is simply the converse side of the medium formed by the 'reception apparatus'. And just as the term *form* comprises certain latent possibilities that remain in the background of the selected variant, so too does the 'receptorium' as a whole comprise both anticipated and unanticipated dispositions. Later, writing in *Lector in fabula*, he returns to the two-category concept proposed by Meyer. When we notice the medium at all (as it appears in latent form) it is by virtue of a disparity between the model and empirical dispositions. The mediality of the media is manifest only in the contact between, and 'short-circuiting' of, variously profiled 'channels' – although there is no reason to consider this aspect as the specific purpose of the narrative text *as medium*.

By relegating the categories of empirical author and empirical reader to the margins of the theory, Eco actually downplays the theoretical significance of mediality, and the word 'model' in his conception of interpretive cooperation suggests both 'a model or example [. . .] intended to serve as a pattern for imitation' and 'a model or representation of something else' (OED). In terms of mediality, the latent aporias presented by Eco's way of thinking in *Lector in fabula* are even more numerous, insofar as it features an ingenious way of describing the essential internal media-semiotic features of the narrative text, especially with regard to the mechanisms of its 'seductions' and dead ends, that allows him to transcend the (classical) semiotic framework. This is especially evident in his differentiation between the first (naïve) and second (critical) reading of the text (Eco 1979: 194–5). What is missing here, however, is any comparative aspect or holistic view of the different media and the various ways they involve the perceiver, raising suspicions that Eco takes the narrative text as a general model for *all forms* of interpretive cooperation (compelled, perhaps, by the theoretical centrality of language in communication). In *Lector in fabula*, mediality seems not much more than an artificial game of sophistication based on a certain (post)modern poetics of the text, rather than reflecting the fundamental characteristics of the literary medium.

Communication models and the birth of the reader

What influence did communication models that emerged in the context of information theory and cybernetics have on the famous 'turn' in literary theory across various different approaches: the birth or 'rehabilitation' of the reader (or as Jonathan Culler puts it, the 'righting of the reader'). In the context of semiotics as it is presented here, and that of phenomenological theories broadly speaking, it is worth noting the following points: The introduction of linearity had a simplifying effect on the (linguistic) study of communication, which was eventually corrected by the adoption of circular, interactive and recursive models. This obscures the fact that the original inspiration for Jakobson's seminal communication model – Bühler's *Organon-Modell* – was not at all linear. The *Organon-Modell*, which both Jakobson and Mukařovský drew on, identifies three communicative functions: in addition to addressee and speaker, it also includes objects and states of affairs (*Gegenstände und Sachverhalte*). Any of these three points of the 'triangle' could become a point of departure for signification. Mukařovský went one step further, designating the *perceiver* as starting point of the work and its complex movement of semantic integration, and to demonstrate that unintentionality – not yet in terms of cybernetic entropy – was an unavoidable condition for the semantic event.[15]

In the progression from Meyer to Eco, we find the emergence of the concept of the open work and application of the idea of the cultural dispositions of perception as a system of channels, as well as a certain interplay between perceiver and work within the information-cybernetics notion of balancing information levels, and several wave forms of different profiles (or probability amplitudes). For the Eco of *The Open Work*, there is a connection between entropy, openness of the source and the unpredictability of its information 'extraction'. For the Eco of *Lector in fabula*, on the other hand, negative entropy places limits on the act of interpretation. What is clear, in the end, is that the principle of feedback tends to downplay the individual perceiver, focusing rather on the whole system of communication in which the recipient is just one of its links; *mutatis mutandis*, the interaction between the work and perceiver also begins to appear as a kind of balancing open system – *and the perceiver is then constructed as its shadow or correlate and cooperation partner* (e.g. implicit reader, model reader).

However, the difficulty of extracting 'useful information' from literary and artistic works can be seen in a certain tension not only between this model of literary communication and real reading and perception practices, but also in the position of literary and artistic communication as such in the context of the 'information age': What purpose is served by this kind of communication, one that hinders and impedes the extraction (or acquisition) of information, rendering it unnatural, demanding repeated reinterpretation and inputs and slowing down communication in general – in a world, moreover, that is becoming more and more connected? Of course – and this is where one of many possible answers have been sought – it draws attention both to itself (subliminally, as a model) and, above all, to the conditions of communication and discursivity in general.

Červenka: The process and organization of a literary work, aesthetic function and focus on the *univers de discours*

We have seen how Jakobson, in his article of 1949, works through the ways in which the word 'Nevermore' moves through a sequence of transmitters and receivers. This description – insofar as it was supposed to provide a universal model of communication – tends to weaken the theoretical importance of the structure of the message (and, in the final analysis, the real ways a particular work resonates and circulates in society).

We also observed how the idea of the 'supersign' in information theory ('information aesthetics') and the code as a system of probabilities in the theory of the open work represent elementary steps towards an assessment of the *meaning* of the 'aesthetic message'. In the 1967 edition of *The Open Work*, Eco indicates how the communication channel corresponds to the dispositions of the perceiver vis-à-vis a given style (rather than to a physical thing made of wires or waves), and that these dispositions are organized in various sets. In *Lector in fabula*, he goes on to suggest (if we read the two works together) that these dispositions constitute certain perceptual competencies in the implementation and interconnection of various sets of subcodes. The significance of these conceptual transformations is best understood in the context of Eco's notion of communication (both aesthetic and literary), which maintains the integrity of the individual work in the way it is read and interpreted, even as he moves towards a systemic concept of communication. The work could thus be interpreted as a changing shape that deviates from the overall set of communication possibilities, while at the same time enriching them, cultivating its own perceiver along predetermined lines (as Eco later conceives it). To the same extent, the work (as modelled by the later concept) is closed once more, and from the dialectic between the original norm and the deviation, a new norm is established.

Another work, this time by Eco's contemporary Miroslav Červenka, must also be included in this context: *The Semantic Organization of a Work of Literature* (1968; first published in 1992), a work at the intersection of the 'revival' of literary structuralism in the 1960s, structural semiotics and information theory.[16] Červenka's work in the field of literary theory comes from the perspective of his previous work in the fields of historical poetics, literary analysis and versology. In broad strokes, the problem on which he refines his concept is this: As information theory would have it, all features related to the order of the text and its stylistic organization tend to increase the predictability of every further use of the sign, thus reducing the novelty of information and entropy. Yet this is contrary to intuition, as well as the traditional concept of a literary work (the poetic text) as a highly organized form that also contains a strong charge of aesthetic information and values.

Červenka proposes the following solution, building on the work of the translatologist and an early proponent of computational analysis of verse, Jiří Levý (1971/1963): Even if predictability and redundancy increase with the high-level organization that characterizes the poetic (artistic) text, this does not mean that entropy and information value decrease in the text regarded as a whole. It is possible for entropy to increase at the same time as redundancy *if they are measured within different sets*. For example, a rhythmically organized message will have high redundancy, but entropy may still increase relative to the whole set of messages that a particular language is capable of producing. This is similar to Eco's idea of measuring order and disorder on the basis of categories of code. Červenka, however, consistently projects this principle of different sets *inside* a literary work and elaborates a category of 'level' (part of a whole). While redundancy may increase in a particular part of a work, the information value may increase at the same time by virtue of *ad hoc emerging relationships* between different parts (including their elements or subsets). For example, a text that is rhythmically organized and that sets up an expectation produces a predictable pattern; however, any seemingly redundant element of the text can in fact multiply the number of relationships both between the individual parts (e.g. the tension between lexical richness and regular rhythm) and between their individual elements (e.g. a cliché that clashes with the incongruity of sentence and verse structure). In this case, the 'elementary signal[s]' (Červenka 1992/1968: 45) become less recognizable, and more dependent on the receptive and interpretive activity of the perceiver.

This illustrates how artistic communication differs from ordinary communication: whereas the non-literary text narrows the channel profile by reducing the number of relevant codes and uniquely identifying them, any element in a literary text can become an element of different sign repertoires, increasing polysemy within the work. Whereas, in ordinary communication, redundancy is enhanced with the aim of distinguishing messages from noise (e.g. the repetitive syntactic constructions and lexical expressions in instruction manuals), the literary work produces a parallel semantic organization based on changes in the hierarchy of semantic parts, and intensification and multiplication of the modality of semantic sets (uncertainty, delay of resolution). This includes cases in which several different elements or parts communicate the same meaning in different repertoires or sets of signs, differing in level (involvement in higher wholes) and/or the way they are constituted (for example, synonyms for various motifs on the compositional and lexical level). 'Properties of speech and the relations among these properties, which may be irrelevant elsewhere, become bearers of meaning in a literary work' (Červenka 1992/1968: 46) and therefore significant.

In this way, information does not grow in width, but in depth. The decisive factor is the overall process that produces meaning – and this process becomes more intricate, and in this intricacy, *exposed*.

According to Červenka, the most enduring value of the high degree of entropy found in a poetic text lies, paradoxically, in the very way of using and reconciling its codes (i.e. bringing them together in a meaningful whole). This exercise becomes a sign in and of itself, bringing to the fore the conventional relationships between communication codes as social institutions, and the communication process as a whole. In this way, a new conception of aesthetic function is revealed: if Červenka's inspiration and teacher Mukařovský defines aesthetic function as an 'empty' function, demonstrating the interconnectedness of all human artistic and 'symbolic' activity, Červenka connects it directly with communication. And if Jakobson understands the poetic function as the propensity of the message to focus on itself (language exercising its expressive potential for its own sake), Červenka diverges here too: for him, the aesthetic function emphasizes – by negating direct denotations and contexts – the relation of speech 'to the basic components of man's position in the universe [world of values] and to the general context, which is the *univers de discours* of humanity' (Červenka 1992/1968: 55): 'literature emphasizes the process itself, actualizes its communication component in the human model of the world, shows how the human world is eminently the world of communication' (Červenka 1992/1968: 12).

We can now try to give precise terms to this shift in the direction of information theory. What the channel represented in the original model of communication (see Diagram 6.1) has become an extended and structured code (or 'code set'). In the original version, the code was situated between the information source and transmitter (as in the case of natural language), and also in the place of the transmitter (as in the case of telegraphy, where the written signs of natural language are converted into sequences of dots, dashes and spaces). The channel existed between the transmitter and the receiver, but no other code appeared on this path. Červenka transforms the notion of the channel (like Eco, but more explicitly) so that it refers to the codes themselves. These changes to the model are necessary before it can be applied beyond the context of communication in its limited technological sense, most importantly to social and cultural communication. Červenka then describes the multi-layered character of the literary work as an extension of the channel's capacity, and the concept of the channel is projected into the work (although not, as Eco had it, into the perceiver) so as to constitute the manner in which its codes and subcodes are related to one another. Having thus situated the channel in the place of the code, Červenka no longer associates it with noise (in opposition to the early Eco). (On my alternative concept of interference, see Chapter 10, esp. pp. 339–40.) However, the combination of channel and noise in information theory still has a particular significance: if noise phenomena inevitably appear on the channel, at the moment when the *channel* becomes *part of the message*, this necessarily leads to mutations and changes in the communication system. In other words, because the codes are mediated, because the codes are *preceded* by messages (or texts), the result is that the codes are *transformed*. We can say that in Červenka's conception, the assumption of a change in the conditions and possibilities of communication *is implicit in the literary work itself*, which can project it yet further in the vagaries of its reception. It does this concurrently with changes in the overall conditions of communication, as well as the various codes running through the social field as a whole; the literary work always works towards them *transversely and simultaneously by a centripetal movement*.

Meanwhile, in his reworking of the concept of literary communication, Červenka delegates all considerations of a technical nature to the fields of textology and editorial work (fields in which Červenka himself had a great deal of interest and experience). No longer limited to problems of undistorted signal transmission, the novelty of the communication process thus comes to the fore, where it can – only under these conditions – become the subject of reflection and play. There remains, however, something fundamental about the *distance* between the 'links of the communication chain' – or, more aptly, in the process of mediation itself. We see this, for example, in Červenka's formulations concerning the aesthetic function: 'The concentration of functions [...] makes the work itself a sign of human communication, of contact between people. [...] It seems that any literary work represents a decision to make contact in a certain situation, so that the very approach to the creative (literary) work amounts to saying: "It's me. Listen, you! We are here!"' (Červenka 1992/1968: 139). It is remarkable that this statement, which could characterize any work to some extent (not just literature) typifies communication of the *phatic* type. According to Červenka, in the case of an otherwise empty aesthetic function, its minimum content is an expression of contact. In this case, *the phatic and aesthetic functions converge to an unprecedented extent*. What we should notice in Červenka's statement above is that it expresses something at once exceedingly elementary and, in the context of the beginning of the 'information explosion', strikingly urgent. After all, Jakobson borrows the term phatic from the anthropological and ethnographical context (Bronisław Malinowski's research), in which a particular form of language use was first identified that did not serve 'as a means of transmission of thought' but instead represented a form of action, establishing bonds of belonging: 'The breaking of silence, the communion of words is the first act to establish links of fellowship, which is consummated only by the breaking of bread and the communion of food' (Malinowski 1949/1923: 315, 314). It is as if literature for Červenka represented the basic sphere of the secondary (cultural) establishment of society and meaning, in a society whose individual messages are otherwise hopelessly scattered, blind and deaf to one another; 'it actualizes its communication component in the human model of the world'.

It is evident that Červenka's concept places great emphasis on the reception and interpretation process of a work, insofar as the set of subcodes forms a structure that changes in the process through which it is perceived. He does not further elaborate his thinking in this direction, but turns instead (with characteristic focus) to the description of the necessary conditions for the semantic organization of the work itself. Here Červenka systematically excludes such categories as technical noise, sensory material and the whole material substrate of communication, except in those cases where it may play a role in the broader meaning of the work, that is, in its semantic structure. From this perspective, literature comes to represent a principally immaterial practice in which the creative process is carried out through the selection of a potentially infinite number of possibilities from a vast complex of codes and a diversity of signifying elements.

This conception of the literary work as a dematerialized, thoroughly semantic organization leads Červenka to make several observations: the graphic record (i.e. typed or handwritten manuscript) does not itself constitute any part of the literary work or its signs (this is true as well for any potential sound recording); rather, the sensory carrier of the work, the *artefact*, is a schematic (imaginary) sound; visual aspects, such as typesetting and graphic layout, is pushed to the boundary that separates literature from visual art. The claim that the sensory-signifying essence of a literary work is not based in graphic representation but in sound (cf. Červenka 1996) is supported by the following arguments: the signifiers of the work are arranged linearly; the identity of the work is preserved in spite of changes to the graphic system, whereas a change in pronunciation alters it; 'sight rhymes' are the product of rhymes based on the repetition of similar sounds which have been lost over time due to shifts in pronunciation; line breaks are sound-based, whereas their graphic equivalent is 'passive'; what distinguishes between different forms of narration (direct, indirect) is not simply a matter of graphics but of intonation. The effective coincidence between the creation of visual/concrete poetry and artistic manifestos that theorized it suggests that this concept may have a certain traditionalist or conservative motivation. Červenka's primary aim is to provide the new developments in communication theory (and semiotics) with a suitable foundation in literary theory. Yet the various trends in experimental poetry called these very characteristics into question (we will return to this in the following part), effectively (re)introducing the openness of the literary system as medium. They systematically borrowed from a variety of artistic disciplines, bringing in such visual elements as lines, surfaces, figures and colours, as well as musical or plastic forms, the narrative potential of typographic forms and other kinds of intermedial relations. At times, they would emphasize the complexity and ambiguity of only one plane of expression – or, in self-referential manner, underline the signification or relationships within the signs – at the cost of impoverishing many or all other forms of content and expression, frequently violating the accepted distinction between form and substance.

After all, if literature can be said in any way to 'put communication on display', then any aspect of its communication 'a priori' – its linear structure, for example – may also be radically negated. This is implicit in Červenka's conception of literary communication.

Any purely 'sign' (i.e. wholly non-material) conception of the literary work is systematically disrupted by the fact that at various levels, and in all the attendant semantic elements and complexes, there are material substrates, or 'substances', that cannot be fully subordinated to the form nor content they carry (neither to their signifiers nor their signifieds).[17] These material complexes include not only the 'lower' sound and graphic substances, but a wide range of heterogeneous compositional and generic substances in the manner of its constitution. Although Červenka examines in detail how elements of these complexes – i.e. poetic rhythm, composition and literary genre – are involved in the work's semantics, his conception of these 'substances' causes a special surplus to enter the literary structure, which is not taken up entirely in the production of meaning within the framework of signification of the literary work as it is traditionally conceived. This has to do with a certain 'objectness' in both the material and socio-cultural sense. Červenka takes into account the general characteristics of language (sound, linearity), the hierarchy of objective language styles, 'possibilities and regularities of human perception' (Červenka 1992/1968: 119) and their changes due to technological advancements, the social status of both the creator and the audience, the set of other arts and the literary tradition itself. It is precisely in the context of these prior factors that we find the nucleus of interference between literature and other media systems, which also causes changes in the 'possibilities and regularities of human perception'.

The media perspective therefore indicates in which directions this theory needs to be advanced. It is necessary, first of all, to reconsider the dematerialization of the work, which is an attendant condition to using the concept of code (a concept that has been adapted from Saussurian linguistics). Not wanting to limit this concept to its purely technical manifestations (which is still, in any case, a *possible* solution), and with the intention of applying it to non-technical systems of conventions and correlations, we need suitable alternatives: an approach, for instance, by which 'communication precedes the code'. The materiality of the sign, as one of the substances underlying the semiotic form in literature, must then be included among the components and factors of perceiving the work. Drawing a sharp contrast between the material process of the work and those that give form to its semantic structure (perception) does not seem justified. These are no more than varying kinds of *mediating processes*. In other words, we must accept the possibility of closer interconnection and continuity of the distribution, reproduction and manipulation *function* of the medium, and the corresponding ways of dealing with it. Materiality is a more or less latent part of the sign processes within a work, while periods of rapid advancement in media give rise to a poetics that draws on materiality as a central feature of its semantic effects. We can even hypothesize (though it is outside the scope of this chapter) that such a process has certain regular features. (Cf. Chapter 10, pp. 341–2 and 350–1, as well as Section 2 in Chapter 1, esp. pp. 33–7.)

For Eco, it is not only the work that is open to the perceiver and to a unique encounter with him (and vice versa), but also the individual materials by virtue of a boundless plasticity in the hands of the artist. Yet Eco ultimately stops short of considering the logical consequences of this move, namely that these materials cannot be fully transposed from one to the other. With Červenka, the concept of dynamic semantic organization (from a certain point of view) sheds light on the media specificity of a literary work. However, this concept also comes up against its own limits concerning the capacity within literature for transformation vis-à-vis the activity of other media and arts.

When Eco (following the example of Meyer) interprets the set of perceptual dispositions as a set of reception channels, he sees a certain value in the discrepancy between two individual reception sets (the creator's and the perceiver's) as one of the characteristics of second-order openness. There are a number of implications of this conceptual shift: the ability to transform human perception by technical means; the concept of the human reception apparatus as the equivalent and partner of a technical device; and the possibility of understanding the communication circuit involving both man and machine by analogy to categories of the unified model.

Červenka's reconceptualization of the notion of a channel, which places it in the category of an extended code structure formed in a unique instance of the (literary) work, can be understood in two ways. On one hand, it is a way of delimiting (and reducing) the technical aspects of literary communication: the problem of the channel is thus confined to its original technical sense as it relates to the practical literary disciplines of textology and editology. On the other hand, it also addresses the 'vertical' layering of the elements of communication in the literary work and (re-)introduces the multidirectional process-oriented nature of individual acts of communication. In these terms, Červenka believes the literary work offers a particularly rich and representative instance in which the *insecurity* of communication is revealed, along with the potential semantic multidimensiality of an individual work, in this way reflecting the *world of communication in general.*

4. The Czech 'poetry of new consciousness' in the Information Age

While Czech poetry of the late 1950s and 1960s that came to be called 'experimental' did not take its only (or even primary) inspiration from foreign trends in concrete and experimental poetics, it was not long before it was taken up as a significant part of this international context. The global dimension of experimental poetry was related to the need, in the post–Second

World War era, for a new poetic language. But this should not obscure the fact that local (vernacular) conditions determine their own distinct views on what is essentially the same phenomenon, and lead to the formulation of somewhat different critical perspectives. Different aspects and genetic lines within experimental poetry are emphasized by different names, too: concrete poetry, visual poetry, poetry of new consciousness, lettrism, evident poetry, artificial poetry, systemic poetry, poetry of the objective model, and others. We will follow the convention of treating 'experimental' as a general term inclusive of visual, concrete, sound (phonic) and performative forms of experimentation (cf. Thiers 2016; Donguy 2007; Jackson, Vos and Drucker 1996; Hartung 1975). Where the word *concrete* is used in place of the general term, this is partly because of the influence of a previous movement in the fine arts (Theo van Doesburg, Max Bill), or in connection to (a clearer version of) its beginnings with Eugen Gomringer and the Brazilian group Noigandres (cf. Solt 1970: 7–16). But it is also because the term experiment can encompass all (historical and contemporary) tendencies in literature and the arts (including the avant-garde) that seek to transcend a broader range of conventions. The terms 'optical poetry' (Dencker 2011) and 'pattern poetry' (Higgins 1987) purposefully seek the continuity of visual poetry across the ages. Other critical approaches (including those collected in Schenk, Hultsch and Stašková 2016, for instance) trace the legacy of experimentation to Symbolism (especially Stéphane Mallarmé) and the avant-gardes (beginning with Marinetti, Apollinaire, Khlebnikov or Joyce), even if it contained a trend that aimed at a radical break from these legacies.

In the theoretical and practical subtext of some forms of experimentation, a significant role is played by the principles of information aesthetics, cybernetics and/or the mathematical model of communication. In these cases, works or installations are just as likely to absorb information-cybernetic ideas as to turn them ironically against themselves. To consider this experimentation as part of the extended context (and cultural foment) of cybernetic thinking and information theory on the one hand, and development of media and genealogy of media thinking on the other, causes it to appear in a particular light, and opens it to a particular approach for assessing its historical significance.

Certain research projects of the time represent another, parallel phenomenon. In 1966–7, for example, Jiří Levý and Karel Pala carried out a machine-generated poetry project at Brno University of Technology, the aim of which was to build the foundations of a generative grammar and poetics. In one form or another, various authors, including Vladimír Burda, Karel Milota, Ladislav Nebeský, Ladislav Novák, Jiří Valoch, Zdeněk Barborka and Emil Juliš, absorbed procedures and principles associated with the fields named above, or their applications – or, more tendentiously, a feel for their implications – and contributed to their practical, in some cases even theoretical (Valoch, Burda, Milota, Jirous) development. This also coincides with a more general tendency to supplement or integrate creations with a 'user manual'. Descriptions of procedure and discovered forms cease to play a mere supporting role and become integral to the creative gesture. Titles, similarly, are elevated vis-à-vis the work as a kind of cryptographic key.

The connection to experimental circles in Germany, Austria, Brazil, France, Japan and elsewhere was especially strengthened by the organizational, translation, editing and creative work of Bohumila Grögerová and Josef Hiršal. The same year (1967) that Emmett Williams's *An Anthology of Concrete Poetry* was published by Something Else Press in New York, two books were released in Prague (by Odeon Publishing House and Czechoslovak Writer): *Experimentální poezie* (Experimental Poetry), an anthology representing a broad range of international works, and *Slovo, písmo, akce, hlas* (Word, Letter, Action, Voice), a collection of neo-avant-garde and experimental art programmes and manifestos from around the world. In this way, certain international authors, groups and trends found an audience in Czechoslovakia, including the Stuttgart Group (e.g. Max Bense, Helmut Heißenbüttel, Reinhard Döhl, Franz Mon), Vienna Group (Gerhard Rühm, Hans Carl Artmann), Brazilian group Noigandres (e.g. Augusto and Haroldo de Campos, Décio Pignatari), French and Japanese Lettrism and Spatialism (Ilse and Pierre Garnier, Henri Chopin, Seiichi Niikuni), Eugen Gomringer, Dieter Roth (Diter Rot), Heinz Gappmayr, Siegfried J. Schmidt, Ferdinand Kriwet, Emmett Williams, and others.

A sense of crisis and cultural breakdown

The experimental tendencies in poetry (and the arts) of the late 1950s and 1960s can be generally defined by their readiness to treat the elements of existing expressive systems as mere materials designated for manipulation, or structural transgressions, or even the creation of new (ad hoc, single-use) systems. The basic defining features also include 'performativeness' (Winter 2010: 26).

In the specific context of Czech literary experimentation, we may also consider (like Astrid Winter) its ideological-political critical dimension. Typescript manipulation (as in Eduard Ovčáček's 'Výslech' (The Interrogation) and Václav Havel's pattern poems in *Antikódy*, 1964, Anticodes) could suggest the conditions of samizdat production, or carry political connotations. Renouncing the central instrument of poetry – i.e. language – and eventually its reduction or semantic transformation could point to the 'everyday schizophrenia of language' (Winter 2010: 27). Representatives of Czech experimental poetry were also united by the fact that they turned their backs on the defiled ranks of civic and engaged poetry. The absence of a jointly formulated programme or unified collective direction also indicates a distance from the connotations associated with the term 'neo-avant-garde', though Czech experimental poets sometimes claimed to be associated with this as well (due partly to their connections with foreign groups); in this way, certain lines of experimental work acquired the signs of a group effort (cf. Hiršal and Grögerová 2007).

With its non-conformist artistic credo and critical attitude, Czech experimental literature of this time came up against the limits of its marginal position in the cultural field, including more limited possibilities for distribution. These same factors, however, gave it a more avant-garde status (exceeding that of its creative intention), and charged it with a stronger ethos of protest, and this in turn gave it significant power to raise major polemics on the essence of poetry. Typescript and Cyclostyle duplication, for example, could be used to suggest the circulation of samizdat – or, more significantly, the entire bureaucratic apparatus and predominance of predetermined (and pre-printed) communication forms and contents, which was *already a more general condition*.

Thus, from the perspective of media development, artistic and literary experimentation might very well aim beyond – or in other directions than – critique of the centrally controlled collectivist society. 'Bourgeois' and 'socialist' poet alike experienced the banalization of language on a daily basis.[18] They thus shared a common feeling that the end – or a turning point – was imminent, that there was a need to disrupt the illusion of universality inherent to linear perspective, and that a *deliberate acceleration* of the *decline* of the existing expressive systems would result in a freeing up of their cultural connotations. Experimentalists and the (second) avant-garde also shared a belief in the need for a world community, notwithstanding their frequent difficulties in understanding one another. In spite of significant differences, the various (neo)avant-garde and experimental directions in the 'West' and 'East' were also confronted with something that was considered a problem on a more common, general level, and which can be better understood precisely from the perspective of media development. To a considerable extent, what 'is now historically called the last international neo-avant-garde' (Grögerová 1997: 21) shared a common socio-critical and ethical horizon.

Inherent problems of media classification

There is a fundamental difficulty posed by classifying these experimental tendencies in terms of their media identity and according to an aesthetic-ideological typology. Such designations as visual, concrete, evident poetry or poetry of new consciousness call to mind a taxonomic identification with literature, even if literature was used only as a source or target system. Other approaches made use of several media systems at once (including music and visual arts, for example), or worked with the connections on various levels that these systems share in common. In some cases, they focused on certain elements or parts in isolation, or something that transcended any one system as such. The word 'poetry' itself may point to an older discourse ('comparison of the arts') or to older philosophical traditions. But it could also be a confusion of terms, or a deliberate and ironic displacement from its appropriate context. Kolář's *chiasmage* works, for example, are made by (mis)applying the figure of 'chiasmus' to one or more printed sources (texts in various scripts, as well as sheet music, star maps, chessboards, etc.). By multiplying the chiasmatic principle, combining a multitude of cut-outs from numerous sources, the 'chiasmata' are emptied of their symmetry, and the merger of content and form is turned inside out (see Figure 6.2). In his object poems, as in the photographs and photograms of Běla Kolářová, we find the application of verse and rhetorical principles: poetic etymology and paronomasia, for example, in the case of objects that appear incidentally to be of the same 'root' (origin, shape, purpose). In Běla Kolářová's photography cycle *Abeceda věcí* (1964, Alphabet of Things), analogies based on shape (meter, hook nail, folding knife, try square, pin with joint) take on a metaphorical character; similar relationships, however, are established at the level of the phonetic alphabet character. At the same time – and more importantly, perhaps – the differential features of these figures blur and shift. In visually similar objects (e.g. a button and a stopper), how can we recognize the difference between, on the one hand, metaphor and metonymy (a metaphorical connection provoked by similarity of shape, or metonymic analogy of purpose) and, on the other, paronomasia and poetic etymology? In the subjects that wander in (and out) of 'evident poetry', what might correspond to paronomasia or other relationships based on word form, or to the articulation of basic (sound and graphic) elements? Is it not the case that the poems in question bring to mind the fact that objects are not articulated in the same way as words, that their ideal 'etymology' and genesis, and so on can hardly be identified?

On the basis of his previous literary practice, Kolář also adapts into an idiosyncratic visual expression that which the reproductive systems of writing and notation have long provided to human civilizations: the possibility of multiple articulations. This procedure paradoxically sheds light on the notational systems explicitly or implicitly referenced, including their pathos, and imbues them with an unprecedented ambiguity (cf. Figure 6.2).

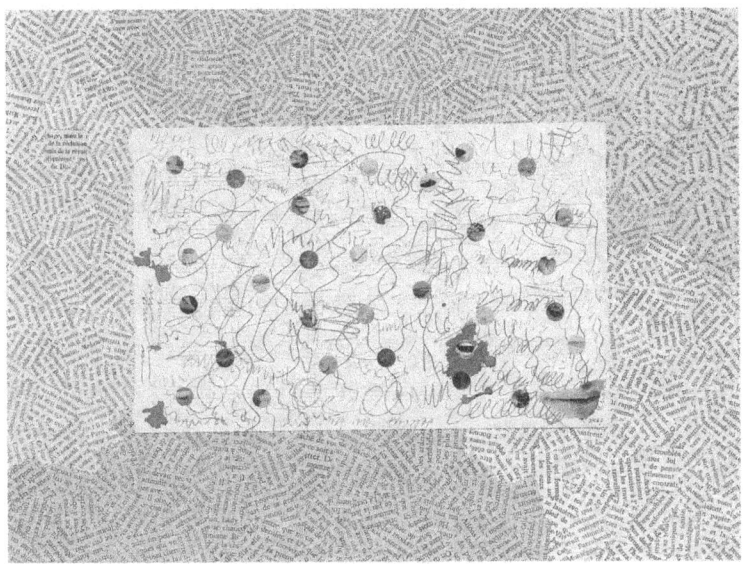

Figure 6.2 Jiří Kolář: *Sólo pro kuličkové pero* (Solo for a Ballpoint Pen), 1982, collage (chiasmage, music sheet), 30 × 40 cm.

The experiments we have discussed here that most took their inspiration from statistical-cybernetic thinking (cf. Hlaváček 2007: 233) tended to 'move more above all systems', although the degree to which the connotations of the original systems or levels came into play varied. We might find a combinatorial game with linguistic expressions, both semantic and non-semantic, or typographical elements and various machine types. Elsewhere, chains of propositions might be arranged according to a certain algorithm, or words and graphic characters distributed into spatial constellations. Error and deviation, programmed or incidental, were common elements. Another similar *information-transmedia* approach was taken by implementing a specific algorithm that performed a coding operation. An operational procedure might include (as in Ladislav Nebeský's works, collected in Nebeský 2022a/1964–72) an elementary code (paradigm), rules for combination and, finally, implementation level (syntagm). The texts then directly provide their key, encouraging not to read, but to decipher the formal procedure and verify its successful execution. These experiments in artificial codes applied to language and its connotations, suggest at times that these connotations cling to words by force of some invisible law, and at other times that they are completely arbitrary. This produces a kind of text that generally tends to refer

```
t š    k ý é    ě r ě č    v g b e z v ě ý é ý
  t̛ t    l z ě    f ř f ď    y h c é ž y f z ě z
    u t̛    m ž f    g s g ď    ý i č ě a ý g ž f ž
      ú u    n a g    h š h e    z í d f á z h a g a
        ů ú    ň á h    i t i é    ž j ď g b ž i á h á
          v ů    o b i    í t̛ í ě    a k e h c a í b i b
            y v    ó c í    j u j f    á l é i č á j c í
              ý y    p č j    k ú k g    b m ě í d b k č
                z ý    r d k    l ů l h    c n f j ď c l
                  ž z    ř ď l    m v m i    č ň g k e č
                    a ž    s e m    n y n í    d o h l é
                      á a    š é n    ň ý ň j    ď ó i m ě ď
                        b á    t ě ň    o z o k    e p í n f e o
                      c b    t̛ f o    ó ž ó l    é r j ň g é ó f
                    č c    u g ó    p a p m    ě ř k o h ě p g ó
                  d č    ú h p    r á r n    f s l ó i f r h p h
                ď d    ů i r    ř b ř ň    g š m p í g ř i r i
              e ď    v í ř    s c s o    h t n r j h s í ř í
            é e    y j s    š č š ó    i t̛ ň ř k i š j s j
          ě é    ý k š    t d t p    í u o s l í t k š k
        f ě    z l t    t̛ ď t̛ r    j ú ó š m j t̛ l t l
```

Figure 6.3 Ladislav Nebeský: from the collection *Zaplňování prázdna* (Filling the Void), 2007.

to its own conversion into code, and *ipso facto* carries itself out, causing a kind of short-circuit between its communicative and meta-communicative levels.

In Nebeský's poem from *Zaplňování prázdna* (Filling the Void, 2022b/2007: 126; see Figure 6.3), diagonal strings of letters in alphabetical order are arranged in a chevron shape, which provides a hint for deciphering the device in bold that runs across the middle – *až sem nyní dohlé[dneme]* ('as far as we can s[ee]') – and which also points to itself as if to the result of the 'process' of the calligram as a whole. It is a miniature example of the birth of order from chaos, one that may also express the limits of our insight into this process ('as far' meaning 'not very far at all').

Typographic experimentation led at times to the abstraction of letters to strokes, lines and colours. Tongue-in-cheek references to non-European written cultures resulted in the creation of new writing systems, with elements of ideograms, pictograms and phonetic alphabets, as well as picture-writing, pseudo-writing and '*quipu* poems' (made of knotted strings). Works based on artificial 'analphabetic' recording systems could take on the character of 'poetry without writing' while also borrowing from the concept of poetry as the highest of creative activities (Kolář), thus situating themselves in a long idealistic tradition of aesthetics and discussions on art. Connections to art (and poetry) were at times dominated by philosophical or cultural-historical and anthropological motivations and associations: the disruption of linear perspective and other perceptual schemes, meanings and values associated with (especially Western) writing cultures, or the feeling of being assailed by impersonal catastrophic forces.

Josef Honys's creations record 'hypnagogic visions' induced by overstrain or psychoactive mushrooms – images conceived on the border between sleep and wakefulness (Honys 2011: 326–30). His drawing *Rozvoj vize* (c. 1964–1968, The Development of Vision), for example, is a simulation of the changing phases, or 'hypnomes', of such a vision: amidst the bizarre metamorphosing shapes, embryonic and fragmentary, the shape-changing representations of what could be masks, animals, people, alien organisms or torture machines, the letter *e* seems to emerge (and disappear) (Honys 2011: 78; see Figure 6.4). The link to

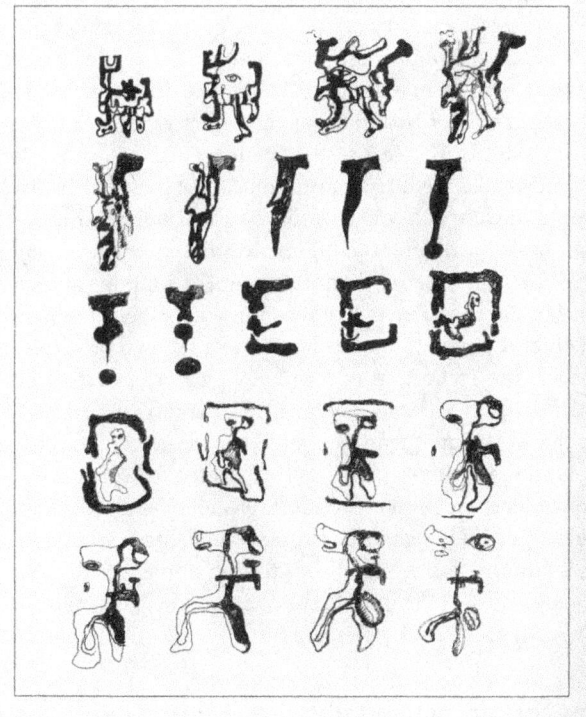

Figure 6.4 Josef Honys: *Rozvoj vize* (The Development of Vision), c. 1964–8, ink drawing, 29.8 × 21.8 cm, private collection in Prague.

the human subject is evidently key here, but not necessarily the *individual*; a necessary precondition of the 'laboratory' nature of Honys's procedure is the relinquishment of rational safeguards. In a series of letters from 1965, where Honys analyses his working method, the importance of medial motivations is unmistakable. He searches for a common basis uniting different sense stimuli and ideas, trying to solve their transposition and the problem of the delay between a 'vision' and its recording (Honys 2011: e.g. 329–30).

In the case of phonic poetry (closely related to the experimentation, described earlier, of the composer Luciano Berio), Ladislav Novák aimed at the creation of a mixed and balanced media form (see Novák 2017: 667). Novák mainly builds on the work of Pierre Garnier, Henri Chopin and Franz Mon.

The targeted pursuit of mixed forms largely prevents us from subordinating individual works to any established initial or final media system. Works can use a form from one media system as basis of expression in another (in Zdeněk Barborka's 'fugues', for example, words or phrases take on the 'syntax' of musical themes in a certain genre or specific composition), or else express a synaesthetic impression through the discovery of a mixed system. The expressive gesture may be carried out as a function of the indefinite space between media or materials, or their interference, or it may draw on materials or media aspects (e.g. visual or audio) with measured disregard for their systemic 'media identity'; on the contrary, it may forcibly isolate them, bring them to the fore and convey a sense of their improper use.

Another basis for differentiation involves the theoretical assumptions of the work in question: whether or not it assumes a unifying authorial subject; whether it implies the existence of a continuous (albeit fragmentary) inner world; whether it points to the realization of a rational principle, or instead to a *parody* of the realization of a principle, or to the actual horizon of a world which is irreducible to any 'principle' or formal analysis; whether it insists on the work's uniqueness or intends precisely for it to be replicated. Similarly, works may be classified by the degree to which they involve an element of chance, the level on which it is applied and the extent to which it is predetermined: total chance (entropy), simulated or controlled chance, chance as an internal principle of the creation of the world, or as part of its representation. This corresponds to the phases of mediality and its modalities (see Chapter 11, pp. 412–15).

Different conceptual and ideational sources and goals

It follows from the previous discussion that the experimental work of the 1950s and 1960s borrowed – both consciously and unconsciously – from the legacy of first avant-gardes (Dadaism, Futurism, Poetism and Surrealism). Various new directions – *Art informel*, abstract expressionism, Lettrism, Neo-Dada, Fluxus, op art, the Situationist International, Constructivism and Neo-Constructivism – also differed from one another in the extent to which they diverged from this legacy, or even the degree to which they 'erased' it from memory.

The interdisciplinary scientific tendencies traced above had their most decisive influence on those directions in art represented by the 'mathematical' and concrete art of Max Bill, information aesthetics of Max Bense and work of the Stuttgart Group. As a conceit, the 'statistical' approach and its scientific aspirations created a certain tension that is best illustrated by the ironic resistance with which it occasionally met – on the part of the Situationists or *Oulipo*, for instance. In 1959, the German Section of the Situationists announced a Bense lecture in Munich, where the audience was played a message from a cassette player, informing them that the author would not speak in person but in 'cybernetic form'; the recording then produced a nonsensical polyphony of phrases in various languages (German, French and Latin), with garbled quotations of Hegel and Marx.

The influence of the information-cybernetic context on the experimental work can be determined by comparing it to certain works of the first avant-garde based on aleatoric principles and the de-semanticization of language. In 'Pour faire un poème dadaïste' (1920, How to Make a Dadaist Poem), for example, Tristan Tzara recommends cutting the words from a newspaper article of the same length as the intended poem and randomly recombining its elements. At first glance, Tzara's method closely resembles the stochastic procedures of later anti-traditionalists, typically carried out without the use of any technical device. With the latter, however, technically automated operations were singled out as a pattern to follow, and the process was not supposed to point to the personality of the originator (not even in an uncontrolled manner). Tzara, by contrast, ends with the dictum (however ironic it may be) 'The poem will resemble you' ('Le poème vous ressemblera'; Tzara 1963: 64). At precisely those moments when the experiment exposes the code and reaches the level of manipulating it, when the code is destroyed and reconstituted, or when the simulation of chance simulates in turn the operation of an impersonal, technical programme – or yet other moments when, in 'dialectical opposition', the exposure of the manipulation of the material, devoid of *a priori* meaning or suddenly equipped only with the symptom of a mute cultural artefact, aims at reality itself – that the connection to the information and cyber 'revolution' becomes unavoidable (in both the positive and negative sense). Language and operational instructions meet on a new level, where they can be bent to new goals: for language, this means (control of) control; for technical code, this means communication (recall Wiener's 'control and communication in the animal and the machine'). Speech and code exchange places – with the implication, however, that language and program code are both artificial constructs.

For a certain element of experimental work in both the Czech and international contexts the crucial difference was that, for the first time, in its conceit, the work was formed by a human creator standing side by side with a machine as an equal partner in all respects.

This same conceit can be found in a certain notion of *reproduction*. With his *Calligrams*, Apollinaire was responding to a crisis in the traditional form of the printed poetic text caused by the rapid rise of new technical media – the phonograph and film – and anticipating the changes that poetic composition would undergo under their influence. The reproducibility of formal procedures in works by the experimentalists of the second half of the twentieth century is of a different kind; its social consequences are ambiguous, and it seems to anticipate the media universality of the computer. It also opens new perspectives on the dialectic of repeatability and singularity. The singularity of the message is denied, paradoxically, by inventing a code that is unique; the repeatability of the code, meanwhile, is called into question by its disintegration, from which a new message emerges.

In connection to this, a new concept of the poetic figure manifests itself. Here, the repeatable constellation of speech material does not (primarily) aim to achieve rhetorical goals, emotional impact, the establishment of rhythm and so on, but is taken beyond its extreme limit to a kind of 'accepted inhumanity': a dehumanizing gesture by which the human individual *humanizes technics at the cost of dehumanizing his or her own speech and self-image.*

We may identify one more specific feature in this context. In the long history of visual poetry – from the figures of Simmias of Rhodes to Baroque meditative calligrams, up to the calligrammatic devices of Apollinaire and Marinetti (see Langerová 2002) – the gesture does tend to avoid a deliberate *contradiction* between form and contents, i.e. between the figure of the poem and its theme. Whatever connotations may be conveyed by the image (a secret language, cipher, esoteric meaning or pun), these works typically involved an *analogy* between the shape of the composition and the subject of the message. In contrast to this: in Havel's Anticodes, the word *vpřed* (forward) is repeated in the form of a circle (parodying the official discourse of progress); in Valoch's *a/z* (1964), the macroform of a capital *Z* is created from the letter *a* (juxtaposing the extreme positions of an entire orthographic system); Běla Kolářová's *Dva čtverce* (1963, Two Squares) features square cut-outs of light drawings of concentric circles (the trace of the medium – light – thus becomes 'meaning', and the relationship between form and content is relativized); Nebeský's *bílý čtverec na bílém pozadí* (1965, white square on a white background) shows a square of blank white paper on the background of a grid formed by the multiplied letters of the word 'white' (an 'empty' content thus emerges between the letters or lines, against the background of that which is written, etc.); Honys's *Humanita* (mid-1960s, Humanitas) presents the image of a skull (perhaps the *memento mori* of an 'alphabetic person') out of the constellation and condensation of typograms in combination with the surface of a blank piece of paper. This process of internal contradiction has parallels (even if fewer) outside the context of the former Eastern Bloc.

In Max Bense's thoughts on artificial poetry, his belief (not unjustifiably) is that the link to the (traditionally conceived) lyrical subject is dissolved, and that this weakens, if not eliminates, the construction of the represented world: 'neither a lyrical I nor fictional epic world can be meaningfully deduced from the linguistic fixing of this poetry. Thus, while for natural poetry an intentional beginning of the semantic process is characteristic, for artificial poetry, there can only be a material origin' (Bense 1967/1962: 121). Even accepting this negation, however, it does not mean all intentionality in the work, all relationship to a human consciousness disappears, which equally applies to the difficulty of 'switching' the positions of author and reader, however analogous they might be. One might say, in fact, that the meta-communicative dimension of the text is thereby strengthened: a commentary on the possibility of transcending existing languages and established spaces of meaning.

Machine poetry and the construction of scienticity: The meaning effect

In case it was not made clear in the preceding argument, let us state explicitly that a certain current within experimental poetry made use of formal and statistical methods (partly inspired by computer processing) in order to convey to these works a certain 'scienticity', by way of approximate parallels and associations borrowed from the scientific context and connected with the possibilities of approaching the text mathematically. At the same time, the statistical implications often left unnoticed the way a source text was selected, the manner in which it was adapted or the associations and connotations it carried outside the context of computer processing, specifically in terms of its perception by the reader and associated effects. (While we have seen that some of the findings associated with the logarithmic approach have led to the modelling of perceptual processes, none of the representatives of experimental poetry, as far as I know, ever dealt with this topic in any detail.) Indeed, these works characteristically took as their subject the application of predetermined and 'rational' procedures that were adapted continuously and in improvised fashion with regard to the effect and meaning of the text.

It could be argued that there was at least one field in which mathematical and statistical processes were not merely approximate, a field moreover in which concrete, verifiable results were actually produced, namely machine-generated and computer-generated poetry. In spite of this – or indeed because of it – these examples seem to support our earlier observations, and compel us to consider what aspects of *communication* they involve.

The earliest case of computer-generated poetry is considered to be the result of a programming experiment by Theo Lutz, a pupil and collaborator of Max Bense at the Technische Hochschule Stuttgart (Lutz studied mathematics, electronics and physics in Stuttgart and Tübingen). An example of the computer-generated text resulting from Lutz's experiment was published in the journal *Augenblick*, an important platform for information-aesthetic thinking and various (more or less) related lines of experimentation. Lutz's article 'Stochastiche Texte', including an example of computer-generated text, appeared in the first issue of 1959. His intention was not to publish a work of 'programmed poetry', but simply to show that automatic computational operations could be applied to language and used for linguistic analysis. He had at his disposal the seventh of Konrad Zuse's computers, the Zuse Z22. Lutz created his 'stochastic text' with the use of a random generator (*Zufallsgenerator*), inputting binary-encoded nouns and adjectives (sixteen of each) from Kafka's novel *The Castle* into the memory cells (*Gedächtniszelle*) and adding a number of articles and pronouns to the program. He also set the basic syntactic form of a single line of verse as two short sentences connected by one of three possible conjunctions – *und*, *oder* and *so gilt* – plus a full stop, and set the frequency with which these would appear (the full stop was five times more likely to appear than each of the conjunctions). Aside from these predetermined settings, the text was processed entirely 'stochastically' – that is, with an even distribution of probabilities of occurrence. In this way, Lutz (1959) imposed a kind of simple syntactic matrix on the text, resulting in sentences like: *Nicht jeder Blick ist nah. Kein Dorf is spaet. / Ein Schloss ist frei und jeder Bauer is fern.* (Not every look is near. No village is late. / A castle is free and every farmer is far.)[19]

Lutz has the remarkable foresight to understand, even in such a rudimentary generative mechanism, that the statistical introduction of uneven distribution into the parent text is enough in itself to produce the impression of meaning. If the number of particular words in the matrix increases and a minimum probability threshold is set for the connection of nouns with predicates, a kind of semantic structure corresponding to the uneven distribution and different frequencies of words in the parent text will arise as well in the randomly generated text.

Lutz does not use the word 'poem' or 'poetry' anywhere. It is evident, however, that the resulting text conveys a certain 'meaning effect'. Lutz's very choice of source text carries significant connotations, and it is no coincidence that he settled on a work that figures among the most important modernist novels of the German literary canon by an author whose attitude to technics should be seen as very ambiguous. (The strategy resembles certain combinatorial techniques carried out in the field of experimental poetry, as well as tactics used to this day by those working in the field of computer-generated poetry to lend an air of legitimacy to their results.) We see then that the intentionality of the text does not disappear; it has merely been displaced. But how to define this meaning effect? If we read the text as a literary work (and not simply with the aim of verifying how it has been processed), we find that the intimate sense of strangeness experienced by K. as portrayed in the novel has effectively been doubled; it is itself estranged and reduced to a randomly generated series of words signalling its disconnection from the original situation and the protagonist's world. The aleatoric quality of the resulting automated 'incantation' – or, what is the same, the high-entropy selection of words from the source text – evokes a sense of repetitiveness, a symptom of meaning. (This is, after all, both a recurring theme in Kafka's work and – more rarely – a characteristic of his own narrative method.) We may consider also that from a West German perspective, the work of a Prague writer would have evoked certain political connotations, along lines of the Western 'critique of totalitarianism', while in the context of the Czechoslovak Socialist Republic, Kafka had come to represent exactly the kind of 'bourgeois' and 'pessimistic' author officially rejected by the institutions of the communist regime. The first Czech translation (by Pavel Eisner) of Kafka's novel *The Trial* had just been published in 1958, and in 1963 a prominent conference on the author's works in Liblice would soon spark heated debate and ideological loggerheads.

All this, of course, would influence the 'communication situation' of the publication of Lutz's scientific demonstration in an anthology of experimental poetry put together by Josef Hiršal and Bohumila Grögerová under the title – inspired by Mallarmé's seminal poem – *Vrh kostek: česká experimentální poezie* (A Throw of the Dice: Czech Experimental Poetry). In 1968, however, as part of the political fallout of the August occupation, the Obelisk publishing house was prevented from releasing the book, and over the next quarter century it would circulate only within a restricted circle of acquaintances before finally being published in 1993. We can see how this too – the circumstances of its non-publication – generates new possibilities for the meaning of Lutz's text. Hiršal and Grögerová, presenting the results of Lutz's experiment as a 'stochastic machine text' alongside an (anonymous) excerpt of his own commentary, implicitly express a certain theoretical view on the notion of authorial instance, leaving aside all discussion of the fact that the text they present is not 'strictly programmed' but instead a Czech translation of Lutz's results (Hiršal – Grögerová 1993/1968: 312). Without calling attention to the fact, they have carried out several additional 'generative operations' on the process Lutz describes. In their adapted version, with deference to the creative potential of the process, the list of 'logical operators' is augmented (adding 'if . . . then', 'if not . . . then'), and additional changes are made to accommodate the specific characteristics of Czech syntax: freer word order, various ways to form the negative and non-existence of the indefinite article. While Lutz is exceedingly precise in the description accompanying the text (he calculates 4,174,304 combinatorial possibilities), the changes made by Hiršal and Grögerová undercut this precision, omitting several details of the original algorithm (e.g. determination of grammatical gender). The result of these global shifts in the communication situation, as a function of both the text itself and the context of its reception, naturally produces far-reaching shifts in the meaning effects of the 'stochastic' experiment.

We thus see among various elements of the neo-avant-garde the hope that artistic experimentation might push the boundaries of scientific knowledge, just as it had in the Renaissance. Along with euphoria, we can imagine they proceeded with a slightly guilty conscience that the initiative is not fully their own in the conditions of current technical civilization. Still, they were able – more or less serendipitously, as a kind of by-product of their efforts – to broaden our understanding of the various mechanisms of human communication by distorting and transforming the more exact (scientific) models to the point where they were unrecognizable. And while they themselves believed to have liberated communication systems by merging them with contemporary scientific and technical knowledge, and by moving them to the field of artistic experimentation, we might say that the result of their efforts was a material more suitable for the discovery of the gaps and limits in information-statistical models of communication.

New modes of reading and perception

With some experimental works, what is presented to the reader is not a single final text but a series: several successive versions of the same text at different stages of its development. This is how Zdeněk Barborka, for example, understands his *processual texts* (included in Barborka 2018). The semantic process might equally engage the configuration of the text on the page, calling for a different, spatial perception of meaning (this is already the case with Eugen Gomringer's *constellations*). This would also suggest the need for a new form of reading, another way to pass through the text, not limited to – or indeed avoiding – a linear movement from beginning to end. In Ladislav Novák's early constellations, for instance, we may look for deviations in the columns or rows of words, and from there try to understand how these deviations relate to the title and theme of the poem. The reader's gaze, as it leaps from one part of the text to another, seems closer here to that of a viewer seeking to visually reconstruct an object, flying from one point to another as it seeks to grasp the whole (as shown by Aumont 1997: 40, for example). At the same time, the 'process' of the gaze seems to imitate the more complex, multi-level and back-and-forth manner in which complex meaning is constructed and gradually projected in the act of reading (as Iser conceives of it; see Chapter 11, Appendix 2, pp. 364–6). Semantics begins to behave visually, 'roving around', while the visual process seems to adapt to the need of reconstructing verbal meaning; a multiple, asymmetrical matrix arises, alienating the acts of reading and seeing in the usual manner.

When we are presented with a text in various stages of disintegration (what Barborka calls *reductions*), a reading from the end suggests itself, confronting these various stages, trying to grasp the logic or dynamics of the text's disintegration. As noted above, the description of the method also becomes part of the creation and affects the way in which it is read. In those cases where we are searching for the logic of a method or procedure (when the description is missing, or only indicated by the title, or perhaps not preserved), we read differently, fleetingly, skipping from here to there, looking for signs and traces of a logic. Conversely, if we already know the method or have already come to discover it (a special code for the composition of a poem may be established 'on the side', as with Nebeský), we may seek instead to verify the method of its application through a systematic reading.

In those kinds of texts that Barborka calls 'penetrage' (*penetráž*), two sections of text gradually merge, one placed at the beginning, the other, at the end, with various stages of their merging in between. One way to read such a text – the 'perceptually friendly strategy' – is through a reconstructive reading of both extreme sections one after the other, followed by a selective 'scanning' of the transitional phases. Textual interstices are not (easily) readable in a linear sense; instead, we are led to look for seams between words (new formations can arise) and sections. At other times – when words are distributed on the page according to a certain principle – these strategies may be associated with spatial perception, an approach suitable to Barborka's *fugues*, for example, or Heißenbüttel's poem 'kommen Möwen Schwänne und Tauben auch an Seen' (1964, gulls, swans and pigeons also come to lakes).

As a result – and this insight would be valid for a broad range of experimental tendencies – what is important here is not interpretation in the traditional sense, or the dynamics of the semantic gesture, but a message that concerns the relationship between tradition and the new age: the metacommunicative aspect of the work, the need to 'say it differently'. Indeed, what is emerging at this stage is a whole new concept of intentionality, along with a new dynamics proper to it, in relation to that which opposes it (unintentionality). This would then confirm that the concept of the semantic gesture – the fluid and increasingly complex dynamics of building meaning, as we talked about with Mukařovský in Chapter 5 – loses its footing in these contexts. In its place arises a different, non-gestural intentionality, along with a new kind of tension between intentionality and chance.

5. The information (cybernetics) moment from the perspective of experimental poetry (and vice versa)

In the context of experimental poetry, a new conception of subjectivity as well as that of text and reading emerges. Its novelty does not lie in the representation of a world that is insurmountably heterogeneous and fragmentary (which, in the end, does not say much), but rather in the fact that the reader is led to a certain intermittent perception and multi-phase process of confrontation and evaluation. However, the emphasis here is not necessarily on interpretation, as Eco maintains, especially insofar as we take this, in more traditional terms, to mean the more or less virtuosic act of making sense of a text.

Experimental works might well call for new systematizing and compare-and-contrast modes of reading, perhaps even – long before the emergence of the internet and media platforms for dispersed communication – non-linear skimming and scanning. Long before the emergence of media platforms designed to provoke and condition similar modes of reception, the 1950s and 1960s experimentation seems to have predicted and actively anticipated them. Unlike the reading practices that would later develop around social networks and internet communication, these experimental works were characterized by artistic gravity, encouraged repeat readings and aimed to lay bare – not only to the eye but also to the very threshold of consciousness – *the new conditions of communication*.

The advent of mechanical printing and dissemination of literature in the early modern period established certain boundaries and gave rise to certain concepts that were then projected into both the past and the future. The conditions of such literary system, from the perspective of literary semiotics, included: the linearity of the text, secondary status of the graphic system, and idealization of the aural (or phonological) nature of the literary artefact and various kinds of discourse (narrators, characters) that make up the text. At the same time that Červenka was formulating his distinctly monomedia-oriented conception of the meaning process of the literary text, works were being created in the field of literature that took these conditions into account. These were works created not only in the context of the experimental poetics itself, but of wider changes in the cultural and media landscape, significantly wider than any one national culture. Contemporary forms of 'inter-field' experimentation had encouraged a very different conceptualization of both reading and the relationship between the text and its originator.

Červenka's *The Semantic Organization of a Work of Literature* is, however, one of the most noteworthy and truly modern theories of the literary work as communication. Not only does it absorb the latest findings in information science, it brilliantly adapts them. Paradoxically, the prototype of the literary work on which he builds his argument is 'traditionally modern' in its conceit, a work that is predominantly representational in its relation to the world. This is in contrast to that element of literary production of the period that had decisively turned its back on the 'represented world' and 'inner consciousness' of the text, even with the practical consequence of a certain 'overflow' or 'information overload' (Leonard Meyer), and of an 'avant-garde aristocracy' or 'neo-capitalist conversion' (Umberto Eco) – or, as in Czechoslovakia, the social marginalization and political persecution of its authors.

Keeping this context in mind, how to evaluate experimental literature from the perspective of media development? To the extent that the literary work was conceived as a meaning-forming whole, a unified structure of concentrated sense,[20] we might consider the rapid development and appeal of visual and concrete poetry at the time in terms of its *resistance* to this conception of the work or as the moment of its opening up and the 'birth' of the reader. From yet another perspective, experimental literature aimed above all to intensify the mediality of the text. The point was not however to renounce 'the sense of sense', as can be seen from the emphasis in post-avant-garde experimental literature on the title and description of method. Similarly, the concept of the text as a free play of codes to which the reader should be open (as in Barthes's *S/Z*, for instance) implies, rather than the renunciation of sense, an essentially intertextual concept of culture. Such a concept is a media legacy of print culture, to which the experimental work, rather than confirming, lends evidence of disintegration and decline. Intertextual play takes place at the level of syntactic recombination rather than deep semantic transformations – the recognition of a signal presupposes that a relationship joins pre-text and post-text without for that matter demanding any extensive interpretive operations. (A concise example of this difference can be found in the multi-level connection of Joyce's *Odyssey* to Homer's epic, on the one hand, and use of Joyce's *A Portrait of the Artist as a Young Man*, on the other, as source material for programmed random selection in the experiment by Josef Hiršal and Bohumila Grögerová.)[21] But what role is played by the intermedia nature of experimental literature and artistic works? We have observed that visualization has returned in the history of writing (not only literature) and that mediality is a characteristic of all human creation, as it is generally of man's relationship to the world insofar as it could be described as 'artificial' or undetermined. Considering the ambiguity of mediality, experimental literature becomes part of the retreat of the cultural rationale for a conception of the work that is medium of condensed meaning. The need for a new conception of the work can be interpreted as a structural response (in the sense of 'structural pairing') to the competing characteristics of communication provided in the contexts of the moving image (film, television) and effective information circulation in the media. At the same time, it seems to corresponds to the need for 'new consciousness' and new senses – and their poetry – in an environment characterized by the intense experience of the fragmentation of meaning, the scattering of minds and bodies, but also by new and emergent realities.

A new feeling? One that would correspond to the form of *chiasmage*, in this case made up of scraps of people and recordings, like so many sound bites played-back and interrupted, collapsible and decomposable pieces, as it were, of man and his 'things'. Or perhaps the feeling of a change of consciousness prompted by a 'dawning' of new conditions (not only) of perception, which should have been obvious to John Glenn or Gherman Titov, peering back from Earth orbit, if not to everyone who shared this perspective vicariously.

If the foregoing analysis set out from the question what the contribution was of the line inspired by information science, and how it differed from other forms of experimental poetry, we might now summarize our answers as follows. To begin with, it involved the 'acceptance of inhumanity', the liberation from all anthropomorphic connotations associated with the links that make up the chain of communication. The act of creation was to consist (only) in the generation of signals and signs drawn from existing source materials, the application of rules, the programming of random output within the limits given by an automated method. The text was considered to be an ongoing operational process, or result of transparent programmed operations; the act of perception like that of reading would be likened to the work of a 'reception apparatus', balancing the information levels of different layers and lines; language was treated as a technical code and code as a type of language. In reality, the new orientation created tensions not only in the context of experimental literature, but within particular works in the first place, insofar as these were created and perceived by real people. After all, neither Červenka nor Eco rid himself of the assumption that the text establishes an important relationship with the creative and perceiving subject and one like the other contributed significantly to the field of communication theory. As we have seen in the case of Lutz's 'scientific' experiment, even machine-generated poetry failed to present itself as purely technical or break free from processes associated with 'natural' codes (connotation, for instance) and subjective 'operations'. It is precisely these tensions that make the information and cybernetics moment in experimental poetry so suggestive, in the same way that its 'dead ends', to this day, seem above all to indicate new starting points and affordances.

Notes

1 Umberto Eco, *Arte programmata* (1962: 18); Miroslav Červenka, *Významová výstavba literárního díla* (1992/1968: 139); **Figure 6.1** Hans G. Markert: Rectangle, square, 1964, concrete poem (in Hiršal and Grögerová 1967: 142); Jiří Kolář, *Slovník metod* (1999: 84).
2 Daniel Lagache, whom Jakobson quotes, defines 'verbal hallucination' by a loss of alertness, anguish, alienation of one's own speech and its attribution to an alter, and a close circumscription of space.
3 See, for example, Kline: 'Where Are the Cyborgs in Cybernetics?' (2009), or Hayles 1999; see also further on the divergent ways of thinking about the relationship between information and entropy.
4 An English translation was published in 1989 (Harvard University Press, trans. A. Cancogni), but we have decided not to use this edition here and all quotations have been translated directly from the Italian original.
5 Insofar as cybernetics was concerned with the whole circuit of communication, it might have seemed appropriate to describe not only the outgoing message but the response as well as part of such system.
6 The term 'zero-order approximation' refers to a situation in which the transition probability of a symbol (discrete sign) is evenly distributed and the symbols are independent of one another. A 'first-order approximation' is when symbols occur independently of one another, but with the same frequency with which they appear in texts in a certain language. 'Second-

order' (digram) is when the first character is random and determines the subset from which the next symbol is selected. 'Third-order' (trigram) is when the third letter is selected from the set determined by the sequence of the first two, and so on. Shannon found that at the level of the trigram, the text began to more closely resemble a text in a certain language. An important, and sometimes overlooked, assumption is the use of quantifiable pre-existing texts (even Shannon talks about approximation to a language instead of text) and their conversion to a *single set*. Shannon gives the following example of a third-order approximation in English: 'IN NO IST LAT WHEY CRATICT FROURE BIRS GROCID PONDENOME OF DEMONSTURES OF THE REPTAGIN IS REGOACTIONA OF CRE' (Shannon and Weaver 1964/1949: 43). Texts can be generated by using word transition probabilities in an analogous manner (Shannon and Weaver 1964/1949: 42, 43).

7   Terry Jo Duperrault was the only survivor of the murder of the crew of the Bluebelle and her immediate family, and spent almost four days and nights in a cork float in the Bahamas. On the third day, she fell into fits of unconscious and delusion, talking continuously. Taking this motif as their framework, the authors of the play represent her speech according to a Shannon approximation process in nine steps, gradually bringing phonetic material closer to real speech (an existing text written in German). As the authors write: 'The fact that there are certain analogies between the initially unconscious state of a girl and the unconscious of a computer seems to justify the use of a program-generated text for the first time in a radio play' (Bense and Harig 1969/1968: 58).

8   Cf. the critique of the first volume of Bense's tetralogy *Aesthetica* (1954) by Eva Schaper (1956; especially the passage on pp. 292–3).

9   All quotations that appear here have been translated from the expanded Czech edition (Bense 1967/1962) and checked against the German original (Kiepenheuer & Witsch).

10 The second edition of 1967 underwent significant changes, absorbing new concepts from the field of structural semiotics (with terms such as signifier and sign, denotation and connotation, as well as references to the works of Jakobson and Barthes), which complemented the integration of information theory and 'American semantics' (Morris, Richards), on which the work relied substantially (cf. Eco 1997/1962: 8).

11 Cf. the parody portrait of Eco created by the left-wing writer and activist Carlo Levi: '*How I love you, young Milanese (how I love you! all of you who are like him). How I love you, [. . .] the mist that envelops you [. . .] The engine roars, the office is nearby; what does the Echo say?*' (Eco 1997/1962: 15).

12 This notion of a 'concrete form' of reproduction is similar to the French Marxist-structuralist conception of Pierre Macherey – the 'theory of literary production' from 1966. Yet it takes into account in more sophisticated terms

the ideological unintentionality of creation, and is prefigured by a certain *conception of history* that aims towards social emancipation (Müller R. 2018).

13   Weaver notes that there are *two types of uncertainty*: one is the amount of information that would have to be known for an information source to be fully described (*equivocation*), the other affects the signals received when the message is known: 'It is therefore possible for the word information to have either good or bad connotations' (Shannon and Weaver 1964/1949: 19).

14   Only an excerpt of the original *Lector in fabula* appears in the English edition of *The Role of the Reader* (1984).

15   The schema of Bühler's *Organon-Modell* is cybernetic (*avant la lettre*) insofar as the situation of signification connects the sender, receiver and world in reciprocal relations of a communication circuit.

16   A German translation of the text was published in 1978 (Červenka 1978).

17   We may recall that in Louis Hjelmslev's model, a sign is a function that emerges between two forms: the *content form* and the *expression form*. While the substance on which they are realized is not itself part of the signs, Hjelmslev treats them as potential forms in themselves that play an important role in all forms of communication. In textual semiotics, these concepts have become tools for the analytical stratification of any 'text' (i.e. of all *media*).

18   Cf. Eco's words on the crisis to which the Italian neo-avant-garde reacts: '[O]ne of the elements of crisis within contemporary bourgeois civilization is the average person's incapacity to escape the systems of acquired forms that are supplied to him from the outside, which he has not developed for himself through a personal exploration of reality. Social diseases such as conformism or heteronomy (*etero-direzione*), gregariousness and massification are precisely the result of a passive acquisition of standards of understanding and judgment which are identified with "good form" in morals as well as in politics, in dietetics and fashion, at the level of aesthetic tastes or pedagogical principles' (Eco 1997/1962: 151).

19   Of the fifty verses produced by Lutz, thirty-five were selected for journal publication.

20   That is to say a 'verbal icon', to borrow the expression of William K. Wimsatt. Three decades later, Monroe C. Beardsley would coin a term that turned away from such visual connotations: 'semantic density'.

21   The authors generated a 'stochastic non-machine text' by selecting every seventh word from every even page of Joyce's first novel, creating a non-syntactic concatenation of words vaguely reminiscent of a fragment-narrative. The experiment is included in the anthology *A Throw of the Dice* mentioned earlier.

7

Technics and media

Tomáš Chudý

In this chapter we elaborate on the conceptual evolution of the medium which has shown its gradual 'technization' and 'instrumentalization' (see Chapter 1). We shall focus on several key points that help complete the picture of the current media paradigm. Our line of enquiry is guided by two aims: first, to identify those forerunners which first indicated the concept's most important aspects; and second, to examine its implications for semiotics and information theory. Proceeding in this way, it will be useful to approach the classics (McLuhan, Kittler) not as a primary subject matter but as background context. We must try to understand, in other words, what still stands in the shadow of McLuhan and Kittler.

1. The technological unconscious as shift in the role of media (Kapp, Thrift, Ihde, McLuhan)

The idea of media as an extension of the organs, or even of the unconscious, is as old as the theory of technology itself.

As Gilbert Simondon rightly predicted in his doctoral thesis *Du mode d'existence des objets techniques* (first published in 1958), new notions of technics in terms of second-order and transclassical machines (Gotthard Günther), as well as non-trivial machines (Heinz von Foerster), had brought about a conceptual shift in the 1950s, exceeding the former unproblematic notion based on simple (hand) tools. Such tools do not compete with their users, and their effect on those users is transparently determined, typically in the sense of a reduction or refinement of simple (manual) actions. At that same time (or perhaps even earlier), a shift was taking place of the quantitative kind. For the first time, technology had come to assume a majority status in civilization and culture. By comparison to its earlier minority status, technology had come to be used by nearly everyone – in any case, by the majority of the economically active part of society. This 'shift', however, consists in the fact that it reveals what has always been at the foundations of culture, namely a techno-logic: the connection of meaning (*logos*) and technology – even if only as the technology of writing. This is also expressed by the increasing importance of recursivity over simple – that is, methodically isolated – operations (Erhard Schüttpelz), and it is this recursivity, in turn, that accounts for the intoxicating effect of media that Marshall McLuhan describes by way of the myth of Narcissus: 'the fact that men at once become fascinated by any extension of themselves in any material other than themselves' (1994/1964: 41). With the difference, of course, that he also identifies – in direct opposition to the activating, stimulating recursivity that spurs the invention of new operating chains in response to the invention of media – an anxious and narcotic aspect. In this way, the cybernetic loop of man and medium may take either a stimulating or narcotic form,[1] or indeed both forms at once, at times in casual connection. We may therefore fall back on an 'ulterior' line of media theory, one that does not begin with McLuhan, or even run through him as its main channel. This one runs through the Franco-German countryside, like the myriad tributaries of the Rhine (Ernst Kapp, Gilbert Simondon, Mark Hansen, Erich Hörl) before flowing on to nourish transplants overseas (Nigel Thrift, W. J. T. Mitchell and again Mark Hansen). At the same time, theories of the 'technical a priori' do not stop at questions of aesthetics or literature, but end with artificial intelligence and anthropological questions connected with posthumanism and postbiologism (Hartmann 2003).[2] Use of media can replace not only the creative act but intelligence itself, even vitality, and it is to the same extent that they can burrow under the skin, upsetting established identities, the paradigm of 'subjectivity', or, more precisely, the 'authorial subject'. What we mean by media is something intrinsically linked to apparatuses: a technics based on scientific knowledge. The fact that media thus defined have been developing into media systems at least since their founding age (the second half of the nineteenth century), as observed by Friedrich Kittler, is self-evident, in the same way as the irreplaceable material nature of recording, communication and dissemination. (We work through these functions in Chapter 1.)

The two basic meanings of the medium, outlined in Chapter 1 – expressed by the instrumental (*by means of, or through which*) and locative (*within which*) cases – correspond to the development of two basic directions in media theory during the twentieth and twenty-first centuries. One is *prosthetic theory*, which can be traced from Kapp to André Leroi-Gourhan, and from there to McLuhan and Bernard Stiegler, and which understands media as an expansion and transposition of human abilities (especially memory) into instruments, through which the range of ever-improving operations also increases. The other is *media ecology*, which can be traced from Simondon to Mitchell,³ and from there to Hansen and Hörl, which explicitly envisages the (technical–) media environment as a habitat thanks to which the human agent (only) becomes an individual. In Kittler, we see both these approaches in combination,⁴ making up the poles of a feedback loop that creates through them an ambient call, in the manner of electroacoustic feedback. In this chapter, we will try to let this connection emerge through the idea of technology as an unconscious projection, which allows us to leave the schema dependent on the human individual and pose the ground of technology as a pre-individual environment.

Ernst Kapp, Nigel Thrift and technics theory after Gilbert Simondon

Technics and media represent essential characteristics of the evolution of Hominidae in the most conspicuous way.[5] We must notice, however, that this connection between man and technology has increased over the course of history, and that it has come to acquire an altogether new quality by virtue of its indispensible status. It is necessary to focus on this as the difference that determines the situation today. With the development of technology and industrial production in the nineteenth century, in periods marked by new discoveries in the fields of mechanics, electromagnetics and chemistry, the paradigms had to change: that of the relationship between humankind and world, humankind and culture, and thus humankind and literature (as Friedrich Kittler writes, 'in the time of Krupp and Armstrong, machine gun and underwater torpedo, it was no longer possible to measure cultural progress only by the development of schools and state, families and the prohibition of incest'; Kittler 2000: 204).

Fortunately, this turning point between the old and new way of thinking is rendered perfectly visible by a single – albeit relatively unknown – work: namely, Ernst Kapp's *Elements of a Philosophy of Technology* (*Grundlinien einer Philosophie der Technik*).[6] The work was published in 1877, sixteen years before Sigmund Freud's earliest publications and more than half a century before *Civilization and Its Discontents*. Even more remarkably, perhaps, Kapp wrote his seminal work eighty-seven years before McLuhan's *Understanding Media* (1964), and even while the nineteenth-century thinker follows his predecessors in regarding artificial creations as a way for humans to adapt to their environment (the Promethean theme), there are other ways in which he anticipates McLuhan's 'extensions'.[7] For Kapp, the essence of man lies in tools and machines that correspond to his prehistory and history.[8] Kittler interprets this as a basic lack (*Mangel*) that Kapp borrowed from Herder's concept, to which he added Benjamin Franklin's notion of man as a 'tool-making animal' – indeed, Kapp directly quotes Franklin's expression (Kapp 1877: 237). We should also note that Kapp, long before Freud, advances a notion of the unconscious[9] (*das Unbewusste*) as a function of the invention of technology.[10]

What we see is that various key elements in the conceptual history were first formulated under a somewhat different (sometimes broader, sometimes narrower) designation; the idea of the medium (or technics in general) as an extension of man serves as a good example, arising from the conception of body parts extended into space. Kapp, a Hegelian, advances such an idea in his philosophy of technics, and the idea is later adopted by numerous theorists of culture (such as Arnold Gehlen in his 1940 work *Man, His Nature and Place in the World*, where he writes on technology as a substitute for and improvement of the human organs). Yet Kapp also saw the possibility of a reciprocal influence or projection of technical creations onto the human form (Kapp 1877: 25–6, 105), and thus was first to outline – albeit in the Hegelian language of an inside mirrored in the outside world – the implicit cybernetic feedback (proto-)mechanism *sub specie technica*. Man thus models its organs as instances fulfilling their respective functions (Hubig 2015: 39).

It was none other than Kittler who first identified the connection between cybernetics and Kapp's philosophy of technics (Kittler 2000). We might take a closer look at Kittler's interpretation, since it also reveals one key pitfall in Kapp's concept. The latter understands tools and inventions as referring back to (i.e. originating in) the hand. This, however, becomes problematic when it comes to the invention of the wheel, which cannot be derived from the hand, or from *any* human organ for that matter. To escape this dead end, Kapp considers a cybernetic projection loop 'of a second order'[11] (the first being between tools and hands/body); here, it is no longer a matter of a tool (*organon*) that serves as projection of an organ, but a tool that serves as a projection of another tool, so that 'one tool engenders another' (Kapp 2018/1877: 5).[12] With further combinations of technical inventions he observes how the Greek expression ὄργανον τῶν ὀργάνων (*organon tón organón*) 'aptly convolutes the concepts of tool and organ', in this way emphasizing 'the affinity between a living organic prototype and its lifeless mechanical after-image, an organ and its technical extension' (Kapp 2018/1877: 142). However, this also allows (thinking about) the assemblage of more complex machines:[13] railway networks and the telegraph, for example, which seem to imitate blood circulation (Kapp 1877: 135–6) and the nervous system (Kapp 1877: 138–45). The outcome is that the inventor of primary tools is no longer able to see the similarity of the following inventions to his own body. Kittler aptly comments on this outcome:

Man as creator of technical culture [. . .] not only does not know that telegraph systems reflect his nervous system; he does not even know what this nervous system is doing. We see without knowing how the eye and the brain can do it, we project our clenched hand into the hand ax, without knowing that and how we project. In this way, it was only the invention of the lens that made it possible to physiologically describe the eye, only the discovery of electricity that made it possible to measure and prove that an electric current also passes through the nervous system. Kapp's philosophy of technology thus leads to the history of science that conceives modern technology as a necessary prerequisite for the natural sciences – and not the other way around, as has been generally assumed since the Enlightenment [. . .] bodies are explained retroactively from their supposed projections: it was Helmholtz who proved that animal nerves work exactly like a telegraph, that is, on the model of the electric cable. From the unconscious of the primitive *homo faber*, which could never understand its own functioning or fabrication, the salvation of science was eventually born. (Kittler 2000: 209)

Because technology is an unconscious projection of human organs, similar projections of a second order may give rise to increasingly complex forms of machines. During conscious projection, the invention of these machines would be hampered by the initial *conscious intention*, or even by the subconscious 'aims', which may in some cases actually get in the way. The projections of a second order might therefore be considered to some extent as being freed also from their initial status as 'unconscious projection' (as a counterpart to the original conscious intention, i.e. as something still owing to the psychological or psychologizing duality of consciousness/unconscious), in this way corresponding to a kind of *unintentionality* whereby the machine is no longer dependent on its creator. With this in mind, we might further generalize unintentionality to the point where it covers *human creation as such*. Art – as defined by Mukařovský, for example – would have a similar reverse effect on people, in common with technology in the Kapp-Kittler interpretation: unintentionality creates new forms (effects on perceivers, interpretations, machines) which otherwise lie entirely beyond the horizon of the conceivable.

It can be added that the thesis about the media as an unconscious extension – or extension of the unconscious – was unconsciously carried over from Kapp through Marshall McLuhan to the 'extended mind thesis', which is formulated by John Sutton as the idea that 'The realm of the mental can spread across the physical, social, and cultural environments as well as bodies and brains' (Sutton 2010: 189).

Technical objects (apparatuses) – indeed, technics in its very essence – thus enable human reality (the individual, as well as his/her organs and organization) to surpass itself as a projection (Hansen 2012: 46), a situation which aptly conveys both the productiveness and 'projectiveness' of technology. McLuhan also notes this transindividual aspect, but for him it is a kind of well into which the human individual inevitably risks falling, hence the 'narcotic' character of technical media and its parallel with Narcissus gazing raptly down at his own image. But this represents a very one-sided vision, and we must take account of the way Narcissus's reflected image takes on a life of its own, conveying more than its original (conscious) investment – to the extent, in any case, that Kapp speaks of *unconscious* projection and that we find here a parallel to the concept of unintentionality as an aesthetic category.

We must be wary, however, of jumping to the conclusion that technical media as unconscious projections open wide the gates of aesthetic unintentionality – though, admittedly this (explicitly or implicitly) is the conclusion of much of the current thinking on e–literature. Yet it does not apply so broadly, nor so straightforwardly, as has been articulated. This is due largely to the fact that even technical apparatuses in the hands of individuals turn into individual instruments, indeed, into conscious projections (i.e. they cease to live up to Kapp's theory). In this sense, they are relegated to the status of a narcissistic mirror image on the surface: a surface, in other words, from which all (unintentional) depth has been evacuated. For example, the conscious use of stochastic series and sequences (designated erroneously as 'entropic') seeks to imprint that which is imbued by impersonality with an individual hallmark (often under an author's name), and so to consciously imitate it.[14] (On unintentionality, see Chapter 5, pp. 135–40 and 150–2.)

We may return here to a simple observation: transindividuation (or impersonal experience) is inevitable, given that every time a new technical medium is invented, it allows a shift in *communication methods*. This has gradually made it possible to disengage communication from initial face-to-face exchange in favour of *global* sharing; yet it has also given rise to a certain retrograde movement in communication methods towards immediacy (the sharing on a global scale not only of audiovisual perceptions, but increasingly of *feelings* – or, more precisely, *affects*), in accordance with the observation by Bolter and Grusin that as mediation evolves, it grows more visible and at the same time more obscure. Thus, transindividuation means re-connecting individuals (more immediately than before), but on a much more impersonal basis than ever, in the sense that it diverges from conscious thought processes. Ever since the invention of writing, communication has involved a form of sending and receiving between two absences. While online communication has indeed expanded and deepened affective (audiovisual) interaction to levels previously unheard of, *it did not cease to have an absent character* (it has not ceased, technically speaking, to be an expression of the projection of the body, and therefore of the unconscious, at least insofar as the connection is provided by electromagnetic waves or optical cables).

In the face of this duality, the post-Simondonian technics theory, with its emphasis on the processuality of the mutual influence between technics and the human, seems to represent particularly fertile grounds. In the age of computer-driven transmission – of 'messages' (Luhmann), 'sensibility' (Hansen) or 'information' (Bateson) – beyond human consciousness,

> the correlation between human-implicating individuation and techniques has moved beyond what we might think of as its objective stage [. . .] and has entered a properly processual stage in which techniques directly intensifies sub-perceptual dimensions of human experience, and thus comes to mediate forms of transindividuation which, by maximizing the potential of the pre-individual, transform the very being of the human. (Hansen 2012: 51)

The question – we believe it to be answered in the affirmative – is whether this processuality has not *always* prevailed, even when it did not so obviously appear as dominant. In other words, is it possible that technology, from its very beginnings, unintentionally (or unconsciously) shaped humanity itself at the level of neurological (and so biological and cultural) development? Hansen's diagnosis of the transition can then be read as a recognition of the most recent manifestation of this process, brought about by the accelerated development of technology in the twenty-first century, to the extent that one can now speak of a technical distribution of human experience (by influencing *how* experience takes form, not just by generating new kinds of experience). In this case, technics is that which compensates for a certain operational blindness on the part of individuals, but which also hides the risk of falling into a 'media trance', where individuality (and everything that has so far characterized it, such as individual expression) completely yields to an 'empty' narcotizing mirroring.

The idea of a technological unconscious then spread among English-language authors, throughout the field of culture theory. These include Nigel Thrift (2005: 212–26), for whom, in a Freudian way, the technological unconscious designates that blind spot in which thinking and action are shaped by unspecified forces. As with Kapp, this is a 'prepersonal substrate of guaranteed correlations, assured encounters, and thus unconscious anticipations' (Thrift 2005: 213). Elsewhere, Thrift speaks of 'Repeated correlations, positionings and juxtapositionings', among human and non-human within technological spaces that assume specific competencies, and of 'powerful infrastructural logic which allows the world to show up as confident'. Environments show up as 'spaces of anticipation', which in turn become 'the way things are' (Thrift 2004: 175–90).[15]

Thus, the technological unconscious predetermines bodies and their environment to the role of a specific set of addresses, without the benefit of any cognitive input.[16] Such are the effects of technical code in the non-linguistic realm captured by Thrift in his concept of the technological unconscious, as N. Katherine Hayles (2006) aptly notes.

Don Ihde and the phenomenology of technics

Let us now return to the historical intensification of the connection between technics and humankind. As it acquires pre-individual dimensions, it makes possible the formation of entire networks, determining individual possibilities – only to the extent, however, that the individual points communicate in some way with one another. In the case of the modern development of communication technologies, for example, we may speak of media 'textures' (as Ihde writes in his book *Technology and the Lifeworld: From Garden to Earth*, 1990; cited in Janson 2014: 275–92), referring to a complex, non-linear and conceptualized symbiosis between man and media. They may at times generate whole new discursive spaces (a form of tourism, for example, based on the circulation of representations of various destinations in the form of postcards, etc.) involving the standardization and organization of social practice as such (daily rhythms of e-mail business communication, reading newspapers, watching TV, smartphone culture, etc.; 2014: 279).

We have still to address the issue of the interface, and of the processes that take place below its surface. Here, we may note that the many social consequences of the theory of technics as unconscious projection (some of which are mentioned earlier), reach even to the phenomenological tradition. In his seminal 1990 study, Don Ihde, the American phenomenologist of technics, distinguishes four different categories of man's relationship to technology. The first is embodiment, or 'technics embodied' (e. g. use of glasses), which he defines as 'the symbiosis of artifact and user within a human action' (Ihde 1990: 74).The second category, 'hermeneutic relations' (Ihde 1990: 86), confirms this interplay, while pushing it towards the border of transparency. This is where 'reading' takes place by means of such technologies as books, telescopes, thermometers, clocks – even the 'reading' of a voice on the telephone. A distinction can be made between perceptual transparency, based on the principle of isomorphism ('iconicity' in semiotic theory), and hermeneutic transparency, which is based on reference, and accompanies the reading of a text (Ihde 1990: 82). Textual transparency thus points in another way to the concept of technics as an unconscious extension, insofar as technics, in the case of reading, only becomes transparent when it is integrated into the natural world, and this is only possible, in turn, if its user has the appropriate hermeneutic skills. Here we deviate from McLuhan, for example, who is not interested in the hermeneutic, or transparent, relation to signs but precisely in the visible technical limits of this relation. This second relationship typically occurs with communication media, but it represents just one of the possible attitudes that the human individual may take vis-à-vis technology. It is typically manifest in the technological difference between spoken and written language (Ihde 1990: 81; cf. Walter J. Ong and Jack Goody, who were among the first to develop the concept).

Ihde identifies the third and fourth categories as 'alterity' and 'background relations'. The first of these will remind us of McLuhan's notion of technology as a 'narcotic' (see herein) that draws attention to itself and ideologically saturates the discourse on media. Technology is thus sacralized or fetishized. Ihde observes that many new technologies were initially received as sacred objects of fascination before gradually becoming items of everyday use (cf. Jansson 2014: 281). In the end, however, such alterity only amounts to a kind of '*quasi-otherness*' (Ihde 1990: 100), which confirms its unconsciously organic origin and foreshadows a recursive loop – a topic we shall return to shortly.

In the last category, the relationship to technology assumes a background or environment status. Rather than 'engagements through, with, and to technologies [which] stand within the very core of praxis', 'background relations' refer to those cases in which technologies 'remain in the background or become a kind of near-technological environment' (Ihde 1990: 108), generating fringe visual, audio or material phenomena that Ihde describes collectively as 'technological texturing' (Ihde 1990: 109). These technologies thus occupy the position of 'a present absence' nonetheless remaining 'part of the experienced field of the inhabitant, a piece of the immediate environment' (Ihde 1990: 111).

This does not mean, however, that they are more neutral or less relevant to the natural world than the technologies on which we typically focus our attention. These background technologies 'transform the gestalts of human experience and, precisely because they are absent presences, may exert more subtle indirect effects upon the way a world is experienced' (Ihde 1990: 112). A prime example can be found in the – unobtrusive, but crucially motivating – background music played at department stores.

That we remain largely unconscious of both the fetishistic relationship and the later hermeneutic phase only confirms the conclusions reached by McLuhan and Ernst Kapp – and even takes them further:

> There is an important common denominator to these four variants, pointing to the very core of the mediatisation meta-process. Ihde's phenomenology of technics [...] clarifies in a systematic way how [...] *the more a particular medium is taken for granted and the more it becomes transparent as technology, the more difficult it is to exclude it from the practices of day-to-day life.* (Jansson 2014: 281)

The recursive loop and Erhard Schüttpelz

So far, we have considered how media represent extensions/projections of human organs and abilities, and how these extensions become independent of the human individual (i.e. the person who interacts consciously with a technology, as its engineer or its user). This has led us to think of technology as an unconscious and pre-individual projection. With the phenomenology of technology, we shifted our focus gradually to the micro level, paying specific attention to the way media perform a certain activity, thus serving to fulfil, at least initially, a certain 'guaranteed' function. Keeping this in mind, we may turn to a question fundamental to the concept of the medium: namely, does it not coincide with the concept of technics, insofar as the achieved form of technics (first as a simple body extension, then scientific technology) prefigures the 'operations' ('techniques') that are expected as well from the medium (Schüttpelz 2006: 88)?

A technical medium does not come to its full use in the first moment of its invention. As suggested in Chapter 1, it always needs a certain modicum,[17] that is, a critical volume of use (or 'critical mass'), in order to develop its effects. We may examine this requirement in more detail. Looking first to Leschke's stages of media development (initial rejection → narrow circle of fans/freaks → wider circle of specialists → even wider group of privileged consumers → broad consumer base), it is easy to see how these 'modica' crystalize in specific social groups during specific historical periods (in certain 'partial' cases, there are even studies that quantify them).[18]

In this way, the medium engages in a range of operations that first exceed it and the original function with which it was endowed. This range can be summed up, broadly speaking, by the term 'cultural techniques' (*Kulturtechniken*), in the sense developed mainly by Bernhard Siegert. According to Erhard Schüttpelz, 'Cultural practices are distinguished from other techniques by having a potential relation to themselves [*potentiellen*

Selbstbezug]. This pragmatics of recursivity is made possible by two other properties of cultural techniques: they perform symbolic work and, in addition, always require a medium, whether as an object/apparatus or as a person' (Schüttpelz 2006: 88).

It would follow that cultural techniques are served by media and the symbolic work they carry out, whose primary aim is for culture to create a concept of itself (and therefore establish the recursivity of culture). We may well ask, however, in the age of intermedia, where media generally refer to one another (and themselves), isn't such an ancillary function obsolete? The function of media at present would seem to be significantly broader, with media taking an active role in pushing the boundaries of culture, insofar as technological development and the effort to create new initially hybrid media conglomerates determines the tone of culture. Schüttpelz refers here to Siegert's double concept of the medium: at once the medium 'in which' (i.e. in which one writes, paints, calculates, etc.) and the medium 'by/through which' (in somewhat looser sense than in Chapter 1, namely as 'the third position between the two poles of the establishing code of culture', such as a door mediating between inside and outside, or a communication medium between signal and noise).

Schüttpelz maintains a conceptual overlap between 'media', 'culture' and of course 'technics', in the sense that each of these concepts is at play alongside the others, and there is no basis on which to delimit one against the other as they arise in the field of human technics (Schüttpelz 2006: 91).[19] Technics is *culturally contingent*, rather than independent or self-sustainable. Had the nursery rhyme *Mary Had a Little Lamb* not come at that moment to Thomas Edison's mind, the first phonographic recording would not have been made. Even more radically: a new technology will not last if, following its invention, it is not taken up as the object of education and upbringing[20] – that is, if it does not become the object of symbolic work.

As Leroi-Gourhan shows, technics – including media – are always preceded by operational chains (*chaînes opératoires*): in other words, it is the gesture which adapts a corresponding technical arrangement to serve it, not the other way around (the technique does not generate gestures). Based on this, Schüttpelz argues that it is much easier to prove the priority of operational chains for media than for non-media technics, because media can be considered as such only when they are used operationally. We would agree with that: the verb precedes the nominal description. Schüttpelz adds, however, that after the Second World War that linked mass media to technological research, this operational use acquired a binding designation, namely, communication (Schüttpelz 2006: 93). Clearly, this way of defining the subject is far too narrow. Still, even if we postulate the plurality of these operating chains and their variability over time, we do not detract from such a theory of technical media any of its original inspiration in French anthropology (Leroi-Gourhan). All we do is account for the element of contingency that has been noted by media historians.

We must see, however, how the connection between an operational chain and the corresponding technics is not a simple link, but something like a closed circuit – or, as Schüttpelz points out, a feedback loop. Recursive operations have priority over simple ones. The notion of a simple linear progress in recording technology consisting in an accumulation of inventions linked to the exteriorization of human abilities is naïve.[21] It must be thought of as a cycle, each new technique bringing with it new 'boomerang effects': repercussions in the form of new specializations and contingent social relations between people and media. 'Exteriorisation happens recursively or not at all', writes Schüttpelz, 'and its consequences cannot be grasped by means of any evolutionary stages – not even when going through the accumulation of inventions, indeed, especially not then' (Schüttpelz 2006: 96).

Another explanatory concept is therefore necessary when reconstructing these relations, even if it is not necessary to abandon the priority of the operating chain altogether. This must be reinterpreted as a greater emphasis on the chaining together of operations, rather than considering each one in isolation – that is, not as a priority over technics itself. This chain must be seen in its cyclical form, whereby the operations are recursively applied to (results of) the same operation (service gestures of exteriorized gestures, programming of programmers and users, domestication of domesticators, memory techniques for artificially augmented memory, mechanization of mechanical acts and machine production, etc.).[22] It is therefore necessary to conclude that the priority of operational chains, with emphasis on the chaining together of operations, can be understood as the priority of recursive over simple (methodically isolated) operations.[23]

This may seem to conflict with certain claims made earlier in this chapter: that technologies may be generated directly by other technologies, or machine extensions by other machines, and so on. In fact, while media do evolve, this evolution does not proceed simply by degrees of exteriorization (as some have understood it). On the contrary, the accumulation of inventions, which gives rise to various unanticipated operations, only confirms the ever-expanding inventory of recursive elements. It's just that we must understand this not as a simple displacement of operations from the domain of the human (organic/interior) to that of technics (machine/exterior), but as the interplay of inside and outside – indeed, of what we mean by the opposition between these designations, and the operations we expect from each side. Rather than developing in linear fashion, the evolution of media thus tends to unfold in the pattern of a many-stranded helix.

This also changes the relation of instrumentality, which is often seen as a characteristic of modern times (see, for example, Charles Taylor's *The Ethics of Authenticity*). In principle, this notion implies a simple scheme of purpose and means, so that, in turn, the 'alienation of the (original) purpose' (*Zweckentfremdung*) or instrumentalization becomes also possible. In reality, however, technical (or media) alienation *precedes* every purpose, given that the scheme as a whole cannot exist without an instrument (or, in the case of communication and recording technologies, without a medium) which develops in a recursive operating chain from the outset. In this way, we see how the priority of recursive operations is a common (not exceptional) principle that makes possible all technical and organizational inventions, transfers and adaptations (including cultural institutions).

One of the important thinkers of the alienation of purpose is the German psychologist Wilhelm Wundt, whose principle of 'heterogony of purposes' (*Heterogonie der Zwecke*)[24] accounts for the unintended consequences produced by (and ultimately determinant of) a chain of actions. We see this principle at work not only at the macro (military, economic, political) level, but also at the micro level of the history of technical inventions and their use (and their users, i.e. their operational chains; Schüttpelz 2006: 98).[25]

The principle of recursive operational chains has far-reaching consequences for literary communication, for example, in the concept of a 'fictitious reader' (which is a recursive application of the operation of literary production to reading, and therefore also to writing). Mukařovský's aesthetics theory, for example, and his notion of unintentionality (alienation of the original intention in a non-ideological sense) grasps the principle of heterogony of purposes as few before him.

In this context, what are the consequences of the emergence of new electronic digital media for literature? According to Riepl's law (see Stöber 2013: 438–43), older media are never fully replaced by new media; and if, additionally, we can broadly apply the law of unintended consequences derived from Wundt's heterogony of purposes, then these older media can (and indeed must) develop new purposes, or, what is the same thing, exapt to other functions. This notion of exaptation may then be postulated also in the context of literature. One way to elaborate it is through media archaeology.[26]

The narcotization of media: McLuhan (and successors inspired by semiotics: Winkler)

Let us now continue with our analysis of technical media at the micro level, with regard to their original purpose and function from which they are gradually alienated. We will focus here in more detail on McLuhan's idea of media narcotization, which illustrates well the recursive loop between operational chains and technics. Here, we will examine the significance of recursivity in the context of media (specifically literary) competence.

The effect of any active media competence comes to the fore every time it works with a medium against its 'hot' nature, in such a way that it shifts the media operation from higher to lower definition (that is, from a high to low quantity of data, accompanied by a rise in unintentionality). But when observing how much these designations depend on the *kind of culture* in which a medium operates, McLuhan eventually sees also media competence as something 'hot', this time on the side of the consumer (McLuhan 1994/1964: 22-3).[27] To compensate for the 'missing data' in the mediated content of the 'cool' medium, a form of writing is used that requires greater participation on the part of the reader by design. Culture and medium thus enter into a mutual dialectic: a hot culture (one that is 'highly literate', as McLuhan says) can dull the effects of a hot medium, and may require a rather cool medium, or it may cool down hot media messages, for example, by compelling them to become elliptical.

The development of mechanized printing and spread of literacy gave rise to a silent and passive mode of reading that, in the centuries that followed, turned into an established competence. This media operation now needs to be cooled, which is to say, interrupted and balanced by active participation, by 'play' (McLuhan 1994/1964: 31). Which is not the same as saying it must be replaced (to extend the thermodynamic analogy, to cool it past a certain limit means thermal death). For McLuhan, as for Leroi-Gourhan, it means a type of (partial) return to the original vision of the world (and communication), which is based on rhythms, synaesthesia, the simultaneous interplay of multiple senses and its dynamics.[28]

Applying the hot and cool media model to the digital synesthetic multimedia of today's world, we may find a general cooling off in the case of both media competences and corresponding media. Properly speaking, this does not represent a return, insofar as its starting point, in Western society, is highly literate culture. For the transition to further media and their proper absorption, it is therefore necessary for culture to be medially 'heated up' to a sufficient degree (the first step of which is to achieve 'modica', as we saw earlier). What is true for whole cultures, in this case, logically applies to their subcultures. Groups of addressees who are not sufficiently educated in deciphering media by existing means have a hard time dealing with new media. The crucial role played by text production in education and acquisition of media literacy generally feeds into a significant side motivation enlarging the Riepl's law of exaptation. Moreover, even if traditional literature is 'hot', this does not mean it cannot gradually turn into a cool medium, insofar as it is a relatively 'low definition' medium compared to digitally processed audiovisual productions.

As we have noted, the hot or cool aspect of media is a matter of data (of its high- or low-definition), which makes it possible to better conceive these changes in terms of a multivector field of hot and cool media whose operation is not a zero-sum game.[29]

The much-discussed narcosis effect of modern media should be understood in this context rather as a defensive reaction to the data flow made possible by the full use of electronic media:

> We have to numb our central nervous system when it is extended and exposed, or we will die. Thus the age of anxiety and of electric media is also the age of the unconscious and of apathy. But it is strikingly the age of consciousness of the unconscious, in addition. With our central nervous system strategically numbed, the tasks of conscious awareness and order are transferred to the physical life of man, so that for the first time he has become aware of technology as an extension of his physical body. (McLuhan 1994/1964: 47)

The paradoxical narcotization does not erase consciousness altogether (as during a surgery); rather, it displaces it into another domain. If each new medium requires 'new ratios or new equilibriums among the other organs and extensions of the body', then the very handling of the associated technologies requires a shift in perception, and it is precisely this shift to the 'Narcissus role of subliminal awareness and numbness' (McLuhan 1994/1964: 46).

In fact, we might say that this notion of the defence mechanism serves as a myth for the origin of media in general: in the beginning, an excessive pressure (stress) is exerted on one of the human organs (on the foot, for example), with the result that

> the central nervous system acts to protect itself by a strategy of amputation or isolation of the offending organ, sense or function [. . .]. The wheel as a counter-irritant to increased burdens, in turn, brings about a new intensity of action by its amplification of a separate or isolated function (the feet in rotation). Such amplification is bearable by the nervous system only through numbness or blocking of perception. (McLuhan 1994/1964: 42–3)

In other words, it is a feedback loop ('servomechanism' or 'closed system'; McLuhan 1994/1964: 41, 46): in response to the introduction of an excessive load, an invention is created whose performance exceeds the performance of the organ it extends, and so ultimately leads to a narcotic numbness.

According to McLuhan, this principle applies as well to communication media, from the advent of language to that of the computer (McLuhan 1994/1964: 43, 124). McLuhan was likely the first to consider the shift in literature (and painting) forced by the new media of recorded reality, namely the turn towards 'inward gestures of the mind by which we achieve insight and by which we make ourselves and our world' (McLuhan 1994/1964: 194). This line of reasoning is logically sound – but is it really possible to proceed logically in the world of media effects, which McLuhan himself later described in his concept of 'media tetrads' as much more contingent than it first appeared?

The transition to internal processes that is induced by narcotization through the medium of literature can be seen in the interpretation of moods. That moods are non-representative does not mean that they are not to be considered as signs at all. According to Hans Ulrich Gumbrecht (2012/2011), for example, moods have a mixed iconic-indexical nature, referring to internal events while also, to a certain extent, depicting them. The same could be said for the 'inward gesture' of literature, in McLuhan's conception.

The narcotization observed by McLuhan – and which Fichte, remarkably, was the first to discuss in connection with reading[30] – is mirrored in the concept of immersion, as described by Frank Rose (2011), for example: 'We know this much: people want to be immersed. They want to get involved in a story, to carve out a role for themselves, to make it their own' (Rose 2011: 8). With each invention of a new medium, from print to film to television, 'the transporting power of narrative' increased, with the result that each new medium inspired both fear and hostility (Rose 2011: 36). This immersion is further enhanced by the fact that – as McLuhan was also probably the first to point out – electricity 'ended sequence by making things instant' (McLuhan 1994/1964: 12). Narcoticization-immersion[31]-instantaneousness therefore represents the complete end of the process that began with the gradual separation of individual extensions, and at the same time represents the starting point for the cooling process. This creates an open-ended dialectic, progressing through phases of narcotization and sobering up, as it were.

In order to move on to further implications of technical mediality for literature, let us turn to those who draw on the 'instrumentarium' of semiotics – that is, beyond the (extensions of) bodily abilities – to extend McLuhan's line of thought. This narrows the scope of enquiry to our main focus, that is, media of communication. In *Docuverse: Zur Medientheorie der Computer* (2002/1997), Hartmut Winkler translates McLuhan's physiological-therapeutic-technical model of narcotic extensions into a model of media as the result of wishes (*Wünschen*): that is, constellations of long-term, unconscious human desires. Man is not master of media development any more than he is master of his wishes; to a certain extent, however, Winkler advances the notion of an anthropocentric (because derived from human desire) media system, which 'inscribes interests, misunderstandings, lies and errors not only into texts but into the material environment as well' (2002/1997: 336). This brings to fruition McLuhan's theory of extensions, insofar as the new technics, arranged in a network, replaces the brain. Yet it does this not in perfect imitation of neural processes, but in such a way that it carries out the function of collective memory, that is, of culture.[32] In this conception, technics thus generates a completely new semiosphere.

It is important to emphasize that even this semiosphere is not detached from individual memories, even if fantasy would have it be so: 'The fantasy of liberating the network of semantic relations from memories and writing them to the outside world must therefore remain a fantasy; and the new text universe does not take the place of "cognition", but remains, like all text universes before it, dependent on a human counterpart' (Winkler 2002/1997: 337). The isolation of aesthetic value in a certain 'external space' (*Aussenraum*), one that is not connected to individual memory – that is, to the cognitive activity of forms recognition – is conceivable only as an illusion.[33]

Winkler also draws on motifs from *Laws of Media: The New Science* (McLuhan and McLuhan 1988): the mosaic-like model that replaces the previous linear model here resembles a musical structure (Winkler 2002/1997: 24). The linearity of print appears as 'narrowing down', which implies, in its positive sense, a certain concentration, but also, in its negative sense, a loss of complexity (Winkler 2002/1997: 25). What if the computer (or 'electronic media', in McLuhan's terms) now promises to combine the previous richness of communication and expression from the period before the advent of (linear) writing with its compactness, clarity and distinctness – that is, to have the best of both worlds (Winkler 2002/1997: 27)?

The historical development cannot be reversed and the diversification of the media cannot be denied. But much depends on the details of media production. The omnipresent digital hypertext structure displayed on plasma screens (allowing also a variety of graphics) replaces traditional forms of printed production: 'The Real (e.g. sound), the Symbolic (e.g. writing) and the Imaginary (images) are integrated on a single display surface' (Bolz 1993: 226). In each case, however, this integration can take place differently, with a different distribution of components and emphases, and this gives rise to a number of new production methods as well as genres.[34] Leaving the intermedial aspects aside for the moment, literature – the original communication medium – must evolve and exapt to these contingent processes, including the way it is written. This exaptation can be seen as a side effect of the recursive operational chains introduced by audiovisual media.

Next, we will focus on processing and manipulation. As Kittler and others have argued, these aspects underwent a revolution with the advent of new media. Even at the level of the text, it has become possible to blend the analytical activity of reading with the synthetic activity of writing by means of certain transitional functions, such as text filtering (thus creating a new text). This way of processing the text may be seen as the harbinger of a new cultural technique, one that relativizes linear coding (Hartmann 2000: 319).

2. Processing, manipulation and discursive economics

Manovich: The persistence of representations

Let us start with a historical gloss. As Lev Manovich observes,

> The year which we remember and celebrate is 1895; it is not 1875 (first television experiments of Carey) or 1907 (the introduction of the fax). Clearly, we are more impressed (or at least, we have been until the Internet) with modern media's ability to record aspects of reality and then use these recordings to simulate it for our senses, than with its real-time communication aspect. If we had a choice to be among Lumiere's first audience or first users of the telephone, we would choose the former. Why? The reason is that the new recording technologies led to the development of new arts in a way that real-time communication did not. The fact that aspects of sensible reality can be recorded and that these recordings can be later combined, re-shaped and manipulated – in short, edited – made possible the new media-based arts which were soon to dominate the twentieth century. (Manovich 2001: 162)

In addition to echoing Kittler's triad of media functions, this passage identifies the crucial points of difference that make it possible to structure the triad: whereas the mere transmission of communication is subject to constant breakdown due to technical problems and the insurmountable difficulty of human interaction in real time, condemning its human agents to interminable melancholy (a predicament aptly described by Kafka, for instance), recording media make possible, and allow sufficient time for, processes of manipulation and transformation – processes which since antiquity (as 'scholé') have characterized acts of thought and creativity. Naturally, this has less to do with a certain quantum of time than with the subversion of the primacy (which had always seemed intrinsic) of instantaneous over delayed communication. Such a delay provides a wider range of possibilities, increasing, but also, in equal measure, decreasing the chances of success.

The purely social aspect of communication is not thereby destroyed; it is only relativized, inserted into a new frame of reference, as we shall later show in the context of Luhmann (see Section 1 of Chapter 9, pp. 303–10). For now, let us focus on the notion of manipulation.[35] It is clear that this third aspect of mediality, discussed by both Kittler and Winkler, offers the most revolutionary potential of all. While Leroi-Gourhan and other classical anthropologists are content to trace the concurrent development of technology and communication with respect to its real-time possibilities, it is only by singling out the aspect of manipulation (which one could trace back to McLuhan) that we may grasp the new complexities and possibilities of creation, beyond the context of transmission. Manipulation also represents the most technical aspect of media, insofar as it requires the most advanced theoretical knowledge, and is last to emerge in every generation of new media. It is precisely this technology of creative complexity that has characterized literature from its earliest beginnings. We may ask then what happens when its primacy is surpassed, especially in the fields of film, audio creation and the digital.

Manovich himself writes, 'Despite persistent experiments of the avant-garde artists with modern technologies of real-time communication – radio in the 1920s, video in the 1970s, Internet in the 1990s – the ability to communicate over a physical distance in real-time by itself did not seem to inspire fundamentally new aesthetic principles the way film or tape recording did' (Manovich 2001: 151). Even though new possibilities emerged from the progress in telecommunications and real-time interaction, Manovich is preoccupied rather with new ways of recording, which has always offered the most fertile ground in the field of aesthetics. This may also be due to the fact that recording makes it possible to 'tinker' with representation (clearly surpassing, in this respect, the possibilities of real-time transmission, through whatever channel and with whatever amount of noise),[36] an endeavour that characterizes all aesthetic mediality. When the media of representation met with the media of communication (in the case of radio and television), we can therefore understand why the aspect of representation held sway from the beginning (with the broadcast of pre-recorded programs, for instance).

The two basic types of modern media are therefore those which convey a fixed and singular referent situated in the past (photography, film and sound recordings, as well as printed texts), and those which convey a simultaneous, current referent in its transformations (telegraphy, the telephone, radar and television, as well as the computer and internet, all of which offer the possibility of update in real time; Manovich 2001: 102). Real-time transmission of change is the counterpart of time axis manipulation, as Kittler puts it.[37] Each of these represents an achievement; when they are combined in a single medium, as in radio or television, the functional paraphernalia of the medium is complete. Even then, however, the transfer of change takes place on the basis of small, imperceptible time intervals of sequential scanning (circular for radar and horizontal for television). Thanks to the minimization of these intervals, manipulation in real time – from the point of view of human perception – is a reality today. Yet the vector of this development is essential: from static recording of past phenomena to dynamic recording of past phenomena, and from there to dynamic transmission of current phenomena. This vector can be interpreted in several ways: as a tendency to suppress the principle of representation (from the perspective of semiology), or as a trend towards the convergence of media and reality (from the perspective of media theory, psychology and epistemology). For the theory of literature, this may all represent a shift towards possibilities that seem to undermine the traditional system of literary communication (from the general to the singular, from the symbolic form to other aesthetic forms, from the static to the dynamic, even interactive, as well as a shift from the constructed to the immediate).

In 2001, Manovich believed that we still live in a society of the screen (Manovich 2001: 114), which suggests that representation has not yet been completely dismantled. Even if a screen is dynamic, real-time and interactive, it is still a screen. But this is not true of devices that can be placed directly on parts of the human body (glasses, headphones, etc.), and Manovich glimpsed the future moment of merging the retina and the screen.[38] At present, imaging technology gradually contrasts more and more with the ongoing tendency to directly grasp and transmit virtual reality. Literature as a representational system of creation (in every possible sense) will thus continue to intermingle with (other) techniques of representation, as well as compete with them.

Kittler: Manipulation without the concept of a sign

Any discussion of the technical aspects of mediality, and especially on the recursivity of technology, would be incomplete without Friedrich Kittler. We will not deal with Kittler in detail here, however, but rather focus on his own latent tendencies towards manipulation vis-à-vis media theory.

First, however, it will be helpful to consider a summary of Kittler's thesis. The well-known pillars of his theory (see, for example, Kittler 1999/1986: 195) are the end of print's monopoly on media, the shift of the centre of gravity to cable, and to radio and optical waves, and from there to the 'securing of traces' and associated new ways of coding, and generally the inexorability of the technological a priori ('Only that which is wireable is at all'). His work also revels in various illustrations of the fact that the diversification of media prepares the way for that of the psychic apparatus (we could say a similar influence stems from Schüttpelz's feedback loop between technics and operational chains).

As Kittler writes (1999/1986: 9), books enjoyed a certain 'power and glory' under the reign of writing which has now been lost. Even if the rise of new media has produced an 'epistemic break', this does not of itself mean the end of media (after all, even Kittler only talks about the end of the *term* 'media' cf. Gitelman 2006 and Belliger, Krieger 2016), due perhaps to the lack of continuity between the analogue and the digital. Instead, it is a matter of singling out those effects which somehow compel us to speak of the media's end, no doubt also to revise (without doing away with) the concept of the plurality of media as formulated by mass media studies, from those which hearken back to older media (most of the features of new media discussed by Manovich (2001), for example, are native already to print, just in a different sense and with a different operational speed).

Kittler is known for his emphasis on the principle of 'the manipulable', which was made possible by new methods for the technical recording and transmission of coded messages. Literature – or more precisely, *writing* – should be considered the first medium involving time axis manipulation (Kittler 2017/1993: 7). In the modern context, 'Editing and interception control make the unmanipulable as manipulable as symbolic chains had been in the arts' (Kittler 1999/1986: 108–9). Which is not to say that every media user becomes an artist.

However, Kittler is wrong to simply equate the flow of spoken language with time, which leads him to make the claim that a sufficient condition for text manipulation, in addition to linearization, is the empty space between letters (Kittler 2017/1993: 6). However, the time created by literature is different from the time of spoken language as it is commonly used to communicate. From the very outset it is different; whether slower or faster, it is always determined by the reading of the text (as a meaningful whole) and is measured according to its own parameters. The reading (and writing) of a text is an *event in time*, which, like other events, can be (almost) as long as you want, depending on a number of variables. To thus confuse the flow of spoken language with time is an error that Jacques Lacan, for example, never commits, and which Claude Shannon wouldn't even dream of when he focused on the logarithmic rate (volume) of data necessary to transmit information.[39]

With analogue media, and even more so with digital, recording media make possible unlimited intervention (*Eingriffsmöglichkeiten*) which allows, in turn, for the elimination during the second playback of nearly all chance elements of any time sequence of data (Kittler 2017/1993: 7–8). However, it is worth pointing out that this is a fictionalization of the recording, not an intervention (*Eingriff*) into the real timeline. It involves the creation of a new time axis that connects to the real through fiction, not interventions on the same axis. The fact that this playback is 'in the domain of the acoustically real' (Kittler 2017/1993: 7–8) changes nothing – it is still a fictional event. Kittler lets himself be guided by his reading of the Lacanian triad real-symbolic-imaginary (RSI), according to which only literature is equated with the symbolic and only the analogue record with the real. The category of fictionality, however, exceeds both, although in terms of its symbolism (in the sense of the semiotics of spoken language) it is paradigmatically linked to literature:[40] 'If reality is produced by language, then fiction is a model of all discourse, since it openly exercises the creative power of its medium' (Ryan 1997: 174–5). The level of distortion/interference/artifice is only a matter of degree, with the initial starting line significantly on the side of distortion in literature, and noticeably less so on the side of the phonograph (which, however, may also feature noise). It would then be possible to call noise not another sound, but the powerlessness of symbols to affect reality (the Real?), and the porosity of the network they form, rather than their garble in a text. In short, these are two different approaches – one keeps the initial heuristic principles (both Lacan and Shannon), the other does not, and ends up confusing the two levels (sign and reference).[41]

Kittler's causal shortcuts should therefore be taken with a pinch of salt: an example can be the sphere of acoustics, which we emphasize here because it is so often neglected. Kittler states, for example, that 'the timbre of individual instruments can be clearly distinguished from each other only during the first one hundred milliseconds of sounding forth, after which the distinguishing features rapidly diminish and vanish into a pure sinus signal devoid of any information' (Kittler 2017/1993: 8).

We know, however, that this is not the case, because the colour of sound is made up of a complex of 'overtones' (or 'upper partial tones'), which are produced by the instrument itself, and which sound for the entire time that the note sounds. Here, Kittler's ideological commitment to the tendency towards 'informationless' chaos effectively manipulates not only data flow but also everyday experience. Gilbert Simondon's formulation is, perhaps, more accurate: 'Information is thus halfway between pure chance and absolute regularity. We can say that form, conceived as absolute regularity, both spatial and temporal, is not information but a condition of information; it is what takes in (*accueille*) the information, the a priori which receives the information. Form has a selectivity function. But information is not a form, nor a set of forms; it is the variability of forms, the contribution of a variation in relation to a form. It is the unpredictability of a certain variation of form, not the pure unpredictability of all variation. We therefore ought to distinguish three terms: pure chance, form and information' (Simondon 1969: 137).

So why does Kittler confuse noise, time and pure media matter (as he likes to say, *Wortsalat*)? Perhaps because he does not use an explicit concept of the sign, regarding as interchangeable the sign and its material carrier (letters with moveable type, the symbolic with the typewriter/computer keyboard, etc.), in striking contrast not only to Lacan, who is his primary inspiration, but also to Nietzsche who also avoids confusing one with the other, considering it rather as a collaboration (cf. Kittler 1999/1986: xxix, 187–8).

It is true, on the other hand, that 'Thanks to the phonograph, science is for the first time in possession of a machine that records noises regardless of so-called meaning. Written protocols were always unintentional selections of meaning' (Kittler 1999/1986: 85). But the question is whether we can still consider it a medium when it assumes this function, that is, whether its medial function does not cease with scientific experiment (unless, however, the result of capturing and playing a primordial sound or verbal mishmash is converted into other units of meaning, about which theorization and even aesthetics are possible; this is largely the case with the 'Real', in Kittler's interpretation). Therefore, it is not quite true that 'notions of frequency are victorious over works, heartfelt melodies, and signifieds' (Kittler 1999/1986: 71),[42] since even if the concept of frequency does come to its directly material realization, this does not mean that it triumphs, only that it is rehabilitated in a certain narrow space. Therein lies the essential difference, the omission of which brings Kittler's interpretation closer to ideology.

In some places, however, Kittler sees a difference between *accepting* randomness (i.e. contingency) and *introducing* it into the material': 'while contingency may be accepted, it cannot be introduced into the material itself, as writers and composers were able to do when dealing with the coded materials of writing or musical intervals' (Kittler 2017/1993: 8; translation modified). Gramophony does not even allow for manipulation, that is, interventions that are dependent on whether or not the material encoding act takes place when recording to the medium. Although Kittler does not mention it here (only elsewhere), the difference between media is whether or not they encode the communicated content and how much. What he is trying to eliminate lies precisely in this moment of coding: a roll of the dice, or rather a series of rolls. Where one is possible, an infinite number of them are possible.

We may now proceed to examine the connection between intervention/manipulation in the mediated material with the psyche. We may best see it with film. In his interpretation of Hugo Münsterberg, Kittler characterizes film simply as a set of technological correlates of unconscious mechanisms revealed by psychotechnics, and also correlates of 'attention, memory, imagination, and emotion' (Kittler 1999/1986: 161). It is evident from this that Münsterberg is the true successor of Kapp, who considers technology to be a manifestation of the human unconscious. Film answers to and elaborates this thesis, and even brings it to perfection.

Psychotechnical analysis in the age of film thus understandably begins with attention, because the media age defines the givens in general by means of their signal-to-noise ratio (Kittler 1999/1986: 161). However, the connection between the key premise of technical communication (signal-to-noise ratio) and attention needs to be understood a bit differently than Kittler likely intended. The point is that attention assumes a crucial role in detecting a signal that is ever closer to noise, whereas such a question could never have arisen in the age of symbolic media, where the role of attention is overlaid and concealed by the role of imagination (which is based on attention), or intellect. In other words, the decoding was so complex (by comparison to the kind of 'deciphering' employed in the context of technical media like the phonograph or film) that a certain degree of attention was naturally assumed, and therefore unremarkable. Münsterberg, on the other hand, considers film to be the embodiment of a kind of unconscious attention referring, as an example, to the close-up, which simulates the manner in which a person focuses on a detail as part of a larger whole; it thus seems to him that the close-up directly presents him with this detail as his unconscious would have done (the same applies to other filmic devices, such as the flashback, etc.).[43] (For the different times of literature and film, cf. Chapter 2, pp. 51–3.) We might observe that this kind of selection also takes place in sound art, which, thanks to the Dolby system, can reduce noise to a minimum and focus the listener's attention on those sound phenomena that the producer wishes to bring to the fore. The nexus of technical media and attention is inseparable because, as Kittler says, 'Close-ups are not just "objectivizations" of attention; attention itself conversely appears as the interface of an apparatus' (Kittler 1999/1986: 162–3).

Note that Münsterberg is talking about art. However, the development of the substitution function of media can already be seen in their genealogy. As Kittler demonstrates, the invention of technical media was motivated primarily by the handicaps either of the inventors themselves or – more often – of their addressees.[44] This applies to the phonograph and typewriter, but also to film, which was originally intended to assist in the treatment of disorders not of organs but of psychic disorders (hysterics and psychotics), and also compensate for the handicap of the human eye when capturing the movement of animals or march of an army. While the beginning of the inventive effort is thus marked by a diagnosis, that is, the recognition of the lack that the medium cures, its unconscious potential is revealed gradually, so to speak, as its narcotic effect is exerted. In this context, the relevant question is: *For what handicap does literature compensate?* (McLuhan would ask: A defense mechanism to what *stress*?) In a way, Plato already revealed the answer in the *Phaedrus*: lack of memory, and more broadly, of the functions of the brain.

Today, however, we are bound to see the starting point in the way the computer replaces intelligence, as well as a number of other higher functions: 'The computer and the brain are functionally compatible, but not in terms of their schematics. Since the nervous system, according to Turing, is "certainly not a discrete-state machine," that is, not infinitesimally precise, all the unpredictabilities of a Laplacian universe loom over it. Thus, "the real importance of the digital procedure lies in its ability to reduce the computational noise level to an extent which is completely unobtainable by any other (analogy) procedure." [. . .] The brain, however, compensates for this loss of transmission through the parallel processing of whole sets of data; statistical breadth (presumably based on majority gates) for which computers can compensate only through serial processing and recursive functions' (Kittler 1999/1986: 249). It is here that the irreplaceable complexity of the brain is revealed, after all. Although Kittler claims that the brain is subject to noise (because it works analogically), this is offset by its unsurpassed capacity and ability to connect processes (which a computer can only perform serially; see Whitworth, Ryu 2009/2005). Yet this indicates precisely a complexity where noise is always already factored in (Luhmann).

Given the importance in Kittler's works of highlighting the role of noise (due to the visibility of the signal-to-noise ratio), we may try approaching the topic from another angle. With advances in the media in general and their synesthetic potential in particular, we also see rising *granularity*[45] related in a way to the evolutionary functional specialization and streamlining of communication. We see here an unprecedented expansion of the possibilities of communication and raster accuracy of transmitted data (including acoustic and visual data),[46] one that, incidentally, also draws our attention to (partial) deficiencies in verbal communication. Thus we suggest a certain reversal of perspective: it is not primarily a question of making communication errors or breakdowns visible (as with Michel Serres, for example), but of a much greater refinement and expansion of the potential for successful communication, one that results in more precise ways to monitor errors and breakdowns (it is on this basis that Shannon sets up his enquiry into how to quantify transmitted information). As granularity of performance increases, inaccuracy become more visible. It is worth pointing out that this principle does not only apply to communication, but also to other areas of scientific and technological progress. (We see this in the automotive industry, for example, where function failures – including partial and secondary functions – must be closely monitored, and in professional sports, where the smallest differences between athlete performances are crucial, and methods for assessing them constantly refined.) Technics first serves to raise the level of functionality; this then makes possible greater attention to detail. We also see here a trend that Hannah Arendt (1958: 585) identifies in connection with the birth of modern science: a shift from *what* to *how*, from objects to processes, that has only continued to grow.

Winkler: Processing and discursive economics

Kittler's emphasis on the manipulation function of media brought new interest and attention to the phenomenon of processing, as one of the paradigmatic ways in which a recursive loop emerges between operational chains and technics. It is in this way that modifications are carried out on various kinds of media content, and that the newly processed content, in turn, has an increasingly stronger feedback (and therefore narcotic) effect on human organs. Simultaneously, the invention of new processing procedures becomes possible: procedures which are all technically possible from the start, but not all of which are required by the other (cultural-organic) side of the loop.

We might now take a closer look at Hartmut Winkler, a theorist of processing who defines this aspect of media as an 'interfering modification' (*eingreifende Veränderung*; Winkler 2015: 29). Winkler considers processing on three different levels: 'transforming' (*Transformieren*), which involves the generation of content; 'transcribing' (*Transkribieren*), which involves the oscillation between creative writing and archiving; and 'translation' (*Übersetzen*), which involves 'metaphoricality', that is, from one experience or medium to another. All of this has already been encompassed, and paradigmatically, by narrative (Claus Pias, cited in Winkler 2015: 19–20), and thus processing is much broader concept than a superficial identification with computer processing might imply.

However, Winkler (2015) runs into various problems arising from his attachment to such outdated conceptual parameters as solid vs. fluid, and this leads him to an almost infinitesimal splitting of processing phases (oscillating between the solid and the changing, which stems from the idea that there must be some kind of subject-matter (*Gegenüber*) of processing, *a perceptible substance upon which this processing is carried out*, as if processing were not possible without tangible products, as if it was possible to perceive (as opposed to conceive) only fixed shapes/forms; Winkler 2015: 150–2). In spite of this, he identifies a key conceptual difference in the context of what the media can do: namely, the difference between syntactic processing (the modification of elements already inscribed with a semantics) and semantic processing (which makes signs, i.e. the process of *darstellen*, or representation). It would seem that the medium – and the computer par excellence – can only combine what is already there (signs) in a different way. However, no medium is ever separate from the specific manner in which it is used, and the computer also models its signs according to external realities. This brings the sphere of semantic processing back into its range of action (Winkler 2015: 114, 150). The restriction to syntactic processing thus only applies to purely technical media, not to expressive media (speech, colour) – and only then if we ignore the context of their use.

However, this means that limitation to syntax never applies fully, and media really are the message. Taken to its extreme, this raises the issue whether processing can only really be carried out by the subject, or whether the anthropomorphization of machines today (for example, within actor-network theory, ANT) already allows us to say not only that they 'work' but also 'process', in the strong sense of interfering modification. Though Winkler does not give an explicit answer, we can infer that processing advances through 'subtotals' (*Zwischensummen*), and that some steps are replaceable while others are not. The technical aspect of processing therefore can only exist as part of a 'network' (Winkler 2015: 191), so that even the influence of technics on content or the quality of communication takes on a different meaning depending on whether the emphasis is on storing, communicating or processing a given message.

It is evident in the last case that technical imperfections themselves can not only present an obstacle, but also serve as a source of processing, or of direct and set boundaries that processing follows and respects (in the sense of the Latin *respicere*: 'to look back at'). Winkler considers both processing and switching (*Schalten*) to be not only a process of selection, but of choice as well. '*Schalter*' is an on/off switch, a relay that is controlled or programmed in some way.

This all may seem to disperse the question about the 'subject' of the processing; at the same time, however, it deepens our insight on the problem. Processing and storage are governed by a fundamental paradox: while what is abandoned to the flow of time becomes irreversible (and therefore fixed), what is captured (stored, written down) as a structure is made available for subsequent change (in the sense of processing, i.e. 'interfering modification'; Winkler 2015: 173, using Luhmann 1981):[47] 'It is in this way that media organize at the same time both stability and circulation. Perhaps one could say that they convert a primary certainty of action into a circulating bond' (Luhmann, cited in Winkler 2015: 173-4). However, the dualism of reversible/irreversible goes further than the question of the stability of forms, and is linked to artistic expression. This, in any case, is how it is understood by Luhmann, whose concept is reminiscent of Aristotle's understanding of 'mimetic actions', which may be unreal but are nonetheless reversible (reversibility here has to do with the decision on which an action is based).[48]

In principle, however, is not *any* capture of phenomena in/by media reversible, insofar as it makes possible the kind of timeline malleability that Luhmann attributes only to storage (*Speichern*)? That seems to be the case. However, Winkler comes to the opposite conclusion, because he imagines processing as 'something connected with time', by which he means the time of manipulation, not of recording. It is as if he had forgotten the substance of his own definition for processing – 'interfering modification' – which, on the contrary, aims to diverge from the irreversible flow of time (and to introduce another dimension), and that the very process by which something – more or less deliberately – is modified also has its correlate, albeit a fluid correlate, which might then be called a 'message'. It is true that the processing *as a process* is irreversible, insofar as it takes place in time. But this is not the case with its content, which is always subject to further modification, even without being 'stored' in the classical sense of the word. Change can take place continuously, without any supports in the form of fixed outputs.

Perhaps it is better to understand processing as a function not of the reversibility of forms but of connecting and disconnecting: after all, Winkler considers media as 'machines for disconnecting from contexts' (*Kontextentbindung*). This should be understood not as generating some kind of extra-contextual layer of signs (which is clearly meaningless), but as carrying out the necessary work of (technically) freeing up signs from their existing contexts. This is precisely what 'technical' media are for. Should we wish to consider the contribution of Winkler's theory to the theory of literature, for example, we must first free up his theses from their original context, and this – somewhat unintuitively – requires certain media (in this case, a computer). So long as we do not juxtapose his theses with others, or change their positions, the kind of decontextualization this implies (the freeing up of signs from a context) is not possible. It is only in the sphere of the 'discursive economy', where (as with commodities) constant de- and recontextualization takes place, do we find the fully developed functioning of media as machines endowed with processing functions. In this sense, the relationship between the symbolic (not in the Lacanian sense but with reference to the articulation of signs in general, as well as their disposal, as expressed by the term 'system of signifiers') and the technical is more essential than it might at first appear. The system of signifiers is always already technical,[49] because only technology ensures its circulation, that is, the circulation of signs through decontextualization and recontextualization. It is impossible to sever the ties that bind signs to their contexts except, as it were, with the sharp blade of technics.

This brings us to the movement that Winkler calls the 'discursive economy', in which he seeks to demonstrate how McLuhan's double pillar of media-message is overly simplistic, to the point of being misleading (Winkler 2004: 256). A closer examination reveals that a number of sublevels exist between the medium (which he identifies with technics) and the message, sublevels which are primarily connected with media use and pragmatics.

The movement of discursive economics represents the key to a dynamic concept of the media, one that nevertheless remains a technical concept:

> A parallel attempt was made for the technical infrastructure of the media. Especially when media studies are centred on a 'materiality of communication', it is important not to reduce the concept of the material. The basic materialistic intuition [*Grundintuition*] goes wrong when it assigns a position to the *acts* – every bit as 'material' as the hardware – at the very edge of the model, as a dependent variable of the technical 'a priori'. Media technology would also have to be understood in terms of circulation; not only as its prerequisite but also as its product. (Winkler 2004: 249–50)

In this case, a recursive loop connects sign operations to the technical hardware.

This loop entails the claim that it is the economy of signs (and discourses) that drives the need for technology, just as much as it is technology that predetermines this economy; it would be impossible to imagine a medium without its (supposed or real) use on signs. From this point of view, the purely technical question of signal-to-noise ratio seems artificially abstract because it is always intertwined with the semiotic plane that exceeds the level of the signal. Shannon's theory of 'information entropy' itself is a distillation that allows us to say how many bits are needed to transmit a certain set of words, but does not say anything about what words or what context. From the perspective of the theory of media, embedded as they are in the social world, the information theory of communication is of little use unless it can be supplemented by questions of semantics, pragmatics, relevance and context. In this sense, Winkler's approach offers an alternative to the mathematical concept of technics (on its early re-evaluation, cf. Chapter 6, esp. pp. 190–1 and 199–206).

By the same token, however, the articulation of spoken language by technical means augments its essential reversibility (and manipulability), understood again as a cycle of recontextualization. It further extends its intrinsic (non-technical) potential for manipulation, not always to a different level (even this, however, is experimentally possible) but in relation to different (media) backgrounds. All of this is processual in nature, running on the verge of the creation of fictional worlds. Yet even in the case of fictional worlds, elements disconnected from real contexts are then integrated into others (constrained by the fact that these too must also be imaginable, thinkable). While this produces a kind of movement that Winkler calls 'symbolic',[50] nothing prevents us from describing it as a kind of proto-fiction that may or may not develop into fiction of the intentional kind (and from there into elaborated, literary fiction).

We see this with communication in the everyday context. In the Internet environment, the same texts appear in multiple versions, yet it is impossible based on their titles to determine whether they are redundant copies, reworked versions or completely new texts (Winkler 2002/1997: 134). In this sense, it is also necessary to understand 'which shift in "content" by comparison to existing media', as Winkler writes, 'is the cause for a new arrangement of signifiers' (Winkler 2002/1997: 338).

Today, the counterpart of context-bound communication is the archive of society, that is, the collective structure.[51] Of course, this is not its very first instance, and we find similar phenomena in the case of the Great Library of Alexandria, for example, or literary canons– or, in a certain sense, the encyclopaedia. Yet it is only with the 'data universe' that discourse begins to align so closely with hardware architecture, making it possible to bridge in real time the gaps that always existed between symbolic processes and technics – or, as Winkler writes, 'between fluid discourses and real social implementations' (Winkler 2002/1997: 127). Such is the new order of signifiers, with its more fluid organization made up of a diversity of discursive styles and texts – all the easier, as a consequence, to carry out basic manipulation (or fiction), to which the use of media architecture inevitably succumbs.

The new order of signifiers is also brought about by another kind of shift, which we are already witnessing: it is not true that *litera scripta manet* – that what is written is given, much less that is permanent. Media carry out the ongoing negotiation of meaning (this is also Lisa Gitelman's definition of media (2006: 6)), and text structures are thrust into motion by an unlimited potential for intervention and breakdown of authorship in its classical conception.[52] The manner in which information is cared for today automatically ensures that outdated information will be replaced by the new, even in an aesthetic sense. The selection and network use of information make it possible to perceive, at every instance, some other element as either redundant or original. The further development of that technics, which first emerged during the first half of the twentieth century and brought to the world an aesthetics born from the spirit of information theory, has also meant the end of a general dialectics of redundancy and originality, which has long served as founding principle of any aesthetics.

A technics built on the notion of information must sooner or later ask itself what that information is about, and as we have already indicated, this leads inevitably to the concept of the sign and its referent.[53] But first there reigns the 'charm' of the early phase, when the issues of signification as such are neglected, so that it is possible to consider technical innovations as an appropriate solution to problems which, strictly speaking, are not of a technical nature, and to lay aside that which was felt to be precarious in the context of the older 'overcome' (*überwundenen*) medium (Winkler 2002/1997: 216–17). Typically, with the invention of audiovisual recording, the imperfection of the symbolic capture of reality (which induced hallucination, as Kittler says) is overcome. However, as Kittler and Winkler add, this leads over time to new (and paradoxically more disturbing) forms of manipulation, which once again raises the question of a new assessment of existing media forms.

It is therefore necessary to return to the historical background, in which, after spoken language had ceased to be perceived as a self-evident reflection or recording of reality,[54] reversibility and manipulability gradually began to be recognized and used (not only theorized), which, however, did not reach its full potential in terms of the practical possibility of editing any perception of reality until the technical inventions asserted themselves. However, this happened in stages, once the conditions for the use of technology had been simplified – the automation of production, standardization of the interface and initially also the layout of positions within the entire system, etc. – and (more crucially) after the public had become more enlightened, their initial prejudices dismantled, and certain habits and corresponding social practices established (as already shown by Siegert's classic breakdown of the history of the postal system).[55] This also involves a certain operational closure (in Luhmann's sense) of the system thus created, but it is still important that this system can only be built with practices that make it possible to actually use the new technologies.

In the era of 'new tertiary media' (as Harry Pross and Werner Faulstich talk about them), which requires the use of technical apparatuses by both sender and receiver, the 'channel throughput' ceases to be the only determinant factor (in contrast to the era of 'secondary' and 'old tertiary' media). Much now depends on the extent to which addressees participate in the processing of mediated content, including manipulation.

As Kittler convincingly demonstrates (in 1999/1986, for example), we must take it as given that the universal and primal potential for manipulation only comes with the advent of new media. Thus, the motivation behind individual cases of manipulation seems unimportant by comparison to the need to clarify its technical and other conditions. Technics is usually thought to be a possibility of manipulation that is at hand, and that may or may not be carried out by the corresponding independent practice (discourse, for instance, in the case of spoken language). In other words, manipulation can be revealed and described. On the other hand, Kittler also attributes a certain autonomous and ever present capacity for manipulation to technics, from which new discourse is derived. In the third approach, which complements Kittler's technical a priori and the autonomy of expressive practice (*Äußerungspraxis*), the question is how to map the influence of this practice on advances in technology (Winkler 2004: 137). This follows up on our previous discussion of the relationship between operations and technics; with Winkler, we are given a micro-analysis of how Schüttpelz's recursive operations loop might appear when applied to a technics dealing with discourse. Building on more robust semiotic foundations than Schüttpelz (and a larger textual 'area' in the material sense), Winkler is able to focus on the main media functions (communication, recording, manipulation).

As a result of expressive practice, codes are produced and technological innovation stimulated. The key to the argument is that the leap from expressive practice to new technologies is only seemingly greater than the leap from this practice to code as its second product. All three have something to do with materiality, and it can even be said that all three engage with material in an arbitrary manner.[56] The difference lies in the fact that air, which the human voice causes to vibrate, is there in the first place, while the copper cable that carries a telephone signal has yet to be produced, arranged and – as Winkler says – *articulated*. The analogy or causal connection between speech and technical operation would therefore consist in the – metaphorical – articulation of materiality. Technics is articulation, and articulation (symbolic discourse) is always already technical. Once more, it is possible to distinguish them using the prepositions *in* and *by/through*, that is, the locative and instrumental cases (cf. Section 3 of Chapter 1, pp. 37–40): 'In this respect, an articulation *in* the signifying material (utterance) would have to be accompanied by a second level, media technology, which articulates the material and functioning of the signifier itself. [. . .] as a consequence, this means that from the beginning, a correlation must be assumed between the use of the signifier and the production/arrangement of the signifier' (Winkler 2002/1997: 139).

Up to this point, it is an obvious and plausible statement, which, however, does not greatly deepen our insight into the production of technology through communication practice. What is the relationship between 'use' and 'arrangement', that is, between 'media content' and 'media standard'? Winkler answers unambiguously: 'power' (*Macht*): 'For one, it is striking that the articulation/formation of media technology takes place in a disproportionately more centralized, controlled and hierarchical manner than the articulation of utterances. For this, the social apparatus has created certain organs, which, moreover, correlate in many ways with more traditional concentrations of power (the state and post office, media corporations, etc.)' (Winkler 2002/1997: 139–40). In this sense, Winkler follows Kittler's (and also Flusser's) interpretation of *pro-grammes* (understood as the first imperative by which the media opens itself to all possible expressions that take place there), with its etymological root in 'pre-scription' (*pro graphein*). Technical standards took over communication and subjugated its 'subjects' (Maresch and Werber 1999: 10, cited in Winkler 2004: 140). We might note how the centralized articulations of material (which predetermine possible arrangements of signifiers) are intrinsically a cause of concern (whether or not we understand their mechanism in terms of power); we find the expression of this in such seemingly distant events as the investigation of Microsoft and Google for the abuse of standardized algorithms, that is, in Winkler's language of articulation of technical material (in legal terminology abuse of a dominant position in the market). In the case of communication media, this also has an obvious influence on discursive practice.

Further discussion of the way this distribution of power is connected to the economy and regulatory economics lies outside the scope of this chapter. From a historical point of view, however, it is worth remembering that spending resources on technological innovation is only possible where a modicum of (purchasable) demand is already being collected on the original investment of a given medium (or its immediate predecessor): starting with the sovereign and army, and later the upper strata of the urban population, and finally lowest strata of the masses.[57] We should speak therefore not only of economic potential, but of economic need – Winkler calls it 'system tension' (*Systemspannung*). This need must be understood as a certain deficit, the inadequacy of the current system, that is, what the discourse would be well to produce, but does not yet do so.[58] In this way, a certain dialectic arises: the existing technical system – its shortcomings – new technology (Winkler 2004: 141–2). The question of whether a certain type of discourse produces a certain medium is therefore badly posed: one should ask rather how a whole media *system* (the mass media system, for example, or film industry system) is created.

At the same time, it is necessary to consider that the various levels – semiotic, institutional, technical and structural-functional – are all equally important (Winkler 2004: 145). Indeed, Winkler claims that they form a 'continuum', with mutual connections joining the demarcation/limitation (*Abrundung/Freistellung*) of individual enunciations and texts (which allows them to circulate), the formation of a system in the transition from discourse to code (accompanied by the emergence of redundancy), and the formation of institutions and inscription/demarcation/encapsulation (*Einschreibung/Abrundung/Einkapslung*) of specifically technical infrastructures (Winkler 2004: 145). Technics does not therefore arise separately but in interaction with a number of other factors, with the result of an operational closure of the system (Luhmann). This also completes the recursive loop, and introduces social factors into it that are crucial to the circulation of signifiers, but also more contingent. It is therefore a three-dimensional or spatial loop. Each of these variants – technics as articulation and discourse as technics – represents a synthetic thesis, presenting a new element to the existing thinking of both, while also allowing us to think of them as a continuum rather than separate systems.

3. Infogenic man and the software explosion

In what follows, let us explore two more ways by which technics may involve human subjects, narcotized, in a recursive loop, by the increasing presence of technical media. The first is the concept of 'infogenic man' coined by Manfred Faßler, the second is the emergence of operating chains at the level of software, which is to say, the articulation of material media (hardware). The first of these traces the emergence of meaning from the materiality of technology, the second the articulation of this materiality itself.

Faßler makes the rather banal claim that a person creates information out of data.[59] This is easily demonstrated using a simple example: the kind of perception that would not lead to the creation of information in the sense of Batesonian difference[60] would not have any use or need for a 'potentially human' (nor 'artificially intelligent') way of interacting with the environment. Where Winkler speaks of a 'layer of signifiers', Faßler describes information as

> wireable (*schaltbar*) [...] encoded intervals of difference (*Unterschiedsintervale*) [...] interactive and communicable decision possibilities [...]

I use information in relation to systems, data in relation to programs. Or, in biological terms, information refers to reproduction, data to replication. To put it another way, information is not the smallest unicity regarding the world, but the smallest ambiguity or equivocality on the agenda. (Faßler 2008: 10–11)

At the centre of Faßler's notion of information is a kind of production chain whereby the original data provides raw material for information, with the result of an increase in the communicability and interactivity – but also of coding and ambiguity. Despite the fact that human information skills aim to minimize data not amass as much of it as possible (Faßler 2005: 64), human civilization falls into the 'curse of complexity' (*Fluch der Komplexität*) as it carries on creating signs out of information, inevitably leading to undefinable mixtures of intentional and unintentional, random, enumerable, justified and unjustified fields (Faßler 2005: 74) – in other words, new areas of 'data', but this time secondary ones, contingent on signs. New means are then created (as already Luhmann argues) to reduce this complexity, including discursive and functional systems, which simplify the data by breaking them down along certain dividing lines – that is, *codes*.

Basic dynamics are thus determined by the factor of complexity, which is inevitable once the sign-coding process begins. This also gives rise to a notion like noise: data is comprised of everything that passes through the channel (including noise), but information already presupposes an effort to shape or group the data (thus abstracting from noise, at least in principle; Faßler 2008: 18–19).[61]

We must now try to understand the implications of these distinctions for communication. Before we get to Faßler's differentiation of interaction and interactivity, it will be helpful to retrace the cascade of signal-data-(sign-)information since it may shed light on the mathematical information theory of communication – and its limits:[62]

it is helpful to distinguish not only between signal (the arbitrary or non-arbitrary form of expression of a subject-matter with no wide-reaching context), data (expectation-bound perception of the dimensions of an object, context or action) and information (bundles of data arising in the course of perception, with which something must be accomplished). [. . .] To undertake this act of self-organization is a major effort, in the course of which the manifold coding of information has to be translated into states of biological, cultural and communication systems. This is not a consistently stable performance, nor is it an outcome. For this reason, a concept of information based on communications technology, as we have known it since Claude E. Shannon, is not sufficient. In addition, it assumes a technical-mathematical control of information flows. The performance of this concept is demonstrated on the transmitter-receiver path or computer-to-computer networking. It does not therefore bring us closer to answering our questions. (Faßler 2005: 200–1)

We find these 'scales of determinacy' elsewhere in the history of thought. Eco (1976; 1999/1968), for example, distinguishes between signal and sign by way of the presence or absence of contexts. With Faßler, the cascading process may be expressed in a single thesis: it involves increases in complexity (*Komplexitätszuwächse*) that arise through integration, in the sense of cooperative evolutionary processes. As a consequence, noise and fuzziness, relevant to the issue of communication, are dimensions of episodic decisions which must be made when consuming information (Faßler 2005: 298). This meaning of noise is somewhat weaker than the one expressed by Michel Serres (1969), for example. Faßler sees noise only as a marginal, albeit necessary aspect of the increase in complexity. It is no longer caused by the signal's passing through the irregularities of the communication channel, and it is evidently *in spite of noise* that complexity increases (otherwise the noise would cause it to stagnate or decrease).[63]

Thus, the anthropologist Faßler describes information as an evolutionary achievement, one that made it possible for human collectives to take account of circumstances other than the individuals immediately present. Information makes possible the emergence of a certain in-between space: a space of interests (as in the double meaning of Latin *inter-esse*). Faßler writes:

> Information bows before the switchability and calculability of the sign [*Schalt- und Kalkulierbarkeit eines Zeichens*], and is at the same time a kind of secret bearer of the uncalculated, the new, and the differently perceptible. *Information serves two masters: calculation and fiction.* With information, a person is able to think a non-objective reality and deal with it cognitively and communicatively. Information promises a reality that in terms of representation it is not obliged to fulfil. (Faßler 2005: 62; emphasis added)

It is this interspace, abounding in complexity, that is generated by data and signal filtering and coding, and the possibilities these practices represent. (It is worth adding, perhaps, that there could not exist a better point of reference for the discussion of fictional worlds.)

The calculability of signs thus opens up a space of more evolutionarily advanced, artificial communication that does not depend on immediately present reality. This is what some theorists call 'culture' or the 'semiosphere' (Lotman), a domain that makes possible fictional worlds, representing more and more independence from matter, from humankind itself, at the same time paving the way for ever-increasing complexity, diversification, artificiality.

The increase in complexity brought about by information is carried out through cooperation, so that the development of technics may be reformulated to a certain degree as a problem of collective knowledge: collective memory (and with it collective knowledge) emerges from the possibilities generated by communication media, and these in turn are determined by conditions that are technological in nature (see, for example, Kittler's tracing of various media to military origins). Under the current technical conditions of network culture, this means on the one hand that cooperative (not authoritarian) procedures prevail, guided by the intention of fundamentally free access and availability. At first glance it may even seem that there are no binding rules or goals. However, the universal accessibility of the internet gives rise to a new (hegemonically developing and therefore neo-Enlightenment) epistemology of public space, the external sedimentation of which is the logic of hypertext. This makes imperative a new dynamic form of representation in the place of the older static form. Producers, products and recipients of the content (author, text and reader) are each situated in a different constellation, where the usual structural principles of linear written culture are weakened (Faßler 2005: 328–9), and where all agents are compelled to adapt.[64]

In this context, Faßler's distinction between interaction and interactivity is particularly salient: 'The conventionally formulated difference between interaction and interactivity is as follows: interaction is primarily sociomorphic; interactivity is primarily technogenic [. . .]. Even though interactivity is machine-supported, extended by a technical network, and partly computer-generated, it remains part of representation and signification processes (visual, discursive, acoustic)' (Faßler 1997: 237). He adds that with the predominance of technically mediated communication, two not so obvious 'selectors' have been identified: the 'willingness of the sender' (*Sendebereitschaft*) and 'interest in involvement' (*Einschaltinteresse*).[65] Interactivity determines the framework of action in media structures with a high proportion of non-human mediators – insurance companies and banks, for example, but also architectural studios, the production, design and distribution of goods and public administration. In this case, communication passes only through the most necessary minimum of shared symbols, in the strong sense of the word – that is, it avoids all redundancy, especially that which arises from pluralism of interpretation.

The aim of this stratification is to free social research from the trouble it gets into when it follows a face-to-face model of interaction and attendant behaviourist types of action, and to make possible the concept of technogenic action in media networks (Faßler 1997: 237–8). According to this concept, as seen from the human perspective, interactivity depends entirely on the audience's interest in involvement (*Einschaltinteresse*). In particular, this is the factor that decides whether and what will be communicated (not necessarily published) in the media; everything else may be technically automated. However, it is only as a function of this basic selector that technogenic *interactivity* ever becomes *interaction*.

These characteristics could be seen as a continuation of the work of McLuhan, with the essential difference that a discrepancy opens up between interaction and interactivity, one that might be characterized as a deficit of meaning: 'At the same time, there are deficits in meaning (including deficits in fiction)[66] in these digital, networked, immersive media worlds. They point to the fact that these electronic-digital media worlds are not (yet) self-evident spaces for orientation, action, perception or interpretation' (Faßler 2005: 176). This deficit is therefore linked to fictions and their potential, namely that of orientation, with respect to communicative interactions.

It turns out that it is not so easy to transfer the psychological metaphor of the network (based on associations) to the technical environment (see Winkler's detailed account, 2002/1997: 47). This also applies to media. As Winkler states, what 'stands as godfather' to computer network structures are not thought associations in general, but their speech output.[67] It is in this particular context that we must place the Faßlerian distinction between interactivity and interaction.

Various theorists (including Faßler himself) have attempted to interpret infogenic activity from an evolutionary point of view as a way of bypassing 'energy-consuming processes' related to data processing, while simultaneously increasing the power of information to create reality (Faßler 2005: 63, 254–5). Media thus make it possible to reduce the amount of energy expended, with the goal of minimizing and reducing the complexity of the data necessary, not of muddying the situation by replacing one mass of data with another. The participation of media in this task is not incidental but purposeful: inventions are ultimately meant to bring about new levels of coordination and cooperation, precisely with regard to those elements that create repeatable precision and an understanding that transcends the limits of individual situations, thereby facilitating evolution (Faßler 2005: 64, 66).

Even though media minimize data flows, they also proceed in a 'dissipative' manner, by temporarily 'wasting' energy on the relatively complex coding (as well as distribution, expansion and subsequent decoding) of communicated content. They therefore oversee both the accumulation and dissipation of communicative energy, without which there could only be a rather contingent circulation of aleatory fragments of gestures – which it seems, according to older social theory, cannot yet be characterized as communication (see, for example, Mead 1934). Thus, in addition to reducing the amount of data, media create states of disequilibrium, and it can thus be tentatively suggested that the dissipativeness that accompanies their operation may also serve as a dividing line between interactivity and interaction – cultural symbolic 'waste', as well as seemingly unintentional or redundant contextual work.

On the other hand, the expansion of the sphere of interactivity involves the increasing displacement of culture-creating intellectual skills into technology: the transposition of the reproduction of visual reality from painting to photography, or of 'thought algorithms' from the human brain to the computer. This, however, frees up capacities for the creation of new culture-creating practices and abilities. Media historians who have compiled the critiques of emerging media (Werner Faulstich, for instance) have shown how these media were ultimately taken to task precisely for expanding those cognitive-psychic possibilities that were its currency.

We may now consider how the materiality of media is articulated in the operational chain of software creation. It is the general case that software culture has overwritten categories of production, distribution and access (consumption) that emerged in the age of mass media (television, etc.) with new formats: client/server, open access/commercial (Manovich 2013: 28). Manovich draws on this example to show that

> 'new media' is 'new' because new properties (i.e., new software techniques) can always be easily added to it. Put differently, in industrial (i.e. mass-produced) media technologies, 'hardware' and 'software' were one and the same thing. For example, the book pages were bound in a particular way that fixed the order of pages. The reader could not change this order [gamebooks being a rare exception to the rule] nor the level of detail being displayed à la Engelbart's 'view control'. Similarly, the film projector combined hardware and what we now call a 'media player' software into a single machine. In the same way, the controls built into a twentieth-century mass-produced camera could not be modified at the user's will. And although today the users of a digital camera similarly cannot easily modify the hardware of their camera, as soon as they transfer the pictures into a computer they have access to endless number of controls

and options for modifying their pictures via software. (Manovich 2013: 92; emphasis added)

It is clear from this concise summary that user flexibility is one of the defining elements of the new software culture. In other words, new operational chains, which previously existed only in the latent potential of the medium, have now become a pillar of its handling and use. The degree to which this is possible is qualitatively different than any similar development in the past (this is also, perhaps, what enables or at least prompts the notion of recursive loop as a many-stranded helix). Of course, the new operational chains carry over laterally into all other areas, including literary fiction. One of the more surprising results of this development is a blurring of the distinction between experimental and conventional works: 'If in modern culture "experimental" and "avant-garde" were opposed to normalized and stable, this opposition largely disappears in software culture' (Manovich 2013: 93).[68] Experimentation in the digital medium is always imminently possible, which corresponds, at least in terms of technical possibilities, to a certain feature of the avant-garde, whose goal was to revolutionize society so that art would permeate all social life. According to Manovich, such a breakthrough means nothing less than a new stage in the history of human media, human semiosis and human communication (Manovich 2013: 46). Every user of software is or can be set in motion, and this also forces us to redefine the limits of experimentation in art.

Let us return briefly to technical development, in relation notably to Engelbart's law: the idea that the intrinsic rate of human performance is exponential – that humans are getting better at getting better. This last notion, also called 'bootstrapping', is something we all know from turning on a computer, which involves a simple programme that serves to activate more complex programmes. This principle inevitably applies to media competence as well, due to the fact that the computer was designed as a universal 'simulation machine' (Turing, von Neumann), not as a 'remediation machine', and therefore does not have its own idiomatic language (which could be taught and learned). While it initially only performed automated computational functions, the gradual development of a graphical user interface essentially meant that users could act as originator of the algorithm. Software can now be created by nearly anyone who wishes, effectively turning the computer into a universal interactive medium – but interaction specifically in the sense of taking part in any modification of what is mediated, or more concisely, what Winkler means by 'processing'.

What the computer makes possible is a much more flexible adaptation of creating a work to the interaction with the addressee. By comparison to the previous potential of intermedial and transmedial phenomena, everything can be carried out more quickly and in the environment of a single meta-media, using filters, techniques and expressive-semiotic means that probably exceed the potential for effective consumption (taking into account bootstrapping, as well as human cognitive and aesthetic limits).

The superficiality of the computer user interface is thus only apparent, being counterbalanced or even outweighed – at least on the conceptual level – by its functional complexity (including its technical implementation in the form of software). Its original task has been replaced by a recursive operation, which assumes a technical reality inter alia in the form of software updates. Whatever human extensions were originally intended, they have melt in the multitude of possible uses, depending on the capabilities of the software.

Conclusion

The technical aspect thus introduces a certain bipolarity into the theory of media. On the one hand, it underscores the aspect of the 'black box' (scientific and technical achievements become more invisible the more they achieve); on the other hand, technology creates more and more opportunities for noise and interference. The gulf between veiling and moments of insight widens, while both somehow remain ever present. The insight, however, pertains rather to how to go about handling the medium than with mediation as such (software-driven). And so technics takes on the character of a black box (or extension of the unconscious) where input-output features are more likely to draw our attention than the internal functioning. To put it another way: the greater the complexity, the greater the demand for simplification (in remarkable, though not coincidental, agreement with Luhmann's theory of communication, testifying to the relationship between complexity and sustainability in the non-linear development of dynamic systems).

It is this development, in turn, which so strikingly mirrors the original media functions: storage, communication and processing. Here we return to Winkler, who ties the development of media complexity specifically with the function of processing, and its reduction with recording (i.e. *Speicherung* or 'storage'; Winkler 2015: 163). The question then is about how the dynamics of complexity relates to communication as a temporal-spatial phenomenon, where meanings are to some extent perpetually in motion, but where a certain degree of permanence is also required. (Let us not forget that *commūnicō* is derived from *commūnis*, or that which is 'common, public, general'. This only makes sense if they can be identified as common, that is, if this is not prevented by an excessive degree of complexity.)

We will deal with this further in the chapter dedicated to the theory of social systems (Chapter 9). In conclusion, let us simply add that the instrumental and locative cases merge together – that media functions intermingle, but do not disappear. The black box of unconscious extension releases its secrets and closes again in uncontrollable cycles. As a function of software, in which the narcotic effect combines with the enduring influence of the folds of expressive practice, the spiral of operating chains and technics is transformed into a kind of universal processing.

Notes

1 To put it another way, media are essentially Promethean: the fire that makes it possible to have more cultural goods is paid for with a part of one's own body, that is, its original nature, which loses its function. This has more to do with physical effects than the message – in other words, with 'massage', and only secondarily with the 'message' (despite the fact that *The Media is the Massage* only appeared three years later than *Understanding Media*, where the original, more recognizable formulation appears). It would be even more accurate to say simply that media erase the difference between the biological and technological, between the natural and artificial.
2 However, the authors mentioned by Hartmann should be supplemented by some others; for example, Bernard Stiegler.
3 Mitchell's concept, however, is connected to the prosthetic concept and emphasizes that the medium is a minimal connection with the environment, a minimal relationality that reflects the nature of man as a fundamentally prosthetic being. Medium means 'form of life', 'general environment for life', 'ontological condition of humanization' (Mitchell and Hansen 2010: xii).
4 To be precise, they also intensify: there is no longer talk of humanisation, but of the opposite movement, the taking of the initiative by technical media, or by their system (*Medienverbund*). This connection of the two lines is therefore not the only possible one, and we find a different (albeit rather sketchy) example in the case of Mitchell.
5 For now, let us take this thesis as a general statement that does not require proof, since its evidence is at first glance all around us.
6 Kapp's 1877 work was published in English in 2018 as *Elements of a Philosophy of Technology* (University of Minnesota Press, trans. L. K. Wolfe). In the present volume, we quote from this translation with occasional modifications, or directly from the original German text, as needed.
7 As Kapp writes: 'science and art take the place of animal instinct in man, whereby he becomes the creator of himself, *even of his physical structure and its refinement*' (Kapp 1877: 29; emphasis added).

8   'Man overcomes this opposition by being able, by virtue of his primordial constitution (*Uranlage*), to productively and receptively extend his endowment with the senses which he shares with the animals, with the support of the mechanisms which are the work of his hands, ad infinitum. He must deal with things, manipulate them, shape matter for his own benefit and subjective needs. [. . .] At the same time, it is a conscious and unconscious activity; the former so as to help himself from a certain momentary lack (*Mangel*), and the latter because the form in which it helps is determined without a definite idea (*ohne deutliches Vorstellen*) and will' (Kapp 1877: 25).

9   The connection here to the psychoanalytic concept of the unconscious is particularly strong; see, for example, Freud's characterization of man in *Civilization and Its Discontents* (1961/1930: 44) as a kind of 'prosthetic God' (*Prothesengott*) who makes use of 'auxiliary organs' (*Hilfsorgane*).

10 'But let us not forget that the unconscious, though it may recede when it comes to executing the particulars of technical engineering, is felt to be all the more operative when we index the organ's disposition to activity to the mechanical construction of forms' (Kapp 2018/1877: 102); 'the defining characteristic of organ projection is that it proceeds unconsciously. Or did the men who first succeeded in sending messages across vast distances by means of electric current consciously intend, even before the first experiments, to dissect a nerve , to make an exact artificial reconstruction of the body's own nervous system and to lay this branching electrical framework over the entire earth' (Kapp 2018/1877: 141; translation modified).

11 Strictly speaking (from the point of view of cybernetics), this is a metaphor or 'retro-projection' of the discovery of the principle of the cybernetic loop (or Turing machine) on the history of technology.

12 He continues: 'If we look at the innumerable forms of primitive implements on the one hand and the innumerable variety of scientifically sophisticated cultural apparatuses on the other, we see a clear line of progress to which the theory of organic evolution with all its assumptions can be applied' (Kapp 2018/1877: 74).

13 'Great inventions (*Erfindungen*) turn out to be products of constant self-discovery (*Sichfinden*), the goal of which was originally always unconscious. [. . .] James Watt knew clearly and distinctly what he was looking for, and therefore succeeded, when the time was right, in inventing what he wanted, but the ground for it had been unconsciously prepared by many attempts, each time advancing a little nearer to the goal. And yet it remained hidden even from him that his invention would in the next phase meet a new improvement by Stephenson' (Kapp 2018/1877: 134).

14 Mukařovský anticipates this as early as 1943, objecting in advance to the (intentional) absolutization or use of the unintentional. For him, the central phenomenon is the mutual relationship and interplay of the intentional and unintentional, not the attempt to instrumentalize the unintentional.

15 However, Thrift does not take over the connection of the unconscious with (tele-)technology from Kapp or Freud, but in an already post-structuralist form from Patricia Ticineto Clough (2000). Referring to Derrida, she focuses on the technical substrates of unconscious memory, from which it is inseparable. Technology is a differentiated unconscious (Ticineto Clough 2000: 40).

16 A few (not very illustrative) examples include GPS, barcodes and more recently the computer network.

17 Here we loosely follow Tristan Thielmann's statement 'every medium needs a modicum' ('Jedes Medium braucht ein Modicum') (Thielmann 2013).

18 I am referring here to the frequency of use. Within the classical paradigm, as in Licklider and Taylor, the task is to use computers to increase the involvement of the masses in democratic process. Rheingold examines more fundamental effects.

19 Therefore, also according to Schüttpelz (2006: 91), 'the term "cultural techniques" is redundant, because all techniques are cultural techniques. Techniques are culturally contingent, they are culturally (not genetically) mediated'. Leroi-Gourhan also refused to distinguish cultural from other techniques.

20 In which, according to Schüttpelz, lies the anthropological element of the dynamics of technology: he refers to Lévi-Strauss's anthropological interpretation of education using binary oppositions. This can obviously be limiting, inasmuch as binary itself is limiting for possible code transformations.

21 'Equating the cumulative history of inventions with progressive "exteriorisation" turns out to be naïve and ultimately deceptive when examining specific sociotechnical organisations and the stories of specific inventions, be it the history of tools, domestication, or media. "Exteriorisation" takes place – if it takes place at all – reciprocally and recursively [...]. If we examine the operational chains that these artefacts have preserved for us, it is easy to prove that with each apparent "exteriorisation" came a *mutual* exteriorisation, and thus the artefacts and their technicians were newly intertwined, forcing these technicians to re-interpret themselves and reorganise their activities as "tools of tools", "gestures of gestures", "motor skills of motor skills", "memory of memory", and "programming of programming", and at the same time to train other persons and organisations for these purposes and equip them in accordance with the principle of division of labour. The exteriorisations postulated by Ernst Kapp and Leroi-Gourhan never took place' (Schüttpelz 2006: 95–6). See Chapter 5, where this finding is decisive – unintentionality has never taken its final toll, for the human subject is always re-entwined in that reorganizing recursivity. This does not mean that he resigns his essence as a subject, but simply that he becomes an involved subject.

22 'The boomerang effects of domestication, memory training of specialists on memory media, mutual "motorisation" of mills, machines, animals, and

slaves, [...] become more plausible if we accept the "priority of the chain of operations" over all the quantities involved in it, admitting also that the "operation" is applied to the results of the same "operation" – and in a different way also to the quantities involved' (Schüttpelz 2006: 97).

23 In this direction, Schüttpelz points to the 'recursive' proofreading of Leroi-Gourhan by anthropologists of a later generation: André Hadricourt, François Sigaut, Bruno Latour and others.

24 In at least two versions, on the one hand in his *Ethik* (*Ethics*, Wundt 1886: 231): 'in the entire field of human free action, the application of the will always occurs in such a way that the effects of the action reach more or less far beyond the scope of the motives, and thereby arise new motives for future actions, which in turn create new effects with similar consequences'; on the other hand in *Völkerpsychologie* ('Psychology of Nations', Wundt 1917: 389): 'that heterogony of purpose in which motives, which are always readily available, give rise to secondary consequences, which in the course of further development, can transform into purposes for which consciousness strives, and finally into main goals, in relation to which those original goals gradually recede into the background, until finally they disappear completely.'

25 Stöber (2013: 447) also works with the double stage of media evolution, when the emergence of new effects must be conditioned by planned features as well as unplanned ones. This also corresponds to Walter Benjamin's remark that the use of technology cannot be directly deduced from its explicit purposes. Cf. also Williams's reflections, discussed in Chapter 8, esp. Section 1 (pp. 280–4); for Williams, the space that mediates all effects of technology is always social and practical (the space of human agency).

26 Cf. Kittler's work or Huhtamo and Parikka 2011.

27 'A cold or low-literary culture [as opposed to e.g. England or America] cannot accept hot media such as film or radio as means of entertainment' (McLuhan 1994/1964: 31). Eduardo Navas (2009) adds to this: 'to consider a certain medium as hot or cold is to perform a social act, influenced by cultural politics'.

28 'As long as our technologies were as slow as the bicycle, the alphabet, or money, it was socially and psychologically okay to deal with being separate closed systems. But now sight, hearing, touch and movement are present simultaneously and on a global scale. And so a certain ratio of interplay between these extensions of our human functions is now necessary on a collective scale, just as it has always been necessary for private and personal rationality' (McLuhan and McLuhan 1988: 226).

29 On the contrary, Navas (2009) believes that there has been a *general* 'cooling', by which he means not only the cooling of hot media, but also the warming of cold ones, within the network culture. This then tends more towards the zero sum, lack of distinguished media competence and thus also critical distance.

30 'And this kind of reading implies in itself and for itself a specific mood of mind different from all other moods, which is something most pleasant and quite easily transmutable into a need we cannot get rid of. And so, like other narcotic means (*Mittel*), it puts us into that carefree state between sleep and wakefulness, lulls us into sweet oblivion, without the need to do anything for it' (Fichte 1806: 191 – sixth lecture). He goes on to point out the connection with tobacco addiction.

31 Here, as in the previous text, we leave it undecided whether the immersion stems more from the imitation of the rhythm of mental processes by the medium (as claimed by Hugo Münsterberg about film), or is the effect of the very disconnection of the time of presentation and the time of representation (regardless of the pace at which the recipient watches the presentation), or whether it is actually two different immersions. On the issue of immersion and interactivity, cf. Chapter 10, Appendix 1.

32 'The new technology is the "brain of the world", precisely in the sense that language was a "brain" and collective memory, and is equally distant from the workings of individual brains' (Winkler 2002/1997: 337).

33 Bolz's harshness is closer to the truth: 'Phrases and rants, advertising and graffiti reflect a change in the media-technical function of speech, which used to be a carrier of experience and now becomes a means of circulation (*Verkehrsmittel*). In these phenomena, an anonymous collective author inscribes the world (*beschriftet*). Thus, not only does writing become mass (because it is addressed to the masses), but the masses themselves write. Typewriters, computers, copiers, spray cans – with all these gadgets man inscribes the world' (Bolz 1993: 196–7).

34 Thus, Stöber (2013) considers the evolutionary model to be beneficial for the development of genres, through which selection and adaptation to changing conditions take place. Leschke's theory of media forms can follow up here.

35 However much 'manipulation', according to the common understanding, suggests an intentional, goal-driven activity, there is no doubt in the context presented here that it includes a fundamental aspect of *unintentionality* and recursion. Indeed, manipulation itself seems to arise by virtue of a recursive operation that was not originally intended. As Kittler points out, the original intention of film, for example, was to break down the movement of animals, bullets and marching soldiers, making it possible to examine them 'scientifically'. To this extent, every aesthetic use of a new medium can be seen as evidence of an originally unintended, recursive use of media, often driven by practical (for example, military) motives.

36 'In short, once we begin dealing with verbs and nouns which start with "tele," we no longer deal with the traditional cultural domain of representation' (Manovich 2001: 150), which is, of course, something of an overstatement. It would be more accurate to say that new media objects may not be created, but even those that are created are not considered to be representa-

tions in the sense of culture (a telephone call does not aim at and does not leave behind cultural creations, but television does).
37 In Manovich's terms, real-time and *representational* media (Manovich 2001: 151).
38 'Dramatic as it is, this immobilization probably represents the last act in the long history of the body's imprisonment. [. . .] Eventually VR apparatus may be reduced to a chip implanted in a retina and connected by wireless transmission to the Net. From that moment on, we will carry our prisons with us' (Manovich 2001: 113).
39 Kittler, however, lets this communication difference slip between the lines: 'Intervals may be distributed across the staves and subjected to all kinds of time axis manipulation, as in the case of Johann Sebastian Bach, who composed a fugue using the letters of his own name B-A-C-H and then reversed the interval sequence to H-C-A-B. But how these four notes with all their overtone features were to sound when played by real instruments, Bach could neither trans-nor prescribe' (Kittler 2017/1993: 6).
40 We may think here of McLuhan, who understands the film shot itself as a 'transportation to another world' (that is, to the world of fiction): 'Our literate acceptance of the mere movement of the camera eye as it follows or drops a figure from view is not acceptable to an African film audience. If somebody disappears off the side of the film, the African wants to know what happened to him. A literate audience, however, accustomed to following printed imagery line by line without questioning the logic of lineality, will accept film sequence without protest.' (McLuhan 1994/1964: 285–6).
41 Compare to Kittler: 'While the retrograde had left the acoustic characteristics of the four tones B, A, C, and H unchanged, the backward replay had a decisive impact on each individual tone' (Kittler 2017/1993: 8).
42 Kittler himself does not distinguish between the experimental and pathological context, or between those contexts and common usage ('The epoch of nonsense, our epoch, can begin' (Kittler 1999/1986: 86)). For him, everyday life is a continuous experiment – a concept which is not unproblematic.
43 As Kittler quotes Béla Balázs: 'the rhythm of montage can reproduce the original speed of the process of association. (Reading a description takes much longer than the perception of an image)' (Kittler 1999/1986: 163).
44 However, we can also see this from the opposite perspective: 'At the same time, however, had language done its job well, there would have been no media history. It was only the systematic defects and limitations of language that triggered what we are confronted with as media history and with what has been described above as a search for ever new signifiers and ever new symbolic-technical arrangements' (Winkler 2002/1997: 332). As can be seen, this is a certain idealization of language, (nostalgically) recalling its former hegemony.
45 See, for example, Manovich's notion of 'deep remixability' (Manovich 2013: 267–77).

46 On the textual level, the increase in granularity is foreshadowed, for example, by the very separation of words in written texts (which Kittler sees as first step towards manipulation), even before they were 'chopped' into moveable letters. Roger Chartier makes this observation regarding the separation of words by Irish and Anglo-Saxon scribes during the high Middle Ages: 'its consequences were considerable, creating the possibility of reading more quickly, and so reading more texts and more complex texts' (Chartier 1995/1993: 16). In this case, it is a recursive influence on a practice (reading) by a certain technique (writing) that was originally motivated by that same practice (reading).

47 To put it another way: process and preservation mutually demonstrate one another. It is a special kind of teleology that answers the question *Why is there structure?* – *To change*, as well as the question *Why is there a process?* – *To create something irreversible*.

48 Cf. Winkler, citing Luhmann: 'this enables that kind of trial action [*Probehandeln*] which, in direct contrast to real action, represents perhaps the most important definition of the symbolic' (Winkler 2004: 220; cf. 49, 253). In Winkler's interpretation of trial we find the same reversible/irreversible distinction. Here, however, trial action never ceases to be real and is therefore irreversible, although it can be understood that working with signs in the case of a test – in a film editing room, for example, or on a computer screen – is reversible in one of its layers in a specifically technical way, which thus differs from the reversal of actions without recourse to machines. On the other hand, the identification of symbolic work with the fictional (that is, virtuality, or in Winkler's words the 'subjunctive' as opposed to the 'indicative') seems plausible. Cf. also Winkler 2015: 59; 2002/1997: 202, 235.

49 Winkler says explicitly that his thought system is in some ways no more than a media-technical reinterpretation of Derrida's critique of the sign and its application to the context of technology (yet another example of decontextualization).

50 Conversely, Bruno Latour (2013/2012: 233–57) refuses to call it symbolic: Beings of fiction (*êtres de fiction*) represent one of Latour's fifteen modes of existence, which, however significant, does not coincide with works of art, although it also includes them. The essential thing is that it is not even what we usually understand under the term 'symbolic world', but a category that precedes it (and which also lends some of its features to other categories), the world 'n', which at the same time immediately gives rise to n+1 (usually mistaken for the author) and n-1 (usually mistaken for the audience) and which takes place in everyday reality (again: not only in art). The sign system as the basis of the symbolic world (or the world of symbolic forms) as opposed to the world of matter is a construct that arises from the exaggeration and hasty identification of the fictitious entities with the world of art (and signs) and from overlooking the rule that none of the categories

exists in itself, but only through others (this follows from Latour's category of network and other categories).

51 '"Communication" had traditionally linked two human communicants, ego and alter; mass communication a central, monological transmitter with a multitude of distributed but still human receivers; and even the medium of writing, despite all irritations, was understood according to the same scheme, that is, as working with a time delay, but ultimately intended for a human reader. With the data universe, a completely different kind of idea prevails. The opposite of "communication" is now the social archive, that is, that overall structure which either coincides with collective memory or represents it at the level of symbolic representations. All symbolic/informational activities go into this archive, questions are addressed to the archive, and it is this archive that, not unlike an oracle, is supposed to answer the questions' (Winkler 2002/1997: 126).

52 'Together with the nature of recording, we must note that computers avoid any material notation and, in direct contrast to writing, present what is stored in constant motion' (Winkler 2002/1997: 128).

53 'A technology that enters the scene under the label of "information" will inevitably be asked what it actually informs us about, i.e. what the object of the information collected is; and if, in any case, empiricism often confuses its "data" with reality – a situation that leads Flusser to observe ironically that it would be better to speak of facts (i.e. of what is made) than of data (i.e. of what is given) – this also indicates that all problems of the sign concept, of meaning and reference, will return once more to the terrain of new media' (Winkler 2002/1997: 216).

54 Cf. Chapter 1, in particular the passage on Bacon and Locke, pp. 24–6.

55 Cited in Winkler (2004: 133–5). See also Jansson (2014: 287–93), especially regarding daily routines.

56 'Is it not that the material of signifiers, in which an utterance is articulated, also appears to have been chosen relatively arbitrarily? A material snatched up from the outer world and made into signifiers? When the sound of oral language emanates through space, it uses the material properties of the air as a carrier medium that ensures articulation, as well as addressing/reaching the addressee' (Winkler 2004: 138–9).

57 It is in this way that interested parties eager for news are catered to. On the process of innovation in its entirety cf. Stöber 2013: 414–32.

58 We find an example of this at the turn of the nineteenth and twentieth centuries in the dilemma of '*Sprachskepsis*' and emergence of film, or even in the spread of mobile phones, which was also caused by an increased demand for general mobility. But it would also be possible to mention the need for a systematic arrangement of texts ('textual positivism', McLuhan), demands for cartography, a new arrangement of social ties ('communal interdependence'), an increased need for authorship, education, etc. in connection with the invention of printing.

59 This is potentially transferable to technogenic interactivity and machines as well: the machine can be considered as an independent communicator, so long as it determines by itself what will be recorded as a coded difference and possibly further communicated.
60 According to Gregory Bateson's well-known definition: information as a 'difference which makes a difference' (Bateson 1987/1972: 199, 229, 271, 321, 323).
61 Even the signal assumes differentiation from noise, but it is accompanied by practically zero contextual determination (see below).
62 At the same time, we are now focusing here, just like Faßler and in contrast to the initial definition, on communication, which can be reborn as signification, i.e. communication between human subjects. Another, broader concept can, of course, refer to communication in the sense of transmitting information between machines. See, for example, Eco: 'So let us define a communicative process as the passage of a signal (not necessarily a sign) from a source (through a transmitter, along a channel) to a destination. In a machine-to-machine process the signal has no power to signify in so far as it may determine the destination sub specie stimuli. In this case we have no signification, but we do have the passage of some information' (Eco 1976: 8).
63 Compare to Faßler's observation on flows of information: 'We are cultivating a kind of blurring [*Geschäft der Unschärfe*], i.e. evolutionary cooperation (!), while at the same time optimizing the fringes of culture, our everyday life, our professions. Economists call it constrained optimization, in science it is known as 'boundary management'. Flows of information promote border-crossings, transit, adaptive transformations' (Faßler 2005: 298). Noise here is not characterized as a definite (and representable) phenomenon, but rather as a management of the boundaries/friction between phenomena.
64 Compare to Chartier's observation: 'The substitution of screen for codex is a far more radical transformation because it changes methods of organization, structure, consultation, even the appearance of the written word' (Chartier 1995/1993: 15).
65 This is Luhmann's concept, parallel to Kittler's dictum: 'Only what is wireable is at all' (Kittler 2017/1993: 5) – suggesting as well its moderation and refinement.
66 It can be recalled that abstract concepts that allow concrete data to be compared work on the basis of operational fictions (Schmidt 2000 – 'we', 'society', 'culture', etc.).
67 'The network metaphor already presupposes what language, as a distinctive force, brings into thinking in the first place; it is not our thinking that is network-shaped/distinctive, but at most our linguistic-semantic system; thinking and language are by no means coextensive, in any case no more than the network metaphor and concept of association coincide' (Winkler 2002/1997: 47).
68 Manovich does not seem to be referring here to the avant-garde as based on its social function (Peter Bürger), but rather with emphasis on experiment and a focus on the medium.

8

Communication, solution and mediality

The paradoxical character of Williams's thinking on the medium

Josef Šebek

Raymond Williams is an enduringly inspirational figure of the second half of the twentieth century in British literary and cultural theory. Yet his position in the intellectual terrain of this period is not unequivocal: for some, he represents the first – now outdated – wave of British cultural theory (Hall 1980), while others criticize his methodological vagueness.[1] Nonetheless, Williams is notable both for his innovative definitions of literature and culture, and for his search for models that would connect text and context in such a way as to overcome the simple dichotomy of work and social 'background' or 'base' and 'superstructure'. He is also notable for his various views on the issue of media and mediality, a topic which for Williams includes literature. His theoretical works – above all *Marxism and Literature* (1977), *Culture* (1981) and the collection of essays *Culture and Materialism* (1980) – illustrate the most characteristic aspect of his thinking: his view that cultural artefacts and social phenomena are not objects but processes or situations, that they are not subject to binary categorizations but distributed on diverse scales. Which is to say, drawing on Williams's own terminology, that these things exist as a 'solution' (not a 'precipitate'), which makes possible the 'lived' actualization of phenomena and convergence of various – sometimes widely diverging – spheres of human life.

This chapter deals with the question of Williams's understanding of the medium and mediality, how this understanding changes from text to text, and whether we can characterize his thinking as a form of media science. Although the concept of the medium was never central to Williams's thinking, his texts repeatedly return both to the medium in a general sense, and to individual media, across a variety of contexts both concrete and conceptual. Not only was he one of the most influential early theorists of 'new media' (cf. Lister et al. 2009/2003: 77–104, 328–43) – one who at times critiqued the very concept of the medium as too narrow and limiting – but the 'medium' and related terms – 'communication', 'transmission' and 'process' – appear with some frequency in his writings. This will lead us at times to consider interpretations of his concepts that are different than those provided by Williams himself, thus confirming a principle that applies throughout the present volume: that we may trace the genealogy of the medium even to those contexts in which the concept as such can only be found in its latency. Williams's work represents a specific case in which the concept of the medium is explicitly named but more narrowly defined, allowing for a genealogical reading of the medium that reveals a rich array of meanings that anticipate the concept as it is defined in contemporary approaches to media and mediality.

I will divide Williams's work here into three phases: (1) the period of his 'trilogy' – *Culture and Society, 1780–1950* (1958), *The Long Revolution* (1961) and *Communications* (1962) – in which he attempts to define and grasp the relationship between culture, the means of communication and society; (2) the period of his increased interest in individual (not only new) media, and greater attention to technics and technology; (3) the period in which he formulates his theory of cultural materialism, and completes the theoretical works *Marxism and Literature* and *Culture*.[2] The second and third periods partially overlap, so that the chronology is supplemented by a focus on two rather different lines of Williams's thought.

The basic thesis of the chapter is that the concept of the medium as such never gained a prominent position in Williams's thinking, and can even be seen to recede into the background over time, or else become an object of critique. This last is due to the particular way in which Williams understands the term, starting in the second half of the 1960s: namely, with an emphasis on its technological dimension, narrowly defined and detached from the contexts of production and reception, and from the wider social framework. This is reflected in his profound disagreement with Marshall McLuhan's concept of the medium – the most influential at the time – which envisages the relationship between media and society as a function of 'technological determinism' and 'aesthetic formalism'. In hindsight, however, we may productively consider how Williams's theory of culture and literature, together with his analyses of individual means of communication, represent an essentially medial way of thinking – in spite of his own explicit rejection of the concept of medium.

1. Culture and communication

In *Culture and Society, 1780–1950*, Williams examines the theories of culture that emerged in the British context, from the late eighteenth century to his day, and their relationship to the concept of society, as well as art, industry, democracy and class (Williams 1976/1958: 13–19). In several places throughout the book, he explicitly lists 'new media', starting with the development of letterpress (e.g. the invention of the steam printing press in 1811), and proceeding to cablegram, telegraph, telephone, film, radio and television (Williams 1976/1958: 290). He emphasizes the process of modernization (and the reaction against it), and thus implicitly aims against the privileging of 'traditional' art forms/media that find themselves in competition with 'new' media. Overall, however, Williams's uses of the terms of 'medium' and 'media' are relatively marginal. He understands all media primarily as means of communication, and 'new' media as means of mass communication. Communication is the key concept here, containing within it all possible conceptions of the medium and media. If, on the one hand, Williams considers the process of modernization to be shaped largely by the expansion, both quantitative and qualitative, of communication and its means, his conception of mass communication is not that of an impersonal system, driven solely by a tendency towards ideological and economic control of the population. On the contrary, communication as a whole plays a role in the creation of human communities, and therefore 'any real theory of communication is a theory of community' (Williams 1976/1958: 301; on the concept of communication in systems theory, see Chapter 9 *passim*).

Here and in later works, it is this conception that is essential to the development of Williams's thinking on the medium and media. It also shapes his view on individual 'traditional' arts. Literature, for example, on which he turns most of his attention, is not an area of aesthetic autonomy or elite values, but precisely a means of communication. Already here, Williams appears to have reservations about any concept of communication determined by its technical means or technical media: 'The techniques are [. . .] at worst neutral [. . .] much of what we call communication is, necessarily, no more in itself than transmission: this is to say, a one-way sending. Reception and response, which complete communication, depend on other factors than the techniques' (Williams 1976/1958: 290–1).

Even in *The Long Revolution*, the concept of the medium is not very prevalent. Yet it is here that Williams develops his theory of communication much more extensively, highlighting in particular the communicative aspect of art (including literature). In order to better grasp the general framework of his understanding of mediality, we should note that he places emphasis on such concepts as 'lived experience' and 'structure of feeling' (see especially Williams 1992/1961: 48–9, cf. Filmer 2003). In other words, Williams broadly conceives of patterns in contemporary culture, as shaped and perceived by contemporary agents. The concept of culture appears here for the first time either as a 'solution' (in its currently experienced, lived form) or as a precipitate (as it is recorded and reconstructed; Williams 1992/1961: 47). The term 'solution' (i.e. a liquid mixture) thus serves as a metaphor that runs through virtually all the texts dealt with in this chapter, and it figures prominently in the argument I will proceed to develop regarding the medial nature of Williams's definitions of culture and literature.

It is also in *The Long Revolution* that Williams clarifies his concept of the relationship between art and communication: 'What we call an art is one of a number of ways of describing and communicating, and most arts, quite clearly, are developments of ways commonly used – as dance from gesture, poetry from speech. [. . .] The distinction of the arts is that in different ways they command very powerful means of this sharing; although again, in most arts, these means are developments from general communication' (Williams 1992/1961: 24). It follows that 'the arts are certain intense forms of general communication' (Williams 1992/1961: 25) and that '[t]o see art as a particular process in the general human process of creative discovery and communication is at once a redefinition of the status of art and the finding of means to link it with our ordinary social life' (Williams 1992/1961: 37). Williams thus dismantles certain binary oppositions and arranges them conceptually as a continuous scale, a tendency that (as mentioned earlier) characterizes his thinking on the relationship between art and social life throughout his works.

In *Communications*, Williams focuses specifically on the role of the means of communication in contemporary British society (except for a few rare occurrences, however, he does not refer to these as 'media' but simply as 'communications').[3] From a theoretical point of view, and in the context of this chapter, there are two ways in which this work is particularly interesting. First, it gives us further insight into the way Williams conceives of 'communications', namely as 'the institutions and forms in which ideas, information, and attitudes are transmitted and received' (we see once more how the means of communication are not limited to technologies or 'techniques'). Communication itself is a 'process of transmission and reception' (Williams 1966/1962: 17), but with much broader social meaning, given that 'society itself is a form of communication through which experience is described, shared, modified, and preserved' (Williams 1966/1962: 18).

Second, it is in *Communications* that Williams exemplifies his conception of communication media (without, however, referring to them in these terms). In his view, the technological aspect of the medium and its specific character do not play a decisive role, even though these are undoubtedly important for the dissemination, scope and impact of what is communicated. Rather, it is necessary to refer back to the history of individual means of communication, and to the two sides of the communication process: production (economic and ideological factors, the overall sociopolitical framework of the system in which the means of communication operate, etc.) and reception (readership and viewership, social strata targeted, im/possibility of feedback, etc.).

We might briefly consider the (limited) degree to which the concept of the medium and general concept of media are present in these three works by Williams. As stated previously, the terms 'medium' and 'media' appear in these works only marginally, limited to the context of mass or new media, or (less often) to the various concrete means of communication. The overarching term here is precisely 'communication' as one of the main factors shaping society. Art is not distinct from communication practice but instead represents the intensification of a creative element that can be found in all communication. The following aspects of communication are particularly important: (1) it shapes communities and society as a whole; (2) technical communication media are means, not goals or determinants, of the communication process; (3) communication is not one-sided, and there is always an active element in reception; (4) culture is not a collection of artefacts but a total communication process. In the works discussed here, we thus recognize three meaning-specific contexts for the term 'medium':

1. Media as historically established means of communication: print (books, newspapers and magazines, which Williams considers as separate media), theatre, radio, television, telegraph, telephone and so on. When studying a particular medium, we must always pay attention to the entire context of communication, the parties involved in sending and receiving, and the relevant social institutions.
2. The medium as an established means or form of communication in the general sense. This context can also be concretely documented, but it is significantly present implicitly, when discussing communication and its specific forms. There is also an aspect of this generally understood medium as a means of storing information.
3. Finally, media can be understood as established types of communication that serve to produce and reproduce society. This third context, which is only implied and therefore difficult at times to identify, follows directly from the fundamental role that Williams attributes to communication, and from his efforts to reconceptualize phenomena conventionally regarded as dichotomies (discrete phenomena, directly opposed to one another) as continuous scales. From a certain point of view, society as such *is* communication. This aspect is related to the level of lived experience and structures of feeling. However culture is recorded, we can only ever encounter it as something lived, which is to say, in the

form of a solution rather than a precipitate. This applies both to the process in which new culture emerges (and is produced and perceived by actual agents) and in the sense of a 'selective tradition', representing an older culture that has 'dissolved' (i.e. it has been activated, evaluated, selected) in culture as it is presently lived. To some degree, it is precisely the various media – that is, historically constituted and socially anchored forms of communication – that enable and realize this 'dissolution'. Williams later elaborates this idea in a number of other works, including 'Means of Communication as Means of Production' (1978), in which he emphasizes that the means of production are both 'general' (comprising but surpassing those narrowly conceived as material) and communicative, *Marxism and Literature*, and *Culture*.

2. Technique, technology and cultural form: The medium and technological determinism

As Williams continued to develop his thinking on media issues in the 1970s, it became more theoretical and his terminology more precise, incorporating a number of new aspects. We see a fundamental shift in his work that involves his coming to terms with the most influential media theory of the time, introduced by Marshall McLuhan in *Understanding Media* (1964). Williams's analysis of the concept of the medium in *Television: Technology and Cultural Form* (1974) is the most thorough of all his works, but it is also shaped by his rejection of McLuhan's concept – or rather Williams's specific interpretation of this concept – and we see him turning away from the concept as such.[4]

While Williams's analysis in *Television* focuses on a single medium, it also raises issues about media and mediality in general, and we find him turning frequently to the concept of medium in the first and second meanings defined earlier. In this chapter, we are primarily interested not in television as a specific medium, but in Williams's approach to this 'exemplary' medium, which is based, in brief, on his understanding of television as a historically embedded social practice that can only be defined by a comprehensive description, ranging from its technological development to its ultimate social use (the concept of 'mobile privatization', fulfilling the needs of spatial and social mobility vis-à-vis the atomization of households), institutions that form the framework of its functioning (both public and private/commercial), as well as its various forms (genres, types of programmes, etc.), fundamental structure (i.e. modulated flow[5]), effects and the possibility of deliberate intervention into this already established but still developing practice.

In the first chapter of *Television*, 'The Technology and the Society' (Williams 2003/1974: 1–25), Williams prefigures his overall conception of television as a medium: according to him, technology is not shaped by isolated technological enquiry, but is 'being looked for and developed with certain purposes and practices already in mind' (Williams 2003/1974: 7). He proceeds to work through nine individual versions of the thesis on causal dependence with regard to the relationship between technology and its (social) consequences; he concludes that television is not *causa prima* of the contemporary world, nor is it merely a symptom of processes that are carried out more forcefully thanks to it. The key concept here is 'intentions', in the context not only of the search for purposes that an existing technology may serve, but also insofar as it motivates the very direction of technological research and discovery (Williams 2003/1974: 3–7).

Williams continues with his general theoretical reflections on the medium in the oft-cited sub-chapter 'The Technology as a Cause' (Williams 2003/1974: 129–32), where he directly confronts McLuhan's theory.[6] According to Williams, McLuhan's concept of the medium is the culmination of an 'aesthetic formalism' that has been projected into social theory. Williams sees this as a celebration of the power of the autonomous technical medium and 'attempted cancellation of all other questions about it and its uses' (Williams 2003/1974: 129). Media are thus understood as extensions of man, which are constitutive of the context of their use. Williams sees this in McLuhan primarily where the latter speaks of 'retribalization' and the global village, understood as a symptom of the latest phase of the 'coolest' media, i.e. media characterized by the highest degree of participation. McLuhan tends in this way to ratify contemporary culture and reduce essential social factors to the effects of the medium. Williams also questions McLuhan's interest in the specificity of individual media, which, according to Williams, McLuhan understands not as diverse historical practices but as aspects of a single extended 'sensorium'. The 'desocialization' of media manifests itself precisely by the transfer of communication to 'physical events in an abstracted sensorium' (Williams 2003/1974: 130). McLuhan's idea of retribalization and the connection of all individuals by communication networks thus neglects, from Williams's point of view, that its form and specific media content are subject to the control of social institutions and authorities, so that we might 'forget ordinary political and cultural argument and let the technology run itself' (Williams 2003/1974: 131). Overlooking this aspect means relegating control of the social space to those who capitalize on the media, in the sense that the means of media production is in their hands. Williams's reading of McLuhan, however, is exceedingly selective: he ignores McLuhan's sensitivity to the manipulative power of the media, both economic and political, as well as a significantly more complicated conception of the relationship between technology and its effects on society, which resist any straightforward characterization as deterministic. To a certain extent, Williams thus seems to use McLuhan as a *pars pro toto* for a certain theoretical position which McLuhan himself does not actually profess (on McLuhan, see Chapter 7, pp. 241–6, or p. 230).

It is significant, in the general context of Williams's concept of the medium as we are dealing with it in this chapter, that this is the point on which his opposition to the identification of medium with technology is most pronounced. By limiting his definition of the medium to its 'reified' technological manifestations, he will ultimately be compelled to abandon the concept altogether. In his works to this point, the concept does not play a central role, and Williams uses it without critiquing or problematizing it in any way, or giving it a clear definition. This changes with his critique of McLuhan's technological determinism or 'aesthetic formalism', and he will make only marginal use of the concept in the works that follow, or else use other terms, or subject it to further critique.

Williams's criticism of McLuhan and the whole 'Williams-McLuhan debate' is perhaps the most well-known intervention by Williams in the context of media studies, one that has not lost any of its urgency or relevance in the age of the next wave of new media (especially the internet and social networks). It can be said that, however – at least in the Anglo-Saxon context – that the argument for technological determinism is today considered to be a rather unsuitable interpretation of the relationship between technics/technology and society. Denis McQuail and Mark Deuze (2020/1983: 161–5) deal with this issue in the chapter 'Communication Technology and Culture' of *McQuail's Media & Mass Communication Theory*, writing that 'technologies are unlikely to have a direct impact on cultural practices' (2020/1983: 162). Their conception of the chain of influence, which they visualize in a schema, is similar to Williams's understanding of the social context, and of the intentions that lead to technical innovation and the eventual expansion of the associated technology (2020/1983: 163). In other works, technological determinism is framed as a concept effectively abandoned by media studies, albeit in a rather precipitous manner, so that it may be necessary to reinterpret it in a more adequate framework (Lister et al. 2009/2003: 78–80; to dominance of the anti-deterministic current, see also Bolter and Grusin 1999: 76 and Mitchell and Hansen 2010).[7]

In *New Media: A Critical Introduction*, Martin Lister et al. analyse the Williams-McLuhan debate in detail, with the aim of rehabilitating some aspects of McLuhan's media theory. They then insert it into the centre of contemporary debates on new media, especially those connected to the use of computers (understood either as a medium or as a platform simulating already existing media) and the internet, in which the determining – or determined – nature of the medium once more becomes an vital question (Lister et al. 2009/2003: 77–99; 327–43). It seems that some kind of rehabilitation of McLuhan's theory is in order, with consideration both for the time in which it was written and for what it might mean vis-à-vis contemporary new media.[8] Particularly apt is the argument that media take on the status of an environment which shapes both perception and what is perceived, often without this mediation itself being (fully) perceived (cf. McLuhan 1969: 22, cited in Lister et al. 2009/2003: 93). In this case, however, there is no reason to draw on the principle of determinism; we may turn instead to the mix of human and non-human aspects that characterizes Walter Benjamin's (2010/1935) thinking on the technical reproducibility of a work of art (his concept of the relationship of the human subject to the photographic and cinematographic apparatus, for example, and the motivations he argues that lead to the creation and development of new technologies; on the relationship between human and technology in Benjamin see Chapter 3, esp. Section 3, pp. 76–7). It is noteworthy that Benjamin too deals with these issues in the context of political critique and crisis of modernity; in this he anticipates Williams's effort to account for the complicated context of intentions, which are often based on the effort to establish or maintain hegemony. However, this conception of media as an environment can also be found to a certain extent in Williams's own writings: in the emphasis he places on the 'world-making' dimension of communication and 'structure of feeling', or in his concept of 'solution', with implications of the imperceptible omnipresence of media and their transparency.

As the subtitle of *Television* implies, Williams makes a distinction between 'technology' and 'cultural form'. The theorist Paul Jones (2006/2004: 166–8) has effectively shown how the term 'cultural forms' in *Television* refers to individual television 'genres' and 'formats', with regard to older media (news, films, sports broadcasts, etc.) as well as 'mixed' and new forms (drama-documentary, education, discussion, etc.). The term 'technology', however, refers to the process of inventing technical devices, as well as the way they are used, their reception, and related institutions. Williams thus distinguishes between 'technique', in the narrow sense of the word, 'technology', and 'cultural form'. In his book *Culture*, Williams will address the same distinction with regard to the printing press: once invented, the technique of printing necessarily required other technologies for its application, for example the expansion of literacy and the practice of reading (Williams 1981: 108–9).

In the article 'Means of Communication as Means of Production' (1978), Williams outlines his own classification of media. Here, however, he presents the concept of the medium in a critical light, and proceeds to replace it with the 'means of communication'. In this way, Williams effectively abandons the concept of the medium in the context of his general thinking on issues of mediality, technique and technology. The central claim of the 1978 article is that means of communication are also – though not exclusively – means of production. In the article, Williams begins by discussing three sets of possible objections to his central claim. The first is related to the fact that means of communication are understood 'only as "media": devices for the passing of "information" and "messages" between persons who either generally, or in terms of some specific act of production, are abstracted from the communication process as unproblematic "senders" or "receivers"' (Williams 1980b/1978: 57). Williams already conceives of media at this point in the narrow sense of tools, reserving the term 'means of communication' for specific means, i.e. historically localized and socially contextualized, among which he mentions writing and printing, as well as radio and television. Another spurious objection, according to Williams, is the distinction between 'natural' (spoken language) and technical ('mass') means of communication. Indeed, the mass means of communication include common language and communication situations; it is, moreover, a particularly diverse category (Williams 1980b/1978: 58–9; on the relationship between speech and technology, see Chapter 5, pp. 147–50). The third possible objection is based on an overly narrow understanding of the terms 'base' and 'superstructure' in some Marxist conceptions, as if 'production' must always refer to the production of objects, and not relations or practices (cf. Williams 1980a/1973).

The most significant contribution of the article, however, is the typology of means of communication, which Williams divides into two categories: those which depend on 'immediate human physical resources' (but not necessarily 'natural' resources), such as spoken language and non-verbal communication – these remain 'the central and decisive communicative means' – and those which require 'transformation, by labour, of non-human material' (Williams 1980b/1978: 61). Williams then divides this use, or transformation, of non-human material into three different types, according to their relationship to immediate human resources: (1) amplificatory, (2) durative and (3) alternative. The amplificatory type is used to strengthen or amplify the immediate means of communication, and comprises a range of means, from the megaphone to radio and television. The durative type, a comparatively recent development, involves ways of storing, and comprises those means which enable the technical recording of sound and images; some kinds of communication are also 'made durable' in painting and sculpture. The alternative type involves the use of physical objects as signs, with writing, as well as the writing system and means of their reproduction, serving as the primary example.

Neither the amplificatory nor durative mode requires any special skills for its encoding or decoding, beyond natural language and an understanding of gestures, and so on. Rather, as Williams argues, it is the accessibility of these means – the opportunity to record or view a recording, for example – that is socially stratifying. This is why the durative use of electronic means of communication, though a fairly recent development, is in many ways closer to the primary modes of communication, which depend purely on human resources, than writing and the printing press. By contrast, the alternative use of means of communication requires specific skills, such as reading and writing. Another essential distinction between the transformative means of the first group is that television and film recording is edited, so that it involves a transformation of the primary communication not merely through its transmission or storage, but through its transformation. The related means of communication thus acquire an alternative character, since they are susceptible to another system of signification superimposed on them, which emphasizes the possibilities of the given medium and at the same time has a potentially manipulative effect. However, these processes are often not very visible, and 'the real activities and relations of men are hidden behind a reified form, a reified mode, a "modern medium"' (Williams 1980b/1978: 69).[9]

Before moving on to Williams's two theoretical books – *Marxism and Literature* and *Culture* – I would like to suggest a certain interpretive turn in the reading of Williams's texts. In the article 'Means of Communication as Means of Production', Williams again rejects the concept of 'media' as technologically deterministic, and as a concept moreover which offers only a narrow and abstract understanding of communication. It is a position he had already taken in his earlier books, *The Long Revolution* and *Communications*, after which it receded to the background in *Television*, before fully manifesting itself once more in this article. In light of more recent developments in media theory, however, I believe we can simply replace Williams's 'means of communication' with the term 'media', keeping in mind that Williams everywhere understands this concept in a social and historical context, and that the technological side of the medium does not define its social functioning, although it undoubtedly participates in it. By doing so, we bring the concept of the medium back into play, and can focus on the remarkable, broadly medial aspects of Williams's theoretical works.

3. Solution: The medium within social signification systems

I will now proceed to apply this interpretive turn to two of Williams's main theoretical works, in a reading that is somewhat 'against the grain' insofar as it involves understanding his 'means of communication' and related concepts instead as 'media', and this leads in several places to a 'reversal' of the express meaning of his works.

This reading – which is designed, at first glance, as a deliberate overstatement and provocation – draws supports from several sources. First, there are a number of sources in which it is argued that the 'means of communication' are in fact 'the absent centre' of Williams's theoretical project (Graham Murdock, cited in Jones 2006/2004: xii, cf. also 157). The idea here is that Williams's own texts contradict his rejection of the medium as a reifying concept, and that he is searching for a middle term between materiality and social practice that the medium may correspond to (Mitchell 2008: 3). The very fact that Williams became one of the main representatives of the early phase of media studies speaks volumes about this tension.

A second, even more significant factor is the way Williams seeks to understand such social phenomena as literature, music, periodicals and television (and numerous others) across a full range of aspects, from their technical character to the internal structuring of their typical forms, as well as their uses and effects, and moreover to grasp them comparatively as diverse phenomena of the same order in their various functions (communication, storage, etc.). The fine arts are plucked out of their traditional context and placed instead alongside other means of communication both 'old' and 'new'. It is difficult to find a more suitable collective name for all these phenomena than the medium.

There is yet another dimension: Williams advances a specific concept of mediality as such (though not by name). The omnipresence of the media, the way they intermingle with both individual experience of the world and 'signifying systems', all this points to their role in world-making, and the way they tend in varying degrees to 'dissolve' other systems (political, economic, etc.) in themselves, and to mediate between the material and the social as a site for 'setting limits' and 'exerting pressures' (cf. Williams 1980a/1973).

For the analysis of media issues in the book *Marxism and Literature* I will begin with a chapter with the rather straightforward title 'From Medium to Social Practice' (Williams 1977: 158–64; Williams deals with a related issue in the chapter 'From Reflection to Mediation' (Williams 1977: 95–100), where the term 'mediation' has the specific meaning of mediating between various spheres of social existence).

The first part of this chapter is devoted to the changing historical meaning of 'medium'. Williams begins by presenting the relevant problematic: cultural practices are commonly described by specifying the medium in which they take place. A literary text, in this sense, is a work in the medium of language; the circumstances of its creation and reception are not taken into account, and all attention is focused on the determination of the medium. The modern semantic aspect of the term 'medium' first appears in the early seventeenth century, when it was used to refer to a 'third' substance – 'phlogiston' or 'caloric' – operating between the organ of perception and object perceived (Williams 1977: 158). This idea was then transferred to human activities, notably language. Francis Bacon thus writes about the 'medium of words', whereby he understands language as a means of expressing ideas already formed in the mind in advance (for the conceptual history of the 'medium', see Chapter 1, pp. 24–5). According to Williams, this results in the abstraction and objectification of 'constitutive human activity' (Williams 1977: 158), a tendency that persists in some contemporary communication technologies. Unsurprisingly, the technological determinism exemplified by McLuhan is also mentioned in this context.

Williams observes how the term continued to develop in the eighteenth century, when it was used to describe 'means of communication', primarily newspapers. Later, in the twentieth century, it became common to refer to the press as an advertising medium, and print, radio and television all came to be known as media. The term is thus used to refer to a 'social organ or institution of general communication', which is different from the older sense of an 'intermediate communicative substance' (Williams 1977: 159). At the same time, however, this older meaning continued to be developed in the context of the visual arts ('the medium of oils' or 'the medium of water-colour', Williams 1977: 159). Having come to refer to certain materials, this notion of the 'medium' was then extended to artistic practice by a process of reification, a semantic development further reinforced by a romantic idealization of art that meant to distinguish it from mechanical work. In this way, two concepts emerged in opposition to one another: on one hand a material medium and on the other an art freed from any connection to the manipulation of the material (Williams 1977: 160–2). Art rid itself of a middle position that Williams considers essential: the materiality of social practice. The art/material dichotomy is therefore misleading, since materiality is inherent in every art form and work of art. To make a special case for the medium hides this essential materiality: 'Necessarily, inside any art, there is this physical and material consciousness', because '[t]he inescapable materiality of works of art is [. . .] the irreplaceable materialization of kinds of experience, including experience of the production of objects, which, from our deepest sociality, go beyond not only the production of commodities but also our ordinary experience of objects' (Williams 1977: 162).

It is not surprising that the concept of media as 'means of communication' does not appear in this text – i.e. beyond the restricted sense of individual 'media' such as print and television – nor in the brief entry for 'media' in

Williams's *Keywords* (1983/1976: 203–4). Looking at the period in which *Marxism and Literature* was written, Williams would have had to refer primarily to McLuhan's broadly inclusive definition of the medium, a definition he had previously rejected. We thus see that Williams rejects any use of the concept of the medium during this period that exceeds the context of mass communication, criticizing it as a reification that serves only to conceal the fact that 'media' is primarily a matter of praxis and practices, rooted in intentions and in the context of production and reception (cf. Lister et al. 2009/2003: 88–9; for the conceptual history of the medium see also Guillory 2010).

A key passage can be found in the chapter on the medium: 'Every specific art has dissolved into it, at every level of its operations, not only specific social relationships, which in a given phase define it (even at its most apparently solitary), but also specific material means of production, on the mastery of which its production depends. It is because they are dissolved that they are not "media"' (Williams 1977: 163). It is thus the 'material means of production' of a given art form that are to be designated as (potential) media – a term he rejects as reifying – and not the art form as such. In his understanding, the concept of the medium is inexorably drawn towards reification and to the (misapplied) concept of determinism. It is clear that all the arts for Williams represent means of communication alongside what is conventionally known as 'the media': press, radio and television. It is here as well that the idea of 'dissolution' appears, with regard to both social relations and material means of production. In view of W. J. T. Mitchell's observation that Williams searches for the 'middle' term while paradoxically refusing to call it 'medium', we may well ask if this concept of 'dissolution' does not represent precisely that missing middle or mediating term – the medium, as it were, by any other name. Moreover, given the nature of the 'solution' (in which the social and the material are dissolved), it behoves us to come up with a more specific term than 'means of communication' with its emphasis on the instrumental, while accounting for the broader sense of 'communication' as it applies in this context. What's more, we are evidently close to the concept of the medium as environment mentioned above (cf. Mitchell 2008: 3; Lister et al. 2009/2003: 95–6). In short: the concept of 'means of communication' does not correspond to the characteristics of the practices that Williams is concerned with here, and it seems more appropriate simply to expand his concept of the medium to cover all these aspects.

Naturally, at this point, the concept of 'mediation' comes into play as a possible model for the relationship between individual spheres of social existence (material production, economy, politics, law, culture, etc.). If a great variety of aspects – everything from material means to social relations

– are 'dissolved' in the medium (as I am proposing it), then this medium also serves as a place precisely where those aspects of social existence are mediated. Williams himself, in *Marxism and Literature*, where he works from the concept of base and superstructure, through hegemony, to the structure of feeling, leaves off with the concept of mediation at some point along the way. Yet it is fully compatible with both his preferred model of hegemony and the structure of feeling, defined precisely as culture *qua* solution.

Grasping Williams's text in its conceptual entirety can be difficult.[10] The thesis presented here about the medial nature of Williams's concept of the 'means of communication', including art, is somewhat at odds with his formulation of the relationship between culture and society in *Marxism and Literature* (and place of literature in this relationship). This medial axis is nonetheless crucial. It is not, of course, that the entire 'social material process' is mediated by media. However, media have a special ability to dissolve within themselves all levels of social experience, including the material side, and thus participate in the structure of feeling, which is a lived and perceived form of culture – in his words, a form of 'social experiences in *solution*' (Williams 1977: 133).

In this way both media, in this conception, and the structure of feeling have the status of a solution, not a precipitate. How do these two kinds of 'dissolution' relate to each other? (It is precisely in the chapters on the structure of feeling and the medium in which the concept of solution appears.) The structure of feeling is a complex formula of 'meanings and values as they are actively lived and felt' (Williams 1977: 132), which assimilates to itself individual cultural creations in a specific and characteristic way, identifying with or rejecting them, exploring or making use of them. The structure of feeling is not limited to artistic phenomena, but also absorbs ideological, economic, political phenomena and so on. The term therefore refers to a lived complex of meanings, attitudes and values, in which phenomena from various spheres of social existence are combined. In this sense, the nature of the solution has to do with the connection between these spheres, and the possibility of their coexistence within a lived experience that transcends individual consciousness. It is precisely in this aspect that the solution of 'media messages' (individual artefacts, such as plays, poems, songs, TV shows, Instagram posts) can enter the solution of the structure of feeling. For Williams, as we have seen, they also dissolve social relations and material means of production.

We can now ask how this solution relates to an overarching concept that, for Williams, speaks to the social dimension in its totality and historical materiality: 'social material process' (or, alternately, 'material social practice'). According to Williams, media – which he calls the 'means of communication' and which he considers to be means of production – play a significant role here. Mitchell draws attention to the fact that by rejecting the medium as too narrow a concept and by expressing the entire issue in terms of social practice, Williams opens a 'Pandora's Box' on the boundless concept of 'social practice' (Mitchell 2008: 12). For all the reasons listed earlier, I believe that if we read 'means of communication' as 'media', we do not need to open this box at all. By doing so, moreover, we may reclaim the mediating role of media between social relations and means of material production, and more broadly between society and art, as well as other means of communication. In each media message, the entire related social context is dissolved, always in a slightly different way, depending primarily on the medium in question (and on the stage of its historical development).

We may think of the book *Culture* as Williams's proposal for a sociological investigation of culture, based in part on terms and concepts from *Marxism and Literature*, but also synthesizing new material. The work returns on occasion to the concept of media, and presents various opportunities for grappling with mediality broadly speaking, but it does not (like *Marxism and Literature*) have a chapter devoted entirely to this concept. I would like to focus here, first, on those moments in *Culture* in which Williams presents greater insight or new perspectives on his thinking about the medium, as he has conceived of it to this point. Then I will proceed to examine the work as a whole from the perspective of mediality. This allows me to redefine the concept of signification in the social context in some surprising ways, as well as the opposing terms 'solution' and 'precipitate', mainly through an examination of the subsection 'Culture as Signifying System' (Williams 1981: 207–14).

In the context of technique, technology, cultural forms and means of communication as means of production, which I addressed in the previous section, the chapter 'Means of Production' is particularly significant. Here again, Williams divides the material means of cultural production into two groups: those which depend on inherent human physical resources (such as dance, song and speech), and those which are based on the transformation of certain non-human material. The second group includes: (1) the combination of human and non-human material (such as costumes); (2) development of instruments (musical instruments), (3) creation of separable objects (painting and sculpture); (4) development of separable material systems of signification (writing) and (5) development of complex technical systems for amplification, extension and reproduction (Williams 1981: 88–97). It is therefore a somewhat different division than in his study 'Means of Communication as Means of Production' with its categories of amplificatory, durative and alternative means (these would probably correspond to the fourth and fifth groups). Williams also observes that the difference between the 'old' medium of writing and new media such as radio, recordings and television is that the latter largely enable the capture of physically grounded means of cultural production (speech, gesture, singing, etc.). In contrast, writing requires a specific skill (not just literacy itself, but also the ability to understand the structure and message of different types of texts, etc.), which creates a certain asymmetry between those with and those without such skills.

A key to the larger problematic concerning media, as I outlined earlier in the case of *Marxism and Literature*, can be found in the chapter 'Organization' of *Culture*, especially in the subsection 'Culture as Signifying System'. Williams refers here to culture as a 'realized signifying system' (Williams 1981: 207). Society and its individual 'subsystems' (economic, political, extended and nuclear family), as well as culture and its subsystems (means of communication, individual arts), all relate to each other in numerous ways. A given system will always contains elements of other systems, not only in the sense that 'big' systems (e.g. culture) always include subsystems (art, literature, music, etc.), but because individual signifying systems 'dissolve' other systems to varying degrees. Williams emphasizes that signification does not exhaust all aspects of social organization or culture, in which case 'all human actions and relationships' would become 'mere functions of signification' (Williams 1981: 207). We can better understand what Williams means by 'signification system' by considering that such a system, though intrinsic to the economic or political system as such, can be differentiated in practice 'as a system in itself: as a language, most evidently; as a system of thought or of consciousness; or, to use that difficult alternative term, an ideology; and again as a body of specifically significant works of art and thought' (Williams 1981: 208). Signification systems are readily apparent in individual artistic systems of signification, for example. Crucially, however, they will inevitably share material with a wider social system of signification. Culture as a realized system of signification therefore maintains vital relations with other systems that are essentially twofold: its signification is dissolved in other 'needs and actions', but these needs and actions, in turn, are 'more or less completely dissolved' in the signification system of culture (Williams 1981: 209; cf. on the differentiation of social systems in Chapter 9, pp. 307–8, 310–11 and elsewhere; on the (social) systemic aspect in cultural semiotics, see Chapter 10, p. 329 and 334).

Williams then demonstrates these scales on several groups of cases, including aspects that do not primarily belong to culture, means of communication and individual arts. For social phenomena, he examines the example of monetary currency, which is first and foremost an economic phenomenon, but exists simultaneously as an independent signifying system of a political and aesthetic nature. This latter signification is secondary, however, and therefore 'dissolved' in Williams's sense. He also presents the example of human dwellings, which represent an 'especially complex solution of socially developed primary needs, which are always at one level dominant, and of a range of significant practices, some of them quite manifest' (Williams 1981: 211). With the telephone, as a means of communication, the need for primary communication is dominant; the case with radio and television represent, however, is much more complicated. Here we find a specific signification system, but it is directly related to the economic and political order, so that it 'cannot be treated as if other kinds of need and action were wholly dissolved in it' (Williams 1981: 212).

Finally, in the case of art, Williams argues that individual arts demonstrate 'relative degrees of solution' (Williams 1981: 212). Literature, for example, shares language as its 'medium' (here Williams uses the term) with numerous other kinds of communication and thus 'takes much of its material from already manifest areas of other kinds of social action and interest' (Williams 1981: 212). Indeed, in the case of literature, the problem arises of how to distinguish the signifying system from other areas at all (the degree to which other systems are dissolved in literature is thus exceedingly low). Music represents a different case, one in which 'the specific signifying system often seems to be a more complete solution of other areas and other signifying systems of action and need' (Williams 1981: 213). Williams therefore concludes that 'the social organization of culture is an extensive and complex range of many types of organization, from the most direct to the most indirect' (Williams 1981: 213).

The passage we have been examining is characterized by certain ambiguities: How exactly is a system of signification defined? How do individual signifying systems relate to each other? Hierarchically? Laterally? What types of signifying systems are there? How do signifying systems relate to other aspects of social and cultural systems? Williams's presentation is characteristically abstract. On the other hand, these notions of solution, and of the scale of dissolution of one area in another, present us with new insight and perspective on the mutual relationship among areas: even in the case of 'absolute music', for example, economics and politics are present, but in a more perfectly dissolved form: that is, we would find it more difficult to isolate their elements (on the politics of form in the neo-avant-garde, cf. Chapter 6, pp. 185–9).

How to relate this idea to the issue of mediality? The very idea of a solution, of mediation by particularly evident 'systems of signification' such as modern media and art, speaks to the constant, ubiquitous mediation of elements of other systems of signification. Media (in the broadest sense) thus mediate other systems of signification and create an environment – a 'solution'. But the converse of this is also important: even phenomena that do not so obviously represent media – food, for example – mediate at least to some extent, dissolving into other systems of signification, other 'needs and actions'. Furthermore, while Williams may write of 'systems of signification', his understanding of the term, especially in connection with this notion of 'solution', seems to go beyond the semiotic concept. Precisely on account of their solubility, the 'dissolved' aspects of other signification systems and practices certainly do not carry out signification in the same way as those which are not dissolved. From a certain perspective, the opposition between 'solution' and 'precipitate' could be read as the opposition between 'non-semiotic' and 'semiotic'.

4. A media theory of literature?

What is the position of literature within Williams's medial conception of culture and communication, as outlined above? Williams offers at least one answer to this question already in *The Long Revolution*, where he analyses literature as a medium in the broadest sense of the word, specifically with regard to British literature of the 1840s (Williams 1992/1961: 54–71). He undertakes this analysis – especially in the case of the novel – in a way that will remind us of his analyses of television in *Television: Technology and Cultural Form* – that is, in the widest possible social and historical context, taking into account technologies (printing, bookbinding, distribution by rail, etc.), changed social needs (literature for railway passengers), prominent themes related to current social issues (poverty, rising wealth, social mobility), and impact on the reader. The subsection on the English novel of the 1840s is part of the chapter 'The Analysis of Culture', suggesting that literature figures as a particular case of culture more broadly (Williams 1992/1961: 41–71). Williams focuses here mainly on literature, but it is evident that his method could be applied to other arts or media.

The subject of literature receives the most attention, from a theoretical point of view, in the first and especially third part of *Marxism and Literature*. It is significant that 'From Medium to Social Practice' (analysed earlier) makes up the third chapter of the third part, and the entire third part deals with the theory of literature, framed once more as an 'exemplary' medium. The question, however, is whether it contains any other considerations approximating or expanding on the concept of medium outlined above.

The main emphasis here is on the continuity between literature and the overall 'social material process'. For this reason, Williams – consistent with his thinking in terms of scales, not binary oppositions – deconstructs the terms 'literature', as well as 'aesthetic' which includes literature as a specific case. According to Williams, the historically constituted concept of literature contains a number of dichotomies: fact/fiction, discursive/imaginative, objective/subjective. In reality, however, the 'factual' and the 'literary' in writing form a fluid, individually and historically variable scale (Williams 1977: 146, 148). Similarly, if we understand 'aesthetic situations' in the context of an overall social material process, the aesthetic/non-aesthetic distinction cannot be maintained, not even within a framework that Williams himself accepts, namely by way of Jan Mukařovský's concept of the 'aesthetic function' (Williams 1977: 152–5). By Williams's account, every artefact, together with the moment of its reception, should be seen instead as a discrete 'situation' in which the literary and non-literary, aesthetic and non-aesthetic are 'mixed' in some specific way; in this sense, the literary and aesthetic will always contain distinct aspects of the non-literary and non-aesthetic. We could therefore consider – following Williams's argument in *Culture* – that the literary and aesthetic are dissolved to a greater or lesser degree in the non-literary and non-aesthetic, and vice versa. While the mutual ratio may vary, both poles are always present. Williams therefore refuses to make a special case for 'aesthetic situations' (including literature) – or for the medium narrowly defined (as we have here) – insofar as these would set them apart from the experience of the individual and from the overall social material process. This corresponds to the concept of media communication as described above: i.e. as a 'solution' dissolving in itself aspects of other spheres of social existence.

Williams subsequently proposes an internal classification for the potentially boundless mass of texts, based on regularities with regard to notations, conventions and genres. Notations is defined here as the reproducible material arrangements of written language (as opposed to 'spoken words'). More specifically, Williams understands this as the recording of certain aspects, attitudes, modalities (the identity of the writer captured in the text; indications of different types of speech – direct, indirect, dialogue; genre; notation of the mutual relationship of parts, pause, transition, emphasis, etc.; Williams 1977: 170–1). The text is then a set of various kinds of notations, depending to a large extent on 'conventions'. This second category represents a wide group of aspects pertaining to literary texts, in which Williams includes, for example, the conventions of theatrical presentation (the distinction between actors and audience, fictional nature of the plot, etc.), conventions of verse or prose, monologue or dialogue, and method of narration. He also considers the variable conventions that bear on the representation of actions (killing, the sexual act and work). Williams places emphasis on the active social significance of all aspects of a literary text based on intersubjective conventions of notations, genres and forms. He understands them primarily as particular social attitudes or points of view, and as part of the overall social material process. Conventionality is a condition for communicability and comprehensibility, but the emphasis is nevertheless on the active transformation and understanding of conventions, and on their wider social significance. Or rather the emphasis is on the fact that they are themselves social, connected with other non-literary aspects as yet another element within 'structures of feeling'. As such, a work of literature is effectively split between reproduction and production, a situation that undermines yet another dichotomy, this time between creation and reproduction. Just as the 'non-aesthetic' realm contains elements of creativity, the 'aesthetic' realm often, or even predominantly (as Williams argues) tends to reproduce rather than create.

This conception of literature clearly illustrates the concept of 'dissolution' analysed above: texts are in no way limited to 'purely' literary aspects, but contain distinctive elements of other areas. This is true not only of specific texts, but also of the individual intermediate stages that mediate between the singular artefact and 'literature' as a whole (notations, genres, conventions, etc.). The totality of 'literature', moreover, is constituted on these interfaces, and dissolves within itself 'the social' in its various manifestations. Every text, understood as a situation, is essentially an act of mediation, as it is always positioned 'in between', in multiple senses: it is a media message.

The aim of this chapter is to present Williams's thinking about the media and the medium from two perspectives: that of its internal development, and that of the interpretative possibilities it offers. There are several issues with Williams's works, including the fact that, without frequently turning to the concept as such, his analyses can hardly be subordinated to any other concept than that of the medium, and to the discourse of media theory within the framework of contemporary thought. The second issue is that Williams proposes a narrower, technologically deterministic understanding of the medium, which he then proceeds to critique, and this further diminishes the importance of the concept in his thinking. What is more, Williams bases this narrow understanding, for his purposes, on a rather synecdochic interpretation of McLuhan's media theory. For these reasons, any successful effort to delineate the medial aspects of Williams's theory must necessarily take a radical approach to his works.

In addition to this somewhat experimental, at times even 'inverted' reading of Williams's main theoretical works, the primary aspect remains: namely, the presentation of his thinking on media and the medium in its developmental logic, and in the relevant texts where he addresses this issue. In this regard, Williams's role as one of the inspirations of contemporary media theory can hardly be questioned. The concepts of 'solution' and 'dissolving' then represent another layer, one that maintains a critical relationship to 'technological determinism', while also indicating the central role played by media vis-à-vis the contemporary world as well as the entire breadth of socially based media-theoretical thinking. This necessarily includes – at times, for Williams, in a rather exemplary way – literature.

Notes

1   For background literature on Raymond Williams, see O'Connor 1989; Eagleton 1989; Eldridge and Eldridge 1994; Drakakis 2001; Milner 2002; 2005/1996; 2006; Milner and Browitt 2002; Turner 2003/1990, Higgins 2013, and especially the seminal work Jones 2006/2004.
2   This division coincides to a large extent with some relatively accepted periodizations of Williams's work. Cf. Milner 2006.
3   Paul Jones thus pauses over the fact that Williams proceeds in this work 'without any systematic reference to the category of "media"' (Jones 2006/2004: 157).
4   A separate question is to what extent Williams misinterprets McLuhan's understanding of the medium, or how McLuhan's thinking, while closely related to the postmodernism that began in the United States in the 1960s, is fundamentally of a different nature. This issue is addressed later in this chapter; also cf. Jones 2006/2004: 161.
5   For the concept of flow, see Allan 1997. Williams speaks of the effect of the flow of television on a viewer in terms similar to those of Marshall McLuhan and other postmodern theorists, such as Jean Baudrillard (Williams 2003/1974: 92–6).
6   This has only ever been done occasionally, especially in Williams's review of McLuhan's *The Gutenberg Galaxy* (Williams 1964), where the divergence of his concept of the medium from McLuhan's is already obvious, especially in his criticism of the alleged historically determinant role of the printing press. Cf. Jones 1998; 2006/2004: 157, 160–1; Lister et al. 2009/2003: 79. *Understanding Media* is the only work by McLuhan cited in Williams's *Television*. On links between McLuhan and Williams, their common intellectual background in literary studies, and interest in the Cambridge circle of F. R. Leavis – that is, his concept of 'organic community' and rejection of popular culture – see Jones 1998. On the continuity of McLuhan's early works in the field of Renaissance studies and his research in media studies, see Guillory 2015.
7   Des Freedman (2002), for instance, further develops Williams's anti-deterministic argument in the context of the internet; also see Stefan Münker (2013: 251), who writes that '[i]n the sphere of social media, media-use generates the media used', which is essentially in line with Williams's approach.

8 Jay David Bolter and Richard Grusin (1999: 75–8) also address this debate in the context of the concept of remediation, partly based on McLuhan, and propose a 'conciliatory' solution: '[W]e can reject McLuhan's determinism and still appreciate his analysis of the remediating power of various media. [. . .] Media do have agency, but that agency is constrained and hybrid' (1999: 77, 78). Also see Lister et al. 2009 /2003: 82–3.
9 Jones (2006/2004: 171) uses a table to summarize Williams's classification of the 'means of communication'.
10 Paul Jones (2006/2004) has attempted to do this using a series of tables to compare concepts from this and other important texts by the theorist. To some extent, however, this way of systematizing Williams's concepts results in the loss of some of the productive ambivalences and tensions that characterize Williams's style of thinking and writing.

9

Social systems theory and the medium

Tomáš Chudý

1. The improbability of communication and double contingency

There is a wide spectrum of semantic variations on the term 'medium', typically emphasizing its technical and perceptual aspects (including 'media of expression'). We may therefore turn to an alternative framing of the concept connecting mediality, namely to a prominent theory linking mediality and social communication: the systems theory of Niklas Luhmann. This thinking has become part of the mainstream theory, especially in – but not limited to – German-speaking countries. We may begin by recalling its central principles and basic elements, before proceeding to consider how it has been applied in the context of the fine arts, and subsequently to Rainer Leschke's logic of media forms – an extension of the theory that can be considered more of an epilogue than a direct development of Luhmann's work.

Let us begin by saying that every system has its own way of dealing with contingency. What do we see in the case of social systems? Given that entropy, as a measure of system indeterminacy, is a state of equilibrium, the social system would inevitably reach this entropic state, and thus total breakdown, if there were no process to bring determinacy into it. This process, for Luhmann, is communication based on differences. It is therefore essential to bring into focus the mechanisms that allow communication to be maintained even under adverse conditions. Unlike those branches of sociology that focus on attitudes, ideas or actions, Luhmann concentrates on communication, in part because attitudes and ideas emerge and change with a frequency that makes them unsuitable for any useful analysis.

We may now take a closer look at the kind of communication Luhmann is concerned with. Where Shannon, for example, conceives of communication as an essentially linear phenomenon, Luhmann takes his inspiration from the non-linear conception of the Palo Alto School.[1] From there he also adopts Bateson's definition of information as 'a difference which makes a difference'

(Bateson 1987/1972: 199, 229, 271, 321, 323). However, nonlinearity is not the main or even most typical postulate. We can grasp this more succinctly if we recall that communication does not arise from the knowledge of information, but rather from its *absence* – that is, the purpose of communication is to convey something which is not yet known (by the addressee). Information – Bateson's difference which makes a difference – can only be communicated if it represents an 'added value' by comparison to what is already known or given in advance. Such value can subsequently take the form not only of content that is communicated and understood, but also of distance or any other pragmatic relationship to the object of communication, as we find in the theory of speech acts, for example (Luhmann 2013/2002: 215, 223–4). Communication can therefore be seen to be a more complex, non-linear process, one that is not limited to the content, or 'message'. And in this process, every aspect is socially relevant.

Luhmann further notices the banal fact that the 'follow-up' of each communication is always susceptible to agreement (consensus) and disagreement (dissent). This brings a certain degree of linearity to what was originally a non-linear model, arising from the emphasis on certain reactions over others in an array of other communications. Communication does not necessarily mean understanding (let alone consensus), but it always means the coexistence of more than one way of experiencing meaning: 'the universal implication of meaningful communication is only that each meaning refers to the co-experiencing of others' (Luhmann 1982: 376–7). On the one hand, this reintroduces the plurality of contexts into communication (complicating the degree of linearity indicated above). On the other hand, Luhmann expands the boundaries of meaning (in explicit opposition to Habermas) to include polemic situations characterized by difference. In other words, the perfect form of communication is defined as much by dissent as it is by consensus, making it possible to describe situations of conflict, revolution and dispute as 'full-fledged'. This way of thinking is more consistent with Bateson's information theory, as well as evolutionary theory.

From this perspective, one of the greatest threats to any functional system of communication is that it will become devoid of information, rendering the vast majority of communication redundant: a circulation of differences that no longer make any difference (that 'don't matter'). Here, the stronger the mechanisms of stabilization within a given system, especially at the level of detail, the harder it is to introduce difference in communication. The autopoiesis of a social system (art, law, religion) can thus languish at any point that it is reduced to the 'rehashing' of redundant statements, so that communication ceases precisely where it should begin – on questions that give rise to further differences.

However, this is not enough. As reflected in its openness to consensus and dissent, communication is conceived as a process of selection, where it is always chosen anew from options determined by contingent factors, even by 'double contingency': that is, factors associated with both sender and receiver (and with each side alternating between these two roles). That the general task of communication is to absorb uncertainty only proves that social autopoiesis emerges from the problem of double contingency: 'it is precisely as a problem that double contingency becomes the autocatalytic factor of the autopoietic reproduction of social systems, to the extent, that is, that it can never be resolved or removed once and for all' (Künzler 1989: 76, cf. also Luhmann 1981: 14, and 1995/1984: 103 f.).

The basis for Luhmann's concept of communication – which has direct consequences for the concept of literary communication – is therefore, paradoxically, that communication, in the sense of follow-up reactions, is inherently improbable (Luhmann 1995/1984: 159–60). The author provides three reasons for this:

(1) '[I]t is, first of all, improbable that ego *understands* what alter means – given that their bodies and minds are separate and individual. Only in context can meaning be understood, and context is, in turn, supplied by one's own perceptual field and memory.'
(2) 'The second improbability refers to *reaching* the addressee. It is improbable for a communication to reach more persons than are present in a concrete situation, and this improbability grows if one makes the additional demand that the communication be reproduced unchanged. The problem lies in spatial and temporal extension. The interaction system of those who are present together at any given time guarantees a communicative attention sufficient for practical purposes. But beyond the boundaries of the interaction system, that system's rules cannot be enforced. Even if communication found meaning carriers that could be transported and would remain temporally stable, it is improbable that it would attract any attention at all beyond the boundaries of the initial interaction. People elsewhere have other things to do.'
(3) 'The third improbability is *success*. Even if a communication is understood by the person it reaches, this does not guarantee that it is also accepted and followed (*angenommen*). [. . .] Communication is successful only if ego accepts the content selected by the communication (the information) as a premise of his own behavior. Acceptance can mean action corresponding to the directives communicated, but also experience, thinking or processing further information under the

assumption that certain information is correct.' (Luhmann 1995/1984: 158–9; cf. Schmidt 1993)

From the point of view of the system, the function of communication can also be expressed as *the reduction of complexity with the help of differences* (*Unterscheidungen*). For Luhmann, this means minimizing the threshold of assumptions for the theory of social action: the level preceding a schematization of the end-means type, for instance. The reduction of complexity is functionally equivalent to the absorption of uncertainty. It is not difficult to see why it is necessary to reduce complexity within everyday communication (and not necessarily at a more advanced level, scientific, artistic or otherwise):

> 'Uncertainty absorption' means that, in the normal course of events, we do not have the possibility of starting from scratch every time and that we cannot ask the speaker every time why he said what he said and not something else, or what his horizon of selection was, and so on. We cannot, time and again, burrow into what is already past. We would run out of time. But we can say 'yes' or 'no'. We do not need investigations into why something came about, why some piece of information became a text or was spoken audibly, why a certain issue is on the agenda right now, how a fact is described, and so on. Perhaps we no longer have to bother about such things and can say instead that we do not believe something or, within reason, ask for additional explanations. To some extent, the process of communication is in a hurry. It depends on sequencing. It cannot continuously get entangled with itself. Thus the 'yes/no' option is an entirely abstract operation that functions as a shortcut and subsequently determines the next steps. One may continue at the level of the 'no' and head for conflict, or one may accept an utterance at face value as the basis for further communication. (Luhmann 2013/2002: 224)

Linearity is therefore desirable in the form of ad hoc sequencing, which allows for a certain degree of balance, and thus the sustainability of communication.

Now comes a medially relevant twist. Based on the analysis above, we see that the degree of contingency increases with the number of relationships and growing complexity, which in turn makes communication even more improbable, so that its case-by-case possibilities (who at a given time can connect with whom, and regarding what topic) become exceedingly narrow. One of the ways that society solves this problem is to represent complexity as a form of meaning (which in turn becomes a medium for functional systems; Luhmann 2012/1997: 82). Due to the fact that communication is primarily applied to itself (and not to the input or output of the system, that is, to any result external to the communication system of a society), it extends its validity to infinity (no statement is final, it can always be denied or accepted on the basis of further communication). Moreover, it must be remembered that meaning is always and exclusively the product of the operations that make use of it, not some property of the world as such (Luhmann 2012/1997: 18). This also means that meaning as a medium of the code of individual functional systems is reproduced with each of their operations.

Starting from the assumption of maintaining the functions of individual social communication subsystems, it follows that in a modern highly interconnected communication-based society more effective means are necessary than what is provided by a 'general medium of meaning'. Luhmann calls these means 'symbolically generalized communication media' or SGCM,[2] which comprise two media aspects: one regarding their (social) meaning, the other their (functional) use.

We are moving now from technology to the field of semantics: that is, individual segments of social communication, among which art and literature figure prominently.

To clarify the role of SGCM, it will first be necessary to turn to the evolution of media in general, looking specifically at the moment when the possibilities of communication expanded to such an extent that the ratio of actual communications to those that are realistically possible radically decreased, leading eventually to the automatic production of messages. To the same degree, these changes brought about an increase in social contingency, and thus the improbability that a given communication will be received and be followed by a (meaningful) response. The invention of new media certainly played a major role in this development, from the printing press, which structurally separates the event of social interaction from communication proper (it is possible to write and read a message independently of face-to-face meetings, setting the conditions for one-way – that is, *mass* – communication from the author to an unlimited number of recipients), to new media. With the rise of digitalization, new media have further distanced communication from immediate social ties (the format of communication is even less dependent on face-to-face meetings, shifting in the final stage to technogenic interactivity), at the same time even further multiplying the possibilities of how, when and what to communicate. Today, thanks to new (technological) media, these possibilities have been extended, in principle, to the communication of everything, at any time, and to anyone – accompanied by the attendant increase in contingency (communication is increasingly contingent). There is one limitation or exception, in this case, which still applies: what Luhmann calls 'sincerity' (*Aufrichtigkeit*), referring to the condition that what is communicated is also meant seriously (Luhmann 2012/1997: 186; cf. Luhmann 1995/1984: 365). The effects of this non-communicative constitutive exception to general communicability, around which everything else is centred, are then multiplied with technological development, thereby widening a gap within the general medium of the social system of communication, which is meaning. This gap, even though it is not *something* in the true sense of the word, can still be bridged (or rather bypassed) with the help of other communication (non-technological) media. At present, these are necessarily only partial, differentiated or plural, and Luhmann names them 'symbolically generalized media' precisely because each of them makes it possible to create an entire order, based on a certain primary, symbolically generalized code.

Where Luhmann points to the improbability of communication due to the complexity of meaning and relations, there are others – Lev Manovich, for example – who point to the computer as source of an unprecedented range of media possibilities, multiplying expression and thus communication. This however has only to do with the *possibilities* of communication, the actual realization of which is not always enough to compensate for the pitfalls of complexity. It implies not only that the resulting vector is not zero, but that the entire communication landscape has been transformed. In the new, more plastic landscape, a number of previously unseen paths have been thrown into relief, while the original single-vector, linear communication equations have been eradicated or transformed. If it was clear before how to distinguish the message from everything else, it now seems that even eccentric or otherwise meaningless behaviour, under certain circumstances, may be perceived as expression. Rather than measuring the signal-to-noise ratio, it would therefore be more suitable to talk about the ratio of symbolic to other kinds of signals made possible by new media: enactive, iconic or acoustic, for example – in short, a mixture of alternatives to which one may resort in case of a misunderstanding at the level of symbolic communication (cf. Chapter 10, pp. 339–42).

However, based on the arguments put forth at the beginning of this chapter, it remains the case that all media communication is improbable. As a preliminary hypothesis, we may argue that new audiovisual media serve *both* as a mitigating factor for shortcomings in communication *and* as intensifiers of its improbability. For the most part, such a claim would run directly counter to the notion that communication possibilities have been expanding alongside advances in media, with improvements in raster accuracy, data granularity, spectrum of data, information and signs that can be communicated. It is therefore appropriate to recall that Luhmann's concept of communication is specifically broader, especially with regard to the third point above regarding the degree of probability that a recipient will respond to communication with communication of his own. It is in this way that the empirical-social concept of communication differs from the technical concept, for which the degree and manner of actual use, in principle, do not represent decisive factors.

Media thus exhibit a dialectical character with respect to the probability or improbability of communication. First, they make it possible to have communication at all – even to have one medium of communication within another (using a telephone to arrange a meeting, for example) – and thereby serve to reduce the improbability of communication events. In addition to introducing new means of expression, depending on technical progress, they also turn communication recursively on itself (as when the news media report on communication events, for instance). In this way they perform a double negation, making the improbable more probable than it was without them (Hörisch 2001: 68).

However, this also has the effect of multiplying the degree of redundancy. In Luhmann's words, 'Dissemination media [...] can be used to confirm social belongingness: people relate what is already known to show their solidarity' (Luhmann 2012/1997: 121). But this by no means serves in all cases to facilitate communication, and may instead, as we have seen, overwhelm and suffocate it. Whether or not it does so depends on contingent factors. Luhmann emphasizes that even while mass media widened the circle of recipients, with the historical expansion of literacy we have entered a state in which no one can know with certainty who has read what texts, and who among them may remember their contents: 'The invention of the printing press and then the advent of modern mass media compounded the anonymization of social redundancy' (Luhmann 2012/1997: 121). From there, he concludes, it should be assumed that, in case of doubt, the communicated information is considered to already be available, and therefore redundant, while not ruling out the opposite.[3] Either way, the anonymized redundancy proceeds to expand throughout the media space to the same degree as uncertainty and contingency arising from the fact that the supposed degree of redundancy is not realized in reality (and far from it).

What role is played here by SGCM? Luhmann's thinking here must be understood in two contexts. First, it is an attempt to better understand social communication – a context that is, after all, rather different from mathematical information theory and the experimental research on which it is based. We should also see them as an effort to address a fundamental paradox at the heart of all technological dissemination media (*Verbreitungsmedien*) as to whether they actually serve the dissemination of communication. This inherent ambivalence (or dialectic) arises due to the principle of double contingency. Having defined social communication on the basis of its ability to engender follow-up communication or actions,[4] Luhmann is compelled to address the exponential increase in the possibilities of dissemination, whereby the exceedingly large number of communicators involved make it impossible to determine what communications actually motivate them to do. This presents a problem for the evolution of social systems, compelling them to come up with a means for reducing redundancy. Their solution – SGCM – combines conditioning and motivation in a new way, in order to raise the 'threshold for the nonacceptance of communication' (Luhmann 2012/1997: 122). SGCM thus provide an answer not only to the problem of double contingency,[5] but also to the problem caused by the boom in technical media.

SGCM remedy the problem caused by the dissemination media precisely by virtue of their *effectiveness* (not *ineffectiveness*). It therefore seems that ever more development in the field of SGCM is necessary: without it, both the functionality of dissemination media and their evolution are inconceivable. The problem that mathematical theory sees from a purely technical point of view of channel throughput and transmission redundancy is thus understood by social theory as already integrated into the functional mechanisms of society, which has its own means for preventing unwanted effects.

It is therefore not primarily a question of improving the quality of the signal, in the case of SGCM, but rather of rebuilding the communication model in terms of content, so that semantics has a better chance to carry out not only transmission of a certain quality, but, more generally, successful communication (hence Luhmann's label for SGCM: *Erfolgsmedien*). Let us once more recall that success, in this case, is measured primarily in terms of effects (and by the degree of continuity of other communications among them). The degree to which communication is exposed to unknown situations increases exponentially with the introduction of modern means of communication, and the role of SGCM in this context is to absorb this uncertainty.

2. The medium of the 'artwork' and the code of art

On the aesthetic level, the SGCM called the 'work of art' was constituted at the same time as the differentiation of functional systems (roughly in the seventeenth century), thus establishing conditions for communication about this particular kind of work as an uncommon object that 'deserves attention' (Luhmann 1987/1986: 109). We could say that what is considered by some theories of literary communication – namely those which are oriented towards the sociology of literary forms – to be the relationship between a set of individual characteristics and a set of norms or conventions that allow these unique features to be recognized (Janusz Sławiński, for example, who uses the biological terms 'phenotype" and 'genotype'), is considered by the theory of social systems to be two sides of the difference of form within the communication medium 'artwork' that circulates in the global environment of social communication.[6]

Although SGCM represents a functional solution for the system as a whole, the 'work of art' obviously supposes a horizon of expectations on the part of individual recipients as well – the reader, for instance, vis-à-vis the literary work – determined by accumulated layers of experience and taste (cf. Hans Robert Jauss), as well as literary competence – the ability, for instance, to identify genre, means of expression, style, etc. We might also think of this as a 'medial' competence; at the very least it is latently medial, insofar as it applies to literature as a specific type of secondary communication system, one that necessarily includes grammatical competence (the competence par excellence required for the perception of literature, cf. Culler 2000/1997: 62, as well as 2002/1975: 132–52).[7] In this regard, it is not only about the recipient's horizon, but about the choice of form already at the origin of such a communication – the fact that the textual medium could be processed (not just read) differently within another functional system (commerce or religion, for example). Literature and its coding is then closely connected with the development of dissemination media, as demonstrated by the use of literary strategies that typically assume knowledge of other referential communication (parody, irony, collage, quotation; Werber and Plumpe 1993: 20). The likelihood that a recipient will have this knowledge increases with the ease of social communication as such.[8]

There are various manners in which the choice of forms comes about. The successors of systems theory Niels Werber and Gerhard Plumpe consider this aspect from a historical perspective, showing how the difference between form and medium offers a continuum of 'system options' (*Systemoptionen*). Differences may be based on the observation of the various approaches to processing the difference between the system (art) and its environment throughout the existence of the modern literature system (which began around the year 1770).[9] At a certain point, a tendency emerges in literature whereby 'technique prevails over content', with the focus of literary production shifting to the novelty of presentation (rather than considering technique and content as two sides of an integrated whole). This is a variation of Arendt's (see Chapter 7, p. 254 ff.) transition from 'what' to 'how', which – as we have already stated – is essentially conditioned by the development of dissemination media. However,

> Aestheticism would eventually arrive at a certain kind of 'thermal death' if it were to base this development only on itself, detached from the environment, since all the 'energy' would be consumed – if it did not, that is, find its permanent counterpart in realism, which brings 'energy' from the environment into the system, importing 'meaning' that can then be re-worn, transformed, sent up or negated within the system. Consolidating the observation that even categorical 'non- or anti-art' is art if it is projected into the SGCM 'work', the modern system of literature has historically exhausted its options. (Werber and Plumpe 1993: 38–40)

We should once more recall that these historical considerations are meant as an investigation into system options resulting precisely from the fact that the social system we are dealing with has a relationship with its environment (and with itself). To speak of the exhaustion of options does not concern the end of art, but the final materialization of all its options. From this follows the second observation concerning the nature of the historical process in question: as always in Luhmann's theory, evolution is not conceived as a single line – as in the Hegelian concept, leading explicitly towards an end (from heroic epic to poeticism, for example) – but instead follows a contingent curve, whose vector is repeatedly altered by the interplay of factors to which the system reacts. Of course, this does not prevent the simultaneous coexistence of multiple options, or the early existence of seeds of system options that will not emerge in full until later. In fact, it is not a matter of linear movement at all but rather the ebb and flow of entire overlapping fields, of regrouping centres of gravity.

The second principle of the systems theory of literature is the notion of a 'code of art', one that distinguishes it from other functional areas. Posing the question in 'Is art codible?' ('Ist Kunst codierbar?', Luhmann 2001a/1974),[10] Luhmann is ambivalent about whether one can really speak of a code of art, given the discordant relations among the systemic features of art, so that tradition (references in relation to the art's own history, ultimately leading to the attitude of *l'art pour l'art*), function (references to society as a whole) and performance (references to other partial social systems, such as that between fashion and the economy, the educational role of art in relation to the education system, or redundant artistic production in relation to religion) no longer sanction each other or operatively interconnect (Luhmann 2001a/1974: 190). Selections in the composition of artistic communication may be guided by only one of these three system references, to the exclusion of the others. This is also the difference between the functional system of art and other systems (religion, economics, law). We should also note that Luhmann's concretization of the functional code of art (ugly/beautiful) has always been perceived as one of the weakest points of Luhmann's theory, and motivated the greatest effort to correct it. What we see as a result is a parade of dualisms, with no less than eleven attempts to define the code of art thus far (cf. Krauss 2012: 53–4). However, the code must also be historically plausible. That is why Werber, for instance, considers that what is 'interesting' is historically connected to a certain aspect of the beautiful ('joli' in Diderot's *Encyclopaedia*), via aspects of surprising and 'singular' – that which attracts attention, or that which stands highest in the hierarchy of aesthetic values (in this sense, it is not a single possible code, but that which prevails over other contending codes) (cf. Werber 1992: 69).

We can also observe a certain crossing of thresholds, from that which 'only' uses the code (the interesting/ordinary, for example) to that which constitutes 'great' art, especially with the requirement of 'connectivity' (*Anschlussfähigkeit*): art's ability to establish itself, discursively, as art. Without it, art is reduced to a private undertaking which does not contribute to the social system. Tradition and orthodoxy no longer play a decisive role, but it is still necessary to identify where art is located according to its 'address in the system of social communication' (Luhmann 2001a/1974: 188). As early as 1974, Luhmann glimpsed a way out of this in art's potential to dissolve and recombine social facts (Luhmann 2001a/1974: 189, Luhmann 2001b/1986: 208), precisely with regard to its need to relate to social reality (Luhmann 2001a/1974: 185). In short, where the founder of the theory of social systems faltered on the issue of the code in 1974, in 1986 – at the peak of the theory of social systems – another way forward was proposed: namely, the medium of art.

But let's not get ahead of ourselves. Given that the basic starting point is the improbability of communication, we can see how the problem of SGCM and their code becomes ever more urgent as literary communication and its works become more contingent. Their fictionality – the principled detachment from everyday contexts – not only doubles this contingency (as with any communication, on the side of both alter and ego, i.e. author and reader), but also amplifies it (a kind of 'contingency squared', insofar as both alter and ego perceive the uncommonness of a work).

Whence the motivation to accept something as art? Let us recall that systems theory interprets communication – including the messages of the work of art – as a chain of selections[11] that leads expressly towards the elimination of contingency. For this to happen, however, it is necessary to provide clues – but not too many, as this would threaten the contingency of selections on the other side to such an extent that it would no longer be a selection at all. This conception of the bipolarity of entropy and redundancy diverges from other theoretical approaches: here, it is necessary to avoid the complete elimination of contingency, leaving room for one's own selections, which consist in favouring one side of a difference, thereby also drawing attention to its existence. In other words, if a message ceases to be visible *as a selection*, it too ceases to be relevant to the selections that follow it.

'The addressee is therefore not influenced by the qualities of a work of art,' writes Luhmann, 'but by their selectivity' (Luhmann 2001a/1974: 165). The point is thus not to single out one side or the other of the code as an individually suggestive feature (what Luhmann calls an 'intrinsic persuader'), because by doing so, we overlook or misconstrue the code *as a selection*, so that it ceases to fulfil its function (which in the *functionalist* theory is both essential and, perhaps, alarming).

With the popularization of cultural forms, art itself then 'increases its improbability, its power to resolve (*Auflösevermögen*)', compelled by the pressure of competition. The production of contingency – that is, conspicuousness, the breaking of expectations – becomes the central aim of art. It does so, however, in order to *show its capacity for recombination* (Luhmann 2001a/1974: 174). Even so, after a certain period of time the horizon of innovation begins to narrow, to the point where the exhaustion of options appears to be only 'a matter of time'. As already stated above, this point does not represent the end of art as an autopoietic system of communication, but rather the moment when it becomes necessary to redefine (the idea of) its code. Here lies the crux of the dilemma: at the same time that the original code falls below the threshold of public attention, the specialized pursuit of eccentricity no longer leads to acceptable results.

Art, however, differs from other systems not only by its greater emphasis on the contingency of the 'problem of reference' (*Bezugsproblem*), but also in terms of its weaker ability to create the system.[12] This allows Luhmann to say that art lags behind other social systems in terms of the associated 'social operation' that would otherwise serve to 'cultivate' it, adapting art to the needs of society through a demand for its 'outputs', for example (Luhmann 2001a/1974: 176). This is primarily because art is not 'for everyone'. It does not create (and should not create) as many opportunities as other social systems for 'follow-up communication' outside its field, which also means that it does not create long follow-up chains. This limitation, Luhmann points out, applies to connections across other systems, and not necessarily on the historical axis (where, on the contrary, art demonstrates strong internal programmatic connections concerning the dialectic between tradition and innovation, discussions about the 'timelessness' of art, etc.).

Yet Luhmann conceives of the work of art as something that demonstrates exceedingly low 'futurizability' (Luhmann 2001a/1974: 177–8). Unlike such media as money, power and faith, which he argues can be separated from their immediate contexts, the abstract medium 'artwork' does not present a viable basis for the functional differentiation of social subsystems ('only mannerisms remain of this work' for further application, compelling him to claim that art 'lives from the negation of its own past', Luhmann 2001a/1974: 177, 179). This however does not exclude frequent 'borrowings' from earlier periods of creation, and the fact that art so often draws its inspiration from them is proof that it is not 'defuturized'. We might therefore accept Luhmann's thesis with a caveat: thanks to its high selection contingency, the medium of artwork does not, in principle, have a fixed form that transcends history, but is rather timeless in its function of dissolution and recombination, or as the basis for discussing the difference between communication and perception (as we will show later). More succinctly, as a consequence of its basic principles, the museum-like tendency of many works of art does not prevent some of them, throughout history, from becoming an inspiration for others.

If, in that case, the key demand does not come from other social subsystems, what influences on the development of a functional system of art are exerted? As we learn in 'The Medium of Art' ('Das Medium der Kunst', 1986), all art, including literature, developed or evolved in a process of functional differentiation, through 'the increase in the capacity for dissolution and recombination, as the development of ever new media-for-forms' (Luhmann 1987/1986: 108). A prime example of the creation of a media-for-forms can be found precisely in written language as a new medium based on (oral) speech (Luhmann 1987/1986: 105–6), making it possible to generate new contrasts, or, *differences*. The original 'strict couplings' (*strikte Kopplungen*) develop in society into a complete system, which can eventually become a certain 'style' (Luhmann 1987/1986: 106): 'A look at the history of art shows that natural media (media of perception) are always presupposed but that art in the process of its development creates additional media of its own in order to introduce new distinctions' (Luhmann 1987/1986: 106). 'Art satisfies the gradually increasing formal requirements, developing its own media for this and therefore taking on its own function; eventually it becomes inevitable that participation in art can no longer depend on universally shared assumptions' (Luhmann 2001b/1986: 206). From this perspective, all media, including technical media, serve as 'fodder' for the escalating demands of art. This is an enticing concept, yet it needs further elaboration: art has a propensity to appropriate for its own purposes everything that may act as a new 'medium'.

Its purposes are always the same: to enrich forms and invent new ways to dissolve and recompose social reality.[13] This mode of operation is further strengthened in the age of technical media, where manipulation is one of the basic functions (see also Chapter 7, esp. pp. 246–8 and 254–7).

In this respect, literature is no different: it breaks down and assembles everyday communication in a way that makes new differences stand out. The final '*non plus ultra*' medium of art is therefore society itself (Luhmann 1987/1986: 108). This may seem at first to contradict previous claims regarding the limited connection of art to social operation. In reality, however, art itself – whose task is to extract forms from the medium of ordinary communication – represents a completely different movement than the subsequent communication about works of art in society.[14] Thus, insurmountable barriers remain, consisting in the inevitability of the media of perception: 'words scattered over the paper must still be legible or at least visibly illegible', just as 'modern music may only transgress the limits of hearability to the extent that this transgression is hearable' (Luhmann 1987/1986: 108). These limits thus involve socially constituted differences (the opposition of music and noise, for instance) without which art could not reproduce itself. This is essential, and it follows from the conception of art (and literature) as a social functional system; the system does not hold unless it refers recursively to itself, in contrast to the environment. Otherwise, art would sink back into the depths of the mundane and everyday (*Alltag*, it is from this notion that Werber likely derived his concept of the code of art as 'interesting'), and, functionally, it would be only a part of another system (an object of religious respect, for example, or economically viable commodity).

As we have just seen, it is one of the unique aspects of the functional system of art to have weaker connections to social operation, an aspect that also implies a certain exemption from the requirement of inclusion, in a situation where indifference towards social operation carries no negative consequences (cf. Helmstetter 2011: 42). In other words, compared to the codes of other functional systems (law, economy, religion), that of art is more acutely disinterested in aspiring to inclusion in 'life', 'praxis' and so on. It is ultimately by virtue of this autonomy, free of all ties to other systems, that we find what Rudolf Helmstetter calls a 'social demand', fulfilling society's desire for a system that would provide for a certain independence *within society* (not outside it). This is not the same, however, as withdrawing into the refuge of an otherwise unproductive autonomy. Nor therefore does it represent the essence of art, but rather the outcome of an evolutionary dynamics of functional differentiation which compels all systems towards autonomy.

We can now return to the question of the essence of communication, recalling that communication theory examines communication operations with the aim of establishing the connection between the *system* of art and *works* of art. It is therefore not concerned (in contrast to aesthetics) with the ontology of the work of art or aesthetic experience, nor with the question of what is actually 'beautiful', but instead with '*how art functions as communication*' (Luhmann 2000/1995: 39): 'The decisive perspective is therefore the *artistic manner of communication* within the medium of a *work of art*, which shapes the material medial substrate (tones, colours, speech), thus creating and stabilizing forms and in this way claiming, occupying, "engaging", "captivating" *perception*' (Helmstetter 2011: 46).

This brings us to a question we have not yet posed: *How does communication take place?* Here, the analytical side of Luhmann's concept of communication offers some insight. His starting point is an elaboration of Bühler's three functions of communication: information (*Information*), conveyance (*Mitteilung*) and understanding (*Verständigung*).[15] (On Bühler's model, see Chapter 2, p. 54.) We have already seen that not every message – not even every *meaningful* message – is information, only a difference that is in some way surprising, a 'difference which makes a difference'. Conversely, not every piece of information constitutes communication, only that which is both communicated *and* received/understood (or misunderstood, without which possibility communication would be reduced to mere behaviour),[16] and which therefore serves as the basis for further selections.

It is art's proper function to problematize the unity (and also distinction) between conveyance and information, or in Bühler's own terms, between expression and representation. Literature in particular does so with specific intent. The author does not wish to create the impression of seeking to provide the reader with information, but rather to irritate the relationship between perception and communication (Helmstetter 2011: 47). We must not forget that words (spoken language) are understood as a medium. Luhmann touches on a definition of the poetic function when he observes that what matters is the choice of words not 'thematic choice' (Luhmann 2000/1995: 26). At the same time, however, it is still information – the additional information – which makes a difference: 'What strikes us in an art form – as, in a different way, does the conspicuous character of acoustic and optic signals – engenders a fascination that turns into information by changing the state of the system – as a "difference which makes a difference" (Bateson). And this is already communication. What else?' (Luhmann 2000/1995: 26).

This striking aspect of art does not, however, preclude meaning; only now it is conveyed more through connotation than denotation, or indications of meanings that mutually unlock one another (Luhmann 2000/1995: 25). The statement that words are a 'medium' means no more than that the emphasis is on their connotative side, that is, on the play of auto-reference and hetero-reference. In other words, 'Text-art organizes itself *by means of* self-referential references that combine elements of sound, rhythm and meaning' (Luhmann 2000/1995: 26; italics added). That which serves as a *'means of'* organization on one occasion can become the object of communication on another.[17] The mediality of the word (or, more precisely, its connotations) thus helps to organize the text in such a way that aspects of sound, rhythm and meaning irritate the usual understanding of the relationship between perception and communication. Let us suggest that this may represent a tacitly assumed code of art, or at least of literature: a connotatively irritating form of communication versus all denotatively standard forms. Or, according to the strict terminology of systems theory: a 're-entry' takes place here, as in other code operations, meaning that the difference in its entirety enters into one side of the code. We find an example of this in passages where epic characters speak 'everyday speech', which is at the same time reinterpreted within the connotative discourse.[18]

As Helmstetter further observes:

> The 'communicative specificity of art' consists in the fact that it communicates the distinction between perception and communication, offers it as a *form* to the perception in special forms, and at the same time denies to the perception the *unity* of this distinction – one can always only perceive *one* side of the form. In crossing the boundary, the boundaries of communication and perception are mirrored in themselves – communication cannot perceive and perception cannot communicate. Therefore, Luhmann sees in the striking observation of the difference between information and conveyance 'the key problem of understanding the work of art'. Art forms turn the usual relationship between information and conveyance on its head – or, indeed, on media-formal feet – they *perplex* (*verdutzen*) the understanding. As 'perplexed communication', it is the 'functional equivalent of speech', the 'alternative of spoken communication'. (2011: 47; quoting Luhmann 2000/1995: 47–8)

We find numerous examples to illustrate the distinction between communication and perception, from visual arts to music, and from dance to literature. We shall limit ourselves, however, to a single theoretical parallel, notably one that overlaps with various attempts in the field of information aesthetics, starting in the 1950s, especially with Moles's and Bense's distinction between aesthetic and semantic information (cf. Chapter 5, pp. 182–4). The informational value of a literary work, which Lotman also examines (see Chapter 10, pp. 333–8), is then only one of its facets, and its aim is not communication in and of itself but rather its mirroring in other communications. The resulting 'perplexed' or irritated perception reminds us, once again, of the perception of unintentionality (Mukařovský) by the addressee of the work.

Luhmann's notion of 'irritation' thus means perplexity, surprise or increase in connotative complexity, all of which can be understood as a possible expression of the code of art. It also explains at least in part why it is so difficult, in the case of art and literature, to grasp the code. The mirroring of communication in perception and vice versa is fluid, and cannot be effectively expressed or summed up in ordinary speech. In this way, the functionalist conception of art also reaches its limit, unable to provide an explicit semantics that would express the basic characteristics of the social system. While the medium 'artwork' disintegrates immediately after it has been established (hence its 'limited futurizability'), some kind of code must remain (the emphatic title of Werber and Plumpe's article: 'Literatur ist codierbar' attests to this), but it is autonomous in society and blurs the very boundary of communication (and perception). The code of art therefore has many forms that are rather symptomatic in nature (unlike most other codes: *pay/not pay* in economics, or *legal/illegal* in the legal system). We have attempted to derive a code of literature – *connotatively irritating/denotatively standard communication* – arising from consideration of one of its essential functions: the problematization of the relationship between perception and communication. With this in mind, we can now reconfirm that each form of code depends in large part on the media landscape.

While we may argue about the concept of art developed by Luhmann and his successors (as they themselves do), we are compelled to recognize, above all, that they are guided by the right questions. Having taken a closer look at the relationship between art and (technical) media in systems theory, we might move beyond the scope of Luhmann's work, to examine one of its more interesting extensions: namely, Rainer Leschke's theory of media forms (and its limits).

Epilogue: Media forms[19]

No sooner had new media gone through technical and economic processes of adaptation and integration than they were subjected to systematic enquiries on their formal-aesthetic conditions, in order to assess their relevance within the context of cultural production (their cultural *Leistungsfähigkeit*, or 'performance capacity', as it were). This resulted, as a rule, in the aesthetic differentiation of individual media.[20] Along with these differentiated aesthetics, the conditions of the corresponding media forms were also given, as well as a central question concerning their transmission – a question that also pertains to the way the meaningful expression of an already established medium could be effectively carried out within the formal-aesthetic conditions of a new medium (Leschke 2010a: 45). 'In fact, media products must play to relatively conservative expectations', writes Leschke, 'while simultaneously exhibiting their innovative aspects, as guarantor of their distinctiveness' (Leschke 2007: 6) – an observation which corresponds to Bateson's definition of information as 'a difference which makes a difference' (pure entropy is nothing more than the total absence of this difference, or, more aptly, a situation in which everything is different from everything else, so that no particular difference is exceptional).

Undoubtedly, the first question that arises is: *What is a medial form?* 'What medial forms have in common is that they are not quotations or material states that copy one another. Rather, they are structures that roam the media[21] and that are transformed, accommodated and adapted in the course of this nomadic journey' (Leschke 2007: 7–8). This view is based on a pre-intermedial paradigm, when there were (emerging) individual media (film, radio, etc.), and is thus essentially historical (and perhaps also historicizing). In spite of this, 'form' seems to refer to recognizable shapes, as opposed to communication *dispositifs* (Werner Wolf), for example; on closer inspection they are also medially unfinished, neutral, so that they appear to cover integrated or combined media formations: 'Medial forms are not identical, but they are certainly distinguishable. They are therefore stable in terms of their basic shape (i.e. the differences of which they are constituted) but exceptionally adaptable in terms of their surface. When medial forms roam media, they therefore establish, as a kind of side effect, totally flexible links between these media' (Leschke 2007: 7–8).

Naturally, differences in semiotic systems (literature vs. audiovisual media) remain, but forms may to a large extent serve to integrate them (as, for example, an advertising poster that appears on the set of a theatre production). In this way, forms bring intermediality to its completion in a period of media integration. We may also think of this in terms of the retreat of individual media as 'cultural resources' (Leschke 2010c: 302) into the role of atavisms. This does not mean that the old media disappear. As Riepl's law tells us, the arrival of new media simply compels the older ones to redefine their function (Riepl 1913: 5). We can furthermore point to the law of remediation, according to which older media persist in the new ones, by 'exaptation', for instance. The retreat of a medium as cultural resource only means that its role of passing down a repertoire of representations based on a certain technology (film, radio and television, but also printing technologies) may become anachronistic (Leschke 2010c: 302). In these cases, strict use of the medium (which can sometimes programmatically exclude intermedial overlaps and parody) may take on a 'retro' or 'artistic' aspect for a certain group of enthusiasts (precisely those who are intermedially educated or more habituated to the practice of looking for intermedial links), whereas the medial system *as a norm* tends more towards integration by means of synapses, mutual references and citations.

This way of presenting the evolution of the medium gives a semblance of regularity to a process that, in reality, is much more prone to contingency. We see this, for example, in the film adaptation (2012) of David Mitchell's novel *Cloud Atlas* (2004), a particularly striking meditation, within the medium, on medial forms. The film presents six intertwined stories and genres revolving around the *idée fixe* of mediality, depicted in each story as a recording of (a fragment of) the story before it. Most of what we have worked through in this chapter regarding the systems theory of mediality and literature can be found in this film, on several levels: the contingency of communication across time (a fragment of the 'moral' of one story invariably reappears in the next to inspire an unlikely hero, and always in an unexpected and unpremeditated way); the influence of the 'medium-work' (the discovery of a written artefact, at times no more than a fragment, corresponding to the discoverer's predicament and medial competence); the subsequent transformation of the material support of the written artefact, from diary and letters to hologram (the specific materials featured in the film are naturally different than those in the original novel). Individual genres appear here similarly as medial forms that speak to the possibility of self-actualization across centuries (the six stories are set respectively in the nineteenth to twenty-fourth centuries), as a function of the 'futurizability' of individual 'exemplifications' of the work of art medium. The variety of forms used (historical fiction, farce, sci-fi) points to the ineradicable difference between perception and communication, ensuring that world events will not be bound to one type of intentional medial form (chronicle, for instance), but will rather depend on the limited capacity of the recipient (the discoverer of the artefact) to adopt content and turn it to a purpose for which it was not originally intended. Jumps in time play a role only vis-à-vis the film as a whole, that is, within the work that connects them. The result is a synchronous image (or figure) made up of diachronic themes. The film, however, presents these in a different manner (each story is presented in no apparent order until the denouement, which builds tension) than in the novel (the first five stories brought one by one to their midpoint, followed by the entire sixth story, and then completion of the first five stories in opposite order).[22] The medium of the work of art thus serves as a material support for the representation of medial forms that have also arisen, in turn, from certain works – a vivid demonstration of the dialectic of mediality and art.

Cloud Atlas, or at least its above-mentioned features, could serve as a banner for the theory of media forms. More specifically, its depiction of contingency makes us think of Leschke's thesis on the universalization of medial forms. For him, forms represent 'an *abbreviation* of expression, representation and context' (Leschke 2010c: 163; italics added) which enables a certain *economization* for the way they are received. Clusters of forms enhance the reduction of complexity, serving as an instrument of aesthetic condenzation (Leschke 2010c: 163) – one, however, that is invariably random, unintentional. However, the upshot of this, precisely, is (more) contingency: the methods of disconnection and reassembly are characterized by variability (as is readily evident in the structural differences between book and film).

Cloud Atlas illustrates the circulation of medial forms on the example of an art form. This, however, begs the question: *What, in this case, is the relationship between art (as a functional system) and media?* It seems to be characterized by what Leschke considers as the dynamics of forms, that is, the movement of their transformation, which is not arbitrary but has its own normative principles. In short: we see a multiplication of forms moving from art to media, with an attendant increase in their redundancy (typified by the pictorial representation on a banknote or postage stamp that is serially reproduced). Conversely, forms that move from media to art undergo a decrease in redundancy, while their individuality (*Vereinzelung*) and reflexiveness increase.

Art is focused on the production of singularity, which means – by the very logic of the system – that redundancy is considered strictly as art's 'cardinal sin' (Leschke 2010c: 163).

With Frankfurt School thinkers, especially Walter Benjamin (see Chapter 3) in mind, it is Leschke's description of a form's *repeated* transition between the two systems, that is strikingly unique: 'To be re-accepted by the art system, a form that has passed through the medial system must solve two problems: disconnection from the medial system and differentiation from its initial presence in the art system' (Leschke 2010c: 269). If the antagonism between the two systems is as marked as Leschke supposes, this transition appears rather 'challenging' indeed. One might argue, however, that with the advent of new media and the corresponding assimilation/adaptation of (artistic, mainly literary) creation, the whole process has largely merged into one, *without for that matter obviating the distinct movements towards redundancy and reflexivity as such*. Indeed, it is possible to see how the one is rendered and mirrored in the other, as we have already seen with *Cloud Atlas*.

For Leschke, each system treats forms in a different manner, and this means that forms are eventually 'worn out' in the medial system, while in the art system they are refined (Leschke 2010c). This also means that art has a unique respect for tradition, so that forms tend to have greater longevity than in a purely media environment. However, none of this changes the basic fact that even art lives only in the media environment[23] and nowhere else (how else would it be communicated?). At the same time, new media show an enormous demand for forms, because in order to be integrated into the medial system, they have to prove more than just their technical capabilities. Insofar as they wish to demonstrate their cultural relevance, they are dependent on a repertoire of already existing forms. There is a clear advantage in those cases where the forms of the new medium are already known, at least to the extent that they are akin to the already established forms. The migration of forms thus provides a double advantage: it provides the new medium with a culturally established and coded repertoire of forms, thereby giving it cultural expressive potential' (Leschke 2010c: 277).

Conversely, even the reflexive, recognizable forms that become art look back retrospectively to unrecognizable media forms (quite explicitly in the case of *Cloud Atlas*).

We may well ask, in this context: *What is the fate of literature and its forms?* It can compensate for its possible 'loss of status as the leading medium by establishing a productive relationship with other media' (Jahraus 2003: 579). In other words, it is capable of a reflexive move that brings added information (difference) into the remaining media production.[24]

New media oscillate between the original function of communication and the new function of experience: they no longer respond to the need to communicate, but offer the possibility of directly experiencing a semiotic space (made up of sound or music, for example) which, even from a literary point of view, is very amorphous. With Helmstetter, we identified the irritation of the relationship between communication and perception as a possible substitute for the code, following Bühler's three aspects of communication. Operative displacements, or shifts (Fuchs 1999: 81, cf. Fuchs 1993) take place among the three components – information, conveyance and understanding – through their distribution in the course of historical changes, and especially in terms of their selectivity – or, as he writes, 'whether communication reacts to acute information, or whether communication [conveyance] behaviour (*Mitteilungsverhalten*) comes to the fore, or whether problems in understanding give rise to metacommunication' (Fuchs 1993: 153, 159). Fuchs identifies the two main operative shifts in the Enlightenment and Romantic modes of communication (Fuchs 1993:

79–104). While the first strives as much as possible to achieve uninterrupted communication without noise, that is, privileging the informational aspect (a concept contested by Michel Serres 1969), the second strengthens its expressive potential, that is, the side of the conveyance (*Mitteilung*). It is clear that we are not dealing with pure historical styles, but with vanishing points, the space between which is filled by a continuum of many diverse operative shifts. What is more, Helmstetter's and Fuchs's approaches could be combined: the irritation of the relationship between communication and perception, which is characteristic of literature (Helmstetter), is achieved precisely through the variability of operative shifts, with the result that we remain uncertain whether we have fully understood them (they are each time different).

If this is the case, and different functional uses of speech are in principle possible in any (modern, post-Renaissance) historical period, polemics against the weaknesses of certain operative displacements become essentially meaningless, because these are not universal, only operative.

Notes

1 The conception of communication put forward by the Palo Alto School represents an alternative to the linear Shannon-Weaver model insofar as it emphasizes the factor of social participation and involvement of a plurality of actors and contexts.
2 Luhmann's examples include such things as power, money, justice, truth, love and faith. Here he extends the concept of the medium far beyond the typical domains of technical apparatuses and social institutions. Yet all his examples have certain common characteristics, especially regarding the functionality of communication.
3 Furthermore, redundancy is defined differently for each addressee: a well-read intellectual, for instance, in contrast to a young child.
4 We might recall here Luhmann's other point regarding social redundancy: 'Not only does time pass faster as the dissemination media generate social redundancy, it also becomes uncertain and finally impossible to ascertain whether uttered information is accepted or rejected as the premise for further behaviour' (Luhmann 2012/1997: 121).
5 The conceptual germ of SGCM can already be seen in the example of direct speech interaction: 'Language alone does not decide whether the reaction to communication is acceptance or rejection. As long as language is used only orally, that is to say, only in face-to-face interaction, there is enough social pressure to say pleasant rather than unpleasant things and to inhibit the communication of rejection' (Luhmann 2012/1997: 122).

6   We might compare this to the metaphor of the art medium as a 'magnet' that attracts to itself a selection differentiating between literary and non-literary communication (Werber and Plumpe 1993: 36). See also Chapter 12.
7   In Culler's (2002/1975: 132–3) interpretation, understanding this choice of form is enabled by conventions, which help to read a given text as fiction, poetry, etc. We find another analogy, however, in the hermeneutically oriented view of Jauss, whose concept of the 'blending of horizons' (*Horizontverschmelzung*) refers to the reception of clashing sets of literary and non-literary norms and their historical dialogue.
8   This is also, however, a matter of social conditions: see, for example, the differentiation of entertainment, and dedication of evening time to pursuits that afford 'pleasure and amusement' (Werber and Plumpe 1993: 33).
9   This rather rudimentary argument defines the gradual appearance of 'system options' in terms of artistic trends (romanticism, realism, etc.). However, they are not a blanket designation covering an empirical body of work, but different possibilities that manifest in the relationship between the system of literature and its 'environment', i.e. the real world.
10 In order to understand Luhmann's concept of the (artistic) code, we must keep in mind that it does not deal only with its 'positive' sense (as we have, for example, in the case of the system of science with its notion of 'truth'), but rather with the disjunction of both values (Luhmann 2001a/1974: 162).
11 Selections also take place, however, at the level of literature as such. Literature is then treated as a (more or less reflected) selectively created canon, where the 99.5 per cent of remaining works that do not enter the canon represent the 'great unread' (Moretti 2000: 207, 225–7). For Moretti, literature is fundamentally a slaughterhouse – loosely reflecting Hegel's notion of history as slaughterhouse of the world.
12 There are countless examples – suffice it to say, as a general rule, that while other fields cannot afford to systematically ignore what society thinks about it (i.e. how it communicates about it), art often elevates this attitude to a programme, as is quite clear in the topos of the (socially) 'unrecognized artist'.
13 This does not mean that it represents reality (see lyrical poetry, abstract painting) but that it allows its addressees to do so indirectly, and this may be seen as yet another mediating function (Luhmann 2001b/1986: 214).
14 This can also be said of abstract art, which responds to commonly communicated patterns, signs, etc., and thus emerges from them.
15 Existing translations of *Mitteilung* in this context use utterance which however indicates specifically verbal communication.
16 See Luhmann 2013/20022013201: 205 ff., 215. It is indeed abstracted from understanding as a necessary condition, but only with regard to the concrete result: that is, it does not matter whether the ego agrees with the message, only whether it provokes a (meaningful) reaction at all, so that here, in

addition to two of the selection points (information and conveyance), there is yet a third. It is in this way that we should read Luhmann's interpretation of Bühler.

17 It is relevant, in this context, to recall Luhmann's *obiter dicta*: 'Every reader of modern literature will know there are texts that are unreadable by design. But this only imposes a limitation on what has always been the case' (Luhmann 2000/1995: 325 n.51; translation modified). It is obvious that the boundaries of what 'has always been the case' cannot be pushed indefinitely.

18 Even in these cases, we are often dealing with carefully constructed speech. Hemingway's dialogues, for example, may seem at first glance like the most natural thing in the world, but you have only to try to mimic their simplicity to understand how carefully arranged and stylized they really are.

19 Cf. Chapter 11, *passim*, for the historical context and pp. 408–10 for an intermedial interpretation of David Mitchell's novel *Cloud Atlas* (2004) and its film adaptation (2012) discussed later in this Epilogue.

20 We also find various attempts to establish 'pure art', in music, painting, literature and so on, in response to new media. Cf. Leschke 2003.

21 'In practical terms, it is no longer conceivable that the medium might somehow remain alone with its forms' (Leschke 2007: 5).

22 It therefore corresponds to the story order scheme 1-2-3-4-5-6-5-4-3-2-1 described by Marie-Laure Ryan (2016: 20).

23 Leschke indirectly confirms this: 'The distinction between art and non-art is a distinction within media' (2010c: 276).

24 Compare again to *Cloud Atlas*, in which a set of six stories constitute these media differences as a whole.

10

Poetics – semiosphere – medium

Lotman's cultural semiotics at the crossroads

Richard Müller

1. Points of departure

In Chapter 6, 'Openness', we saw that the cybernetic and information 'turn' in semiotics indicated some of the media limits of semiotic thinking while obscuring others. Indeed, semiotics had a media-related blind spot that the discipline failed to recognize until recently: it used language as its underlying model, presuming it to be the only universal and foundational communication system (this may be useful in some cases but it is often misleading). The emerging media features of semiotics included a reconsideration of the reception process (as a model process). Differences between different sign systems and semiotic codes were gradually formulated in growing detail, as were the connections between these systems and codes and their cultural effects. It was this line of thought that played a determining role in the transformations of Yuri Lotman's thinking. Lotman was a leading representative of 'cultural semiotics'. In this chapter I will focus on selected features of these developments. In the context of reflecting on his own work and that of the Tartu-Moscow School, Lotman understands these transformations as marking a shift from structural poetics towards a semiotics of cultures and from examining sign systems towards studying their history.[1] The 'historicizing' of semiotics primarily brought with it an interest in the 'semiotic mechanism of memory'. Lotman and Boris Uspensky began to speak about the memory function of 'semiotic objects' or cultures as one of their basic functions; sometimes texts were seen as elements in a code that was maintained as time progressed, recoded in a new context (this process could be compared with Williams's concept of selective tradition; see Chapter 8, pp. 283–4), and culture in general began to appear as 'nonhereditary memory of the community' (Lotman and Uspensky 1978/1971: 213).

Here, the job of the memory function is conceived as the direct opposite of the process of accumulating information; this function engages in selection that varies with the context changing in time, bringing (in interaction between the individual subtexts of a text) sets of textual elements into a latent state. (This concept is also very close to Eco's later idea of the text as a 'tool for forgetting', Eco 2014/2007: 89.)

We will have to take a more detailed look at the theoretical implications of this shift, in which codes, texts and systems 'are returned memory' (i.e. destined to processes of selection and forgetting). Several questions arise at the outset: If at first glance the recording and reproducing function of media seems clear, to what extent, if at all, can the concepts of the sign system and medium overlap? And this question leads us to others: As Lotman's later semiotics focus directly on the relationships between different sign systems, to what extent can these relationships be characterized as 'intermedia' relationships? From here, it is just a short step away to a related question, one that is, however, not at all apparent in earlier semiotic thinking: To what extent is the (latent) notion of media, or the development of media technologies, involved in the historical and cultural turn of this current in semiotics? And at the same time how have understandings of literature and the literary system changed?

If we take as our starting point the suggestion contained in our 'unapparent' question, then three evolutionary factors that appeared in media culture from the 1960s to the 1980s stand out. First, there is the coexistence of many various types of media – printed, analogue, electronic. Related to this fact, of course, is the development of film and television semiotics.[2] Second, the full interconnection between developments in computer and media technology,[3] that is, the convergence of all forms of media on a digital (binary-numerical) platform, was slowly beginning, generally under experimental conditions, although at the time it had yet to become a common reality. (In the 1986 book *Grammophon Film Typewriter* (*Gramophone, Film, Typewriter*, 1999) Kittler seems to derive a certain eschatological rhetoric from this near certainty). Third, the large-scale application of automated technological processes in art and the development of creative artificial intelligence (AI), which in the 1940s and 1950s seemed to be just beyond the horizon, never really occurred and, where it did, did not produce convincing results. Margaret Boden notes how, as AI developed in the 1960s, there was a 'schism' between the cybernetic approach, based on modelling adaptive behaviour, and the symbolic approach, most often based on logical and linguistic-logical principles. As she recounts, the cybernetic/connectionist approach fell out of favour in the following three decades, with the situation only reversing itself in the second half of the 1980s with the development of parallel distribution processing systems (neural networks).[4] (We shall return to a discussion of AI in light of Lotman's semiotics in Section 3.)

Related to this is another impetus for the cultural reorientation of semiotics: inspiration from 'second-order' cybernetic theories and theories of self-organizing systems (of consciousness and communication, human and non-human). In short, the transmission model that both information theory and cybernetics initially worked with changes significantly if the position of the observer is recognized as participating in communication and, therefore, also in the transformation of the message and the system; complex, non-linear, cyclical and recursive communication processes that also include meta-communication emerge. The notion of information may, from a semiotic perspective, seem to be inadequate because in its original context it neglected meaning and interpretation. But when we say that information is always already coded and interpreted, we find ourselves in the realm of communication theory. This point of view can be applied to the whole cultural system so that we start to see culture as a sort of peculiar mechanism or organism that observes itself for which it uses 'texts' as 'input' and 'output'. Some currents in semiotics concur with theories of (self-organizing) systems that individual messages relate to the system as the system relates to its disordered environment. (On systems theory, see Chapter 9.) At the same time, however, the text transcends the system; the latter is never self-sustainable. It changes, 'mutates' and 'recoded', re-enters the text again.[5]

In Chapter 6 we explored both inspirations and the dead ends (those prevailed) of transferring the principles of information theory directly to literary studies, aesthetics and to experimental works. We saw that in the contexts of social and cultural situations (communication) the need for correcting technical models appeared immediately. The disregard for meaning in statistic models here was unacceptable as was the lack of consideration for the context in which a work or text is created and received; when various semiotic codes were projected into the original notion of 'channel' in the field of literary semiotics, or conversely when codes were defined as channels of various profiles, the primary result was not that the entire technical concept was metaphorized, although that is not without significance.

Perceivers, with their expectations and dispositions, appeared, but more as *abstracted correlates of the individual system*. In the cultural-systemic semiotic approach some doubts related to these conceptual transpositions and corrections gain special emphasis, and the questions have changed significantly: What are the ramification of assuming that a text is always composed of multiple codes or subtexts, which at the same time introduce tension and extraneity to the text? If uncertainty is not just technical noise, what role does it play in communication? Does uncertainty mean the degradation or the growth of the system, and how do various ways of 'coding', and their mutual translations, partake in the *increase – or reduction – of certainty*? What is the relationship between a text and a culture (as a system or a whole)?

Thus, if we read certain hints correctly, in the context of the emergence and development of cultural semiotics we run up against media boundaries or dividing lines, even though the concept of media might not be explicitly addressed by cultural semiotics. The causes and above all the implications of this conceptual latency and the question of to what extent they are specific to cultural semiotics will be thoroughly addressed in this chapter once the stage has been set.[6]

The starting points of some aspects of Lotman's semiotics, upon which we have touched, can be placed in yet another interpretive framework, one that corresponds with its spirit. No less important was the environment in which his semiotics emerged. After completing his studies at Leningrad State University in 1950, Lotman arrived in Tartu, on the Soviet Union's periphery, that is, the very area of the semiosphere about which he would later write was particularly semiotically charged and the scene of intense semiotic activity, the semiosphere's border.

The following factors, which also reveal glimpses of semiotic boundaries or friction points, influenced the dynamics of Lotman's development as a thinker (and of the Tartu-Moscow School in general): (1) Lotman's move to Tartu was influenced by his Jewish background, which contributed to his not getting a recommendation after graduating from Leningrad State University. (2) Tartu already had a long university tradition: Baudouin de Courtenay, a proponent of synchronic linguistics and the theory of phoneme and phonetic alterations, worked in Dorpat (as Tartu was formerly known) from 1883 to 1893; Jakob Johann von Uexküll, whose notion of the *Umwelt* and certain biocybernetic principles influenced a wide range of academic fields and approaches, including philosophy, biosemiotics and system theories, studied here. (3) Lotman (gradually) came to realize his dual role as a persona non grata arriving in the borderlands and as a Russian occupier; as he recalls in his 'non-memoirs', during the war he served in the Red Army, which 'liberated' Estonia.[7] (4) From the perspective of the official lines of Soviet science, semiostructural poetics and cultural semiotics seemed suspicious; Lotman's pragmatic and rhetorical abilities were, in this context, put to use in the development of the Tartu School as a kind of clique or secret society (see Waldstein 2008). (5) The second half of the 1950s marked a turning point for cybernetics in the USSR; translations of Norbert Wiener's and Ross Ashby's works were published, and semiotic and cybernetic currents claimed for themselves the position of a universal scientific discourse. (6) In this context, contacts between the humanities and formal sciences were fostered (influential works include those by Andrey Nikolaevich Kolmogorov, mathematician Vladimir Andreevich Uspensky was the brother of Boris Andreevich Uspensky, and so on). (7) In the 1970s, state and institutional supervision put such pressure on academia that Alexander Piatigorsky, Boris Gasparov and Alexander Zholkovsky, among others, emigrated. (8) The relationship between 'West' and 'East' appeared to be 'functionally asymmetric' (cf. Lotman 2005/1984: 225). In all these points (and in several others), we can identify sites of friction and interfaces that are retroactively interpretable in Lotmanesque semiotic categories. Relevant to the topic of this chapter is the interpretive possibility that from Lotman's sense for cultural polysemy and multilingualism grew his sense for the principle of incompatibility – between at least two languages, two means of coding, between image and word – as a fundamental mechanism of semiotics. Just as Lotman found a way to Estonian culture, Estonians, too, grew to love Lotman and his regular television programmes about seventeenth- and eighteenth-century Russian culture (Heczková 2013: 9): in a country that in 1920 had still been a stateless nation and which in 1944 was once again (and for many years) connected to Soviet Russia. These circumstances, too, make questions of translation and intercultural relations germinal for Lotman's semiotics. As we will see, incompatibility is not resolved through transfer, bridging gaps or understanding; it is generative. Lotman – a Russian literary and cultural historian of Jewish descent born in Saint Petersburg, living and working on the periphery of Soviet Russia in Tartu, Estonia – provides a convincing meta-language for grasping the dynamics of the history of intercultural relations and the dynamics of the semiosphere as the *ex definitione* dynamics and history of misunderstanding and incongruity.

2. Lotman's crossroads and borders

Prologue: Uncertainty and the dream as a (pre-)media phenomenon

The first hint towards explaining the media dimension of Lotman's thinking[8] is provided by his sketch of the dream as a phenomenon. Lotman's book *Kul'tura i vzryv* (1992, *Culture and Explosion*, 2009), the last published in his lifetime, contains a chapter titled 'The Dream – a Semiotic Window', in which Lotman essentially understands the dream to be a pre-media phenomenon, as an independent reaction to a certain impulse, an expression of a stage in the history of consciousness in which the mechanism of reaction loses immediacy and acquires sufficient independence and complexity. The dream thus enters between impulse and instantaneous reaction, becoming complex and independent as a delayed reaction of sorts. However, it cannot be controlled and remains physiologically conditioned. On the one hand, dreaming appears to be a peculiar reproduction mechanism, enabling the uncontrolled creation of maximally indeterminate signs; on the other hand, its reproduction remains tied to the inner circuit of the consciousness. The dream is a kind of sign 'in pure form', a sign with enormous indeterminate meaning that creates pressure for its translation into an understandable language. This is the reason not only for its importance but also the diverse ways in which it is understood in different cultures and periods: as a foreign prophetic word, an oracle, a riddle, a mysterious utterance, an inner truth, the voice of supressed conscience, an expression of repressed sexuality.

If in dreams the possibility of developing a specific sphere of an independent consciousness opened up, then, according to Lotman, this possibility was suppressed by the concurrent development of speech and gestures. A similar logic affected the culture of spoken language: 'the degradation of oral culture' (Lotman 2009/1992: 143) – in the spheres of mnemonics, and the memory functions of rhythm and intonation – went hand in hand with the development of writing. (The word *degradation* must be taken with a grain of salt; for example, the invention of the printing press could have taken many paths, including one leading towards the stimulation of a rich manuscript production as a practice complementing the new printed forms of communication, as Roger Chartier notes, or towards new conceptions of the forms of oral culture, towards 'the invention of the oral' and towards the mutual defining of cultural forms and functions of printed production and spoken language, as Paula McDowell (2017) demonstrates in her historical work *The Invention of the Oral*.)

The connection between the dream and uncertainty is critical:

> The dream is characterized by polylingualism: it does not immerse us in visual, verbal, musical and other spaces but rather in the space of their coalescence which is analogous to real space. [. . .] The translation of the dream into the languages of human communication is accompanied by a decrease in the level of uncertainty and by an increase in the level of communicability. (Lotman 2009/1992: 145)

Boris Uspensky, exploring the dream, analysed the process through which the diffuse semantic clusters present in dreams are, through a retroactive impulse, transformed into a syntactic order, a narratable sequence of signs. According to Uspensky, this happens especially in dreams in which amorphous images are retroactively linked together on the basis of an external stimulus (e.g. a sound or touch) ending the dream and creating a narrative sequence. (It was on the basis of this type of dream that Russian theologian and mathematician Pavel Alexandrovich Florensky concluded that time flows backwards in dreams; Uspensky, therefore, gives a different explanation.)[9] Lotman writes that the dream is 'the reserve of semiotic uncertainty, a space which must, of necessity, become filled with meaning. This renders the dream an ideal *ich-Erzählung*, capable of being filled up with diverse interpretations, both mystical and aesthetical' (Lotman 2009/1992: 146). We encounter here a remarkable connection between the dream and the history of communication and recording devices. According to Lotman, ancient and shamanic cultures possessed a more developed culture of the dream, which included (as ethnographic research has demonstrated) techniques for controlling dreams and, of course, systems for retelling and interpreting them. The ancient culture of dreams, however, withered under the pressure of more successful means of communication that reduced uncertainty;[10] the dream was unsuitable for relaying messages. Writing brought with it a similar shift in the communicative functions of the seemingly 'redundant' acoustic features of language (which were also in part a premedia phenomenon) – primarily rhythm and intonation patterns. These sound features are moved away from mnemonics and mythology to 'poetry'; meters, in particular, were created, to which, as Lotman observes elsewhere (1977/1970), there is no analogy in the practical functions of language. Furthermore, and this is for us another hint of the distinct media dimension of theories of cultural dynamics, here the anthropological disposition to dream is explained as a sort of ur-model of the uncertainty of visual and verbal messages, a still premedial model in which the spheres of the senses mix or where they appear before being separated out of the common continuum.

Towards cultural dynamics

The three functions of intelligence and incongruity as a semiotic driver

In the preface to *Universe of the Mind*[11] Lotman defines three functions of minimally functioning semiotic structures: transmitting, creating, and preserving and reproducing information (i.e. texts),[12] that is, a transmissive (information) function, a creative (poetic) function and a memory function (Lotman 2000b/1996: 151). All three work in conjunction, for they must if semiotic objects – as well as intelligence – are to function. The introduction of a 'memory function' is clearly an important step towards a media dimension and an answer to the general problem of contextualizing the paradigm of information theories in the humanities. Conceptually, this can also be translated into the problem of code: code – unlike language and culture (and intellect) – does not have memory. As we will see, not only 'people' but also 'semiotic objects' have memory. But before we proceed to explain how Lotman understands the job of the memory function, we may have certain doubts about the aforementioned distinction.

First: What are these 'semiotic structures'? Lotman nearly freely switches between this phrase and others: *culture, text, intelligence, semiotic object*. It is as if these terms were embedded in each other, as if hypernyms could trade places with their hyponyms, and vice versa. This though is not the result of the arbitrariness of Lotman's thinking and meta-language. Instead, we can observe the following line of reasoning here: The complexity of culture, that is, the system in which the text is created, is on one hand greater than the complexity of an individual text; the system responds to its surroundings, which in the broadest sense comprise its natural environment and other cultures, in such a way that it translates their stimuli into its own 'language'. On the other hand, the individual text transcends this system (in the sense of a set of codes used for this 'translation'); from this perspective the text is then a certain adapting system, and if it is to successfully adapt, it must possess requisite variety, that is, at the very least the same variety as is found in its environment (the cybernetic concept of requisite variety was originally developed by Ross Ashby). In other words, unlike pre-semiotic communication processes (e.g. within a single biological organism), semiotic formations are structurally autonomous and function only secondarily within more complex units. What links semiotic formations of different levels is, from certain stages of Lotman's thinking on (beginning approximately in the 1970s), the notion of text: 'what turns a culture into a Text is internal polyglottism' (Lotman 1979b: 507).

Worth noting is that the boundary between the categories of the 'literary' and the 'extraliterary' may be in such a conceived semiotics less significant than other types of borders, without ignoring the nuances of how the literary text is constructed. Lotman does away with the tendency to build literary scholarship mainly upon such a distinction (literature/non-literature, fiction/non-fiction, the autonomy of literature, etc.) and in the context of historical semiotics, he draws examples from literature as a source of historical knowledge about the logic of certain phenomena (just like he reflects on the phenomena of the everyday life of the nobility through Pushkin's *Eugene Onegin*). In this line of reasoning what is primary is the translation between various kinds of coding; it is only in these 'in-between spaces' and collisions that something emerges that in some respects could indicate what is found outside of semiosis, in the clash between two or more semiotic processes that are not fully mutually transposable.

When Lotman speaks about 'generating new information and texts', he is building upon Jakobson's communication model and the poetic function it contains. Moreover, Lotman, in his consideration of which function of code is, from the perspective of the development of the system, primary, whether the transmissive or creative function, refers to Ferdinand de Saussure and Roman Jakobson as coming from opposite positions, with de Saussure's point of departure being information and signification as opposed to Jakobson's focus on the artistry and iconicity of language. Jakobson's explanation of the poetic function, however, has its shortcomings (and not just from a media perspective). Above all, Jakobson takes the poetic function out of the context of reception; this comes to the fore especially in comparison with Mukařovský's notion of the aesthetic function (see esp. Section 3 of Chapter 2, pp. 54–9).

Lotman holds that semiotics had invariably taken as its starting point the methodical reduction of semiotic phenomena to a single isolated case (a sign, a communication act). Lotman claims that this fundamental premise needs to be transcended, even turned inside out.[13] The linguocentrism and the contextlessness of these models are features that Lotman turns into negative inspiration for his own solution: 'the ensemble of semiotic formations functionally precedes the singular isolated language' (Lotman 2005/1984: 205); the incompatibility of different types of codes is the 'beginning' of the semiotic process.

Or to put it another way, in Lotman's eyes the birth of cultural semiotics is conditional upon the upheaval of the model in which the communication act is viewed as *an exchange of equivalent values*: 'in trade, the exchange of equivalent goods, in marriage relationships, the exchange of equivalent women, in the structure of semiotic relations, the exchange of equivalent signs' (Lotman 1979a/1977: 86; a line of thinking that includes Ferdinand de Saussure, Marcel Mauss, Claude Lévi-Strauss and Roman Jakobson).[14]

According to Lotman, at the start of culture as a tremendous semiotic mechanism stands incompatibility; he presents three basic patterns of incompatibility in *Universe of the Mind*: (1) incompatibility between two languages (see Diagram 10.1); (2) incompatibility between two differently constructed channels – a discrete one and a continuous one; and (3) incompatibility between two different directions of communication, the 'I–s/he' direction and the 'I–I' direction (autocommunication). Lotman transcends the linguocentric, monolingual, literature-centric and art-centric tendencies of semiotics through several interconnected 'negations':

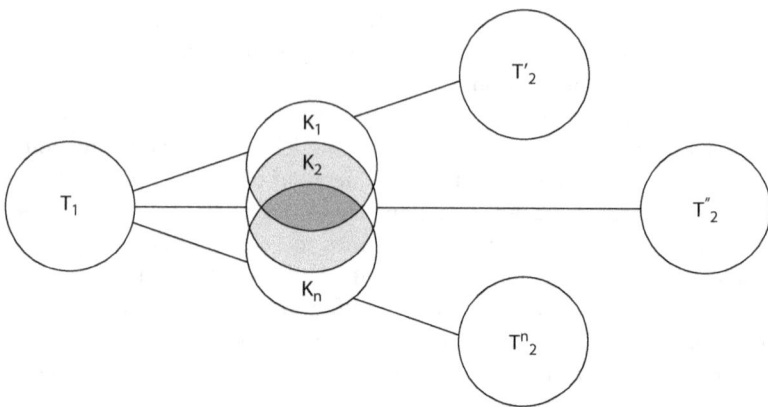

Diagram 10.1 The transformation of text T1 within the space of conventionally correlated codes (K{1, 2, ..., n}). *Source*: Lotman 2000a: 159.

a communication model cannot be built upon a single, isolated language; cultural dynamics cannot be modelled only on the conflict between natural languages, when communication 'directions' and 'differently constructed channels' have the same theoretical importance; meaning-making cannot be attributed to only works of art,[15] even though the creative function may be concentrated in this sphere.

Autocommunication and interference

According to Lotman, autocommunication is made up of two semiotic processes occurring in opposite directions at the same time. On one layer, already known information is communicated to oneself, as in mnemonic forms of communication (notebooks, notes). But in the second layer something else is happening: above the semantic dimension of the message forms a supplementary, asemantic code by the linking up of unexpected, and from the perspective of information, disruptive elements. Unanticipated interference occurs, during which 'the rank of the message is raised' (Lotman 2000b/1996: 164). According to Lotman, autocommunication begins with the occurrence of an unexpected distortion, of the 'counter-magnetization' of the message at the syntagmatic level (recurring rhythmic figures, patterns, ornaments), of the emergence of unintended isorhythm, which causes a qualitative transformation. At the same time, not only is the message itself restructured but so too is the subject of the addresser. In the autocommunication system 'the addresser inwardly reconstructs his/her essence, since the essence of a personality may be thought of as an individual set of socially significant codes, and this set changes during the act of communication' (Lotman 2000a/1990: 22). The formation of an additional asemantic layer of the message organizes free associations of the speaker and changes the identity of the communicator.[16]

This already suggests the cultural-semiotic significance of autocommunication. If 'I–s/he' communication serves for transmitting information while preserving the code, autocommunication (I–I) results in an increase in information, the transformation of the message and the code, and a change in the addresser (Lotman 2000a/1990: 29); both typological submodels of communication respond to two opposite ways of 'constructing channels'. According to Lotman, the primal forms of autocommunication can be found in myths, proverbs and parables, whose typically repetitive forms were not perceived as aesthetic but instead played a mnemonic and moralistic function. Lotman explains their redundancy and tendency towards pure syntagmatics and rhythmicity by the fact that their original connection to ritual had been lost ('the semantics of the magic tale evidently was a function of its relationship to ritual'; Lotman 2000a/1990: 34). What is said about an individual text is also true of culture as a whole: culture is first the sum of messages circulated by different addressers (I–s/he), and second it is a single message that the collective communicates to itself; 'From this point of view human culture is a vast example of autocommunication' (Lotman 2000a/1990: 33).

For Lotman to come to such conclusions, he needed to transform the idea of the 'channel' (*kanal*). This may seem to be at first glance to be of minor importance, but in fact it is significant for the transformation of technical models of communication in the context of the study of culture. In Jabkobson's model the word *channel* was understood as a 'physical channel' (Jakobson 1981b/1958: 21) enabling a connection between the addresser and the addressee to be established and communication to be initiated and sustained. If Shannon understood the channel as 'merely the medium used to transmit the signal from transmitter to receiver', Jakobson saw contact as occurring through such a 'physical channel' and a 'psychological connection', ideas that introduce the question of interpreting meaning. Lotman, whose interest lies in the semiotics of culture, further expands the concept of the channel. It includes not only a physical link and a psychic connection but also the very structure and orientation of the message.

Upon closer inspection, however, it is striking that the secondary organization of the message in Lotman's examples are concentrated around two opposing poles. In some examples, the inspiration for new meaning is the rhythmicized and quantifiable background (the rhythm of a horse's hooves, a stone park), thanks to which subjective associations are reorganized. In other examples, though, the background is comprised of random waves (such as the flickering of a fire). In Tyutchev's poem 'Son na more' (Dream at Sea), the background for the visions contained in dreams is not rhythm, but 'the chaos of sounds', unpredictable waves and tremors, indicating a high degree of entropy, where it is impossible to determine the next state of the system. In one example, the graphical dimension unexpectedly plays a role in the transmission process. In other examples, across the semantic layer, other, differently organized messages are formed: from a semantic perspective, interference occurs (an asemantic layer), but in terms of its own organization, this asemantic layer forms a regular pattern.[17] Thus, on one hand we find examples connected with randomness, interference and disturbance, and on the other, we observe the emergence of isorhythm, secondary syntagmatic patterns and a high degree of organization. How should we interpret the cultural-semiotic and media-genealogical significance of this bipolarity of interference, of the opposing nature of Lotman's examples of autocommunication?

The significance of interference

In the book *Le parasite* (1980, *The Parasite*, 2007) Michael Serres reflects upon a phenomenon that we could refer to as the bipolarity or the bivalence of interference.[18] Here he describes a particular situation, a dialogue held in a busy room: The sounds in the background are mere noise; one of the communicators shifts his attention and the situation suddenly changes; what was originally noise becomes communication, and what was originally communication, noise. According to Serres, critical is the moment of transition and indecision as to what is noise and what is information, what is a disruption and what is a message: 'Noise [...] has at least two values [...]: a value of destruction and a value of construction. It must be included and excluded' (Serres 2007/1980: 67).

In various areas of the dynamics of production – in agriculture and land management, economics, thermodynamics, communications, art and seafaring – Serres finds a similar series of relations, a 'cascade' in which it is demonstrated that every production or communication relationship is founded on the exploitation of resources, which are provided from elsewhere, tracing all the way back to those most general of resources for humankind – the natural world and solar energy, and in the case of communication, human culture in its entirety. Both the technical understanding of noise and the idea of entropy originally emerging out of the natural sciences became for Serres impulses for reflecting on the ambiguity and indeterminacy (openness) of human cultural activities and evaluating information in the process of perception and cognition. Technical communication is used as a metaphor; at the same time, however, a certain irreducible foundation of communication is made visible (see also Serres 1969).[19]

This brings us back to Lotman, who generally limits the idea of noise to the technical sphere and grasps uncertainty more clearly as a semiotic relationship.[20] The text, as Lotman notes in his earlier work *The Structure of the Artistic Text*, is a realization (*vÿrazhennost'*, *expression*) of a system, which also means that it bears non-systematic elements as 'an inevitable consequence of materialization' (Lotman 1977/1970: 52). Materialization, however, is not meant as technical noise or the effects of a material substance, that is, variations in concrete, perceivable material; materialization is instead the result of the verbalization of the text, the fact of its being expressed, and its substance is thus primarily the relationships that the text establishes in the semiotic process.[21] The 'realization of the system' in a certain sense always means a departure away from the system and its disruption, due to which the text can switch to another system or code.

The concept of the semantic gesture, discussed in Chapter 10 (see pp. 138–40 and 149–50), is well applicable to texts of this complex, self-reflective kind. They induce the movement of perception in a certain anticipated direction, while the collision with a non-systemic element can paradoxically elicit effort to submit to this movement. This only applies when this non-systemic element is correlated with another semantic field or code, which then 'presupposes a description of the *type of culture which we take as the observer*' (Lotman 1977/1970: 75; emphasis added). The perceiver must have this description at their disposal to a certain extent, as culture can observe itself through the perceiver. A statue moved from a park to a rubbish heap (Lotman's example) can affect the perceiver because it elicits the shock of encountering extrasemiotic reality (Mukařovský) and it may reflect 'the fantastical non-systemic order of the surrounding world' (Lotman 1977/1970: 77); in a specific cultural context (e.g. a postmodern installation) the potential of the semantic or affective resonation of such a work may increase.[22] This also marks another transformation of 'noise' into 'information'. From this point on, however, it will be better to use the term *(cultural) interference* for this phenomenon (cf. the line of argument in Chapter 6, pp. 195, 202 and 204–5). Here, let us repeat, 'noise' – interference – does not refer to the physical, measurable characteristics of a dataset but to the effect of observation and perception, or to the effect of the subsequent communication.

The sign system is therefore given in relation to other systems; at the same time, any expression or realization of the system in the semiotic process moves the system forward. This was already justified by Sergei Karcevsky when he proposed the concept of the asymmetric dualism of the sign and described the mechanisms through which the language system is modified and develops in discourse. What does this entail if we take into consideration the multiplicity of relations of thusly understood sign systems? Transposition between channels may rearrange the relationship between systemic and non-systemic elements, so that that which seemed to be noise can be expressed in terms of the system and vice versa (cf. the different effect of a documentary photograph of the statue on the rubbish heap, which fixes the point of view, concentrates perception along a visual channel, emphasizes facticity and distance, etc.). In this case, interference becomes part of cultural communication, a position it can maintain over the long term if it contains the potential to clash and resonate with other levels of the text, semantic fields, codes and cultural spheres. This state of agitation, which introduces a foreign semiosis to the text (e.g. through confrontation with a different sign system or the use of a different code), can also be understand as an *effect of the real* (the real as that which is inaccessible to any symbolization and representation).[23]

This change of perspectives suggests that it is necessary to re-evaluate the concept of the text so that it preserves its heterogeneity and variability in translation and transfer, when its 'immanent structure' (Lotman 1981b: 9) is re-organized. From Lotman's formulation it is clear that what motivates his view on the generation of new meanings and unanticipated semiotic processes is not materiality itself but rather (pure?) mediality. In this sense the text is coded many times over and the structure and hierarchy of its codes are rearranged whenever they are activated, in contact with 'heterogeneous consciousness' – the text, too, is in such a semiotic approach a type of consciousness – transferred to a different time, code, textual sequence or culture; and generally when

> The introduction of an alien semiosis (Введение чуждого семиозиса), which is in a state of untranslatability to the "mother" text, brings the latter into a state of excitation. [. . .] In these conditions, its constituent subtexts may begin to act in relation to each other as alien (чужие) and transform themselves according to laws alien to them, forming new messages. (Lotman 1981b: 10)

The intermedial extension of rhetoric

Elsewhere, Lotman refers to the structural unity of two or more subtexts constructed 'with the help of several, mutually untranslatable codes' as the rhetorical text (Lotman 2000a/1990: 57; a linguistic code may or may not be one of them). In the case of a rhetorical text – unlike a non-rhetorical text – this *internal inconsistency* is part of its design. The mutual untranslatability – between channels, codes and languages – that is, their limited structural compatibility that urges creative solutions (or causes incomprehension) is here a critical condition for the creative function to 'work'.

In the several chapters in *Universe of the Mind* focused on such 'rhetoric', Lotman specifies these codes as being verbal, pictorial, acoustic and gestural ones. For example, in eighteenth-century portrait paintings, theatre acquires the function of a code mediating between painting and fashion (or etiquette); the use of theatrical stylization and contemporary theatre costumes allowed the artists to depict the subjects of their portraits in the manner of certain historical or mythological figures. The form migrated further: portraits painted by Élisabeth Vigée Le Brun contributed to the popularity of the Empire style 'à la grecque' in Saint Petersburg,[24] and thus 'the Empress Maria Feodorovna appeared at an intimate supper on 11 March 1801 (the last in the life of her husband Paul I!) in a proscribed "antique" dress' (Lotman 2000a/1990: 59). Numerous examples of various types illustrate the definition of the rhetorical text involving transitions between discrete and continuous sets of signs and codes: the translation of a libretto into an opera or of a screenplay into a film is conceived as a perceptible expansion of the dimensions of the semiotic space and an increase in the number of coordinates in this space (cf. the intermedial system of Werner Wolf, as mentioned in Chapter 11, pp. 395–400). The palindrome (Lotman 2000a/1990: 78–9), an example of a strictly symmetrical sequence, is a case of the creative incompatibility of coding insofar as its creation is dependent on oscillation between perceiving the order of signs and their combined whole (an image).

In this intermedial rhetoric, the mutual transformations of discrete and continuous coding, whether they are realized in a sequence of signs or in a single combined sign as the result of a deep generative transformation, concentrate around the relationships between image and verbal sequence. Tropes as the core of the rhetorical transformation of a text, however, surpass the boundaries of art and they include 'all attempts to create visual analogues for abstract ideas, to depict continuous processes in discrete formulae [. . .], to construct spatial physical models of elementary particles, and so on' (Lotman 2000a/1990: 37; here too we see another difference with most theories of intermediality and their precursors). As Lotman writes, 'A trope is a figure born at the point of contact between two languages, and its structure is therefore identical to that of the creative consciousness itself' (Lotman 2000a/1990: 44).

At this point, intermediality can be understood as a network of possibilities for rearranging the systemic and non-systemic that is made up of the communication and representation *dispositifs*. It is surely paradoxical that something like meaning should be born out of such in-between spaces, emerging from the cracks, where from the perspective of a single medium pure chaos reigns.

However, there are questions suggested by assuming the perspective of media development that are only tacitly implicit in Lotman's work, extractable only fragmentarily or by way of further exploration. What happens when this network grows denser or when it becomes more firmly intertwined? Does the degree of uncertainty increase or, in contrast, decrease when relationships between media multiply or when they become more stably interwoven? What role do their media *dispositifs* play for the cultural functions of various sign systems and for cultural dynamics in general? How do these media *dispositifs* – a term that Lotman does not use – fulfil a creative and memory function? It seems that before these questions can be answered, the problem of the different layers of media needs to be clarified. It depends where exactly in the media network the mentioned processes (increasing density, loosening, separating) occur: whether in the technological reality, as happens in digitization, or during processes in which the transposition work lies on the shoulders of human actors and how these operations are stratified. For these reasons, we have chosen the term *media dispositif* and – beyond Lotman's reasoning – apply it to such a notion of media (i.e. the communication or representation *dispositifs*), which, besides sign and material parameters, also take into consideration the mode of technical mediation as a part of the specific potentiality of fulfilling the information, memory and/or creative functions of semiotic objects.

Another question that might occur to us today is whether a model of creativity founded on the incompatibility of two codes is also applicable when they are transformed automatically by some kind of technical apparatus.

Some questions on the dynamics of culture

In *Culture and Explosion* Lotman reflects on the idea that the unexpected layering of 'text', or that which stands in opposition to information (noise/ secondary organization), can be found both on the level of the individual message as well as that of culture as a whole and its dynamics. Here, we read the following about the relationships between organization and explosion in culture: 'The dynamic processes of culture are constructed as a unique pendulum swing between a state of explosion and a state of organisation which is realized in gradual processes. The state of explosion is characterized by the moment of equalisation of all oppositions. That which is different appears to be the same' (Lotman 2009/1992: 158). What Lotman says here about organization and explosion is analogical to what he writes about the work of art and intense moments of perception and contemplation in *Universe of the Mind*: the moment of explosion is a moment in which noise and secondary coding are indistinguishable, a black box in which it is impossible to determine whether the system will subsequently descend into chaos or whether it will achieve a higher degree of organization. Thus, interference may become new information; it all depends, of course, on the selection and length of the sequence into which it is incorporated: 'One and the same event, depending on the sequence (ряд) within which it falls, may change its degree of predictability' (Lotman 2009/1992: 125; translation modified).

How can we better understand the analogy between a work and an unpredictable event? In his writings on historical semiotics and his conception of cultural dynamics, Lotman is inspired by Ilya Prigogine and Isabelle Stengers's theory of dynamic processes.[25] The problems of the predictability of a system's development and the transformation of uncertainty (chaos) into organization can be generalized insofar as we speak about dynamic systems that are, like historical cultures, irreversible in time. The closer a system or structure comes to achieving balance, the more predictable the next step in its development will be. In contrast, the farther a system grows from equilibrium, the more it fluctuates, following a sinusoidal pattern, until it reaches what Prigogine and Stengers call the 'bifurcation point'. At this point, all determinism is lost: the possibilities are now open, and the factor of *randomness* takes on first-order significance, as does, from another point of view, the issue of choice. As Lotman writes, *where there is consciousness, there is always choice* (Lotman 2009/1992: 234). At the critical point where the trajectory of a structure's development branches, according to Prigogine and Stengers as well as Lotman, the system begins to behave like an intelligent organism.

Thus, the predictability of a structure's development stretches between two poles of a spectrum: on one end there is interference of the creative consciousness (of a thinking creature, but also random interference), and on the other the ironclad predestination of the historical processes viewed in retrospect. If seen retrospectively, historical development seems predetermined, while from a predictive perspective it appears highly unstable, especially if it involves the intervention of a single creative actor or a culture in a high state of disequilibrium, at the moment of 'explosion'. For Lotman's theory of cultural dynamics, the most important insight is this conflict between consciousness and historical process; and in his model of semiotic reconstruction, past events are conceived as intersections of probability functions surrounded by clusters of unrealized possibilities. Two paradigms in French history scholarship correspond with these two same poles. The French new history (e.g. Marc Bloch, Fernand Braudel, Jacques Le Goff, Jean Delumeau, Michel Vovelle) focuses on the *longue durée*, shifts of inexorable weight occurring on a nearly geological timescale, moving imperceptibly comprised as they are of an enormous sets of vectors and data; this notion of history corresponds with the pole of predetermination. On the other hand, the older 'great men' theory proceeds from explosive moments in history. The irreversible nature of the historical process is vividly illustrated in Lotman's objection to Marc Bloch's use of the film as a metaphor for history (in the essay 'Apologie pour l'histoire ou métier d'historien', 1949). In Bloch's metaphor the only clear frame in the 'film of history' is the last one, the most recent one, and if the historian wants to restore the faded features of the previous frames, they must progress backwards, as if unwinding a film reel. Lotman, however, aptly notes that history 'is a strange film that, when it is run backwards, will *not* get us back to the first frame (кадру)' (2000b/1996: 347).

The semiosphere and the mediality of memory

These lines of thought would interconnect and be incorporated under the banner of Lotman's late notion of the semiosphere. Culture is organized in a certain semiotic time-space; this time-space though emerges, is created and develops at the same time with culture. The semiotic continuum precedes any communication act, sign or designation, every language and code – and only within this continuum are semiotic operations possible. Here, Lotman draws a connection to Vernadsky's notion of the biosphere, a continuum of all life on Earth that forms a special geological element having a fundamental influence on all other geological forces on Earth ('[w]ithout life, the crustal mechanism of the Earth would not exist', Vernadsky 1998/1926: 58). When Lotman read Vernadsky's *The Biosphere* (several decades after it was first published), he wrote in a letter to his colleague Uspensky that he was particularly drawn by the idea that live organisms come from live organisms and could not have evolved out of non-living matter (Semenenko 2012: 112); he then tended to think in similar terms about human cultures and intelligence. Only in the continuous semiospace can meanings and information emerge, circulate and be formed in languages and codes, which, when they come into contact with each other, increase the pressure on their translation.[26] 'Lotman,' as Vladimír Macura writes, 'has in mind a construct completely detached from the contrast of the part and the whole and one that in fact directly cancels this opposition. [. . .] A fundamental concept for semiotics should rather be the idea of this semiotic universe, a holistic idea' (Macura 1995: 10).

Contributing to the same principle – the fundamental incompatibility of discrete and continuous coding – Lotman includes processes connected to modelling culture, particularly narrative, myth and memory. At the level of self-description and interpretation of cultures, a variant of the relationship between the discrete and the continuous is when continual, cyclical and sinusoidal fluctuations of a culture's development are transposed into the parameters of discrete periods. (This resembles an instrument recording a natural process, whose continuous values fall outside the instrument's sensitivity threshold). Likewise, 'Only when narrative forms came into being could people learn to distinguish the plot aspect of reality, that is, to divide the non-discrete flow of events into several discrete units, linking these units together by semantic interpretations, and organizing them into ordered chains by syntagmatic interpretations' (Lotman 2000a/1990: 170). The semiosphere can also 'exude' its spatial models, expressed, unlike verbal and discrete channels, in the continuous dimensions of 'iconic texts' (architecture, dance, painting, drawings): 'This image of the universe can better be danced than told, better drawn, sculpted or built than logically explicated' (Lotman 2000b/1996: 334). A meta-linguistic description and interpretation of these spatial models increases the complexity of the semiosphere by the fact that the thresholds between spatial images and discrete language are crossed. In contrast, the tendency towards the extension of a certain 'grammar' over other subareas of the semiosphere is associated with the semiosphere's stabilization and complexity reduction; it is the same in cases of exerting influence in intercultural relationships. For example, the dialect of Florence became the literary language of Italy, the legal norms of Rome became the laws of the entire Roman Empire and the etiquette of Louis XIV's court became the etiquette of courts across Europe (Lotman 2000a/1990: 128).

In the context of historical semiotics, the fundamental importance of the opposition between discrete and continuous channels is demonstrated in Lotman's ideas on the memory function in non-literate cultures, such as those of the highly developed pre-Incan cultures of Peru. Through comparison, Lotman once again arrives at two opposing poles of mnemonic coding and differing 'syntax', where on the one hand is the syntagmatic dependence associated with discrete signs, the grapheme and the hieroglyph, and on the other hand, the cyclical nature of spatial constellations and the free combinability of symbols in the ritual context (idols, tumuli, amulets, monuments, structures, natural landforms); their involvement in many different rituals gives rise to their ambiguity. Their memory function is activated in the context of the ritual, the song, the legend, storytelling, and is dependent on the recurring structures of oral 'texts'.[27] Lotman also mentions well-known written sources from the Classical period and the Old Testament documenting the ambiguous impact of writing in oral cultures, that is, the Book of Exodus and Plato's dialogue *Phaedrus*. Friedrich Kittler also refers to Chapter 20 of Exodus to demonstrate the monopoly writing holds yet at the same time how it radically reduces sensory experiences to words and the notion of history that springs from this reduction (Kittler 1999/1986: 7).[28] Plato's *Phaedrus* is also mentioned by Walter J. Ong (2002/1982) to demonstrate the structure of resistance at the moment a new medium is introduced, acquires new functions or usurps those that older technologies fulfilled. Lotman interprets the same sources as illustrating opposite manners of coding and the fulfilment of the mnemonic function. An idol, a sculpture, places in the landscape outside Athens' gates about which Phaedrus and Plato's Socrates converse in *Phaedrus*, a ritual of a cyclical nature – these are all continuous signs. Writing, however, which works with discrete, non-continuous signs,[29] 'will atrophy people's memories'. 'Trust in writing will make them remember things by relying on marks made by others, from outside themselves, not on their own inner resources' (Plato 2002: 69). Writing, as Phaedrus convinces Socrates, makes people 'seem to be men of wide knowledge, when they will usually be ignorant' (Plato 2002: 69). The defence of dialogical thinking here remarkably resonates with critical views on the accessibility of information and ways of disseminating it in today's 'networked' global contexts, with critiques of the 'post-fact' era. The confrontation between Moses and Aaron and the camp of the Israelites below Mount Sinai is a clash between different ways of fulfilling the mnemonic function, two differently constructed channels and mechanisms of cultural memory, represented on the one hand by written tablets of testimony and on the other by ritual dance, writhing around the golden calf: the antithesis between writing and sculpture (Lotman 2000b/1996: 368). A characteristic anthropological subtext is also evident in Lotman's emphasis on the complexity of non-literate cultures and his efforts to understand the different laws according to which they were arranged (see also earlier Lotman's ideas about the greater culture of dreams in archaic and shamanic societies and his analyses of mediative and contemplative situations).

The concept of the semiosphere is without question a media concept; the question remains unanswered of how the consequences of the long absence of the media concept are inscribed in Lotman's cultural semiotics and whether this semiotics, despite its focus on memory and collisions between different kinds of coding, is perhaps 'technologically blind' after all.

Commentary from a media-genealogical perspective

Although the extension of Lotman's theory to media semiotics is one of the most significant currents in contemporary thinking about Lotman,[30] the critical implications of the latent presence of the media concept in this context have yet to be thoroughly reflected upon – and this despite the fact that otherwise substantial attention has been devoted to Lotman's legacy and the institutional and conceptual history of the Tartu-Moscow School. It is as if the current omnipresence of the media concept justified overlooking the history of theoretical discourse. One of the leitmotifs of this book is that such an approach is harmful for understanding both older stages in media thinking and how media thinking is currently evolving.

Now, we would like to show in greater detail that Lotman's theory belongs to a recent stage in the genealogy of media thinking, thanks to substantial transformations of the semiotic paradigm that have occurred to explain the principles of cultural dynamics, and that his theory includes a certain residual conceptual inclination or resistance. Lotman uses the term *text* to express a universal notion that applies to all media kinds and for entire cultures, just as he generally applies linguistic categories to non-linguistic media. The persistence of his use of the concept of *text* (*language*) can be understood as follows:

1. The universalist claim of the concept originates from a monomedia bias (i.e. thinking predating the emergence of the media concept; see Kittler 1999/1986; Guillory 2010) or from a linguocentric perspective (e.g. the 'grammar' of film). From the beginning, Lotman *rejects* monolingual thinking; however, his tendency to adapt non-language systems to concepts from linguistic semiotics, present at least in a certain stage of his work, is linguocentric. One example is his notion of secondary modelling systems presented in *The Structure of the Artistic Text*. He claims these systems emerge out of a natural language system in two variants: a) one that uses natural language as a prototype for modelling (such systems 'are constructed *on the model of language*'; Lotman 1977/1970: 9) and b) one that uses natural language as both a prototype and a material (literature). Hence come the 'syntagmatic' arrangement of music, 'syntagmatic' and 'paradigmatic' relations in fine art and in film, and so forth. Human consciousness 'is a linguistic consciousness' (Lotman 1977/1970: 9).

Historically, this type of projection had goals and forms that were in nature ethnographic and colonialist (people who do not speak our language do not constitute a nation and are not fully human), educational and psychiatric (the speech of children and madmen is not worth studying or recording). Over time, language comes less and less to model Lotman's semiotic theory, and he explicitly deconstructed the historical 'logocentric' forms of semiotics.

2. Text is a concept that is medially heterogeneous; it has both discrete and continuous aspects. If divided into modalities – for instance, material, sensorial, spatiotemporal and semiotic modalities – text is not medially uniform (see Ellestrӧm 2010). It is exactly the medial heterogeneity of 'text'

that allows Lotman to use it – although the motivation is latent and not addressed – as an essentially media concept. Therefore, paradoxically, 'text' applies to those cultural artefacts that in principle stand in direct opposition to the traditional understanding of text as a message made up of discrete signs, arranged linearly, and so forth. Thus, Lotman's 'text' is both discrete and continuous (cf. e.g. the spatial features of the page, such semantic phenomena as metaphor, the visual aspects of writing, 'suprasegmental' sound features). As he would write in a later commentary on this concept,

> Culture as a whole may be considered as a text. However, it is exceptionally important to emphasise that this is a complex text, which consists of a hierarchy of 'texts within the texts' and which, moreover, generates a complex network of texts. Since the word 'text' itself includes the etymology of something that is woven together, we can say that in this interpretation we are returning the concept 'text' to its original value. (Lotman 2009/1992: 77)

At the same time the concept of code, which originated in information theory, semiotics, post-war structuralism and cybernetics, seems to be unsuitable for many reasons: its difficult-to-remove technical connotations evoke strict, or invariable, correspondence between the signifying and signified units or sets of units. It is also inadequate for describing the nature of both ordinary conversation and artistic communication, which cannot be, at least not meaningfully, 'decoded'. Code is equally inappropriate for describing continuous, non-discrete systems of expression. Nonetheless, Lotman partially frees the word from these connotations. First, he introduces here a complementary perspective, in which text precedes code (Lotman 1981b: 4–5). Second, a text fulfilling the creative function appears to be internally heterogeneous and consisting of multiple codes. He then demonstrates that a code is defined by conflict with other codes,[31] by correlation with the memory of texts (with the communities of the code's users), by the tension between the tendency to resignify and the inclination towards redundancy and by situations of instability and reinterpretation. The code is simultaneously headed towards disintegration and restoration; it is in contact with other codes, submerged in semiotic experience as if in a bath from which it cannot be pulled out. Characteristic of the retreat of residual categories in Lotman's writings, in his last work, *Culture and Explosion*, he attributes to the concept of code only a transmissive function, and he explains its limitations by saying that code, unlike language, has no memory (Lotman 2009/1992: 4).

We might continue in this genealogical critique of Lotman's meta-language.[32] However, if we examine the intermedial shift of his conceptualization of rhetoric and more generally how Lotman's theory began to relate to the phenomena of boundaries and untranslatability and dynamic processes, its medial nature comes to the surface. Lotman replaces 'technical noise' with the medially polyvalent concept of uncertainty, understanding it as a phenomenon related to the interstices and contrasts between various kinds of 'coding'. Technical noise, therefore, is not the same as 'cultural noise'; the transformation of technical noise into cultural interference can only happen by chance, under favourable circumstances and in the context of a certain set of cultural codes, poetics (see Khlebnikov's typographical errata or Cage's sound experiments) or a type of perception. This approach may also better explain Serres's 'bivalence' of noise.

Despite a certain underestimation of the self-referential capabilities of non-linguistic media, Lotman's theory also significantly contributes to the recognition of the media logic of self-reference ('self-interpretation', 'self-description') and its direct connection with the cultural dynamics of the semiosphere. Lotman demonstrates that literary criticism is medially *isomorphic* to literature; in this seeming concordance though, we might already sense medial tension. Artistic literary expressions enable the media dimensions of written speech that usually remain latent (potential pictorial, sound aspects, etc.) to come to the surface more clearly; literary critical style can adapt to these dimensions and make them available to all kinds of commentary. In contrast, the concept of *heteromorphy* enables the grasping of referential relationships between different media morphologies. Inevitably, the issue of self-referential expressions of non-linguistic (and non-written) media emerges, as we saw in our examination of competition and reciprocal delimitation between certain cultural models that the semiosphere emanates. At the same time, media transformation (e.g. adaptation) may appear to be a type of commentary revealing the latent media dimensions of the primary medium. Despite a certain rudimentariness, this distinction (isomorphic/heteromorphic) can be used as a basis for further reflection, for instance, on how these relationships are typically arranged, what happens when different media morphologies temporarily align when one medium imitates another, and how iso-/heteromorphism affects cases when media reference one another – and how all this determines the dynamics of the semiotic space. The argument that natural language is the core of the semioshpere and a model of the meta-linguistic (meta-communication) function (Lotman 2000a/1990: 128) is justified. It may, however, result in neglecting the abilities of different media to relate to themselves and the power that non-linguistic or non-written modes of self-reference can have on cultural dynamics. It is a testament to Lotman's insightfulness that we can apply his own remarks on this theoretical neglect of his. Is it not the tendency of a certain sphere of the semiosphere, of a certain cultural 'dialect', to project the grammar it self-descriptively created onto other areas of the semiosphere, to become a meta-language for describing the broadest cultural space possible (Lotman 2000a/1990: 128)?[33]

3. Lotman's semiotics and technology

The memory function and the technological *dispositif*

The memory function of media is undoubtedly correlated to its technological parameters and distribution potential (compare with the passages on the techniques of 'collective memory' and the triad of media functions in Chapter 7, pp. 244–7); this, however, has deeper implications, which Lotman's theory takes no particular notice of.

Lotman, for instance, demonstrates that a text may be constructed between the poles of a general, widely shared memory within a given culture or, in contrast, it may refer to an individualized memory. Both poles may become elements in its structure. If we take a literary text as an example, a composition in a published collection may address a close friend-poet; letters between friends may be published later; a personal code may be imitated or, in contrast, be hidden to various extents; and so forth. Let us notice, however, that *the memory and distribution functions become components in the structure of a work*; they may be addressed and implied in any number of ways, but at the same time, they form the conditions for their own possible involvement in the structure. The availability of a work in space and time is directly dependent on the distribution potential of the given media kind (distribution potential is not purely technically determined but is inseparable from technology) and at the same time may create semantic tension with how a perceiver or certain group of perceivers is projected into the work. In contrast to Kittler, Lotman associates technology and the realization of scientific ideas with the pole of slow, long-term, successive and predictable processes of cultural evolution, whereas theoretical science and great scientific ideas are linked to explosive, unpredictable events. But considering Kittler's history of technology, this assumption does not seem to be justified. Lotman's observation that both types of dynamics are mutually dependent on each other, and that one cannot exist without the other, seems to be a corrective to Kittler's technological 'paranoia' – despite or rather because of the fact that 'in the conventional phrase "science and technology" the conjunction [. . .] in no way signifies an ideal harmony. Rather, it rests on the edge of a deep conflict' (Lotman 2009/1992: 7).

We can hypothesize that the correlation between the technological aspect of the media *dispositif* and memory or creative function gains greater significance when the slowly occurring evolutionary changes in the development of technology turn into a moment of 'explosion'. Here, we find support in Kittler's theory in which armed conflict is understood as a node where technology increases its involvement in 'determining the situation' by leaps and bounds. A similar moment arises not when a new medium emerges but in the process during which a new medium begins to expand its functions. It is at this same moment that the network of media relations becomes volatile.

The creative function and text generation by neural networks

This brings us to questions about contemporary new media and the impact of computer-facilitated communication on (not just literary) culture and the prospects of cultural semiotics.

How did the evolution of computer-based hypermediality test Lotman's notions? Did it make them – particularly the idea that the dissimilarity between two types of channels represents the seed and model of creativity – obsolete?

Today's diverse deep learning techniques in the field of AI provide particularly fertile ground for a discussion of this question. Deep learning today is notorious for being tested and used in an astounding number of areas of automated information processing and labour. Examples include diagnosing breast cancer, testing self-driving cars, predicting protein structures, playing the game of Go (and beating the best humans), discovering innovative hide-and-seek strategies in digital simulations or controlling finger movements in neuroprosthetic hands. It has also found innumerable applications in interlinguistic translation as well as text, video, graphics and sound generation. All this happens through and in digital environments, but what is most striking is the ability of neural network techniques to autonomously learn to transpose messages between different media channels including different languages (as in DeepL), from text to image (Dall-E or Midjourney), from image to video (as in Deep Nostalgia), from video to video (as in 'deep fakes') or from sound to image (as in Speech2Face). Large language models (LLMs) have made apparent the possibility of extrapolating partial solutions (for instance, a learned subset of parameters) from one domain to another (for instance, from interlinguistic translation to sentiment analysis). Strikingly, pre-training enables these large models to perform a variety of tasks without any specific training, fine-tuning or gradient updates (this has never been possible before), being able to adapt based on a few prompts from a human user (Brown et al. 2020).

Lotman's ideas are particularly relevant in this context due to their foundation in both the *semiotic theory of communication* (a line which goes back to the Prague School; see Chapter 2) and the *semiotics of culture*. I argue that this framework provides key insights into understanding the implications of deep learning models, which are currently the most dynamic area of research and development in AI.

Three main preconditions render such an approach suitable: First, Lotman's theory leaves open the question of whether the actor communicating is human or non-human and whether there was a certain intention in the mind of the communicator, and shifts the focus to the effects and assumptions of communication. The division of the communication act into three interconnected components (in the sense of message, effect and interpretation) means that 'understanding' (Peircian interpretation) is always present within the act of communication, and thus constitutes a situation of signs within that act. Second, Lotman explains that the assumption of perfectibility does not apply to communication phenomena (Niklas Luhmann thinks along similar lines in his systems theory of communication, as explained in Chapter 9). Third, any communication contains ambiguity and relationships to multiple codes as well as an ability to change the structure of its functions, which links back to the capacity of intelligence itself.

Given the ability of various deep learning models to transpose information from one media channel to another, we are reminded of Lotman's 'test' of creativity. According to Lotman, creativity requires the irreversibility principle – by translating a message from one code to another and back we do not get the same message (Lotman 2000a/1990: 14–19, 74–81). While transposition based on one and the same code (binary numerical code) corresponds to the *transmissive* function of texts and culture, generating new meanings requires an asymmetrical mechanism, as exemplified by *dialogue* and *translation*. The creative process is defined by irreversibility, which means that we do not receive the same result when translating in reverse.

Given these premises, let us briefly touch upon current LLMs, which run tools such as Google.Translate, DeepL or ChatGPT, and consider what perspective Lotman's semiotics offers to assess this form of AI that attracts so much attention today.

First, we can see that the architecture of models such as Generative Pre-trained Transformers (GPT) or Google Neural Machine Translation indeed fulfils the requirement of irreversibility. If an output is subjected to reverse processing through the neural network, it certainly does not regain its original (input) form. Since the network is layered and each layer has a different autonomously learned set of parameters (weights, biases, functions), processing an image (for instance) in the opposite direction can never transform the image back into the original. If we reverse a complex function (a function of functions), we receive a different processing effect on the data.[34] This can be also illustrated by such applications as feature visualization or DeepDream, where a set of parameters of a certain layer is made to work upon the input image, allowing us to imagine what the networks 'see', or where an output is used as input in a trained network to produce 'psychedelic', 'hallucinatory' images (increasingly so depending on the number of iterations the input is processed through the network); a network with parameters fixed to distinguish fish will 'hallucinate' fish in any image whatsoever.

Irreversibility is also reflected on the more surface level of LLM translators, when outputs are processed back as inputs. In this environment, automatic back translation from the target language to the original language does not produce the same text. The point of 'Lotman's test' of creativity, however, is not that the message is distorted beyond recognition, but on the contrary that while the syntax is altogether transformed, an analogous meaning remains. It is easy to show that LLMs will frequently fail to properly translate messages that demand creative solutions, most notably puns, but also less usual or, on the contrary, more traditional phrases (less prone to be adequately reflected in the training dataset).

Here are several examples of flawed multiple reverse translations and chatbot translations between Czech and English and vice versa using DeepL, Google Translate and ChatGPT (Default and GPT-4):[35]

Vyfoukli mu boty pod nosem. – *They blew his shoes out from under his nose.* – *Vyfoukli mu boty před nosem.* – *They blew his shoes off in front of his nose.* – *Odfoukli mu boty před nosem.* (DeepL) [The meaning of the phrase is, 'They pinched his shoes right from under his nose.']

Kdyby se na hlavu postavila, nemohla to opravit. – *She couldn't fix it if she stood on her head.* – *Nemohla to opravit, kdyby se postavila na hlavu.* (Google Translate) ['No matter what she did, she couldn't fix it.']

Zajít na úbytě – *Go to accomodation* or *Go to the lodging* (GPT-4), or *To go bankrupt* (ChatGPT Default) ['To wither away.'][36]

The Importance of Being Earnest – *Důležitost být vážen* / *Důležitost být Ernest* / *Důležitost mít jméno Poctivý* – *The Importance of Having the Name Honorable* (ChatGPT Default)

The Great Switcheroo – *Velká výměna* / *Velká výměna rolí* / *Velká permutace* / *Velká záměňačka* – *Big confusion* or *Great mix-up* (ChatGPT Default)[37]

What are the implications of these failings? If at times, LLMs fail Lotman's test of creativity, while still incorporating the irreversibility principle, does it say anything about LLMs and deep learning in general? It is here that Lotman's definition of intelligence is helpful (see Lotman 1979a/1977). Lotman understands intelligence as an 'apparatus' capable of creating new messages in changed conditions, that is, messages that cannot be derived from any existing set of languages. Therefore, intelligence should have the ability to invent a new code for a situation to which no existing code can be assigned; this corresponds to the traditional definition of an intelligent organism as one that can behave in a new and purposeful way in radically altered environments. This delineation is however reworked in the framework of 'textual' production (so that transformed environments mean those for which there exists no decoding stereotype or its variant).

Here we need to broaden the scope of our discussion to include text generation. With deep learning (whether its outputs are visual, textual or something else), we certainly find solutions that have (at least) the semblance of creativity. The problem, in my opinion, is the *direct dependence* of the process of learning – and thus of the trained ability of the network – *on the given dataset*. This dependence is at the base of the approach. No matter how much the architecture of the large model or the learning techniques (such as word embeddings) reflect or even uncover some of the fundamental structural characteristics of language (see Gastaldi 2021),[38] the relationship between the message and the dataset is fixly reflected in the trained parameters. However vast the space of possible messages is, it will always be derived from the training dataset whose essential feature is immutability – it remains the same until the next time training occurs. Thus, the training dataset does not allow *in principle* for the creation of new messages independent of the given set of codes, even if, or rather especially if we concede that the model has recognized its organization (or part thereof) as a system of coding (as Gastaldi argues). Once the *corpus* acquires the function of a *(language) system*, the relationship between message and system is transformed, as is that between text and context – this relationship, in a sense, is reversed.

Four features can be extrapolated to describe the new status of text in the field of natural language processing (NLP) using deep learning and LLMs:

- Instead of an individual text there is a potentially endless series (series in place of a fixed text were already anticipated in modernism, but also in the pre-literary and pre-professional eras);
- Context is represented by the training dataset, an immense collection of texts – materials diverse in terms of genre, context and form – converted into a digitally homogenized set that is further structured for the

purposes of training (data curation, modulating batch size, fine-tuning, etc.);
- The text–context relationship is reversed: The network gradually adapts to the context during training, but once it is adequately trained (avoiding the problem of under- or overfitting), processing acquires a stochastic nature and the context remains unalterable. The selections (correlations of patterns) within the network can be shown and visualized, but only in terms of its design, not in terms of the logic of representation; the network, indeed, creates its own 'logical' organization;
- Output in the form of words has no reference; these symbols do not represent any entities in the world (neither actual nor possible or fictional), but rather representation itself, or more specifically, representation makes the stuff of further representation. Access to the material form of representation, so to say, creates an imitation effect (cf. Bender et al. 2021). Following semiotic tradition (the 'secondary semiotic systems' or 'secondary modelling systems' concept), such systems can be called tertiary or n-order representational systems, with the caveat that these 'systems' are static and derivative: they are derived from a vast corpora of data as a result of *collected human labour* (cf. also Zuboff 2019).

A secondary modelling system[39] is such a modelling (semiotic) system that builds on top of a primary system using its coding and its logic of signification as the material for a different 'encoding'. The primary system might assume the role of a signifying subsystem within the secondary system (myth, according to Barthes), of a signified subsystem (meta-language, according to Barthes) or of both planes of signification (conceded by Lotman). With LLMs, fragments of various secondary modelling systems – as well as various groups of forms and genres of texts – become part of the training dataset and integrate into the functioning of the network. Everything becomes enmeshed here to the point where distinguishing 'levels' becomes impossible (that is why I use the expression 'n-order representational systems').[40] It is the mechanism of attention built within the (GPT) architecture and reactivated by prompts that guides the network to 'locate' the relevant representational spaces in the training data (Vaswani et al. 2017). The relationship between the space of possible messages and the architecture of the network, which is in a specific way capable of reflecting the space of the dataset, becomes 'stochastically static'. This is another aspect of 'n-order' logic.

The communication framework perspective is indispensable as well. If we admit, for example, that GPT-3 or ChatGPT have some form of consciousness (Chalmers 2020), to what extent can we assume its communicability? This question is related to asking what type of text we are dealing with in these cases. The following line of thought gives us a sense of a possible answer: ChatGPT creates an impression of communicative adaptability by instantly conforming to the prompts to change its outputs from a factual standpoint or due to its self-contradictions. However, it does not reflect that a complete transformation of basic assumptions requires *effort* in terms of the *continuity of consciousness*. By continuity of consciousness, I mean the fundamental need for self-conception as a continuous self. By contrast, the logical errors in reasoning that we inevitably encounter in conversation with the bot invalidate its sometimes 'stubborn' resistance to changing positions. On one hand, there is the peculiar subservience and flexibility of the system or, in other words, its artificial (non-resistant) adaptability to entirely new assumptions, which resembles a lack of integrity; on the other hand, there is the blatant irrationality or rhetorical shamelessness of logical inconsistency. The two types of behaviour in combination belie the demands of the philosophy of the mind and phenomenology of consciousness, and both fail the Turing Test, for that matter; however, this is mostly problematic from the viewpoint of communication. As Ian Bogost (2022) writes: 'I was starting to feel like I was negotiating with a student who had come to office hours to complain about their grade.' In other words, the 'communication' that takes place here is of a very peculiar kind; it makes a loop beginning and ending in the human, while it is as if the network's outputs gave us the opportunity to misrecognize ourselves and our creations and tools, or to distinguish a logic alien to us – the logic of data and data patterns. All of the aforementioned features – logical inconsistency, incoherence (see also Marcus and Davis 2020), especially of larger textual units, discontinuity of the self, failure to recognize that a total change of starting points and assumptions encounters resistance in terms of the continuity of the self – point to the fact that we are dealing with very powerful digital tools, which remain, nonetheless, exactly *tools*. Their *mediality* might lie, however, in their specific ability for falsification, of setting up a distorted mirror. I will return to this point briefly at the end of this section.

We might argue that radical inconsistency works to invalidate the communication of both human *and* non-human actors; however, the only guarantee of the continuity of consciousness is the assumption that we are dealing with a human.

With ChatGPT, we thus have no reason to assume a gap between competence and performance – between intention and expression. As with media products, the original intent cannot be made clearer by further questions. The potential to express the same intention differently in a specific situation relates precisely to the continuity of consciousness. The aforementioned characteristics (inconsistency, unrealistic compliance) confirm that I cannot rely on the assumption that there is an analogy between me and the consciousness of the chatbot (or the communicator).[41] The artificial seems again implicated at the core of the natural: Might we not say that organic or human communicators behaving in this way resemble a poorly constructed AI? It appears, complicating matters further, that the communication environment, platform or media system itself may legitimize personal inconsistency (as we see in the case of some protest politicians' communication, on social media and the like). (The development of language in children provides another ground for comparison.) In other words, the determining factor may ultimately be the *willingness* to communicate, which, on the human side, stems from a socio-anthropological need but has a certain capacity and psychological limits, and on the chatbot side, from its settings. This willingness then entails phenomena such as *interpretative charity* (Brown and Yule 1983), that is, the need and ability to complete utterances and, above all, entire texts and communication acts so that they 'make sense', including those that are, at first glance, incoherent, fragmented, incomprehensible, encrypted, and so forth, including metaphors (cf. also Dobrzyńska 1984).[42] The willingness to participate in communication, the principle of cooperation, albeit fulfilled indirectly and by way of various substitutions (as discussed by Paul Grice in the context of communication pragmatics), seems primary and takes precedence over any requirements for consistency and coherence of the text. With the help of a general disposition to create meaning, we can find various meta-levels and contexts of communication acts and thus remedy all disruptions, including those related to the continuity of consciousness.

Most AI philosophers and researchers today will agree that we are still far away from creating a general AI, but there is disagreement on whether LLMs and similar tools are a step in that direction or not, and how far that step might be taking us (cf. Mitchell 2021). From Lotman's point of view, LLMs as such do not constitute *intelligence* per se, since communication between two minds that are mutually untranslatable is not involved. What is missing is not untranslatability, however, but the continuity principle, or, from another angle, the principle of asymmetry, which would be tied to an autonomous agency, an ability and urge, also, to initiate an interchange (cf. also Lotman 1979a/1977). Quite simply, the principle of dialogue is missing here. In all these regards, Lotman's thinking supports the notion of LLMs as stochastic parrots (Bender et al. 2021), instead of signifying a major leap towards general AI.

As far as we can generalize, even today's most successful forms of AI in practice, such as deep learning and LLMs in the field of speech, do not represent a 'switched-on' consciousness, but rather a model of a *certain set* of dispositions of the *general mind*, based on its artificial construction as a multi-level equilibration process. This process seems to be more sub-perceptual or subconscious in nature (if we want to find a real parallel for it). ChatGPT cannot assign itself a task, and it derives its abilities from an enormous corpus of texts, which is partly evaluated automatically but, of course, is created by humans. It seems that, for the time being, we need to proceed from the mutually alien character of artificial and human intelligence and the incomparability of human and computational mechanisms of creating abstraction (Fazi 2019).

This does not mean that these models do not uncover something about the nature of data and our naturalized ways of 'processing', language being the prime example, which we have had no access to by other means – quite to the contrary. AI is becoming both the subject of and a tool for testing (including testing creativity) and part of the communication and creative process (assisted creativity). With this development, it helps open up new perspectives, new definitions and comparative mappings – on the functioning and system of language, on the nature of creativity, on the structures of genres and styles, on the nature of consciousness and understanding.

LLMs thus represent an extremely interesting theoretical problem, as they realize forms of sign generation that neither posthumanist nor antihumanist literary theories or philosophies – nor a significant part of the traditional, symbolicist approach to AI – anticipated.

The hope in presenting this brief excursus is to demonstrate how Lotman's thinking – despite its romanticizing tendency, perhaps related to his interest in great Romantic authors or the 'Russian cult of the poet' (Emerson 2011: 265) – helps to demystify the futuristic inclination with which AI *creativity* is sometimes discussed today. Should this be deemed creativity, it is certainly a very mild (derivative) form of it. Even so, an insight into the different functioning of deep neural networks might open new windows into how we understand language, texts, genres and forms.

Appendix 1: The phantom of interactivity and the dimensions of immersion (Marie-Laure Ryan)

In a related context, literary critics have recently dealt with questions associated with the programmed yet unpredetermined transformation of a textual artefact (a literary hypertext). This discussion gave birth to the contemporary understanding of the term *interactivity* in literary criticism. Marie-Laure Ryan's theory presented in *Narrative as Virtual Reality:*

Immersion and Interactivity in Literature and Electronic Media (2001) provides us here with a certain opportunity to think about the limitations involved in projecting contemporary technology into the conceptualizations of older media and their evolution and how its projection into the future may narrow our horizons.

Marie-Laure Ryan was primarily interested in how reading as well the experience of art change as literature and art, their creation and reception, move into the realm of computer technology. At the turn of the twenty-first millennium, when Ryan developed her theory, the entire world was becoming rapidly computerized,[43] and thus, unsurprisingly, her starting point is a metaphorical model. Virtual reality as a 'metaphor for total art' provides her with a hypothetical model of experience that is both *immersive* and *interactive*. She theorizes that being in a computer-generated environment is interactive, as this environment is transformed through the physical gestures and sensorimotor activities of the perceiver (and in utopian visions, through his or her thoughts), and at the same time immersive, as the virtual stimuli that are being simultaneously created fully engulf perception of the real environment. The real technological progress lagged behind technological visions, just as in the head-mounted displays from this period there was a delay between the user's head movements and the visual response. This futurological metaphor is nonetheless an interesting idea that supports Ryan's entire concept.

Here arises the general dichotomy between the aesthetics of illusion (immersion) and interactivity (game), which is then applied to the history of art and literature. Thus, Ryan draws a portrait of their dialectic, 'their rises and falls' (and syntheses). Up to a certain point, this seems convincing, especially as Ryan associates each with particular historical periods. The idea of immersion in art reached its zenith earlier than in literature, beginning in the Renaissance with the discovery of linear perspective and later in Baroque optical illusions, whereas the rise of immersion in literature is associated with the nineteenth-century novel. The interactivity in text is said to have culminated – although this claim raises doubts – with postmodernism and in fine art with conceptual schools and digital installations, which incorporate immersivity and bring us closer to the technological (technological-phenomenological) ideal of the future.

The first problem with the idea of immersion in literature lies in the fact that it is primarily based on a model produced for the fine arts and the effect of linear perspective. Such perspective makes the surface of the painting 'invisible' as the point of view is projected into the observer's body, whereas his or her virtual body is drawn 'into' the painting. There is a similarity to Bolter and Grusin's immediacy, understood as one of the two basic principles of the paradoxical logic of remediation. The concept of immersion therefore relies on the metaphor of 'invisibility' (the transparency of media) and (unlike immediacy)[44] is based on the perceiver's experience.

The analogy between literary and visual immersivity, however, has its flaws, which in light of Lotman's theories should come as no surprise to us. The 'vanishing of the medium' in literature and works of fine and visual art are very different processes, depending on the medium in question, in terms of perception, signs, technologies and the material 'surface'. As Marie-Laure Ryan is well aware, the vanishing of the medium in literature, connected with the process of reading, is 'hard-won and significant property that plays a crucial role in shaping the experience of the appreciator' (Ryan 2001: 176). Given the precarious nature of these parallels, it will be instructive to return, as we do in the following section, to Iser's classic work, in which we find revealing comparative passages distinguishing between the construction of images in literary texts and in film.

The other method of engaging the perceiver – interactivity – is built upon the prototype of the hypertext (Ryan 2001: 6 and elsewhere). According to Ryan, the literary hypertext is where three sets of features intersect and combine: interactivity, where the user determines the text his or herself (on the distinction from interaction, see Chapter 7, pp. 265–7); electronic support; and ergodic design, through which a text can change the way it is arranged over time (examples of printed, non-electronic works include books with unbound pages by B. S. Johnson and Marc Saporta or texts designed so that chapters can be read in any order). The 'effectiveness' of the hypertext's ergodic design, which Ryan emphasizes, is a contentious issue: it consists in the fact that a feedback loop exists that closes off or, in contrast, opens up access to some fragments (*lexias* to use Landow's term). Electronic support or new media are not necessary to do this. New media only facilitate and automate this possibility – which is generally not particularly attractive for the perceiver.

A hologram or the simultaneity of media (un)awareness?

The distinction between these two poles is nonetheless blurred thanks to the observation that immersion is conditioned upon 'a subtle awareness of the medium' and that media awareness and a medium's 'invisibility' act simultaneously, that is, that perceiving a medium – especially art – has this duplicity inscribed in it. This, however – and this is the first objection – suggests that awareness and unawareness of the medium do not stand in opposition; in reality they are complementary and may both have an effect at the same time.

Ryan touches on this insight, but regularly suppresses it: 'language behaves like holographic pictures: you cannot see the signs and the world at the same time' (Ryan 2001: 284). The *tertium comparationis* of this comparison (between language and holographic image) once again relies on visuality; awareness, however, is not modelled only visually. Instead, we find that the 'substance of language' (Ryan 2001: 192) may be invisible but at the same time the reader may be aware of it (not that in immersive texts words are transparent signs, whereas in interactive texts the material substance of the media is made present), that keeping a certain distance from the fictional world may go hand in hand with the suspension of disbelief (and not that they are in 'stark contrast'; Ryan 2001: 194) and that both dimensions of experience can be experienced at the same time, with one being temporarily suppressed and the other coming to the forefront, and vice versa.[45]

Elsewhere the author speaks in similar terms about signs (as well as signifiers). But the terms *media* and *sign*, and this is a second objection, imply different scopes and stratifications. What aspects of signs and what aspects of medium does Ryan mean when she speaks about 'interactivity'? The construction function of signifiers evoked through the signified (such as in Kundera's and Calvino's novels); the intertextual aspects of signs (such as in Eliot's *The Waste Land*); the etymological and philological dimensions of verbal signs (such as in the appreciation of a good translation); the rhythmic, metric or genre aspects of a text (when we appreciate the transformations of the sonnet form in Shakespeare, for instance); the technological aspects of a medium (such as in programmed hypertexts), its distribution-related aspects (e.g. when a historian is aware of the print run of a text or the local availability of a manuscript); or its material aspects (as in *Tristram Shandy*)? Not to mention the fact that in different types of media, as we already mentioned, in/visibility implies various processes and different social conditions for cultivating perceptual and cognitive dispositions. Just consider the long-term process of internalizing writing and making it invisible, which is so effective that it may surprise us when in a written text we 'see' or 'hear' something other than the conceptual meaning. Or, in contrast, consider the hardly perceptible processes through which we initially learned to perceive images, processes that suppress or support the disposition to perceive and express rhythms, and so forth.

Media diversity as a corrective of the dichotomy of 'interactivity' and 'immersion'

Marie-Laure Ryan, however, certainly meant to go beyond the limitations of modelling literary immersion on a visual basis. Perhaps this is why she associates immersion with the 'world', and interactivity with 'game', and why she draws conceptual inspiration, in a move that is to a certain point beneficial, from the ideas of Maurice Merleau-Ponty and his analyses of the phenomenology of perception. Ryan then begins to understand immersion as an experience stemming from the embodiment of consciousness, thanks to which a virtual body can be projected into a depicted or fictional world. That which should be possible in a virtual environment – 'to modify the environment through either verbal commands or physical gestures', '[to] adopt new identities', '[to] experience an expansion of our physical and sensory powers' and '[to] apprehend immaterial objects through many senses' (Ryan 2001: 1) – is that which we do and experience in reality, in our minds or through various media (or through the use of psychotropic substances). For the sake of consistency, however, Ryan must necessarily understand interactivity as 'a purely cerebral involvement with the text' (Ryan 2001: 21) and 'the experience of a pure mind that floats above all concrete worlds in the ethereal universe of semantic possibility' (Ryan 2001: 354–5). It is at this point that her conception is stretched to the limits of probability.

First, Merleau-Ponty's phenomenology of the embodied situatedness of the consciousness, which Ryan notably relies upon when she presents her conceptualization of virtual reality in the second chapter, aims at overcoming this dichotomy. Second, and perhaps more importantly, in an electronic environment, interactivity is more often associated with physical action (even minimal actions, such as clicking on a link) and immersion, with mental activities and the imagination.

Projecting this dichotomy onto the general development of media is also problematic. If textual interactivity culminated alongside postmodern thinking and writing, what status can we then attribute to literary modernism? Kafka's 'The Judgement', written in 1912, can provide us with some background for our study. At first, the story builds an illusion of a coherent world, one in which readers can 'immerse themselves'; but the story itself begins to counter this construction with increasing intensity. The communicability of the minds and the information possessed by the characters (Georg and his father) and the cohesiveness of the entire fictional world is gradually disrupted and eventually falls apart; conflicting statements and words clash, oscillating between figurative and literal meanings, and the consequences are fatal (for both Georg and his father). But such tendency to contradiction can hardly be called interactivity. To describe a text provoking such an act of reading, Marie-Laure Ryan might stick to using the term *self-reflexivity*,[46] which she occasionally uses in connection with postmodern interactivity. However, it cannot become a central category for her because the model she applies and her starting point are the mechanisms of computer technology and the protocols of human-computer interface. When she wants to explain the active nature of reading and briefly turns to the phenomenologist of reading par excellence Wolfgang Iser, she suddenly speaks about the 'interactive nature of the reading experience' (Ryan 2001: 17) and emphasizes it in places where, following her theory, she should be speaking about immersion. Therefore, her claim that 'the feature of interactivity conferred upon the text by electronic technology came to be regarded as the fulfilment of the postmodern conception of meaning' (Ryan 2001: 5) is not overly convincing. Instead, it seems that for certain types of media – for example, many interactive (and at the same time immersive) computer games – the concept of meaning is secondary.

Her remarkable and detailed reading of Michael Joyce's hypertext 'Twelve Blue' serves as an example of an experience with a fully interactive text. Ryan enumerates possible entryways into the text and from there reconstitutes links and layers of the hypertext, based on her many (always different) re-readings. She is no longer reading but mapping, restructuring possible narrative links and reconfiguring the text's layers; she builds a certain semantic set of sets (in a mathematical sense). With this, one reconstructs the story and its possible facets, and it makes one feel almost sorry that it has not been told in the 'normal' way and published by Joyce.

The immersion-interactivity dichotomy, however, traces its origins back to McLuhan's distinction between hot and cool media (Ryan 2001: 347–8). For McLuhan, and this is one of his most interesting ideas, media are, however, not just extensions of the senses but they are simultaneously 'amputations'. The space between an organ and its extension is one of irritation, an irritation which the nervous system resists by refusing any response just as extreme sensations temporarily numb our perceptive capabilities. For McLuhan, electric media – and this claim applies all the more so to *electronic* media – are nothing less than extensions of the entire nervous system, a relocated and living model of the central nervous system, and hence the narcissistic numbness that overpowers people in environments in which such media is omnipresent: like Narcissus looking at the creature reflected on the water's surface, a person becomes a closed system adapting to his or her own extended image. It is now their 'servomechanism'. This is, however, a very different image of 'interactivity' (on McLuhan's concept, see Chapter 7, pp. 241–4). Ryan's conception is unsustainable due to the incompatibility that characterizes the structure of modalities of the basic media types and domains in question; by moving from print to electronic form, literature and the experience of it may change relatively little, which is at least still the case for most parts of such transmediations, quite substantially (as in an audiobook) or fundamentally (as in the case of hypertext):[47] these contradictions and differences can hardly be grasped within the same technologically modelled duality. Ryan's project of 'narrative as virtual reality' can be interpreted as a symptom of a phase in which the symbolic meaning of automatic and computing processes in literary or artistic media creation outreaches their actual cultural function, possibilities and results.

Appendix 2: A return to Iser: Reading, image and indeterminacy

Wolfgang Iser's classic work, which I have mentioned several times, is still a model analysis of the internal complexity characterizing the reading process. Iser substantially diverges from the way in which Roman Ingarden, an inspirational figure in literary phenomenology, understood *places of indeterminacy* in a literary work of art. Iser locates indeterminacy in the shifting gap that arises between the reader and the text, in the interplay between the two, which is dependent upon the reader's cognitive activities.[48] Iser's references indicate that he knew the concept of uncertainty and the way Umberto Eco grasped the notion in the context of information aesthetics. Unlike early Eco, however, he gives uncertainty a phenomenological twist. A critique of Ingarden's places of indeterminacy, which oscillate between mechanical completion and excessive determination of the text's schematic aspects that threaten the polyphonic unity of the work, leads Iser to subtle reflections on gaps as shifting lacunae between different perspectives and levels of a text and about various types of *negation*.[49] In direct connection with Eco's openness (Eco speaks about a second-order openness in modern works), Iser begins his detailed discussion of the two basic structures of indeterminacy in the text (gaps and negation) and surpasses Ingarden's static notion of places of indeterminacy by referring to modernist works by William Faulkner, James Joyce and Virginia Woolf, which are not very compatible with Ingarden's central aesthetic idea of *polyphonic harmony*. This modernist and subsequently information-theory context leaves its mark here.

Iser claims that, in the course of reading, signifieds and signifiers are constantly changing. The signified in one section of the text is created through changes made based on later sections, which is then followed by further corrections, meaning that the reader 'had to modify the signified, which he himself had produced' and that these dynamic changes are 'cybernetic in nature' (Iser 1978/1976: 67). The interaction between the reader and the text is a self-propelled, self-regulating mechanism of feedback loops. It would be only later that Lotman expressed the idea that 'The aesthetic effect arises when the code is taken for the message and the message as a code, i.e. when a text is switched from one system of communication to another while the audience keeps awareness of both' (Lotman 2000a/1990: 30).

The image as *metaxy* and the reading process

According to Iser, imagination (*Vorstellung*) is the embryonic layer of the process of reading and creating meaning; following in the vein of Husserl, he describes it using the term *passive synthesis*, whose fundamental element is the image (*Bild*). In this idea of passive synthesis we can sense potential seeds of misunderstanding if the 'immersive' reading of literary fiction is taken as 'passive' in nature. Following Husserl, Iser understands passive synthesis as a subconscious act but one that above all is a necessary attendant consequence of the 'wandering' viewpoint that the reader's consciousness takes in the text. What though is a 'textual image' and what isn't? Here, an image is not a percept derived from the sensorial qualities of an object (not even of an imagined object), nor is it a concept. According to Mikel Dufrenne, the image is a *metaxy*, the third component found between a sensorial percept of an empirical object and the meaning of the represented object. The literary image in a text – that is, an idea based on the evocation of some reality, not figurative expression – is never isolated and always evolves in different ways over time; this feature is something it has in common with the film image (sequentiality; Iser 1978/1976: 195). Unlike the film image, the literary image is based on the absence or non-existence of its subject because an image in a literary text is provided to the reader as a sum of conditions for creating a mental image, as a set of schematized aspects. Thus, the absence of an object results, on the one hand, in the diffusiveness and indeterminacy of a textual image, and, on the other hand, in its openness and close connection with the reader's consciousness; the image is always for the reader, and it is constructed in his or her mind. Hence springs disappointment and the paradox of the comparative *poverty* of the film image in adaptations, when the reader confronts his or her own image with a film image meant to visually supplement and enrich an existing literary image. Here, we can add to Iser's ideas that the opposite process also takes place: visual images become firmly stuck in the mind and difficult to 'erase', even when the reader returns regularly to the literary text. Mental images are fragile. In contrast, visual sensations provide a great volume of data, and as a result, open, diffuse images are easily pushed aside. One of the reasons that a visual adaptation of a literary text may seem to be so poor is that the perceiving subject is visibly excluded from the active creation of the image (an idea put forward by American philosopher Stanley Cavell). Photographic and film images entail the vanishing of the subject; the world and the self are not both present at the same time. In contrast, the textual image is immersed (embedded) in the reader's consciousness, and as an image it lives solely off it, indivisible from it.

Moreover, in the literary text an image is in no way pre-given; it is reconstructed as both an image and as a meaning; it is of a 'hybrid nature', always in a state of motion and transition, relative to the other layers of the text, relative to the presupposition of the whole, and finally, relative to its own aspects, which develop with the text in time. It is also always constituted simultaneously as a theme (or part thereof) and as a meaning, or the theme and meaning are co-constituents of the image. The act of selecting 'schematized aspects' rises to the surface, and those moments in which, in the continual process of synthesis, we encounter the unpredictable (e.g. when a character behaves differently then we assumed they would), when selection (e.g. of the description of an object or character) is unexpected or, in contrast, 'mechanically' repeated (in Robbe-Grillet, for instance), and so forth, gain importance. The temporal nature of reading and the fact that meaning develops in time also mean that time cannot be made present as a referential framework of meaning.

A key feature of the literary text is therefore its call for interaction and the simultaneous transformation of the subject into a reader, who, by definition, completes the text through the self-propelled motion of consciousness, confronting what is revealed against the backdrop of his or her expectations and attitudes, even ones (initially) latent. At the same time, attitudes expressed in the text appear only in the context of the series of selections made and the activity of sense.

The spontaneous acceptance of an outside thought process as one's own (the wandering viewpoint), which of course only takes place against the background of one's own 'orientations', corresponds to the simultaneous interconnectedness of 'immersion' and 'interactivity'. We could refer to it as a double consciousness, a consciousness of travelling through the world of text, which is interwoven with the always-present consciousness of sign mediation. According to Iser, 'the unique value of literature' lies in its ability to make accessible new experiences through one's own mental constructions stimulated by a text.

For Iser, the literary text represents a particularly prominent model of meaning formation and its temporal and continual nature, a model highlighted by the fact that its objects are constructed without empirical objects as templates, and only thus become meaningful. Iser understands literature as an essential medium for re-orienting the subject and the mutual reconstitution and verification of the relationships between percepts and sense. We can experience this 'double consciousness', however, in other types of media. Iser thus neglects the secondary, mediating effect of media, creating a *'secondary' breeding ground* for the perceptive and cognitive activity of the perceiver. We *learn* to perceive and imagine differently with and in (different) media. These film-related asides suggest that from a historical perspective we can read Iser's argument for literature's privileged position as an expression of the media-hierarchy logic, as a response trying to return literature to the places (i.e. the media functions) that it is slowly losing. If we were to insist on Iser's definition of literature's mediality, then we would have to predict the inevitable, long-term corrosion of its privileged position among media and the arts. But the breeding ground or substrate underlying this, as Iser understands it, regenerating activity is not given once and for all and invariable. This 'corrosion' might mean on one hand the necessity to change the conceptualization of literature as a medium and on the other the possibility of transforming literature itself, for instance, by highlighting its, broadly speaking, *discursive functions* (its material is 'speech'), which give literature a 'competitive advantage' over other types of media and which indeed it has fulfilled over the long-term in modern European cultures. Another obvious consequence of the evolution of media, one that calls for a conceptual change – and this relates to the mentioned 'secondary' media sensory substrates – is the increase in *intermedial links* within literature as a medium.

Notes

1 Lotman 1987. On the history of Tartu semiotics, see also Gasparov 1994; Waldstein 2008; Salupere, Torop and Kull 2013; Pilshchikov and Trunin 2016.
2 The semiotic thinking of the Tartu-Moscow School and of Lotman himself was built in part on an interest in film (cf. the film studies papers published in *Trudy po znakovým sistemam*, Sign Systems Studies, or Lotman's book *Semiotika kino i problemy kinoestetiki*, 1973, *Semiotics of Cinema*, 1981).
3 Manovich 2001: 20; Friedrich Kittler thinks along similar lines.
4 Since the beginning of the twenty-first century, these two approaches have re-found mutual respect and even began to envisage convergence in some places, for example, within the sphere of deep learning (Boden 2016; see also Buckner and Garson 2018).
5 For the contextualization of literary theory within systems theory and second-order cybernetics, see Hayles 1990; 2000; Paulson 1988. For more

on neo-cybernetics and attempts at its application to literary criticism, see Clarke 2014.
6   Cf. the different lineage of intermedia studies in Chapter 11, esp. pp. 373–9.
7   Lotman's autobiographical notes were published posthumously in a volume titled *Ne-memuarȳ* (1995/1992, *Non-memoirs*).
8   The aim of our partial, latent genealogy is not to determine the phases in the evolution of Lotman's thinking or to present a comprehensive picture in terms of thematic areas.
9   The question was: How is it possible that a random stimulus interrupting a dream and becoming in changed form the last element of the dream's material seems to be the necessary culmination of all previous elements towards which the entire dream was inexorably headed?
10 If in Freudian analysis the dream is conceived as 'suppressed speech', here speech and its reproduction appear as a gag placed on the dream.
11 *Vnutri mȳslyashchikh mirov* contains works from the 1970s and 1980s. It was published posthumously in 1996 with the subtitle *Chelovek–tekst–semiosfera–istoriya* and was included in an extensive collection titled *Semiosfera* also published posthumously (2000). An English version, translated by Ann Shukman, titled *Universe of the Mind: A Semiotic Theory of Culture*, was first published in 1990. I generally cite the English version (2000a/1990) and where necessary the Russian original as well (2000b/1996).
12 For now, let us accept Lotman's choice of terms (*text, information*, etc.) as they are and leave a commentary on their media genealogy for later.
13 Some of the features of Jakobson's thinking (especially his later interest in 'intersemiotic transposition') transcend this tradition. For more on Jakobson's influence on intermedia research, see Chapter 11, p. 389.
14 Among concepts of the economy of values criticizing the assumption of equivalence in exchanges is Bourdieu's field theory and concept of the symbolic economy, which focuses on the processes of accumulation and the unequal distribution of capital (see Müller 2017).
15 Cf. Lotman's interpretation of the dream presented above: '[The dream] is extremely well suited to the generation of new information' (Lotman 2009/1992: 144).
16 For example, identifying with the protagonist while reading a fictional text or imitating a fictional character is an autocommunicative process during which the text is used as a kind of code.
17 In a manuscript of one of Pushkin's poem we find a note in roman letters that reads 'ettenna eninelo / eninelo ettenna': the text is an anagram of the first name and surname of a girl (Anna Alekseevna Olenina) Pushkin was courting and about whom he was thinking in French (Annette Olenine); the playful reversal of the letters in her name established a unique rhythm.
18 *Le parasite*, a word that entered modern European languages in the sixteenth century from Latin, traces its etymology to the Greek *para-sitos*:

one who sits at another's table, one who feeds 'besides' (*sitos* means 'food', 'grain'). Later, the French word's semantic field expanded to include a technical meaning: noise, interference, malfunction.

19 Serres, like Lotman, strove for a dialogue between the formal sciences and the humanities. For example, the mathematical topological method is reflected in his interpretive style (see Serres and Latour 1995/1990: 105 ff.). Perloff (2000) has developed some of the principles contained in Serres's thinking (a well as some critical comments about them) from a literary interpretive perspective.

20 Cf. here: '[I]t is important to emphasize that a degree of non-understanding cannot be interpreted only as 'noise' – a harmful consequence of an imperfection of the system, which is not present in the idealized schema. The growth of nonunderstanding and/or inadequate understanding may bear witness to the technical defects in the system of communications, but it may also be an indicator of the increased complexity of this system, its capacity to fulfil ever more complex and important cultural functions' (Lotman 1979a/1977: 90).

21 We will address the disadvantages of a certain neutralizing of the 'reverse' material facet of the semiotic process in Lotman later.

22 The motif of a rubbish heap evokes the bizarre lack of system in the world; it could also call to mind the social and ecological consequences of 'overproduction' culture.

23 In contrast, Kittler *identifies* the real with technical noise.

24 A popular portrait painter (1755–1842) during the reign of Louis XVI and Marie Antoinette; she spent six years altogether in Russia.

25 This theory was originally developed in the context of (bio)chemistry, biology and physics, but Lotman builds on its potential universality.

26 To what extent this feature applies in technically based cyberspace is an unanswered question. In my opinion, the direct parallel between it and cyberspace, which we find in contemporary readings of Lotman's semiosphere, is unconvincing.

27 Again, the universalist application of the term *text* is startling here.

28 Up to this point, Lotman agrees with him: 'We could even say that history is one of the by-products of the emergence of writing' (Lotman 2000a/1990: 246).

29 And it puts them together in verifiable, and later easily navigable messages: according to Kittler, one radical turning point in the evolution of media technology was the transition from the scroll to the codex, which attributed to every place in the text a certain set of 'addresses', making information more rapidly accessible.

30 Cf. the special edition of the *International Journal of Cultural Studies* 18 (1), 2015.

31 This problem is solved to a limited degree by its overlapping with the concept of channel ('pictorial channel', etc.).

32 For example, the translation model evokes a linguistic essence, which, however, cannot be imposed on visual or musical forms of media; the distinction between discrete and continuous code is only approximate if we want to take into account the sensory and perceptive variety of media modalities.
33 Lotman's legacy is currently being richly developed, with currents focusing on mediation, the digital sphere and cyberspace, biosemiotics, ecosemiotics, the cognitive sciences, or the concepts of transmediality, intermediality and 'cross-mediality'. Scholars contributing to the latter trend include Peeter Torop, Maarja Orama, Indrek Ibrus, Winfried Nöth and Nicola M. Dusi. For other research building upon Lotman's ideas, see works by Mihhail Lotman, Kalevi Kull, Timo Marana, Marina Grishakova and others, including Tamm 2019, Monticelli 2019, Gramigna and Salupere 2017, a special edition of *Recherches sémiotiques* 35 (1), 2015, Frank, Ruhe and Schmitz 2012, Schönle 2006, Andrews 2003.
34 For an introduction to the principles underlying deep learning systems, see Kelleher 2019.
35 The testing was carried out in February and March 2023.
36 I was able to elicit a close enough answer from ChatGPT Default in one instance (*to go to decline, to come to nothing*).
37 With ChatGPT (both versions), the prompts tried to guide the tool to take into account the ambiguity of 'earnest' in the sense of 'sincere', 'honest' and 'Earnest' as the character's name. A creative solution might be to change the name of the character to correspond to an existing Czech phrase with a fitting meaning; the traditional translation 'Jak je důležité mít Filipa' (the importance of having Philip) relies on 'to have Philip', a Czech phrase meaning 'to be smart'. The prompts to translate the title of Roald Dahl's story 'The Great Switcheroo' were explaining the playful connotations of the noun and its less usual place in the vocabulary. The solidus indicates different outputs (a selection of them) in the sequence of prompts. 'The Great Switcheroo' has been translated (by humans) as 'Velká rošáda', because the Czech 'rošáda' (castling) also means 'a swap', or, as 'Velká šoupaná', since 'šoupat' means 'to shuffle' but is also a colloquial expression for 'to have sex' (which corresponds to the theme of the story).
38 Gastaldi (2021) provides a number of interesting points in his 'Why Can Computers Understand Natural Language?'. He claims that *word embedding*, an NLP technique by which the vocabulary of a raw corpus is transformed (by training) into dense word vector representations in a continuous space of a fixed number of dimensions, corroborates a half-forgotten structuralist conception of language whereby semantic relationships are concurrently formed with syntactic ones. Interestingly, he claims that insight into this 'image' of language is independent of the neural network architecture and can be achieved by other models (such as matrix models) as well.
39 See, in particular, Lotman 1977/1970 and Monticelli 2016.

40 Cf. Lee-Morrison 2023; presented at Digital Theory Lab, NYU, on 7 May 2021.
41 On this, touching upon embodiedness of consciousness, see Husserl 1960. Cf. Sartre 2016/1948, who raises the issue of answerability.
42 '[T]he essence of figurative language lies in the fact that, in order to eliminate deviation arising on the syntagmatic axis, a certain meaning must be conceived, which can be put in place of the used word and which allows the expression to regain coherence' (Dobrzyńska 1984: 13).
43 The World Wide Web was launched in 1991; beginning in the mid-1990s USB ports came standard with personal computers and enabled the connection of peripherals (cameras, printers, modems, external storage devices, etc.).
44 Immediacy is based on the evolutionary principle that new media technologically triumphs over old media in its ability to fulfil users' desires to achieve unmediatedness and presence, which by necessity turn out to be nothing more than illusionary.
45 We find a similar idea in Bateson: 'In primary process, map and territory are equated; in secondary process they can be discriminated. In play, they are both equated and discriminated' (Bateson, cited in Iser 1993/1991: 248–9). Lotman (2000a/1990: 32) also happens to support this idea.
46 Compare Iser's argument in *Der Akt des Lesens* (1976, *The Act of Reading*, 1978) on Joyce's *Ulysses*: repertoires of social norms and literary references form 'the communication medium' of text. Iser demonstrates how the interwovenness of both systems makes it impossible to subject the simultaneity of literary-mythological and 'everyday' life to a single referential framework, and thus its effect 'as a communication medium' becomes self-reflexive.
47 This is why Roger Chartier, for example, distinguishes between digital and digitized communication (Chartier, Wögerbauer and Müller 2018).
48 Unlike an actor in interpersonal communication, a text cannot be asked questions.
49 For example, the selection of certain socio-ethical norms leaves awareness about the repertoire from which these norms were selected somewhere in the background. A different case is the negation of one's own socio-ethical expectations and their transformation in the course of taking positions in the text.

The theory of intermediality

Apparentness of relations, elusiveness of medium

Stanislava Fedrová and Alice Jedličková

1. The genealogy of intermediality

The genealogical approach suggested by John Guillory (2010) and used throughout this book proves to be particularly suitable for studying the evolution of intermedial thinking. This becomes obvious as soon as we take a closer look at the stage that preceded the theory of intermediality, interart studies. Beneath the surface of this discipline dating back to the 1980s we get fleeting glimpses of a deep prehistory of examining the relationships between different kinds of art that draw from classical thought: the traditions of *ut pictura poesis* and *paragone*, the paradigm of the 'sister arts', and the Enlightenment-era pre-semiotic study of the semiotic character of the individual arts. As it was establishing itself as a discipline, intermedial studies legitimized its existence by referring to older lines of scholarly enquiry that compared the forms and effects of different forms of artistic representation. We shall follow this pattern in our genealogic explication while also anticipating some of the future effects of these processes in order to make visible individual lineages of intermedial thinking. The questions of why and how members of the intermedial family tree referenced concepts from the past – especially pre-modern ones – appear sometimes even more important than the particular content of these concepts.

In mapping the ideas (and ideals) that led to relating and comparing cultural representations since antiquity, we wish to outline germinal processes of what may be understood as the *prehistory of intermedial thinking*. Concepts that imply the media specificity of arts in one way or another may be considered *proto-intermedial* modes of observing cultural phenomena. Despite having resulted from the *epistémé* and the cultural needs of the period they were developed in, they may have retained their importance for current intermedial research (Gotthold Ephraim Lessing's 'limits of arts' being one of the most conspicuous examples). Others, such as Oskar Walzel's 'mutual illumination of arts', may be included under 'historically legitimizing' and inspiring approaches in our genealogy though they were not followed by direct successors. The term *pre-intermediality* has been introduced here to denominate disciplines (such as the above-mentioned interart studies) which, while inquiring into the relations and transformations of cultural representations, employed methodological approaches (e.g. semiotics) that lie at the basis of intermedial studies.

Outlining a genealogy of intermedial thinking could also help clarify several aspects of the current state of intermedial studies and its prospects. For example, why was the conceptualization of medium itself put off for so long in intermedial thinking? One possible reason lies in the fact that for a long time, the subject of study was not the medium itself, but the apparent *relationships* between different media, whose *constitutive* features were taken as self-evident. This self-explanatory nature stems from the historical preference for observing *art* (whose different forms we today recognize as media) – and defining it was not considered a problem. As Guillory (2010: 321) explains, traditional art did not need to be referred to in terms of media, at least not until this concept first emerged in response to the expansion of new technological media. Moreover, the direct predecessors of intermedial theory were primarily guided by *the status of the work of art* until the 1990s. This is despite the fact that the debate on the concept and definition of art had been going on for decades, mainly within the fields of aesthetics and art history (cf. Danto 1964, Dickie 1974). The comparative pre-intermedial line and interart studies did not pay attention to the general questions posed by aesthetics, and what makes art 'art', was long taken for granted. Thus, we encounter the first blind spot in the evolution of intermedial thinking.

Prehistory: The paradigm of art and the concept of *ut pictura poesis*

The traditions of *ut pictura poesis* and *paragone* belong to intermedial thinking's prehistory. They initially emerged as devices debated among artists and scholars, but eventually were transformed into paradigms or conceptualizations of art. In the historical discourse on art, they often intertwined, sometimes complementing and sometimes contradicting each other. They also have a place in the contemporary intermedial discourse, another good reason to explore the diachronicity of these seemingly antiquated concepts.

Both interart studies and intermedial studies, in their early days, claimed these two ideas to be their precursors (e.g. Wagner ed. 1996), although such references were often just gestures legitimizing these newly forming disciplines (e.g. Lund 2002: 14). Some typological studies that were created after intermedial theory was codified in the 2000s also returned to these ideas; for example, Uwe Wirth included in his hierarchical model of intermedial relations the terms *ut pictura poesis* and '*poetische Malerei*', without specifying what either meant or comparing them to other terms (Wirth 2006: 33). Wirth was motivated to include these archaic concepts into his own model because intermedial studies, at this stage in its development, was fixated on the history and prehistory of intermedial thinking.

In retrospect, the concept of *ut pictura poesis* may seem like an attempt to make absolute the mutuality of these two arts, poetry and painting. In diachronic perspective, however, the meaning and sense of this concept has changed fundamentally. Its beginnings are always traced back to a pre-Aristotelian tradition, according to which painting is *speechless poetry* and poetry is *speaking painting* (attributed to Simonides of Ceos from the fifth century BCE). We also find hints of the relationships between the arts in Aristotle's *Poetics* (c. 325–323 BCE), according to which all arts, and thus also painting and poetry, are connected through *the act of mimesis of the object world* (cf. Whalley 1997: 1448, 1450a, 1460b). This analogy was put to even greater use in Horace's *Ars Poetica* (c. 19 BCE). Interpreting the phrase *ut pictura poesis* (l. 361), traditionally translated into English as 'as is painting, so is poetry', poses several problems. If we read this phrase in the broader context of Horace's treatise (following Wesley Trimpi 1973, or Eleanor W. Leach 1988: 5), it is clear that it does not indicate that both arts are *identical* but rather that they are *analogous*. By using a metaphorical comparison to painting, Horace was attempting to distinguish different rhetorical styles, for example, a style that is appropriate for longer narratives, or a style that accents its own impressive details. With an understanding of classic rhetoric, it is clear that styles can be distinguished based on the intended effect on the recipient, and therefore, Horace was most interested in the spectator's impression of the work.

Later though, Horace's verse was detached from its original context, and in the discourse of the following millennia was used as a formulation referring to the similarity or even the identicalness of these two arts. His thesis casts a long shadow on the entire tradition of Western thinking about art. Medieval theologians used it to support arguments in favour of the greater value of the spoken word (Markiewicz 1987: 536–8). It was extremely popular among humanist thinkers and would later be taken up by artists themselves. Around the mid-1600s, in the commentaries to editions of Aristotle's and Horace's writings, we find that the topos of similarity became a *prescriptive* rule: poetry should be similar to painting, it should mimic its methods and features.[1] Up until the eighteenth century, in texts preceding the establishment of aesthetic thought, we can trace how the original topos of the effects of the poem was treated at first as an axiom and then later as an artistic programme (cf. Lee 1940; Abrams 1971/1953: 33). From the seventeenth to the mid-eighteenth century, authors such as John Dryden, Hildebrand Jacob, Joseph Spence and Daniel Webb continued to adhere to a notion derived from Horace, and to describe it using terms such as *parallels* and *correspondence*, or metaphorically referred to poetry and painting as *the sister arts*.[2]

In the early 1800s, with the erosion of the certainty of Aristotelian imitation as a principle shared by all kinds of art, the idea that poetry and painting were parallel nearly disappeared from Romantic aesthetics. It was replaced by the idea of the relationship between literature and music and the concept of music as the high art to which all the other arts should aspire – as Arthur Schopenhauer or, in the 1870s, aesthetician Walter Pater were convinced. Or, music replaced painting as the art that could express human passions with the greatest immediacy and that could most effectively evoke an emotional response from the recipient. In such debates, the kinship of the arts served as an argument employed to legitimize the potential of the individual arts. Thus, *this kinship was conceived of as a certain value rather than a general trait of the arts*. Although the concept of *ut pictura poesis* was temporarily pushed aside during Romanticism, it did not disappear completely. As Henryk Markiewicz (1987: 543–55) demonstrates, this concept continued to influence debates about the essence of poetic imagery in twentieth-century literary theory and appeared in both defences and refutations of the old thesis that the capacity of the image to induce the effect of the sensorial presence of its subject in the recipient and 'internal perception' are not only qualities of poetry but are also fundamental in determining its value. The concept of *ut pictura poesis* would re-appear again in the programmatic principles of nineteenth-century art movements. The pre-Raphaelites and their theorists (e.g. John Ruskin) returned to the idea that poetry and painting are related or even one and the same art. The Parnassians were also fond of this notion of parallelism between arts, influenced particularly by the ideas of Théophile Gautier and his term 'the transposition of art'. As Anne Hofmann (2000: 79–86) notes, Gautier's theory of the parallelism between arts is grounded in the dialogue with the tradition of *ut pictura poesis*.

Finally, the modern revival of interest in ekphrasis (Spitzer 1955) builds upon this long tradition, bounded by, on one end, classical authors and, on the other, Gautier. This theme would become central in interart studies. But drawing on ancient predecessors in the emerging theory of intermediality had its pitfalls: for example, when Jürgen E. Müller (1998: 33) interpreted the Aristotelian idea of the inseparability of poetry from music as 'indivisible media unity'. Such an artificial unifying approach though could be rightly seen as an expression of 'media blindness' (Hausken 2004: 392).

At the other end of the spectrum of the possibilities of inter-relating arts, we find *paragone*, which highlights the advantages of one kind of art over another. This popular Renaissance-era topos eventually developed into a full-fledged genre. It arose out of scholars' and artists' interests in classical culture and knowledge, which they applied to their current day: in *paragone* they drew from the works of classic philosophers on the essence of art and from the traditional hierarchical understanding of human creations and the senses that mediate their perception. The argument derived from the nature of *perception* proved to be particularly strong: in the writings of Albrecht Dürer's and especially Leonardo da Vinci's, seeing is associated with verisimilitude and truthfulness (von Einem 1968; Dürer 1966: 109, 112, 151–2). With his belief that sight was the most sublime of the senses, Leonardo was joining a debate about the importance of sight and seeing as the sources of truth that classical philosophers and rhetoric theorists had started long before and was reflected in the rhetorical device of *sub oculos subiectio* or *hypotypósis* (Quintilian IX, II, 40; cf. Führer and Banaszkiewicz 2014: 56, 61–2; Fedrová and Jedličková 2016: 124–38). Thus, Leonardo interprets painting as being truer at depicting the world, as well as being capable of depicting totality and abstract, unnameable things, whereas the poet can only capture the 'conversation of people' (Farago 1992: 177, 200–3). For Leonardo painting (*pittura*) is a broader concept: it includes generally representation in space. What was originally a mental representation, that is, an idea in the artist's mind (which makes painting a *cosa mentale*, 'a mental thing'; cf. Chastel 1991), then becomes a form of visual representation, one perceivable by the senses. More generally in the language of sixteenth-century art theory, imitating the world or nature did not mean representation in the sense of imitating reality but rather the permeation of artistic creation with the principles of nature, through which a new reality emerged. The humanistic revision of the trivium in the university education system emphasized the role of poetry – and this is the reason that the burgeoning visual arts compared themselves to poetry in a bid to gain recognition. To gain entry into the exclusive club that was the seven liberal arts, fine arts placed its bets on the discourse of the *sister arts* – that is, considering visual art and poetry to be sisters in the same family and emphasizing their close connections. The development of this thesis determined the basic direction of most theoretical writings on painting until the eighteenth century (Lee 1940). At the same time, pointing out the close relationships between these arts was also motivated by something unrelated to media, as it served as a *means for negotiating these arts' social position* and was a manifestation of the burgeoning process of artistic individualization.

Sixteenth-century visual art theorists, however, moved on from the idea of sororal equality to a quest for primacy. Leonardo's followers wanted to replace music with visual arts as holding the highest position among the arts (e.g. debates on vocal music; Gess 2010: 141). The mannerist concept of *disegno* encapsulates the idea of visual art's primacy: the foundation of *disegno* is drawing, the purest expression of artistic virtuosity and at the same time the essence of all visual arts.

This perspective was after the mid-eighteenth century changed with the emergence of aesthetics, when the paradigm of the *mechanic* and *liberal arts* (the concept of *techné*) was replaced by the paradigm of the *fine arts* (the concept of *ars*). Thus, not only was everything associated with mechanical creation expelled from the world of art, but so too were the liberal arts as developed in antiquity (e.g. rhetoric, arithmetic, astronomy). We should add that from a retrospective intermedial perspective, this removal of the *techné* aspect from the idea of art resulted in the marginalization of *materiality* in thinking about art.

In aesthetics, this idea of hierarchal order was maintained as a tool to distinguish the arts. For example, Friedrich Schlegel claimed that poetry occupied the highest position among the arts and that it was 'the art of arts' (quoted in Markiewicz 1987: 541), Walter Pater, as we have seen, claimed the same for music. Then, in the pages of *Atheneum* the Schlegel brothers praised the idea of the *synthesis* or *symbiosis* of all arts and sciences as an expression of the human spirit. The typologies of the arts presented by Baumgarten and Hegel were also the result of hierarchization and a historical comparison. Hegel's aesthetic system differentiated arts based on the *material* they worked with. In keeping with the spirit of *paragone*, however, Hegel ranked them according to their ability to express the spiritual as absolute. This was a consequence of employing one parameter of hierarchy rigidly. At the bottom of his hierarchy stand architecture (whose material is the matter itself) and sculpture (which inserts a spiritual content into a bodily human form that is perceptible by the senses). Above these two, we find an art whose material enables it to better express the spiritual as absolute: painting as the most accessible art to the senses thanks to the material of colour. Even higher in the pyramid still is music, which translates the sensorial into ideas. At the top stands poetry, primarily because it is closest to the conceptual thinking of philosophy and science (Hegel 1998/1835: 82–90).[3] Hegel's idea that poetry and philosophy are related and his attributing them both the highest station are likely the result of his logocentrism. From an intermedial perspective, however, it seems more likely to be the result of recognizing their medial essence, that is, that they both share the same linguistic medium. Even though for Hegel, materiality is a critical factor distinguishing the arts, poetry as the highest art means *emancipation from matter*. We can also encounter a contemporary approach that was antithetical to Hegel's: the idea that the visual arts held a higher position than literature, as they were truer, mimetically more faithful depictions of reality (for more, see Krieger 1992: 82–90).

The paradigm of the sister arts and both the topoi associated with it – *ut pictura poesis* and *paragone* – were still current and intertwined in interart studies: Calvin S. Brown refers to these ideas in his seminal work *Music and Literature* (1948), Jean H. Hagstrum, in *The Sister Arts* (1958), bases his study of 'literary pictorialism' in English neo-classical poetry on the reflection of the concept of *ut pictura poesis* from antiquity to the seventeenth century. Hagstrum's definition of ekphrasis is akin to the understanding of *paragone*: for him, ekphrasis animates a silent work of art, which is finally given speech by poetry. The influence of both traditions is clearly visible in the work of Leo Spitzer (1955): according to him, ekphrasis is characterized by the transcendence of temporality. Similarly, James Heffernan sees ekphrasis as a contest between 'rival modes of representation: between the driving force of the narrating word and the stubborn resistance of the fixed image' (Heffernan 1993: 6), thus displaying traces of the *paragone*-like struggle for primacy between word and image. The concept of *ut pictura poesis* has been addressed repeatedly as well (Praz 1970, Steiner 1982, Krieger 1992).

In the germinal stage of intermedial studies, scholars understandably drew links to the ideas from the past in an attempt to legitimize their new methodology. This, however, sometimes led to historical concepts being treated almost as labels. For example, Peter Wagner (1996: 5) in his historical survey identifies the evolution of intermedial thinking with the notions of *ut pictura poesis*, *the sister arts* and Walzel's *gegenseitige Erhellung der Künste*. Once the theory of intermediality was introduced and the term *medium* defined, intermedial studies began to examine the historical nature of these concepts.[4] However, a thorough revision of how these historical concepts have been interpreted, uncontrolled by the field's current needs, is still a major challenge facing intermedial scholars.

Proto-intermediality: An overlooked member of the family tree

A more urgent challenge, however, is presented by a new reading of Lessing's *Laocoon or, The Limits of Poetry and Painting* (1766). In a recent volume titled *Rethinking Lessing's Laocoon* (2017), published in celebration of the

250th anniversary of this essay, *Laocoon* was subjected to rethinking from the perspectives of various disciplines and in different contexts. From the many fields represented in this work perhaps only one is missing: intermedial studies. In the discourse of intermedial theory, the significance of Lessing's essay has thus far been generally reduced to the normative delineation of the 'borders' between the arts. As a result, Lessing is often described as having sparked the 'violent' ripping apart of what had once been interconnected arts. We, however, view his essay as a cornerstone in the prehistory of intermedial studies.

Throughout the twentieth century, Lessing's ideas were often subject to superficial generalization. But scholars used the core of his ideas to argue in favour of very diverse opinions, first and foremost, about what a given kind art is or should be. Literary critic Irving Babbitt (*The New Laocoon*, 1910) rejected the 'confusion' of the arts, which for him was embodied by the pre-Raphaelites or the Parnassians. In the manifesto 'Towards a Newer Laocoon' prominent American art critic Clement Greenberg (1992/1940) subscribes to Lessing's claim that each type of art is *media specific* and rejects any hybrid forms. Like Lessing before him, Greenberg used this idea to support his own critique of art, that is, the denouncement of the European avant-garde and the endorsement of American abstract expressionism. In Greenberg's opinion only the latter could achieve *medium purity*. Painting could become 'pure' only when it moves away from any form of imitation, including imitation of the three-dimensionality of the depicted, and from the subject of representation – all that remains are the means of expression specific to abstractionism: basic colours and an acknowledged flatness. Painting therefore represents nothing else but itself as a medium. In his essay, Greenberg does not use the term *medium* as a simple synonym for *art*. Under this term he includes the traditional meaning of *material* used in specific forms of artistic expression and typical *methods* (e.g. those that lead to creating an illusion). Importantly, the 'Greenbergian' definition of *medium* had a long-lasting influence on how this term was used and the relationship between art and medium was understood in art history (see also Schröter 2008: 581–3) – at the very least until the media concept was reformulated and Dick Higgins's concept of intermedia was introduced in the 1960s.

Lessing's main thesis is often simply reduced to the notion that painting is a spatial art and poetry a temporal one; an attendant idea is that he also rejected literary description. A careful reading, however, reveals that Lessing criticizes redundancy and the weak aesthetic effect of description in the poetry of some of his contemporaries. Literary theorist Murray Krieger (1967) accused Lessing of denying literature the 'space form' typical of visual art. According to Krieger, the *ekphrastic principle*, which he understands as *stasis*, or the stopping of time, can 'return' space to literature. W. J. T. Mitchell (1994: 154–5, 179) blames Lessing for dishonouring ekphrasis and rejecting all descriptivism, before using a nearly psychoanalytical approach to reveal the source of Lessing's 'fear of literary emulation of the visual arts' as the fear of the irrational power that paintings and visual signs embody and lastly a fear of 'castration'.

Interart scholars tended not to study Lessing's ideas in greater depth and merely simplified them in certain theses: that he left a lasting negative mark on the debate about the sister arts, that he sparked the schism between painting and poetry. Lessing is even accused of being obsessed with the purity of art, a manifestation of 'petit bourgeois aesthetics' (e.g. Lund 2002: 16; Wagner 1996: 6). The editors of a handbook on the relationship between literature and visual culture (Benthien and Weingart 2014:17) seem to mention Lessing merely in order not to omit his name; yet, one of the contributors, historian of aesthetics Sabine Schneider (2014), who examines Lessing's thought in the context of Enlightenment-era semiotics develops Karlheinz Stierle's (1984) suggestion that *Laocoon* was the first consistent treatise on *media aesthetics*.

In the semiotics discourse, Lessing's essay is recognized as a germinal 'semiotic' work, in which the difference between arts is interpreted as the difference between *distinct sign systems* (Todorov 1984/1973, Wellbery 1984, Gebauer 1984). Meir Sternberg (1999: 333–51) views Lessing's approach as having been inspirative for interart studies. Nora Krausová (1999: 101) assesses Lessing's essay in the context of other 'proto-semiotic' works: for Lessing, just like for classicist aesthetics in general, the understanding of art as the imitation of reality still played a role. At the same time though, he contributed to the end of this era, which came with the acceptance of the sign concept. In 1719 aesthetician Jean-Baptiste Dubos built his reworking of the *ut pictura poesis* concept on the idea that painting works with natural signs, simultaneously present, whereas poetry works with artificial signs, presented successively. Hence, Dubos argues that paintings can evoke stronger emotional responses. Lessing, however, claims that the difference between literature and painting does not lie in the difference between artificial and natural signs: he demonstrates that a poetry sign can be arbitrary and natural and that not all signs of painting are natural.[5] For example, a thin cloud shrouding a divine figure signalizes the figure's invisibility (divine 'different' corporeality), or tells the observer that he or she should imagine the invisibility of the figure. Therefore, this is a symbolic sign (and thus conventional) and not a natural one (Lessing 1989/1766: 185). The editors of an interdisciplinary volume rethinking Lessing's essay (Lifschitz and Squire 2017: 20) point out that as the motto of *Laocoon*, its author chose an epigraph from Plutarch; according to this Greek philosopher, painting and poetry 'differ in their medium and manners of mimesis' (Lifschitz and Squire 2017: 20). Whereas for Aristoteles both arts' mimetic forms were identical, Plutarch saw a difference in how they relate to time. From the thesis about the spatial simultaneity of the signs of painting and the temporal succession of the signs of poetry, Lessing comes to use the concept of 'successiveness' as that which defines the limits of each art. We could translate this idea into the language of intermediality theory as *the distinctive media traits* of individual arts.

Keeping in mind the limits of the eighteenth-century normative poetics in which Lessing's essay is grounded, we can still find other arguments in favour of including Lessing in the intermedialist family tree. In *Laocoon* Lessing drew clear lines not so much between the arts themselves but between the disciplines that study them. Lessing's critique of seeking out interrelationships between the arts was mainly an objection *to the mechanical transfer of the methods used to study art from one discipline to another*. The epistémé of Lessing's day was to a certain extent defined by the gradual transformation of discourses into independent disciplines and the shaping of their methods and vocabularies. Taking this process into account may prevent us from under- or overinterpreting the nature and impacts of Lessing's explication. Lessing states that with artworks that were produced at roughly the same time and feature the same subject matter, it is sometimes difficult to determine which work or works are the source and which are the receiving ones. Using several realizations of the Laocoon story in different media as examples, Lessing explains the necessity of differentiating a situation in which one work of art is depicted in another from a situation in which a poet and painter share the same subject matter (when both 'imitate nature'; Lessing 1989/1766: 45). Lessing's identification of the fact that various media share the same subject can be understood as a seminal concept of the *text of culture*; Wolf (1999, 2002a) and Rajewsky (2002) refer to such coexistence of media-non-specific themes and forms in different media as *transmediality*.

Lessing's defining of the individual features of different arts also presages the debate on *media specificity*. When he says that epic poetry tends to prioritize representation of action (Lessing 1989/1766: 78), he does not mean that he wants to eradicate description, but he is pointing out what he considers to be the optimal *media affordances* in intermedial terms (cf. Bruhn and Schirrmacher 2021: 12). Lessing does not wish the arts to compete; he calls upon them to make full use of their representation potential. He believes that poetry tends to have a suggestive effect on the recipient's senses and therefore requires the poet to choose devices that evoke images but without calling attention to themselves:

[The poet] wants rather to make the ideas he awakens in us so vivid that at that moment we believe that we feel the real impressions which the objects of these ideas would produce on us. In this moment of illusion *we should cease to be conscious of the means* which the poet uses for this purpose, that is, *his words*. (Lessing 1989/1766: 85; emphasis added)

By this, however, he does not mean the recipient's illusive identification of a poetic representation with reality but that in the process of simulating sensorial information through poetry the language medium becomes transparent, producing an effect that approximates the recipient's experience with reality. The ability to distinguish between evoked mental images and reality – that is, *aesthetic distance* – is preserved (for more, see Fedrová and Jedličková 2010: 78–81, Lifschitz 2017, Grethlein 2017).

To summarize: Lessing identifies arts as sign systems that possess media-specific affordances; in Werner Wolf's words, Lessing's thinking is directed towards distinguishing arts as *distinctive communication dispositifs* (2002a: 165). At the same time, it is clear that Lessing not only describes the *media-specific properties* of poetry and painting, but he also considers the different *effects* they have. Thus, we must acknowledge in his ideas a latent awareness of *art's communicative nature*. For all these reasons, *Laocoon* can certainly be considered a proto-intermedial work.

Pre-intermediality: Comparative arts, interart studies

In the early days of intermedial studies, Oskar Walzel was referred to as the founder of the modern approach to studying the relationships between the arts. There were two main reasons for this: first, because intermedial thinking grew out of comparative literature studies; and second, it was cultivated in large part by German-speaking scholars (e.g. Wagner 1996: 6; Weisstein 1992: 17; Paech 1998: 18; Lund 2002: 15; Rajewsky 2002: 8; Wolf 2018: 174).

Walzel's lecture 'Wechselseitige Erhellung der Künste' (1917) builds on Heinrich Wölfflin's concept of stylistic polarities. Wölfflin (2015/1915) tried to capture the difference between the art of the High Renaissance and of the seventeenth century through a set of paired opposite concepts (linear/painterly expression, plane/recession, tectonic form/a-tectonic form, etc.). Walzel then noted linear and painterly methods in poetry and also distinguished tectonic and a-tectonic motifs in poetry. He found inspiration in Wölfflin's emphasis on forms of representation, which cast aside all interest in the mental predisposition of the artist. Only through such objectification could a specialized vocabulary for describing works of art and principles for observing them be developed. Walzel primarily understood the application of Wölfflin's system to poetry as objectifying the approach to different arts and clarifying the vague terminology used in early-twentieth-century literary criticism.

Jan Mukařovský (1977c/1941: 213) criticized this approach, claiming that Walzel's elimination of features specific to individual arts 'reduces the unity of the arts to the undynamic parallelism of artistic configurations'. Mukařovský understands the opposites of linearity and painterliness that Walzel finds in poetry as a loose *analogy*. Mukařovský compares Art Nouveau painting and Symbolist poetry. Some scholars have proposed understanding this study by Mukařovský as a precursor to intermedial thinking (e.g. Šlaisová 2014), but we do not agree. First, here Mukařovský is essentially limiting himself to comparing *motifs* (cf. Schmid 2004), and thus is only engaging in *intermedial thematization* (Wolf 2002a), which today is generally not considered a mark of intermediality (cf. Wirth 2006). Second, the foundations of Mukařovský's methods, based on defining the semiotic essence of a work, were introduced into *general* semiotics, and thus became applicable to other arts, only in Roman Jakobson's post-war work. Nonetheless, we must admit that Mukařovský here introduces the important topic of *material* or the *materiality of media*. For him, material is what makes the fundamental difference between literature and painting; it is through material that the *specific nature* of individual arts can be identified. Whereas language as the material of poetry is a sign system per se, the material of the visual arts is a natural phenomenon and only acquires the character of a sign in the work of art (on the concept of material, see Chapter 2, pp. 50 and 53).

In the 1940s, René Wellek also took a critical view of Walzel's distinction of art-specific methods and generally of the possibilities of comparing literature with other kinds of art: '*relationships* [of various arts] are not *influences* which start from one point and determine the evolution of other arts' (Wellek and Warren 1949: 135). Wellek (1941) rejects seeking out forced analogies and in particular the idea that a 'time spirit' could be identified that permeates all types of art from a given period. He is convinced that each of the arts goes through its own development and at different speeds. We should add that he observes these transformations primarily in literature, whereas he sees styles of visual arts as having greater temporal homogeneity. Wellek's mindset is typical of early intermedial thinking: he takes a reductionist approach to the 'other' art, the one that is not his specialization. He, however, argues that for the relationships between arts to be studied it would be necessary to rethink the poetics and terminological system of the individual kinds of art, while respecting their specific features (Wellek and Warren 1949: 124–35).

In the 1950s, a new approach began to appear at American universities among comparative literature scholars who also compared different kinds of art. It eventually developed into its own field, *comparative arts*. A degree programme was established at Indiana University in 1954, where Ulrich Weisstein and later Claus Clüver worked (for its history, see Weisstein 1974/1968: 184–9; Weisstein 1993: 1). In the texts of these scholars, literature logically remained the reference point for comparison; other traditional arts occupied the position of the 'other medium'. Northrop Frye and Calvin S. Brown studied the relationship between literature and music/sound, whereas Wylie Sypher examined the relationship between literature and the visual arts. Unsurprisingly, these comparative approaches were often based on the traditional concept of *influence* (which would eventually, and very gradually, be pushed to the margins of debates about the relationships between arts with the development of intertextuality). Terms used to describe the findings of such *comparison* are already familiar to us, for example, *parallel* and *analogy*. Sypher (1955) firmly advocated the idea of analogy, and, like Walzel, he applied Wölfflin's set of opposing concepts and basic principles found in art to study literature from the Renaissance to the Baroque period.[6] Comparative arts as a new subdiscipline of comparative literature also made references to the past in an attempt to legitimize its existence (from the axiom of *ut pictura poesis* up until its reflection in pre-aesthetic texts from the seventeenth and eighteenth centuries). Walzel is always named as a pioneer in this field. Today, we can still hear echoes of Walzel in comparative arts (e.g. Corbineau-Hoffmann 2004; Zymner and Hölter 2013).

Ulrich Weissstein's (1974/1968: 150–66) well-respected introduction to comparative literature contains a chapter whose title is a clear reference to Walzel's 'mutual illumination'. In it, Weisstein outlines the direct and hidden connections between Walzel's method and comparative arts (even referring to Sypher as Walzel's American 'disciple'). Comparative literature in the 1960s – in part due to the dismissive attitude of Paul van Tieghem, a leading theorist in the field – avoided dealing with questions about the relationships between the arts. Weisstein, however, calls for gaining an analytical grasp of phenomena such as 'double talent' (*Doppelbegabung*) and the functioning of what he calls *mixed forms* (*Mischformen*: opera, film, song, the emblem) and *transitional forms* (*Grenzformen*: ekphrasis, visual poetry) (1974/1968: 162–3; for the same terms, see, e.g. Schmeling 1981).

Weisstein (1993: 3, 7) also recognized the inadequacy of the terms *parallel* and *analogy*. Later, in retrospect, he considered terms grounded in semiotics, such as *transmutation* and *transposition* to be the most useful for comparative arts, mainly because they enable describing the transfer of artistic techniques and methods. Nonetheless, even today the comparative arts has yet to give up its traditional vocabulary, as we confirmed by analysing the terminology contained in introductions to comparative literature (e.g.

Corbineau-Hoffmann 2004) as well in recent handbooks (Zymner and Hölter 2013). Comparative arts still studies subject matters, motifs and themes, their coexistence, and the transformations of their *contents* (e.g. Corbineau-Hoffmann 2004: 202), that is, phenomena that are referred to in intermedial theory as manifestations of *transmediality*.

Pre-intermedial research's grounding in comparative literature also explains why it continued to focus on the traditional 'high' arts and the relationships between them. This focus would be disrupted by the rethinking of the concept of art and its replacement with a cultural construct, a process that has been ongoing in the humanities since the 1980s. Another source of change was the shift of methodological focus of the most prominent proponents of comparative arts, Weisstein and Clüver, towards semiotics in the late 1980s. Both theorists began to use the term *intersemiotic translation*, and this new discipline began to be called *interart studies*.

Several different interdisciplinary methodologies existed in the late 1980s and early 1990s that shared the focus on the same subject matter, but nonetheless differed. In addition to the broadly conceived interart studies, two further subdisciplines, *word and image studies* and *word and music studies* were established and institutionalized in academic associations (1987 IAWIS/AIERTI, 1997 WMA). Characteristic of this stage in the evolution of intermedial thinking was the postponement of the revision of some fundamental concepts. The 'paradigm of art' and the long tradition of seeking out kinship between the arts clearly shine through in the terms these two subdisciplines use as well as in their very names. Yet in introducing the terms *image* and *music*, they tried to avoid the notion of *art*. Unlike in interart studies, in other fields (e.g. aesthetics, art history), a thorough rethinking of the concept of art was coming to a close (1994, the *pictorial turn* of W. J. T. Mitchell and the *iconic turn* of Gottfried Boehm, visual studies, and 'Bildwissenschaft') at the roughly same time. Under the influence of this conceptual rethinking and also under the influence of the representation potential of new media, the realm of art expanded, and the terms used in related discourses changed (art vs. image).

To illustrate the rich pre-intermedial genealogy we have selected one branch of research to describe in a more detailed way the relationship between 'word and image'. (For the prehistory and history of research into relations between 'word and music', see especially Wolf 1999.) The link to the past and tradition explains why, at first, word-and-image studies held a strongest position; this preference was also reflected in interart studies. In retrospect, we see that three genres associated with the relationship between verbal and visual media were prominent focuses in interart studies: ekphrasis, the emblem and visual poetry. This is why many texts that we could consider to be of an intermedial nature interpret not only modern art but also from pre-modern art. In fact, we encounter such phenomena at the very beginnings of literature, in Homer's ekphrasis of Achilles' shield in the *Iliad*. Whereas the emblem had been a dead genre since the eighteenth century, interart scholars found visual poetry and ekphrasis very tempting subject matters, for they could examine their current forms, trace their history and examine their transformations. For example, the visual poems of Ferdinand Kriwet or Jiří Kolář from the 1960s and 1970s, which came in the shape of mazes, were interpreted in the context of similarly arranged poems from the Middle Ages and especially Baroque experimental poetry. Interart scholars thus created a microhistory of a very specific type of visual poetry, which was presented as a 'constant in European literature' (Ernst 1990). Similarly, microhistories of ekphrasis could be written that examined this form from antiquity to the ekphrastic poetry of the second half of the twentieth century (Heffernan 1993; Boehm and Pfotenhauer 1995).

Interart studies were characterized by their diversity of methodological approaches and concepts, which prevented the development of a systematic theory. Due to the diversity of initial specializations that interart scholars had, the field featured a broad range of methodological approaches: ekphrasis studied from the perspective of literary criticism or classical philology (e.g. Heffernan 1993 and Webb 1999), and other subjects investigated using the methods of comparative literature, iconography (emblem studies), new historicism, visual studies or the theory of representation. When commenting on the proceedings of the conference held at Lund University in 1995, Stephen Greenblatt (1997: 15) aptly grasped the situation as a 'cacophony of methods'; his description applies also to other volumes from this period (e.g. Harms 1990; Hoesterey and Weisstein 1993; Wagner ed. 1996). Nevertheless, the Lund conference succeeded in firmly establishing the term *interart studies* (Lagerroth, Lund and Hedling 1997) in the scholarly discourse, which until that point had been used rather freely. The notion nailed down some of the main currents in intermedial research that had been developing in different academic communities, primarily those in German-speaking countries and Scandinavia, but also in Brazil, where interart perspective was introduced by Claus Clüver and developed further.

Interart studies began as a 'literature-centred' discipline in the sense that it mainly concentrated on the relationships between literature and other arts. Literature gradually ceased to be the reference point for comparison, but the use of the term *text* to designate any media product persisted for years (on the notion of text, see Chapter 10, p. 347–8). In interart studies, a *text* is a structured unit created based on one or more codes with a concrete communicative intent – the text is a *supersign*. The semiotic conception of interart studies gradually came to dominate, but its focus began to shift away from an understanding of text as representation towards accenting of communication.

Comparative arts and interart studies played an integral role in the genealogy of intermediality theory, first, because it was from these subdisciplines that the institutional contours of intermedial studies began to take shape. Second, it is here that we find the first attempts at producing classifications and typologies and systematic terminology.

The growing number of analytical studies on the relationships between different kinds of arts led to the need to classify the subjects being studied. Literary critic Áron Kibédi Varga (1989) tried to introduce a systematic perspective to the discourse on the relationships between text and image. He first distinguished the meta-level, containing indirect relationships between arts: the phenomenon of the double talent of the author and the relevance of contacts between writers and artists (like between Zola and Cézanne), and so forth. Kibédi Varga classifies direct relationships based on the following three criteria: First, the criterion of *time* poses the question of whether an author was inspired to create a work by an already existing work in another medium (an ekphrasis, illustration), or whether both works emerged at the same time as a unit. Second, the criterion of *quantity* addresses whether a work is a single object (an emblem) or a series or group of interconnected objects (a book of emblems connected by a certain topic). Third, the criterion of *form* is primarily central to visual poetry and forms experimentally combining word and image from the Middle Ages until the twentieth century. As a result, Kibédi Varga distinguishes three types of interactions between forms:

- The *coexistence* of forms in a defined space (e.g. an advertising poster);
- *Interreference*, where forms within a defined space are visually separated but connected through a meaning-making relationship (emblem, illustration);
- *Coreference*, in which the forms do not share the same space but refer to the same represented entity (ekphrasis).

Even though Kibédi Varga's typology covered only a part of what interart studies was interested in, it was still frequently applied in the 1990s. It presaged the next stage in intermedial research, which focused on developing a systematic classification of the relationships between 'arts' and 'media'. The persistent lack of clarity of the exact relationships between these two terms, or what they actually mean, is one of the reasons that the definition of *medium* was put off for so long in intermedial thinking.

The first study aimed at theorizing the relationships between literature and other arts was based in semiotics. In it, Claus Clüver conceptualized the transformation of the contents of one medium into another as *intersemiotic transposition*. There a fundamental change in methodological perspective took place; the focus was no longer on the product of transposition but on the *process* through which the product was created. In a later stage of intermedial studies, especially in the discussion sparked by Roberto Simanowski, it would become clear just how significant this change in emphasis was.

We encounter the notion *transposition* even earlier, in the work of Gisbert Kranz (1981), who built it upon Théophile Gautier's use of the term *the transposition of art*. While Kranz describes a very broad range of phenomena and includes them under the term *Bildgedicht*, Clüver adapts this notion within semiotic thinking; he understands transposition not as a process of transfer from one kind of art to another but as a process of *translation*. Here, Clüver's idea converges with that of *intersemiotic translation*, which Jakobson distinguishes from *intralingual* and *interlingual* translation (for a recent examination of this concept, see Aguiar and Queiroz 2009). Jakobson understands intersemiotic translation as the 'interpretation of verbal signs by means of nonverbal sign system' (Jakobson 1966/1959: 233); to shore up the idea that it involves transformation, he introduces *transmutation* as a synonymous term. Jakobson claims that a semiotic system always functions as a code, that is, it includes the rules for its use, and is thus indelibly connected with communication. Here, let us recall Guillory's (2010: 351–3) thesis about the latent presence of the media concept; in Jakobson's work it is revealed through its contact with the communication model and the process of mediation (more on this latency in semiotics, see Chapter 6, pp. 183–4, 191–2 and 202).

Although Clüver did not develop a full-fledged theory of transposition, he did state that interart studies should deal with questions related to those posed by semiotics: What kind of *code* makes the recipient read a text as a transposition of a painting? What expectations might induce readers to approach a verbal text as a transposition? What features of the text and what contextual restraints might prevent them from such a reading? (Clüver 1989: 62). Clüver treats individual kinds of arts as sign systems in which meaning is conferred 'by readers according to the codes, conventions and interpretative norms endorsed by their interpretative communities' (Clüver 1989: 84). All these points reveal that Clüver was actively building upon Jakobson's ideas. Wendy Steiner's ideas (1982) might have played a mediating role here. Clüver claims that he essentially agrees with her, with the exception of her proposed terms: Steiner rejects the term *translation*, instead preferring *structural imitation*. However, when interpreting William Carlos Williams's ekphrastic poem 'The Hunters in the Snow', they both seem to mean basically the same thing despite their different use of terms (Steiner 1982: 90; Clüver 1989: 68). Steiner highlights the *structural* and *material* correspondences between the painting and the poem (Steiner 1982: 17, 53, 87–9). Her approach stems from Jakobson's semiotics and an elaboration of the ideas of the Prague School, including Mukařovský's concept of *material* as the factor differentiating arts. Steiner sees material correspondences between Brueghel's reduction of the chromatic scale of colours to shades of black and white with other colours used for accent and Williams's reduction of vowels and diphthongs and their distribution in the text. Significantly, this use of the term *material* was, at this nascent stage of interart studies, obviously difficult for Clüver to accept, and he therefore employs the term *technical features* in its place. In contrast, in his latest rethinking of the concept of ekphrasis he confidently works with the distinction between the materiality of a medium (lines, shape, colour and texture in painting) and the techniques it uses (Clüver 2017: 31).

In the early 1990s, Clüver's concept of intersemiotic transposition enabled him to distinguish it from the overly broad definition of the term *Bildgedicht* suggested by Kranz (1981), in which relationships of various orders merged: imitation, influence, commentary, contemplation, criticism, interpretation. From the retrospective perspective it was also very important that Clüver included in his concept the opposite direction of creation, that is, from text to image, starting with traditional illustration all the way up to contemporary artistic artefacts understood as 'visual equivalents' to the poem (Clüver 1989: 69, 80). Even though he declares his efforts to develop a concept encompassing the different relationships between arts (semiotic systems), Clüver does not deny that his primary interest lies in ekphrasis. This preference of themes may be the reason why the term *intersemiotic transposition* did not catch on to a greater extent. During the transition from interart studies to the theory of intermediality, Clüver (1997) tried to show ekphrasis as a concept essentially synonymous with intersemiotic transposition (in recent texts he has replaced this term with *intermedial transposition*, Clüver 2017). There were two consequences to this: First, extending the concept to include, among other things, the idea of mimetic representation, means that essentially anything can be called ekphrasis. Logically, other authors responded by trying to narrow the definition of ekphrasis again. Second, this put a stop to the further elaboration of the concept of intersemiotic transposition. The main contribution of this concept still lies in the fact that it implies the *processuality* of meaning-making, which would become an explicit topic of debate only at the end of the 2010s.

2. Intermediality: The systemization of theory and the establishment of the discipline

Motivations for change: The state of culture and the academic discourse

The transformation of interart studies into intermedial studies was motivated by broader changes in culture. The individual arts had been in extremely close contact with each other since the earliest days of the avant-garde, when they were forced to come to terms with newly introduced technologies (especially reproduction technologies and the significant expansion of film) that complemented but also competed with 'old' media. The avant-garde no longer differentiated between 'high' and 'low' art, but instead cultivated the idea that art is for the wider public. This state of culture shook the foundations of art's privileged status. Another stage in this process came with the emergence of complex artistic projects in the 1960s, which erased the borders not only between individual kinds of arts but also between the creator of a work and its recipients (see also Chapter 6, e.g. pp. 188–9). Since the late 1980s and early 1990s, with the rise of digital media, society and cultural studies have been forced to deal with this truly new way of representing reality, including virtual reality, which has fundamentally altered human experience. Literature, as an art form, has had to come to terms with the fact that it now forever finds itself in 'complex media configurations' (Schröter 1998: 129) and as a result is in a constant state of merciless competition with other 'media offers' (Schmidt 2008: 9 ff.). This change has affected both the writing of literature and the forms of its distribution, reception and criticism. Literary criticism has been forced to respond to these changes for other reasons as well, ones related to the nature of the humanities and the paradigm shifts towards interdisciplinary research. Whereas in the natural sciences changes were made in response to rapid technological development on the one hand and the growing need to share research with global impacts globally, on the other, the humanities lost their academic exclusivity and now must constantly prove their relevance to society, whether by cooperating with the social or other sciences. Great emphasis on the social grounding of cultural phenomena is also the result of 'methodological fatigue' caused by the domination of structuralism and its universalism. The humanities have turned away from seeking out universality and pattern, and now focus their attention on the diversity of cultural phenomena in their historical context, their communication functions and their relationship to human experience.

The interdisciplinary context provided fertile ground for the institutionalization of intermedial studies. Incubation sites were often comparative literature institutions (e.g. Weisstein's and Clüver's departments). Research groups were formed in Utrecht, Graz and Lund, and academic associations have been established (1995 in Lund 1996 in Växjö 1997 in Montreal). As part of this process, degree programmes were established at universities: in 2001, the first master's programme in interart studies (later changed to intermedial studies) was opened at Lund University, followed by post-graduate programmes in Belo Horizonte and Montreal. One branch of intermedial studies, which we will examine in greater detail, was primarily based on literary criticism (e.g. Hans Lund, Claus Clüver, Werner Wolf, Irina O. Rajewsky, Gabrielle Rippl, Lars Elleström), whereas another branch was grounded more in media theory (e.g. Jürgen E. Müller, Joachim Paech, Jens Schröter).

The background of intertextuality: An expanding scope under the influence of visual studies

One of the major inspirations of intermedial research was visual studies, which developed rapidly in the 1990s, when scholars began to look beyond the borders of the traditional arts, seeking out various forms of visual representation with aesthetic functions. At the same time, as we have already mentioned, important concepts were being rethought. W. J. T. Mitchell's books *Iconology* (1986) and *Picture Theory* (1994) were responses to interpretations based in comparative art (in American thought, from Ulrich Weisstein to Wendy Steiner), and he argued against the use of terms from comparative literature (e.g. *comparison, analogy*). At the same time, he opposed the assumption made in semiotic and intersemiotic analysis that there is a unifying concept (sign, semiosis). His thought though was based on another unifying concept, that of representation (Mitchell 1994: 84–107). Mitchell uses the term *medium* without questioning it. He proposes classifying media based on the senses used to perceive them. He, however, rejects the idea that there are clear-cut borders between media, arguing that all media are *mixed media*. The problem of image and text in 'synthetic forms' (e.g. comics, film, illuminated manuscripts, the works of William Blake) for him means 'the heterogeneity of representational structures within the field of the visible and readable' (Mitchell 1994: 88). He then carefully distinguishes between two terms he has coined, *imagetext* and *image-text*: *imagetexts* are composite, synthetic works/concepts, whereas an *image-text* is a matter of the *relations* between visual and verbal media (Mitchell 1994: 89).[7] From recognizing that the nature of media relations is inherently mixed (film), Mitchell comes to the conclusion that the same method should be applied to analysing 'unmixed' media, and that this is not something constructed *between* arts or media but an unavoidable issue *within* the arts/media. Because all media combine 'codes, discursive conventions, [and] channels, sensory and cognitive modes', Mitchell claims that medium is 'a heterogeneous field of representational practice' (Mitchell 1994: 94–5, 100). We should emphasize once again his main interest of study – according to Mitchell, media are mixed from the *perspective of perception*. The influence of Mitchell's concepts of imagetext and image-text and his theory that all media are mixed media can be seen in certain sections of interart studies in the 1990s (especially in the work of Peter Wagner); it persists today in word-and-image studies (cf. Louvel 2011). This thesis about *mixed media* and the consequent irrelevance of distinguishing media has been accepted mainly by the current in intermedial studies that draws from media theory, media philosophy and performance theory.

The theory of intertextuality is another source of changes in the way the relationships between arts are thought about. Intersemiotic concepts examine the relationships between arts through the prism of sign systems and they usually do so through the analysis of individual works of art. Intertextuality, however, changes the concept of what a work is; although it views all works of art as unique, it also sees them as points where networks of intertextual relationships intersect (Kristeva 1980/1967). From here, it is only a short step away to proposing that a work of art is the intersection point of the relationships between media.

This step was taken by Slavicist Aage Hansen-Löwe (1983) in a study on the relationships between literature and the visual art in Russian modernism: he coined the term *intermediality* as an analogy to intertextuality. But this new term had to wait another twenty years before it became a theory or underwent codification. For comparison with Clüver's contemporaneous vocabulary, we should add that Hansen-Löve (1983: 88) works with the term *intermedial correlation* between word and image, and refers to individual forms of these media as *configurations*. Intertextuality conceptualizes a literary work of art as the result of different ways of absorbing and transforming a set of other texts contained in verbal culture: from the cultural proximity of the text to the pre-text to a direct, historically documented genetic relationship. In structuralist semiotics, bound like structuralist narratology to linguistics, the term *text* was, particularly under the influence of Yuri Lotman, fundamentally expanded to encompass any cultural entity created *on the basis of a distinctive semiotic system* (see Chapter 10, esp. p. 334).

In the 1980s and 1990s intermedial relations were already playing a role but one subordinate to intertextuality and the broader understanding of the text. Horst Zander (1985) and Heinrich Plett (1991) speak about intermediality as a particular type of intertextuality; they primarily focus on the adaptation of literary texts and the range of relationships that can arise by borrowing or sharing themes and motifs. In any case though, they examine a concrete relationship between a text and its pre-text: a Shakespearian drama as a radio play, the use of a motif from Hamlet in one of Picasso's graphic works (Zander 1985: 190). The inclusion of a wide range of cultural phenomena leads Peter Wagner (1996: 18) to prefer the term *intermediality* over *intertextuality*, inspired by, among other things, Norman Bryson's and Mieke Bal's (1991) study on semiotics and art history. The discussion about the relationship between intertextuality and intermediality at this time was mainly held between Horst Zander, Manfred Pfister, Jürgen E. Müller, Ulla-Britta Lagerroth, Peter Wagner, Werner Wolf and Claus Clüver. Around the mid-1990s, we encounter more references to intermediality, but this term was often used as just a synonym for *interart* (Lagerroth, Lund and Hedling 1997: 7, 12).

The process of establishing intermedial studies as a field should be understood as a *process of emancipation*: liberation from the dominance of linguistics as a universal science and the understanding of text as the universal semiotic form, but also from the historically taken-for-granted notion of art. Jürgen E. Müller (1996: 297) pointed out that the word *medium* as the basis of the new term *intermediality* still did not have a fixed meaning and could therefore still be easily applied to content that corresponds to traditional art. For Müller, the introduction of the term *medium* is what allows for the distinction between intertextuality and intermediality. He claims that intermediality does not present a primary challenge to intertextuality or literary criticism but rather to media studies because it is capable of grasping new forms of cultural communication and becoming one of them. It is even capable of developing into a new scientific paradigm (J. E. Müller 1996: 98–102; J. E. Müller 1998: 135).

Werner Wolf (2002a: 165) prefers to re-narrow the concept of text as the universal semiotic activity to a *linguistic* sign complex and to consider it a sub-class of *medium*. This allows him to divide the field of intersemiotic relationships into the sphere of *intermedial* relationships, which are characterized by crossing the borders between media, and *intramedial* relationships in which (through allusion, citation, paraphrase) relationships are established within a single semiotic system: we can talk about intertextual, intermusical or interfilm relationships.[8]

Seeking a perfect model: Literature-centred intermediality

At the turn of the twenty-first century, as intermedial studies were becoming institutionalized and their scope expanded, the time had come for introducing a theory including a system of categories. Four of the most influential studies (by Claus Clüver, Hans Lund, Werner Wolf and Irina O. Rajewsky) share a perspective that Wolf called *literature-centred intermedial research* (*literaturzentrierte Intermedialitätsforschung*). The identifying features of this approach are a predominantly semiotic methodology, a focus on literary works and an interest in developing a typology that may include as many forms of intermedial relationships as possible. Intermediality refers to the inner features of a work or to relationships between works in which we can identify manifestations of more than one type of medium, defined as a semiotic system. Like the interart studies that preceded it, intermedial studies inquire into *relationships*. The *mediality* of works of art became evident as a consequence of studying them from a *comparative* perspective, which attributed them the status of *media products*.

Clüver proposed a classification of intermedial phenomena in the 1990s. He considers *multimedia* to be media whose components, such as the libretto and music of an opera or the screenplay and soundtrack of a film, retain their legibility even when separated from each other, while the components of *mixed media* cannot function independently (e.g. comics; Clüver 1993, 2000-1: 25-8). Clüver's suggestion of a typology of relationships between text and image was developed by Leo H. Hoek and Eric Vos (1997), who present a broader range of media relationships. A fundamental role is played in this model by Clüver's concept of intersemiotic transposition and the emphasis on his processual understanding of intermedial relationships, which enables these two scholars to distinguish several such forms: *transposition, juxtaposition, combination* and *fusion* (Table 11.1).

The process of meaning-making was the basis of Hans Lund's model, whose classification of media relationships as the *transformation, integration* and *combination of media* is essentially close to that of Clüver (Lund 2002: 20) (Table 11.2).

At the turn of the twentieth century, Werner Wolf referred to intermediality as a provocation of or a challenge to literary criticism (2002a). His systematic theory of intermedial relationships was developed in close connection with his research into word and music relations (Wolf 1996, 1999) and his narratological research (Wolf 2002b). Wolf (2002a: 165) defines medium primarily as a *communication dispositif*, which is distinguished by the specific use of one or more semiotic systems. On the one hand, Wolf expands the definition by attributing to the medium the *role of a cognitive frame of reference*, whose recognition is necessary for the recipient's understanding because it evokes in her expectations of communication strategies that she knows from previous experience. On the other hand, Wolf narrows his concept of medium, relegating the material vehicles of the media product and

Table 11.1 Claus Clüver, Leo H. Hoek and Eric Vos 1997

SCHEMA OF WORD-IMAGE RELATIONS	transmedial relation [relation transmédiale]	multimedia discourse [discourse multimédial]	mixed-media discourse [discours mixte]	intermedial discourse [discours syncrétique]
distinctiveness [séparabilité]	+	+	+	−
coherence/self-sufficiency	+	+	−	−
polytextuality	+	−	−	−
simultaneous production	−	−	+	+
simultaneous reception	−	+	+	+
process	transposition	juxtaposition	combination	union/fusion
schematized text-image relation	text > image image > text	image	text	image + texte	i t m e a x g t e
examples	ekphrasis art criticism photonovel	emblem illustrated book painting & title	poster comic strip postage stamp	typography calligramme concrete poetry

Source: Clüver 2007: 26.

the technological necessities for distributing it to the margins. This exclusion of media as object and channel was certainly one of the reasons that media theory (which has several concepts of medium at its disposal; see Section 3 of Chapter 1, pp. 37–40, and Chapter 7, pp. 232, 238–9 and *passim*) expressed little interest in intermedial studies.[9] Yet there was a good reason for such narrowing: it allows Wolf (2002a: 165) to bridge the gap between arts and media that opened up throughout the long history of studying the relations between arts, and makes it possible to include under the concept of medium 'traditional arts and their mediation forms as well as new communication forms'. This, of course, also applies to literature, which, as a result, begins to be understood as a verbal medium. Wolf's definition of medium also allows him to define intermediality as the crossing of the borders between media. He observes its manifestations in proportionally different relationships between the part, the autonomous whole and the system. Intermediality may manifest itself as a complex relationship between two individual works, between a work and a part of another work, between a work and a group of works (e.g. within a genre or artistic movement), or between an individual work and a semiotic system. It is this multitude of relationships that is the starting point of Wolf's typology. 'Extracompositional' (*werkübergreifend*) intermediality is recognizable only when we compare two media products, or a media product and a medium. 'Intracompositional' (*werkintern*) intermediality denotes a situation in which more than one medium is incorporated into the meaning-making structure of a single work (Diagram 11.1).

Wolf (2002a: 170–1) differentiates two sub-forms of *extracompositional* intermediality. Making reference to Rajewsky (2002: 11–15), he explains *transmediality* as a sum of cultural contents and established constellations of their sub-components (e.g. mythological and biblical themes but also archetypes and master plots) travelling between media without it being possible to identify specific genetic, that is, transpositional relationships. According to Wolf and Rajewsky, complex phenomena parallelly observable in different media from one period can also be viewed as transmedial (e.g. the sentimental expressivity characteristic of the eighteenth-century sensibility). This notion is very similar to Mary Ann Caws's (1981) (diachronic) concept of *architexture*: it includes both themes that were characteristic of a period and modes of conveying these themes. Conventional structures like the story and modes of representation such as dialogue and description also have a transmedial nature. Studying these modes from a transmedial perspective can contribute to understanding them both from the synchronic and diachronic perspective (cf. Wolf's concept of description as a macromode of representation, 2007; cf. also Fedrová and Jedličková 2016, Jedličková 2014).

The second sub-form of Wolf's extracompositional intermediality, *intermedial transposition*, corresponds with Clüver's definition of *intersemotic* transposition. Unlike transmediality, intermedial transposition is characterized by an always detectable *genetic connection* between two works realized in sequence in different media (e.g. a film or opera adaptation of a literary work). Wolf, in keeping with the theory of intertextuality, refers to the relationship between such works as a relationship between the *pre-medium* of the original work and the *post-medium* of the follow-up work. In intermedial transposition, individual media manifest their particular representation potential. Wolf reminds us that for the recipient to grasp the sense of the post-media product it is not necessary to know the pre-product. The intermedial relation may – if at all – be referred to only in the margins (such as in a note reading 'based on the novel by . . .' or in film credits). Media transposition, Wolf (2002a: 171) claims, results in an *autonomous configuration* of signs organized according to the principles of the post-medium. In other words, it is completely legitimate for a recipient to consume a product of media transposition without thinking, or even knowing, about its genetic relationship to the source product. This, of course, does not necessarily lead to the elimination of knowledge of the source medium in the reception process; it only means that it is not necessary for such knowledge to be applied directly in this process. Nevertheless, we agree with Elleström

Table 11.2 Hans Lund 2002

	Combination	Integration	Transformation
Interreference	Coexistence	Concrete poetry	Verbal ekphrasis
		Sound poetry	Musical ekphrasis
Illustration	Advertising visuals	Typography	Program music
Emblems	(Postage) stamp	Calligram	Novel mediates film
Image & title	Song/ditties	Ideograms	Word mediates music
Music & title	Video	Sprechgesang	Film mediates novel
Photojournalism	Cartoon strips	Conceptual art	Dramatization of text
Picture-book	Opera	Picture alphabet	
	Liturgy	Iconicity	
	Poster	Verbal signs in images	

Source: Lund 2002: 21.

(2010) that the *mediality* of one medium can manifest itself thanks to the (latent) presence of other media and our knowledge of them.

Intracompositional intermediality includes intermedial reference and plurimediality. Plurimediality represents a number of phenomena that can be located on the axis between the additive *combination* of media and the *mixing* of media. In a product resulting from the mixing of media, the elements of the source media cannot be separated.

A reference to another media or media product can be made *explicitly* or *implicitly*. In his 2002a study, Wolf mentions as an implicit form of intermedial reference the *musicalization of fiction* as an example of *media imitation*. In a recent rethinking of this idea (2019), he presents a detailed scale of references stretching from evocation to reproduction. But for studying the evolution of intermedial thinking, another modification is more important: Wolf introduces the term *performance*, placing it besides *work* to make it clear that intermediality applies to fixed, closed works as well as performance-based works (Wolf 2019: 31; see Diagram 11.1).

The mere *mentioning of a medium* in a work has been subject to several discussions; many intermedialists, including the authors of this analysis, favour its exclusion from the classification of intermedial relations. Differentiating between *covert* and *overt* intermediality (suggested in Wolf 1999: 39–42), while the latter is supposed to be discernible on the 'surface layer of the work' (*Werkoberfläche*; similarly understood also by Paech 1998: 23), has become subject of critique by Elleström (2014: 8–9). He questions the notion of 'surface' itself, provided that according to Wolf, intermediality is recognizable at the *signifying layer*, which appears to be *hetereogenous* or even *hybrid* in nature, 'he delimits overt intermediality to a narrow category'

The Theory of Intermediality

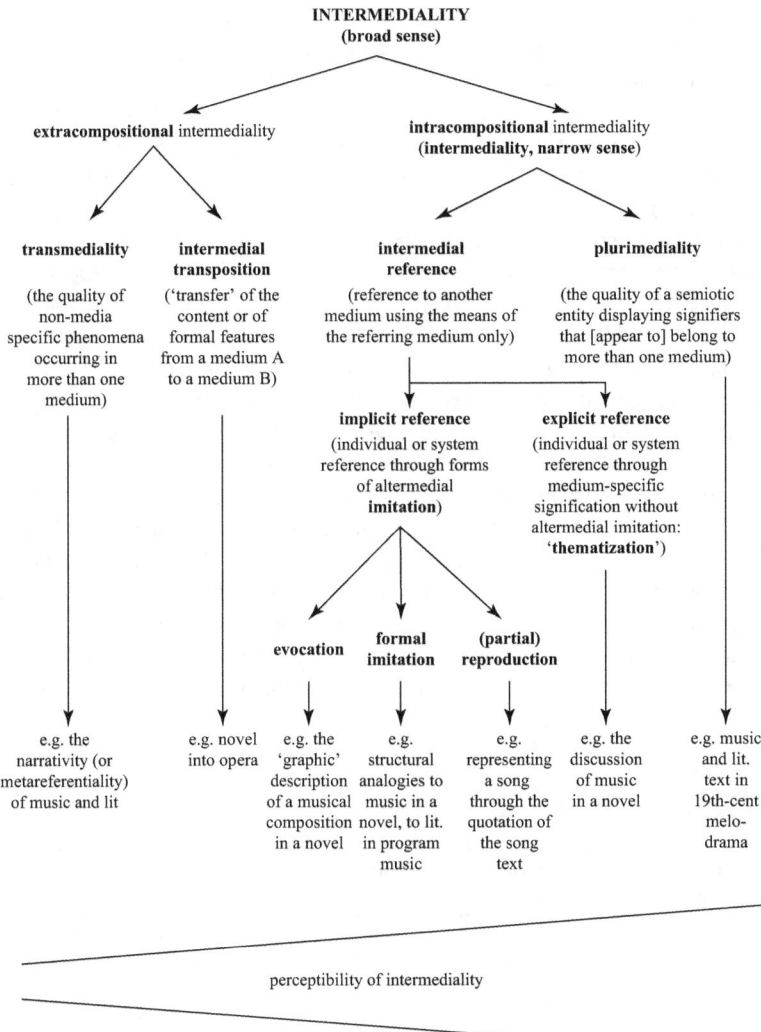

Diagram 11.1 Werner Wolf 2002, revised 2018. *Source*: Wolf 2018: 143.

(Elleström 2014: 8). Even though we may argue that Wolf's concept of medium as a *cognitive frame* implies the act of a recipient's discerning cultural representations from each other as products of various media, and thus, Wolf expects the recipient to possess the capacity to detect the heterogeneity of a representation, Elleström objects that the differentiation between cases of overt and covert intermediality actually requires a very clear perception of 'the exact end' (Elleström 2014: 8) of structures resulting from employing means of distinct media.

Elleström raises an even more foundational objection to Wolf's *subordination of intermedial transposition to extracompositional intermediality* (Elleström 2014: 8–9). These different attitudes are partly of a historical nature (cf. Jedličková 2017): Wolf's concept of intermediality still draws from the idea of interart (word and music) studies, in which the mediality of a cultural representation emerges mainly as the result of a specific comparative perspective of observation, which reveals intermediality as a *relationship*. Unlike Wolf, Elleström (2014) may rely on 'evident', academically studied mediality, and he suggests the concept of 'media transformation', based on media representation and transmediation as key notions.

Irina O. Rajewsky whose concept resulted from a dialogue with Wolf also relates intermediality to intertextuality and employs the same definition of medium as well as the trio of basic notions: *intramediality, intermediality, transmediality*. She defines three fundamental categories of intermediality (Rajewsky 2002: 15–18): media combination (*Medienkombination*), including representations in which different media are co-present; media transformation (*Medienwechsel*), which occurs with a change of the semiotic system; and intermedial references (*intermediale Bezüge*), in which a media product is related to another product in another medium or another medium as a system (Table 11.3).

Table 11.3 Irina O. Rajewsky 2002

Media transformation	Combination of media	Intermedial references
Intermedial transposition	Multi- or plurimediality/media interplay/*co-presence*	One media product refers to another or to another media system (or sub-system)
e.g. filmic adaptation of a novel, *novelization*	e.g. theater, opera, film; illuminated manuscript; photonovel, performances, comics, graphic novel, sound art (multimedia, mixed media, intermedia)	e.g. a literary text refers to a certain film, to a cinematic genre and/or to the film as media system (such as through evocation or simulation of certain cinematic techniques; 'filmic writing')

Source: Rajewsky 2019: 57.

Rajewsky stipulates that the primary task of intermedial analysis is to establish the criteria for distinguishing between an intentional, truly intermedial phenomenon and such one that results from the internal evolution of the medium or appears to be a partial imitation of a device used by another medium. Thus, her classification begins with the single mentioning of another medium as a system (*Systemerwähnung*). Unlike in Wolf's understanding, according to Rajewsky, mentioning another media does not necessarily affect the structure of the media product: for example, in a verbal narrative it might have an impact only at the story level. Nevertheless, Rajewsky, like Wolf, assumes that the semantic effect of explicitly mentioning the system results from the process of the recipient's interpretation. A more complex phenomenon is the *simulation* or *imitation of the methods of another medium* (Rajewsky 2002: 85). The essence of simulation is creating the illusion of the presence of another medium in the recipient's mind through the use of the media-specific elements and devices of that medium. This type of media relations was the initial focus of Rajewsky (2003) in her monograph on the Italian postmodernist fiction: her aim was to differ between merely metaphoric and descriptive use of terms such as 'filmic writing' or 'cinematic modes of narration' encountered frequently in literary criticism. The third type of reference (*teil-reproduzierende Systemerwähnung*) is based on the 'reproduction' of components of the source media system that may be genre-typical but are media-non-specific; an example would be the literary use of characters or plot constructs typical of the film genre of 'Hollywood melodrama' (Rajewsky 2002: 104–6). To put it another way, seemingly transmedial thematic components (e.g. a scene of lovers kissing) are presented in such a way that they call to the mind of the recipient a device typical of another medium (e.g. slowed-down literary narration corresponding to a slow-motion sequence in a romance film in which the faces of two lovers get closer to each other).

Rajewsky refers to intermedial relations that manifest themselves constantly throughout the receiving media as *system contamination*. The difference between the source (contacting) and receiving (contacted) medium is preserved, but the recipient is directed towards an illusory feeling of the other media system's presence (to illustrate this point Rajewsky uses Wolf's example of the *musicalization of fiction*, e.g. using the compositional principles of the fugue in a text's structure; Rajewsky 2002: 122–4).

Rajewsky's subtle, more-or-less descriptive classification is useful for systematically describing, comparing and sorting intermedial phenomena at the intersection point of two axes: the first axis includes phenomena ranging from *a simple singular reference* to *a complex representation*, and the second axis indicates their meaning-making potential. This classification's subtlety was subsequently subjected to criticism, and the author would later modify it (Rajewsky 2019; see Table 11.3). Wolf (2019), maintaining the relation between both concepts, included these two axes in his recent revised typology (see Diagram 11.1).

Lars Elleström (2014: 9) would later object to distinguishing between *media representation* and *intermedial reference*, arguing that the distinction between them could not be pinpointed in practice; moreover, he claims that intermedial references include excessively heterogeneous phenomena. In general, we have to take into account that Rajewsky aims at a subtle classification of media relationships, while Elleström is interested in identifying media traits that make media transformation and representation possible, and the mechanisms aligned with these processes. If we concede that Rajewsky's *references* are – to a certain degree – *representations* (which Elleström also implies in an enumeration of representations in which he included citations, allusions, etc.; Elleström 2014: 28), then we can offer some reconciliation: What Elleström calls *the complex representation of a medium* (such as *ekphrasis*) may be compared to *the maximum* (complex) *reference form* in Rajewsky's scheme, and vice versa: what Rajewsky calls 'media mentioning' (*Systemerwähnung*) may be considered an equivalent to 'minimum representation' in Elleström's terms.

3. An established discipline

Critiques of existing models and new emphases

At the beginning of the twenty-first century, intermedialists concentrated on finding a 'perfect' model that would make it possible to grasp and classify the vast amount of diverse intermedial phenomena. These classifications were then subjected to critique and revision in a process comparable to the one that narratologists subjected Genette's subtle classification of the temporality of narrative discourse to: minor objections did not prevent the application of the main concepts in analytical practice. The same goes for the mentioned models of intermediality, which provide suitable tools for analysing and interpreting concrete media configurations (cf. Berndt and Tonger-Erk 2013; Maiwald 2019). The rethinking of intermedial models in the 2000s led to a proliferation of terms, which often overlapped without bringing anything new to the table. Therefore, we have selected only those that offer something novel. Although Wirth (2006) and Simanowski (2006) remain grounded in semiotics, they still attempt to incorporate technological aspects into the media concept.

Literary critic and media theorist Uwe Wirth views the intermedial approach as a transdisciplinary interface between literary, cultural and media studies. He distinguishes between *soft* and *hard intermediality* (Wirth 2006: 33–4): soft intermediality is typically studied by scholars with a literature-centred approach, whereas examining hard intermediality requires studying the *technological aspects* of differences between media (which Wolf and Rajewsky intentionally push to the margins when they prioritize the semiotic system in their definitions of *medium*).

Wirth distinguishes three levels of intermedial relationships: the first level, and a fundamental condition for intermediality to occur, is the reconfiguration of the original sign system, for example, the transposition of a dramatic text into a theatre performance (Wirth 2006: 32). The second level involves the *combination* (not the mere coexistence) of differently configured sign systems, for instance, a combination of text, image and sound. This *integrative* reconfiguration requires a certain transformation in media technology: Wirth refers to it as *media grafting* (*mediale Aufpropfung*). *Conceptual grafting* is the foundation upon which the third level of intermedial relations is built: it involves the transfer of a media configuration from one sign system to another, for example, the transfer of film editing techniques to writing experimental literature (cf. *filmic writing*, Rajewsky 2003). According to Wirth, levels one and three are *soft forms* of intermediality, or intermediality in the broad sense, whereas level two with its technological dimension is a form of *hard* intermediality. In addition, here Wirth also includes – in a move that we consider to be anachronistic – ideas from the prehistory of intermedial thinking: the concepts of *ut pictura poesis* and 'poetic painting'.

We have deliberately left out Wirth's 'zero level', the mentioning of another medium (Wolf 2002a refers to it as *intermedial thematization*). Wirth (2006: 31–2) claims that this phenomenon is more of an indication of implicit intermediality but is not an actual form of intermediality. We cannot but agree with Wirth's singling out of this mentioning of media (unlike in Wolf's system): our main argument is that merely mentioning another medium does not capture its properties, its 'mediality'. If a novel explores the actions of its characters, such as making telephone calls or painting a portrait, it can only have an impact at the story level; at the discursive level addressing such subject matter can at most act as a signal paving the way for further (inter) medial meaning-making.

In Wirth's notion of 'grafted medium', the 'rootstock medium' is affected by the function of the old medium and thus redefined; this is not just the resulting product of intermedial relationships but is also a process that he calls *transmedial transition* (2006: 33). Wirth claims that this form of intermediality opens the way to *transmediality*, which he refers to as the main new paradigm of media relations. Therefore, he uses an umbrella term that Wolf and Rajewsky employ to refer only to a limited set of phenomena.

Searching for an umbrella term

Irina O. Rajewsky (2002) coined *intermediality* as an umbrella term for several phenomena at a time when the meaning of this term was a topic of debate (e.g. Ochsner and Grivel 2001: 4; Gumbrecht 2003; Helbig 2008), in which other competing terms also appeared. To understand this matter, we need to return to the past once again, first to the neo-avant-garde art of the 1960s: Fluxus, happening, experimental computer art and so forth. American Fluxus artist Dick Higgins (1984:18) used the term *intermedium* in his seminal essay on just that topic. In the oft-cited first sentence of this manifesto he expresses his belief that 'much of the best work being produced today seems to fall between media'. About twenty years later he would add that he was introduced to the term *intermedium* by Romantic poet Samuel Taylor Coleridge, who used it as far back as in 1812 (1984: 23). Coleridge, however, was not writing about media or the concept of art, but about allegory; the poet used this unusual term to refer to a mediator 'between person and personification' (J. E. Müller 1998: 33). Higgins, however, wanted to create a name for a new type of art, one that was a response to the emergence of various new media and mass-produced culture. Higgins's own art, based in happenings and performance, relied on a method that in intermedial terms we could call *media fusion*. In the 1980s Higgins tried to draw a line between intermedia and mixed media: traditional *mixed media* include more than one medium (opera or 'paintings which incorporate poems within their visual fields', Higgins 1984: 24); the individual forms they contain are not indelibly connected, but they function side by side and the recipient can tell them apart. As Wolf (1999: 40, 50) might say, they are 'discernible on the surface of the work'. According to Higgins, *intermedia* are hybrids of different artistic forms or media whose conceptual *fusion* gives birth to something new, such as visual poetry, concrete poetry or performance art (on Czech experimental poetry, see Section 4 of Chapter 6, pp. 206–22).

In the 1990s, the term *fusion* was adopted by Clüver and other scholars who incorporated Higgins's concept into the model of intermediality. They distinguish traces of the media process contained in a work based on a scale ranging from 'mere' juxtaposition (multimedia discourse: e.g. an illustrated book), through combination (mixed-media discourse: e.g. a poster) to a fusion of the arts or media involved (intermedial discourse: e.g. concrete poetry, calligrams; Vos 1997; Clüver 2007: 34; see Table 11.1).

Besides the 'literature-centred' understanding of intermediality, an approach more closely related to media studies, was also taking shape. Scholars practising this approach follow Higgins in their understanding of media fusion (and the fusion of art forms) as the main theme of intermediality. Müller, for example, writes that 'a media product [. . .] becomes intermedial when it transforms the *multimedial juxtaposition of media citations into conceptual co-existence*, whose (aesthetic) refraction and deformation open new dimensions of experience' (1998: 31–2; emphasis added). Yvonne Spielmann also delineates multimedia as the 'simultaneous occurrence of different art forms in an integral medium, as in theatre, opera, or film' (2000: 61). She claims that intermediality emerges from the intersection and *transformation* of the expressive forms specific to individual media.

Media theorist Jens Schröter (1998; 2008) takes a position that is somewhere in between these approaches. He uses *intermediality* as an umbrella term, distinguishing between *synthetic* intermediality (a fusion of various media into a super-medium, inspired by the Wagnerian concept of *Gesamtkunstwerk* and Higgins's intermedium), *transmedial* intermediality ('structures' or 'forms' not specific to individual media, e.g. narrative construction, as well as seriality, fictionality, etc.) and *transformational/ ontological* intermediality (the representation of one medium through another medium – this concept draws from the 1980s theory of representation and the concept of *re-representation*, i.e. it is built on similar foundations as Mitchell's ideas, as we examined). Schröter, however, does not come to these categories by observing concrete intermedial phenomena, but mainly through studying different concepts of intermediality. His conclusions are partly comparable with Wolf's and Rajewsky's categories: multimediality, transmediality and intermedial reference (cf. Schröter 2008: 585–90).

From the start of the new millennium onwards, we also find concepts that derive the differences between intermediality, multimediality and transmediality from developments in media technology, for example, in the work of media theorist Gundolf Freyermuth. He defines intermediality as 'the mutual relationship between media, which is the aesthetic consequence of materially separated storage by mechanical means', whereas multimedia is 'the aesthetic consequence of automated re-production through industrial means' in the time of analogue media, and finally, he defines transmediality as 'the integration of media, which is the aesthetic consequence of software realization, virtualization' (Freyermuth 2007: 8). Even though in the broader social discussion about culture multimediality is generally connected with digital technology, this understanding is barely present in the academic debate about intermediality. The reason is the field's association with tradition and efforts not to shut out from interpretation artefacts created before the digital era and those that are still created independently outside the sphere of digital technology.

McLuhanesque media theory, unlike the theory of intermediality, is not overly interested in the relationships between media. In this approach, media are classified mainly based on their *effects on the recipient*; a (concrete) *medium* takes the place of, or rather is put in the place of, *representation*. Various concepts of mediality arise out of the different focuses, and indeed, the different natures of research disciplines: while intermedial studies is more of an idiographic discipline, media and social systems theory is nomothetic. Social systems theory works with the basic concept of 'symbolically generalized communication media', defining them only for the individual functional systems of social communication (Luhmann 1997: 203–4; see also Chapter 9, pp. 307–10). Luhmann's concept of the *medium of the work of art* (see Section 2 of Chapter 9, pp. 310–19) is the most directly applicable to literature. Other theories work with the term *artefact* or *autonomous entity*.

Niklas Luhmann and his successors in social systems theory, Niels Werber and Gerhard Plumpe (1993: 38–40), suggest the concept of *medium of the artwork* as the framework in which the status of an art is negotiated. Social systems theory prioritizes the social function and how 'successful' a medium is at communicating. This concept of the media of artwork brings the understanding of art as media closer to Foucault's concept of discourse (1971) or Bourdieu's theory of the field of cultural production (1992) rather than to intermedial relations.

The fact that for Werber and Plumpe mediality is of a completely different nature is revealed in their comments on the evolution of the (social) *system of literature*: at a certain phase, literature exhausted its capacity for representation and began to shift towards a preference for self-reference and absolute aestheticism, and in this process transformed itself into a *medium for forms*. When these scholars claim that the ability to project what is clearly 'non-art' or 'anti-art' into the general framework of the *medium of the work of art* demonstrates that the system of literature is exhausted, they are essentially declaring the end of art. This view reveals their incomprehension of art's transformative potential, and it thus proves unfruitful for intermediality.

Stimuli and competition: Narratology, transmedia storytelling and adaptation studies

Narrative theory gradually became one of the stimuli contributing to the further growth of intermedial studies. While in the second half of the 1990s the methods and concepts of narrative theory played virtually no role in intermedial theory or in interpretations of cultural artefacts (cf. Wagner

1996; J. E. Müller 1996; 1998; Helbig 1998), the situation changed at the turn of the millennium. It is evident that Paech (1998) had come into contact with narratology while Wolf's narrative studies preceded and intermingled with intermedial studies (2000b). Also, several scholars in ekphrasis studies applied narratological analysis: Tamar Yacobi (1995) focused on the occurrence of ekphrasis in prose using narratological analysis. She was followed by Gabriele Rippl (2005), who wrote a monograph on ekphrasis in Anglo-American literature, and Laura M. Sager Eidt (2008), who studied film and tried to create a system that would be applicable to all types of media (poetry, novels, drama, film).

Post-classical narratology also includes research on media, an issue that classical narratology had already proclaimed interest in to confirm the universality of the story, but which generally remained unaddressed. In the same year, 2002, when at the very least three influential systematic intermedial studies were published (Lund; Wolf; Rajewsky), narratologists Ansgar and Vera Nünning edited a volume reflecting narrative from interdisciplinary perspectives including the intermedial one (cf. Wolf 2002b).

In the 1960s structural narratologists were already talking about the story as a structure independent of any medium of representation. According to Claude Bremond, there is a

> layer of autonomous significance, endowed with a structure that can be isolated from the whole of the message: the story (*récit*). So any sort of narrative message [. . .], regardless of the process of expression which it uses, manifests the same level in the same way. It is only independent of the techniques that bear it along. It may be transposed from one to another medium without losing its essential properties: the subject of a story may serve as argument for a ballet, that of a novel can be transposed to stage or screen, one can recount in words a film to someone who has not seen it. (cited in Chatman 1978: 20)

This example is a small demonstration of the hibernation that the term *medium* went through: narratologist Seymour Chatman added the word *medium* (without indicating he had done so) to his translation of this citation from Bremond's 1964 article. It is in Chatman's work that we find the first faint traces of intermedial thinking, evidently limited, however, by the current dominance of the concept of *text*. This can be seen, for example, in Chatman's (1978: 34) analysis, or we could call it 'reading', of a painting representing different stages in the story of Salome: he does not consider the compositional demands of visual representation or the way depicting certain subjects has changed throughout history. Chatman (1990) focused his attention on medial transposition of literary narrative, a film adaptation; however, narratology would only begin to study the story as a transmedial structure systematically as late as in its post-classical phase in the 1990s.

Media-sensitive narratology was forming essentially in parallel to intermedial studies and began to specialize on subjects where the interests of intermedial theory, narratology, possible worlds theory, new media theory, interactivity and even cognitive science intersected. Narratology gradually freed itself from investigating the verbal narrative, considered to be the default medium and therefore the most thoroughly studied, and overcame the hurdle that Liv Hausken (2004: 392) calls 'medium blindness', that is, the constraints arising from fixating on the text as the dominant narrative structure. Sometimes narratological research on intermedial relations would do with commenting on intermedial terms (cf. Grishakova and Ryan 2010), some scholars tended to work out their own theory of intermediality, replacing the initial concept of 'narrative across media' (Ryan 2004) by transmedia storytelling or even transmedia narratology.

The boom in digital media and their broader application in cultural representation, and also in the media industry, has intensified the migration of themes, characters and subject matter across media; this trend ballooned as a result of the *branding* of characters and the real places associated with fictional plots and their further *franchising* (or *repurposing* in Bolter and Grusin's terminology, 1999). Henry Jenkins refers to this as *transmedia storytelling* and to the current state of culture as *convergence culture* (the title of his 2006 book). Jenkins uses the term *convergence* to describe the flow of content between different media platforms that adapt to each other and are also adapted by audiences, which cease to consist of passive consumers and actively contribute to circulating content and optimizing these platforms (*participatory culture*). The evolution of media has led to the transformation of culture and influences not only how we perceive things but also how we think and live our everyday lives.

According to Marie-Laure Ryan, Jenkins's term *transmedia storytelling* captures well the media plurality of narratives related to the same fictional world; she refers to transmediations of the same story as *narrative proliferation* (2016: 12). Ryan explores these phenomena in an examination of the film adaptation of David Mitchell's novel *Cloud Atlas* (2004; film 2012, dir. Tom Tykwer and Lana Wachowski) and uses it to demonstrate the difference between understanding a fictional world as a cognitive and ontological concept. Considering that the relationship between the novel and film has been explored elsewhere in this book from the perspective of the evolutionary relationship between media and the concept of intermedial (literary) genres as *media forms* (see Chapter 9, pp. 321–2), we would like to add an intermedial interpretation. The reader of the novel receives many clues indicating that, with one exception, the numerous stories contained in the book are about one world, but take place in different times. The reader first recognizes individual ways of verbally presenting experience, or rather individual genres of literary narrative (the memoir, the novel), based on her 'readerly' memory in which typical structures are stored as cognitive frameworks that can be applied. By tapping into these frameworks, the reader can realize that the fourth story reveals the third to be written in the style of a novel – and thus is able to distinguish its unique storyworld from the storyworlds of the other stories. When the character from this inserted story meets a character from the main storyworld, two ontological spheres intersect and narrative *metalepsis* occurs. The chapters in the book are sequenced following a certain pattern, which, once detected, leads the reader to putting the stories together and revealing their shared (unsurprising) meaning: 'everything is connected to everything else'. In the film adaptation, the signals indicating connections between stories are too weak to overpower the changing sequence of individual stories that lacks any obvious organizing principle and makes it difficult for the viewer to find coherence. Familiarity with the source medium, however, is not necessary for understanding the film: recall that even the 'literature-centred' intermedialist Wolf (2002a) fully legitimizes film adaptations as autonomous works. The medium of film, or digital film here, makes full use of its technological potential, from manifestation to self-reference (*media foregrounding* in intermedial terms). The film's intoxicating visuality and the distinctive way of life of the characters in each story make the viewer inclined to projecting an autonomous storyworld for each story – even though the conditions present in what are assumed to be different worlds are not mutually exclusive and the narrative provides hints to their temporal continuity. In other words, the dominant representation of the storyworld and how it works relegates the viewer's cognitive process of understanding to the background. Ryan (2016: 23) presents *Cloud Atlas* as an illustrative example of a *world-centred narrative*. Such narratives (e.g. in fantasy, sci-fi), thanks to their variety of populations and the diversity of their worlds, can attract the recipient's attention even when using an unoriginal story (or idea, e.g. that everything is connected with everything else). Ryan places at the other end of the spectrum narrative genres that can 'make do' with minimalist world building (tragedies, jokes). We should add that *Cloud Atlas* is also an illustrative example of *transmedia storytelling*, in which a substantial *change in controlling the recipient's understanding* occurs as a result of *media transformation*. Digital film's media potential increases the attractiveness of the storyworld(s), but at the same time it also detracts from the story's *tellability* – the same devices (digital visualization, editing, partly using sci-fi variations on 'post-something' stories) lead to the fragmentation of narrative and thus reduce the work's 'readability'. The disparate genres contained in Mitchell's literary version are unified by the narrative transmission of experience. Although this narrative uses strategies of defamiliarization, it still provides a compositional legend for achieving *narrative coherence*.

While transmedia storytelling has a good relationship with intermediality, its relationship with adaptation studies is much tenser. The latter has always somewhat resisted proclaiming an affinity with intermedial studies, not to mention Elleström's efforts (2017) to integrate the two approaches – at first, out of fear that intermediality in its initial literature-centred form would contribute to the idea that a source literary text would always be superior to any film adaptation, thus weakening the adaptation's autonomy, and later out of fear that adaptation studies would be classified as a sub-discipline of intermedial studies. Indeed, Elleström (2017) even proposes this idea, whereas adaptation studies scholar Sarah Cardwell (2018) suggests understanding adaptation as a specific form of intertextuality because intertextuality is a necessary condition for adaptation, although not a sufficient one. Also important is that adaptation studies, unlike intermedial studies, studied popular culture social contexts as an important factor in analysing adaptations long before intermedial studies did the same (Dudley 1980, Cartmell et al. 1996, Murray 2012).

The bone of contention, however, is the issue of media specificity, which, together with the transmediation capacity (which we could call *transmediability*; see below) that is derived from it, remains important for intermedialists, who do not lose sight of 'old' media. Proponents of media fusion object to such notions as they believe that it is now impossible to distinguish between the uses of different media. Likewise, the question of media specificity has lost meaning for adaptation studies scholars (cf. Cardwell 2018). To explain why this gap in the otherwise shared interests between these fields cannot be bridged, let us turn to Rajewsky (2010), who admits that the point of performance art and installations, whose effects are created in the process of interaction between media components, is not to rigidly 'construct' borders between media. She does reiterate, however, that the recipient's awareness of distinctive media, which provides him or her with a *frame of understanding*, is required for media configurations to work. This cognitive framework is also applied when people perceive medially homogeneous artefacts, which use their own devices to convincingly evoke in the recipient an experience with another medium and give the illusion that he or she is observing a different kind of media product (e.g. a photorealistic painting evokes an impression of 'quasiphotography'). Although identifying media may seem to indicate conservative ontological essentialism, according to Rajewsky, this is a requirement for observing creative processes that do not result in 'boundaries' but in interesting transitional zones.

Elleström's reconciliatory proposal (2017) that an area of shared interest between intermedial and adaptation studies could be research on *the mechanisms of media transformation* is grounded in the idea that both methodologies have a comparable thought process. This assumption may apply to some theorists of film adaptation from the 1990s, when adaptation studies continued soaking up ideas from literary criticism and narratology. For example, Brian McFarlane (1996: 13) distinguishes between *transfer* and *adaptation proper*: 'Transfer is the process whereby certain narrative elements of novels are revealed as amenable to display in film', whereas adaptation is a 'process by which other novelistic elements must find quite different equivalences in the film medium, when such equivalence are sought or are available at all'. For McFarlane, transfer is about structures that are essentially *transmedial*, whereas adaptation proper explains the necessity of replacing elements tied to the source semiotic system by choosing other ones available in the post-medium.

In other words, employing Elleström's suggestion is plausible as long as adaptation is still understood as a transformation process (e.g. Voigts-Virchow 2009). Any such efforts, however, are pointless if adaptation studies wants to view adaptations exclusively as original, independent works and sees no need to examine the pre-text. Recently, some scholars in adaptation studies suggested to give up on defining what *adaptation* means at all (cf. Leitch 2017); others focus on the ideological and economic conditions of artistic production under which film is made.

After intermedial studies was established as a discipline at the beginning of the millennium, scholars tried to open it up to other research currents, such as adaptation studies and narratology. In the book *Changing Borders*, the editors express their conviction that intermedial studies has already become 'the discipline underlying any conceivable study of cultural artefacts' and can therefore fill the anachronistic gap between disciplines (Arvidson et al. 2007: 14). This universalist methodological claim may remind us of the one made by narratologists who proposed structuralist narratology as a humanities super-discipline in the 1960s. The advantage of narratology was that it related to (seemingly) clear generic objects of study, the *story* and the *narrative discourse*, from the very beginning; the discipline also managed to recast the universalist claim into 'post-classical' methodological plurality in the 1990s. Due to the genealogic evolution of intermedial studies, which encompassed many attitudes and interests during its long prehistory, proto-history and history, the phenomena of *mediation* (inherent not only in narration but in cultural communication in general) and the fundamental notion of *medium* were able to manifest themselves as late as in the period of the established discipline. Nevertheless, it is exactly the process of mediation that calls for interdisciplinary cooperation (cf. Johansson 2021).

Finally, a definition of *medium*: The concept of modality

A definition of *medium* long remained a blind spot in intermedial modes of thinking. This is evidently a result of the various conceptualizations of 'medium': some include forms that were traditionally referred to as kinds of art, whereas others also include representation techniques (cf. Elleström 2014: 2). Although some prominent intermedial theorists were aware of this shortcoming and called attention to why defining *medium* was so difficult or what criteria need to be taken into account (e.g. Paech 1998: 23–5), they did not offer a definition of their own or they suggested a preliminary one (cf. Wolf 2002a). We see two reasons that defining *medium* was put off for so long. The first lies in the long (pre)history of intermedial studies focused on examining the relationships between arts, whose properties are considered self-evident. This may be why scholars interested in the relationships between arts neglected shifts that were occurring in other disciplines, such as aesthetics, art history and sociology, where the concept of art was being redefined following its modes of institutionalization (cf. Danto 1964; Dickie 1974); later on, ideas such as Bourdieu's (1992) concept of social field, in which the position of art has to be negotiated, were taken into account by intermedialists. The second reason for the delayed definition lies in the initial focus on refining typology and terms to cover the broad spectrum of intermedial relations. In an attempt to remedy this situation, Lars Elleström (2010, 2021a) offered and later revised a tool for describing and comparing different media in his system of *modalities*, which he presents as a platform for sharing in a broad spectrum of media research.

The idea of modalities or the application of certain criteria to determine a medium's constituent parts was not entirely new. W. J. T. Mitchell, for instance, primarily based his definition of *medium* on the criterion of sensorial perception. Media theorist Knut Hickethier, following McLuhan's definition of media (1964) as 'extensions of man', distinguishes between different media based on different criteria: based on the medium's function, the technology used, and the relationship between the medium and the meaning it mediates (for broader context on McLuhan, Luhmann and Kittler, see Chapter 1, pp. 19–20). Thus, Hickethier divides media into 'media of observation' (of general perception), which assist the human sense organs (e.g. the microscope, the megaphone); 'media of storage and processing' (writing, the film camera); and 'media of transmission', which enable 'the transport of information, news, content, etc'. There is also 'media of communication', which combine the basic forms and enable the functional structuring of interpersonal communication (cf. Hickethier 2003: 21–2). Although including this level of communication identifies mediality as a capacity resulting from the cultural use of a medium, the mediality of 'old media' or art remains elusive here.

Elleström (2010) considers Wolf's defining of media (2002a) based on a semiotic system to be limiting because this approach cannot capture the material aspect of a medium or how it is perceived. Elleström, working with the assumption that every medium is created by a certain complex of basic properties and is intermedial in the sense that it is *evident and explainable in relation to other types of media*, defines general criteria that can help determine the constitutive traits of media and which at the same time create the preconditions for communication and cooperation between different media. He identified these traits shared by all media as *media modalities*: Identifying *material modality* means describing what the products of a given medium are created from (e.g. the spoken word and music share as their material modality sound waves carried by air). *Sensorial modality* is the sum of the ways the products of a given medium can be perceived, that is, it describes with which sense or combination of senses we receive them (e.g. we perceive the printed word and paintings with sight). *Spatiotemporal modality* reveals how the products of a given medium are realized in time and space (e.g. dance and film in an inevitably coherent temporal sequence). Finally, *semiotic modality* determines which sign system is dominant in or typical of the products of a given medium, and allows us to describe the interplay of signs that take relations of indexical, iconical and symbolic nature in various mediation practices such as education (the prominent iconicity of illustrations in a children's encyclopaedia) or instruction for use (the icons on a computer's desktop meant to facilitate its use in referencing a set of items formerly used for non-digital office work; currently, these icons may rather be seen as symbolic).

Individual *basic* media are determined by the constellation of these four modalities. Let us illustrate the constellation of modalities in print: two-dimensionality, the flatness of the material base of sensorially perceptible configurations of linearly arranged signs, the semiotic system is language as a system of symbolic signs. The printed text shares flatness and two-dimensionality as a manifestation of material modality with painting; the printed text, however, must be perceived continually over time, similarly to the song. Such distinction makes it possible to separate the inherent properties of a media product (e.g. a verbal narrative imitating the techniques of visual media, such as imitating camera motion in representing the space of the storyworld) from the effects resulting from the reception process (mental visualization).

Whereas in other systems we saw technology as a criterion, Elleström (2010: 32) does not include it in his modalities and, besides basic media, defines *technical media* as devices that display and distribute the products of individual media. He calls the relationship between basic and technical media *mediation*.

The last component of Elleström's system includes a diachronic dimension and implies a social dimension: in developing both their communicative and social functions, individual basic media gradually 'qualified' for a certain status under certain historical, cultural and technological circumstances. For instance, they acquired the status of a kind of art (with the domination of the aesthetic function) or that of a form of mass media (with the dominance of rapid and widespread distribution of information, as in the case of television). Elleström (2010: 17–24) therefore calls historically and culturally grounded, institutionalized media with a relatively fixed structure of functions *qualified media*.

Specifying modalities provides tools for identifying and comparing the properties of media and is one of the substantial advantages of intermedial studies: Elleström does not say what a medium is per se, but he does say how to determine if *something is a medium*. In doing so he also facilitates describing how a particular set of modalities 'qualifies' in an individual socio-historical context. [10]

Some authors address the issue of socio-historical context in suggesting the addition of social modality to Elleström's concept, for example Kay O'Halloran (2022), a digital media specialist. She argues that even sensory input from the environment is conditioned by social factors, culture, beliefs and values, and is thus filtered. In doing so, she also questions the capability of the modality system to grasp the changes occurring as a result of digital media technologies and their impact on social structures and the human condition in general. Here, we might object that although the social aspect of how media work is indeed undeniably crucial, we can only analyse it when we are studying a concrete media product or the mutual relationships between concrete media that are historically and culturally grounded, as well as anchored in *qualified media*. Only then can the social norms that exercise influence upon the creation of the media product be identified. In other words, social modality is difficult to grasp as a general quality. The other modalities (i.e. those identified by Elleström) defining *basic media* are much easier to describe and some – at least for the time being – are nearly invariable (e.g. sensorial modality).

A certain set of social norms undoubtedly underpin social modality, but determining factors include not just a change in these norms but also the current political situation. Sometimes, it could be what we might call collective experience and the resulting 'emotional atmosphere'. We can illustrate this through an analysis of social factors associated with the installation of several replicas of a memorial to the victims of the Utøya island massacre installed in various Norwegian communities and locations (Maagerø and Veum 2019). The prototype monument itself as a 'memorial of a national trauma' is an object of the complex intermedial process of meaning-making (a stone, manifestly spatial, hollow object with symbolic shapes has on one side the date of the event and on the other, a literary text). More than the design of the monument itself, it was the selected locations and the symbolic spatial relations associated with them that provoked debate in the affected communities. Thus, the authors of the study focus greater attention on the semiosis of the 'work in the process of installation' than on an analysis of the artefact and its modal components. They apply an alternative, in some aspects similar, methodology of *multimodality*. Like intermedial studies, this field has an evolutionary connection with semiotics, but its focus is on the social context of meaning-making. Thus, it is worth comparing the two methodologies to understand the potential of the social modality suggested to complete Ellestrom's system. The comparison also makes it easier to outline the prospects of intermedial studies.

4. The identity of research: Flexibility and continuity

Parallel disciplines: Intermediality and multimodality

From Ellestrom's perspective, *multimodality* may be considered an inevitable property of every medium: in his system, a *basic medium* comprises a constellation of modalities as its constitutive features. In multimodality studies, however, the term has a different meaning.

Despite the shared semiotic foundation of both disciplines, multimodality studies draw from a different line of research; it is much younger than that of intermedial studies and is related to functional linguistics. Multimedia studies' theoretical basis is the '*social semiotic theory* of language and communication based on the idea of choices between available options' (Ledin and Machin 2020/2007; emphasis added), which is derived from the theory of linguist Michael A. K. Halliday (1978). If we claim that the theory of intermediality is underpinned by the theory of intertextuality, likewise we can say that the idea of multimodality is based on the transfer or expansion of the concept of *language* and *grammar* to other domains, such as advertising, television or design (O'Halloran and Smith 2011: 3). From linguistics and verbal communication (or from literature in the case of Paul J. Thibault 1991), in the 1990s the field of semiotic research began to expand to address the practices and contexts of cultural communication, especially in the work of Gunther Kress and Theo van Leeuwen. At first, based on a critical analysis of Barthes's visual semiotics (1957, 1977, 1981/1980), they focused in particular on visual representation (Kress and van Leeuwen 1996; O'Toole 1994), and gradually they began to study other areas such as advertising (van Leeuwen and Jewitt 2001) and digital media and its application in the educational process and in developing creativity (Kress 2005). According to these scholars, multimodality can be found in 'any text whose meanings are realized through more than one semiotic code' (Kress and van Leeuwen 1996: 177). Thus, this viewpoint entered the cultural studies discourse at roughly the same time as Mitchell's (1994) thesis that 'all media are mixed media'. Obviously, linguists Kress and van Leuwen share a semiotics background with literary critic Wolf; despite the common starting point and the affinity of their subjects, that is, the mixed nature of cultural representations, the multimodalists extended the scope of enquiry by taking into account further agents of the process of meaning-making and mediation, for example communication practices in various structures of power and communities.

The dialogue between intermediality and multimodality scholars has seemed limited until recently. Intermedialists refer to the multimodal research of visual representation, whereas multimodalists (e.g. Bateman, Wildfeuer and Hiippala 2017) touch upon Elleström's concept of modalities. Elleström (2021a: 41–2) appreciates the pragmatic advantages of the multimodal approach yet finds that multimodal studies seems to circumscribe rather than define its key categories and suggests a systematic (possibly comparative) analysis of the methodology.

What obstacles have thus far prevented the two disciplines from growing closer?[11] The first difference stems from history: both methodologies were developed in the 1990s, and for scholars in both fields it was critical that they build an identity and make a name for their discipline. In this regard, Joachim Paech (1998: 14) aptly speaks about intermedial research as 'a marketplace for connecting aging humanities', which were beginning to be frightened by their isolation and were trying to keep up with the times, whether by gaining control of 'the broad field of intermediality' (Wolf 2002a), expanding their scope of subjects to cover popular culture or adopting paradigms from other disciplines. The adoption of other paradigms often leads not only to desirable innovations in method and the interdisciplinarization of research but also to a paradoxical result, to the establishment of further, often overlapping disciplines. In a certain sense this applies also to intermediality and multimodal studies.

Whereas intermediality's identity is built to a large extent on its genealogical lineage, which we have described here, multimodality tries to capitalize on its relative 'methodological youth' and presents itself as a discipline that views cultural representations as social phenomena and that flexibly responds to their changes. O'Halloran and Smith (2011: 1) see as a challenge for the field 'sophisticated multimodal practices within interactive digital media'. In fact, all disciplines related to cultural studies view the digital sphere, which is gradually consuming all forms of representation and communication, as a perspective field of study. Whereas intermedial studies has always exhibited its methodological ambitions and also inheres the intermedial observation of phenomena that may seem medially homogenous at first sight (cf. also Bruhn's intermedial reading of narrative literature, 2016), multimodal studies often presents itself as a field of interdisciplinary collaboration based on shared interests. Jewitt (2009: 54) argues that 'multimodality [. . .] refers to a field of application rather than a theory' (cf. also Kress 2009, O'Halloran and Smith 2011). Multimodalists enquire into advertising, interior decorating, social networks, communication in the classroom and so forth (cf. O'Halloran and Smith 2011); that is, they tend to focus on configurations of signs and discourses in which the aesthetic function is secondary or auxiliary. Yet they also pay attention to 'multimodality and aesthetics' (Tønessen and Forsgren 2019) in analyses of artistic creations that in particular alter and develop the relationship between *public space* and *cultural communication*. The alternative approach to the same issue in intermedial studies differs in the fact that it remains acceptable – although no longer typical – to bracket the physical and social context and to deal with an artistic representation's semantic structure or to observe similar media products in synchronic or diachronic perspective.

In fact, cooperation between related concepts such as intermediality and multimodality may facilitate the study of the complex nature of representation in today's digital world and the specific phenomena that occur not only as a result of the development of technology and software but also under the influence of radically changing societal needs, attitudes and values. For example, digital deepfake technology that may be useful in entertainment and education has become a tool of 'alternative truth' in the political arena, especially during election season. The 'emergency' replacement of in-person debates with online conferences and the substitution of classroom learning with virtual education during the Covid-19 pandemic have been established as the standard or preferred communication form in some contexts.

Cooperation between experts on digital technology, media studies and sociology will make studying these phenomena easier.

The approach of intermedial studies, interconnected with cultural tradition by the field's own history, provides a safe background for explaining phenomena such as the medial transformation of artistic forms, which presuppose contact between the public and the performance space or the place where artefacts are presented (theatres, galleries), into virtual remote forms, as occurred during the pandemic from 2019 to 2021. The complete lockdown led to the further proliferation of digital forms for representing traditional art, whether at the level of mere remediation or through complex transmediation. One of the strategies for compensating for the forced distance between recipients and art was to encourage people to be creative at home. For example, in the Getty Museum Challenge people were asked to materially imitate or physically recreate famous paintings at home (cf. Waldorf and Stephan 2020). How exactly we approach these creations depends on the point of view we choose (let us recall that already in the early days of intermedial studies Wolf drew attention to the flexible application of the method; 2002a: 166). If the Getty Museum Challenge interests us as a kind of advertisement for classical art, then we will take a medial-rhetorical approach. However, if we are interested in comparing such creations as manifestations of the attitudes of non-experts towards 'high' art, then social semiotics would be the optimal tool. If we want to examine how these amateur artists relate to the material nature of the originals through the material and structuring of their artefacts and to what extent they relate to the historical meanings of the work and its current reception, then both discussed methodologies could compete. Both intermedial and multimodal studies absorbed theories of representation and meaning-making as reflected in various disciplines (Panofsky 1955, Goodman 1968, Barthes 1957, 1977, 1981/1980). Intermedial studies, however, has an advantage: its elaborate descriptive system of classification enables the distinction in inter- and intramedial relations between different levels of transformation, imitation or 're-creation' of the media pre-product or the medium itself. The subtle system of classification not only facilitates analyses but also makes it possible to introduce a typology of similar intermedial phenomena.

Moreover, some of the differences between the two disciplines have already faded or are slowly fading away due to internal methodological changes or external ones, such as the growing permeability of the artistic and non-artistic spheres, and the convergence of 'old' and 'new' media. There seems to be one persisting difference: a media product arising out of the transformation of a pre-product (*transmediation*) does not interest multimodalists, at least not as a primary subject of analysis. On the contrary, it has become one of the crucial phenomena investigated in intermedial studies. Lars Ellestrōm (2014) has even suggested that transmediation could become a central concept in theories of media relations.

A concept as an argument: Media transformation

We can analyse Ellestrōm's choice of transmediation and media representation as basic concepts from two perspectives. From the perspective of the previous history of intermedial thinking, this step seems like a change in the main focus of study, that is, a shift from the relationships between media observed as *states* of media products towards the processes of *media transformation* (Ellestrōm 2014: 11–35). The second possible perspective is to focus on the *essence of mediality*. It can be understood as the capacity of medium to create and distribute meaning as well as its inevitable 'relatedness' to other media. Let us recall that for Mitchell, mediality lies in the heterogeneity of all media. For Ellestrōm it is the ability of media to transfer among themselves structured contents, a capacity we might call *transmediability*. Ellestrōm's starting point is similar to Mitchell's main thesis: Ellestrōm claims that 'all media are multimodal and intermedial in the sense that they are composed of multiple basic features and are understood only in relation to other types of media' (Ellestrōm 2014: 2). He presents the following argument in favour of taking a genetic approach to research and thus of prioritizing transmediation: 'mediality is the key to understanding how meaning is created in human interaction and that basic research in the area of media transformation [...] is vital for further progress in *understanding communication in general*' (Ellestrōm 2014: 1; emphasis added). His goal is to create a conceptual framework for a series of thus far unduly separated areas of investigation that may facilitate a detailed analysis of transfers of media characteristics. Ellestrōm generalizes *media characteristics* as medially distinctively structured semantic wholes of various extents. In doing so, he tries to avoid the idea that media are 'containers' that hold and, thus, form certain contents. Unlike other systems (especially Wolf's, which he explicitly addresses), Ellestrōm includes both transmediation and media representation as types of media transformations. In generalizing these processes, Ellestrōm applies Peirce's sign theory: when something represents, it makes something else – the represented – present in the mind of the recipient (in intermedial terms, a medium, which is something that represents, becomes itself represented). Transmediation is explained in the following terms: 'the representamen of the target medium conjures up in the mind of the perceiver both the representamen and the object of the source medium' (Ellestrōm 2014: 17). Or, in other words, if certain *sensory configurations* mediated by a technical

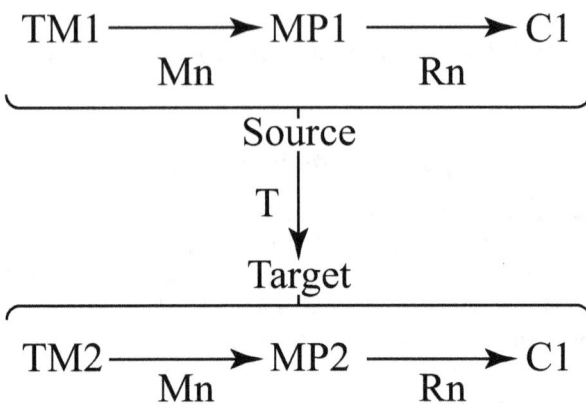

Diagram 11.2 Lars Elleström's model of transmediation. *Source:* Elleström 2014: 55. TM1 = technical medium, MP1 = media product, C1 = represented compound media characteristics, TM2 = a new technical medium, MP2 = a new media product, Mn = mediation, Rn = representation, T = transfer

medium are capable of introducing a representation equivalent to the configuration performed in another media previously, it means that they are *transmediated* (Diagram 11.2).

Though Elleström wished to avoid (mis)understanding medium as a 'container', it is not easy to avoid the pitfalls that may lie in describing the complex process of mediation. Elleström defines mediation as a material process through which a technical medium, as a material vehicle and means of distribution, facilitates *pre-semiotic sensory configurations* (Elleström 2014: 14): for example, a printed page in a book can possess visual configurations that the reader can recognize as a poem or diagram. However, separating out this 'pre-semiotic' component is artificial because it would – if only in a generative model – temporarily deny the semiotic nature of the media product. (In 2010, Elleström called the relationship between technical and basic media *mediation without significance*.)

Elleström illustrates transmediation using a fictional account of a film scene that recreates an image from an existing painting in which a man is picking red flowers. A film scene can be a mere transmediation of the content of the media pre-product (a scene, an event): this means that the media-non-specific traits of the media characteristics (such as composition and colour scheme in Elleström's example, cf. 2014: 25–6) that the film scene shares with the painting are transmediated. Logically then, the intermedial relationships can only be recognized by a film viewer who associates the scene with a specific famous painting (to name an example, *The Cook, the Thief, His Wife & Her Lover*, dir. Peter Greenaway, 1989). If, however, media-specific characteristics are transmediated, such as brushwork with the help of a digital filter (*Loving Vincent*, dir. Dorota Kobiela and Hugh Welchman, 2017) or the composition of the figures in the painting and the lighting of the scenes (e.g. in Greenaway's film *Nightwatching*, 2007), the film scenes elicit associations of individual paintings, and thus we have a clear case of *media representation*. Elleström himself acknowledges that transmediation always actually includes some amount of media representation. On the other hand, it could be argued that what Rajewsky (2002) called *media reference* through *the imitation of the source medium's method* is actually a certain degree of media representation. Thus, the two systems may be considered complementary: a detailed classification of intermedial relationships based on their differences (Wolf, Rajewsky), which facilitates a cultural and/or historical typology, and a general scheme of processes of representation and transmediation that facilitates the explication of how they work together in any media product.

The simple transmediation of qualified media corresponds with the transfer of the simple contents of one medium to another. (Again, we encounter the problem of content and form that Elleström wished to avoid.) As an example of simple transmediation Ellström (2014: 22) presents the transfer of a story 'about a lucky person who turns unlucky'. Nevertheless, the presence of such a plot-pattern in an individual story allows us to assign it to a certain set of *media non-specific* entities and structures (often timeless themes and stories that migrate between cultures), which Rajewsky and Wolf subsume under the term *transmediality*. This means that it is usually impossible to discern the influence of a single, specific pre-product or pre-medium in a given media product (cf. Wolf 2002a: 170); various media representations of the same content simply coexist. This comparison provides another opportunity for 'methodological reconciliation': Ellström himself concedes that media characteristics might 'circulate among several qualified media' (2014: 23).

In contrast, the *complex transmediation of a qualified medium* assumes the transmediation of numerous aspects of the source medium into another medium or media product. Ellström, however, presents very different examples of this process. *Musicalized fiction* results from the verbal transmediation of media- and (genre-)typical rules for the construction of a musical work, but this relation becomes obvious only through a close reading by a recipient educated in music. Ellström's second example, an acrylic painting that imitates the properties of photography, however, displays its *resemblance* to the source media product, sometimes to such a degree that it could confuse the uninitiated viewer, like a modern *trompe l'oeil*, whether being viewed in situ or in reproduced form (i.e. in *remediated* form). An institutional context (i.e. an exhibition of a painter's work in a gallery) can usually prevent such misunderstanding. From the perspective of classifying inter- and transmedial phenomena, however, we get no clues for how to safely tell such transmediation apart from a *representation* of the source medium. During the process of reception something occurs that we could call 'manifest mediality', both of the producing (painting) and transmediated medium (photography). Elleström's semiotic explication still applies here: the representamen of transmediation conjures up in the mind of the recipient basically *the same object* as the representamen of the source medium. We could observe this dual manifestation of medium in the behaviour of visitors (including ourselves) to a retrospective exhibition of Gerhard Richter's work (National Gallery Prague 2017): many of them evidently knew these paintings only from reproductions and went to the exhibition to experience a truly 'close' sensory encounter with the paintings as material artefacts and to observe the techniques used to create them.

Elleström concludes his study with a subtle analysis of the methods Czech surrealist filmmaker Jan Švankmajer used in animated shorts inspired by Bach's *Fantasy in G Minor*, Carrol's 'Jabberwocky' and Arcimboldo's paintings. He convincingly demonstrates the intermediality of Švankmajer's creations and the analytical potential of his own method, but he will hardly succeed in convincing film theorists to understand films as media transformations. Potential disagreement between Elleström and film or adaptation scholars can be illustrated by the film adaptation of Jane Austen's novel *Pride and Prejudice* (dir. Joe Wright, 2005): the methods used to compose scenes can be interpreted both as the spatial transmediations of the writer's verbal representation of the social hierarchy of early-nineteenth-century society and typical devices of *heritage cinema*, which relishes in showing Georgian architecture but also alludes to it, for example, in the visual compositions of interacting characters.

In foregrounding media transformation and creating models of transmediation and media representation, Elleström provided a methodological basis for and shifted the focus of intermedial research.

Processuality and materiality: Latency and presence once again

Elleström's prioritization of media transformation and thus of the processual nature of media relations bridged a major gap in intermedial studies. His predecessor Roberto Simanowski (2006) revised Wirth's (2006) model of *hard* intermediality, replacing the *combination* of differently configured sign systems with the concept of the *transformation* or *transfer* (*Übergang*) of such systems.

The breadth of scope here plays a principal role: Wirth's perspective remains semiotic while Simanowski adds the technological aspects of media. Thus, his definition of *medium* contains both a material and a technological level, forming the complex of sender – channel – receiver. Transmedial processes may occur both between different semiotic systems (from text into image, from image into text; for an example contained here, cf. the methods developed by Běla Kolářová or Jiří Kolář, as explained in Chapter 6, p. 210) and between different presentation technologies (Simanowski gives as an example the transformation of internet chatrooms into theatre performance in Tilman Sacks's 'chat theatre' concept). The accent here is not on the results of such combinations, that is, on a work itself, but on the *transfer*, which takes place at a specific *process of perception* (Simanowski 2006: 5). This is characteristic of a situation that usually does not arise in ordinary reception, or rather, that arises only in 'new' media (e.g. the transformation of digital data into another form of media – music, image or performance – into the currently fashionable form referred to as *mapping*, Simanowski 2006: 20–6). Thus, to identify ongoing transformations the source and target media must both be present. This fundamental distinction that Simanowski makes between intermedial and transmedial relationships essentially puts all the weight on *reception* as the recognition of transmediality, as opposed to searching for or applying transmedial strategies.

As much as Simanowski's concept introduces new accents into the debate, which should be further elaborated, from our genealogical perspective on intermediality, its weakness is the nearly exclusive focus on new media and new representation technologies. It primarily draws from Higgins's concept of intermedium, which is related to the displacement of 'old' media or at the very least weak interest in them. This is typical of discussions developing out of the positions of media studies.

The processual nature of media transformation has been a theme present in the intermedial discourse for quite some time – although partly latently. Interest in the process of a work's construction is encompassed in the concept of *intersemiotic transposition* (Clüver 1989). Also, we can trace the idea of 'transformation' in intermedial thinking all the way back to the concept of intertextuality, in the work of Julia Kristeva (1980/1967: 66), who wrote that 'any text is the *absorption and transformation* of another'. Following this, in the mid-1990s Yvonne Spielmann explicitly emphasized the processual nature of the *transformation* (*Übergang*; *passage* in Kristeva) of elements from one sign system to another (Spielmann 1995; 2004: 80). Spielmann then understands intermediality as a 'process of differentiation', and in doing so clearly distinguishes it from multimediality, which means the mixing (*Vermischung*; Spielmann 2004:: 60) of forms articulated by originally different media. Her concept, derived from the theory of intertextuality, intersects with Higgins's distinction between intermedium and mixed media. According to Spielmann, the transformation process takes place as a kind of interpretation of a work in a new context (*Aktualisierung*), and the space between the medium and its potential as a *symbolic form* she calls *intermediality* (1995: 113; in a reference to Erwin Panofsky's concept of 'symbolic form', Panofsky 1955). Spielmann (1995: 115) rejects the idea that intermediality emerged with the rise of new media or that new media somehow caused it to develop. The transformation process occurs not only in new media but also between 'old' media, and thus, according to Spielmann, intermediality has more of an effect on old media's form and materiality.

Materiality is another relatively new focus of intermedial studies. The impetus for introducing this topic came from the recent debate on the (cultural, social, experiential) impacts arising from the transition from analogue to digital media. These changes have also led to questioning the sustainability of intermedial categories in the digital age, and even the need to rethink the entire theory of intermediality (such ideas are largely contained in two edited volumes, Paech and Schrötter 2008 and Blättler 2010). *Virtualization*, and thus the 'dematerialization' of media forms in the digital age, is one of the focal points of this debate. This concept enables us to compare the current state of affairs with 'conventional' concepts of mediality, based on studying the relationships between existing analogue media, and their emphasis on meaning and media forms.

Jürgen E. Müller took an extreme position in this debate, convinced that intermedial processes are vanishing in the 'general virtuality of the material' (2010: 18). In contrast, other scholars posit that these processes will attract greater attention because in their transformed, virtual form they still remain effective. According to Jens Schröter (2008: 585), through conventional *representations* (*Vorstellungen*), which are combined with corresponding analogue media, media forms remain recognizable as 'clearly discernible effects in the multimedial surface layer' (cf. Wolf's '*Werkoberfläche*' and Elleström's critique of this concept mentioned earlier). To exemplify this point, Schröter notes that we still distinguish the 'material substrate' (media specificity) of film, sound and image tracks in different data formats (2008: 584, 587). Thus, this also marks a significant refocusing on the materiality of media. If we take Schröter's observations one step further, we realize that today we often observe intermedial effects in digital media and through such mediation we understand them (e.g. visual representations such as photorealistic paintings are often perceived as digital reproductions) and that this may have a fundamental impact on reception and interpretation.

This also reveals a shift in perspective in the debate on the significance of the materiality of media practices. For example, J. E. Müller (2008: 36) proposed that materiality is a basic assumption of all considerations about 'interaction between different media'. Later, however, he relativized the importance of materiality in the context of the 'digital age', pointing to 'new, remediated forms of intermediality' in the context of reality-simulating digital media, which he claims are one of the biggest challenges facing (media-oriented) intermedial research today (J. E. Müller 2010: 18). Digital forms can be de-formed or re-formed in a new way thanks to the fact that they are separated from their materiality (Schröter 2008: 584). For the same reason, in the monograph *Hybridkultur* (2010), Spielmann advocated for the *remediation of intermediality* in the context of digital technologies and in connection with the *hybridization of culture*. Intermedial studies, therefore, should do what media do: absorb approaches associated with interpreting new media.

From a genealogical perspective, this debate is thought-provoking because today's virtualization and dematerialization of media forms have resulted in a renewed interest in the materiality of media in the intermedial discourse. It is more a reaction to the current state of affairs than an attempt at building on the earlier (semiotic) debate. In our diachronic perspective, we were able to observe an accent on materiality already in proto-intermedial research from the 1980s; for example, Wendy Steiner (1982) identified materiality as an important aspect of arts/media. Had it been further developed, its explication could have prevented many misunderstandings in today's intense debate. Thus, the materiality of media was an issue in proto-intermediality, if only latently, certainly before the dawn of the digital era and even before 1988, when the editor of the volume *Materialität der Kommunikation*, Hans Ulrich Gumbrecht, presented *materiality* as a new topic permeating all humanities research and even as a 'new paradigm' (Gumbrecht 2003). Materiality has long been omitted in the semiotic- and communication-focused debate in intermediality, only to return in full strength in recent years as a concept contributing to renewed discussion about the essence of intermediality.[12]

Prospects for the future: Across, inter, in-between, in?

There is no doubt that intermedial studies has been forced to reflect upon itself by competition from within cultural studies, the dynamic growth of media and the emergence of socially relevant issues, which acting together have put pressure on developing a method that has to retain its capacity to react to new tasks. Unfortunately, this strain is also leading to the weakening of intermediality's interest in 'old media', including literature, and in the 'aging' disciplines that study them. In other words, the current object of research in the discourse of cultural studies has become a symptom of the current method, hence the keen interest of scholars in digital visualization and the discourse of social media. Intermediality, however, may become for literary studies and education a tool for describing the position of literature in contemporary culture and even propose ways of strengthening it (indeed, in intermedial and multimodal studies there is great interest in education; cf. Kress and Burn 2019; Costa Vieira, Führer and de Paiva Vieira 2021). Thus, the intermedial approach can contribute to the changing understanding of literature and literary studies. As Siegfried J. Schmidt (2008: 9) states, since the late 1970s, literature has been interpreted not only as a set of texts but also as a social system (cf. Schmidt 1989, Bourdieu 1992) in which products considered to be literature are produced, distributed, received and processed. Let us recall again his claim that in the 1980s at the latest 'it already seemed undeniable that literary texts are media offerings that compete with the offerings of other media' (Schmidt 2008: 9). This, he argued, brought about the gradual expansion of the subject of literary studies and its potential transformation into media cultural studies. And what else is literature-centred intermedial research then a variant of such a transformation?

This concept of intermediality, however, soon proved to be unsustainable. Rajewsky (2019) offers up a shift in perspective in a revision of her own system: the focus is no longer on the literary work but intermediality itself, and thus, she speaks of the term *literature-related intermedial research* (*literaturbezogene Intermedialitätsforschung*). Though literature is no more a privileged medium, literary scholars may profit from its remaining an inevitable aspect of research, for example, in enquiries into transmediations of literary pre-texts or *post-autonomous writing* (Ludmer 2007/2006) that crosses the boundaries of artistic and popular genres, of fiction and non-fiction, and also of different media. For example Brazilian author Teresa Montero's 2018 novel *O Rio de Clarice* is staged as a walk through the city during the lifetime of the protagonist. Readers can scan QR codes in the book to supplement verbal representations with digital ones. As a result, such writing suggests also new ways of reading (Domingos 2020).

The multigenre and multimedia nature of contemporary works of art is, besides omnipresent digital representation, one of the stimuli for intermedial studies' methodological self-reflection. Many arguments based on the study of contemporary art and newly proposed theories were presented at an international roundtable of intermedialists in 2021, especially by theatre scholar and narratologist Janine Hauthal and film scholar Ágnes Pethő (Hauthal, Pethő and Rajewsky 2021). They both suggest that intermedial phenomena need to be reconceptualized based on the interpretation of works that were not created through contact with other media or media transformation but result from (and are performed in) the space 'in-between' (the parallel with the post-structuralist theory of meaning emerging from the space between signs is obvious here). The two scholars illustrated medial 'in-betweenness' by examining complex media projects dealing with the socially urgent topics of endless armed conflict (Milo Rau: *Orestes in Mosul*, 2019) and political protests under dictatorships (Radu Jude: *Tipografic majuscul*, 2020). The two works (Rau's resulting in a theatre performance, Jude's in a film) are composed as collages of representations alternating between the cinematic and the theatrical, the poetics of a fictional video clip and a real television show, the action on stage and the recording of a theatre performance in a real location, involving the spoken and written word and actors of different nationalities speaking different languages. The recipient therefore must reconstruct the story from this intermedial, intergeneric, intercultural and interlingual conglomerate while employing the cognitive frame of theatre and cinema. Believing that multimodalists would concur, we suggest that the in-betweenness of these complex creative processes, which blend performance and reality, be understood as an instance of multimodality.

Pethő refers to the *overt mediacy* of the many representations in Jude's film as the *unmasking of media* and suggests *multiple mediatedness* as an umbrella term indicating the insertion of one media representation into another. We might object that such multiple insertion of a medium into another was already introduced by Bolter and Grusin (1999) as *hypermediacy*; it also includes the *unmasking of media* (the text in a text editor can be displayed as a page or sheet of paper). If such unmasking is conspicuous or manifest, it can also be referred to by the established term of *media foregrounding*. Pethő, however, does not consider Jude's film to be an example of a composite medium that works with a collage of representations in other media but claims it exemplifies the current *state of media in general* (cf. Pethő 2011, expanded in 2020a, 2020b). She also relates the phenomena of in-betweenness to the existing paradigms of intermedial research: descriptions of intermedial relations (e.g. in the works of Rajewsky and Wolf) assume the existence of 'borders'. Given the in-between state of the medium, Pethő considers it more productive to return to Higgins's *intermedium* and to apply the ideas of post-structuralist philosophers. This is reflected in her substitution of the term *intermediality* with her reconceptualization of a *rhizomatic set of interconnections*.

We could argue that this 'rhizomaticity' is already contained in the concept of intertextuality, which has historically served as a matrix for grasping the forking of intermedial relations. Furthermore, we may also object that Pethő's suggested reconceptualization was inspired by media products typical of today's multimediality but resulting nonetheless from exclusive projects. This should be taken into account prior to stereotyping these projects as exemplifications of the 'general state of the medium'. We could argue that media products continue to be created, distributed and successfully consumed that, although they were created in the context of other media, remain clearly established in one 'old' medium (such as painting), and therefore, it does not make sense to relate them to the concept of 'intermedia'. Even the ever-changing field of intermedial phenomena has a relatively stable base that lies in cultural continuity. And provided there are no more borders between media, why speak of 'intermedia' then? The term itself concedes the existence of distinctive media as 'communication *dispositifs*'.

We can only agree with Rajewsky, who in this debate (Hauthal, Pethő and Rajewsky 2021) insisted on preserving the concept of transmediality, which can grasp one persistent aspect of culture: in the current *convergence culture*, audiences always appreciate media remakes of popular subjects in different genres and value modes that are compilations of many historical versions. Thus, it no longer makes sense to relate the target media product to its genealogically related pre-texts. The strategies aimed at target audiences are what makes these transmediations interesting for intermedial enquiry. Exploring media products that return to their traditional materiality in response to digitalization (i.e. the remediation and hypermediation of 'old' media) also seems promising: for example, there is a growing number of books involving visual representations, including traditional artistic and decorative techniques (e.g. embroidery), in a fundamental meaning- and story-making function. Rajewsky therefore proposes dealing with new forms and the new essence of 'bookishness'. Such themes seemingly take us back to the beginnings of intermedial research, but that is not true. Since the advent of mass printing, the book as an artistic artefact has always regularly returned as a response to mass-produced publications often of inferior quality. Today, an essential aspect of such books is their communication and aesthetic function of inducing or restoring sensorial experiences in recipients who are used to digitally mediated texts.

Around fifteen years ago, when intermedial studies was making its way into the Czech scholarly community, we thought of it as a typical example of a 'humanistic discipline' (in terms of Panofsky 1955): the origins of intermedial thinking lie in antiquity; in its evolution, it was capable of transforming the germinal comparison of arts into a systematic explication of media affordances and functional analyses of interrelated media representations; and, above all, it seemed to keep relying on the individuality and freedom of communicating subjects. Today, when media are no longer just 'extensions of man' but a continuum that surrounds us, when social networks have transformed into a spiderweb in which the identity of the individual is spun, intermedial thinking has inevitably begun to distance itself from a humanistic conception. It is beginning to become akin to other cultural disciplines in understanding medium as an active agent of representation and communication. This is also evident in the growing interest among intermediality scholars in general social issues, whether they have been brought to the fore by the focusing of other research areas (e.g. memory studies), media evolution (social media), or the current state of the public debate and political culture. *Poetics* and *politics* have become an inseparable pair in intermedial research – both in individual studies and in comprehensive projects that demonstrate the analytical and interpretive potential of the intermedial approach (e.g. Bruhn and Schirrmacher 2021).

It will be interesting to follow how intermedial studies continues to fare on the 'marketplace of discourses', whether it will lean more towards research on widespread societal and media phenomena from an interdisciplinary perspective or whether it will retain some of its characteristic features, such as taking into account the diachrony of the phenomena, attempting to differ and classify them, and refining the heuristic tools required for conducting subtle analysis – including analysis of 'old media' products like literature. The question is whether intermedial studies will become one of many cultural disciplines or whether it will be 'an augmented science of literature' that can approach its main subject matter as 'one of several current media offerings'.

Notes

1 E.g. in 1541 in a commentary on Horace, Pomponius Gauricus writes that poetry and painting *should* resemble each other, Francesco Luisini in 1554 recommended poets 'imitate good painters' (cf. Hagstrum 1958: 59–60, 94–5).
2 Such terms often appeared in the titles of their writings: 'parallel' (John Dryden, 1695), 'sister arts' (Hildebrand Jacob, 1734), 'agreement' (Joseph Spence, 1747), 'correspondence' (Daniel Webb, 1766).
3 When Zima (1995: 2) takes a retrospective look at aesthetics through the lens of intermedial thinking, he criticizes Hegel's neglect of the 'specific nature of the medium, which makes poetry, poetry; music, music; and painting, painting'.
4 E.g. by putting Shakespeare's poem 'The Rape of Lucrece' into the context of the humanistic discourse of *paragone* (Rouse 2015).
5 From the point of view of modern semiotics and its evolution, Lessing's conception of the sign appears important: according to him, the signs of a work of art must have a 'suitable relation' (*bequemes Verhältniss*) to the thing signified (Wellbery 1984: 11, 191, 203; Lifschitz and Squire 2017: 43–5; 200, 220; for the historical background of this notion see Lifschitz and Squire: 200, 220).

6   Wölfflin's method of studying opposing pairs in different arts and Walzel's 'mutual illumination' informed also the work of other authors (e.g. Fritz Strich, Kurt Wais; cf. Hermand 1971/1965: 16–20).
7   Independently, Nerlich (1990) developed the concept of *iconotext* to interpret modern and postmodern works based on the montage and collage of verbal and visual sign systems. In contrast, Mitchell always included older media forms (the emblem, ekphrasis) (cf. Wagner 1995).
8   Isekenheimer's *interpictorality* (2013) is derived from intertextuality and seeks to replace the traditional art history concept of *influence*, thus involving intramedial relations.
9   So far there has been very little overlap between the interests and modes of thinking of the literature-centred branch of intermedialists and those of media historians and 'new' media theorists. Although (new) media theorists sometimes recognize literature to be a medium, they are not particularly interested in it. This may be illustrated in the work of Jay David Bolter and Richard Grusin (1999), who include among examples of remediation a database of literary texts; nevertheless, literature is mentioned here only to represent 'textuality'. In order to facilitate an 'understanding of new media' these authors try to grasp the typical mechanisms of media evolution by introducing several general concepts (*remediation, hypermediacy*, etc.; cf. Rajewsky 2005; see also Chapter 1, pp. 32–3). They focus on media that tend to or are meant to suppress the mediatedness of representations of reality (hence the terms *immediacy, transparency of media*), and evoke in the recipient the illusion of perceiving, or even being immersed in the represented world (e.g. perspective painting, photography, film, television, VR; cf. Chapter 10, pp. 359–60).
10 After Elleström suddenly passed away in 2021, to honour his memory his model was subjected to systematic analysis and revision by the intermediality and multimodality academic community (Thomas Leitch, Kamilla Elliot, Joao Queiroz, John Bateman, Mieke Bal, Kay O'Halloran, Marie-Laure Ryan, Nafiseh Mousavi) in the 'Meeting Media Minds: Critical Legacies of Lars Elleström' series, organized by the Linnaeus University Centre for Intermedial and Multimodal Studies in 2022 and 2023.
11 However, the Centre for Intermedial and Multimodal Studies (IMS, Växjö) and the graduate programme MIDWorld launched in Växjö and Örebro recently engage in regular scholarly exchange to help bridge this gap.
12 Materiality and mediality are now issues dealt with in semiotic works (e.g. Genz and Gévaudan 2016).

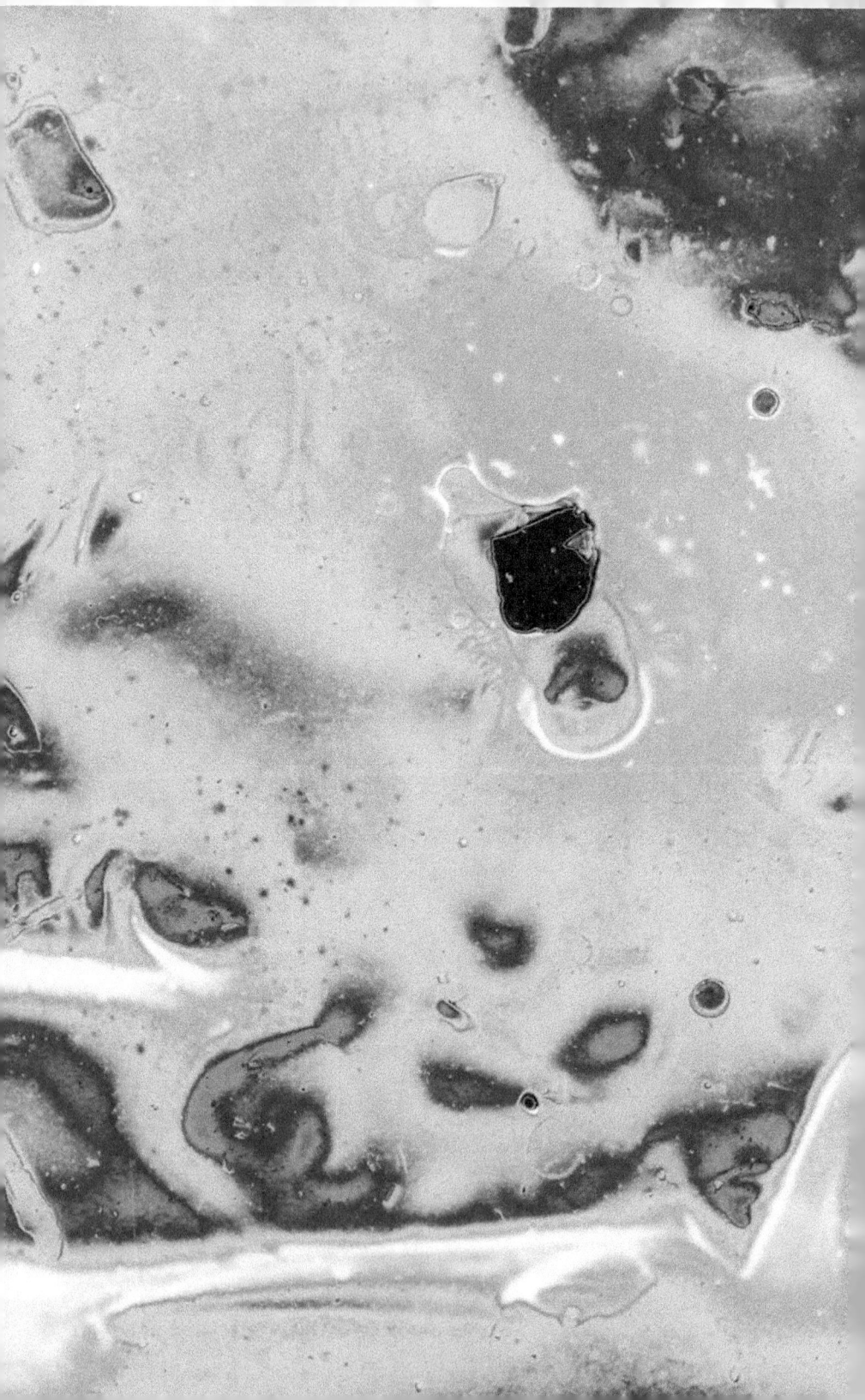

Polylogue

Steps to a media theory of literature

Richard Müller, Tomáš Chudý, Alice Jedličková, Josef Šebek and Stanislava Fedrová

How to make literary theory coherent with media thinking? What prospects are offered by the idea of a medial literary theory, and what challenges faced by any effort to carry it out? Leaving aside for a moment the historical reasons for the 'late discovery' of the mediality of literature (we will return to this later), what we see now is rather the consequence of this delay: namely, that literature receives little interest by those studying of media in other fields. There is, in other words, a reluctance to count literature (like other traditional arts) as a medium, and it remains noticeably under-represented in media discourse. Literary scholars, on the other hand, can argue that the study of literature was doing quite well without the category of mediality – until the advent of *new media* that is, and the fundamental transformation of the way of writing and distribution of text that came with it – both in the study of plurimedial artistic experiments with a basis in literature, and later, with research into the practices of reading and cultures of the written word, for instance, which evidently deal with rather important questions of mediality (in those cases, for example, when this research is able to bridge the conventional division between the textuality of the book and materiality of the text). Should we not then consider the concept of the medium to be effectively redundant? There are, moreover, certain obstacles that arise out of its fundamental polycontextuality, and from the related heteromorphy of media theories. Attempts at codifying the medium concept by various individual authors and schools of thought have tended to be rather narrowly conceived, with only partial overlap among them, and there is no generally accepted definition.

Here, however, we may consider the emergence of alienation within a certain discourse as a starting point. At those moments when literature began to reveal itself as a medium in critical reflections specific to it, this was most often, as we have seen, the result of stimuli foreign to its own mediality, mainly related to – and often as an excursus from – the development of new media and technologies. Marshall McLuhan wrote *Understanding Media* at a time when

Western and other societies had already been transformed by the medium of television, and Friedrich Kittler his *Gramophone, Film, Typewriter* when the world had already begun to reorganize itself, never to return, with (and in) the 'universal medium' of the computer. Both pioneers of media discourse treated literary texts primarily as ornaments and symptoms of technological-media development, and their literary analyses can best be understood precisely as symptoms – symptoms of the revolutionary nature of their own media approach. Yet we must not overlook what they brought to light: an unusual and hitherto obscure tradition of media discourse, stored within the literary works themselves. Above all, and in a peculiar way (and each in a different way), their work touches on what today might be considered an axiom of all media theory: namely, that the mediality of each medium, its creation and use, and the context of its effects and reception can only be understood in relation to other media.

A first step is therefore to recognize that media establish their identity through mutually differential relations. This would compel us to ask: Is this process connected to the principle of difference that is foundational to Ferdinand de Saussure's model of the linguistic system, with its two planes of the signifier and signified? It is not without reason that we raise this question here. Indeed, it represents one of the most persistent errors of pre-media thinking: the tendency to project the principles of language systems, and more generally of any one medium, onto diverse other media types. By critically reflecting on this propensity, we are more likely to proceed on the premise that media differences are themselves of various kinds, the Saussurian one being no more than one of them, and this only in a rather attenuated sense.

Media and media processes, defining 'medium' and conceptual genealogy

So what is a 'medium', and do the differential qualities of media have implications for a general definition?

A dive into the etymology of the term, and above all into the genealogy of the semantic field of the concept, reveals the evolution and layering of a number of interpenetrating and contradictory aspects: the medium as a means; environment; tool; the space of mediation into which this process simultaneously intervenes; *organon tón organón* ('instrument/organ of organs/instruments'). At the most general level, we find it possible to distinguish two meanings – though quite difficult to reconcile, of the concept of the medium. These can aptly be described as *instrumental* and *environmental*, corresponding to the questions *by what means?* and *in what?* Is it possible, however, to completely transpose individual concepts formulated on the basis of the instrumentality of the medium to those emphasizing its all-encompassing nature, and vice versa? Or is it not rather the case that these concepts, in their connotations, are diametrically opposed, especially as regards the relative ease with which the medium may be controlled or used? While it seems that mediality cannot be limited to media in the traditional sense (as means of communication), it is precisely the evolution of various means of communication, representation and appearance generally speaking, that reveals and above all makes it possible to reflect on mediality in the most general sense (even if at other times and in other aspects it may obscure or conceal it). The medium can be anything from means to form, from wheels to clothes, from 'ether' and vacuum to paper and canvas. Lest such conceptual limitlessness undermine all possibility (or pursuit) of understanding, it is the study of these means – means of creating an environment, means of configuring the parameters of communication and representation, means even of self-reflexivity – that represents our best chance at grasping everything contained within the word 'mediality', including that which media causes to disappear, makes absent or makes appear as absence (and how it does so). In other terms, 'mediality' could imply transitions, breakdowns and frictions between media and modes – modalities, phases or degrees – of perception. Everything points to the fact that the definition of the medium will always be provisional and incomplete, that the medium always extends to modes of perception, to the environment in general (blurring the division between artificial and natural, internal and external, etc.), but also that communication media and technological *dispositifs* establish certain characteristic medial and communication situations in relation to which *the most general medial phenomena should be formulated, or at least compared* (the mediality of photography on one hand and the face of the deceased on the other; remembering and the forms of memoir literature; etc.).

With regard to the conceptual genealogy and evolution of media (and its theory), it has been possible to focus on the operations that typify the media (developmentally and systemically); these include affecting, communicating, visualizing, storing, modifying, processing, 'cutting' (editing), decomposing, reproducing, distributing, and so on. This affords us with certain possibilities for classifying media. First, media make possible the undertaking of various activities (which can be further divided into those which emphasize representation versus real-time communication); second, media processes take place in different ways at different levels (e.g. technical-articulatory, material, combinatorial and semantic); third, different media (to varying degrees) fulfil the same functions, for example, transmission, recording and manipulation (generation). The medium, as that which determines the parameters of communication (and in that sense as a means or even a tool), but also the medium as a 'solution' (in the sense of a liquid mixture) or 'decontextualization machine', an environment or habitat, a way of organizing perception and so on.

On the one hand, there seems to be an essential 'deflectivity' (or 'metaphoricality') in media that cannot be permanently compensated for, since shifts in meaning (e.g. function) are the determination of every mediation (not only by language) and every medium carries traces of previous shifts in the possibilities of expression and communication. On the other hand, however, it is precisely those processes which emerge as a function of media that make it possible, in retrospect, to determine what the medium actually is, along with those operations and performances for which it *disposes* itself, other media and man. The 'metaphorical deflection' of media would then consist in their inability (as perceived by humans) to provide perfect mediation – of such perfection that the medium would effectively erase itself in the act. Yet this inability on the part of the media becomes a source of desire, serving as ground for their further development. Mediality would thus appear as something that always happens or occurs 'between' (perhaps even between words, but especially between media), and of course on different levels or between incomparable 'regimes', and by that token in a transverse manner, or 'obliquely'. Examining processes that occur due to media incompatibility – this is where a focus on media functions and operations may offer a way out – would then lead to the most general description of mediality, as that which media have in common.

It is therefore crucial to directly contend with media-related operations and processes. And here conceptual genealogy offers a particularly helpful method. By tracing the genealogy of the term, we see how those meanings that are definitional for the theory and philosophy of media today – as a tool, or that with which something is conducted; as a middle and mediating means (already in Aristotle and in the tradition of *medium diaphanum*); and as a *Khôra*, substance or environment that surrounds or intervenes – first appeared or were reinforced through the gradual development of communication and technical media as they acquired increasingly important communication, cultural and socially constitutive functions. With this development, the most general contradiction arose between two aspects of the medium: as that, on the one hand, which disappears during mediation (content, form, information, data) and ceases to be visible or perceptible (like Plutarch's messenger who dies upon delivering news of the Athenian victory), and as that, on the other hand, which essentially determines, embodies and performs both content and form, a feature that tends to characterize art but is ultimately inherent to all media. Paradoxically, this is made evident precisely through artistic methods of manipulating various media materials or forms: an advertisement brought to the outer limit of art in pop art; Giacometti's *Cube* that calls to mind a death mask, with its links to the Roman *imago* (image of the ancestors), the theatrical mask and the absent human face; or the cutting and mixing of different voices, stylistic layers and references to other discourses in the modern poetic text (Eliot's *The Waste Land*).

Art and media, and the veiled mediality of literature: A lesson in (and to) intermediality

The arts tend to be neglected, however, or even excluded in media discourse, so that the split between (mass) media and art, which has deeper roots, persists.

We can best explain why the mediality (and materiality) of literature has so long been neglected by looking to the field of intermedial studies and its history, or indeed its prehistory and the way this prehistory was worked through in the process of the discipline's development. While some of the reasons for this neglect are closely tied to the development of intermedial thinking itself, most of them arise from the legacy of a general understanding of the position of art in the development of culture, its critique and gradually developing scholarship on the arts. A major role was played by the hierarchization of individual arts on the basis of their placement in the material and/or spiritual sphere, and related issues of perception. Similar influences can be found in the changing relationship between art and reality, that is, the oscillation between the concept of literature as a mimesis of reality, artistic transformation and a self-reflexive sign. The consequences of the long-standing and historically rooted hierarchy of the arts can be found as well in their relationship to the modes of representation, which primarily arise in the form of new technologies for recording, scientific modelling of reality and mediation of information, with the function and status of art being explored only as an afterthought (photography, film, television). However, art itself may or may not contribute to the disclosure or admission of its own mediality.

Uncertainty around the differentiation of art and media (i.e. the conditions under which a special theory of intermediality began to take shape in the 1990s) has its root, paradoxically, in the certainty of the historical starting points of the discipline. The subject of research had long been the arts, or rather the mutual comparison of their forms of representation and effects on the perceiver. The constitutive properties of art, within this tradition, were simply taken for granted. We might summarize the long-term influence of this tradition with the notion of the arts paradigm, which manifests itself in the emblematic concepts of individual development phases or of entire epochs (*ut pictura poesis, paragone*, sister arts). One of the key moments for the future awareness of the mediality of art was the consistent differentiation of media according to their representation potential as a function of their specificity. It was Gotthold Ephraim Lessing who pointed this out during the Enlightenment in the context of his poetics. Yet it is because of his normative approach, so difficult to extricate from the Enlightenment discourse on arts, that Lessing has often been understood as a liquidator of the interrelationship of artistic disciplines, rather than a proto-intermedial scholar. Another medial aspect of his thinking consists in his recognition that representation by signs functions as a means of producing a certain effect on the perceiver. What is essential here for Lessing is the suggestive power of a given representation, which can be achieved by rendering it in such a way that it allows for a transparency of the sign system, however momentary, in the process of reception. However, it is precisely the progressive 'sign character' of art and emphasis on the *transparency of the medium* within the modality of *sense perception* that lead to a certain (regressive) counter-movement as they deny the 'presence' of the medium and marginalize its materiality.

Aesthetics, a field that began to form in the mid-eighteenth century, has also restricted the premises to some extent for identifying the mediality of art. The paradigm of the mechanical and liberal arts was replaced by that of the fine arts, effectively excluding production of a mechanical nature, with the likely result that the interpretation of art moved yet further away from the context of its materiality. What is certain is that the hierarchization of the arts contributed to this situation, with poetry – a thoroughly 'immaterial' expressive medium as in Romantic aesthetics – often presiding at the top. Even Hegel's aesthetic system, which hierarchizes the arts according to their capacity to express the spiritual, contributes to this tendency, notwithstanding that one of the parameters of his distinction of art is precisely its material. Here again, poetry is given the highest place, as a form of artistic expression that is capable of working only with concepts. With Hegel, it is emancipation from matter that distinguishes the 'highest art'.

Somewhat surprisingly, the vigorous initiatives of the interwar avant-garde did little to draw attention to the mediality of literature or other artistic media, despite a marked aptitude to cross the high and low, the traditional and new, despite all their efforts to democratize artistic production, to integrate various materials and procedures – despite even their willingness to adopt the new technologies of photography and film, their fascination with modern technology in general. Rather than an interest in mediality as such, what these commitments revolved around was the thing itself (whether a 'found object' or technical object) as expression of modern times, and the individual as an engaged agent working within a new reality. In the 1940s, with the trend towards abstraction in the arts, the essayist and art critic Clement Greenberg brought concepts of mediality and materiality to the fore in his article (and manifesto) 'Towards a Newer Laocoon' (1940). His argument is that the power of abstract expressionism lay in its emancipation not simply from the imitation of reality but from representation in general, thereby arriving at a kind of self-representation of the medium and mediality of painting in its materiality. In those approaches that still represent the genealogical forebears of intermediality – 'comparative arts' and 'interart studies', for example – the basic paradigm of the arts remained. Notions of the materiality of literature only arise with the early beginnings of the theory of intermediality, focusing on the transmediations that characterize the experimental work of the 1960s (visual poems), but also looking back at works of the first avant-garde. Various forms of intermediality were then defined at the turn of the millennium under the influence of certain trends in artistic creation labelled 'multimedia' (or 'intermedia'). Digital media also contributed significantly to this change: ironically, it might be as a result of the *dematerialization* of the text in the virtual environment that attention (and not only in the academic context) began to turn to the corporeality and materiality of physical writing, and to the influence of technology not only on writing techniques in speech representation but on literary forms and way of thinking. However, alongside this new sensibility in contemporary intermedial theory, we find another tendency. While research on creative transmediation as result of the franchising of media-tested content (cf. Henry Jenkins's concept of 'convergence culture') provides favourable conditions for new insight into the mediality of cultural phenomena and has the potential to integrate literature as a medium, it unfortunately takes little interest in its media specificity.

Media archaeology, media evolution?

There are further indications that support connecting theoretical reflections on literary mediality with communication (and signs) and the notion of 'bridging distance', as well as materiality (or embodiment): namely that, looking to the past, those aspects of the medium which we now consider to be part of the modern concept seem to arise precisely in those moments, in which the aim was to invent a not yet existing language or sign system, often as universal as possible, that is, one that would correct the confusion of languages, enable everyone to understand each other, overcome the apparent 'imperfection' of communication or distance between people. For centuries – more noticeably since the dawn of the modern age – some of the most inventive thinkers (John Wilkins, Athanasius Kircher, Claude Chappe, Samuel Morse and Claude Shannon) seem to have stumbled upon the fact that the very thing which impedes language and perception, the very thing that stands in their way, makes it possible to some extent to discover the laws that govern their construction, thus raising the prospect for the invention of a universal code. With regard to the findings of the archaeology and history of media, it follows that a medium is only regarded as such when it is confronted with another, usually newer medium; this arises wherever the newer medium has exceeded the status of a mere invention to attain more significant cultural functions that are broader and more profound in their scope. Why is this so? It seems that an inculturated (qualified) medium may temporarily fall into 'media oblivion' (*Medienvergessenheit*), that it becomes an invisible, unconscious entry condition for cultural perception, but that the mutual pressure of newer and older media provokes a reconfiguration of the network of media relations, bringing the mediality of older media once more to the fore (less 'taken for granted'). Evidence of the mutual influence of older and newer media can be found, for example, upon the initial use of a certain technical invention at a stage when it has not yet become a (developed) medium. What would individual inventions be (as Rudolf Stöber points out) if they did not become media? Letterpress would serve as a perfect tool for scriveners, wireless telegraphy to connect individual end users with a more efficient infrastructure, photography as a substitute for sitting models in painting, television as an improved telephone (with visual component), computers as clusters of machines designed for more efficiently sharing computing tasks in real time. A technical invention becomes a medium (also conceptually) only at the moment the various layers or groups of its compilers and users, and perhaps administrators, are differentiated.

Another feature of media evolution (in the sense of an obvious increase in complexity and operative possibilities) is that older (developed) media do not disappear: they may be affected to varying degrees by a decline in prestige, anachronization or periods of inactivity, but they do not go extinct or disappear altogether. This also means that they can once more assume a significant, though apparently not dominant, position (simple contemporary examples include the record player and analogue photography). This principle also applies – and above all – to practices and functions associated with media. As shown by Roger Chartier, for example, even in a time when silent reading had become common practice for educated readers (i.e.

between the sixteenth and eighteenth centuries), reading out loud remained dominant, serving as the connecting link for various forms social interaction. Moreover, the older media stubbornly impose their physiognomy and forms of use and representation on the newer ones; in codices (bound books), the division into 'books' (*libri*) corresponded to individual scrolls, which also long remained the dominant visual representation of the text. Keyboards, computer interfaces, electronic representations of text derive and evolve from connections to the typewriter, desktop, page layout, flipping through the pages of a book and so on.

There is yet one more feature of media archaeology that should be taken into account: it is precisely the media, it seems, that shape the very manner in which the past is processed, which is related to the creation of an 'environment' but also to their functions. If media give rise to the very environment in which certain forms of meaning are discernible, we are confronted with one more special question or aspect of the matter: To what extent do media create – and recursively transform – what we call history? To what extent do media grasp and record their own history and development?

Communication, its aporias and limits, literature, medium and culture

Given the importance of the concept of communication in literary studies, and its increasing importance in the history of literary criticism, we are compelled to connect with it our thoughts on media. This is in spite of the fact that it is precisely in (discussions on) literature and the arts that those aspects of mediation are evoked which go beyond 'mere' communication, or that those features of language and communication become visible which in ordinary situations remain below the threshold of the differential dispositions of the communicators, lie beyond the scope of further discussion or are considered in purely instrumental terms. These are the features that account for the ability to more permanently evoke a memory, impression or experience, including rhythmic and sound aspects of spoken language, visual aspects of writing and print, and so on. Among the most interesting contributions from the field of literary theory to the theory of communication are those of Roman Jakobson and Jan Mukařovský, who alongside the communicative functions of language that were recognized by modern linguistics of the time, discover a function oriented around the sign itself, on its structuring, the message or communication 'in and of itself'. They call this the 'poetic' or 'aesthetic' function. It is a function they are compelled in all cases to define negatively, and in opposition to the more common functions or models: at times against scientific language (the Vienna Circle and Slovak structuralism), at times against the 'usual' communicative functions of language, and at still other times against *all* functions, so that the aesthetic function comes to be defined, paradoxically, as a function denying (ordinary) functionality – or else as a function that allows for the mediation between all functions or all layers of a material or medium given its most rudimentary social and anthropological uses. Among the various attempts by Mukařovský to define the aesthetic function, the most enduring seems to be that it serves as a mediating function, one that establishes a relationship between functions – and values – that are otherwise difficult to connect in the broader social reality.

Is it not the case, however, that some of the more utopian aspects of avant-garde projects have left their traces in this concept? And does this not, paradoxically, give rise to a certain tendency to preserve the status quo, especially in view of a field of literary production that seems to have developed considerable resistance to the development of media, and remains (albeit only seemingly) beyond their reach? Could it not be the case that these models remain largely bound by the concept of literature as art, and to a definition of the medium directly borrowed from the field of art theory?

In addition to this line of enquiry, which is essentially connected to the aesthetic tradition, several other approaches may provide important insight on media communication models and our understanding of literature as a medium, namely those which proceed from perspectives of the social system, culture as a semiosphere, culture as a signifying system and *society as communication*. These last two examples are taken from the cultural theory of Raymond Williams, which has come to be known for its critique of the concept of 'media', and which therefore might appear anachronistic from the point of view of media theory. Yet it is precisely through this term that his cultural theory can be read more productively. On the one hand, Williams convincingly argues why it is misleading to separate art from other media, and shows that this division has often been historically associated with certain hegemonic tendencies. This seems to match with the finding of media historians: in eleventh-century China, for example, letterpress technology was already in use but only in the imperial court and monasteries. The developmental phase of a given medium can also be classified according to the degree of expansion: from specialists to a small privileged class of consumers, and from there, by social differentiation of the circle of users and opening access to 'editing', to wider layers of society. The aesthetic function, to return to Williams's critique, always constitutes only a certain concentrated, provisionally defined situation; similarly, creativity is historically derived from artistic practices, but in reality it is also present to a greater or lesser extent in other communication situations. Nevertheless, for Williams as for us, the conceptual emphasis on communication and means of communication (that is, against Williams's dictum: media) is key, since all communication contributes to the creation of human communities (so that every theory of communication is at the same time the theory of a certain community), in both the material and purely semiotic sense. What is more, society itself is a form of communication through which experience is grasped – that is, described, shared, preserved and modified. In this sense, communication is literally a world-making phenomenon, a fact that is all the more evident in modern societies where more and more aspects of life and 'production' are shifting to communication processes. (One might add, however, that technology is also moving more and more into prehension and pre-communication processes, the unconscious or directly imperceptible settings of their parameters and protocols.)

A fundamental implication of this shift from art to media is the necessity of examining the limits of the semiotic character of media-specific messages. It is a question, in other words, of the materiality of the medium, including its non-signifying dimension. Williams effectively accounts for this through an emphasis on the 'lived experience' of culture, and in the metaphorical contrast between 'solution' and 'precipitate'. Culture – in the broadest sense of the word – is always activated, evaluated, selected by the actors who experience it in a lived and perceived form ('structures of feeling'); it is in the truest sense a 'solution'. This truly medial concept draws attention to one aspect that is often overlooked in contemporary media theories. Every medium and every message simultaneously dissolves phenomena of a different order within itself (the economic order, or specific economic aspects in a musical composition, for example, where the degree of dissolution is typically higher than in the case of literature). This 'dissolving' of phenomena of various orders is one of the essential properties of media, and does not necessarily take place on the semiotic level, or in any case, can be carried out by very diverse ways of signification.

It is the tension between different ways of signifying that is at the core of Yuri Lotman's thinking and his theory of cultural dynamics and the semiosphere. Lotman proceeds from the observation that common communication models, even if they include various components of communication (speaker, addressee, context, channel, code), tend to suppress the existence of *other* codes and languages, of differently constructed 'channels', and of other directions of communication (towards the other, but also towards oneself), all of which can be regarded as components of the medium. A set of semiotic formations, as Lotman keenly observes, functionally precedes language when considered in isolation. This suggests that a perfectly independent intelligence or communication, a solitary code, language or culture is inconceivable: not only empirical but (primarily) theoretical fictions. We see this axiom most readily in the very thing that appears to violate it, namely autocommunication. Indeed, if the notion of autocommunication is scalable without limits – if culture itself may be understood as one enormous autocommunication process – then it is a semiotic process in which one language is supplemented by *at least one additional 'foreign' language*. Moreover, and perhaps more importantly, if ever something outside the semiotic process is revealed, it is precisely when two or more *mutually untranslatable* languages, codes, channels or 'texts' collide. The fact that the dissonance between *at least two different media* plays this culturally generative as well as sensorially and cognitively disruptive role (according to Lotman, semiotic objects, like consciousness, have three functions: creative, information and memory) is of fundamental importance for any media theory.

Analysis of Lotman's approach together with a discussion on the limits of the information-theoretical communication model, which have been made visible by attempts to extend this model to more complex communication situations (including both the production of art and literature and their criticism), leads us to several conclusions. Instead of 'noise', as defined in the context of the technical understanding of communication (information transmission), it is advisable to work with the category of 'cultural interference', which implies the action of various types of coding (or sets of conventions) and the possibility of transposition. This transposition is never 'complete', yet its results are distinguishable in terms of their cultural-communicational relevance.

Information-theoretical uncertainty can also be redefined in terms of the different potentialities of expression in different forms and types of media. Media transposability, together with the translatability of linguistic expression into other languages, need to be considered as a condition that is primal to semiosis (the very condition of its possibility) (as corroborated by the concept of the 'mythogram'). We accept Lotman's thesis that the dream represents a model of communication which best captures the potentiality of polymediality, and in which the sensory spheres exist before their separation from the common continuum; as such, the dream may serve as mechanism for the return to a germinal unity of media spaces that will later diverge. The effectiveness of communication means, expressed in terms of such factors as unambiguity, speed and general comprehensibility, works against this communicative (medial) indeterminacy of the dream. Yet the development of media and their interaction brings that potentiality and ambiguity once more to bear, which suggests that this kind of ambiguity represents a fundamental condition of media development, not only from a psychological-anthropological point of view, but also from the perspective of communication.

The idea of incompatibility, of difference, is also of key importance in those theories of communication which speak not only to the plurality of media and cultural forms but to their general technical aspect. We are particularly interested here in the works of Niklas Luhmann, who (in express opposition to Jürgen Habermas) argues that communication conveys a difference that matters – or, as Gregory Bateson so aptly puts it, 'which makes a difference'. In this way, the notion of communication expands to an unprecedented level to include all events that are not *in*different, that is, not only matches but also imperfect matches, disagreements, and for that matter also noise insofar as it may be thematized in those cases where it serves as a stimulus to establish another communication (as selected from an equally broad spectrum).

Communication is subject to radical contingency (on the side of both sender and receiver). As far as communication is not prevented from occurring altogether by technical obstacles, the incompatibility or absence of a second consciousness, or risk of communication as such ceasing even when technical and cognitive obstacles are overcome, it will be sparked by the smallest of causes.

Luhmann's theory helps to explain why communication processes tend to evolve. The underlying situation in which communication arises is not the presence of knowledge of information but its absence; acts of communication can then be understood as selections that aim somehow to absorb this underlying uncertainty. The function of communication is also to reduce (data) complexity by means of differences. With the increasing number of relationships and growing (technical, informational) complexity, the level of contingency also increases, making communication more and more improbable. This suggests that more effective means are needed than a general medium of meaning, and this need is met by symbolically generalized communication media (including 'art' and mass media with their forms).

Communication thus prevents the attainment of a state of entropy within the social system, a situation that would lead to its termination if it were not – and it is difficult here to disagree with Luhmann – for a process that introduced some degree of certainty back into it in the form of the communication of differences.

Luhmann's concept of communication thus acquires a new significance in that it can grasp, differentiate and even help to explain the dichotomy of technogenic and natural communication. Otherwise put, we find that it still provides a valid conceptual framework for understanding the data-signal-message-information continuum, in spite of the marked increase in technogenic processes, due in large part to the fact that Luhmann advances a concept of selection (and follows a systemic approach) that is neutral with regard to the human-machine dichotomy. What differs in the case of human selection can only be intimated here: the question of sincerity, which entails the question of the intentional ambiguity of signs, the generation of information as differences that make a difference, or eventually, both extremes: the dissipativeness of communication and its non-programmable reductiveness (the possibility of answering by a simple 'yes' or 'no').

Technics

So what constitutes the specificity of media? In the final account, is it not to be found in their technical side? It seems symptomatic that technics and technology remain a blind spot in literary theory (whether latently and overtly medial) until the last possible moment.

The conceptualization of the relationship between technology and man has gone through a number of changes, with the question of influence oscillating between one and the other in various ways. Does man have a decisive influence on the form of technology, which he constructs in his own image? Or is it precisely in the service-orientation of technics that the reverse influence is hidden, as a result of which technics itself comes to dictate – more or less evidently – the terms of its own use? We seem to be witnessing the generation of one technology out of another, the cybernetic projection of a second order, a situation that is breaking down the intuitive anthropocentric media system based on human demands. And if man and technics is not a simple one-way relationship, what does this mean for the concept of 'creation'? As technical limits tighten, does this not present the opportunity to bring the fact of that complicated relationship to the fore? In other words, how may we extract unintentional consequences and alienation from original purposes, as the stimulus for a similarly unintentional way of communication that could be called art? Is it not unconscious human wishes (*Wunschkonstellationen*, as Hartmut Winkler calls them) that are at stake, after all? Such a framework does not of itself imply a return to the notion of man in absolute command of his technics, and is well conceivable with man acting as one of the nodes in an 'actor network', as Bruno Latour calls it. In any case, we are not pressed to decide the matter now.

The 'discovery' of technics (by Erik Havelock, Jack Goody or Walter J. Ong) as a difference that splits spoken and written language seems particularly significant for the theory of literature. This is not only about the obvious technological nature of literature, but recognition of the limits of a certain type of medium, one that produces its own type of logic or view of reality (oral versus written cultures). Are there any technological limits to literature? What is the (historically specific) ratio between what is given and what remains variable, with regard to materials, distribution channels or procedures? Once more we come across the changing differential nature of media and mediality, and the difficulty of formulating the timeless features of the literary sphere, to say nothing of prognosticating on its future. However, we should at least take into account a certain alternative character of the medium of literature, and of the hermeneutic relationship between man and technology that is suggested in this case: namely, the specific capacity for literature to work with a certain self-referential or meta-communicative disclosure, which requires of the recipient a higher level of media competence in order to make the medium transparent. It is necessary to consider the processes of user inculturation, acquisition of various media competences, mutual social effects of media processes and, in relation to technics, unconscious projections. In the case of art and literature, following Mukařovský's proposal, we would need to assess the systemically integrated 'unintentionality' of the work.

Literature and the medium of speech, culture and (contemporary infogenic) society

The need to explain the relationship to technics thus allows us to establish a perspective in which the media of art and literature appear as unintentional projections not (only) of consciousness, the body or the senses, but also of those 'natural' (actually mediating) sources – sources so complex in themselves that they produce autonomous (and apparently inexhaustible) spaces of desire, as well as settings for manipulation. We are speaking here of *gesture and speech*. Even at the risk of artificially introducing the trace of an ill-suited anthropomorphic humanism, we can say that among all media, gesture and speech, with their connection to the human body, occupy a key articulating and transitional position.

The notion that the material of literature is speech in all its levels, stylistic layers and forms – a rather late-developing insight with revolutionary significance for the modern theory of literature in general – thus remains valid. At the same time as the rise of 'tertiary' media in the 1950s and 1960s, certain semiotic theories took a markedly medial turn, namely those which recognized literature as a secondary semiotic ('mythological' or modelling) system that allows for the symbolic treatment of language, which in and of itself serves as a complex and culturally constitutive system of expression. In addition to attempts to define literature itself as a medium, as with Oliver Jahraus for example, it must be assumed that literature makes visible the medium of speech in a special way. At least two aspects of making a medium visible can then be distinguished: its materiality (spatiality, temporality) and its function (making visible the possibilities of semantic complexity, and demonstrating *how meanings are formed in a given medium*). Can any more be added to them? Perhaps, yes. In any case, literature is a medium of the 'second order' that works with the production of ordinary (medial) communication as if with an already given value, and which is in this sense similar to the other arts.

If we have criticized the position taken by Jakobson in his extremely influential communication model, and the organization of semiotics around a 'single universal' system, we also need to acknowledge that speech (along with gesture, which Jakobson, however, marginalizes) is in fact situated in a special 'transitional' position, as mentioned above. Even in a media-saturated culture characterized by highly competitive media relations, literature, as a system based primarily on writing, can play an important role as a recognized meaning-making medium, so long as it retains its capacity to make mediality 'speakable' as well as 'readable'. Literature, after all, is isomorphic with language; this is in contrast with other media, which (to date) require speech-gestural commentary. Yet this represents both an advantage and a disadvantage. So long as it retains its medial nature, the literary process is well-positioned to make other media and mediality in general 'speakable', as the articulation of the mediality of memory, for example. We may recall, in this context, the concept of 'realistische Fantastik', born in the nineteenth century as *ars oblivionalis*. According to Renate Lachmann, this genre represents the 'opposite side of culture' and 'a space made possible by counter-memory in which *imagines* of the unseen and unthinkable are stored'. We might wonder, for example, in a media-convergence culture, what is it that allows for differently constructed media images to acquire orientation in linguistic form?

However, the condition of speakability/readability (understood as a reflected understanding of things by abstracting them in speech and fixing them in a written record) may not be universal to all communication. It is possible that interest in these aspects of communication will be on the wane in a world where other media offer different and increasingly dominant ways of modelling experience, meaning and above all, sharing and communicating. (Compare, for example, the possibilities offered by Instagram, and 'meme culture' – the combination of a simple paratext or icon with a digitally manipulated photo – and an exceedingly wide circle of users who are only superficially engaged.)

Perhaps 'literature' will retreat from many of its media-social roles or become something else altogether, like scattered islands in a media sea – or perhaps the mainland of literature, properly so-called will be understood as such only for a certain period of time, before breaking up into several parts.

There are indeed both long-lasting and current aspects of literature that separate it from the order of media – or which suggest, conversely, that it will be absorbed by media altogether. Revolutionary technologies do not only introduce new dimensions of representation (virtual reality) and communication, but also contribute to the creation of a complex information exchange environment, one that does not connect to the external environment but gradually grows through it (metaphor of the World Wide Web), eventually replacing it in part, in some cases almost entirely (as in the case of social networks; the notion of total replacement finds its cinematic treatment in the *Matrix* film series), or in a state of superposition (as with the concept of 'alternative truth' in the current field of media information). It is possible that some effects of the literary system, by sheer inertia, will prove to be virtually ineradicable: Literature, which can still be represented metonymically by the object of a book, does not and perhaps cannot have the nature of a ubiquitous and continuously updated network of interconnected information. Its basic form, still dominant and functioning in literary communication, remains closed: a story with a beginning and an end (as in a novel or a play), or a human situation culminating in the moment of utterance (as in a lyrical poem). Such formations, relatively closed in nature, cannot but remain a closed and alien 'input' vis-à-vis that universal environment.

All the more striking then are the examples of a countertrend: experiments with hypertext (remarkably short-lived today), shared digital creation with varying degrees of participation by a human subject and finally, to a certain extent, the digitization, by various methods, of traditional texts (with any number of consequences – liquidity, fragmentation, virtualization, combinability, interchangeability of the roles of creator and addressee, 'phenomenology' of the mobile screen, etc.). Another example, of course, is artificial poetry, which still conforms to the presentation of a quasi-human performance even if the interaction with artificial intelligence lacks the principle of dialogue (as Yuri Lotman would aptly say) – hence the emergence of such concepts as 'assisted creativity' and the successful 'collaborative' involvement of various kinds of AI in literary creation. In the current situation, there seems to be an acute contradiction between, on one hand, deriving AI from the simulation of the largest possible set of dispositions of human intelligence, and, on the other, the way it actually functions (especially in the case of 'deep learning' architecture), which may not have any direct analogies with the mechanisms of the human mind.

Computer-based creativity in literature is still limited by its existing source data: a human-created corpus of texts and data (or, in any case, the need for their anthropomorphic presentation). Yet that too may change.

Given this observable shift towards non-signifying medial modalities, we must therefore analyse their interaction with the current hegemonic model. Semiotic models, which inevitably enter into a dialectic with media theory, must also adapt to the new reality. The mainstream of media theory adapted a long time ago, turning to the question of the essentially fictional nature of media and related ways of shaping social reality, that is, the question of how to free up individual cognitive abilities from their contexts (e.g. memory). The media field appears to be multivector, and this also has an impact on artistic communication. If, as Hartmut Winkler convincingly argues, media are primarily 'decontextualization machines' (*Maschinen der Kontext-Entbindung*), then the issue is not about the audience's involvement within the framework of 'interactivity', but about the possibility of the emergence of mediality by way of complementing media contexts along more than one vector.

We might return here to one of literature's more important 'vectors', namely its disposition to model the form in which an experience or memory is shared (in a medially self-reflective manner) as an experience or memory expressed by language. We may then make the (seemingly self-evident) observation that content manipulation, which in turn presupposes the ability to record, attracts more attention than real-time communication. (This brings us back to the discussion that began with the functions of the media, that is, to questions about what the media are capable of doing.) Can we account for this by the fact that manipulation increases the complexity of communication, which in turn nurtures higher cognitive abilities? Or perhaps not even this is a decisive factor, and manipulation occurs simply because it is possible in the media environment, and because it is an operational option of the system, which will make use of it regardless of whether anyone wants it. Is the fundamental unavailability of reality reflected in literature as inseparable from the desire to merge with reality? *Nostalgia – that desire to return / where we have never been.* (Ivan Blatný)

What, then, is so quintessential about the possibilities of 'kinetizing' recorded contents, making them liquid, subjecting them to change? It is rather difficult to grasp this quality using categories independent of the older paradigm of representation. But there are certain exceptions: the term 'editing', for example, may acquire new meaning, shifting from its connotations of 'correction' to (what we have called here) transformation or manipulation. In short, technology points to the materiality of media because it makes use of the possibilities of materiality. Just as technological advances are accompanied by the increasing articulation of material (as we see with the development of microchips), they also establish, in a non-trivial way, new possibilities for making (and theorizing) technical choices. If creation consists in a sequence of selections, then it follows that multiplying these choices should also multiply the possibilities of creation. This, in turn, leads to more profound insight into mediality itself, which allows one – and this is key – to productively alienate and sever oneself from original intentions, or to search for and experimentally engage those uses envisaged as marginal. We should also take into account that the concept of creativity has thus far been associated, on anthropological grounds and perhaps not by chance, with the notion of difficulty – that is, the overcoming in each instance of a certain *resistance*. The ease with which we may now transfer materials, use forms in a binary-numerical environment and engage users, the increasing possibilities for reorienting and integrating communication tools, all this, paradoxically, may have a negative influence on the preconditions for creative intervention and its reception, insofar as these have hitherto consisted in a certain concentration – of shape, attention and effects. The mutual alienation of the black boxes of technology (including artificial intelligence) and human destiny can then begin once more to create new starting points and drive the transformation of existing essences – not only of 'media specificities' but of cultural processes in general.

References

Abrams, M. H. (1971/1953), *The Mirror and the Lamp: Romantic Theory and the Critical Tradition*, Oxford: Oxford University Press.

Aguiar, D. and J. Queiroz (2009), 'Towards a Model of Intersemiotic Translation', *The International Journal of the Arts in Society*, 4 (4): 203-10.

Allan, S. (1997), 'Raymond Williams and the Culture of Televisual Flow', in *Raymond Williams Now: Knowledge, Limits and the Future*, ed. J. Wallace, R. Jones and S. Nield, 115-44, Basingstoke and London: Macmillan.

Ambros, V. (2001), 'Přesýpací hodiny – Aneb pražská sémiotika divadla a dramatu v kontextu soudobých sémiotických teorií', in *Česká literatura na konci tisíciletí II: Příspěvky z 2. kongresu světové literárněvědné bohemistiky*, ed. D. Vojtěch, 457-70, Praha: Ústav pro českou literaturu AV ČR.

Anders, G. (1985/1956), *Die Antiquiertheit des Menschen: Über die Seele im Zeitalter der zweiten industriellen Revolution*, München: C. H. Beck.

Andrews, E. (2003), *Conversations with Lotman: Cultural Semiotics in Language, Literature and Cognition*, Toronto: University of Toronto Press.

Arendt, H. (1958), 'The Modern Concept of History', *The Review of Politics*, 20 (4): 570-90.

Arvidson, J., M. Askander, J. Bruhn and H. Führer, eds (2007), *Changing Borders: Contemporary Positions in Intermediality*, Lund: Intermedia Studies Press.

Aston, E. and G. Savona (1999), 'Czech Performance Theory', in *The Performance Text*, ed. D. Pietropaolo, 113-25, New York and Ottawa: Legas.

Aubert, M., P. Setiawan, A. A. Oktaviana, A. Brumm, P. H. Sulistyarto, E. W. Saptomo, B. Istiawan, T. A. Ma'rifat, V. N. Wahyuono, F. T. Atmoko, J.-X. Zhao, J. Huntley, P. S. C. Taçon, D. L. Howard and H. E. A. Brand (2018), 'Palaeolithic Cave Art in Borneo', *Nature*, 564: 254-7.

Aumont, J. (1997/1990), *The Image*, London: British Film Institute.

Babbitt, I. (2013/1910), *The New Laokoon: An Essay on the Confusion of the Arts*, Cambridge: Cambridge University Press.

Bachofen, J. J. (1958), *Die Unsterblichkeitlehre der orphischen Theologie auf den Grabdenkmälern des Altertums: Gesammelte Werke VII*, Stuttgart and Basel: Verlag Benno Schwabe & Co.

Bal, M. and N. Bryson (1991), 'Semiotics and Art History', *Art Bulletin*, 73 (2): 174-208.

Barborka, Z. (2018), *Hommage: Básně a prózy*, Praha: Dybbuk.

Barthes, R. (1957), *Mythologies*, Paris: Seuil.

Barthes, R. (1977), *Image – Music – Text*, ed. and trans. S. Heath, Glasgow: Fontana-Collins.

Barthes, R. (1981/1980), *Camera Lucida*, trans. R. Howard, New York: Hill and Wang.
Batchen, G. (2018), *Apparitions: Photography and Dissemination*, Sydney and Prague: Power Publications and Academy of Performing Arts in Prague.
Bateman, J. A., J. Wildfeuer and T. Hiippala (2017), *Multimodality: Foundations, Research and Analysis: A Problem-Oriented Introduction*, Berlin and Boston: De Gruyter.
Bateson, G. (1987/1972), *Steps to an Ecology of Mind: Collected Essays in Anthropology, Psychiatry, Evolution, and Epistemology*, Northvale and London: Jason Aronson.
Belliger, A. and D. J. Krieger (2016), 'The End of Media: Reconstructing Media Studies on the Basis of Actor-Network Theory', in *Applying the Actor-Network Theory in Media Studies*, ed. M. Spöhrer and B. Ochsner, 20–37, Hershey: IGI Global.
Belting, H. (2001), *Bild-Anthropologie: Entwürfe für eine Bildwissenchaft*, München: Wilhelm Fink.
Bender, E. M., T. Gebru, A. McMillan-Major and S. Shmitchell (2021), 'On the Dangers of Stochastic Parrots: Can Language Models Be Too Big?', in *Proceedings of the 2021 ACM Conference on Fairness, Accountability, and Transparency (FAccT '21)*, 610–23, New York: Association for Computing Machinery. Available online: https://doi.org/10.1145/3442188.3445922 (accessed 5 May 2023).
Benjamin, A. and B. Hanssen, eds (2002), *Walter Benjamin and Romanticism*, London and New York: Continuum.
Benjamin, W. (1979a/1916), 'On Language as Such and on the Language of Man', in *One-Way Street, and Other Writings*, ed. and trans. E. Jephcott and K. Shorter, 107–23, London: NLB.
Benjamin, W. (1979b/1928), 'One-Way Street', in *One-Way Street, and Other Writings*, ed. and trans. E. Jephcott and K. Shorter, 45–104, London: NLB.
Benjamin, W. (1979c/1933), 'Doctrine of the Similar', trans. K. Tarnowski, *New German Critique*, 7 (17): 65–9.
Benjamin, W. (1979d/1933), 'On the Mimetic Faculty', in *One-Way Street, and Other Writings*, ed. and trans. E. Jephcott and K. Shorter, 160–3, London: NLB.
Benjamin, W. (1996a/1918), 'On the Program of the Coming Philosophy', in *Selected Writings I, 1913–1926*, ed. M. Bullock and M. W. Jennings, 100–10, Cambridge, MA: Harvard University Press.
Benjamin, W. (1996b/1919), 'The Concept of Art Criticism in German Romanticism', in *Selected Writings I, 1913–1926*, 116–200, ed. M. Bullock and M. W. Jennings, Cambridge, MA: Harvard University Press.
Benjamin, W. (1996c/1923), 'The Task of the Translator', in *Selected Writings I, 1913–1926*, ed. M. Bullock and M. W. Jennings, 253–63, Cambridge, MA: Harvard University Press.
Benjamin, W. (1996d/1930), 'Theories of German Fascism', in *Selected Writings II, 1, 1927–1930*, ed. M. W. Jennings, H. Eiland and G. Smith, 312–21, Cambridge, MA: Harvard University Press.

Benjamin, W. (1996e/1932), 'Excavation and Memory', in *Selected Writings II, 2, 1931–1934*, ed. M. W. Jennings, H. Eiland and G. Smith, 576, Cambridge, MA: Harvard University Press.
Benjamin, W. (1996f/1940), 'On the Concept of History', in *Selected Writings IV, 1938–1940*, ed. M. Bullock, H. Eiland and G. Smith, 389–400, Cambridge, MA: Harvard University Press.
Benjamin, W. (2010/1935), 'The Work of Art in the Age of Its Technological Reproducibility', 1st version, trans. M. W. Jennings, *Grey Room*, 11 (39): 11–37. Available online: https://doi.org/10.1162/grey.2010.1.39.11 (accessed 27 April 2023).
Benjamin, W. (2011/1915), 'The Rainbow: A Conversation about Imagination', in *Early Writings (1910–1917)*, ed. and trans. H. Eiland, 224–7, Cambridge, MA: Harvard University Press.
Benjamin, W. (2019/1924), 'Epistemo-Critical Foreword', in *Origin of the German Trauerspiel*, trans. H. Eiland, 1–39, Cambridge, MA: Harvard University Press.
Bense, M. (1967/1962), *Teorie textů*, trans. B. Grögerová and J. Hiršal, Praha: Odeon.
Bense, M. and L. Harig (1969/1968), 'Der Monolog der Terry Jo', in *Neues Hörspiel: Texte, Partituren*, ed. K. Schöning, 57–91, Frankfurt am Main: Suhrkamp.
Benthien, C. and B. Weingart, eds (2014), *Handbuch Literatur & Visuelle Kultur*, Berlin and Boston: De Gruyter.
Bergson, H. (1963/1932), *The Two Sources of Morality and Religion*, trans. R. Audra and C. Brereton, University of Notre Dame: Notre Dame Press.
Berndt, F. and L. Tonger-Erk (2013), *Intertextualität: Eine Einführung*, Berlin: Erich Schmidt.
Bernhard, P. (2007), 'Plessners Konzept der offenen Form im Kontext der Avantgarde der 1920er Jahre', *Arhe: Časopis za filozofiju*, 4 (7): 237–52.
Blanchot, M. (1982/1955), *The Space of Literature*, trans. A. Smock, Lincoln: University of Nebraska Press.
Blättler, A., ed. (2010), *Intermediale Inszenierungen im Zeitalter der Digitalisierung: Medientheoretische Analysen und ästhetische Konzepte*, Bielefeld: transcript Verlag.
Blumenberg, H. (1990/1979), *Arbeit am Mythos*, Frankfurt am Main: Suhrkamp.
Blumenberg, H. (2001a/1964), 'Sokrates und das "objet ambigu": Paul Valérys Auseinandersetzung mit der Tradition der Ontologie des ästhetischen Gegenstandes', in *Ästhetische und metaphorologische Schriften*, 74–111, Frankfurt am Main: Suhrkamp.
Blumenberg, H. (2001b/1966), 'Die essentielle Vieldeutigkeit des ästhetischen Gegenstandes', in *Ästhetische und metaphorologische Schriften*, 112–19, Frankfurt am Main: Suhrkamp.
Boden, M. A. (2016), *AI: Its Nature and Future*, Oxford: Oxford University Press.

Boehm, G. and H. Pfotenhauer, eds (1995), *Beschreibungskunst – Kunstbeschreibung: Ekphrasis von der Antike bis zur Gegenwart*, München: Wilhelm Fink.
Bogatyrev, P. (1940), *Lidové divadlo české a slovenské*, Prague: Fr. Borový.
Bogatyrev, P. (2008/1938), 'Disney's *Snow White*', trans. K. B. Johnson, in *Cinema All the Time: An Anthology of Czech Film Theory and Criticism, 1908–1939*, ed. P. Szczepanik and J. Anděl, 277–80, Prague and Ann Arbor: National Film Archive and Michigan Slavic Publications.
Bogatyrev, P. (2016a/1936), 'Clothing as Sign: The Functional and Structural Concept in Ethnography', trans. Y. Lockwood, in *Theatre Theory Reader: Prague School Writings*, ed. D. Drozd, T. Kačer and D. Sparling, 441–7, Prague: Karolinum Press.
Bogatyrev, P. (2016b/1938), 'Theatrical Signs', trans. B. Kochis, in *Theatre Theory Reader*, ed. D. Drozd, T. Kačer and D. Sparling, 99–114, Prague: Karolinum Press.
Bogost, I. (2022), 'ChatGPT is Dumber Than You Think', *The Atlantic*, 7 December. Available online: https://www.theatlantic.com/technology/archive/2022/12/chatgpt-openai-artificial-intelligence-writing-ethics/672386/ (accessed 5 May 2023).
Böhme, H. and Y. Ehrenspeck (2007), 'Nachwort: Zur Ästhetik und Kunstphilosophie Walter Benjamins', in *Aura und Reflexion: Schriften zur Ästhetik und Kunstphilosophie*, ed. W. Benjamin, 445–88, Frankfurt am Main: Suhrkamp.
Bolter, J. D. and R. Grusin (1999), *Remediation: Understanding New Media*, Cambridge, MA: MIT Press.
Bolz, N. (1993), *Am Ende der Gutenberg-Galaxis*, 196–226, München: Wilhelm Fink.
Bondanella, P. (1997), *Umberto Eco and the Open Text: Semiotics, Fiction, Popular Culture*, Cambridge: Cambridge University Press.
Bourdieu, P. (1992), *Les Règles de l'art: Genèse et Structure du Champ littéraire*, Paris: Édition du Seuil.
Boyd, B. (1991), *Vladimir Nabokov: The American Years*, Princeton: Princeton University Press.
Breton, A. (1999/1933), 'Picasso in His Element', in *Break of Day*, trans. M. Polizzotti and M. A. Cawsin, 111–22, Lincoln: University of Nebraska Press. Available online: https://archive.org/details/breakofdaypointd0000bret (accessed 29 April 2023).
Brown, G. and G. Yule (1983), *Discourse Analysis*, Cambridge: Cambridge University Press.
Brown, T. B., B. Mann, N. Ryder, M. Subbiah, J. D. Kaplan, P. Dhariwal, A. Neelakantan, P. Shyam, G. Sastry, A. Askell, S. Agarwal, A. Herbert-Voss, G. Krueger, T. Henighan, R. Child, A. Ramesh, D. Ziegler, J. Wu, C. Winter, C. Hesse, M. Chen, E. Sigler, M. Litwin, S. Gray, B. Chess, J. Clark, C. Berner, S. McCandlish, A. Radford, I. Sutskever and D. Amode (2020), 'Language Models are Few-Shot Learners', *Advances in Neural Information Processing*

Systems, 33. Available online: https://arxiv.org/abs/2005.14165 (accessed 16 August 2023).
Bruhn, J. (2016), *The Intermediality of Narrative Literature: Medialities Matter*, London: Palgrave Macmillan.
Bruhn, J. and B. Schirrmacher, eds (2021), *Intermedial Studies: An Introduction to Meaning Across Media*, London: Routledge.
Buckner, C. and J. Garson (2018), 'Connectionnism and Post-Connectionist Models', in *The Routledge Handbook of the Computational Mind*, ed. M. Sprevak and M. Colombo, 76–90, London and New York: Routledge.
Bühler, K. (1990/1934), *The Theory of Language: The Representational Function of Language*, trans. D. F. Goodwin, Amsterdam: John Benjamin's Publishing Company.
Bunz, M. (2019), *On the Misunderstanding of AI* [paper presented at the Center of Data Science], New York University, 1 October.
Burian, E. F. (2016/1936), 'The Function of Photography and Film in the Theatre', trans. E. Daníčková, in *Theatre Theory Reader: Prague School Writings*, ed. D. Drozd, T. Kačer and D. Sparling, 497–8, Prague: Karolinum Press.
Bydžovská, L. and K. Srp (2007), *Jindřich Štyrský*, Praha: Argo.
Caesar, M. (2009), 'Eco and Joyce', in *New Essays on Umberto Eco*, ed. P. Bondanella, 141–56, Cambridge: Cambridge University Press.
Cardwell, S. (2018), 'Pause, Rewind, Replay: Adaptation, Intertextuality and (Re)defining Adaptation Studies', in *The Routledge Companion to Adaptation*, ed. D. Cutchins, K. Krebs and E. Voigts, 7–17, New York: Routledge.
Cartmell, D., I. Q. Hunter, H. Kaye and I. Whelehan, eds (1996), *Pulping Fictions: Consuming Culture across the Literature/Media Divide*, London: Pluto Press.
Cassirer, E. (1993/1939), 'Naturalistische und humanistische Begründung der Kulturphilosophie', in *Erkenntnis, Begriff, Kultur*, ed. R. A. Bast, 231–63, Hamburg: Felix Meiner Verlag.
Cassirer, E. (2004), *Aufsätze und kleine Schriften (1927–1931): Ernst Cassirer Werke. Hamburger Ausgabe XVII*, ed. B. Recki, Hamburg: Felix Meiner Verlag.
Caws, M. A. (1981), *The Eye in the Text: Essays on Perception, Mannerist to Modern*, Princeton: Princeton University Press.
Červenka, M. (1973), 'Die Grundkategorien des Prager literaturwissenschaftlicher Strukturalismus', in *Zur Kritik literaturwissenschaftlicher Methodologie*, ed. V. Šmegač and Z. Škreb, 137–68, Frankfurt am Main: Athenäum S. Fischer Verlag.
Červenka, M. (1978), *Der Bedeutungsaufbau des literarischen Werks, Theorie und Geschichte der Literatur und der schönen Künste 36*, ed. F. Boldt and W. D. Stempel, München: Wilhelm Fink Verlag.
Červenka, M. (1992/1968), *Významová výstavba literárního díla*, Praha: Karolinum.

Červenka, M. (1996), 'Literární artefakt', in *Obléhání zevnitř*, 40–78, Praha: Torst.
Chalmers, D. (2020), 'GPT-3 and General Intelligence', *Dailynouns*, 30 July. Available online: https://dailynous.com/2020/07/30/philosophers-gpt-3/#chalmers (accessed 5 May 2023).
Chartier, R. (1995/1993), *Forms and Meanings: Texts, Performances and Audiences from Codex to Computer*, Philadelphia: University of Pennsylvania Press.
Chartier, R., M. Wögerbauer and R. Müller (2018/2017), 'Three Textual Cultures: With Roger Chartier on Manuscripts, Books and Digital Media', *Ústav pro českou literaturu AV ČR*, 15 June. Available online: https://ucl.cas.cz/ceska-literatura-blog/three-textual-cultures-with-roger-chartier-on-manuscripts-books-and-digital-media/ (accessed 5 May 2023).
Chastel, A. (1991), 'Peinture et Science', *Monuments et mémoires de la Fondation Eugène Piot*, 72: 107–13.
Chatman, S. (1978), *Story and Discourse: Narrative Structure in Fiction and Film*, Ithaca and London: Cornell University Press.
Chatman, S. (1990), *Coming to Terms: The Rhetoric of Narrative in Fiction and Film*, Ithaca: Cornell University Press.
Chudý, T. and R. Müller (2023), 'Intermediality, Semiotics and Media Theory', in *The Palgrave Handbook of Intermediality*, ed. J. Bruhn, A. López-Varela and M. de Paiva Vieira, Cham: Palgrave Macmillan. Available online: https://doi.org/10.1007/978-3-030-91263-5_18-1.
Chvatík, K. (1970), *Strukturalismus und Avantgarde*, trans. H. Gaertner, München: C. Hanser.
Clarke, B. (2014), *Neocybernetics and Narrative*, Minneapolis: University of Minnesota Press.
Cloud Atlas (2012), [Film] Dir. L. Wachowski, T. Tykwer and L. Wachowski, Germany/UK/USA: Warner Bros. Pictures.
Clüver, C. (1989), 'On Intersemiotic Transposition', *Poetics Today*, 10 (1): 55–90.
Clüver, C. (1993), 'Interartiella studier: En inledning', in *I musernas tjänst: Studier i konstarternas interrelationer*, ed. U.-B. Lagerroth and H. Lund, 17–47, Stockholm: Brutus Östlings bokförlag Symposion.
Clüver, C. (1997), 'Ekphrasis Reconsidered: On Verbal Representations of Non-verbal Texts', in *Interart Poetics: Essays on the Interrelations of the Arts and Media*, ed. U.-B. Lagerroth, H. Lund and E. Hedling, 19–33, Amsterdam and Atlanta: Rodopi.
Clüver, C. (2000–1), 'Inter/textus, Inter/artes, Inter/media', *Komparatistik: Jahrbuch der Deutschen Gesellschaft für Allgemeine und Vergleichende Literaturwissenschaft*: 15–50.
Clüver, C. (2007), 'Intermediality and Interart Studies', in *Changing Borders: Contemporary Positions in Intermediality*, ed. J. Arvidson, M. Askander, J. Bruhn and H. Führer, 19–37, Lund: Intermedia Studies Press.
Clüver, C. (2017), 'A New Look at an Old Topic: Ekphrasis Revisited', *Dossi*, 19 (1): 30–44.

Coleridge, S. T. (1912), *The Complete Poetical Works of Samuel Taylor Coleridge: Including Poems and Versions of Poems Now Published for the First Time. Volume I, Poems*, ed. E. H. Coleridge, Oxford: The Clarendon Press.
Conard, N. J. (2009), 'A Female Figurine from the Basal Aurignacian of Hohle Fels Cave in Southwestern Germany', *Nature*, 459: 248–52.
Condorcet, J. A. N. de (1796/1795), *Outlines of an Historical View of the Progress of the Human Mind*, Philadelphia: M. Carey, H. & P. Rice & Co., J. Ormrod, B. F. Bache and J. Fellows.
Conrad-Martius, H. (1923), 'Realontologie: I. Buch', *Jahrbuch für Phänomenologie und phänomenologische Forschung*, 6: 159–333.
Cooley, C. H. (1909), *Social Organization: A Study of the Larger Mind*, New York: Charles Scribner's Sons.
Corbineau-Hoffmann, A. (2004), *Einführung in die Komparatistik*, Berlin: Schmidt.
Costa Vieira, E. V., H. Führer and M. de Paiva Vieira, eds (2021), *Letras & Letras: Literatura, intermidialidade e ensino*, 37 (1), Special issue.
Crary, J. (1990), *Techniques of the Observer: On Vision and Modernity in the Nineteenth Century*, Cambridge, MA: The MIT Press.
Culler, J. (2000/1997), *Literary Theory: A Very Short Introduction*, Oxford: Oxford University Press.
Culler, J. (2002/1975), *Structuralist Poetics: Structuralism, Linguistics and the Study of Literature*, London and New York: Routledge & Kegan Paul.
Daneš, F. (2001), 'Analýza zdrojů pražského lingvistického funkcionalismu', in *Funkcionalismus ve vědě a filosofii*, ed. J. Nosek, 11–20, Prague: Filosofia.
Danto, A. (1964), 'The Artworld', *The Journal of Philosophy*, 61 (19): 571–84.
Därmann, I. (1995), *Tod und Bild: Eine phänomenologische Mediengeschichte*, München: Wilhelm Fink.
Debray, R. (1991), *Cours de médiologie générale*, 16–535, Paris: Gallimard.
Debray, R. (1996/1994), *Media Manifestos*, trans. E. Rauth, 534–5, London and New York: Verso.
Dencker, K. P. (2011), *Optische Poesie: Von den prähistorischen Schriftzeichen bis zu den digitalen Experimenten der Gegenwart*, Berlin: De Gruyter.
Derrida, J. (1993/1990), *Memoirs of the Blind: The Self-Portrait and Other Ruins*, trans. P.-A. Brault and M. Naas, Chicago: The University of Chicago Press.
Derrida, J. (1998/1967), *Of Grammatology*, Baltimore and London: Johns Hopkins University.
Derrida, J. (1999/1997), *Adieu to Emmanuel Levinas*, trans. P.-A. Brault and M. Naas, Stanford: Stanford University Press.
Derrida, J. (2000/1997), *Of Hospitality*, trans. R. Bowlby, Stanford: Stanford University Press.
Derrida, J. (2001), *The Work of Mourning*, Chicago and London: The University of Chicago Press.
Derrida, J. (2014/1987), *Cinders*, trans. N. Lukacher, Minneapolis: University of Minnesota Press.
Derrida, J. and B. Stiegler (2002/1996), *Echographies of Television: Filmed Interviews*, trans. J. Bajorek, Cambridge: Polity Press.

Deuber-Mankowsky, A. (2009), 'Umspielende Massenbewegungen: Zum Verhältnis von Medium und Wahrnehmung nach Benjamin', in *Techniken der Übereinkunft: Zur Medialität des Politischen*, ed. H. Blumentrath, K. Rothe, S. Werkmeister, M. Wünsch and B. Wurm, 57–78, Berlin: Kulturverlag Kadmos.

Dickie, G. (1974), 'What is Art? An Institutional Analysis', in *Art and the Aesthetic: An Institutional Analysis*, 19–52, Ithaca and London: Cornell University Press.

Diderot, D. and J. le R. D'Alembert (1765), *Encyclopédie, ou Dictionnaire raisonné des sciences, des arts et des métiers VIII*, Paris: Le Breton, Durand, Briasson and David.

Didi-Huberman, G. (1992), *Ce que nous voyons, ce qui nous regarde*, Paris: Éditions de Minuit.

Didi-Huberman, G. (1998), *Phasmes: Essais sur l'apparition*, Paris: Éditions de Minuit.

Didi-Huberman, G. (2001), *Génie du non-lieu: Air, poussière, empreinte, hantise*, Paris: Éditions de Minuit.

Didi-Huberman, G. (2015/1993), *The Cube and the Face: Around a Sculpture by Alberto Giacometti*, trans. S. B. Lillis, Zürich and Berlin: Diaphanes.

Dobrzyńska, T. (1984), *Metafora*, Wrocław: Zakład Narodowy Im. Ossolińskich.

Doležel, L. (1995), 'Roman Jakobson as a Student of Communication', in *Studies in Poetics: Commemorative Volume: Krystyna Pomorska (1928–1986)*, ed. E. Semeka-Pankratov, 27–38, Columbus, OH: Slavica Publishers.

Domingos, A. C. M. (2020), 'Intermidialidade na literatura brasileira contemporânea', *Letras de Hoje*, 55: 14–26.

Donguy, J. (2007), *Poésies expérimentales, zone numérique (1953–2007)*, Dijon: Presses du réel.

Drakakis, J. (2001), 'Cultural Materialism', in *The Cambridge History of Literary Criticism 9: Twentieth-Century Historical, Philosophical and Psychological Perspectives*, ed. Ch. Knellwolf and Ch. Norris, 43–58, Cambridge: Cambridge University Press.

Drozd, D., T. Kačer and D. Sparling, eds (2016), *Theatre Theory Reader: Prague School Writings*, Prague: Karolinum Press.

Dudley, A. (1980), 'The Well-Worn Muse: Adaptation in Film History and Theory', in *Narrative Strategies: Original Essays in Film and Prose Fiction*, ed. S. Cogner and J. Welsch, 9–17, Macomb: Western Illinois University Press.

Dürer, A. (1966), *Albrecht Dürer: Schriftlicher Nachlass I*, ed. H. Rupprich, Berlin: Deutscher Verein für Kunstwissenschaft.

Eagleton, T., ed. (1989), *Raymond Williams: Critical Perspectives*, Cambridge: Polity.

Eco, U. (1962), '[Introduzione]', in *Arte programmata: Arte cinetica, opere moltiplicate, opera aperta*, exhibition catalogue, ed. B. Munari and G. Soavi, Milano, Venezia and Roma: Olivetti.

Eco, U. (1976), *A Theory of Semiotics*, Bloomington: Indiana University Press.

Eco, U. (1979), *Lector in fabula: La cooperazione interpretativa nei testi narrativi*, Milano: Bompiani.
Eco, U. (1987/1977), 'The Influence of Roman Jakobson on the Development of Semiotics', in *Classics of Semiotics*, ed. M. Krampen, K. Oehler, R. Posner, T. A. Sebeok and T. von Uexküll, 109–27, New York: Plenum Press.
Eco, U. (1989/1962), *The Open Work*, trans. A. Cancogni, Cambridge, MA: Harvard University Press.
Eco, U. (1994/1990), *The Limits of Interpretation*, Bloomington: Indiana University Press.
Eco, U. (1997/1962), *Opera aperta*, Milano: Bompiani.
Eco, U. (1999/1968), 'Vom Signal zum Sinn', in *Kursbuch Medienkultur: Die massgeblichen Theorien von Brecht bis Baudrillard*, ed. C. Pias, L. Engell, O. Fahle, J. Vogl and B. Neitzel, 192–5, Stuttgart: Deutsche Verlags-Anstalt DVA.
Eco, U. (2014/2007), *From the Tree to the Labyrinth: Historical Studies on the Sign and Interpretation*, trans. A. Oldcorn, Cambridge, MA: Harvard University Press.
Einem, H. von (1968), 'Das Auge, der edelste Sinn', *Walraff-Richartz-Jahrbuch*, 30 (1): 275–86.
Eldridge, J. and L. Eldridge, eds (1994), *Raymond Williams: Making Connections*, London and New York: Routledge.
Elleström, L. (2010), 'The Modalities of Media: A Model for Understanding Intermedial Relations', in *Media Borders, Multimodality and Intermediality*, ed. L. Elleström, 11–48, Basingstoke and New York: Palgrave Macmillan.
Elleström, L. (2014), *Media Transformation: The Transfer of Media Characteristics Among Media*, Basingstoke and New York: Palgrave Macmillan.
Elleström, L. (2017), 'Adaptation and Intertextuality', in *The Oxford Handbook of Adaptation Studies*, ed. T. Leitch, s. 509–27, New York: Oxford University Press.
Elleström, L. (2021a), 'The Modalities of Media II: An Expanded Model for Understanding Intermedial Relations', in *Beyond Media Borders: Intermedial Relations among Multimodal Media 1*, ed. L. Elleström, 3–91, Cham: Springer International Publishing.
Elleström, L., ed. (2021b), *Beyond Media Borders: Intermedial Relations among Multimodal Media 2*, Cham: Springer International Publishing.
Emerson, C. (2011), 'Review of Maxim Waldstein: The Soviet Empire of Signs: A History of the Tartu School of Semiotics', *Kritika: Explorations in Russian and Eurasian History*, 12 (1): 262–8.
Ensslin, A., J. Round and T. Bronwen (2023), *The Routledge Companion to Literary Media*, Abingdon and New York: Routledge.
Ernst, U. (1990), 'Labyrinthe aus Lettern: Visuelle Poesie als Konstante europäischer Literatur', in *Text und Bild, Bild und Text*, ed. W. Harms, 197–215, Stuttgart: J.B. Metzler.
Fabian, J. (2005), 'Ruku v ruce s básnictvím: Roman Jakobson a Umělecký svaz Devětsil', *Slovo a smysl*, 2 (4): 74–95.

Fadiga, L., L. Craighero, M. Fabbri Destro, L. Finos, N. Cotillon-Williams, A. T. Smith and U. Castiello (2006), 'Language in Shadow', *Social Neuroscience*, 1 (2): 77–89.
Farago, C. J. (1992), *Leonardo da Vinci's Paragone: A Critical Interpretation with a New Edition of the Text in the Codex Urbinas*, trans. C. J. Farago, Leiden: Brill.
Faßler, M. (1997), 'Informationelle Poiesis: Elemente einer Theorie der Mensch-Computer-Interaktivität', in *Differenz und Integration: Die Zukunft moderner Gesellschaften. Verhandlungen des 28. Kongresses der Deutschen Gesellschaft für Soziologie im Oktober 1996 in Dresden II: Sektionen, Arbeitsgruppen, Foren, Fedor-Stepun-Tagung*, ed. K. S. Rehberg, 234–9, Opladen: Westdeutscher Verlag.
Faßler, M. (2005), *Erdachte Welten: Die mediale Evolution globaler Kulturen*, Wien and New York: Springer.
Faßler, M. (2008), *Der infogene Mensch: Entwurf einer Anthropologie*, München: Wilhelm Fink.
Faulstich, W. (1997), '"Jetzt geht die Welt zugrunde . . ." "Kulturschocks" und Medien-Geschichte: Vom antikem Theater bis zu Multimedia', in *Multimedia-Kommunikation: Theorien, Trends und Praxis*, ed. P. Ludes and A. Werne, 13–36, Opladen: Springer.
Faulstich, W. (2006), *Mediengeschichte von 1700 bis ins 3. Jahrtausend*, Göttingen: Vandenhoeck & Ruprecht.
Fazi, B. (2019), *The Incommensurable: Explainability and the Autonomy of Computational Automation* [paper presented at the Graduate Center], City University of New York, 12 November. Abstract available online: https://www.gc.cuny.edu/events/incommensurable-explainability-and-autonomy-computational-automation/ (accessed 5 May 2023).
Fedrová, S. and A. Jedličková (2010), 'Why the Verbal May Be Experienced as Visual', in *The Aesthetic Dimension of Visual Culture*, ed. O. Dadejík and J. Stejskal, 76–88, Cambridge: Cambridge Scholars Publishing.
Fedrová, S. and A. Jedličková (2016), *Viditelné popisy: Vizualita, sugestivita a intermedialita literární deskripce*, Praha: Akropolis.
Fichte, J. G. (1806), *Grundzüge des Gegenwärtigen Zeitalters in Vorlesungen (1804–1805)*, Berlin: Realbuchhandlung.
Filmer, P. (2003), 'Structures of Feeling and Socio-Cultural Formations: The Significance of Literature and Experience to Raymond Williams's Sociology of Culture', *British Journal of Sociology*, 54 (2): 199–219.
Foucault, M. (1971), *L'ordre du discours*, Paris: Gallimard.
Frank, S., C. Ruhe and A. Schmitz, eds (2012), *Explosion und Peripherie: Jurij Lotmans Semiotik der kulturellen Dynamik Revisited*, Bielefeld: transcript Verlag.
Freedman, D. (2002), 'A "Technological Idiot"? Raymond Williams and Communicative Technology', *Information, Communication and Society*, 5 (3): 425–42.
Freud, S. (1961/1930), *Civilization and its Discontents*, trans. J. Strachey, New York: Norton.

Freyermuth, G. S. (2007), 'Einleitung', *Figurationen: Gender – Literatur – Kultur*, 7 (2): 6–8.
Fuchs, P. (1993), *Moderne Kommunikation: Zur Theorie des Operativen Displacements*, Frankfurt am Main: Suhrkamp.
Fuchs, P. (1999), *Intervention und Erfahrung*, Frankfurt am Main: Suhrkamp.
Führer, H. and B. Banaszkiewicz (2014), 'The Trajectory of Ancient Ekphrasis', in *On Description*, ed. A. Jedličková, 45–75, Praha: Akropolis.
Gamm, G. (2000), *Nicht nichts: Studien zu einer Semantik des Unbestimmten*, Frankfurt am Main: Suhrkamp.
Gamm, G. (2004), *Der unbestimmte Mensch: Zur medialen Konstruktion von Subjektivität*, Berlin and Wien: Philo & Philo Fine Arts.
Gamm, G. (2006), 'Kunst und Subjektivität', in *Subjekt und Medium in der Kunst der Moderne*, ed. M. Lüthy and Ch. Menke, 49–67, Zürich and Berlin: Diaphanes.
Gasparov, B. M. (1994), 'Tartuskaya shkola 1960-ch godov kak semiotičeskiĭ fenomen', in *Y. M. Lotman i tartusko-moskovskaya semioticheskaya shkola*, ed. A. D. Koshelev, 279–94, Moskva: Gnozis.
Gastaldi, J. L. (2021), 'Why Can Computers Understand Natural Language?', *Philosophy and Technology*, 34 (1): 149–214.
Gebauer, G., ed. (1984), *Das Laokoon-Projekt: Pläne der semiotischen Ästhetik*, Stuttgart: Metzler.
Genz J. and P. Gévaudan (2016), *Medialität, Materialität, Kodierung: Grundzüge einer allgemeinen Theorie der Medien*, Bielefeld: transcript Verlag.
Geoghegan, B. D. (2011), 'From Information Theory to French Theory: Jakobson, Lévi-Strauss, and the Cybernetic Apparatus', *Critical Inquiry*, 38 (1): 96–126.
Gess, N. (2010), '"Intermedialität Reconsidered": Vom Paragone bei Hoffmann bis zum inneren Monolog bei Schnitzler', *Poetica*, 42 (1–2): 139–68.
Giesecke, M. (1999), 'Geschichte, Gegenwart und Zukunft sozialer Informations-verarbeitung', in *Alle möglichen Welten: Virtuelle Realität – Wahrnehmung – Ethik der Kommunikation*, ed. M. Faßler, 185–205, München: Wilhelm Fink.
Gitelman, L. (2006), *Always Already New: Media, History and the Data of Culture*, Cambridge and London: The MIT Press.
Goodman, N. (1968), *Languages of Art: An Approach to a Theory of Symbols*, Indianapolis, New York and Kansas City: Bobbs-Merrill Comp.
Gramigna, R. and S. Salupere (2017), 'Umberto Eco and Juri M. Lotman on Communication and Cognition', in *Umberto Eco in His Own Words*, ed. T. Thellefsen and B. Sørensen, 248–57, Berlin and Boston: De Gruyter Mouton.
Greenberg, C. (1992/1940), 'Towards a Newer Laocoon', in *Art in Theory 1900–1990: An Anthology of Changing Ideas*, ed. Ch. Harrison and P. Wood, 554–60, Oxford: Blackwell Publishers.
Greenblatt, S. (1997), 'The Interart Moment', in *Interart Poetics: Essays on the Interrelations of the Arts and Media*, ed. U.-B. Lagerroth, H. Lund and E. Hedling, 13–15, Amsterdam: Rodopi.

Grethlein, J. (2017), 'Lessing's Laocoon and the 'As-If' of Aesthetic Experience', in *Rethinking Lessing's Laocoon*, ed. A. Lifschitz and M. Squire, 307–26, Oxford: Oxford University Press.
Grishakova, M. and M.-L. Ryan, eds (2010), *Intermediality and Storytelling*, Berlin and Boston: De Gruyter.
Grögerová, B. (1997), 'Počátky a vývoj konkrétní a vizuální poezie', in *Báseň, obraz, gesto, zvuk: Experimentální poezie 60. let*, exhibition catalogue, 15–21, Praha: Památník národního písemnictví.
Guillory, J. (2010), 'Genesis of the Media Concept', *Critical Inquiry*, 36 (2): 321–62.
Guillory, J. (2015), 'Marshall McLuhan, Rhetoric, and the Prehistory of Media Studies', *Affirmations: Of the Modern*, 3 (1): 78–90.
Gumbrecht, H. U., ed. (1988), *Materialität der Kommunikation*, Frankfurt: Suhrkamp.
Gumbrecht, H. U. (2003), 'Why Intermediality – If at all?', *Intermédialitiés/Intermediality*, 2: 173–8.
Gumbrecht, H. U. (2012/2011), *Atmosphere, Mood, Stimmung: On a Hidden Potential of Literature*, trans. E. Butler, Stanford: Stanford University Press.
Hagen, W. (2008), 'Metaxy: Eine historiosemantische Fußnote zum Medienbegriff', in *Was ist ein Medium?*, ed. S. Münker and A. Roesler, 13–29, Frankfurt am Main: Suhrkamp.
Hagstrum, J. H. (1958), *The Sister Arts: The Tradition of Literary Pictorialism and English Poetry from Dryden to Gray*, Chicago: University of Chicago Press.
Halas, F. (1957), *Básně*, Praha: Československý spisovatel.
Hall, S. (1980), 'Cultural Studies: Two Paradigms', *Media, Culture and Society*, 2 (1): 57–72.
Halliday, M. A. K. (1978), *Language as Social Semiotic*, London: Edward Arnold.
Hansen, M. B. N. (2012), 'Engineering Pre-individual Potentiality: Technics, Transindividuation, and 21st-Century Media', *SubStance*, 41 (3): 32–59.
Hansen-Löve, A. A. (1983), 'Intermedialität und Intertextualität: Probleme der Korrelation von Wort- und Bildkunst am Beispiel der russischen Moderne', in *Dialog der Texte: Hamburger Kolloquium zur Intertextualität*, ed. W. Schmid and W.-D. Stempel, 291–360, Wien: Wiener Slawistischer Almanach.
Harms, W., ed. (1990), *Text und Bild, Bild und Text*, Stuttgart: J.B. Metzler.
Hartmann, F. (2000), *Medienphilosophie*, Wien: Wiener Universitätsverlag.
Hartmann, F. (2003), 'Techniktheorien der Medien', in *Theorien der Medien: Von der Kulturkritik bis zum Konstruktivismus*, ed. S. Weber, 49–79, Konstanz: UVK Verlag.
Hartung, H. (1975), *Experimentelle Literatur und konkrete Poesie*, Göttingen: Vandenhoeck & Ruprecht.
Hausken, L. (2004), 'Coda: Textual Theory and Blind Spots in Media Studies', in *Narrative Across Media: The Languages of Storytelling*, ed. M.-L. Ryan, 391–403, Lincoln: University of Nebraska Press.
Hauthal, J., A. Pethő and I. O. Rajewsky (2021), 'Roundtable of Researchers In Intermediality, Colóquio Internacional Leitura e Cognição', *Universidade*

de Santa Cruz do Sul – Unisc. Available online: https://www.unisc.br/site/coloquio2021/en/index.html (access 28 March 2023).

Havránek, B. (1938), 'Jazyk Máchův', in *Torso a tajemství Máchova díla: Sborník pojednání Pražského linguistického kroužku*, ed. J. Mukařovský, 279–331, Praha: Fr. Borový.

Hayles, N. K. (1990), *Chaos Bound: Orderly Disorder in Contemporary Literature and Science*, Ithaca and London: Cornell University Press.

Hayles, N. K. (1999), *How We Became Posthuman: Virtual Bodies in Cybernetics, Literature, and Informatics*, Chicago: University of Chicago Press.

Hayles, N. K. (2000), 'Making the Cut', in *Observing Complexity: Systems Theory and Postmodernity*, ed. W. Rasch and C. Wolfe, 137–62, Minneapolis: University of Minnesota Press.

Hayles, N. K. (2006), 'Traumas of Code', *Critical Inquiry*, 33 (1): 136–57.

Heczková, L. (2013), 'Jurij Lotman: Etika možností', in J. Lotman, *Kultura a exploze* , 7–12, Brno: Host.

Heffernan, J. (1993), *Museum of Words: The Poetics of Ekphrasis from Homer to Ashbery*, Chicago and London: University of Chicago Press.

Hegel, G. W. F. (1998/1835), *Aesthetics I*, trans. T. M. Knox, Oxford: Clarendon Press.

Heidegger, M. (1997/1991), *Kant and the Problem of Metaphyisics*, trans. R. Taft, Bloomington and Indianapolis: Indiana University Press.

Heißenbüttel, H. (1972/1965), 'Keine Experimente? Anmerkungen zu einem Schlagwort', in *Zur Tradition der Moderne: Aufsätze und Anmerkungen 1964–1971*, 126–35, Berlin: Luchterhand.

Helbig, J. (1998), 'Vorwort', in *Intermedialität: Theorie und Praxis eines interdisziplinären Forschungsgebiets*, 6–11, Berlin: Schmidt.

Helbig, J. (2008), 'Intermedialität – Eine spezifische Form des Medienkontakts oder globaler Oberbegriff? Neue Überlegungen zur Systematik intersemiotischer Beziehungen', in *Media Encounters and Media Theories*, ed. J. E. Müller, 77–85, Münster: Nodus Publikationen.

Helmstetter, R. (2011), 'Autonomie – Bertolt Brecht und F. W. Bernstein', in *Systemtheoretische Literaturwissenschaft: Begriffe – Methoden – Anwendungen*, ed. N. Werber, 39–58, Berlin and New York: De Gruyter.

Henshilwood, C. S., F. d'Errico, K. L. van Niekerk, L. Dayet, A. Queffelec and L. Pollarolo (2018), 'An Abstract Drawing from the 73,000-Year-Old Levels at Blombos Cave, South Africa', *Nature*, 562: 115–18.

Hermand, J. (1965/ 1971), *Literaturwissenschaft und Kunstwissenschaft: Methodische Wechselbeziehungen seit 1900*, Stuttgart: J.B. Metzler.

Hickethier, K. (2003), *Einführung in die Medienwissenschaft*, Stuttgart: J.B. Metzler.

Higgins, D. (1984), *Horizons: The Poetics and Theory of the Intermedia*, Carbondale: Southern Illinois University Press.

Higgins, D. (1987), *Pattern Poetry: Guide to an Unknown Literature*, Albany: State University of New York Press.

Higgins, J. (2013), *Raymond Williams: Literature, Marxism and Cultural Materialism*, London and New York: Verso.
Hildebrandt, T. (2011), 'Bild, Geste und Hand: Leroi-Gourhans paläontologische Bildtheorie', *Image: Zeitschrift für interdisziplinäre Bildwissenschaft*, 7 (2): 76–88.
Hiršal, J. and B. Grögerová (2007), *Let let: Pokus o rekapitulaci*, Praha: Torst.
Hiršal, J. and B. Grögerová, eds (1967), *Experimentální poezie*, trans. J. Hiršal and B. Grögerová, Praha: Odeon.
Hiršal, J. and B. Grögerová, eds (1993/1968), *Vrh kostek: Česká experimentální poezie*, Praha: Torst.
Hlaváček, J. (2007), 'Vizuální a konkrétní poezie, lettrismus', in *Dějiny českého výtvarného umění VI, 2*, ed. R. Švácha and M. Platovská, 232–9, Praha: Academia.
Hoek, L. H. and E. Vos (1997), 'The Eternal Network: Mail Art, Intermedia Semiotics, Interart Studies', in *Interart Poetics: Essays on the Interrelations of the Arts and Media*, ed. U.-B. Lagerroth, H. Lund and E. Hedling, 325–37. Amsterdam: Rodopi.
Hoesterey, I. and U. Weisstein, eds (1993), *Intertextuality: German Literature and Visual Art from the Renaissance to the Twentieth Century*, Columbia: Camden House.
Hoffmann, S. (2002), *Geschichte des Medienbegriffs*, Hamburg: Felix Meiner Verlag.
Hofmann, A. (2000), 'Formen der transposition d'art bei Théophile Gautier: Artefaktreferenz im Lichte des poetischen Systemwandels', in *Jenseits der Mimesis: Parnassische "transposition d'art" und der Paradigmawandel in der Lyrik des 19. Jahrhunderts*, ed. K. W. Hempfer, 77–120, Stuttgart: Steiner.
Homer (1999/1967), *The Odyssey of Homer*, trans. R. Lattimore, New York: Harper Perennial.
Honys, J. (2011), *Nesmelián aneb Do experimentálních textů vstup nesmělý*, ed. J. Šulc, Praha: Dybbuk.
Honzl, J. (1940), 'Objevné divadlo v lidovém divadle českém a slovenském', *Slovo a slovesnost*, 6 (2): 107–11.
Honzl, J. (2016/1940), 'The Mobility of the Theatrical Sign', trans. I. R. Titunik, in *Theatre Theory Reader: Prague School Writings*, ed. D. Drozd, T. Kačer and D. Sparling, 129–46, Prague: Karolinum Press.
Honzl, J. (2018/1935), 'Contribution to the Discussion of Speech in Film 1', trans. K. B. Johnson, in *Cinema All the Time: An Anthology of Czech Film Theory and Criticism, 1908–1939*, ed. P. Szczepanik and J. Anděl, 205–8, Prague and Ann Arbor: National Film Archive and Michigan Slavic Publications.
Hörisch, J. (2001), *Der Sinn und die Sinne: Eine Geschichte der Medien*, Frankfurt am Main: Eichborn.
Hörl, E. (2013), 'The Artificial Intelligence of Sense: The History of Sense and Technology after Jean-Luc Nancy (by Way of Gilbert Simondon)', trans. A. de Boever, *Parrhesia: A Journal of Critical Philosophy*, 8 (17): 11–24.

Hubig, C. (2015), *Die Kunst des Möglichen III: Macht der Technik*, Bielefeld: transcript Verlag.
Huhtamo, E. and J. Parikka, eds (2011), *Media Archaeology: Approaches, Applications, and Implications*, Berkeley, Los Angeles and London: University of California Press.
Husserl, E. (1960), 'Fifth Meditation: Uncovering of the Sphere of Transcendental Being as Monadological Intersubjectivity', in *Cartesian Meditations: An Introduction to Phenomenology*, trans. D. Cairns, 89–151, Dordrecht: Springer.
Husserl, E. (2001/1966), *Analyses Concerning Passive and Active Synthesis – Lectures on Transcendental Logic*, trans. A. J. Steinbock, Dordrecht: Kluwer Academic Publishers.
Husserl, E. (2006/1980), *Phantasy, Image Consciousness, and Memory (1898–1925)*, trans. J. B. Brough, Dordrecht: Springer.
Ihde, D. (1990), *Technology and the Lifeworld: From Garden to Earth*, Bloomington: Indiana University Press.
Imorde, J. (2005), 'Schleier aus dem Nichts: Materialisationsphänomene und ihre Dokumente', in *Ikonologie des Zwischenraums: Der Schleier als Medium und Metapher*, ed. J. Endres, B. Wittmann and G. Wolf, 361–84, München: Wilhelm Fink.
Ingold, T. (1999), '"Tools for the Hand, Language for the Face": An Appreciation of Leroi-Gourhan's Gesture and Speech', *Studies in History and Philosophy of Biological and Biomedical Sciences*, 30 (4): 411–53.
Isekenheimer, G. (2013), *Interpiktorialität: Theorie und Geschichte der Bild-Bild-Bezüge*, Bielefeld: transcript Verlag.
Iser, W. (1978/1976), *The Act of Reading: A Theory of Aesthetic Response*, Baltimore: Johns Hopkins University Press.
Iser, W. (1993/1991), *The Fictive and the Imaginary: Charting Literary Anthropology*, Baltimore: Johns Hopkins University Press.
Iser, W. (1998), 'Mimesis Emergenz', in *Mimesis und Simulation*, ed. A. Kablitz and G. Neumann, 669–84, Freiburg i. Breisgau: Rombach Verlag.
Iuli, C. (2013), 'Information, Communication, Systems: Cybernetic Aesthetics in 1960s Cultures', in *The Transatlantic Sixties: Europe and the United States in the Counterculture Decade*, ed. C. Juckner, G. Kosc, S. Monteith and B. Waldschmidt-Nelson, 226–55, Bielefeld: transcript Verlag.
Jackson, K. D., E. Vos and J. Drucker (1996), *Experimental – Visual – Concrete: Avant-garde Poetry since the 1960s*. Amsterdam: Rodopi.
Jahraus, O. (2003), *Literatur als Medium: Sinnkonstitution und Subjekterfahrung zwischen Bewußtsein und Kommunikation*, Weilerswist: Velbrück.
Jakobson, R. (1966/1959), 'On Linguistic Aspects of Translation', in *On Translation*, ed. R. A. Brower, 232–9, Cambridge, MA and New York: Harvard University Press and Oxford University Press.
Jakobson, R. (1971a/1952), 'Results of a Joint Conference of Anthropologists and Linguists', in *Selected Writings II: Word and Language*, 554–67, The Hague: Mouton.

Jakobson, R. (1971b/1968), 'Language in Relation to Other Communication Systems', in *Selected Writings II: Word and Language*, 697–710, The Hague: Mouton.
Jakobson, R. (1971c/1970), 'Linguistics in Relation to Other Sciences', in *Selected Writings II: Word and Language*, 655–96, The Hague: Mouton.
Jakobson, R. (1976/1933), 'Is the Cinema in Decline?', trans. E. Sokol, in *Semiotics of Art*, ed. L. Matejka and I. R. Titunik, 145–52, Cambridge: MIT.
Jakobson, R. (1981a/1949), 'Language in Operation', in *Selected Writings III: Poetry of Grammar and Grammar of Poetry*, 7–17, The Hague: Mouton.
Jakobson, R. (1981b/1958), 'Linguistics and Poetics', in *Selected Writings III: Poetry of Grammar and Grammar of Poetry*, 18–51, The Hague: Mouton.
Jankovič, M. (1985), 'Svébytná koncepce individuálního stylu', in J. Mukařovský, *O motorickém dění v poezii*, 123–45, Praha: Odeon.
Jankovič, M. (2005), 'Dění smyslu jako teoretický a interpretační problém', in M. Červenka, J. Holý, Z. Hrbata, M. Jankovič, A. Jedličková, L. Jungmannová, M. Kubínová, M. Langerová, Z. Mathauser and N. Vangeli, *Na cestě ke smyslu: Poetika literárního díla 20. století*, 821–964, Praha: Torst.
Jansson, A. (2014), 'Indispensable Things: On Mediatization, Materiality, and Space', in *Mediatization of Communication*, ed. K. Lundby, 273–96, Berlin and Boston: De Gruyter.
Jedličková, A., ed. (2014), *On Description*, Praha: Akropolis.
Jedličková, A. (2017), 'Jeden model, různé zájmy: Konvergence a divergence intermediálních studií', *Bohemica litteraria*, 20 (1): 98–125.
Jenkins, H. (2006), *Convergence Culture: Where Old and New Media Collide*, New York: New York University Press.
Jewitt, C. (2009), *Technology, Literacy and Learning: A Multimodal Approach*, London: Routledge.
Johansson, Ch. (2021), 'YouTube Podcasting, the New Orality, and Diversity of Thought: Intermediality, Media History, and Communication Theory as Methodological Approaches', in *Digital Human Sciences – New Objects, New Approaches*, ed. S. Petersson, 253–84, Stockholm: Stockholm University Press.
Jones, P. (1998), 'The Technology is not the Cultural Form? Raymond Williams's Sociological Critique of Marshall McLuhan', *Canadian Journal of Communication*, 23 (4). Available online: https://cjc-online.ca/index.php/journal/article/view/1058/964 (accessed 8 May 2023).
Jones, P. (2006/2004), *Raymond Williams's Sociology of Culture: A Critical Reconstruction*, 157–71, Basingstoke and New York: Palgrave Macmillan.
Kafka, F. (1988/1913), 'Unhappiness', trans. W. Muir and E. Muir, in *The Complete Stories*, 390–4, New York: Schocken Books.
Kalivoda, R. (1984), 'Cesta estetického myšlení Jana Mukařovského', in *Miroslavu Drozdovi a Jiřímu Honzíkovi k šedesátinám: Sborník*, ed. J. Franěk, 198–218, Praha, [typewritten copy].
Kapp, E. (1877), *Grundlinien einer Philosophie der Technik*, 25–145, Braunschweig: George Westermann.

Kapp, E. (2018/1877), *Elements of a Philosophy of Technology: On the Evolutionary History of Culture*, ed. J. W. Kirkwood and L. Weatherby, trans. L. K. Wolfe, 5–142, Minneapolis: University of Minnesota Press.
Kassner, R. (1951/1932), *Physiognomik*, Leipzig: Insel-Verlag.
Kelleher, J. D. (2019), *Deep Learning*, Cambridge and London: The MIT Press.
Kibédi Varga, Á. (1989), 'Criteria for Describing Word-and-Image Relations', *Poetics Today*, 10 (1): 31–53.
Kim, H. K. (2014), 'Die Geste als Figur des Realen bei Walter Benjamin', in *Bild und Geste: Figurationen des Denkens in Philosophie und Kunst*, ed. U. Richtmeyer, F. Goppelsröder and T. Hildebrandt, 107–25, Bielefeld: transcript Verlag.
Kircher, A. (1673), *Phonurgia nova*, Kempten: Rudolph Dreherr.
Kittler, F. (1988), 'Signal-Rausch-Abstand', in *Materialität der Kommunikation*, ed. H. U. Gumbrecht and K. L. Pfeiffer, 342–59, Frankfurt am Main: Suhrkamp.
Kittler, F. (1993), *Draculas Vermächtnis: Technische Schriften*, Leipzig: Reclam.
Kittler, F. (1995/1985), *Aufschreibesysteme 1800/1900*, München: Wilhelm Fink.
Kittler, F. (1999/1986), *Gramophone, Film, Typewriter*, trans. G. Winthrop-Young and M. Wutz, Stanford: Stanford University Press.
Kittler, F. (2000), *Eine Kulturgeschichte der Kulturwissenschaft*, München: Wilhelm Fink.
Kittler, F. (2017/1993), 'Real Time Analysis, Time Axis Manipulation', trans. G. Winthrop-Young, *Cultural Politics*, 13 (1): 1–18, Durham: Duke University Press.
Kline, R. R. (2009), 'Where are the Cyborgs in Cybernetics?', *Social Studies of Science*, 39 (3): 331–62.
Kline, R. R. (2015), *The Cybernetics Moment: Or Why We Call Our Age the Information Age*, Baltimore: John Hopkins University Press.
Kokeš, R. D. (2018), 'Strukturalismus a film', in *Slovník literárněvědného strukturalismu*, ed. O. Sládek, 661–8, Brno: Host.
Kolář, J. (1999), *Slovník metod: Okřídlený osel*, trans. B. Kolářová, Praha: Gallery.
Kouřil, M. 'Dvě lidové suity E. F. Buriana', *Český lid*, 65 (4): 207–17.
Krämer, S. (2006), 'The Cultural Techniques of Time Axis Manipulation: On Friedrich Kittler's Conception of Media', *Theory, Culture & Society*, 23 (7–8): 93–109.
Krämer, S. (2015), 'Methodological Considerations: Is a Metaphysics of Mediality Possible?', in *Medium, Messenger, Transmission*, trans. A. Enns, 27–38, Amsterdam: Amsterdam University Press.
Kranz, G. (1981), *Das Bildgedicht I: Theorie, Lexikon*, Köln: Böhlau.
Krausová, N. (1999), 'K začiatkom moderného semiologického uvažovania (Lessingova estetika)', in *Poetika v časoch za a proti*, 99–113, Nové Zámky: Literárne informačné centrum.
Krauss, S. W. D. (2012), *Die Genese der autonomen Kunst: Eine historische Soziologie der Ausdifferenzierung des Kunstsystems*, Bielefeld: transcript Verlag.

Kress, G. (2005), 'Gains and Losses: New Forms of Texts, Knowledge, and Learning', *Computers and Composition*, 22 (1): 5–22.
Kress, G. (2009), *Multimodality*. London: Routledge.
Kress, G. and A. Burn (2019), 'Multimodality, Style and Aesthetic: The Case of the Digital Werewolf', in *Multimodality and Aesthetics*, ed. E. Seip Toenessen and F. Forsgren, 15–36, New York and London: Routledge.
Kress, G. and T. van Leeuwen (1996), *Reading Images: The Grammar of Visual Design*, London: Routledge.
Krieger, M. (1967), 'Ekphrasis and the Still Movement of Poetry; or *Laokoon* Revisited', in *The Poet as Critic*, ed. F. P. W. McDowell, 3–26, Evanston: Northwestern University Press.
Krieger, M. (1992), *The Illusion of the Natural Sign*, Baltimore and London: Johns Hopkins University Press.
Kristeva, J. (1980/1967), 'Word, Dialogue and Novel', in *Desire in Language: A Semiotic Approach to Literature and Art*, trans. T. Gora and A. Jardine, 64–91, New York and London: Basil Blackwell.
Kučera, J. (2008/1933), 'Film and Building', trans. K. B. Johnson, in *Cinema All the Time: An Anthology of Czech Film Theory and Criticism, 1908–1939*, ed. P. Szczepanik and J. Anděl, 183–6, Prague and Ann Arbor: National Film Archive and Michigan Slavic Publications.
Künzler, J. (1989), *Medien und Gesellschaft: Die Medienkonzepte von Talcott Parsons, Jürgen Habermas und Niklas Luhmann*, Stuttgart: Ferdinand Enke Verlag.
Kupsch, K. (2010), 'The Extra-ordinary Art of "The Vane Sisters"', *The Midwest Quarterly*, 51 (3): 300–11.
Lachmann, R. (1998), 'Phantomlust und Stereoskopie: Zu einer Erzählung aus dem Spätwerk Ivan Turgenjevs', in *Mimesis und Simulation*, ed. A. Kablitz and G. Neumann, 479–514, Freiburg im Breisgau: Rombach.
Lachmann, R. (2002), *Erzählte Phantastik: Zu Phantasiegeschichte und Semantik phantastischer Texte*, Frankfurt am Main: Suhrkamp.
Lachmann, R. (2004), 'Literatur der Phantastik als Gegen-Anthropologie', in *Positionen der Kulturanthropologie*, ed. A. Assmann, U. Gaier and G. Trommsdorff, 44–60, Frankfurt am Main: Suhrkamp.
Lagerroth, U.-B., H. Lund and E. Hedling, eds (1997), *Interart Poetics: Essays on the Interrelation of the Arts and Media*, Amsterdam: Rodopi.
Langerová, M. (2002), 'Vizuální aspekty básnického díla', in M. Červenka, M. Jankovič, M. Langerová and M. Kubínová, *Pohledy zblízka: Zvuk, význam, obraz. Poetika literárního díla 20. století*, 377–474, Praha: Torst.
Largier, N. (2008), 'Gefährliche Nähe', *Magazin 31: Das Magazin des Instituts für Theorie*, 12–13: 43–8.
Latour, B. (2013/2012), *An Inquiry into Modes of Existence: An Athropology of the Moderns*, trans. C. Porter, Cambridge, MA: Harvard University Press.
Latour, B. (2014), 'Technical Does Not Mean Material', *Journal of Ethnographic Theory*, 4 (1): 507–10.

Leach, E. W. (1988), *The Rhetoric of Space: Literary and Artistic Representation of Landscape in Republican and Augustan Rome*, Princeton: Princeton University Press.
Ledin, P. and D. Machin (2020/2007), *Introduction to Multimodal Analysis*, London: Bloomsbury Academic.
Lee, R. W. (1940), 'Ut pictura poesis: The Humanistic Theory of Painting', *The Art Bulletin*, 22 (4): 197–269.
Lee-Morrison, L. (2023), 'Machinic Landscapes: Aesthetics of the non-human', *Media + Environment*, forthcoming.
Leeuwen, T. van and C. Jewitt (2001), *Handbook of Visual Analysis*, London: Sage.
Leitch, T. (2017), 'Against Conclusions: Petit Theories and Adaptation Studies', in *The Oxford Handbook of Adaptation Studies*, ed. T. Leitch, 698–709, New York: Oxford University Press.
Lemonnier, P. (2012), *Mundane Objects: Materiality and Non-Verbal Communication*, Walnut Creek: Left Coast Press.
Leroi-Gourhan, A. (1993/1964, 1965), *Gesture and Speech*, trans. A. B. Berger, Cambridge, MA: The MIT Press.
Leschke, R. (2003), *Einführung in die Medientheorie*, München: Wilhelm Fink.
Leschke, R. (2007), 'Mediale Formen zwischen Intermedialität und Vernetzung'. Available online: https://web.archive.org/web/20220618144630/http://www.rainerleschke.de/downloads/pdf/Mediale%20Formen%20&%20Vernetzung.pdf (accessed 3 May 2023).
Leschke, R. (2010a), 'Die Figur als mediale Form: Überlegungen zur Funktion der Figur in den Medien', in *Formen der Figur: Figurenkonzepte in Künsten und Medien*, ed. R. Leschke and H. Heidbrink, 29–52, Konstanz: UVK Verlag.
Leschke, R. (2010b), 'Einleitung: Zur transmedialen Logik der Figur', in *Formen der Figur: Figurenkonzepte in Künsten und Medien*, ed. R. Leschke and H. Heidbrink, 11–26, Konstanz: UVK Verlag.
Leschke, R. (2010c), *Medien und Formen: Eine Morphologie der Medien*, Konstanz: UVK Verlag.
Lessing, G. E. (1989/1766), *Laocoon: An Essay Upon the Limits of Painting and Poetry*, trans. E. A. McCormick, Baltimore: Johns Hopkins University Press.
Lévinas, E. (1974), *Autrement qu'être ou au-delà de l'essence*, Den Haag: Martinus Nijhoff.
Lévinas, E. (2007/1961), *Totality and Infinity*, trans. A. Lingis, Pittsburgh: Duquesne University Press.
Levý, J. (1971/1963), 'Teorie informace a literární proces', in *Bude literární věda exaktní vědou? Výbor studií*, ed. M. Červenka, 31–70, Praha: Československý spisovatel.
Lifschitz, A. (2017), 'Naturalizing the Arbitrary: Lessing's Laocoon and Enlightenment Semiotics', in *Rethinking Lessing's Laocoon*, ed. A. Lifschitz and M. Squire, 197–220, Oxford: Oxford University Press.

Lifschitz, A. and M. Squire, eds (2017), *Rethinking Lessing's Laocoon*, Oxford: Oxford University Press.
Lister, M., J. Dovey, S. Giddings, I. Grant and K. Kelly (2009/2003), *New Media: A Critical Introduction*, London and New York: Routledge.
Locke, J. (1689), *An Essay Concerning Human Understanding*, London: Thomas Basset.
Lotman, Y. M. (1977/1970), *The Structure of the Artistic Text*, trans. R. Vroon, Ann Arbor: University of Michigan.
Lotman, Y. M. (1979a/1977), 'Culture as Collective Intellect and Problems of Artificial Intelligence', trans. A. Shukman, in *Dramatic Structure: Poetic and Cognitive Semantics*, ed. L. M. O'Toole and A. Shukman, 84–96, Oxford: Holdan Books.
Lotman, Y. M. (1979b), 'The Future for Structural Poetics', *Poetics*, 8 (6): 501–7.
Lotman, Y. M. (1981a/1973), *Semiotics of Cinema*, trans. M. E. Suino, Ann Arbor: University of Michigan.
Lotman, Y. M. (1981b), 'Tekst v tekste', in *Trudy̆ po znakovy̆m sistemam XIV, Tekst v tekste*, ed. Y. M. Lotman, 3–18, Tartu: Tartuskiĭ gosudarstvennȳĭ universitet.
Lotman, Y. M. (1987), 'Ob itogakh i problemakh semioticheskikh issledovaniĭ', in *Trudy̆ po znakovy̆m sistemam XX, Aktual'nȳe problemȳ semiotiki kul'tury̆*, ed. Y. M. Lotman, 12–16, Tartu: Tartuskiĭ gosudarstvennȳĭ universitet.
Lotman, Y. M. (1995/1992), 'Ne-memuary̆', in *Lotmanovskiĭ sbornik 1*, ed. E. V. Permyakov, 5–53, Moskva: IC-Garant.
Lotman, Y. M. (2000a/1990), *Universe of the Mind: A Semiotic Theory of Culture*, trans. A. Shukman, Bloomington: Indiana University Press.
Lotman, Y. M. (2000b/1996), 'Vnutri my̆slyashchikh mirov', in *Semiosfera*, 149–390, Sankt-Peterburg: Iskusstvo-SPB.
Lotman, Y. M. (2000c), *Semiosfera*, Sankt-Peterburg: Iskusstvo-SPB.
Lotman, Y. M. (2005/1984), 'On the Semiosphere', trans. W. Clark, *Sign Systems Studies*, 33 (1): 205–29.
Lotman, Y. M. (2009/1992), *Culture and Explosion*, ed. M. Grishakova, trans. W. Clark, Berlin and New York: Mouton de Gruyter.
Lotman, Y. M. and B. A. Uspensky (1978/1971), 'On the Semiotic Mechanism of Culture', trans. G. Mihaychuk, *New Literary History*, 9 (2): 211–32.
Louvel, L. (2011), *Poetics of the Iconotext*, trans. L. Petit, Farnham and Burlington: Ashgate.
Ludmer, J. (2007/2006), 'Literaturas postautónomas: Otro estado de la escrictura', *Ciberletras: Revista de crítica literaria y de cultura – Journal of Literary Criticism and Culture*, 8 (17): 236–44. Available online: https://www.lehman.cuny.edu/ciberletras/documents/ISSUE17.pdf/ (accessed 1 April 2023).
Luhmann, N. (1981), *Soziologische Aufklärung III: Soziales System, Gesellschaft, Organisation*, Opladen: Westdeutscher Verlag.
Luhmann, N. (1982), 'Autopoiesis, Handlung und kommunikative Verständigung', *Zeitschrift für Soziologie*, 11 (4): 366–79.

Luhmann, N. (1987/1986), 'The Medium of Art', trans. D. Roberts, *Thesis Eleven*, 18 (1): 101–13.
Luhmann, N. (1995/1984), *Social Systems*, trans. J. Bednarz Jr. and D. Baecker, Stanford: Stanford University Press.
Luhmann, N. (1997), *Die Gesellschaft der Gesellschaft*, Frankfurt am Main: Suhrkamp.
Luhmann, N. (2000/1995), *Art as a Social System*, trans. E. M. Knodt, Stanford: Stanford University Press.
Luhmann, N. (2001a/1974), 'Ist Kunst codierbar?', in *Aufsätze und Reden*, 159–97, Stuttgart: Reclam.
Luhmann, N. (2001b/1986), 'Das Medium der Kunst', in *Aufsätze und Reden*, 198–217, Stuttgart: Reclam.
Luhmann, N. (2012/1997), *Theory of Society I*, trans. R. Barrett, Stanford: Stanford University Press.
Luhmann, N. (2013/2002), *Introduction to Systems Theory*, trans. P. Gilgen, ed. D. Baecker, Cambridge: Polity Press.
Lund, H., ed. (2002), *Intermedialitet: Ord, bild och ton i samspel*, Lund: Studentlitteratur.
Luther, M. (1912), *Werke, kritische Gesamtausgabe: Tischreden, 1531–46, I*, Weimar: Böhlau.
Lutz, T. (1959), 'Stochastische Texte', *Augenblick: Zeitschrift für Tendenz und Experiment*, 4 (1): 3–9. Available online: https://www.netzliteratur.net/lutz_schule.htm (accessed 11 October 2019).
Maagerø, E. and A. Veum (2019), 'Memoria of a National Trauma', in *Multimodality and Aesthetics*, ed. E. S. Tønessen and F. Forsgren, 65–80, New York and London: Routledge.
McDowell, P. (2017), *The Invention of the Oral: Print Commerce and Fugitive Voices in Eighteenth-Century Britain*, Chicago: University of Chicago Press.
McFarlane, B. (1996), *Novel to Film: An Introduction to the Theory of Adaptation*, Oxford: Oxford University Press.
McLuhan, M. (1969), *Counterblast*, London: Rapp and Whiting.
McLuhan, M. (1994/1964), *Understanding Media: The Extensions of Man*, Cambridge, MA: The MIT Press.
McLuhan, M. and E. McLuhan (1988), *Laws of Media: The New Science*, Toronto, Buffalo and London: University of Toronto Press.
McQuail, D. and M. Deuze (2020/1983), *McQuail's Media and Mass Communication Theory*, London: Sage.
Macura, V. (1995), 'Lotmanova „jiná" dekonstrukce', *Tvar*, 6 (1): 10–11.
Maeterlinck, M. (1917/1894), 'Alladine and Palomides', in *A Miracle of Saint Anthony and Five Other Plays*, 161–207, New York: Boni and Liveright.
Maiwald, K., ed. (2019), *Intermedialität: Formen – Diskurse – Didaktik*, Baltmannsweiler: Schneider Verlag Hohengehren GmbH.
Malinowski, B. (1949/1923), 'The Problem of Meaning in Primitive Languages', in *The Meaning of Meaning: A Study of the Influence of Language upon Thought and of the Science of Symbolism. With Supplementary Essays by*

B. Malinowski and F. G. Crookshank, ed. Ch. K. Ogden and I. A. Richards, 296–336, New York: Harcourt, Brace & World.
Manovich, L. (2001), *The Language of New Media*, Cambridge, MA: The MIT Press.
Manovich, L. (2013), *Software Takes Command*, New York: Bloomsbury Academic.
Marcus, G. and E. Davis (2020), 'OpenAI's Language Generator Has No Idea What It's Talking About', *MIT Technology Review*, 22 August. Available online: https://www.technologyreview.com/2020/08/22/1007539/gpt3-openai-language-generator-artificial-intelligence-ai-opinion/ (accessed 7 May 2023).
Maresch, R. and N. Werber (1999), 'Vorwort', in *Kommunikation, Medien, Macht*, ed. R. Maresch and N. Werber, 7–18, Frankfurt am Main: Suhrkamp.
Marin, L. (1993), *Des pouvoirs de l'image*, Paris: Éditions du Seuil.
Markiewicz, H. (1987), 'Ut Pictura Poesis . . . : A History of the Topos and the Problem', *New Literary History*, 18 (3): 535–58.
Matejka, L. and I. R. Titunik, eds (1977), *Semiotics of Art: Prague School Contributions*, Cambridge, MA: The MIT Press.
Mead, G. H. (1934), *Mind, Self and Society*, Chicago: University of Chicago Press.
Menke, B. (1991), *Sprachfiguren: Name – Allegorie – Bild nach Walter Benjamin*, München: Wilhelm Fink.
Menninghaus, W. (1980), *Walter Benjamins Theorie der Sprachmagie*, Frankfurt am Main: Suhrkamp.
Mersch, D. (2010), 'Meta / Dia: Zwei unterschiedliche Zugänge zum Medialen', *Zeitschrift für Medien- und Kulturforschung*, 2 (2): 185–208. Available online: http://dieter-mersch.de/.cm4all/iproc.php/Medienphilosophie/Mersch_Meta_Dia_Zwei%20unterschiedliche%20Zuga%CC%88nge%20zum%20Medialen_2010.pdf?cdp=a (accessed 6 May 2023).
Meyer, L. (1957), 'Meaning in Music and Information Theory', *The Journal of Aesthetics and Art Criticism*, 15 (4): 412–24.
Milner, A. (2002), *Re-Imagining Cultural Studies: The Promise of Cultural Materialism*, London: Sage.
Milner, A. (2005/1996), *Literature, Culture, and Society*, London: Routledge.
Milner, A. (2006), 'Raymond Williams', in *Modern British and Irish Criticism and Theory: A Critical Guide*, ed. J. Wolfreys, 75–83, Edinburgh: Edinburgh University Press.
Milner, A. and J. Browitt (2002), *Contemporary Cultural Theory*, London: Routledge.
Minkowski, E. (1999/1936), *Vers une cosmologie: Fragments philosophiques*, Paris: Payot & Rivages.
Mitchell, D. (2004), *Cloud Atlas*, London: Sceptre.
Mitchell, M. (2021), 'What Does It Mean for AI to Understand?', *Quanta Magazine*, 16 December. Available online: https://www.quantamagazine.org/what-does-it-mean-for-ai-to-understand-20211216 (accessed 23 March 2023).

Mitchell, W. J. T. (1986), *Iconology: Image, Text, Ideology*, Chicago: University of Chicago Press.
Mitchell, W. J. T. (1994), *Picture Theory: Essays on Verbal and Visual Representation*, Chicago: University of Chicago Press.
Mitchell, W. J. T. (2008), 'Addressing Media', *Media Tropes* 1: 1–18. Available online: https://mediatropes.com/index.php/Mediatropes/article/view/1771 (accessed 8 May 2023).
Mitchell, W. J. T. and M. B. N. Hansen (2010), 'Introduction', in *Critical Terms for Media Studies*, ed. W. J. T. Mitchell and M. B. N. Hansen, vii–xxii, Chicago and London: University of Chicago Press.
Monticelli, D. (2016), 'Critique of Ideology or/and Analysis of Culture? Barthes and Lotman on Secondary Semiotic Systems', *Sign Systems Studies*, 44 (3): 432–51.
Monticelli, D. (2019), 'Borders and Translations: Revisiting Juri Lotman's Semiosphere', *Semiotica*, 230: 389–406. Available online: https://www.researchgate.net/publication/334548165_Borders_and_translation_Revisiting_Juri_Lotman's_semiosphere (accessed 1 April 2021).
Moretti, F. (2000), 'The Slaughterhouse of Literature', *Modern Language Quarterly*, 61 (1): 207–27.
Morin, E. (2005/1956), *The Cinema, or The Imaginary Man*, trans. L. Mortimer, Minneapolis: University of Minnesota Press.
Mukařovský, J. (1933), 'Otakar Zich: Estetika dramatického umění. Teoretická dramaturgie', review, *Časopis pro moderní filologii*, 22 (19): 318–26.
Mukařovský, J. (1966/1938), 'K noetice a poetice surrealismu v malířství', in *Studie z estetiky*, ed. K. Chvatík, 309–11, Praha: Odeon.
Mukařovský, J. (1971a/1936), 'Estetická funkce, norma a hodnota jako sociální fakty', in *Studie z estetiky*, ed. K. Chvatík, 7–65, Praha: Odeon.
Mukařovský, J. (1971b/1946), 'Člověk ve světě funkcí', in *Studie z estetiky*, ed. K. Chvatík, 283–91, Praha: Odeon.
Mukařovský, J. (1977a/1936), 'Poetic Designation and the Aesthetic Function of Language', in *The Word and Verbal Art*, ed. and trans. J. Burbank and P. Steiner, 65–72, New Haven and London: Yale University Press.
Mukařovský, J. (1977b/1940), 'On Poetic Language', in *The Word and Verbal Art*, ed. and trans. J. Burbank and P. Steiner, 1–64, New Haven and London: Yale University Press.
Mukařovský, J. (1977c/1941), 'Between Literature and Visual Arts', in *The Word and Verbal Art*, ed. and trans. J. Burbank and P. Steiner, 205–34, New Haven and London: Yale University Press.
Mukařovský, J. (1978a/1934), 'Art as a Semiotic Fact', in *Structure, Sign and Function*, ed. and trans. J. Burbank and P. Steiner, 82–8, New Haven and London: Yale University Press.
Mukařovský, J. (1978b/1935), 'Dialectical Contradictions in Modern Art', in *Structure, Sign and Function*, ed. and trans. J. Burbank and P. Steiner, 129–49, New Haven and London: Yale University Press.

Mukařovský, J. (1978c/1937), 'On the Problem of Functions in Architecture', in *Structure, Sign and Function*, ed. and trans. J. Burbank and P. Steiner, 236–50, New Haven and London: Yale University Press.

Mukařovský, J. (1978d/1942), 'The Place of the Aesthetic Function among the Other Functions', in *Structure, Sign and Function*, ed. and trans. J. Burbank and P. Steiner, 31–48, New Haven and London: Yale University Press.

Mukařovský, J. (1978e/1943), 'Intentionality and Unintentionality in Art', in *Structure, Sign and Function*, ed. and trans. J. Burbank and P. Steiner, 89–128, New Haven and London: Yale University Press.

Mukařovský, J. (1985/1926–7), *O motorickém dění v poezii*, ed. M. Jankovič, Praha: Odeon.

Mukařovský, J. (2000/1943), 'Umění', in *Studie I*, ed. M. Červenka and M. Jankovič, 185–207, Brno: Host.

Mukařovský, J. (2001a/1938), 'Sémantický rozbor básnického díla: Nezvalův Absolutní hrobař', in *Studie II*, ed. M. Červenka and M. Jankovič, 376–98, Brno: Host.

Mukařovský, J. (2001b/1939), 'Významová výstavba a kompoziční osnova epiky Karla Čapka', in *Studie II*, ed. M. Červenka and M. Jankovič, 451–80, Brno: Host.

Mukařovský, J. (2008a/1933), 'Time in Film', trans. K. B. Johnson, in *Cinema All The Time: An Anthology of Czech Film Theory and Criticism, 1908–1939*, ed. P. Szczepanik and J. Anděl, 262–9, Prague and Ann Arbor: National Film Archive and Michigan Slavic Publications.

Mukařovský, J. (2008b/1939–40), 'Estetika architektury', in *Umělecké dílo jako znak: Z univerzitních přednášek 1936–9*, ed. M. Jankovič, 119–32, Praha: Ústav pro českou literaturu AV ČR.

Mukařovský, J. (2016a/1931), 'An Attempt at a Structural Analysis of an Actor's Figure (Chaplin in *City Lights*)', trans. P. Steiner and J. Burbank, in *Theatre Theory Reader: Prague School Writings*, ed. D. Drozd, T. Kačer and D. Sparling, 192–8, Prague: Karolinum Press.

Mukařovský, J. (2016b/1933), 'A Note on the Aesthetics of Film', trans. P. Steiner and J. Burbank, in *Theatre Theory Reader: Prague School Writings*, ed. D. Drozd, T. Kačer and D. Sparling, 272–83, Prague: Karolinum Press.

Müller, C. (2018), 'Gesture and Sign: Cataclysmic Break or Dynamic Relations?', *Frontiers in Psychology*, 9: 1651. Available online: https://www.frontiersin.org/articles/10.3389/fpsyg.2018.01651/full#h11 (accessed 28 April 2023).

Müller, J. E. (1996), *Intermedialität: Formen moderner kultureller Kommunikation*, Münster: Nodus.

Müller, J. E. (1998), 'Intermedialität als poetologisches und medientheoretisches Konzept: Einige Reflexionen zu dessen Geschichte', in *Intermedialität: Theorie und Praxis eines interdisziplinären Forschungsgebiets*, ed. J. Helbig, 31–40, Berlin: Erich Schmidt.

Müller, J. E. (2008), 'Intermedialität und Medienhistoriographie', in *Intermedialität Analog/Digital: Theorien – Methoden – Analysen*, ed. J. Paech and J. Schröter, 31–46, München: Wilhelm Fink.

Müller, J. E. (2010), 'Intermedialität digital: Konzepte, Konfigurationen, Konflikte', in *Intermediale Inszenierungen in Zeitalter der Digitalisierung: Medientheoretische Analysen und ästhetische Konzepte*, ed. A. Blättler, D. Gassert, S. Parikka-Hug and M. V. Ronsdorf, 17–40, Bielefeld: transcript Verlag.
Müller, R. (2011), 'Autorský subjekt jako gesto, stopa, hypotéza', PhD diss., Faculty of Arts, Charles University, Prague.
Müller, R. (2017), 'Distance, iluze, prokletí zisku: Problémy (nejen) novohistorické symbolické ekonomie', *Svět literatury*, 27 (56): 22–54.
Müller, R. (2018), 'Souběžná míjení: Marxismus a zlom v pojetí literární "struktury"', *Česká literatura*, 66 (2): 153–81.
Munari, B. and G. Soavi, eds (1962), *Arte programmata: Arte cinetica, opere moltiplicate, opera aperta*, exhibition catalogue, Milano, Venezia and Roma: Olivetti.
Münker, S. (2013), 'Media in Use: How the Practice Shapes the Mediality of Media', *Distinktion: Scandinavian Journal of Social Theory*, 14 (3): 246–53.
Murray, S. (2012), *The Adaptation Industry: The Cultural Economy of Contemporary Literary Adaptation*, London: Routledge.
Nabokov, V. (1958–9), 'The Vane Sisters', *The Hudson Review*, 11 (4): 491–503.
Nabokov, V. (1975), *Tyrants Destroyed and Other Stories*, New York and Toronto: McGraw-Hill.
Nabokov, V. (1989), *Selected Letters, 1940–1977*, ed. D. Nabokov and M. J. Bruccoli, San Diego: Harcourt Brace Jovanovich.
Navas, E. (2009), 'After Media (Hot and Cold)', *Remix Theory*. Available online: http://remixtheory.net/?p=400 (accessed 10 May 2023).
Nebeský, L. (2022a/1964–72), *Experimentální poezie 1: Kombinatorické hry (1964–72)*, Praha: Tomáš Nosek.
Nebeský, L. (2022b/2007), 'Zaplňování prázdna', in *Experimentální poezie 2: Neviditelnost a prázdno (1992–2010)*, 109–26, Praha: Tomáš Nosek.
Newton, I. (1730/1704), *Opticks, or, A Treatise of the Reflexions, Refractions, Inflexions and Colours of Light*, 195–209, London: William Innys.
Novák, L. (2017), *Dílo II: –1999*, Praha: Dybbuk.
Nünning, A. and V. Nünning, eds (2002), *Erzähltheorie transgenerisch, intermedial, interdisziplinär*, Trier: WVT.
O'Connor, A. (1989), *Raymond Williams: Writing, Culture, Politics*, Oxford: Blackwell.
O'Halloran, K. L. (2022), '"Everything is Intermedial"', lecture in the series Meeting Media Minds: Critical legacies of Lars Elleström, 20 April.
O'Halloran, K. L. and B. A. Smith (2011), 'Multimodal Studies', in *Multimodal Studies: Exploring Issues and Domains*, ed. K. L. O'Halloran and B. A. Smith, 1–14, New York: Routledge.
O'Toole, M. (1994), *The Language of Displayed Art*, Leicester: Leicester University Press.
Ochsner, B. and Ch. Grivel (2001), 'Einleitung', in *Intermediale: Kommunikative Konstellationen zwischen Medien*, ed. B. Ochsner and Ch. Grivel, 3–9, Tübingen: Stauffenburg.

Ong, W. J. (2002/1982), *Orality and Literacy: The Technologizing of the Word*, London and New York: Routledge.
Orth, E. W. (1991), 'Philosophische Anthropologie als Erste Philosophie: Ein Vergleich zwischen Ernst Cassirer und Helmuth Plessner', *Dilthey-Jahrbuch für Philosophie und Geschichte der Geisteswissenschaften*, 7: 250–74.
Orth, E. W. (1996), 'Orientierung über Orientierung: Zur Medialität der Kultur als Welt des Menschen', *Zeitschrift für philosophische Forschung*, 50 (1–2): 167–82.
Orth, E. W. (2006), 'Der Mensch als Medienereignis – Im Lichte der Philosophie Max Schelers', in *Solidarität: Person und Soziale Welt*, ed. Ch. Bermes, W. Henckmann and H. Leonardy, 29–42, Würzburg: Königshausen & Neumann.
Paech, J. (1998), 'Intermedialität: Mediales Differenzial und transformative Figurationen', in *Intermedialität: Theorie und Praxis eines interdisziplinären Forschunggebiets*, ed. J. Helbig, 14–30, Berlin: Erich Schmidt.
Paech, J. and J. Schröter, eds (2008), *Intermedialität Analog/Digital: Theorien – Methoden – Analysen*, München: Wilhelm Fink.
Panofsky, E. (1955), *Meaning in the Visual Arts: Papers in and on Art History*, Garden City: Doubleday.
Paulson, W. R. (1988), *The Noise of Culture: Literary Texts in a World of Information*, Ithaca: Cornell University Press.
Perloff, M. (2000), '"Multiple Pleats": Some Applications of Michel Serres's Poetics', *Configurations*, 8 (2): 187–200.
Pethő, A. (2020a), *Caught In-Between: Intermediality in Contemporary Eastern European and Russsian Cinema*, Edinburgh: Edinburgh University Press.
Pethő, A. (2020b/2011), *Cinema and Intermediality: The Passion for the In-Between*, Newcastle: Cambridge Scholars.
Petříček, M. (2006), 'Svět jako analogon obrazu', *Svět literatury*, 16 (33): 33–8.
Petronius (2000), *Satyricon*, trans. S. Ruden, Indianapolis: Hackett Publishing Company.
Picard, M. (1921), *Der letzte Mensch*, Leipzig, Wien and Zürich: E. P. Tal & Co. Verlag.
Picard, M. (1937), *Die Grenzen der Physiognomik*, Erlenbach, Zürich and Leipzig: Rentsch Verlag.
Picard, M. (1951/1934), *The Flight from God*, trans. M. Kuschnitzky and J. M. Cameron, Chicago: Henry Regnery Company.
Picard, M. (1955/1929), *Das Menschengesicht*, Erlenbach, Zürich and Stuttgart: Rentsch Verlag.
Picard, M. (1988), *Wie der letzte Teller eines Akrobaten . . . : Eine Auswahl aus dem Werk*, ed. M. Bosch, Sigmaringen: Jan Thorbecke Verlag.
Pilshchikov I. and M. Trunin (2016), 'The Tartu-Moscow School of Semiotics: A Transnational Perspective', *Sign Systems Studies*: 44 (3): 368–401.
Plato (2002), *Phaedrus*, trans. R. Waterfield, Oxford: Oxford University Press.
Plessner, H. (1985/1924), 'Die Utopie in der Maschine', in *Gesammelte Schriften X*, ed. G. Dux, O. Marquard and E. Ströker, 31–40, Frankfurt am Main: Suhrkamp.

Plessner, H. (2019/1928), *Levels of Organic Life and the Human: An Introduction to Philosophical Anthropology*, trans. M. Hyatt, New York: Fordham University Press.
Plett, H. F. (1991), 'Intertextualities', in *Intertextuality*, ed. H. F. Plett, 3–29, Berlin and New York: De Gruyter.
Pöggeler, O. (2002), *Bild und Technik: Heidegger, Klee und die Moderne Kunst*, München: Wilhelm Fink.
Praz, M. (1970), *Mnemosyne: The Parallel between Literature and the Visual Arts*, Princeton: Princeton University Press.
Preisendanz, W. (1977), *Wege des Realismus: Zur Poetik und Erzählkunst im 19. Jahrhundert*, München: Wilhelm Fink.
Propertius, S. (2004), *The Complete Elegies of Sextus Propertius*, trans. V. Katz, Princeton and Oxford: Princeton University Press.
Pross, H. (1972), *Medienforschung: Film, Presse, Fernsehen*, Darmstadt and Wien: Habel.
Rajewsky, I. O. (2002), *Intermedialität*, Tübingen: Francke.
Rajewsky, I. O. (2003), *Intermediales Erzählen in der italienischen Literatur der Postmoderne: Von den giovani scrittori der 80er zum pulp der 90er Jahre*, Tübingen: Francke.
Rajewsky, I. O. (2005), 'Intermediality, Intertextuality, and Remediation: A Literary Perspective on Intermediality', *Intermédialités/Intermedialities*, 6 (6): 43–64.
Rajewsky, I. O. (2010), 'Border Talks: The Problematic Status of Media Borders in the Current Debate about Intermediality', in *Media Borders, Multimodality, and Intermediality*, ed. L. Elleström, 51–68, Basingstoke: Palgrave Macmillan.
Rajewsky, I. O. (2019), 'Literaturbezogene Intermedialität', in *Intermedialität: Formen – Diskurse – Didaktik*, ed. K. Meiwald, 49–76, Baltmannsweiler: Schneider Verlag.
Rautzenberg, M. (2009), 'Resonanzen zwischen Medientheorie und Ästhetik: Medialität als Un-mittelbarkeit bei Walter Benjamin', in *Resonanz: Potentiale einer akustischen Figur*, ed. K. Lichau, V. Tkaczyk and R. Wolf, 339–52, München: Wilhelm Fink.
Riepl, W. (1913), *Das Nachrichtenwesen des Altertums, mit besonderer Rücksicht auf die Römer*, Leipzig and Berlin: Teubner.
Rippl, G. (2005), *Beschreibungs-Kunst: Zur intermedialen Poetik angloamerikanischer Ikontexte (1880–2000)*, München: Wilhelm Fink.
Ritter, M. (2007), *Filosofie jazyka Waltera Benjamina*, Praha: Filosofia.
Ritter, M. (2016), 'Co říká duha?', *Svět literatury*, 26 (54): 28–35.
Rose, F. (2011), *The Art of Immersion: How the Digital Generation Is Remaking Hollywood, Madison Avenue, and the Way We Tell Stories*, 8–36, New York and London: W. W. Norton & Company.
Rouse, M. (2015), 'Text-Picture Relationships in the Early Modern Period', in *Handbook of Intermediality: Literature – Image – Sound – Music*, ed. G. Rippl, 65–81, Berlin: De Gruyter.
Ryan, M.-L. (1997), 'Postmodernism and the Doctrine of Panfictionality', *Narrative*, 5 (2): 165–87.

Ryan, M.-L. (2001), *Narrative as Virtual Reality: Immersion and Interactivity in Literature and Electronic Media*, Baltimore: Johns Hopkins University Press.
Ryan, M.-L. (2016), 'Texts, Worlds, Stories: Narrative Worlds as Cognitive and Ontological Concept', in *Narrative Theory, Literature, and New Media: Narrative Minds and Virtual Worlds*, ed. M. Hatavara, M. Hyvärinen, M. Mäkelä and F. Mäyrä, 11–28, New York and London: Routledge.
Ryan, M.-L., ed. (2004), *Narrative Across Media: The Languages of Storytelling*, Lincoln: University of Nebraska Press.
Sager Eidt, L. M. (2008), *Writing and Filming the Painting: Ekphrasis in Literature and Film*, Amsterdam and New York: Rodopi.
Salupere, S., K. Kull and P. Torop, eds (2013), *Beginnings of the Semiotics of Culture*, Tartu: University of Tartu Press.
Sartre, J.-P. (2016/1948), 'Préface', in N. Sarraute, *Portrait d'un inconnu*, Paris: Gallimard.
Schaper, E. (1956), 'The Aesthetics of Hartmann and Bense', *The Review of Metaphysics*, 10 (2): 289–307.
Schenk, K., A. Hultsch and A. Stašková (2016), *Experimentelle Poesie in Mitteleuropa: Texte – Kontexte – Material – Raum*, Göttingen: V&R Unipress.
Schmeling, M., ed. (1981), *Vergleichende Literaturwissenschaft: Theorie und Praxis*, Wiesbaden: Athenaion.
Schmid, H. (1997), 'Das Problem des Individuums in tschechischen Strukturalismus', in *Prager Schule: Kontinuität und Wandel. Arbeiten zur Literaturästhetik und Poetik der Narration*, ed. W. F. Schwarz, 265–303, Frankfurt am Main: Vervuert.
Schmid, H. (2004), 'Oskar Walzel und die Prager Schule', in *Felix Vodička 2004*, ed. A. Jedličková, 18–47, Praha: Ústav pro českou literaturu AV ČR.
Schmidová, H. (2011/1997), 'Přístupy k subjektu v pražské strukturalistické antropologii a v genetickém strukturalismu Ernsta Cassirera', trans. M. Šimečková and J. Schwarz, in *Struktury a funkce: Výbor ze studií 1989–2009*, 68–85, Praha: Karolinum.
Schmidt, S. J. (1989), *Die Selbstorganisation des Sozialsystems Literatur im 18. Jahrhundert*, Frankfurt am Main: Suhrkamp.
Schmidt, S. J. (1993), 'Kommunikationskonzepte für eine systemorientierte Literaturwissenschaft', in *Literaturwissenschaft und Systemtheorie: Positionen, Kontroversen, Perspektiven*, 241–68, Opladen: Westdeutscher Verlag.
Schmidt, S. J. (2008), *Přesahování literatury: Od literární vědy k mediální kulturní vědě*, trans. Z. Adamová, Praha: Ústav pro českou literaturu AV ČR.
Schnädelbach, H. (1999/1983), *Philosophie in Deutschland 1831–1933*, Frankfurt am Main: Suhrkamp.
Schneider, S. (2014), 'Die Laokoon-Debatte: Kunstreflexion und Medienkonkurrenz im 18. Jahrhundert', in *Handbuch Literatur & Visuelle Kultur*, ed. C. Benthien and B. Weingart, 68–85, Berlin and Boston: De Gruyter.

Schönle, A., ed. (2006), *Lotman and Cultural Studies: Encounters and Extensions*, Madison: University of Wisconsin Press.
Schröter, J. (1998), 'Intermedialität: Facetten und Probleme eines aktuellen medienwissenschaftlichen Begriffs', *montage AV: Zeitschrift für Theorie und Geschichte audiovisueller Kommunikation*, 7 (2): 129–54.
Schröter, J. (2008), 'Das ur-intermediale Netzwerk und die (Neu-)Erfindung des Mediums im (digitalen) Modernismus', in *Intermedialität Analog/Digital: Theorien – Methoden – Analysen*, ed. J. Paech and J. Schröter, 579–601, München: Wilhelm Fink.
Schröter, J., ed. (2014), *Handbuch der Medienwissenschaft*, Stuttgart: Metzler.
Schüttpelz, E. (2006), 'Die medienanthropologische Kehre der Kulturtechniken', in *Archiv für Mediengeschichte 6: Kulturgeschichte als Mediengeschichte (oder vice versa?)*, 87–110, Weimar.
Schüttpelz, E. (2010), '"Get the Message Through": From the Channel of Communication to the Message of the Medium (1945–60)', trans. B. Pichon and D. Rudnytsky, in *Media, Culture, and Mediality: New Insights into the Current State of Research*, ed. L. Jäger, E. Linz and I. Schneider, 109–38, Bielefeld: transcript Verlag.
Sedlmayr, H. (1957), 'Pieter Bruegel: Der Sturz der Blinden. Paradigma einer Strukturanalyse', *Hefte des Kunsthistorischen Seminars der Universität München*, 2: 1–48.
Semenenko, A. (2012), *The Texture of Culture: An Introduction to Yuri Lotman's Semiotic Theory*, New York: Palgrave Macmillan.
Serres, M. (1969), *Hermès I: La communication*, Paris: Éditions de Minuit.
Serres, M. (2007/1980), *The Parasite*, trans. L. R. Schehr, Minneapolis: University of Minnesota Press.
Serres, M. and B. Latour (1995/1990), *Conversations on Science, Culture, and Time*, trans. R. Lapidus, Ann Arbor: University of Michigan Press.
Shannon, C. E. and W. Weaver (1964/1949), *The Mathematical Theory of Communication*, Urbana: University of Illinois Press.
Siegert, B. (2014), 'Cacography or Communication? Cultural Techniques of Sign-Signal Distinction', in *Cultural Techniques: Grids, Filters, Doors, and Other Articulations of the Real*, trans. G. Winthrop-Young, 19–32, New York: Fordham University Press.
Siegert, B. and K. Krtilová (2016), 'Dějiny médií a média dějin: Rozhovor s Bernhardem Siegertem', in *Medienwissenschaft: Východiska a aktuální pozice německé filosofie a teorie médií*, ed. K. Krtilová and K. Svatoňová, 157–70, Praha: Academia.
Siegert, B. and G. Winthrop-Young (2015), [radio programme], 'Material World: An Interview with Bernhard Siegert', *Artforum*, 53 (10): 25. Available online: https://www.artforum.com/print/201506/material-world-an-interview-with-bernhard-siegert-52281 (accessed 3 May 2023).
Simanowski, R. (2006), 'Transmedialität als Kennzeichen moderner Kunst', in *Transmedialität: Zur Ästhetik paraliterarischer Verfahren*, ed. U. Meyer, R. Simanowski and Ch. Zeller, 39–81, Göttingen: Wallstein.

Simondon, G. (1969), *Du mode d'existence des objets techniques*, Paris: Aubier.
Šlaisová, E. (2014), 'The Prague School's Contribution to the Theory of Intermediality', *Theatralia*, 2: 41–9.
Šlaisová, E. (2016), 'Spojité nádoby: Etnologie, pražský strukturalismus a česká divadelní avantgarda', *Theatralia*, 19 (1): 65–85.
Solt, M. E. (1970), *Concrete Poetry: A World View*, Bloomington: Indiana University Press.
Somaini, A. (2016a), 'Walter Benjamin's Media Theory and the Tradition of the Media Diaphana', *Zeitschrift für Medien- und Kulturforschung*, 7 (1): 9–25.
Somaini, A. (2016b), 'Walter Benjamin's Media Theory: The Medium and the Apparat', *Grey Room*, 17 (62): 6–41.
Spielmann, Y. (1995), 'Intermedialität als symbolische Form', *Ästhetik und Kommunikation*, 24 (88): 112–17.
Spielmann, Y. (2000), 'Aspekte einer ästhetischen Theorie der Intermedialität', in *Über Bilder sprechen: Positionen und Perspektiven der Medienwissenschaft*, ed. H. B. Heller, M. Kraus and T. Meder, 57–68, Marburg: Schüren Verlag.
Spielmann, Y. (2004), 'Intermedialität und Hybridisierung', in *Intermedium Literatur: Beiträge zu einer Medientheorie der Literaturwissenschaft*, ed. R. Lüdeke and E. Greber, 78–102, Göttingen: Wallstein.
Spielmann, Y. (2010), *Hybridkultur*, Berlin: Suhrkamp.
Spitzer, L. (1955), 'The Ode on a Grecian Urn or Content vs. Metagrammar', *Comparative Literature*, 7 (3): 203–25.
Srp, K. (2014), *Bohumil Kubišta: Zářivý krystal*, Praha and Ostrava: Arbor Vitae and Galerie výtvarného umění v Ostravě.
Stehlíková, E. (2016), 'Strukturalistická stopa Olgy Srbové', *Theatralia*, 19 (1): 181–200.
Steiner, W. (1982), *The Colors of Rhetoric: Problems in the Relation between Modern Literature and Painting*, Chicago and London: University of Chicago Press.
Štěpánek, F. (1912), 'T. A. Edison a několik jeho myšlenek o budoucnosti', *Epocha: Časopis pro popularisování vědy vůbec, zvláště pak věd technických a přírodních*, 17 (2): 21–3. Available online: https://www.idnes.cz/technet /technika/edison-navsteva-praha.A181005_130927_tec_technika_mla (accessed 7 May 2023).
Sternberg, M. (1999), 'The Laokoon Today: Interart Relations, Modern Projects and Projections', *Poetics Today*, 20 (2): 291–379.
Stiegler, B. (1998/1994), *Technics and Time 1: The Fault of Epimetheus*, trans. R. Beardsworth and G. Collins, Stanford: Stanford University Press.
Stierle, K. (1982), 'Babel und Pfingsten: Zur immanenten Poetik von Apollinaires Alcools', in *Lyrik und Malerei der Avantgard*, ed. R. Warning and W. Wehle, 92–104, München: Wilhelm Fink.
Stierle, K. (1984), 'Das bequeme Verhältnis: Lessings Laokoon und die Entdeckung des ästhetischen Mediums', in *Das Laokoon-Projekt: Pläne der semiotischen Ästhetik*, ed. G. Gebauer, 23–58, Stuttgart: Metzler.

Stöber, R. (2004), 'Re: R. Stöber: Mediengeschichte: Die Evolution "neuer" Medien von Gutenberg bis Gates', *H / SOZ / KULT: Kommunikation und Fachinformation für die Geschichtswissenschaften*, 15 July. Available online: https://www.hsozkult.de/publicationreview/id/rezbuecher-4626 (accessed 6 May 2023).

Stöber, R. (2013), *Neue Medien. Geschichte: Von Gutenberg bis Apple und Google. Medieninnovation und Evolution*, 413–47, Bremen: Edition Lumière.

Straus, E. W. (1965/1963), 'Born to See, Bound to Behold: Reflections on the Function of Upright Posture in the Esthetic Attitude', *Tijdschrift Voor Filosofie*, (27) 4: 659–88.

Štyrský, J. (1970), *Sny (1925–1940): Zrození díla ze zdrojů psychických modelů polospánku, prostřednictvím věrných ilustrací snových objektů a autentických záznamů snů*, Praha: Odeon.

Štyrský, J. (1992/1946), *Poesie*, Praha: Československý spisovatel.

Štyrský, J. (1995/1933), 'Kraj markýze de Sade', in *Život markýze de Sade*, 51–4, Praha: Kra.

Štyrský, J. (1996), *Každý z nás stopuje svoji ropuchu: Texty 1923–40*, Praha: Thyrsus.

Štyrský, J. (1997/1933), *Emilie Comes to Me in a Dream*, trans. I. Irwin, New York: Ubu Gallery.

Sutton, J. (2010), 'Exograms and Interdisciplinarity: History, the Extended Mind, and the Civilizing Process', in *The Extended Mind*, ed. R. Menary, 189–225, Cambridge, MA: The MIT Press.

Švácha, R. (1994/1985), *Od moderny k funkcionalismu: Proměny pražské architektury první poloviny dvacátého století*, Praha: Victoria Publishing.

Švácha, R. (1998), 'Karel Teige jako teoretik architektury', *Acta Universitatis Palackianae Olomucensis, Facultas philosophica: Philosophica – Aesthetica*, 16: 145–56.

Sypher, W. (1955), *Four Stages of Renaissance Style: Transformations in Art and Literature 1400–1700*, Garden City: Doubleday.

Szczepanik, P. and J. Anděl (2008), *Cinema All the Time: An Anthology of Czech Film Theory and Criticism, 1908–1939*, trans. K. B. Johnson, Prague and Ann Arbor: National Film Archive and Michigan Slavic Publications.

Szondi, P. (1978), 'Zone: Marginalien zu einem Gedicht Apollinaires', in *Schriften II*, 414–25, Frankfurt am Main: Suhrkamp.

Tamm, M. (2019), 'Introduction: Juri Lotman's Semiotic Theory of History and Cultural Memory', in J. Lotman, *Culture, Memory and History: Essays in Cultural Semiotics*, ed. M. Tamm, 1–26, Basingstoke: Palgrave Macmillan.

Teige, K. (1994/1949), 'Bohumil Kubišta', in *Výbor z díla III: Osvobozování života a poezie. Studie ze 40. let*, ed. J. Brabec and V. Effenberger, 345–86, Praha: Aurora.

Thibault, P. J. (1991), *Social Semiotics as Praxis: Text, Social Meaning Making, and Nabokov's Ada*, Minneapolis: University of Minnesota Press.

Thielmann, T. (2013), 'Jedes Medium braucht ein Modicum: Zur Behelfstheorie von Akteur-Netzwerken', *Zeitschrift für Medien- und Kulturforschung*, 4 (2), *ANT und die Medien*: 111–27.
Thiers, B. (2016), *Experimentelle Poetik als Engagement: Konkrete Poesie, visuelle Poesie, Lautdichtung und experimentelles Hörspiel im deutschsprachigen Raum von 1945 bis 1970*, Hildesheim: Georg Olms Verlag.
Tholen, G. Ch. (2005), 'Medium/Medien', in *Grundbegriffe der Medientheorie*, ed. A. Roesler and B. Stiegler, 150–72, Paderborn: Wilhelm Fink.
Thrift, N. (2004), 'Remembering the Technological Unconscious by Foregrounding Knowledges of Position', *Environment and Planning D: Society and Space*, 22 (1): 175–90.
Thrift, N. (2005), *Knowing Capitalism*, London and Thousand Oaks: Sage.
Ticineto Clough, P. (2000), *Autoaffection: Unconscious Thought in the Age of Teletechnology*, Minneapolis and London: University of Minnesota Press.
Todorov, T. (1984/1973), 'Ästhetik und Semiotik im 18. Jahrhundert: G. E. Lessing: Laokoon', in *Das Laokoon-Projekt: Pläne der semiotischen Ästhetik*, ed. G. Gebauer, 9–22, Stuttgart: Metzler.
Toman, J. (1995), *The Magic of a Common Language: Jakobson, Mathesius, Trubetzkoy, and the Prague Linguistic Circle*, Cambridge, MA: The MIT Press.
Tønessen, E. S. and F. Forsgren, eds (2019), *Multimodality and Aesthetics*, New York and London: Routledge.
Trimpi, W. (1973), 'The Meaning of Horace's Ut Pictura Poesis', *Journal of the Warburg and Courtauld Institutes*, 36 (1): 1–34.
Turner, G. (2003/1990), *British Cultural Studies: An Introduction*, London: Routledge.
Tzara, T. (1963), *Lampisteries, précédées des Sept manifestes Dada*, Montreuil: Jean-Jacques Pauvert.
Ulver, S. (1991), 'Estetika filmu Jana Mukařovského', in *Filmový sborník historický II*, ed. I. Klimeš and J. Rak, 241–51, Praha: Československý filmový ústav.
Valéry, P. (1960/1923), 'Eupalinos ou l'architecte', in *Oeuvres de Paul Valéry II*, ed. J. Hytier, 79–147, Paris: Gallimard.
Vančura, V. (2008/1935), 'Contribution to the Discussion of Speech in Film 2', trans. P. L. Garvin, in *Cinema All the Time: An Anthology of Czech Film Theory and Criticism, 1908–1939*, ed. P. Szczepanik and J. Anděl, 209–14, Prague and Ann Arbor: National Film Archive and Michigan Slavic Publications.
Vaswani, A., N. Shazeer, N. Parmar, J. Uszkoreit, L. Jones, A. N. Gomez, L. Kaiser and I. Polosukhin (2017), 'Attention is All You Need', in *NIPS'17: Proceedings of the 31st International Conference on Neural Information Processing Systems*, ed. U. von Luxemburg, I. Guyon, S. Bengio, H. Wallach and R. Fergus, 6000–10, Red Hook: Curran Associates. Available online: https://dl.acm.org/doi/10.5555/3295222.3295349 (accessed 7 May 2023).
Veltruský, J. (1994/1981), 'Divadelní teorie Pražské školy', in *Příspěvky k teorii divadla*, 15–24, Praha: Divadelní ústav.

Veltruský, J. (2016/1940), 'People and Things in the Theatre', trans. P. Steiner and
J. Burbank, in *Theatre Theory Reader: Prague School Writings*, ed. D. Drozd,
T. Kačer and D. Sparling, 147–56, Prague: Karolinum Press.
Vernadsky, V. (1998/1926), *The Biosphere*, trans. D. B. Langmuir, New York:
Copernicus.
Vidman, L. (1997), *Od Olympu k Panteonu: Antické náboženství a morálka*,
Praha: Vyšehrad.
Voigts-Virchow, E. (2009), 'Metadaptation: Adaptation and Intermediality –
Cock and Bull', *Journal of Adaptation in Film & Performance*, 2: 137–52.
Vojvodík, J. (2004), 'Ĺavant-garde retrouvé? Poznámky k problematice recepce
české avantgardy v USA a Německu a k několika jejím opomíjeným
aspektům, především k Teigovi', *Slovo a smysl*, 1 (2): 229–41.
Vojvodík, J. (2011), 'Structuralism, Phenomenology and the Czech Avant-
Garde', in *A Glossary of Catchwords of the Czech Avant-garde:Conceptions
of Aesthetics and the Changing Faces of Art 1908–1958*, ed. P. A. Bílek, J.
Vojvodík and J. Wiendl, 361–78, Prague: Faculty of Arts, Charles University.
Volek, E. (2004), *Znak – funkce – hodnota: Estetika a sémiotika umění
Jana Mukařovského v proudech současného myšlení. Zápisky z podzemí
postmoderny*, Praha: Paseka.
Wagner, P. (1995), *Reading Iconotexts: From Swift to the French Revolution*,
London: Reaktion Books.
Wagner, P. (1996), 'Introduction – The State(s) of the Art(s)', in *Icons – Texts
– Iconotexts: Essays on Ekphrasis and Intermediality*, ed. P. Wagner, 1–42,
Berlin and New York: De Gruyter.
Wagner, P., ed. (1996), *Icons – Texts – Iconotexts: Essays on Ekphrasis and
Intermediality*, Berlin and New York: De Gruyter.
Waldorf, S. and A. Stephan (2020), 'Getty Artworks Re-created by Geniuses the
World Over', *Getty*, 30 March. Available online: https://www.getty.edu/news
/getty-artworks-recreated-with-household-items-by-creative-geniuses-the
-world-over/ (accessed 6 February 2023).
Waldstein, M. (2008), *The Soviet Empire of Signs: A History of the Tartu School of
Semiotics*, Saarbrücken: VDM Verlag Dr. Müller.
Walzel, O. (1917), *Wechselseitige Erhellung der Künste: Ein Beitrag zur
Würdigung kunstgeschichtlicher Begriffe*, Berlin: Reuther – Reichard.
Webb, R. (1999), 'Ekphrasis Ancient and Modern: The Invention of a Genre',
Word & Image, 1: 7–18.
Webern, A. (1959), *Briefe an Hildegard Jone und Josef Humplik*, ed. J. Polnauer,
Wien: Universal Edition.
Weingart, M. (2008/1935), 'Zvukový film a řeč: Čtyři zásadní kapitoly', in *Stále
kinema: Antologie českého myšlení o filmu 1904–1950*, ed. P. Szczepanik and J.
Anděl, 228–46, Praha: Národní filmový archiv.
Weischedel, W. (1960a), 'Abschied vom Bild', in *Wirklichkeit und Wirklichkeiten:
Aufsätze und Vorträge*, 158–69, Berlin: De Gruyter.
Weisstein, U. (1974/1968), *Comparative Literature and Literary Theory: Survey
and Introduction*, trans. W. Riggan, Bloomington: Indiana University Press.

Weisstein, U. (1992), 'Literatur und bildende Kunst', in *Literatur und bildende Kunst: Ein Handbuch zur Theorie und Praxis eines komparatistischen Grenzgebietes*, ed. U. Weisstein, 11–31, Berlin: Erich Schmidt.
Weisstein, U. (1993), 'Literature and the (Visual) Arts: Intertextuality and Mutual Illumination', in *Intertextuality: German Literature and Visual Art from the Renaissance to the Twentieth Century*, ed. I. Hoesterey and U. Weisstein, 1–17, Columbia: Camden House.
Wellbery, D. E. (1984), *Lessing's Laocoon: Semiotics and Aesthetics in the Age of the Reason*, Cambridge: Cambridge University Press.
Wellek, R. (1941), 'The Parallelism of Literature and the Arts', in *English Institute Annual 1942*, 29–63, New York: Columbia University Press.
Wellek, R. and A. Warren (1949), *Theory of Literature*, New York: Harcourt – Brace.
Werber, N. (1992), *Literatur als System: Zur Ausdifferenzierung literarischer Kommunikation*, Opladen: Westdeutscher Verlag.
Werber, N. and G. Plumpe (1993), 'Literatur ist codierbar', in *Literaturwissenschaft und Systemtheorie: Positionen, Kontroversen, Perspektiven*, ed. S. J. Schmidt, 9–43, Opladen: Westdeutscher Verlag.
Whalley, G. (1997), *Aristotle's Poetics: Translated and with a Commentary by George Whalley*, ed. J. Baxter and P. Atherton, Montreal and Kingston: McGill-Queen's University Press.
Whitworth, B. and H. Ryu (2009/2005), 'A Comparison of Human and Computer Information Processing', in *Encyclopedia of Multimedia Technology and Networking I, A–Ev*, ed. M. Pagani, 230–9, Hershey and London: IGI Global.
Wiener, N. (1961/1948), *Cybernetics, or Control and Communication in the Animal and the Machine*, New York: The MIT Press.
Wiesing, L. (2005), *Artifizielle Präsenz: Studien zur Philosophie des Bildes*, Frankfurt am Main: Suhrkamp.
Wilde, O. (2006/1891), *The Picture of Dorian Gray*, ed. J. Bristow, Oxford: Oxford University Press.
Wilke, T. (2010), 'Tacti(ca)lity Reclaimed: Benjamin's Medium, the Avant-Garde, and the Politics of the Senses', *Grey Room*, 11 (39): 39–55.
Wilkins, J. (1694/1641), *Mercury: Or the Secret and Swift Messenger*, London: Richard Baldwin.
Williams, R. (1966/1962), *Communications*, London: Chatto and Windus.
Williams, R. (1964), 'A Structure of Insights', *University of Toronto Quarterly*, 33 (3): 338–40. Reprinted in G. E. Stearn, ed., *McLuhan: Hot and Cool*, 188–91, Harmondsworth: Penguin.
Williams, R. (1976/1958), *Culture and Society, 1780–1950*, Harmondsword: Penguin.
Williams, R. (1977), *Marxism and Literature*, Oxford: Oxford University Press.
Williams, R. (1980a/1973), 'Base and Superstructure in Marxist Cultural Theory', in *Culture and Materialism: Selected Essays*, 35–55, London: Verso.

Williams, R. (1980b/1978), 'Means of Communication as Means of Production', in *Culture and Materialism: Selected Essays*, 57–70, London: Verso.
Williams, R. (1981), *Culture*, London: Fontana Paperbacks.
Williams, R. (1983/1976), *Keywords: A Vocabulary of Culture and Society*, New York: Oxford University Press.
Williams, R. (1989/1983), 'Culture and Technology', in *The Politics of Modernism: Against the New Conformists*, 119–39, London: Verso.
Williams, R. (1992/1961), *The Long Revolution*, London: Chatto & Windus.
Williams, R. (2003/1974), *Television: Technology and Cultural Form*, London: Routledge.
Winkler, H. (2002/1997), *Docuverse: Zur Medientheorie der Computer*, München: Boer.
Winkler, H. (2004), *Diskursökonomie: Versuch über die innere Ökonomie der Medien*, Frankfurt am Main: Suhrkamp.
Winkler, H. (2008), 'Zeichenmaschinen: Oder warum die semiotische Dimension für eine Definition der Medien unerlässlich ist', in *Was ist ein Medium?*, ed. S. Münker, 211–21, Frankfurt am Main: Suhrkamp.
Winkler, H. (2015), *Prozessieren: Die dritte, vernachlässigte Medienfunktion*, Paderborn: Wilhelm Fink.
Winner, T. G. (1994), 'Jakobson a avantgardní umění', *Estetika*, 31 (2): 1–12.
Winner, T. G. (2015/1994), *The Czech Avant-Garde Literary Movement Between the World Wars*, ed. O. Sládek and M. Heim, New York: Peter Lang.
Winter, A. (2010), 'Jiná estetika: Konceptualismus a transmedialita v české literatuře po druhé světové válce', in *Česká literatura v intermediální perspektivě: IV. kongres světové literárněvědné bohemistiky. Jiná česká literatura (?)*, ed. S. Fedrová, 25–38, Praha: Ústav pro českou literaturu AV ČR.
Wirth, U. (2006), 'Hypertextuelle Aufpropfung als Übergangsform zwischen Intermedialität und Transmedialität', in *Transmedialität: Zur Ästhetik paraliterarischer Verfahren*, ed. U. Meyer, R. Simanowski and Ch. Zeller, 19–38, Göttingen: Wallstein.
Wolf, W. (1996), 'Intermedialität als neues Paradigma der Literaturwissenschaft? Plädoyer für eine literaturzentrierte Erforschung der Grenzüberschreitungen zwischen Wortkunst und anderen Medien am Beispiel von Virginia Woolfs "The String Quartet"', *AAA: Arbeiten aus Anglistik und Amerikanistik*, 21 (1): 85–116.
Wolf, W. (1999), *The Musicalization of Fiction: A Study in the Theory and History of Intermediality*, IFAVW Internationale Forschungen zur Allgemeinen und Vergleichenden Literaturwissenschaft 35, Amsterdam: Rodopi.
Wolf, W. (2002a), 'Intermedialität: Ein weites Feld und eine Herasuforderung für die Literaturwissenschaft', in *Literaturwissenschaft: Intermedial – interdisziplinär*, ed. H. Foltinek and Ch. Leitgeb, 163–92, Wien: ÖAW.
Wolf, W. (2002b), 'Das Problem der Narrativität in Literatur, bildender Kunst und Musik: Ein Beitrag zu einer intermedialen Erzähltheorie', in

Erzähltheorie transgenerisch, intermedial, interdisziplinär, ed. A. Nünning and V. Nünning, 23–104, Trier: WVT.

Wolf, W. (2007), 'Description as a Transmedial Mode of Representation: General Features and Possibilities of Realization in Painting, Fiction and Music', in *Description in Literature and Other Media*, ed. W. Wolf and W. Bernhart, 1–87, Amsterdam and New York: Rodopi.

Wolf, W. (2018), *Selected Essays on Intermediality by Werner Wolf (1992–2014): Theory and Typology, Literature-Music Relations, Transmedial Narratology, Miscellaneous Transmedial Phenomena*, Leiden and Boston: Brill and Rodopi.

Wolf, W. (2019), 'Das Feld der Intermedialität im Überblick', in *Intermedialität: Formen – Diskurse – Didaktik*, ed. K. Meiwald, 23–48, Baltmannsweiler: Schneider Verlag.

Wölfflin, H. (2015/1915), *Principles of Art History: The Problem of the Development of Style in Early Modern Art*, trans. J. Blower, Los Angeles: The Getty Research Institute.

Wundt, W. (1886), *Ethik: Eine Untersuchung der Tatsachen und Gesetze des sittlichen Lebens I*, Stuttgart: Enke.

Wundt, W. (1917), *Völkerpsychologie: Eine Untersuchung der Entwicklungsgesetze von Sprache, Mythus und Sitte VII*, Leipzig: Kröner.

Wutsdorff, I. (2011), 'Aesthetic Function and Functionalism', in *A Glossary of Catchwords of the Czech Avant-garde: Conceptions of Aesthetics and the Changing Faces of Art 1908–1958*, ed. P. A. Bílek, J. Vojvodík and J. Wiendl, 71–83, Prague: Faculty of Arts, Charles University.

Yacobi, T. (1995), 'Pictorial Models and Narrative Ekphrasis', *Poetics Today*, 16 (4): 599–649.

Zander, H. (1985), 'Intertextualität und Medienwechsel', in *Intertextualität: Formen, Funktionen, anglistische Fallstudien*, ed. M. Pfister and U. Broich, 178–96, Tübingen: Max Niemeyer.

Zich, O. (1931), *Estetika dramatického umění: Teoretická dramaturgie*, Praha: Melantrich.

Zielinski, S. (2006), *Deep Time of the Media*, Cambridge, MA: The MIT Press.

Zima, P. V. (1995), 'Ästhetik, Wissenschaft und "wechselseitige Erhellung der Künste"', in *Literatur intermedial: Musik, Malerei, Photographie, Film*, ed. P. V. Zima, 1–28, Darmstadt: Wissenschaftliche Buchgesellschaft.

Zuboff, S. (2019), *The Age of Surveillance Capitalism: The Fight for a Human Future at the New Frontier of Power*, New York: Public Affairs.

Zymner, R. and A. Hölter, eds (2013), *Handbuch Komparatistik: Theorien, Arbeitsfelder, Wissenspraxis*, Stuttgart and Weimar: J. B. Metzler.

Index

Abrams, Meyer Howard   376
Aguiar, Daniella   389
Allan, Stuart   300 n.5
Ambros, Veronika   60
Anděl, Jaroslav   49
Anders, Günther   12, 83, 84, 87, 98–100, 168
Andrews, Edna   370 n.33
Apollinaire, Guillaume   100, 207, 216
Aquinas, Thomas   23
Arcimboldo, Guiseppe   134, 422
Arendt, Hannah   254, 312
Aristotle   22, 23, 31, 42 n.34, 78, 256, 375, 436
Armstrong, William George   231
Artmann, Hans Carl   208
Arvidson, Jens   411
Ashby, Ross   177, 330–1, 334
Askander, Mikael   411
Assmann, Aleida   39
Aston, Elaine   60
Aubert, Maxime   143
Aumont, Jacques   221
Austin, John Langshaw   79
Avicenna (Ibn Síná)   23

Babbitt, Irving   380
Bach, Johann Sebastian   275 n.39, 422
Bachofen, Johann Jakob   113, 114
Bacon, Francis   8, 24, 25, 28, 41 n.15, 277 n.54, 291
Bal, Mieke   394, 430 n.10
Balázs, Béla   275 n.43
Balzac, Honoré de   122
Banaszkiewicz, Bernadette   377
Barborka, Zdeněk   207, 214, 220–2

Barthes, Roland   85, 86, 104, 150, 176, 196, 223, 226 n.10, 355, 416, 418
Batchen, Geoffrey   151
Bateman, John Arnold   416, 430 n.10
Bateson, Gregory   170, 178, 235, 278 n.60, 303, 304, 317, 320, 371 n.45, 445
Baudelaire, Charles   81 n.7
Baudrillard, Jean   98, 300
Baumgarten, Alexander Gottlieb   63, 378
Beardsley, Monroe C.   227 n.20
Belliger, Andréa   249
Belting, Hans   12, 87, 90–3
Bender, Emily M.   355, 357
Benjamin, Andrew   81
Benjamin, Walter   12, 14, 42 n.21, 49, 69–81, 124 n.6, 128, 148, 150, 273 n.25, 287, 322
Bense, Max   13, 182–4, 208, 215, 217, 218, 226 nn.7–9, 318
Benthien, Claudia   381
Bergson, Henri   38, 162 n.5
Berio, Luciano   185, 214
Berndt, Frauke   402
Bernhard, Peter   88
Bigelow, Julian   177
Bill, Max   207, 215
Blake, William   392
Blanchot, Maurice   106, 107
Blatný, Ivan   450
Blättler, Andy   424
Bloch, Marc   343, 344
Blumenberg, Hans   95, 96, 113
Boden, Margaret Ann   328, 367 n.4
Boehm, Gottfried   386, 387

Bogatyrev, Petr   59, 61, 62, 66 n.5,
  67 n.18, 67 n.22
Bogost, Ian   356
Böhme, Hartmut   70, 74, 80 n.4, 81
  n.6, 81 n.7, 148
Bolter, Jay David   32, 33, 234, 286,
  301 n.8, 359, 408, 427, 430
  n.9
Boltzmann, Ludwig   179
Bolz, Norbert   245, 274 n.33
Bondanella, Peter   185
Bonnet, Charles   24, 41 n.13
Boulainvilliers, Henri de   24
Boulez, Pierre   188
Bourdieu, Pierre   176, 368 n.14,
  406, 412, 426
Boyd, Brian   161
Bradbury, Ray   2
Braudel, Fernand   343
Brecht, Bertolt   186
Bremond, Claude   407
Bremond, Henri   132
Breton, André   135
Březina, Otokar   122
Brillouin, Léon   181
Bronwen, Thomas   3
Browitt, Jeff   300 n.1
Brown, Calvin S.   379, 385
Brown, Gillian   357
Brown, Tom B.   352
Brueghel, Pieter, the Elder   167, 390
Bruhn, Jørgen   382, 411, 429
Bryson, Norman   394
Buckner, Cameron   367 n.4
Bühler, Karl   54, 198, 227 n.15, 317,
  323, 326 n.16
Burda, Vladimír   207, 208
Bürger, Peter   278 n.68
Burian, Emil František   66 n.5, 67
  n.22
Bydžovská, Lenka   115

Caesar, Michael   185
Cage, John   349

Calvino, Italo   361
Campos, Augusto de   208
Campos, Haroldo de   208
Cancogni, Anna   225 n.4
Capa, Robert   150, 151
Čapek, Karel   132
Cardwell, Sarah   410
Carey, George R.   246
Carpenter, Edmund   177
Cartmell, Deborah   410
Cassirer, Ernst   54, 87–9, 122 n.1
Cavell, Stanley   366
Caws, Mary Ann   397
Celan, Paul   122
Červenka, Miroslav   13, 57, 171,
  193, 194, 199–206, 223,
  225, 225 n.1, 227 n.16
Cézanne, Paul   388
Chalmers, David John   355
Chaplin, Charlie (Charles
  Spencer)   49–51
Chappe, Claude   28, 440
Chartier, Roger   35, 276 n.46, 278
  n.64, 332, 371 n.47, 440
Chastel, André   377
Chatman, Seymour   407
Chopin, Henri   208, 214
Chudy, Joseph   27
Chudý, Tomáš   176
Chvatík, Květoslav   66 n.3
Cicero, Marcus Tullius   41 n.9
Clarke, Bruce   368 n.5
Clüver, Claus   385–7, 389, 390,
  392–7, 404
Coleridge, Samuel Taylor   156, 157,
  165 n.31, 404, 423
Conard, Nicholas J.   143
Condorcet, Jean Antoine Nicolas de
  25, 27
Conrad-Martius, Hedwig   116
Cooley, Charles   30–2, 42 n.21
Corbineau-Hoffmann, Angelika
  385, 386
Costa Vieira, Erika Viviane   426

Courtenay, Baudouin de   330
Crary, Jonathan   105
Cros, Charles   29
Culler, Jonathan   198, 311, 325 n.7
Dahl, Roald   370 n.37
D'Alembert, Jean le Rond   24, 25
Dalí, Salvador   134
Daneš, František   54
Dante Alighieri   156
Danto, Arthur C.   374, 412
Därmann, Iris   91
Davis, Ernest   356
Debray, Régis   30, 35, 36, 40
Deleuze, Gilles   39, 141
Delumeau, Jean   343
Dencker, Klaus Peter   207
Derrida, Jacques   83, 86, 99–102, 116, 120, 121, 141, 144, 145, 164 n.19, 272 n.15, 276 n.49
Descartes, René   24
Deuber-Mankowsky, Astrid   75, 81
Deuze, Mark   286
Dewey, John   32
Dickie, George   374, 412
Diderot, Denis   25, 313
Didi-Huberman, Georges   92, 93, 102–4, 112, 113, 118, 122 n.2
Dobrzyńska, Teresa   357, 371 n.42
Doesburg, Theo van   207
Döhl, Reinhard   208
Doležel, Lubomír   66 n.4
Domingos, Ana Cláudia Munari   426
Donguy, Jacques   207
Dovey, Jon   279, 286, 287, 292, 300 n.6, 301 n.8
Drakakis, John   300 n.1
Drozd, David   66 n.3, 66 n.4
Drtikol, František   106
Drucker, Johanna   207
Dryden, John   376, 429 n.2
Dubos, Jean-Baptiste   381

Dudley, Andrew   410
Dufrenne, Mikel   365
Duperrault, Terry Jo   226 n.7
Dürer, Albrecht   92, 122 n.2, 377
Dusi, Nicola M.   370 n.33
Eagleton, Terry   300 n.1
Eco, Umberto   13, 171, 175, 178, 181–200, 202, 205, 206, 222, 223, 225, 225 n.1, 226 n.10, 226 n.11, 227 n.18, 264, 278 n.62, 328, 364
Edison, Thomas Alva   239
Ehrenspeck, Yvonne   70, 74, 80 n.4, 81 n.6, 81 n.7
Einem, Herbert von   377
Eisenstein, Sergei   50
Eisner, Pavel   219
Eldridge, John   300 n.1
Eldridge, Lizzie   300 n.1
Eliot, Thomas Stearns   85, 156, 165 n.30, 361, 437
Elleström, Lars   41 n.3, 347, 392, 397–400, 402, 410–16, 419–24, 430 n.10
Elliot, Kamilla   430 n.10
Emerson, Caryl   358
Engelbart, Douglas   267, 268
Ensslin, Astrid   3
Ernst, Max   134
Ernst, Ulrich   387
Eupalinos   123 n.4

Fabian, Jeanette   66 n.3
Fadiga, Luciano   162 n.3
Fahs, Charles   173
Farago, Claire J.   377
Faßler, Manfred   14, 30, 31, 37, 262–6, 278 n.62, 278 n.63
Faulkner, William   364
Faulstich, Werner   22, 31, 32, 34, 259, 267
Fazi, Beatrice   358
Fedrová, Stanislava   377, 383, 397

Feuerstein, Bedřich   57
Fichte, Johann Gottlieb   71, 72, 244, 274 n.30
Ficino, Marsilio   41 n.10
Filmer, Paul   281
Florensky, Pavel Alexandrovich   333
Flusser, Vilém   98, 261, 277 n.53
Foerster, Heinz von   170, 229
Forsgren, Frida   417
Foucault, Michel   5, 406
Frank, Susi K.   370 n.33
Franklin, Benjamin   231, 232
Freedman, Des   300 n.7
Freud, Sigmund   231, 232, 235, 271 n.9, 272 n.15
Freyermuth, Gundolf   405
Froissart, Jean   41 n.12
Frye, Northrop   385
Fuchs, Peter   323-4
Führer, Heidrun   377, 411, 426
Fyodorov, Vasily Fyodorovich   66 n.8

Gamm, Gerhard   93-7
Gappmayr, Heinz   208
Garnier, Ilse   208
Garnier, Pierre   208, 214
Garson, James   367 n.4
Gasparov, Boris Mikhailovich   331, 367 n.1
Gastaldi, Juan Luis   354, 370 n.38
Gautier, Théophile   376, 389
Gebauer, Gunter   381
Gebru, Timnit   355, 357
Gehlen, Arnold   232
Genette, Gérard   402
Genz, Julia   430 n.12
Geoghegan, Bernard Dionysius   171, 173
Gess, Nicola   378
Gévaudan, Paul   430 n.12
Giacometti, Alberto   13, 92, 93, 112, 113, 437
Giacometti, Giovanni   92

Giddings, Seth   279, 286, 287, 292, 300 n.6, 301 n.8
Giesecke, Michael   32, 33
Gitelman, Lisa   36, 249, 258
Glenn, John   167, 224
Gočár, Josef   65
von Goethe, Johann Wolfgang   122 n.1
Goldin-Meadow, Susan   127
Gomringer, Eugen   161, 207, 208, 221
Goodman, Nelson   418
Goody, Jack   237, 446
Gramigna, Remo   370 n.33
Grant, Iain   279, 286, 287, 292, 300 n.6, 301 n.8
Greenaway, Peter   421
Greenberg, Clement   380, 439
Greenblatt, Stephen   387
Grethlein, Jonas   383
Grice, H. Paul   357
Grishakova, Marina   370 n.33, 408
Grivel, Charles   404
Grögerová, Bohumila   208, 209, 219, 220, 224, 225 n.1
Groos, Karl   133
Grünewald, Matthias   124 n.5
Grusin, Richard   32, 33, 234, 286, 301 n.8, 359, 408, 427, 430 n.9
Guattari, Félix   39
Guillory, John David   8, 23-6, 29, 46, 148, 292, 300 n.6, 347, 373, 374, 389
Gumbrecht, Hans Ulrich   3, 244, 404, 425
Günther, Gotthard   183, 229
Günther, Hans   65
Gutenberg, Johannes   34

Habermas, Jürgen   304, 445
Hadricourt, André   273 n.23
Hagen, Wolfgang   23
Hagstrum, Jean H.   379, 429 n.1
Halas, František   119-21

Hall, Stuart 279
Halliday, Michael A. K. 415
Hansen, Mark B. N. 230, 231, 234, 235, 270 n.3, 286
Hansen-Löve, Aage A. 47, 393
Hanssen, Beatrice 81
Harig, Ludwig 182, 226 n.7
Harms, Wolfgang 387
Hartmann, Frank 230, 246, 270 n.2
Hartmann, Nicolai 84
Hartung, Harald 207
Hausken, Liv 4, 377, 408
Hauthal, Janine 426, 428
Havel, Václav 208, 216
Havelock, Eric 446, 162 n.4
Havlíček, Josef 56, 57
Havránek, Bohuslav 64, 67 n.20
Hayles, Katherine N. 171, 181, 225 n.3, 236, 367 n.5
Heczková, Libuše 331
Hedling, Erik 387, 394
Heffernan, James 379, 387
Hegel, Georg Wilhelm Friedrich 4, 45, 55, 182, 215, 325 n.11, 378, 379, 429 n.3, 438
Heidegger, Martin 102, 110
Heißenbüttel, Helmut 187, 208, 222
Helbig, Jörg 404, 407
Helmholtz, Herrman von 233
Helmstetter, Rudolf 316–18, 323, 324
Henshilwood, Christopher S. 143
Herder, Johann Gottfried 231
Hermand, Jost 430 n.6
Hickethier, Knut 412, 413
Higgins, Dick 207, 380, 404, 405, 423, 427
Higgins, John 300 n.1
Hiippala, Tuomo 416
Hildebrandt, Toni 164
Hiršal, Josef 208, 209, 219, 220, 224, 225 n.1
Hjelmslev, Louis 227 n.17
Hlaváček, Josef 211

Hoek, Leo H. 395, 396
Hoesterey, Ingeborg 387
Hoffmann, Stefan 8, 41 n.16
Hofmann, Anne 376
Hofmannsthal, Hugo von 98
Hölderlin, Friedrich 122
Hölter, Achim 385, 386
Homer 159, 224, 387
Honys, Josef 213, 214, 217
Honzík, Karel 56, 57, 59, 66 n.11
Honzl, Jindřich 51, 53, 61, 62, 67 n.22
Horace (Quintus Horatius Flaccus) 375, 376, 429 n.1
Hörisch, Jochen 20, 31, 33–5, 309
Hörl, Erich 164 n.15, 230, 231
Hošek, Arnošt 67 n.13
Hostovský, Egon 119, 121
Hubig, Christoph 232
Huhtamo, Erkki 273 n.26
Hultsch, Anne 207
Hunter, I. Q. 410
Husserl, Edmund 87, 99, 101, 102, 104, 365, 371 n.41

Ibrus, Indrek 370 n.33
Ihde, Don 229, 236–8
Imorde, Joseph 124
Ingarden, Roman 194, 364
Ingold, Tim 163 n.13
Isekenheimer, Guido 430 n.8
Iser, Wolfgang 16, 84, 85, 194, 221, 225, 360, 363–7, 371 n.45, 371 n.46
Isou, Isidore 161
Iuli, Cristina 171, 177, 187

Jackson, Kenneth David 207
Jacob, Hildebrand 376, 429 n.2
Jahraus, Oliver 323, 448
Jakobson, Roman 7, 13, 21, 46, 47, 49–51, 53, 59, 66 n.5, 66 n.6, 127, 132, 168–76, 178,

198, 199, 201, 203, 225 n.2,
226 n.10, 335, 337, 368
n.13, 384, 389, 390, 441,
448
Janet, Pierre   132, 138
Jankovič, Milan   131, 133, 162 n.5
Jansson, André   237, 238, 277 n.55
Jauss, Hans Robert   311, 325 n.7
Jedličková, Alice   377, 383, 397, 400
Jenkins, Henry   408, 439
Jewitt, Carey   416, 417
Jirous, Ivan Martin   208
Johansson, Christer   412
Johnson, Brian Stanley William   360
Jonas, Hans   84
Jone, Hildegard   191
Jones, Paul   287, 290, 300 n.1, 300
n.3, 300 n.4, 300 n.6, 301
n.9, 301 n.10
Jousse, Marcel   132, 162 n.4
Joyce, James   156, 157, 182, 185,
207, 224, 364, 371 n.46
Joyce, Michael   363
Jude, Radu   427
Juliš, Emil   207
Jünger, Ernst   124 n.6

Kačer, Tomáš   66 n.3, 66 n.4
Kafka, Franz   83, 128, 218, 219, 246,
362
Kalivoda, Robert   57, 65
Kant, Immanuel   45, 63, 80 n.2, 89,
122 n.1
Kapp, Ernst   14, 229–35, 238, 252,
270 n.6, 270 n.7, 271 n.8,
271 n.10, 271 n.12, 271
n.13, 272 n.15, 272 n.21
Karcevsky, Sergei Iosifovich   339
Kassner, Rudolf   98, 99, 124 n.6
Kaye, Heidi   410
Kelleher, John D.   370 n.34
Kelly, K.   279, 286, 287, 292, 300
n.6, 301 n.8
Kendon, Adam   127

Khlebnikov, Velimir (Viktor
Vladimirovich)   207, 349
Kibédi Varga, Áron   388
Kilpatrick, Franklin Peirce   193
Kim, Hyun Kang   128
Kircher, Athanasius   27, 41 n.16,
440
Kittler, Friedrich   1, 2, 5, 6, 14, 20,
21, 24, 27, 31, 32, 35, 36,
39, 41 n.4, 42 n.22, 42
n.23, 42 n.27, 43 n.35, 182,
229–33, 246–54, 259–61,
265, 273 n.26, 274 n.35,
275 n.39, 275 nn.41–3, 276
n.46, 278 n.65, 328, 345–7,
350, 351, 367 n.3, 369 n.23,
369 n.29, 412, 434
Klages, Ludwig   87
Klee, Paul   116
Kline, Ronald R.   173, 177–9, 225 n.3
Kobiela, Dorota   421
Kohout, Eduard   62
Kokeš, Radomír D.   49, 66 n.4
Kolář, Jiří   6, 18, 210–12, 225 n.1,
387, 423
Kolářová, Běla   210, 216
Kolmogorov, Andrey
Nikolaevich   331
Kouřil, Miroslav   67 n.22
Kracauer, Siegfried   75, 124 n.6
Krämer, Sybille   41 n.4, 79, 81 n.10
Kranz, Gisbert   389, 390
Krausová, Nora   381
Krauss, Sebastian W. D.   313
Kress, Gunther   416, 417, 426
Krieger, David John   249
Krieger, Murray   379, 380
Kristeva, Julia   176, 393, 423
Kriwet, Ferdinand   208, 387
Krtilová, Kateřina   67 n.12
Krupp, Alfred   231
Kubišta, Bohumil   13, 85, 106–9,
113
Kučera, Jan   56, 66 n.5

Kuhn, Roland   125 n.9
Kull, Kalevi   367 n.1, 370 n.33
Kundera, Milan   361
Künzler, Jan   305
Kupsch, Kenneth   155

Lacan, Jacques   39, 249–51, 256
Lachmann, Renate   47, 83, 104–6, 124 n.8, 125 n.9, 448
Lagache, Daniel   225 n.2
Lagerroth, Ulla-Britta   387, 394
Landow, George P.   360
Langerová, Marie   216
Largier, Niklaus   109
Latour, Bruno   141, 163 n.13, 273 n.23, 276 n.50, 369 n.19, 446
Lautréamont, Comte de (Isidore Lucien Ducasse)   113, 115
Leach, Eleanor W.   375
Leavis, Frank Raymond   300 n.6
Le Corbusier (Charles-Édouard Jeanneret)   58
Ledin, Per   415
Lee, Rensselaer W.   376, 377
Lee-Morrison, Lila   371 n.40
Leeuwen, Theo van   416
Le Goff, Jacques   343
Leitch, Thomas   411, 430 n.10
Lemaître, Maurice   161
Lemonnier, Pierre   7, 163 n.13
Leonardo da Vinci   87, 122 n.2, 377, 378
Leroi-Gourhan, André   7, 13, 129–31, 140–9, 162 n.3, 163 n.13, 163 n.14, 164 n.15, 164 n.16, 164 n.18, 230, 239, 240, 242, 247, 272 n.19, 272 n.21, 273 n.23
Leschke, Rainer   15, 34, 35, 238, 274 n.34, 303, 319, 320, 322, 323, 326 n.20, 326 n.21, 326 n.23

Lessing, Gotthold Ephraim   4, 374, 379–83, 429 n.5, 438
Levi, Carlo   226 n.11
Lévinas, Emmanuel   117–20
Lévi-Strauss, Claude   6, 176, 272 n.20, 335
Levý, Jiří   200, 207
Licklider, Joseph Carl Robnett   272 n.18
Lifschitz, Avi   381–3, 429 n.5
Lister, Martin   279, 286, 287, 292, 300 n.6, 301 n.8
Locke, John   25, 26, 277 n.54
Lotman, Mikhail   370 n.33
Lotman, Yuri Mikhailovich   5, 8, 15, 16, 42 n.24, 139, 176, 265, 318, 327–55, 357, 358, 360, 365, 367 n.1, 367 n.2, 368 n.7, 368 n.8, 368 n.12, 368 n.15, 369 nn.19–21, 369 n.25, 369 n.26, 369 n.28, 370 n.33, 375 n.39, 371 n.45, 393, 443, 444, 449
Lotz, John   127
Louis XIV, king of France   345
Louis XVI, king of France   369 n.24
Louvel, Liliane   393
Ludmer, Josefina   426
Luhmann, Niklas   15, 20, 28, 38, 39, 42 n.25, 235, 247, 253, 255, 256, 259, 262, 263, 269, 276 n.48, 278 n.65, 303–19, 324 n.2, 324 n.4, 324 n.5, 325 n.10, 325 n.13, 325 n.16, 326 n.17, 352, 406, 412, 445, 446
Luisini, Francesco   429 n.1
Lumière, Auguste Marie Louis Nicolas   246
Lumière, Louis Jean   246
Lund, Hans   375, 381, 383, 387, 392, 394, 395, 398, 407
Luther, Martin   25, 32
Lutz, Theo   218–20, 225, 227 n.19

Lyotard, Jean-François 171

Maagerø, Eva 415
McCulloch, Warren 170, 177
McDowell, Paula 332
McFarlane, Brian 411
Mácha, Karel Hynek 67 n.20, 131, 132, 137
Macherey, Pierre 226 n.12
Machin, David 415
MacKay, Donald MacCrimmon 402
McLuhan, Eric 245, 273 n.28
McLuhan, Marshall 1, 9, 14, 15, 20, 23, 28, 29, 32, 33, 36, 38, 39, 41 n.1, 42 n.23, 42 n.32, 84, 129, 177, 192, 229–31, 233, 234, 237, 238, 241–5, 247, 253, 257, 266, 273 n.27, 273 n.28, 275 n.40, 277 n.58, 280, 284–7, 291, 292, 299, 300 nn.4–6, 301 n.8, 363, 406, 412, 433
McMillan-Major, Angelina 357
McNeill, David 127, 128
McQuail, Denis 286
Macura, Vladimír 344
Macy, Josiah 173
Maeterlinck, Maurice 122
Maiwald, Klaus 402
Makovský, Vincenc 109
Malinowski, Bronislaw 203
Mallarmé, Stéphane 103, 188, 207, 219
Manovich, Lev 14, 42 n.26, 246–9, 267, 268, 274 n.36, 275 n.37, 275 n.38, 275 n.45, 278 n.68, 308, 367 n.3
Mantegna, Andrea 139
Marcus, Gary 356
Maresch, Rudolf 261
Mari, Enzo 185
Maria Feodorovna, empress of Russia 341

Marie Antoinette, queen of France 369 n.24
Marin, Louis 86, 102
Marinetti, Filippo Tommaso 207, 216
Markert, Hans G. 225 n.1
Markiewicz, Henryk 375, 376, 378
Marten, Miloš 113, 114
Marx, Karl 38, 215
Matejka, Ladislav 66 n.4
Mathesius, Vilém 64
Mauss, Marcel 335
Maxwell, James Clerk 181
Mayerová, Milča 47
Mead, George Herbert 32, 267
Mear, Margaret 128, 173
Menke, Bettine 80 n.3, 81 n.14
Menninghaus, Winfried 80 n.3
Merleau-Ponty, Maurice 362
Mersch, Dieter 19–21
Mersenne, Marin 24
Meyer, Leonard B. 194, 195, 197, 198, 223
Michelangelo (Michelangelo di Lodovico Buonarroti Simoni) 87
Milner, Andrew 300 n.1, 300 n.2
Milota, Karel 207, 208
Minkowski, Eugène 109
Mitchell, David 15, 321, 408, 410
Mitchell, Melanie 355, 357
Mitchell, W. J. T. 29, 42 n.33, 230, 231, 270 n.3, 270 n.4, 286, 290, 292, 294, 381, 386, 392, 393, 405, 412, 416, 419, 430 n.7
Moles, Abraham André 182, 189, 318
Mon, Franz 208, 214
Montero, Teresa 426
Monticelli, Daniele 370 n.33, 370 n.39
Moretti, Franco 325 n.11
Morin, Edgar 85–7, 100

Morris, Charles William   183, 226 n.10
Morse, Samuel   26, 28, 440
Mousavi, Nafiseh   430 n.10
Mukařovský, Jan   7, 12, 13, 46, 48–52, 54–65, 66 n.1, 66 n.5, 66 n.6, 66 n.8, 66 n.10, 67 n.16, 67 n.17, 67 n.21, 117, 128–41, 146, 149, 162 n.8, 163 n.11, 179, 198, 201, 222, 233, 241, 271 n.14, 298, 319, 335, 339, 384, 390, 441, 442, 447
Müller, Cornelia   127
Müller, Jürgen E.   377, 392, 394, 404, 405, 407, 424, 425
Müller, Richard   176, 196, 227 n.12, 368 n.14, 371 n.47
Munari, Bruno   185
Münker, Stefan   300 n.7
Münsterberg, Hugo   252, 274 n.31
Murdock, Graham   290
Murray, Simone   410
Musil, Robert   109
Muther, Richard   139, 140

Nabokov, Vera   161
Nabokov, Vladimir   13, 124 n.7, 131, 152–8, 160–2, 164 n.22, 164 n.23, 164 n.25, 165 n.32, 165 n.39, 165 n.42
Navas, Eduardo   273 n.27, 273 n.29
Nebeský, Ladislav   207, 211, 212, 217, 221
Němcová, Božena   131
Nerlich, Michael   430 n.7
Neumann, John von   31, 170, 268
Newton, Isaac   24
Nezval, Vítězslav   47, 66 n.2, 132–4, 140
Nietzsche, Friedrich   251
Niikuni, Seiichi   208
Nora, Pierre   90
Nöth, Winfried   370 n.33

Novák, Ladislav   207, 214, 221
Nünning, Ansgar   407
Nünning, Vera   407

O'Connor, Alan   300 n.1
O'Halloran, Kay   414, 416, 417, 430 n.10
O'Toole, Michael   416
Obrtel, Vít   55, 57, 64, 65
Ochsner, Beate   404
Ogier, Pascale   100, 101
Oktaviana, Adhi Agus   143
Olenina, Anna Alekseevna   368
Ong, Walter. J.   148, 162 n.4, 237, 346, 446
Orama, Maarja   370 n.33
Orth, Ernst Wolfgang   88–90
Ovčáček, Eduard   208

Paech, Joachim   383, 392, 398, 407, 412, 416, 424
de Paiva Vieira, Miriam   426
Pala, Karel   207
Panofsky, Erwin   418, 424, 428
Paracelsus (Philippus Aureolus Theophrastus Bombastus von Hohenheim)   23
Parikka, Jussi   273 n.26
Parmiggiani, Claudio   118
Parry, Milman   162
Paspa, Karel Maria   47
Pater, Walter   376, 378
Paulhan, Frédéric   138
Paul I, emperor of Russia   341
Paulson, William R.   367 n.5
Peirce, Charles Sanders   183, 352, 419
Penone, Giuseppe   123–4 n.2
Perloff, Marjorie   369 n.19
Pethő, Ágnes   426–8
Petříček, Miroslav   145
Petronius (Gaius Petronius Arbiter)   85, 86, 165 n.30
Pfister, Manfred   394
Pfotenhauer, Helmut   387

Piaget, Jean   67 n.17, 193
Pias, Claus   254
Piatigorsky, Alexander
    Moiseyevich   331
Picard, Max   87, 97–9, 124 n.5, 124 n.6
Picasso, Pablo   135, 394
Pignatari, Décio   208
Pilshchikov, Igor   367 n.1
Pitts, Walter   170, 177
Plato   73, 81 n.6, 157, 159, 253, 345, 346
Plessner, Helmuth   87, 88, 95, 123 n.3
Plett, Heinrich F.   393, 394
Pliny the Elder   107
Pliny the Younger   41
Plumpe, Gerhard   311, 312, 319, 325 n.6, 325 n.8, 406
Plutarch   382
Poe, Edgar Allan   168–70
Pöggeler, Otto   116
Pomponius Gauricus   429
Pousseur, Henri   188
Praigg, Noble T.   42
Praz, Mario   379
Preisendanz, Wolfgang   104
Prévert, Jacques   86
Prigogine, Ilya   343
Propertius, Sextus   159
Pross, Harry   34, 259
Pushkin, Alexander
    Sergeyevich   334, 368 n.17

Queiroz, Joao   389, 430 n.10
Quintilian (Marcus Fabius
    Quintilianus)   377

Rajewsky, Irina O.   382, 383, 392, 395, 397, 400–5, 407, 410, 411, 421, 426–8, 430 n.9
Raleigh, Walter   41 n.13
Rank, Otto   118
Rau, Milo   427

Rautzenberg, Markus   79
Regnault, Henri Victor   102–4, 106
Rheingold, Howard   272 n.18
Ribemont-Dessaignes, Georges   86
Ribot, Théodule-Armand   132, 138
Richards, Ivor Armstrong   226 n.10
Richter, Gerhard   422
Riepl, Wolfgang   32, 33, 241, 242, 320
Rilke, Rainer Maria   99
Rippl, Gabriele   392, 407
Ritter, Martin   70, 80 n.3
Robbe-Grillet, Alain   366
Rose, Frank   244
Rosenblueth, Arturo   177
Ross, Harold   155
Rössler, Jaroslav   106, 107
Roth, Dieter (Diter Rot)   188, 208
Round, Julia   3
Rouse, Margitta   429 n.4
Ruhe, Cornelia   370 n.33
Rühm, Gerhard   208
Ruskin, John   376
Ruttmann, Walter   67 n.14
Ryan, Marie-Laure   16, 250, 326 n.22, 358–64, 408, 409, 430 n.10
Ryle, Gilbert   79
Ryu, Hokyoung   253

Sack, Tilman   423
Sager Eidt, Laura M.   407
Salupere, Silvi   367 n.1, 370 n.33
Sapir, Edward   127
Saporta, Marc   360
Sartre, Jean-Paul   371 n.41
Saussure, Ferdinand de   53, 174, 205, 335, 434
Savona, George   60
Schaper, Eva   226
Scheler, Max   89
Schenk, Klaus   207
Scherpe, Klaus R.   148
Schirrmacher, Beate   382, 429

Schlegel, August Wilhelm 378
Schlegel, Friedrich 71, 378
Schmeling, Manfred 385
Schmid (also Schmidová),
   Herta 54, 58, 384
Schmidt, Siegfried J. 208, 278 n.66,
   306, 391, 426
Schmitz, Alexander 370 n.33
Schnädelbach, Herbert 98
Schneider, Sabine 381
Schönle, Andreas 370 n.33
Schopenhauer, Arthur 376
von Schrenck-Notzing, Albert
   124 n.7
Schröter, Jens 8, 23, 27, 36, 41 n.14,
   42 n.31, 380, 391, 392, 405,
   424, 425
Schüttpelz, Erhard 7, 14, 176, 177,
   230, 238–41, 249, 260, 272
   n.19–21, 273 n.23
Sedlmayr, Hans 113
Seifert, Jaroslav 66
Semenenko, Aleksei 344
Serres, Michel 253, 264, 324, 338,
   339, 349, 369 n.19
Setiawan, Pindi 143
Shakespeare, William 153, 361,
   394, 429 n.4
Shannon, Claude 170, 173, 177–82,
   226 n.6, 226 n.7, 227 n.13,
   249, 250, 253, 257, 264,
   303, 324 n.1, 337, 440
Shukman, Ann 368 n.11
Siegert, Bernhard 6, 66 n.12, 163
   n.13, 182, 238, 239, 259
Sievers, Eduard 133
Sigaut, François 273 n.23
Simanowski, Roberto 389, 402,
   422, 423
Simmias of Rhodes 216
Simondon, Gilbert 229–31, 250,
   251
Simonides of Ceos 375
Šlaisová, Eva 66 n.4, 67 n.22, 384

Slaviński, Janusz 311
Smith, Bradley A. 416, 417
Smith, Tony 93
Snow, G. 42 n.17
Soavi, Giorgio 185
Socrates 123 n.4, 346
Solt, Mary Ellen 207
Somaini, Antonio 70, 78
Soto, Jesús Rafael 188
Sparling, Don 66 n.3, 66 n.4
Spence, Joseph 376, 429 n.2
Spielberg, Steven 42 n.30
Spielmann, Yvonne 405, 423–5
Spitzer, Leo 376, 379
Squarcione, Francesco 139
Squire, Michael 381, 382, 429 n.5
Srbová, Olga 61
Srp, Karel 106, 115
Stašková, Alice 207
Stehlíková, Eva 61
Steiner, Wendy 379, 389, 390, 392,
   425
Stengers, Isabelle 343
Štěpánek, František 36
Stephan, Annelisa 418
Stephenson, George 271 n.13
Sternberg, Meir 381
Stiegler, Bernard 42 n.33, 83,
   99–101, 163 n.13, 230, 270
   n.2
Stierle, Karlheinz 100, 381
Stöber, Rudolf 31–4, 36, 42 n.28,
   241, 273 n.25, 274 n.34,
   277 n.57, 440
Straus, Erwin W. 83
Strich, Fritz 430 n.6
Štyrský, Jindřich 13, 85, 109–19,
   122, 134
Suetonius Tranquillus, Gaius 42 n.8
Suino, Mark E. 66 n.7
Sutton, John 233
Švácha, Rostislav 57, 67 n.15
Švankmajer, Jan 422
Sypher, Wylie 385

Szczepanik, Petr 49
Szilárd, Leó 179
Szondi, Peter 100

Tamm, Marek 370 n.33
Taylor, Charles 241
Taylor, Robert 272 n.18
Teige, Karel 47, 106
Thibault, Paul J. 416
Thielmann, Tristan 272 n.17
Thiers, Bettina 207
Tholen, Georg Christoph 8, 21, 148
Thomas Aquinas 23
Thrift, Nigel 229–31, 235, 236, 272 n.15
Ticineto Clough, Patricia 272 n.15
Tieghem, Paul van 385
Tinguely, Jean 188
Titov, German 167, 224
Titunik, Irwin R. 66 n.4
Todorov, Tzvetan 381
Tolstoy, Leo (Lev Nikolayevich) 152
Toman, Jindřich 47, 66 n.3
Tønessen, Elise Seip 417
Tonger-Erk, Lily 402
Torop, Peeter 367 n.1, 370 n.33
Toyen (Marie Čermínová) 118
Trimpi, Wesley 375
Trnka, Bohumil 54
Trunin, Mikhail 367 n.1
Turgenev, Ivan Sergeyevich 104, 105
Turing, Alan 31, 253, 268, 271 n.11, 356
Turner, Graeme 300 n.1
Tykwer, Tom 408
Tyutchev, Fyodor Ivanovich 338
Tzara, Tristan 215

Uexküll, Jakob Johann von 330
Uldall, Hans Jørgen 145
Ulver, Stanislav 66 n.4
Uspensky, Boris Andreevich 327, 331–3, 344

Uspensky, Vladimir Andreevich 331

Valéry, Paul 95, 96, 123 n.4
Valoch, Jiří 207, 208, 216
Vančura, Vladislav 66 n.5, 132
Varchi, Benedetto 109
Vasari, Giorgio 139
Vaswani, Ashish 355
Veltruský, Jiří 60, 62, 66 n.4
Vernadsky, Vladimir Ivanovich 344
Vertov, Dziga (David Abelevich Kaufman) 50, 67 n.14
Veum, Aslaug 415
Vidman, Ladislav 165 n.28
Vigée Le Brun, Élisabeth 341
Virgil (Publius Vergilius Maro) 156
Virilio, Paul 98
Voigts-Virchow, Eckart 411
Vojvodík, Josef 48, 66 n.3
Volek, Emil 66 n.4
Vos, Eric 207, 395, 396, 404
Vovelle, Michel 343

Wachowski, Lana 408
Wagner, Peter 375, 379, 381, 383, 387, 393, 394, 406, 430 n.7
Wais, Kurt 430 n.6
Waldorf, Sarah 418
Waldstein, Maxim 330, 367 n.1
Walzel, Oskar 374, 379, 383–5, 430 n.6
Warren, Austin 384
Watt, James 271 n.13
Weaver, Warren 173, 178–80, 194, 226 n.6, 227 n.13, 324
Webb, Daniel 376, 429 n.2
Webb, Ruth 387
Webern, Anton (von) 191
Weingart, Brigitte 381
Weingart, Miloš 66 n.5
Weischedel, Wilhelm 84
Weisstein, Ulrich 383, 385–7, 392
Welchman, Hugh 421

Wellbery, David E.   381, 429 n.5
Wellek, René   384
Werber, Niels   261, 311–13, 316, 319, 325 n.6, 325 n.8, 406
Whalley, George   375
Whelehan, Imelda   410
White, Katharine   155, 157
Whitworth, Brian   253
Wiener, Norbert   170, 171, 173, 177, 179, 181, 183, 216, 330
Wiesing, Lambert   91
Wilde, Oscar   152, 155, 156
Wildfeuer, Janina   416
Wilke, Tobias   81 n.13
Wilkins, John   25–7, 41 n.16, 440
Williams, Emmett   208
Williams, Raymond   14, 15, 24, 39, 148, 273 n.25, 279, 301, 327, 442, 443
Williams, William Carlos   390
Wimsatt, William K.   227 n.20
Winkler, Hartmut   14, 36, 41 n.1, 41 n.4, 42 n.20, 42 n.24, 42 n.26, 43 n.35, 148, 241, 244, 245, 247, 254–62, 266, 268, 269, 274 n.32, 275 n.44, 276 n.48, 276 n.49, 277 nn.51–53, 277 n.55, 277 n.56, 278 n.67, 446, 450
Winner, Thomas G.   66 n.3
Winter, Astrid   208, 209

Winthrop-Young, Geoffrey   163 n.13
Wirth, Uwe   375, 384, 402, 403, 422, 423
Witasek, Stephan   138
Wittgenstein, Ludwig   79, 183
Wögerbauer, Michael   371 n.47
Wolf, Werner   320, 341, 382–4, 386, 392, 394–405, 407, 409, 412, 413, 416, 418, 419, 421, 424, 427
Wolfe, Lauren K.   270 n.6
Wölfflin, Heinrich   383–5, 430 n.6
Wundt, Wilhelm   241, 273 n.24
Wutsdorffová, Irina   54

Yacobi, Tamar   407
Yule, George   357

Žák, Ladislav   65
Zander, Horst   393, 394
Zholkovsky, Alexander Konstantinovich   331
Zich, Otakar   59, 60, 62
Zielinski, Siegfried   27
Zima, Peter V.   429
Zola, Émile   388
Zrzavý, Jan   106
Zuboff, Shoshana   355
Zuse, Konrad   218
Zymner, Rüdiger   385, 386

www.ingramcontent.com/pod-product-compliance
Lightning Source LLC
Chambersburg PA
CBHW070005010526
44117CB00011B/1432